The Scope of Renaissance Humanism

THE SCOPE OF
Renaissance Humanism

Charles Trinkaus

ANN ARBOR • THE UNIVERSITY OF MICHIGAN PRESS

*To my students at Sarah Lawrence College
and the University of Michigan*

Library of Congress Cataloging in Publication Data

Trinkaus, Charles Edward, 1911–
    The scope of Renaissance humanism.
    Includes bibliographical references and index.
    1. Renaissance—Addresses, essays, lectures.
    2. Humanism—Addresses, essays, lectures.   I. Title.
CB361.T74   1983   001.3'09'024   83-6650
ISBN 0-472-10031-9

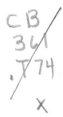
068945

Acknowledgments

My intellectual debt to scholars in the Renaissance fields is enormous and international—American, English, Italian, German, French. Some of my more particular debts are discussed in the following Introduction. Foundations, learned societies, colleges, and universities have also contributed to the support of my work in large and smaller ways, all generous and essential: the American Council of Learned Societies, the National Endowment for the Humanities, the John Simon Guggenheim Foundation, the Horace H. Rackham School of Graduate Studies of the University of Michigan with research grants, subventions, and fellowships on a major scale; Sarah Lawrence College, the University of Michigan College of Literature, Science and the Arts with leaves of absence and sabbaticals. To all of them I am deeply grateful. Other universities and learned societies have provided many occasions for composing or presenting these papers. Mention should be made of the following institutions: the Columbia University Seminar on the Renaissance with whom I have long been associated and to whom a number of these papers have been read; the Renaissance Society of America and its regional conferences; the Center for Medieval and Renaissance Studies of the University of California, Los Angeles; and the American Historical Association. My students, undergraduate and graduate alike, have not so much suffered from neglect as provided stimulation with their interest, for the largest part of these studies were written during regular teaching terms. I dedicate this book to them.

I must thank, too, many journals, publishers, sponsoring societies, and editors for their generous and unfailing permissions to reprint various studies here: the McGraw-Hill Book Company and the Istituto per la Collaborazione Culturale for two essays from the *Encyclopedia of World Art;* the Renaissance Society of America for four essays from *Studies in the Renaissance* and for the long passage in the following Introduction from *Renaissance Quarterly;* Manfredi Editore of Palermo for one essay; E. J. Brill Publishers of Leiden and the editors of the respective Brill volumes where three essays first appeared; the *Journal of the History of Ideas* for one essay; the American Society for Reformation Research for an essay published in *Archiv für Reformationgeschichte;* Columbia University Press for an essay from *Essays in Medieval Life and Thought;* Charles Scribner's Sons for an essay from the *Dictionary of the History of Ideas;* Editore Laterza and Methuen & Co. Ltd. for an essay in its Italian and English versions; the editors of the forthcoming Benjamin Nelson memorial volume for the essay on Thomas More; James J.

Murphy for an essay in *Renaissance Eloquence,* edited by Professor Murphy; and Marcel Tetel, editor of *The Journal of Medieval and Renaissance Studies* for the final essay. Where first publication was made or copyright is held by any of the above, I gratefully acknowledge this.

Finally, I owe a more specific debt for scholarly hospitality and provision of working facilities to the Warburg Institute of London, to the American Academy in Rome, and to the Harvard University Center for Italian Renaissance Studies and its Biblioteca Berenson at Villa I Tatti. My thanks to all three institutions are heartfelt.

Contents

Introduction

The following essays and studies were written over a period of nearly forty years. They are offered in a single collection because they are, in my mind, a coordinated series of investigations or expositions of the character and extent of Renaissance humanism. They are also inevitably an effort to evaluate the historical importance of this movement both in the context of the Italian and Northern Renaissance and in the larger perspective of its place in the history of Western civilization. I should like in this introduction to present some sense of where I would place my own work as a Renaissance historian in relation to the needs and problems of this discipline as I encountered them as a graduate student at Columbia in the thirties and as a young Ph.D. in the forties and fifties. After this I should, of course, want to clarify some of my ideas and intentions as a so-called mature scholar in the sixties and seventies.

For an exposition of how my thinking was formed in the early decades, but also reaching into the later period, I can think of nothing more appropriate than to incorporate here the first part of a paper written as a report to the Fourteenth International Congress of Historical Science in 1975: "Humanism, Religion, Society: Concepts and Motivations of Some Recent Studies" (*Renaissance Quarterly* 39 [1976]). The second part, which was a review of then recent publications in the Renaissance area seems no longer relevant or of sufficient interest to be reprinted. At the end of the section, which now follows, I shall attempt to relate my own more recent work, including the bulk of the papers in this volume, to the approaches and the positions set forth here.

History, as other scholarly disciplines, tends always to look inward at its own work and the publications within its particular national and language boundaries. But at the same time more inventive minds within the discipline constantly feel a dissatisfaction with provincialisms of various sorts and seek to open their thinking and their work to wider influences. Yet this may happen very slowly. For example the famous essay of Lucien Febvre, 'Une question mal posée,' first appeared in 1929 (*Revue historique,* 161), found an Italian counterpart in Delio Cantimori's *Prospettive di storia ereticale italiana* of 1960, and was cited for its parallels with Pre-Reformation German piety in Berndt Moellers' 'Frommigkeit in Deutschland um 1500' of 1965. And now both Moeller's and Febvre's essays have appeared in English translations, though, to be sure, the influence of these three master-historians was felt outside their own language areas long before 1960 and 1965 and also in the English-speaking world.

Renaissance studies in Britain and America, like Reformation studies, have had to bear an analogous burden to that Febvre deplored in the study of sixteenth-century religious developments under the aegis of sectarian religious interests. It was Febvre's plea to throw off this burden of sectarianism for the historically serious goal of regarding these religious attitudes and practices with a more universal and human perspective, to see them no longer as quarrels over dogmas but as the thought, sensibility, and actions of specific groups of peoples and individuals—*histoire religieuse* rather than *histoire ecclésiastique*. If Protestant and Counter-Reformation sectarianism was the burden of the epoch of 'Reform,' free-thought (*libre-pensée, libertinisme*) and the Enlightenment (*Aufklärung, Illuminismo*) were those of the Renaissance. Enlightened, anticlerical, humanistic liberals of the eighteenth, nineteenth, and twentieth centuries thus saw themselves as the heirs of a Renaissance which had originated the qualities and values they cherished. There were, of course, other burdens—the dispute between romanticism and its cousin neo-classicism, the formation of the modern sovereign-state with its 'Machiavellian' *real politik, fin de siècle* aestheticism (sharing its favors with the so-called Pre-Raphaelite painters of the Trecento and early Quattrocento), and so on. Yet a major distortion in Renaissance historiography continues to be the contemporary effort to locate the beginnings of rationalism and political liberalism in that period.

If a retrospective historiography, looking for paradigms and seedbeds of admired contemporary developments, or even of deplorable ones, has become an obstacle to authentic understanding of the Renaissance, Renaissance studies have suffered even more from the Renaissance's own myth that it alone brought about a rebirth of classical antiquity. For although the Renaissance did, indeed, add importantly to our knowledge and understanding of antiquity, certain major works of the literature and philosophy of the classical world were also known and possessed by the writers and thinkers and men of learning of those previous centuries which we have learned from the Renaissance humanists to call the *Medium Aevum*. Now it seems as though the men of the Renaissance who gave us that name of the Middle Ages have, by their distortions or memory-lapses or simple ignorance—or much more likely their disgust with the more traditional scholastic and legistic professions and intellectuals of their own day—also created our modern partisanship and rivalry between Renaissance scholars and medievalists. The latter, who championed the cause of medieval culture against humanistic exaggeration, have in the early twentieth century engaged in what Wallace Ferguson has characterized as a 'revolt' against those Burckhardtians and others who seemed to take the humanists too much at their own word.

The danger for historians always is to identify their own partisanships with those of the past. The real enemies of these medievalists were not the men of the Renaissance but certain of their own contemporaries. Those were to be found not among the enlightened liberals so much as among the late nineteenth-century aesthetes and the dilettantes, or the *Macht-politiker* and the Neo-Nietzscheans. Those, largely Anglo-American, medievalists, who considered themselves enlightened liberals, were not prompted to their defense of the 'medieval' world by the nationalistic literary and linguistic concerns of the earlier romantics who combatted what they regarded as the effete, archaic Latin-classical revivalist tendencies of the humanists. Nor were they affected by the nostalgia of Catholic neo-scholastics. On the contrary, they took a sober, empirical, professional, pro-scientific, post-Protestant point of view, democratic and anti-élitist perhaps, and one even more impatient with the literary, the artistic, the amateurish, and with—above all—what, in surprising agreement with Burckhardt, seemed to be the morally dubious and intellectually shallow, rhetorical character of humanist culture.

Believers in professional learning, in science and progress both in the Middle Ages and in the modern world, but also sympathetic to popular cultures such as the early-medieval Germanic or the early Italian communes were assumed to be, the modern medievalists found even the world of antiquity to be characterized by magic and superstitions, wholesale erotic indulgence, tyranny, hypocritical moralism and pseudo-responsible legalism, and other such negative qualities that were felt to dim the lustre of what was once thought to be the world's happiest centuries. And thus for them the epigones of twelfth- and thirteenth-century learning began to be regarded not so much as Bernard of Chartres' dwarfs standing on the shoulders of giants as giants elevating dwarfs. Scholastic theology and an oppressive ecclesiastical hierarchy were no longer viewed with fear in consideration of the great architectural works, both the buildings and the scholastic *summae,* which fed and depended upon an awakening interest in the natural world, in mathematics and natural philosophy, and even in rudimentary experimental science. The modern world, they suggested, rather than originating in the Italian Renaissance, began in the twelfth century with its earlier Renaissance, its translations of Greek scientific works, and found its first peak in the universities of the thirteenth. These scholastic university centers manifested the first organized, rational application of learning and intelligence to human problems, and with their tough-minded teachers were more likely candidates to be forerunners of the modern technical bureaucratic world emerging over the last hundred years than the more non-utilitarian, beauty- and pleasure-loving playboys (and girls) of the 'so-called Renaissance.'

One cannot, of course seriously criticize the magnificent researches of Charles Homer Haskins or of Lynn Thorndike (and many others), whose evaluative attitudes toward their historical periods have been, I hope, not unfairly characterized. (And lest I be misunderstood, let me say that I have no quarrel with serious study of any historical epoch, including most definitely the Middle Ages, but only with partisan-ship concerning the past in all its forms—medievalist, 'Renaissance-ist,' liberal, Protestant, conservative, Neo-Catholic, or whatever.) Yet the revolt of the medievalists nearly won the day, and a kind of bitterness remains among their heirs, many of them even students of these two great American medievalists, at the return of the pendulum. More than anything else the revival of Renaissance studies and the present extraordinary retrospective admiration for this period has been effected by the transplantation of early twentieth-century German scholarship to England and the United States as a tragic consequence of the Hitlerian whirlwind. One could speak of many great figures, but perhaps two, neither of whom were professional historians, may stand for all the rest: Erwin Panofsky, who extended the history of art to a general history and periodization of culture, and the philosopher-philologist Paul Oskar Kristeller.[1] (The influence of a third great figure, in this case a historian, Hans Baron, we discuss below.) Signi-ficantly, both Kristeller and Panofsky were rather more empirical scholars, endowed with a vast erudition, than representatives of the Anglo-American *bête noir*, German idealist philosophy. Even though they were in some respects 'Neo-Kantians,' and certainly admirers of Ernst Cassirer's many works, and especially his *Individuum und Kosmos in der Philosophie der Renaissance* of 1927 (Eng. trans., 1963), still their concerns were primarily with Renaissance culture in its relationship to its medieval and classical pasts. And it was not so much the original researches of Panofsky and Kristeller as their erudition and wide knowledge of ancient, medieval, and Renaissance culture, together with their gift for apodictic formulation and statement, that for a time at least restored the Renaissance to historical respectability in the English-speaking world. Undoubtedly it needed no such rehabilita-tion in Italy and Germany, and probably not in France, where Febvre was busily creating his own *revision*.

The dates are important, as well as the structure of their solutions. Critical articles were published in English in 1944—Panofsky's lecture 'Renaissance and Renascences' in the *Kenyon Review,* eventually expanded into his *Renaissance and Renascences in Western Art* (Uppsala, 1960; Harper Torchbook, 1969); Kristeller's key statement, 'Humanism and Scholasticism in the Italian Renaissance,' in *Byzantion, XVII* (1944–45), reprinted in 1956 in his *Studies in Renaissance Thought and Letters* and again in 1961 in *Renaissance Thought: The Classic, Scholastic and Humanist Strains,* which incorporated his *The Classics and Renaissance Thought* of 1955. We have thus now [1974] had thirty years in which to absorb the perspectives of these two great influences (need I say that I use their work as representative of many others' valuable contributions along sympathetic lines who will not be mentioned here). What they accomplished—and for this it is perhaps important to mention also the influence of E. R. Curtius' seminal notebook, *European Literature and the Latin Middle Ages* of 1948, English translation 1953—was to establish the continuity of the classical traditions (emphatically plural) from antiquity, through the medieval periods, on into the Renaissance with the critical variations and transformations that took place over this enormous timespan of roughly two millennia.

Panofsky with his notion of a series of classical revivals in the Middle Ages, both artistic and literary-philosophical, which he called 'Renascences,' ended by establishing a qualitatively and quantitatively different Italian 'Renaissance' on the basis of its self-perceptions and historical consciousness that was possibly the most important novelty he succeeded in identifying for this phase in the history of Western culture.

The 'Renaissance,' he claimed, through its historical consciousness was able to or at least strove to see the ancients in their authenticity. Thus he not only offered an acceptable key to understanding the Renaissance in terms of its own characteristics with no need for invidious comparisons over the degree of knowledge of antiquity, but unleashed a flood of studies, both art-historical and intellectual-historical, of Renaissance modes of perception—visual and literary-historical—which became of course simultaneously comparative with the various phases of medieval, ancient, and post Renaissance modes of perception. Again the parallel influence of Cassirer's interpretive study of Renaissance thought and philosophy along these lines needs emphasis. By seeing Renaissance classicism and Renaissance perspective as two interrelated aspects of at least that part of Renaissance consciousness which we have designated 'modes of perception,' Panofsky also established a link with the study of the history of science, then dominated by both Thorndike's and Sarton's (later revised) rejection of any significant Renaissance contribution. Thus they, with Duhem and others, created the problem of continuity of medieval and modern science, of how to move from Buridan's and Oresme's important but clearly scholastic physics to the new science of Copernicus, Kepler, and Galileo. But now after Panofsky, Kristeller, and Cassirer, the problem is more likely to be formulated as a movement from Alberti to Galileo, though the former's dependence on Biagio dei Pelacani's optical conceptions establishes links with at least some aspects of medieval science. In fact, what was missing, but is now under way, was an understanding of the parallels and even interconnections of late medieval 'nominalistic' scholastic thought (both theology and natural philosophy) and Renaissance thought, humanistic and scientific.

But first the basic divisions and broad historical relationships of Renaissance thought had to be placed in true perspective, and this was the great contribution of Kristeller. Reacting in part to the Italian periodization of the history of philosophy or of intellectual history into successive phases designated as *scolasticismo, umanesimo, rinascimento,* Kristeller demonstrated that both scholasticism and humanism were late growths in Italy and came in the fourteenth century side by side, humanism emerging from the medieval *ars dictaminis* and scholasticism developing independent traditions in such fourteenth-century universities as Bologna, Pavia, and Padua. Renaissance Aristotelianism, particularly in the area of natural philosophy, dominated university learning, with theology being taught and cultivated primarily in the schools of the mendicant orders. Thirteenth-century Italian learning had remained primarily concentrated in jurisprudence, the major Italian theologians being active in Paris. Thus a differentiation was made between a high medieval northern French scholastic and literary culture and a later Trecento and Quattrocento Italian culture divided between scholastic natural philosophy at the universities and the humanities, at first at schools and courts and in chanceries, but soon also within the universities. The term 'Renaissance' simply indicated, spatially and temporally, the phase of the late medieval culture that occurred at this time in Italy.

But Kristeller also stressed the importance of the successive phases of a rhetorical tradition—Greek, Roman, medieval, Renaissance humanist—and did the same for the Aristotelian and Platonic philosophical traditions, indicating in each instance the classical phases, the Byzantine, the Arabic, and the Western medieval and the ways in which they were brought to bear on Renaissance Aristotelianism and Platonism. Thus he contributed a very badly needed, large-scale chart of the basic contours of the history of the Western cultures—Greek, Roman, Hebraic, Early Christian, Islamic, Byzantine, medieval Latin, Renaissance. It became very clear through his writings that Renaissance culture could not simply be a revival of an undifferentiated classical antiquity but that antiquity itself was received in its own widely differing, complex schools and historical phases, and that they were in turn screened through their history in the three intervening successor cultures in highly differentiated ways. Thus a much more refined and articulated conception of the history of thought emerged.

Although his background and training was in philosophy, classical philology, medieval intellectual history, and he had little knowledge or sympathy for the modern social sciences as for instance anthropology, Kristeller's work also made an important contribution to a mode of understanding the Renaissance in terms of the multiple and complicated layers of historical traditions that diffused earlier learning and operated within it, a perspective that in fact paralleled certain basic anthropological conceptions of the process of diffusion. However, this methodology, traditional but still highly valuable, rested on a thorough knowledge of the basic texts of philosophy and rhetoric, of the historical cultures mentioned, combined with a knowledge of the textual history (or 'fortuna') of the key works written within the period under study.

Moreover, Kristeller's sensitivity to the religious concerns of the humanists and philosophers of the Renaissance, reflected in his recognition of the importance of centers of lay piety such as he thinks Ficino's Platonic Academy was, underlined the importance of intellectual developments for certain aspects of the social history of the Renaissance. To the increasing interest in the religious aspects of Renaissance humanist thought Kristeller also contributed his emphasis on the revival of Augustinianism and of patristic thought generally as Christian 'classics' among the humanists and in the emerging Renaissance Platonism.

Thus, Kristeller (and Panofsky to a lesser extent) contributed to a clarification of the relationships of the Renaissance and of humanism to their pasts, ancient and medieval, but basically left open the question of their relationships to and influence upon the historical genesis of the future. Certainly the weight of Cassirer's thinking, and, because of the similarity of some of his ideas, by inference Panofsky's, looked forward to the Enlightenment, to early modern science, to German idealist philosophy. It was, perhaps, also difficult for Kristeller as historian of philosophy and Neo-Kantian to escape from this tendency altogether; but it is notable that the thrust of his work was toward the goal of understanding the Renaissance in terms of autonomous qualities authentically its own, though derived in a complex historical process from the past, and no doubt leading in an equally complex but unpredictable way toward the future. What he emphatically did not wish to do was to confuse one period or phase of the history of thought with another by loose characterizations linking the two.

The work of Panofsky and Kristeller (and others) has thus reestablished the distinctiveness of the Renaissance by clarification of the nature of its classicism, humanism, Aristotelianism, Platonism, Christian thought, and historical consciousness in comparison with previous medieval ones. There is no doubt in my mind that, while to some degree 'correcting' the polemical emphasis of such historians as Haskins and Thorndike, work of this sort has also vindicated it. Distinctiveness, continuity with past and future, parallelism and connection with other contemporary developments—all three qualities were present and must be affirmed.

Continuity and change are of the essence of the historical process so that it becomes even banal and obvious to discuss the question. It is the concrete continuities and changes that are of moment; yet what has plagued Renaissance studies has been the persistence in Western historical thinking of the far too sweeping distinction between the 'medieval' and 'modern' made so emphatically by so many Renaissance thinkers and the consequent search for the 'medieval' or the 'modern' within the Renaissance. If 'modern times' began with the Renaissance, then the stage is set for the long tradition of historical investigations of what aspects of modern culture took their beginnings in the Renaissance. But the very fact that the medieval-Renaissance controversy broke out as early as the seventeenth century is evidence that something was wrong with this historical scenario. It forgot, of course, that the Renaissance meta-historians were saying that their age was or could be more like antiquity than the *saecula recentiora* which would then become a *medium aevum,* that in fact they saw their own times as regrettably closer to the previous period than to the ancient glories. The medieval-modern quarrel was, of course, shaped also by the sectarian historiography of Protestants and Catholics who identified the medieval with either religious decay or triumph and, reversing the roles of the modern, with somehow both developing a certain ambivalence about the Renaissance. Basically the argument is about when the modern European world began and whether the Middle Ages was an intervening 'middle' period or in fact is the very *tempus* within which the modern world takes its start.

Yet at that very moment when the effect of work such as Kristeller's and Panofsky's was to dampen the medieval-modern quarrel, a renewed assertion of the contrast and a location of the critical turn within the Italian Renaissance was presented by Hans Baron with the assistance of such epigones of modern, liberal enlightenment as Professors Walter Ullmann of Cambridge University and Peter Gay of Columbia and Yale. One should not underestimate the collective appeal of the work of all three, nor their profound influence on comtemporary historical thought in England and America, nor their roots in the frustrated liberalism of modern Germany (Bismarckian, Wilhelmian, as well as of Weimar), but for the comprehension of recent Renaissance historiography we must undoubtedly turn to that of Hans Baron.

Baron's *The Crisis of the Early Italian Renaissance* was first published in 1955 (revised edition in 1966), exactly twenty years before this Congress (though he had formulated his ideas as early as 1932). Just as Kristeller and Panofsky emphasized the distinctiveness of Renaissance classicism in art history and intellectual history, Baron, also of the same generation of Weimar emigrés, stressed the uniqueness of the political attitudes of the Italian humanists—or at least of those whom he was able to include in his magic circle of 'civic' or *bürgerlich* humanists. But whereas for Kristeller and Panofsky the distinctiveness of the Renaissance is embedded in an even stronger sense of the historical continuity and connection with the ancient, medieval, and Byzantine pasts, Baron in his well-known thesis conceives of the Renaissance as a 'crisis,' a critical turning away from or break with medieval culture and also a break with the regressive elements of classical culture which were regarded more favorably in the medieval period. His emphasis is forward-looking and definitely 'modernizing.'

Apart from the many valuable analyses of particular datings and other such subsidiary problems that Baron has made in order to support his argument, the basic appeal and value of Baron's work is that it put Italian Renaissance studies into a context of historical significance that the period would seem to have lost if it had not in fact, as Burckhardt claimed, revived classical learning and given faith to modern individualism, and as a consequence was absorbed into a notion of a declining medieval culture. Baron made Renaissance republicanism the antechamber of the eighteenth-nineteenth-twentieth-century secularist, liberal, constitutional ideal.

Baron's conception has attracted several of the most important intellectual historians working today, and he has also inspired a remarkable number of potent social and institutional historians, as is evidenced by the festschrift *Renaissance Studies in Honor of Hans Baron,* edited by Anthony Molho and John Tedeschi in 1971. Yet to my mind, his work, however valuable the new data and interpretive analyses of detailed portions of it, suffers excessively from the traditional genetic-modernist bias that at the same time is so prevalent among contemporary social and political scientists and those historians whom they have influenced. The trouble is that in this genetic-modernizing kind of history which has flourished in recent years (and not only with respect to the Renaissance) we tend to look for ancestors and not for understanding of the way things were, that we do in fact tend to impose our reading of universal history on a period that may have had a very different historical consciousness from our own. The consequence is that we can all-too-easily impose issues and a line-up of forces and parties that essentially do not correspond with the true concerns of the period in question, which are frequently much more complex and problematical than we, in our quest for clarity, sometimes make them.

All historiography is by definition retrospective; it is totally impossible to escape one's own cultural values altogether. Historical periodizations are bound to be to some extent self-reflecting and arbitrary. Nonetheless, it is also not impossible to be critical or to attempt to be critical, to attempt to acquire a sufficient understanding of the wholeness of a past period to be able to grasp it in its own terms. It seems to me that the need to revise our most basic historical assumptions concerning the place of the Renaissance within the whole Western tradition has now arrived and that an increasing number of historians are becoming aware of this. I should like to sketch out my own views of this problem in close relation to an evaluation of the recent historical studies on the Renaissance I have set out to discuss. What I have said about Kristeller and Panofsky is not a diversion because they have set the stage for the kind of thinking that must now go on—indeed has in many respects already begun to go on, and, if we can refer back to Lucien Febvre's essay mentioned at the beginning, already some time ago. No doubt the French *Annales* school has contributed heavily to this kind of revisionist thinking, but it is by no means the only or the most important source.

Modern western European history might better be seen as beginning in the eleventh and twelfth centuries with the formation of the French and English monarchies, the medieval German empire, and the Italian communes, with the attempted consolidation of the papacy with the Gregorian reforms. At least as far as the central institutional and legal continuities are concerned that is where it begins. As far as culture was concerned, both its Christian and classical elements were inherited; but it begins, in a sense that was not true of the earlier Middle Ages, to have a history of its own, and one where new professional classes of intellectuals assume a certain responsibility within society as a whole and create their own institutions for training, study, and debate, the medieval universities with theologians, canon and civil lawyers, notaries and rhetoricians, natural philosophers and physicians. All the most important constitutional and intellectual developments of the modern world have evolved directly from these beginnings—divided regionally sometimes in protest and revolt, but always with a sense of relationship to and the assumption of responsibility for the culture as a whole, sometimes in a shamelessly self-centered and corrupt manner, but always with at least lip-service to the wider common interest. By whatever definition of a civilization, a culture, a polity, a social order we wish to make, the historical facts fit a phasing such as this.

But as Haskins, Thorndike, Panofsky, and Kristeller knew, more significant by far than the established institutions—political power-centers, ecclesiastical temporalities, professions, economic organizations (all drastically and sometimes catastrophically important)—were the elements of consciousness: ideas, purposes, feelings, behavior, beliefs, hopes, and fears; the characters and differences of urban and rural communities; individualism and community-identifications; conceptions of and believed relations with supernatural beings and forces; technologies, habits, and skills. For all of these, too, not only have their structures, their differentiations, and their phasings, sometimes regional, frequently totally individual, but do in fact comprise the sum-total of the culture itself. And they must be grasped not taxonomically but dynamically because they are evanescent and only exist in relation to and interaction with experience. Institutions, power-concentrations, statuses of privilege exercise a continuing influence, inhibiting or releasing, on the conduct of life, as does the provision of means of subsistence and material wealth, the presence of famine, prosperity, and business depression; but only through conceptions, purposes, moods, feelings of the living humans who enact and suffer them can they be understood.

To my mind the most important phasing of the history of this European culture did not occur between the medieval and Renaissance-Reformation periods but later. Yet there is no doubt but that the way was prepared by what had gone on before. It would not be excessively original to think that the gradual impact of the new sciences of the seventeenth century, the technological and industrial revolutions from the eighteenth to the twentieth centuries, the emergence of large-scale mass political movements beginning with the abortive seventeenth-century English Puritan revolution were the elements that brought about a drastic transformation of the older

European modes of consciousness, but this did not happen suddenly or without great confusion.

What, however, was central to them was the gradual development of a 'deification' of man, or a displacement of the consciousness of God as the prime directive force in the universe by a notion of human powers and of 'natural' forces, which indeed begins in the Italian Renaissance. What I am asserting, of course, is the historical centrality of the displacement of religion which occurred very gradually in the course of modern history. The roles of the earlier phases of European culture within this process have been very badly misinterpreted—those of twelfth-century humanism, of twelfth- and thirteenth-century scholasticism, fourteenth- and fifteenth-century 'nominalism,' Petrarchan humanism, Aristotelian natural philosophy, fifteenth- and sixteenth-century Platonism, religious conflict and reform, sixteenth- and seventeenth-century science. For the secularization of culture and the 'deification' of man grew directly out of the movements and attitudes that were present within medieval-Renaissance-Reformation Christianity itself rather than being the program of a secularist opposition movement to 'medieval' Christianity within this first great phase of the history of the modern West.

Unquestionably the relationship of the sacred and the secular became a critical problem in our period of the Late Middle Ages, Renaissance, and Reformation; and the major cultural innovations—nominalism, mysticism, humanism, reformation theologies—should perhaps be seen as varied attempts to clarify the relationship of secular and religious values while somehow preserving both. The revival of Augustine or 'Augustinianism' should be equally seen as a recourse to a thinker who seemed so centrally to be trying to resolve the same problem. This is a matrix for the study of the self-consciousness of our period—not the assertion of a dichotomy between the sacred and the secular, the cleric and the layman, the mystical and the rational which generated factions and multifarious parties, but a search for ways of trying to bring together and reconcile the apparently conflicting values. Let us propose that what was going on was a tendency to secularize the sacred while simultaneously sacralizing the secular.

Obviously polarizations did occur, some solutions chosen were more satisfactory to some groups than others, sometimes to such an extent that persecution, war, massacre seemed the only answer to the danger of the false solution embraced by others. Obviously also the solutions ranged from complete separation and isolation of the modes of thinking and acting within the two spheres to complete identification. Whatever the degree of rational thought applied to carefully isolated problems (which in the case of Machiavelli could be intense), the divine, the supernatural, the magical, the daemonic remained palpably real and had to be accepted in some form or another—even in Galileo's and Newton's universe, even in politics, history, or fortune.

Within this context of enormous confusion concerning the relationship of sacred and profane, divine and human, the individual sought to possess power, again in some form or other—divine, daemonic, political, social, magical, scientific, mechanical, sacramental, moral. Particularly moral—for virtue is personal moral power, and the individual sought it by his own free will, or trusted it would come to him by grace, sufficiently, that is, to render him 'just' as well as 'justified.' Or his meritoriousness was debated, not only in a theological context but in terms of secular or sacred status. Was nobility a matter of birth or could it be seized by virtue, by action, by achievements? Was the monk or friar, 'religious' by vocation, especially sacred and thus meritorious because he was bound over to God by his vows (thus contributing to the treasury of holiness in which his less meritorious neighbor might by indulgence participate)? Or was the spontaneously, graciously emitted act of charity or love by the layman or secular cleric more saintly and salvation-bringing (or salvation-signifying)? Is it too daring to call this sacral power that all sought—from the Impruneta Virgin's secret smile and the king's thaumaturgic touch to the prince's seizure of fortune's occasions—by that odd old anthropological term 'mana'? At least what we are talking about has some of the qualities of 'mana.'

And then there is the matter of human thought and culture itself—its power, its effectiveness, its reliability, its veracity. Certainly here was one of the foci of the debates between humanists and scholastics and of the concern with the power of words and language—rhetoric as opposed to dialectic, the former enchanting and the latter compelling. Certainly the validity of the Word, of revelational knowledge against the humanly conjectured, becomes of great issue between *nominales* and *reales*. How much of this is connected with the great debates concerning God's *potentia absoluta* against his *potentia ordinata,* his philosophically conceived limitless power and the seemingly much closer and more tangible decreed power of his commandments and covenants? How much of the ancient doctrine of reification in which a deeply intellected thought is itself the substance of its object was being asserted by the earlier scholastic's philosophical realism or how much reification was there in the uttered word of the sacrament, the written word of the Scripture (or of Aristotle), and later the *ipse dixit* of the printed word? All of these were conceptual counters in the efforts to discover the validity of thought and language—not to mention the visual language in the painting or sculpture, on or off the altar. And positions and solutions are multiple.

Individuals sought 'power' in a vast variety of ways, but the problem of 'power' must be grasped collectively and socially as well. Charity, which binds men to each other as well as to God, is seen as pure affect and emotional power, fierce and fortitudinous, by Valla. It both binds and sends men forth as *milites Christiani* against their enemies, charged or not with daemonic power. And the collectivity of the community, divinely endowed and providentially directed, seeks a new fulfillment of the Christian vision of brotherhood in apocalyptic movements and civic religions. For Machiavelli the question of justice and morality as the constituted source of political power becomes entangled with the brutal assertion of princely power in the corrupt community. It is not only the individual, the class, the religious status that is endowed with virtue, but also the community, the universal condition and dignity of mankind. It is in this process that the 'deification' of man that looks forward to the later modern culture begins to emerge in writings of the time.

Such, loosely stated, are some of the problems that need more systematic exploration in any effort to develop an anthropological consideration of the history of the Italian Renaissance and its cousin-cultures, the northern Late Middle Ages, and the Reformation epochs of both Italy and the North. To approach the study of the Renaissance in this way does not necessarily contradict and certainly does not supersede or cancel the importance of the genetic-modernizing type of study exemplified by Baron and others. A number of historians working today clearly subscribe to both approaches and probably would not agree that they are even separate or different. Nevertheless, from my point of view as I have stated it, a much more radical effort at a critical 'then-mindedness' seems called for, one that does not fall into the extreme of historicism seeking to think entirely within the concepts and perceptions of a past age but one which seeks to see that age in the fullness of its internal interconnections, including its reconstructions of its past and its anticipations of its future, as an autonomous sub-whole of the totality of human experience. Thus, hopefully, the ideological partisanship of the historian with a fragment of the past, which tends to be utilized as a counter in his own ideological battles of the present, may be avoided, and fuller and deeper understanding of a past phase of history may be attained.

What I stated more impersonally in the above section of my report for the 1975 International Congress applied to my own development as Renaissance historian many decades earlier. I was a student of Austin P. Evans and of Lynn Thorndike at Columbia in the early thirties, and I wrote my dissertation under the chairmanship of Professor Thorndike. From Evans I derived an interest in the social aspects of religious thought, particularly those of the Catharist heretics of the thirteenth century and those of the sixteenth-century Protestant reformers. From Lynn Thorndike I acquired a research methodology and a sense of the complexity and paradoxical character of intellectual history. I also developed a lasting respect for the originality of this indefatigable researcher of what then seemed the odd subject of magic and a sense of the potency of a close adherence to positivistic empirical study in bringing forth revisionary conceptions of hitherto superficially held historical dogma.

Thorndike, of course, though he knew the period in great detail from his researches in the manuscript sources, repudiated not only the notion but the very term *Renaissance.* I learned eventually from the work of Panofsky and Kristeller, as I describe it above, that their evidence and structuring of Western history required that I return to the notion of Renaissance but, as has been indicated, in a totally different sense than the one Thorndike had been rejecting.

My dissertation developed out of a paper written for Thorndike's seminar, a collection of pessimistic treatises and statements in fifteenth and early sixteenth-century European thought. The dissertation itself was sensibly confined to writings of the Italian humanists on the sense, modes, and conceptions of human happiness and the limitations imposed upon it (*Adversity's Noblemen, The Italian Humanists on Happiness,* New York: Columbia University Press, 1940. Reprinted with new preface and corrections, New York: Octagon Books, 1965). I learned from writing the dissertation that my interest was in the history of attitudes more than of ideas. I attempted to study the specific content of the humanists' ethical thinking as well as the mode of consciousness of this given group of writers. Rather than stressing their importance for the originality or unoriginality of their contributions to a field of learning, I looked for the possible connections of their thought to the general history of the period. Thus I regarded the moral thought of the Italian humanists (and Platonists) of importance in its manifestation of the attitude of these intellectuals toward themselves and the culture, society, and history of the Italian Renaissance. I was not concerned with it as something either surpassing corresponding aspects of medieval thought or anticipating those of the high (i.e., eighteenth- to twentieth-century) modern world. However, I also found clearly medieval elements and outlooks enduring in humanist thought which was built around traditions derived not only from the schools of classical philosophy but from St. Augustine and St. Thomas as well.

What I developed as part of my own historical thinking by means of this experience prepared me for ready acceptance and approval of the conceptions of the place of the Renaissance in the development of Western intellectual traditions that I encountered in Panofsky and Kristeller. Thus I found a way of transcending the strictures on the level of fifteenth- and sixteenth-century learning I had learned from Lynn Thorndike and at the same time was able to incorporate them into the new perspective. The Italian "Renaissance," I became convinced, did exist as a viable historical concept, not as the rediscovery of classical antiquity after centuries of darkness, but rather as a transformation of attitudes toward antiquity which did indeed lead to a fuller and more accurate knowledge of ancient thought, letters, and art, and to a greater awareness of the historical differences between antiquity, the medieval centuries, and the *recentior aevum* of the late middle ages. In the forties I also acquired a close knowledge and a deep appreciation of the importance of Kristeller's work from my participation as a translator in the preparation of *The Renaissance Philosophy of Man* volume and as an early member and regular attendant at the University Seminar on the Renaissance founded at Columbia University in 1944. Properly, and not invidiously, defined, *Renaissance* became no longer an opprobrious word.

Three continuing aspects of my approach to Renaissance studies grew out of these early experiences as a student of Lynn Thorndike and as a collaborator and University Seminar colleague of Paul Oskar Kristeller: (1) I acquired an enduring interest in the question of the intellectual nature, the historical derivation, and the cultural role of Italian—and also Northern—humanism. (2) I became perennially concerned with the religious elements in the thought of the humanists which seemed to derive, not so much from their Ciceronian or antique commitment to the subject matter of rhetoric as from their involvement in the religious thought of their time and the ecclesiastical and religious crises of the late Middle Ages. This involvement necessarily turned them toward a critique of the practices and attitudes of the traditional institutions of the medieval church as well as its modes of defining and propagating doctine and belief. And this critical stance made it important to consider the relationship of their specific approaches to the church and religion with those of their medieval predecessors and with those of the much more radical and forceful taking of positions of the sixteenth-century religious reform movements, Protestant and Catholic alike. (3) I developed a far-ranging awareness of the possible significance for the general shaping of Renaissance culture of their conceptions of man. I saw the humanists' philosophy of man as emerging out of both the profound influence of ancient rhetoric on their thinking and their posing of the problems of the powers of man and their relationship to the divine.

In short, for a period of close to fifty years, but with ever increasing intensity I have been exploring the scope of Renaissance humanism, and I have been doing this within the three closely integrated categories reported. Although it will be obvious that what I wrote and published in the forties and fifties is not identical with what happened in the sixties and seventies, I believe the three subdivisions of this book do correspond to my permanent interests, which I again emphasize are overlapping. At the same time it would be well to point out that four of the six essays of part one—"Renaissance Humanism, Its Character and Influence"—appeared in the early sixties, because of the importance at that time, as it seemed to me, of setting forth the Kristellerian conception of the Renaissance as the more fundamental approach but at the same time one that was compatible with the emphasis of Hans Baron on "civic humanism" which was then so vigorously influencing historical thought. The two other papers were both written in the seventies and reflect my more recent explorations of the intellectual aspects of Renaissance humanism—its relation to the ancient sophists and to natural philosophy and science.

The essays of part two—"Renaissance and Reformation"—are interspersed but derive actually from three phases of my career. The early contribution of a translation of Lorenzo Valla's *Dialogue on Free Will* with an introductory essay in the well-known *Renaissance Philosophy of Man* led directly to the paper on "The Problem of Free Will in the Renaissance and the Reformation" of 1949 in which references to Valla's work by Erasmus, Luther and Calvin were reported. The paper on Calvin naturally enough followed in 1954. A paper of the same vintage (1955) on Luther's social views and their correspondence to his religious thought has been included. But a quite recent essay on Luther's anthropology as expounded in his *Lectures on Genesis,* something that clearly derives from my emphasis on the dignity of man and the human condition generally in humanist thought in my volume of 1970 (*In Our Image and Likeness*), and which is also related to my more recent concern to move from the genres and forms of humanists' discussions of human nature and God to an examination of the structural and anthropological features of their thought, has been included in part three. The other essays of part two are closely associated with the preparation of *In Our Image and Likeness* or with attempts to bring out or clarify some of the undeveloped implications of the studies contained in it—the essays on the status of the religious, the Italian humanists and the Reformers, Erasmus and the nominalists. Yet there seems to me to be sufficient continuity in subject matter and approach to justify grouping papers written over a period of thirty years.

The third part—"Renaissance Philosophy of Man"—is topically differentiated from parts one and two but closely related in my mind. The anthropological thought of Renaissance humanism was central to its general and historical character. Moreover, the religious thought of the humanists was also constructed around their conceptions of the position of man in history and the cosmos, and of human nature in its recalcitrance or susceptibility to salvation. The first essay on the dignity of man is built out of researches for a part of *In Our Image and Likeness* focusing on this topic. The essay "Themes for a Renaissance Anthropology" is an attempted rethinking of the subject matter of the same volume. New material is presented in the first section on *Humanitas* and *genus humanus*. Consideration is given to the significance of humanist activism manifested in discussions of *Conditio hominis*. And an exploration of polarized religious themes in their rhetorical thought—*Theologia rhetorica*—constructs a more generalized conception of the humanist contribution to Renaissance cultural structures. The essays on Luther and Thomas More are further developments of the search for new thinking in the preceding essay. The final paper from the early seventies is a conclusory statement on the general historical significance and influence of humanism.

Mention should perhaps also be made of other recent work necessarily related to the later essays and particularly to part three. I had a central part in planning, organizing, and managing a conference on Late Medieval and Renaissance Religion which met in April, 1972 at the University of Michigan. The conference brought together a number of scholars who were actively researching religious aspects of the medieval, Renaissance and Reformation periods from the points of view of several traditions, including the nominalist, the humanist, the sacramental theological, and the reformation. With Heiko A. Oberman I edited the papers and interventions in *The Pursuit of Holiness in Late Medieval and Renaissance Religion* (Leiden: E. J. Brill, 1974). More immediately connected with the last part of this volume was the small book written mainly in the midseventies (but including one earlier essay published in 1954) entitled *The Poet as Philosopher: Petrarch and the Formation of Renaissance Consciousness* (New Haven: Yale University Press, 1979). It, too, should be considered part of my recent efforts, illustrated in this present volume, to explore the intellectual aspects and impact of Renaissance humanism.

Although if I were to rewrite the earlier papers in this collection today I should inevitably state many things differently, and even possibly sharply disagree with what I said then, I have preferred not to revise them and to keep them historically intact for scholars' references, except for minor anachronisms of referential indications. Occasional recent and definitive editions or studies have been added to the notes.

NOTE

1. Of course Renaissance studies also retained some vitality in the United States in the early forties, and Panofsky and Kristeller, as the latter reminds me, found a

warm reception from such figures as B. L. Ullman, Lester Bradner, and, among historians, Wallace K. Ferguson, at that point writing his important historiographical survey and evaluation of Renaissance history, *The Renaissance in Historical Thought* (Boston, 1948). Activities of such American scholars on the Committee on Renaissance Studies of the American Council of Learned Societies led eventually a decade later to the foundation of the Renaissance Society of America. Myron P. Gilmore and the present writer had recently published dissertations in the area of Renaissance history.

PART ONE

Renaissance Humanism, Its Character and Influence

Renaissance Humanism,
Its Formation and Development

Among the great and influential achievements of the Renaissance period must be included the scholarly and cultural activities of the humanists, chiefly carried on in Italy, although important contributions were made in northern Europe as well. The term "humanism," used historically and empirically, will refer to the Renaissance humanist movement as such, without any of those preconceptions as to its doctrinal content which are present when it is defined as a universal philosophical position. The word itself is of early 19th-century origin (coined by the German pedagogue, F. J. Niethammer, in 1808), and it has acquired such a range of meaning since then that, as it is used today, its meaning is extremely ambiguous. Niethammer originally used it to designate a philosophy of education favoring classical studies in the school curriculum, a meaning literally closer to the Renaissance phenomenon than subsequent usages. It was linked early in the 19th century with the humanitarian attitudes that were a heritage of the 18th-century Enlightenment. It has subsequently been identified with such diverse political tendencies as the libertarian ideas of John Stuart Mill and Marxian socialism. In the 20th century the term, which seems to have connotations inherently pleasant to the contemporary temperament, has been variously associated with the attempt to develop a nontheistic religio-ethical movement, with currents of Roman Catholicism which favor the study of classical philosophy (including Neo-Thomism), with a trend of literary criticism deploring emotionalism and romanticism, and with other points of view almost ad libitum. The conceptually chaotic character of this usage stems primarily from the tendency of the modern self-designated "humanist" to identify the Renaissance humanist movement with his own particular brand of humanism, a practice which can only

This article originally appeared, along with the second essay, as the first part of a two-part article in *The Encyclopedia of World Art*, vol. 7 (New York: McGraw-Hill Book Co., 1963), cols. 702–21, "Humanism" and "Humanism and Renaissance Art." This first part was originally subtitled: "Humanism as a Literary and Philosophical Movement"; it is here retitled as above. The bibliographies for both parts, though extensive, ran only up through 1962; for this reason they are omitted here and in the following essay, and because too much important further work on both these questions has been published in the meantime. They may be consulted, for what they are worth, in the original publication.

3

generate distortion and confusion. In so far as possible this discussion will be confined to what occurred in the Renaissance, taking humanism to be the sum total of the activities, ideas, and direct influence of the Italian humanists, eschewing all notions of it as the forerunner or counterpart of any modern movement or philosophy labeling itself "humanism."

Medieval Antecedents

Renaissance humanism did not spring forth full-armored from the head of Zeus. Necessarily, as it developed out of, as well as in reaction to, certain medieval cultural traditions, it had to correspond to needs and find support in the general historical conditions of late medieval Italy. Essentially centered around an interest in the literature of classical antiquity, the humanist movement had its (for the most part) unacknowledged predecessors in previous medieval movements of antique revival. The Carolingian renaissance through its zeal for transcribing works of classical authors provided the Italian humanists with copies of many ancient works they were to seek so eagerly half a millennium later when the originals were no longer available. It was, however, the 12th-century renaissance (now a thoroughly accepted historical concept) that provided the more immediate historical antecedent. Although its influence continued through the 13th century as a latent, but almost moribund, tradition of classical studies, a gap of almost a century and a half separated the declining days of this northern French enthusiasm for the old pagan authors and the stirring of Italian activities in this field.

As Jean Seznec, Erwin Panofsky, and others have shown, there were significant differences between the intellectual content of the earlier medieval "renascences" and that of Renaissance classicism. It will be essential to examine these, however briefly, in order to understand the actual nature and significance of Renaissance humanism. Moreover, there were equally important differences between the environment and professional attachments of the medieval scholars and those of the humanists of the Renaissance. It is well to remember in an age when universal education is the ideal that during the Middle Ages and much of the Renaissance, literacy and learning were marks of specialized professions. And, indeed, if the ideal of general education was itself a product of Italian humanism, this may well have been due to the fact that the acquisition of culture was already becoming a goal not only of the lay professional but of the well-to-do laity in general.

Perhaps the strongest motivating factor in the Carolingian effort to revive the study of the classics was the need to provide an administrative staff for the centralized regime that was Charlemagne's aim. It was natural enough that with his notions of restoring the Roman Empire the attempt to establish an educational program for its administrators should look to the Latin rhetorical tradition. The abortive character of Charlemagne's efforts, imperial and cultural, left literacy and learning once again in the care of the monasteries, whence he had drawn the leaders of his program. For the next three centuries in northern Europe a feudal monarch who sought to establish some sort of centralized administration in place of the universal feudal tendency toward localism had necessarily to find support from the abbeys, a support both material, in the sense of being financial and political, and intellectual, in the individuals sufficiently educated to act as administrators. This was the case in the so-called "Ottonian," or 10th-century renaissance. The 12th-century renaissance (which had its beginnings in the 11th and extended into the 13th century) was primarily an urban and episcopal affair, having its chief centers at such cathedral schools as Tours, Chartres, Laon, and Orleans in France, and (to a lesser extent) Canterbury in England. It may be considered a part of the restoration and consolidation of the episcopal administrative hierarchy that was one of the accompaniments of the Hildebrandine reform and strengthening of the papal monarchy within the Church. Latin literary classics, late-antique grammars, and the Latin rhetorical tradition were still the principal educational resources at hand, and the study of the humanities through the *auctores* and the *artes liberales* was the usual method of training the host of clerical administrators needed by an expanding ecclesiastical hierarchy. The cathedral chapters, whose Canons Regular (Augustinian Canons) were supported by agreed shares of the episcopal revenues, maintained schools and supported scholars and teachers. John of Salisbury, the outstanding figure of this movement, was bishop of Chartres at his death in 1180.

The scholarly and intellectual achievements of these 12th-century centers of rhetorical and classical tradition were by no means slight. While the movement as a whole did not have the exact shape nor the same impetus as later Italian humanism, it ventured into several areas that roughly parallel later developments. John of Salisbury maintained the traditional rhetorical emphasis on "civil philosophy" in the *Policraticus,* an outstanding example of medieval political thought. Thierry of Chartres, in his *De sex dierum operibus,* found a basis in Chalcidius' 4th-century commentary and translation of Plato's *Timaeus* for a consideration of the physical aspects of the divine creation. Bernardus Silvestris of Tours put forth the notion of man as a microcosm mirroring the universe in his *Cosmographia,* an allegorical-philosophical work based on the *Asclepius* attributed to Apuleius, thought to be a Platonist.

The literary and rhetorical studies in the classical tradition of the 12th century never became the full-fledged *studia humanitatis* of the Renaissance, however, despite John of Salisbury's belief that the liberal arts serve *ad cultum humanitatis.* Subordinated strongly and ultimately to the study of theology and the education of clerics, their practitioners could not help being drawn toward the new logic of Aristotle and the canon law. As a consequence this movement was overwhelmed by the rush toward the higher faculties of theology and law at the emerging universities. The trivium and the classics were relegated to preparatory grammar school subjects; new, more practically oriented textbooks of grammar and rhetoric replaced the classical and late classical ones that had prevailed until then. Dialectic and logic, together with the naturalistic emphases of the quadrivium prevailed among the arts faculties in the north.

Thus medieval humanism, which was centered in northern France and radiated into England and Spain, and to a lesser extent into Germany and Italy, was eclipsed and forced into temporary oblivion by the new university organization of learning and scholasticism in the late 12th and 13th centuries. What remained of the written texts of this movement had only a limited influence on the revival of classical studies by the Italian humanists in the 14th century, but some of the manuscript copies that it had produced of works of classical authors were to find their way into the hands of Petrarch and other humanists.

Scholasticism and the Historical Purposes of the Humanists

The revival of humanistic studies by Petrarch and Boccaccio in the mid-14th century had its immediate roots in an Italian protohumanism, but it was also a reaction against scholasticism. That, fundamentally, this reaction was against contemporary 14th-century Italian tendencies in scholasticism, Paul Kristeller has made abundantly evident. It is equally apparent that the major development of the great 13th-century scholastic theologies at the northern universities of Paris and Oxford tended to cut off Italian humanism from the medieval classical and rhetorical traditions. Both factors contributed to the self-awareness of the early humanists and led them to regard themselves as having something particularly significant and revolutionary to contribute to civilization in their time. However persistent and intermittently strong the Latin rhetorical tradition had been in the Christian Latin west from the 6th to the 12th centuries, it was the consensus of the humanists both that they desired and that they could establish a more genuinely antique program of studies.

Certain historians have with reason regarded the great influx of Aristotelian and other Greek scientific, logical, and metaphysical texts into the Latin west during the 12th and 13th centuries, together with the establishment of the universities and the development of scholastic procedures, as the true, or first, revival of learning and the only cultural renaissance of major significance in European history. In part this judgment has been evoked by the seeming excesses of the Italian humanists' apprehension and evaluation of their own historical role. Thirteenth-century scholasticism, nourished by the translations from Arabic and Greek and centered in the universities, did, indeed lay the foundations of systematic, orderly, logical, and internally self-correcting thought, establishing the principal communities of organized intellectual activity that together have been so vital in highly organized, scientifically oriented modern civilization. By mid-14th century, when the humanist movement was on the threshold of a rapid and solid development, university-centered intellectual activity and professional research and training were already well-established, powerful institutions and enduring elements of culture.

In the face of this preexistent situation, the humanists, beginning with Petrarch, sought to bring about and, in fact, accomplished four essential aims: First, they wished to establish literary and historical scholarship (the humanities) as a respectable and valued learned profession with a place in the scheme of higher education and organized intellectual activity. Second, they wished to assert the importance of their kind of studies in the education of the layman, as distinguished from the highly trained professional; as professionals themselves they wished to maintain a close and friendly relationship with the educated laity. Third, and closely connected with the second aim, they wished to claim for their disciplines a special moral and civic importance by the eloquent presentation of broad truths of human experience as gathered from the study of literature and history and from esthetic inspiration. Moreover, this moral vocation might best be effected through the active employment of their particular learned skills in the service of the community or the body politic. Fourth, they themselves possessed in varying degree a sense of historical and cultural identity, which they wished to propagate among others, feeling that men should be conscious of their own time and culture in relation to their own past traditions and to the cultures and traditions of other peoples and religions. Along with this went an insistence on the importance of an individual's own sense of identity and of his achievement, his striving after fame.

It is impossible to say exactly why these underlying purposes, so vaguely held during the time of quickening medieval interest in classical studies, came to fruition with the Italian humanists. The period of high scholasticism was marked (as Panofsky suggests) by a "passion" for clarification combined with synthesis, or "concordance of opposites." The Aristotelian logic of classification embodied in the very schema of organization and procedure of the scholastic *Summae,* together with the use of dialectic to explain away apparent discrepancies by consideration of time, place, speaker, occasion, purpose, and so on, were the effective instruments of this passion. The resulting image of the universe, with its clearly defined, hierarchically subordinated and articulated place for every type of being and activity, denied the status the humanists sought for themselves. More important, it was the encyclopedic, abstract, logic-based, unhistorical, and impersonal character of this image that most seemed to offend the humanists.

It is perfectly true that such medieval Franciscans as St. Bonaventura and Duns Scotus sought to reassert an Augustinian mysticism that would leave scope for personal spirituality, and subsequently some of the humanists expressed themselves in ways more sympathetic to St. Augustine. It is also true that the logical-analytical procedures of the scholastics had more in common with the grammatical-syntactical analysis of texts by humanists than the latter cared to recognize. The Ockhamists in the 14th century not only disintegrated the vast Thomistic synthesis by their demonstration that the universal categories essential to its metaphysical structure could be examined primarily as problems in terminology, but they also focused discussion on the analysis of language and on a syntactical logic, thus dealing with philosophical texts in a way that was analogous to the humanists' treatment of literary, rhetorical, and historical texts. Moreover, the effect of nominalism was to reduce all intellectual activities and theories to the same level, since a metaphysical hierarchy of values could no longer have a logical or an epistemological status. In Ockham's view religious knowledge rested ultimately on the individual's own faith. Although these late scholastics never expressed it, there was in nominalism an implied historical and cultural relativism of the sort the humanists came to favor. It was without doubt the highly technical language and mode of discussion of these *moderni* that kept Petrarch from becoming aware of these implications and which led him to regard the influence of Ockham and the British "barbarians" with such disdain.

The highly specialized and professional character of the university curriculum in Trecento Italy was in itself an additional incentive to humanistic studies. There was no theological faculty dominating the scene, as in the French and English universities. Some theological courses were offered in the arts faculty, but theological training was largely in the hands of provincial schools established by the two leading mendicant orders, the Franciscans and the Dominicans, who utilized the *Summae* and other writings of their great 13th-century brothers as texts for study. The dominant university faculties at such centers as Pavia, Padua, and Bologna were those of arts and of law. Medical education was under the jurisdiction of the arts faculty, and part of the course of training involved the study of Aristotelian logic and natural philosophy, the chief occasion for laymen (though as part of a course of professional training) to study philosophy. Prominent among the texts studied and analyzed were the writings of Avicenna and of Averroës, particularly the latter's commentaries on such Aristotelian works as the *Physics, Metaphysics,* and *De anima.* It was this practice that gave rise to the charge of heresy and "Averroism" on the part of Petrarch and other humanists. It was in fact the highly intricate methods of the Aristotelians' discussions of questions involving the nature of man and the goals of human existence as well as the "pure" character of these discussions (i.e., not applied to theological and ethical exposition and doctrine), which offended the humanists. The very great historical importance of these Italian Aristotelians (misnamed "Averroists") of the 14th through the 16th centuries is becoming increasingly recognized through the work of Bruno Nardi, John Herman Randall, Jr., and other scholars. Moreover, the views of the Aristotelian Pomponazzi in the early 16th century concerning the nature of man were such as some humanists might have reconciled to their own if they had accepted the source.

Historical Origins of Italian Humanism

It is in the context of the study of law at the Italian universities, however, that the historical origins of Italian humanism become most concrete. The enormous importance of the legal profession in the economic and political life of the expanding Italian communes cannot be exaggerated. The quickening legal studies from the time of Pepo in the late 11th and Irnerius in the 12th centuries had not only drawn a flood of ambitious young men away from other professions and studies (including literature) to law courses, but had made possible an organized and orderly regularization of the burgeoning commercial economies of the cities. The law courses had provided a corps of trained civil servants for the expanding governments of the cities to draw upon, and leading legal commentators had ultimately adapted the precepts of Roman law (both private and public) to the needs of a different civilization. The autonomous self-government of the cities, achieved "illegitimately" from former feudal overlords (usually the Holy Roman Emperor), was given legal justification by such jurists as Bartolus of Sassoferrato. Adjunct to the advocate and judge was the notary, trained also by the law faculties of Bologna and elsewhere, who had important functions in drawing up legally viable contracts and instruments, both commercial and governmental. The influence and prominence of the legal and notarial professions are attested by the fact that the guild of Giudici e Notai (Judges and Notaries) was among the seven dominant guilds (*arti maggiori*) in Florence by the middle of the 13th century. Physicians trained at the arts faculties and lawyers and notaries trained at the law faculties of the universities were the first learned lay professionals of the Middle Ages. Moreover the legal profession developed a branch within the Church in the parallel emergence of a canon law utilizing concepts and procedures of the Roman law, a response to the increasingly organized, bureaucratic character of the expanding ecclesiastical hierarchy. Not only in Italy but also in northern

Europe, the popularity of legal study contributed to a decline in rhetorical-classical studies in the 12th and 13th centuries.

An important subject that traditionally had been closely associated with law, indeed had been the mother of law in the earlier Middle Ages, was the *ars dictandi,* or *ars dictaminis,* the rhetorical study of letter writing. Under the influence of the strongly practical and professional bent of the 12th- and 13th-century emergence of Roman law and the medieval jurist and notary, the *àrtes dictandi* as taught at the universities were reformed by purging them of their emphasis on classical Latin style in imitation of Quintilian and Cicero. Because of men like Buoncompagno in Bologna, this originally humanistic subject was subordinated to the practical needs of the legal professions. On the other hand, the study of the Code and the Digest could not help prompting an interest in Roman civilization and moral philosophy on the part of many jurists.

The birth of humanism in the 14th century was in a sense a rebirth of literary and classical rhetoric as a profession—a rebirth that recognized the aegis of the legal profession, out of which it was emerging, while it criticized and rejected the strongly utilitarian and anticlassical character it had acquired during its tutelage to the law. Among the so-called "prehumanists" of Italy were men of the generation born about 1260, active in the closing decades of the 13th and in the first quarter of the 14th centuries. Centered in Padua, Verona, and Vicenza in the north, and at Arezzo and Florence in Tuscany, many of these men were students of the *ars dictaminis,* or notaries, lawyers, or judges. Many were active in governmental affairs— Lovato dei Lovati (1241–1309), Albertino Mussato (1261–1329) and Geremia da Montagnone (ca. 1260–1321), all of Padua; even earlier Brunetto Latini (ca. 1220–94), notary, communal orator, commentator on and translator of Cicero's *De inventione,* and Dante's teacher at Florence; Francesco da Barberino (1264–1348), Florentine jurist; Geri d'Arezzo (ca. 1270–ca. 1339), *advocatus communis* at Florence. Their reputations and their surviving writings reveal a revived interest in the classical authors, with attempts to write letters, moral dialogues, Latin poems, tragedies modeled on Seneca, and histories, all in imitation of antiquity. In 1321 Giovanni del Virgilio of the Paduan circle, who exchanged poetic epistles with Dante and wrote his epitaph, was appointed to lecture on Latin poetry at the University of Bologna. While these men, and others like them, were not fullfledged humanists, it is significant that they were laymen, not clerics, and that they aroused the interest and support of prominent lay circles and of ruling families such as the Carraras in Padua and the Angevins in Naples.

The newly developing taste for the study and imitation of classical Latin poetry, history, and morality within the legal professions may well have been stimulated by the very nature of attempts to interpret and apply the Roman legal Code and the Digest of the Roman jurists to the juridical problems of their own age. At the same time there was a renewed interest in classical studies in certain ecclesiastical circles. The cathedral chapter at Verona, whose library possessed a superb collection of 9th-century classical manuscripts, was the setting for the activities of several scholars. The outstanding figure in the first quarter of the Trecento was Giovanni Mansionario, who made a critical use of corrupted classical texts in composing his *Historia imperialis,* and whose most striking work was the *Adnotatio de duobus Pliniis,* demonstrating the existence of and differences between the two Plinys who had previously been confused as one.

The papal court, removed to Avignon in 1309, was the most important ecclesiastical center for reviving classical studies. Among those drawn to this interest were certain Italian clerics who had close connections with the Angevin court of Robert, king of Naples, which was in turn linked with the Florentine circle of legal humanists during the sojourn of Robert's son Charles, the duke of Calabria, in Florence as Signore in 1326–27. The father of Petrarch, Pietro di Parenzo, or Ser Petracco (a Florentine notary before he was forced to flee in 1302), who had himself been interested in Cicero and had commissioned the famous Milan manuscript of Vergil later possessed by his son, settled in Avignon in 1312. Petrarch acquired many friends and patrons with a taste for the classics among the Avignon clerics: such men as Raymond Subirani, Giovanni Cavallini, and most importantly Cardinal Giovanni Colonna. Another Avignon churchman, who commented on Boethius and Seneca, was the English Dominican Nicholas Trevet. Moreover, the Augustinian Dionigi da Borgo San Sepolcro, whose gift of Augustine's *Confessiones* Petrarch treasured, composed important commentaries on Latin authors such as Valerius Maximus and traveled back and forth between Avignon and Naples. A further important feature of this Franco-Italian connection in the development of humanism was the link with the earlier 12th- and 13th-century French tradition of humanistic studies, particularly through the accessibility of library collections of classical authors, such as the Sorbonne library utilized by Petrarch. Moreover, Dionigi da Borgo San Sepolcro lectured at Paris prior to 1329, and another friend of Petrarch, the Florentine Roberto de' Bardi, was a professor and subsequently chancellor of the university from 1336 to 1349.

Petrarch as Chief Founder of Humanism

The historical origins of Renaissance humanism were multifarious and obscure, with definite roots in the medieval past. Its basic character, however, was established not by these anticipatory currents and lesser forerunners but by the strongly defined character, single-minded energy, genius, and inspiring influence of Petrarch (Francesco Petrarca, 1304–74). Although some of those who came shortly after him were aware of the importance of men like Mussato and Geri d'Arezzo, to most humanists he alone was founder of their studies and chief reviver of antique literary eloquence. Unlike most of his successors, who were teachers in schools or universities or held established positions in the service of republics, princes, or the papacy, Petrarch (along with his friend Boccaccio) was a free-lance writer, only on rare occasions performing a service for a patron, able to devote himself fully to his studies, discovering and propagating the texts, literary styles, and notions of the classical Latin authors. A student of law at Montpellier and Bologna, he abandoned this profession at his father's death. His income, which was considerable, derived from a number of ecclesiastical benefices, which he did not personally serve. Ordained to minor clerical orders, he lived and thought as a layman. His success despite the lack of a profession is evidence not only of the great impression his devotion to humanism made on his contemporaries but of the high value that classical studies already had among churchmen and the lay rulers who sought his friendship and supported him.

Unable or unready to appreciate Dante, his great predecessor as an Italian poet, Petrarch himself was not primarily valued for his Italian lyrics until the late 15th century. He regarded his historical study of the achievements of the Romans, *De viris illustribus,* and his Latin epic poem on Scipio Africanus, *Africa,* as his most important writings. When he was crowned with laurel at the Capitol in Rome in 1341, it was as a Latin poet and historian. His search for works of the classical authors for his collection was important as a future example, although the Paduan and Veronese protohumanists had also looked for classical manuscripts. The fact that these humanists "discovered" not originals but medieval copies of the classics in medieval and monastic libraries should not detract from the importance of these finds, since it was in this way that long-forgotten works were restored to circulation and many copies were made, ensuring their transmission to the modern world with their incorporation into the extant body of ancient writings available for study and enjoyment. Petrarch also contributed significantly to the spreading interest in humanism in his letters.

His outlook on life was fundamentally Christian and in many respects medieval. By no means a profound thinker or in any strict sense a philosopher, Petrarch was, nevertheless, a man of uniquely independent and original mind, whose attitudes, developed and elaborated by succeeding humanists, typified Italian humanism. He himself was heavily dependent on Livy, Cicero, and Seneca and on those late-classical, Ciceronian-Christian, Roman thinkers, Lactantius and St. Augustine. But, as is true in all humanists, his thought cannot be tightly linked with a single school or tendency. Even where there was a close identity, as with those influenced by Neoplatonism, Renaissance humanists used their sources eclectically in their synthesis of classical and Christian elements.

Perhaps it was the completeness of Petrarch's self-revelation which made his life and thought so much a model for emerging humanism and which has led modern historians to find in him in so many ways the key to understanding the Renaissance. Although there had been strikingly acute analyses of moral motivation on the part of medieval Christian thinkers such as Gregory I's *Regula pastoralis,* Bernard of Clairvaux's *De gradibus humilitatis,* Bonaventura's *De triplici via,* these treatments were general in nature rather than highly personal and autobiographical. Petrarch's *Secretum* properly went back to the late-classical Christian work, the *Confessiones* of St. Augustine. Yet Petrarch departs from both the classical and the medieval Christian spirit by viewing himself as confronted by the demands of both Christian religious authority and classical moral authority, blended together in the dialogue in the role of Augustinus, who is not the saint of the *Confessiones* (whose vicissitudes Petrarch more closely identifies with his own in the role of Franciscus) but the voice of Christian orthodoxy speaking in the language of Seneca's stoicism and preaching rational control of one's emotions, on the model of the *De tranquillitate animi.* Petrarch was able to view himself in a highly subjective way, in detachment from history and culture, which he viewed objectively. He saw himself faced with the problem of making an intellectual and artistic achievement worthy of the admiration of posterity while at the same time living in accord with both classical moral wisdom and Christian revelation. This characteristically modern outlook, which combined a strong sense of subjective selfhood (a result of the Christianization of European culture) with an externalized conception of history and society, was manifested in his *Epistle to Posterity,* letters to classical authors, *De vita solitaria,* and elsewhere.

Petrarch originated the concept of the "Dark Ages," viewing European history from the 5th century to his own time not as the transfer of the Roman Empire to German-Christian successors, but as the residue of a decline and fall of a once great civilization. It was the task of his own day to recapture the virtue, and thus the glory, of the Roman past. Whatever romanticism about antiquity and distortion of plain facts of medieval history may be involved in this value judgment, in it must be recognized the humanists's conception of their own age as a renaissance, attained, or programmatically to be attained, through the recapture of a true understanding of classical antiquity and through a reshaping of the present in accord with antique esthetic, moral, and political values.

Consistent with a more objective consideration of history—more objective despite Petrarch's admiration of the antique and censure of the medieval—was a new view of man as striving to attain virtue on the antique model although faced with the vicissitudes of fortune. Indeed, history in different ages has been the result of striving or not striving for virtue. But for Petrarch virtue is not merely moral and is no longer the Christian state of grace as Augustine and the Middle Ages viewed it; it is, rather, the sum total of the individual's resolve to leave his mark on his time, to combat fortune with his achievements, whether military and political, as in the case of his hero Scipio Africanus and other illustrious Romans; literary, as in the case of Vergil, Livy, and Cicero; or piety in living, as in the case of St. Augustine or even Petrarch's own brother Gherardo and his fellow Carthusian monks. These ideas permeate the treatises and letters (setting the style for his successors), but they were especially emphasized in Petrarch's *De viris illustribus, Africa, De remediis utriusque fortunae,* and *De vita solitaria.*

It is essential to stress, moreover, that Petrarch, however much he admired the classical Roman, or Ciceronian, outlook, never failed to recognize that it was not Christian. His view of the relationship of the Roman pagans to Christianity, in fact his conception of the historical role of the Renaissance humanist, is most clearly expressed in *De sui ipsius et multorum ignorantia.* Here, turning the slur that was so wounding to an old man's retrospective image of himself—"Petrarch is a good man but not very learned"—into a defense of the moral earnestness of humanism and an attack on the amoral erudition of the contemporary Aristotelians at the universities, he again set the pattern for subsequent humanist polemic against the study of natural philosophy in the medical course. (Petrarch also composed *Invectivarum contra medicum quendam libri.*) Charging that Aristotle may give an intellectual comprehension of virtue but cannot produce a motivation for a good life, and averring that "it is better to will the good than to know the truth," Petrarch asserts: "He teaches what virtue is, I do not deny that; but his lesson lacks the words that sting and set afire and urge toward love of virtue and hatred of vice. . . . He who looks for that will find it in our Latin writers, especially in Cicero and Seneca, and, what may be astonishing to hear, in Horace, a poet somewhat rough in style but most pleasing in his maxims." He wrote, "If to admire Cicero means to be a Ciceronian, I am a Ciceronian. . . . However, when we come to think or speak of religion, that is, of supreme truth and true happiness, and of eternal salvation, then I am certainly not a Ciceronian, or a Platonist, but a Christian."

Petrarch's relationship to and influence on the visual arts in his own lifetime was small but significant. He was a friend of Simone Martini, owned a painting by him, and commissioned from him a neoclassical scene including Aeneas, Vergil, and Servius to illustrate the frontispiece of the Vergil made for his father. An ardent admirer of the paintings of Giotto, Petrarch possessed a Madonna by the painter. In subsequent generations Petrarch's works, especially his *Trionfi,* were to inspire numerous representations; one of the writings from the last years of his life provided the theme and the details for a large fresco, which was actually executed under his direct supervision. Toward 1367 he was commissioned by Francesco Carrara (il Vecchio), duke of Padua, to complete his *De viris illustribus* and to prepare a compendium of it. The figures of Roman statesmen and military leaders whom Petrarch felt worthy of emulation were then represented on the walls of a room of the palace which was known as the Sala Virorum Illustrium. Beneath each figure was a scene from Petrarch's biography in which antique Roman buildings formed the background. The figures in the scene, however, wore 14th-century costume. In these paintings the combination of classical form and content present in some of Petrarch's writings was only partially manifested. By 1379 Petrarch's history was completed by Lombardo della Seta, whose portrait was included along with Petrarch's in the Sala. The paintings, variously attributed to Altichiero, Jacopo Avanzo, Guariento, and Ottaviano Prandino, were destroyed by fire about 1500; knowledge of them derives from a contemporary manuscript copy (Darmstadt, Landesbibliothek, Cod. 101). This series made a decisive break from the medieval-feudal tradition of representing the *Neuf Preux* (Nine Worthies), an assortment of classical and medieval heroes, on walls and tapestries in the houses of the prominent and set a precedent for other Italian examples of halls of famous men of a more strictly classical and humanistic provenance.

Boccaccio, Salutati, and the Consolidation of Humanism

The most important link between Petrarch's pioneering phase of humanism and its later development as a widely diffused, increasingly favored cultural movement in the Quattrocento was Giovanni Boccaccio (1313–75). The fact that both Petrarch and Boccaccio were equally important as authors of vernacular literature and as humanists (i.e. classical Latin scholars and authors) contributed enormously to the influence and prestige of humanism itself. The relationship between authorship in the vernacular and in Latin was complex and, as Petrarch's attitude toward Dante shows, sometimes hostile, but it no longer seems possible to emphasize, as historians once did, the opposition between the two traditions. Instead there is increasingly convincing evidence of the continuous association and mutual support of the history of Italian literature and the development of the humanist movement.

Boccaccio's Italian tales and *novelle,* and especially, of course, *The Decameron,* indicate the growth of a secular outlook in a lay audience of the middle and upper classes in urban Italy. It was the same social element whose enthusiastic acceptance of the values and activities of the humanists and whose taste for a revival of classical antiquity ensured the great vogue for humanism and its penetration into almost every aspect of culture including, most significantly, the visual arts. Both Petrarch and Boccaccio made contributions of specific and practical importance to the artist who was called upon to depict a classical scene or an antique deity. Although the writings of Vergil and Ovid as well as various late-classical and medieval collections were available as iconographical sources, the third canto of Petrarch's *Africa* (verses 138–262) gave a succinct and visual description of the pagan deities with a concentration on essentials that especially appealed to the artist. Boccaccio's lengthier and more encyclopedic *De genealogia deorum,* with its literal, moral, and allegorical interpretations, its undiscriminating dependence on classical and medieval compendiums, was, nevertheless, the most important handbook of mythology until the appearance in the mid-16th century of L. G. Giraldi's *De deis gentium,* Natale Conti's *Mythologiae,* and Vincenzo Cartari's *Le imagini degli dei.* Equally popular and influential were Boccaccio's collections of biographies, *De claris mulieribus* and *De casibus virorum illustrium,* which repeated in a less profound way Petrarch's theme of the conflict of virtue and fortune. Boccaccio also contributed to the restoration of ancient texts, most notably a manuscript of the *Annals* and the *Histories* of Tacitus, which he found at the monastery of Monte Cassino.

It was Boccaccio's prestige as a citizen and resident of Florence that led to the appointment of Coluccio Salutati (1331–1406) as chancellor, or Latin secretary, of the Florentine Republic in 1375. Salutati, trained as a notary at Bologna, by his signal contribution as a humanist to Florentine public affairs created the precedent and demand for appointing humanists as chancellors, secretaries, and writers in the employ of the major states of Italy. With the great prestige that accrued to Florence through the state papers and official correspondence written by Salutati, particularly in connection with the struggles with the papacy and with Milan under the Visconti, Florentine rulers saw the value of continuing to employ humanists as chancellors after the death of Salutati. In the course of the Quattrocento, Milan, Naples, Venice, the papal *curia,* and many of the lesser signorial courts followed suit. While the entrance of Ciceronian Latin into the major Italian chanceries, and the vogue for stating the case of a particular power in terms of Roman precedent must assume the prior growth of a state of mind to which such appeals would seem persuasive, this development was strategic for the further influence and cultural dominance of humanism. Not only did the prestige and emoluments of office make a humanistic career seem a lucrative one, but even more attractive was the fact that humanists were placed in positions to advise the powerful and wealthy to undertake major scholarly, educational, architectural, and artistic programs. The major impact of humanism on the arts may be dated from the establishment of such connections.

The advancing influence and prestige of humanism during the generation of Salutati may also be seen in the provision of facilities for the education of humanists and for the propagation of humanism. While the minor practitioners of the *studia humanitatis* in the generation of Petrarch and Boccaccio and in that of Salutati may not be discounted, even though they have not been adequately studied, certain more important figures formed a link between the work of Petrarch and Boccaccio and the brilliant generation of the first third of the Quattrocento, particularly in the two centers of Padua and Florence. Giovanni Conversino da Ravenna (1343–1408), wandering teacher of the humanities, was professor of rhetoric at the University of Padua in 1392 and twice chancellor of Padua (1379–82 and 1393–1404). His pupils included many leading humanists of the early Quattrocento. Gasparino da Barzizza (1359–1431), professor of rhetoric at Padua (1397–1421), was succeeded by his protege, Vittorino da Feltre (1373–1446). Barzizza maintained an important private school for humanists during these years. Giovanni Malpaghini da Ravenna (1346–1417), Petrarch's copyist, who was active as a teacher in the north, was appointed professor of rhetoric at the University of Florence (ca. 1395). Luigi Marsili (ca. 1330–94), Augustinian monk as well as correspondent and friend of Petrarch, established a circle for the discussion and study of the humanities at the Monastery of Santo Spirito in Florence. A similar but more distinctly lay and social group met at the villa of a leading Florentine, Antonio degli Alberti. Such men as these propagated the learned skills and spiritual enthusiasm which sustained the new generation.

The striking fact is that several means of giving practical support to a new profession, linked to the medieval past but distinct in character, were well established by the beginning of the 15th century. Humanism, as a profession, had now been permanently established in four institutions: in the civil service and emerging diplomatic service of the Italian states (the common word for envoy was *orator*); in education, with university appointments in poetry, eloquence, and sometimes moral philosophy, as teachers or directors of communal or private schools, or as private tutors; in ecclesiastical or monastic centers, where churchmen enamored of the humanities studied or gave support and blessing; in princely courts and private households, where the wealthy and powerful frequently were not only patrons but practitioners of these studies.

Another fundamental achievement of the generation of Salutati was the establishment of the study of ancient Greek on a sufficiently solid basis for it to become part of the normal education of a humanist and for the study and translation of Greek literature to be a normal activity of the Italian humanist. Facility in Greek in the Latin west during the Middle Ages, and into the 14th century, was perhaps more widespread than was once assumed, but at its best, it was regarded as (and in fact was) an exceptional feat, thanks to which a considerable number of Greek scientific and metaphysical texts had been translated directly from the Greek by westerners, mainly Italians, although some came from the north (William of Moerbeke).

With the appointment of Manuel Chrysoloras to the University of Florence in 1397, his subsequent teaching in northern Italy, and the advent of a long series of Byzantine Greek teachers in the first half of the Quattrocento (as well as after 1453), the linguistic barrier to full knowledge of the extant works of classical antiquity was breached. While this was to have its initial impact on the literary, historical, and moral-philosophical interests of the humanists, and on humanistic circles of both clergy and laity who eagerly translated the Greek patristic writings, the more traditional university subjects of logic, metaphysics, and natural philosophy also benefited from the spreading capacity to study original Greek texts. Near the end of the Quattrocento, Politian, introducing his university course on Homer, boasted that the Attic tongue, torn from its own soil by barbarians, now echoed in the mouths of youths of the most noble families of Florence. Between the faltering efforts of Petrarch and Boccaccio to acquire the language and the common study of Greek literature as a university subject, the appointment of Chrysoloras was the most important step.

By the 15th century humanism had evolved, not into an old profession with new style, tastes, and standards, but into a new group of scholarly and creative literary activities which was based on a tradition of learning and education that reached back at least to the Greek Sophists but which had also acquired an outlook and contemporary flavor that distinguished it from all historical precedents. The men who carried on these activities, which they called *studia humanitatis,* did so for the sake of literary creation and advancement of learning in these fields as well as for carrying on their several professions. Their motives were both pure, in devotion to their disciplines through which they hoped to contribute to moral or civic well-being, and impure, in seeking and welcoming rewards for creative efforts or paid employment for particular learned skills. In the fluid situation during the Renaissance, these elements were continually changing. Beginning with the new generation of the early 1400s, ideas concerning the content of the *studia humanitatis* underwent a change. In the 14th century the *studia* comprised a varying list, but it was mainly thought of as poetry and eloquence, or rhetoric. University appointments were usually for studies titled "Poetry and Eloquence," and such listings continued into the 15th century. Moral philosophy was occasionally designated as a subject. History also was mentioned as when Petrarch was crowned poet-laureate. Paul Kristeller, who perhaps wishes to emphasize the traditional professional character of the *studia humanitatis* more than their diffuse practice seems to justify, has cited the license granted to Petrarch by King Robert of Naples: "for reading [or teaching], disputing and interpreting the ancient writers both in the said poetic discipline and in the said historical discipline *and* [italics added] for himself composing new [or modern] books and poetry," a document which is accurately descriptive of the activities of the humanist. Thus there was, and there continued to be, an important distinction between the interpretation of classical literature (in this case poetry and history are specified) and the composition of modern works in these genres. Both activities, the scholarly and the creative, are comprised in the *studia humanitatis.* Ordinarily history was subsumed as a branch of rhetoric, following Cicero's conception.

From the early Quattrocento frequently not two but five *studia,* which may be taken as ultimately definitive of humanism, were specified: grammar, including not only usage and sentence structure of the Latin language and of Greek, but philological and historical interpretation of all texts; rhetoric, the study of stylistic and literary aspects of all genres of texts by ancient authors as well as composition of orations and letters; history, increasingly separated from rhetoric and including both study of ancient historians and the writing of historical works about the classical and the recent past; poetry, study of Roman and Greek poets and composition of Latin verse; moral philosophy, including study, exposition, and interpretation of the moral thought of Cicero, Seneca, Aristotle, and other ancient writers and composition of numerous treatises on the ethical, domestic, and civic life of man. Thus by the Quattrocento it is possible to arrive at a full definition of humanism according to the professional activities in which the humanists engaged and the disciplines they claimed. This definition, as was proposed, is historical and empirical, but while it is fundamental, it is too formal to be completely satisfactory. However, efforts to go beyond this, although essential, inevitably become involved in the controversial character of the historical and philosophical interpretations not only of Renaissance humanism but of the Renaissance itself. The interpretations which follow are based on recent studies which seem most significant to the author as well as most relevant for an understanding of the relationship of humanism to art. It must be borne in mind that humanism was a most complex historical phenomenon: not only did the humanists attempt to combine in shifting patterns their pursuit of scholarly and creative literary disciplines with their employment in both traditional medieval and newly developed institutional situations, but they also attempted to apply a variety of classical moral-philosophical and literary-esthetic positions to the problems of their times. All this made for polemic and controversy within the humanist movement and between its members and other groups and individuals—that was begotten not only by jealousies and professional rivalries but also by genuine intellectual and artistic disagreement. Moreover, there was quite clearly a vitality among the humanists, a sense of mission that related itself in a complicated way to the many other historical currents of the Renaissance. Furthermore, the relationship of humanism and humanists to religion, so firmly established both as an institution and in popular conviction in western Christendom, was inevitably highly controversial, however daringly new or devotedly pious a humanist considered his ideal to be. In addition to the question of how the *studia humanitatis* agreed or clashed with religion and clergy was the question of the humanists' relationship with the increasingly powerful lay forces of their time. What should be remembered, though frequently forgotten, is that humanism must inevitably be studied individual by individual, generation by generation, region by region, and aspect by aspect.

Representative Humanists
of 15th-Century Italy

It is beyond the scope of this discussion to deal in detail with the subsequent history of humanism; certain broad lines only can be suggested. The 15th century marked its high point, and its development falls into three roughly defined periods corresponding loosely to the period of maturity of three generations. The first generation, initiated into humanism under the influence of the contemporaries of Salutati, included many notable figures. One such was Niccolò Niccoli (1364–1437), the wealthy Florentine collector of manuscripts and antiquities, who left no writing himself but had nonetheless a profound influence on the cultivation of a taste for the literature and art of antiquity among the upper classes of Florence and created an important library of classical works. Another, Pier Paolo Vergerio (1370–1444), was a student of Conversino, Chrysoloras, and Malpaghini and a friend of Salutati and Bruni. Vergerio was active in Florence, Padua, and Verona, serving as secretary to Innocent VII, and to Cardinal Zabarella at the Council of Constance. Later he was court orator to the emperor Sigismund. Vergerio died at Buda in 1444. Vittorino da Feltre and Guarino da Verona (1370–1460), as founders of important humanistic schools at Mantua, Verona, and Ferrara, were responsible for the spread of humanism at the courts and in lay circles of northern Italy. Vergerio, Vittorino, and Guarino's son Battista wrote important treatises delineating the humanist educational ideals. Perhaps of greater stature was Leonardo Bruni (1374–1444), who gave long service as chancellor of the city of Florence, and whose works included important translations from the Greek (Plato, Demosthenes, Plutarch, Aristotle, St. Basil), historical writings that ranged from plagiarizing quasi translations of the ancients to histories of his own time that were outstandingly original, treatises on the *studia humanitatis,* and defenses of Florentine republicanism that prove him unquestionably the principal so-called "civic humanist." Poggio Bracciolini (1380–1459), long apostolic secretary and at the end of his life Florentine chancellor, was the most important discoverer of classical manuscripts, principally in European monasteries. His moral treatises show a sharp and critical view of the institutions and mode of life of his time. Most important to art historians is the description of Roman ruins in his *De varietate fortunae.* Poggio was apparently one of the few humanists to be genuinely sensitive to the esthetic values of antique monuments rather than prizing them as historical and literary documentation. Ambrogio Traversari (1386–1439) became prior of the Camaldolese Convent of S. Maria degli Angeli in Florence and turned it into a center for humanistic discussion of the sort Santo Spirito had been. He was the most important humanist translator of the Greek fathers and an active spirit in the attempt to reconcile the Greek Orthodox and Roman Catholic Churches at the Council of Basel-Ferrara-Florence. Krautheimer has shown the influence of Traversari's iconographical and religio-historical ideas in Ghiberti's Doors of Paradise. Traversari probably prepared the program of this Christian-humanist masterpiece.

The generation active in the middle years of the century overlapped, of course, with the older humanists of the preceding generation, which included many outstanding figures. Francesco Barbaro (1390–1454) was among the first of the prominent Venetians to become a classical scholar. Cyriacus of Ancona (Ciriaco de' Pizzicolli, 1391–ca. 1457) was not a scholar but a merchant and adventurer with a passion for traveling, who collected inscriptions and made remarkably accurate descriptions and drawings of ancient Roman and Greek monuments in the course of his wanderings in the eastern Mediterranean—Greece, the islands, and Asia Minor. His notebooks, which were of great importance for Renaissance artists, remain so today for classical archaeology. His depiction of the remains of the polyandrion in Delos, dated 1445, is among the earliest examples of 15th-century pictures of ruins. An archetype of the Renaissance explorer, "I go," said he, "to awaken the dead." The historian, geographer, and commentator on Roman antiquities, Flavio Biondo of Forlì (1392–1463), is also remembered for his attempts to collect Roman inscriptions. The Milanese humanist Pier Candido Decembrio (1392–1477) served for many years as chancellor of Milan under the Visconti, the republic of 1448, and the Sforzas. Antonio Beccadelli, called "Panormita" (1394–1471), a Latin poet and historian, worked in many centers of Italy but especially in Naples. Giannozzo Manetti (1396–1459), of a prominent Florentine family, had an outstanding reputation as an orator, was active as a statesman and diplomat, and was the author of important treatises revealing a combination of piety and thorough pride in human achievements, including those of his contemporaries. Manetti's *De dignitate et excellentia hominis* was a striking statement showing both a positive evaluation of the life and actions of man and a dependence on the views of Cicero and of Lactantius, the so-called "Christian Cicero." Manetti was an early Hebrew and Biblical scholar who translated the Psalter as well as the Greek New Testament. His life of Nicholas V is an important record of the building projects of this humanist pope.

Of even greater importance to the arts was, of course, Leon Battista Alberti who was not only the most influential art theorist of the 15th century and an outstanding Renaissance architect but an important exponent of humanist moral ideals. Alberti's role as a mediator between humanism and the arts will be dealt with below. Francesco Filelfo (1398–1481) had a long and checkered career as manuscript collector, translator, teacher, impetuous polemicist, and philologist. Enea Silvio Piccolomini (1405–64), known as Aeneas Sylvius, after a career as historian, geographer, orator, and diplomat became Pope Pius II (1458–64). An outstanding figure was Lorenzo Valla (1407–57), who wrote the most influential philological treatise of the Quattrocento, *Elegantiae linguae latinae*. Valla challenged traditional approaches to law, logic, history, theology, and ethics. His *De voluptate ac de vero bono* long gave him the reputation of being an epicurean and sensualist and therefore antireligious. Today however, despite its antirational and its historical emphasis, his philosophy is regarded as unquestionably Christian but uniquely original in its affirmation of the moral autonomy of the individual. Finally, there were three spokesmen of the Florentine ideal of the humanist civic-patriot: Carlo Marsuppini (1398–1453), Florentine chancellor after Bruni; Matteo Palmieri (1406–75), author of the *Della vita civile* and admired orator, who revived in his *Città di vita* the Origenist heresy, that mankind was created to replace the fallen angels; and Benedetto Accolti (1415–66), Florentine chancellor after Poggio, who maintained the superiority of his contemporaries over the ancients in his *Dialogus de praestantia virorum sui aevi*. There were, of course, hosts of other less important or little-known figures in both of these vigorous generations of humanists.

The last four decades of the Quattrocento saw humanism thoroughly established in court and literary circles in all parts of Italy—not only in Medicean Florence, the papal *curia,* the court of Alfonso V at Naples, in Sforza Milan, and at Venice, but in the minor princely courts of the Gonzaga at Mantua, the Este at Ferrara, the Malatesta at Rimini, and the Montefeltro at Urbino. Humanists were active as private tutors and as teachers in the schools and universities; as secretaries, orators, and diplomats; as consultants on classical mythology, tombs, inscriptions, and architecture; as court poets and historians. They were active in the service of states and of powerful individuals; they were available to assist men of lesser rank and wealth. Their methods and their historical and philological understanding of classical antiquity had become increasingly firm and professional; in many instances their standards approached those of modern scholarship.

In late Quattrocento humanism there were three chief developments. The first was the increasing integration of humanism, that is to say, classical scholarship, with literary composition in the vernacular. Politian, whose real name was Angelo Ambrogini (1454–94), was an outstanding scholar and commentator on Greek and Latin philosophical and literary texts and was highly regarded both as a Latin and as an Italian poet. Another such figure, active at the Neapolitan court, was Giovanni Pontano (1426–1503), whose Latin verse achieved a fusion of classical with modern Italian lyrical style. A similar figure in Naples was Jacopo Sannazzaro (1456–1530), author of the *Arcadia,* which was to inspire representations of pastoral life in late Renaissance art, and of *De partu virginis,* a poem in classical form and language on the life of the Virgin. The mingling of the traditions of classical scholarship and popular literature found such figures as Politian and, later, Pietro Bembo frequently serving as bridges to the visual arts.

The second, and almost dominant, development was the translation of Plato and the principal Neoplatonists by Marsilio Ficino (1433– 99), with the penetration of his characteristic version of Platonism into humanist circles not only in Florence but elsewhere in Italy. Prior to the vogue for Platonism there had been an interest in Aristotelian moral philosophy in Florence following the appointment of the Byzantine Aristotelian John Argyropoulos to the university in 1457. His pupil and follower Donato Acciaiuoli (1428–78), became a venerable image to the humanists of Ficino's day. Another Florentine Aristotelian, Alamanno Rinuccini (1419–99), who acquired a reputation as an orator and civic humanist, composed an anti-Medicean dialogue *De libertate.* Ficino's Neoplatonism will be discussed below in its relationship both to humanism and to the arts. In general the impact of Platonism, which Kristeller distinguishes from humanism, was to bring about not so much a literal adoption of Ficino's philosophy as a free adaptation of his allegorical interpretations and of many individual ideas. For instance, Cristoforo Landino (1424–1504) and Politian, who professed to act as humanist spokesmen of Neoplatonism, drew encouragement for the construction of a sort of Neoplatonic philology rather than a complete adherence to Ficino's philosophy. In some ways a more daring thinker than Ficino but in other respects less of a humanistic scholar and less important as a founder and expounder of Renaissance Platonism, Giovanni Pico della Mirandola (1463–94) followed the precedent of Giannozzo Manetti both in his interest in Hebrew and in his pronouncement on the dignity of man (*De hominis dignitate*). Both Ficino and Pico, who were exposed to scholastic Aristotelianism in their youthful studies, supplied, or attempted to supply, a much needed bridge between humanism and traditional scholastic and Christian thought.

The third development was the spread of the new invention of printing to Italy, and the rapid employment of the philological knowledge and skills of humanists as editors of classical texts. Not only did this provide a new means of support for the humanists, but it led to a further diffusion of humanist thinking and scholarship through their commentaries, which were frequently included with printed editions of the ancient writers. Printing also led to a shifting of the leading center of humanism from Florence to Venice toward the end of the century, because of the preeminence of the new printing trade in Venice and the particular encouragement given to humanists by the great Venetian printer, Aldus Manutius.

In the 16th century Venice, which managed for some time to maintain its prosperity and its grandeur despite the cataclysmic changes elsewhere in Italy, in Europe, and in the trade routes, came into its own as a center of art, literature, and humanism. But it was symbolic of the fate of Italian humanism in the age of its decline that the career of Venice's outstanding humanist and poet, Pietro Bembo (1470–1547), led him to the society of the Este court at Ferrara and the Montefeltro at Urbino, as well as to the Vatican. Not only was he an important literary exponent of the Neoplatonic doctrine of love, as in *Gli Asolani* and as portrayed by Baldassare Castiglione in the last book of *Il Cortegiano,* but he became perhaps the most ubiquitous humanist adviser of painters such as Giovanni Bellini, Raphael, and Titian. Bembo, like Jacopo Sadoleto (1477–1547) and Girolamo Aleandro (1480–1542), was one of the humanists whom Leo X, the first Medici pope, dignified as cardinals. Under the worldly rule of Alexander VI, Julius II, Leo X, and Clement VII, until the Sack of Rome (1527) and the onset of the Counter Reformation, Rome was a powerful magnet for humanists, who found themselves favored and in demand as advisers on the great artistic programs.

By 1500 humanism had become a European phenomenon. It is not possible to discuss the history of northern humanism here, except to indicate that after the great generation of Erasmus, Budé, Lefèvre d'Étaples, Colet, More, Reuchlin, and Vives, all intimately involved in the religious crosscurrents preceding the Reformation, there was a continuation of the humanist tradition in Europe at least into the 18th century. By reason of the similarity of their ideas and activities to those of Renaissance Italian humanists, many outstanding figures in the history of European culture may properly be thought of as belonging to the same tradition as the humanists, even though they are not ordinarily so designated: men such as Michel de Montaigne, Justus Lipsius, John Milton, and the Earl of Shaftesbury.

Because the Italian humanists of the late 14th, the 15th, and the early 16th centuries constituted a self-conscious movement of innovation, because they were centrally important in Renaissance culture, society, and politics, and in their influence on Renaissance art, and because of the formative character of their ideas and intellectual activities, the following discussion will concentrate on the humanist movement in the Quattrocento.

Moral and Religious Concerns of Humanism

There is more to humanism than is revealed in a historical consideration of the intellectual and professional activities of the humanists, more also than the extensive additions to western European knowledge of ancient Latin and Greek culture contributed by the humanists through their "second revival of learning." Almost to a man the humanists regarded themselves, or their studies, more as making a general contribution to the well-being of mankind than supplying an expert, encyclopedic knowledge of antiquity. In their emphasis on "letters" and "speech," on accurate and elegant diction, on precise historical and philological understanding of textual meanings, they were not merely asserting that the beauty and precision of what was said might sometimes render the statement more graciously acceptable or factually clearer. They were, or maintained they were, as interested in *what* was said as in *how* it was said.

It has been suggested that properly the humanists fall into the western rhetorical tradition that began with the Greek Sophists, was sustained by the Hellenistic rhetorical schools, was expanded by Cicero into the theoretical basis of Latin culture, and, adapted and adopted by the Latin Fathers, was passed on by medieval grammarians and rhetoricians in a series of renascences. But the principal spokesmen of this tradition rarely considered it to be concerned with forms alone. Definite claims to wisdom along with eloquence had been put forth from Protagoras on; Cicero had placed the knowledge of philosophy within the sphere of the orator; rhetoric in the Middle Ages had frequently been associated with "civil philosophy," and as late as the mid-14th century Jean Buridan in his commentary on Aristotle's *Ethics* considered moral philosophy to be closely connected with rhetoric, which he called *logica moralis.* Thus the humanists' assertion that the student of letters and eloquence was properly concerned with moral philosophy coincides with this tradition, and not only because ethics involves action to which eloquence moves men, as Petrarch suggested.

Besides the prose text, which could, as in orations and letters on the model of Cicero and Seneca, be directly rhetorical and persuasive; in histories, exemplify moral and political virtue and convey wisdom drawn from past human experience; or in treatises, bear directly upon man's ethical life; the humanists were deeply concerned with poetry. The medieval *ars dictaminis* had recognized both poetic (metrical and rhythmical) composition and prose, as well as a composite of the two. There had been a tendency toward a rhetorical conception and practice of poetry, which the humanists were to carry even further. But what seems most significant in the Trecento were the series of defenses of poetry by Mussato, Petrarch, Boccaccio, and Salutati, all setting forth an exalted conception of poetry as theological writing. In part this may have been a defense against clerical criticism of the study of pagan authors. In the case first of ancient Latin, and later on of Greek, poetry with its references to pagan deities and to amatory episodes (as well as modern Latin poetry composed in imitation of the ancients), the resort to theology through allegory may well seem necessary to escape censure. But it should also be remembered that the notion of a poetic theology, classical in origin, had prevailed throughout the Middle Ages until poetry was downgraded into a "lower discipline" by Thomas Aquinas and other scholastics. Thus, as E. R. Curtius has shown, the humanists sought to restore poetry's lost status.

Not only a reassertion of a traditional position was at stake, however. A wider claim was asserted: that divine knowledge and divine insight should be not a technical speciality of the university theologian but, as poetic theology would make it, accessible to others. According to Hans Baron, the humanists of the early Quattrocento turned against this "medieval" conception of their literary activities to a more worldly, direct service of the civic community. In fact there were two concurrent developments. In one, poetry and the *studia humanitatis* generally were assimilated to the Ciceronian rhetorical notion of letters as the instrument of civility or of *urbanitas,* with poetry serving the same utilitarian functions of persuasion, edification, and pleasure that writing in general possessed. In the other, as Dante's *Divine Comedy* became increasingly the subject of humanist study, the vernacular (and vernacular poetry) acquired equal acceptability with Latin, and Dante's opus, in accord with his own view of it, attained recognition as the classic example of poetic theology. In line with the first of these tendencies Horace's *Ars poetica* came more and more to be interpreted according to rhetorical canons from Cicero or Quintillian, a practice possibly not too alien to Horace's poem itself. Thus the 15th century would seem to have converted the earlier *theologia poetica* into *theologia rhetorica,* only to return later in the century (with Landino's *Commentary on the Divine Comedy,* as well as his study of Vergil, and with Pico's project of a *Poetic theology*) to a viewpoint not too dissimilar to that of Pierre Bersuire, in his *Ovide Moralisé.*

There are today three broad tendencies in the interpretation of humanism, each of which brings out a highly significant aspect of the movement but at the same time seems to place too severe restrictions on the other interpretations. One group of scholars (Douglas Bush, Augustin Renaudet, Giuseppe Toffanin, and their disciples) tends to see a primarily religious meaning in the rise of the *studia humanitatis,* emphasizing the reconciliation of Greek and Latin culture with Christianity and finding support for this view in the humanists' revival of patristic Christian thought and in their opposition to Aristotelian natural philosophers. In Toffanin's extreme view the humanists are the forerunners of the Counter Reformation. Another group strongly emphasizes what its members (Hans Baron, Eugenio Garin) call "civic humanism," or placing of the *studia humanitatis* at the service of the community, but they wish to confine this very important aspect of humanism to Florentine and Venetian republicanism, considering the fact that humanists also served in papal and princely courts as something of a perversion of their true vocation. To the humanists is attributed "the conscious design to break with tradition for the sake of a renewal which takes antique culture as the model which incarnated in paradigmatic form the ideal of the free man in the free city." (Eugenio Garin, *Il pensiero pedagogico dello umanesimo.*) The third group (Paul Oskar Kristeller, Walter Ruegg) prefers to see humanism rather strictly as the practice of the learned disciplines legitimated as *studia humanitatis;* but in its restraint, generated by the inclination of the first two to include only those aspects of humanism which fit their particular images, it risks a failure to grapple with the question of the broad significance of humanism in Renaissance culture generally and in the arts in particular. A broader view of humanism sees no necessary contradiction between these three tendencies and the possibility of genuine synthesis. For humanism did consist of the devotees of the *studia humanitatis,* who laid claim to special importance in a Christian culture where the ecclesiastical, legal, and medical professions had become technically proficient and overspecialized at the very time that laymen were acquiring a taste for learning and culture. This fact underlay the combination of religious, moral, and civic interests that humanists variously found to be coherent aspects of their literary and rhetorical studies. As Salutati replied to the criticisms of Giovanni Dominici, "Connexa sunt humanitatis studia; connexa sunt et studia divinitatis, ut unius rei sine alia vera completaque scientia non possit haberi" ("Both the *studia humanitatis* and the *studia divinitatis* are so connected that true and complete knowledge of one cannot be gained without the other").

In understanding Renaissance humanism the significant distinction is between theory and practice and not between the contemplative and the active life. Much of the trouble and disagreement that exists in the interpretation of humanism derives from the fact that some humanists espoused the *vita contemplativa* while others urged the *vita activa.* Moreover, certain humanists saw the value of each as dependent upon circumstance, and certainly in their dialogues many of them were able to state the arguments for each very effectively. Petrarch, as has been seen, admired the illustrious Roman men of action, who were models for moral emulation; on the other hand, no humanist more eloquently and sincerely praised the values of contemplation than he in his *De vita solitaria* and *De otio religioso.*

But in both cases it was the attainment of moral wisdom, or prudence, for the sake of the good life that concerned him.

This sense of a moral vocation to guide their contemporaries in making the proper practical decisions on how to live virtuously was what drew men to the tradition of the *studia humanitatis* and attracted them particularly to the most thorough-going statement of the values of a philosophy of practice embodied in rhetoric, namely the writings of Cicero. Renaissance humanism cannot be understood without accepting as historical fact the genuine need of a more informal and practical basis for making decisions of a domestic, civil, or even spiritual nature than was afforded by the inherited institutional machinery of the Middle Ages. In the Renaissance towns, whether the government was republican or despotic, men of leisure or those engaged in business, administrative, or political activities found various images of life with which they could identify in the study of classical literature, oratory, poetry, and history that the humanists urged on them. The moral-philosophical aspects of humanism were therefore an essential ingredient in the emergence of a lay culture.

It was also essential that the emerging culture of the laity find a *modus vivendi* that did not stand in contradiction to the Catholic faith. The evidence is strong that, except during the religious upheavals of Savonarola and of the 16th century, the humanists were convinced that there was nothing intrinsically antireligious, heretical, or contrary to Christian morals in their studies and activities. But at many points, particularly when they were accused or challenged, they felt compelled to defend this view, to indicate the special moral role humanism might play, to criticize the inadequacy of traditional means of meeting the moral needs of the laity of the middle and upper classes. It was not accidental that they so consistently favored patristic statements of Christian views over medieval and contemporary scholastic and mendicant pronouncements, nor that both Leonardo Bruni, the most explicitly "civic" humanist, and Lorenzo Valla, who served under despots, could criticize the mendicant conception of moral behavior as living up to (or hypocritically seeming to live up to) ascetic vows and could advocate, instead, individual responsibility and reliance on conscience. Lorenzo's oration praising the historical role of the Roman Catholic Church in transmitting the Latin language and facilitating the revival of the *studia humanitatis* reveals his conviction that the Church and the humanists had a like responsibility for the moral and cultural conditions of mankind.

Humanism and Renaissance Platonism

It was conceptions such as these which, fusing classical ethics and the Biblical tradition, lent themselves to artistic representation. In many instances the programs of art works of the late Quattrocento and the early Cinquecento have been attributed to Neoplatonism; the existence of some of these ideas even in the writings of humanists prior to the publication of Ficino's works should be carefully examined to determine the relationship of Platonism to the purposes of the humanists. Particularly relevant is the often exalted conception of both the earthly achievements and the heavenly destiny of man that evolved among the humanists. It is quite clear that, while the humanists could not and did not separate their philosophies of man from the Christian relevation of his ultimate destiny, the tendency from the mid-Quattrocento on was to view human destiny as exclusively and ineluctably heavenly and glorious. Instead of an emphasis on the human in place of, or in preference to, the divine, there was a decided tendency to emphasize not only that human dignity rested in the fact that man was created in the image of God but that the perfection of humanity would be realized in equality with divinity. Valla in the third book of his *De voluptate* described the Christian's entry into the celestial life in the image of a triumph, and in his sermon *De mysterio Eucharistiae* he declared, "Nor is it only that He himself is more similar to us than to the angels. From this it may also be known that God reveals to pious and believing minds that, as he transforms that bread, so he will transform us in the day of judgment, into God." Giannozzo Manetti in *De dignitate et excellentia hominis* proclaimed that the incarnation would have occurred even if Adam had not sinned, "so that man, through this humble assumption of human flesh, might be miraculously and incredibly honored and glorified." It was not without precedent, then, that Ficino, thirty years after Valla and twenty after Manetti, said in his *De Christiana religione* concerning the incarnation, "the divine sublimity was not depressed to the human, as if by some defect, but rather the human was elevated to the divine."

From the time of Petrarch the underlying motive of the humanist movement, to achieve recognition of the *studia humanitatis* for the benefits they might be expected to confer on mankind, found expression in the defense of poetry for its allegorical-theological content and in the praise of rhetoric for its inherently moral or civic content. Both arguments implied, and were accompanied by, criticisms of scholastic subject matter and methods. When humanism had gained solid recognition at least from the established social, political, and ecclesiastical authorities by the mid-Quattrocento, the need to discover a doctrinal reconciliation with both the traditional scholastic Aristotelian outlook and with Christian theology—a reconciliation that would grant the fullest value to the classical studies of the humanists and to their views on the nature of man and society—became more pressing than the need to defend and criticize. Some, such as Acciaiuoli, sought this reconciliation in a new but not entirely unscholastic approach to Aristotle; to many, Ficino's approach to Platonism proved more acceptable.

Whatever richness and complexity Ficino was able to gain for this own thought from his monumental humanistic achievement of translating Plato, the philosophy which he elaborated as a "Platonic theology" contained many elements that had been anticipated by humanists before him or that they had long hoped to discover in Platonism. In its relationship to humanism Ficino's Platonism had three important characteristics. First of all, as a philosophy it sought, as the 13th-century scholastics had sought, a synthesis of Christianity and pagan thought, but between the broad range of pagan moral and religious anticipations of Christianity and the teachings of the Church and not, as in the 13th century, between dialectic and revelation. With the acceptance of the oracular nature of the Greek mysteries, and of Plato and the Greek and Latin poets, any estrangement between Christianity and humanism could be bridged. Moreover, the emphasis on the universality of truth, whatever its source, reflected the fundamental eclecticism of humanism if, indeed, it was not identical with it. And this synthesis included those of the earlier medieval scholastics.

The second feature of Ficino's philosophy which appealed to the humanists was the clear recognition of the value of beauty alongside of truth and goodness. This gave the esthetic aspect of the humanist interest in poetry and rhetoric the prospects of sanctification and could provide a bridge between the literary vision of humanism and the sensibility of the visual artist. Intimately connected with the valuation of beauty as a revelation or intimation of divinity was the adaptation to Christian purposes of the Platonic love dialogues, the *Symposium* and *Phaedrus.* Moreover, Ficino's assertion of the divine madness of the poet, based on the *Phaedrus* and *Ion,* reaffirmed the prophetic and theological character of poetry which Ficino especially recognized in Dante.

Third, by the reinstatement of the allegorical mode of interpretation it became possible, in combination with the two previous conceptions, to deal with classical themes in literary compositions or to represent them visually in such a way that the more strictly humanistic emphasis on historical validity, preserving classical form and classical content, could be retained, while at the same time, by placing the themes in a Christian-Platonic philosophical context, a Christian meaning could be read into them. It was possible to treat a pagan literary *topos* or philosophical statement in its own historical perspective and with scholarly precision and yet see it as part of a movement of the spirit toward the subsequently revealed Christian truth. Ficino's philosophy was thus compatible with humanist values.

The Ficinian synthesis was not formal and methodological, as 13th-century scholastic syntheses had been, but was philosophically more coherent and spiritually more profound. Despite a capacity to comprehend and include Aristotelian viewpoints, it was fundamentally Augustinian in strategy and values. Its success within the Church was for the most part limited to the period of humanist influence in the papacy and was greatest at the Fifth Lateran Council, during the pontificates of Julius II and of Leo X (son of Lorenzo the Magnificent and, of all popes, the most favorably disposed to humanism). Ficino's ideas (and Pico's), although reduced to lay status by the lack of interest of the Counter Reformation, had a pervasive and persistent influence, in close attention with humanism, on literature, art, and philosophy, both in Italy for the remainder of the Cinquecento and in the rest of Europe from the 15th century on. Renaissance Platonism was, however, a culmination of many basic tendencies that were stimulated by humanism, and whatever its importance in the general history of Platonism, it must be regarded historically as most influential through its intimate involvement with humanism. It was not "the philosophy of humanism" as such, since humanism by its rhetorical nature more easily operated on antimetaphysical, eclectical, and skeptical premises similar to Cicero's. But it satisfied the humanists' underlying desire for a metaphysical justification of their activities, solved many of their disturbing conflicts, and, as St. Augustine had, accepted rhetoric within a religious context.

Humanism and Renaissance Art

Preliminary Definitions

The relationship of humanism to the visual arts during the Renaissance was complex and necessarily problematic. Yet art historians have been tempted to apply the term "humanist" to artists and their works as loosely as have intellectual historians to phenomena in the history of thought. Discretion, precision, and restraint are necessary qualities for valid discussion of this question. Nonetheless, it cannot be denied that the developing intimacy of humanism and the arts during the Renaissance was a fact of major importance. Mediators between the Quattrocento and a revered antiquity, the humanists were instrumental in transmitting the spirit of the antique to their own times. However, as Richard Krautheimer (1956) has noted, a distinction must be made between the literati—scholars, orators, poets, rhetoricians, philosophers, historians, and antiquarians—and the artists and collectors of art. A literary approach to antiquity permeated the former group in contrast to the artists' visual approach to antique works of art. The former regarded the antiquities of the Eternal City as relics of the past, as testimonies of the lives of great men, and, above all, as a source of inspiration and guidance, providing an affirmation of the humanist belief in man's potential. On the other hand, the artist found in antiquity models of craftsmanship and excellence, standards of beauty, and a repertory upon which he could draw to enrich his own work. As Giovanni Doldi says of antique figures in a letter to Petrarch, written in 1375 from Rome: ". . . if they had but the spark of life, they would be better than nature."

Frequently it is not possible to document the influence of a humanist, although it seems evident in the work of an artist; indeed, it may often be equally possible to assume that the artist arrived at the point of view he expressed without the influence of the humanist. Although it has generally been inferred that certain Quattrocento paintings are based on programs drawn up by humanists—the most notable being Botticelli's mythologies—documentation is often lacking. Paride da Ceresara's instructions to Mantegna and Perugino for the painting of Isabella d'Este's *studiolo* are

This article is the second part of the article "Humanism" and "Humanism and Renaissance Art," from *The Encyclopedia of World Art*, vol. 7, cols. 721–34 (described in source note to the previous essay). As indicated there, the bibliographies have been omitted here as well. I wish to thank Naomi Miller for her contributions to this article.

among the few recorded. In the absence of documentation, a direct influence can be assumed only in the presence of a particular fact or symbolic meaning, such as would be known only to an accomplished classical scholar familiar with a literary text or an inscription. But one must always bear in mind that humanists and artists shared in and expressed many ideas, attitudes, and purposes simply because they were common to the age. The development of a style *all'antica* with classical forms and classical motifs took place in the history of art independent of but parallel to the focus on antiquity that was an integral part of the *studia humanitatis*. There can be no doubt that the two movements each stimulated interest in the other, that contacts and mutual assistance between artists and scholar-writers were plentiful, and that in given settings both groups shared a common outlook, but it would be a misconception to make either responsible for the other.

Humanism was deeply concerned with the dignity of man, giving new importance to human values while taking full account of human limitations. This approach, which was central to the Renaissance, gave expression to a renewed interest in man in his historical setting and to a heightened appreciation of the qualities and achievements, the "wonders" of man, without any repudiation of the Creator in whose image man was wrought. The fact that a special concern for the nobility and affective eloquence of the human figure in an increasingly natural environment was a central characteristic of the paintings of Giotto (contemporary with the protohumanists of the time of Mussato) led later humanists (Boccaccio, Aeneas Sylvius) to suggest that, as Petrarch had revived the study of letters, Giotto had revived the arts. But this should not lead to the conclusion that Giotto must in any sense have been connected with the literary humanist movement. Just as Ambrogio Lorenzetti's frescoes of Good Government and Bad Government (1337–40) in the Palazzo Pubblico in Siena utilized current Thomist notions of justice and the common good—at the same time providing evidence of the absorption of antique artistic elements—so Giotto's humanizing tendencies had reflected contemporary Gothic developments. But when in 1414 in the Siena Palazzo Pubblico, Taddeo di Bartolo executed a fresco cycle emphasizing the same civic vitues as had Lorenzetti, his program of Roman military heroes and statesmen, defenders of the Republic, was clearly of humanist devising. And, though undocumented, a connection is rightly suspected between the late Trecento work of the Hercules Master executed in a definitely antique manner on the Porta della Mandorla of the Florence Cathedral, and Salutati's *De laboribus Herculis*, which included the first complete modern treatise on the ancient hero and helped make the Labors of Hercules a favorite theme in Renaissance art. In the solidly established Florentine humanist circle of the early Quattrocento there were definite but rather aloof relationships between Bruni, Niccoli, Traversari and other humanists and the striking group of artists working in the new antique manner—Brunelleschi, Ghiberti, Donatello, Luca della Robbia, and Masaccio. Both groups were supported by elements of the leading citizens but moved in essential independence. It should be noted, however, that their lack of social standing tended to put the artists at a disadvantage in Florentine humanist circles. Bruni, in his introduction to the program for the Florentine Baptistery doors, emphasized the eminence of those learned humanists and theorists who has charted the program for the artist to follow. However, a somewhat different attitude was evidenced by Poggio Bracciolini, who was interested in the esthetic aspects as well as the content of the art of antiquity—so much so that he sought Donatello's judgment on the quality of a piece of ancient sculpture.

The account of possible connections between humanism and art which follows is meant to illustrate the impact of the humanist movement, especially as conceived by Alberti, on Renaissance art. It will be concerned chiefly with Italy between 1430 and 1530 and will not attempt to provide more than a sampling of the artists who showed classical, rhetorical, or allegorical elements in their works.

Alberti and His Influence

With Leon Battista Alberti appeared a humanist with artistic yearnings, who developed, moreover, a fully humanist theory of art, as well as an interpretation of the nature of ancient art. His knowledge of the art of the ancients was based to a great extent on his reading of Greek and Roman works, such as Seneca's description of the Three Graces and the *Imagines* of Philostratus the Elder. But it was primarily because he had studied surviving monuments in great detail that Alberti's notions of antiquity have such visual force. Although the humanist treatises of Alberti have been most effectively dealt with by Eugenio Garin, as those on art have been by Luigi Mallè, the decidedly humanist character of Alberti's approach to art needs further stressing, since it illuminates the way in which Renaissance humanism penetrated into the arts.

In his *Della pittura* (1435–36) Alberti emphasized three necessary elements in a painting: the evocation of spatial and historical actuality by a combination of artificial perspective and a system of proportion and scale based on the human figure; the invention of an *istoria* (theme, dramatic situation, or historical episode to be depicted); and its elaboration through the use of appropriate color, light, proportion, composition, and affective movement in such a way as to communicate a living, moving visual drama that would edify, terrify, instruct, or please the viewer. In advocating a knowledge of geometry and optics to achieve perspective (which, as will be seen, springs from a viewpoint analogous to the humanists' new attitude toward history), in expressing the notion of a transformation of poetic into visual beauty, and in urging the goal of moving the viewer to appropriate insight, emotion, and action, his treatise embodied a historical, literary, and rhetorical—in short, a truly humanist—conception of art.

Panofsky has emphasized the analogy between the development by the humanists of a new view of history (in which time, the moral and cultural character of men, and men's actions are seen as objectively detached from the present) and the creation by Renaissance artists of a new "historical" notion of space (viewed in linear perspective, like a stage setting populated by seemingly real, three-dimensional human figures). There are further parallels between the artists' search for a mathematical and "scientifically" valid method of creating an illusion of reality on a two-dimensional surface and the humanists' pursuit of scholarliness and accuracy in historical and philological interpretation. Alberti's desire to achieve a literary, narrative quality in painting, the effectiveness of which could be measured by its emotional and moral impact, and his detailed and resourceful suggestions for accomplishing this (such as acquiring a knowledge of history and poetry and associating with poets and orators), clearly demonstrate that he was trying to point a way by which painters could lift themselves from the status of craftsmen and mechanical artists to practitioners of an intellectual discipline. To this end he thought that the education of the humanist artist should be based on a study of both antiquity and nature. Moreover, Alberti clearly felt that this new "liberal art" should have the scholarliness (or mathematical precision), the rhetorical persuasiveness, and the sense of high moral purpose of the humanist. He reinforced this conception of the artist by references to ancient art drawn from Pliny, Vitruvius, and Lucian, and even more by his constant citation of anecdotes concerning ancient artists, drawn from Cicero and Quintilian, to instruct the painter, although they were originally intended for the orator. Although his emphasis was more rhetorical and Ciceronian (his definition of painting as *circumscriptio, compositio,* and *lumina* may be compared to Cicero's *inventio, dispositio,* and *elocutio*), it was manifested in terms of the formula adapted in reverse from Horace's *Ars poetica, ut pictura poesis* ("as is painting, so is poetry," was to be understood: "as is poetry, so is painting"), which, as Rensselaer Lee has shown (1940), became a central tenet of art theory in the 16th–18th centuries.

Alberti's views, although by no means universally known or observed by painters, did establish a new, increasingly accepted concept of art and of the purposes of the artist. He directed attention to the rapprochement between humanists and artists that was already in the process of developing. Whether or not Alberti's thoughts on art were largely original—a question which has been frequently debated—he forged tangible bonds between the new trends in the arts and humanism by supplying a purely humanist interpretation and rationale.

Perhaps the most immediate reflection of Alberti's ideas can be detected in certain panels of Ghiberti's Doors of Paradise in which Alberti's concepts—the handling of space based on mathematically correct perspective, the human figure *all'antica,* the handling of drapery and over-all composition within fantastic architectural settings—seem to have left their mark. It has been suggested (Krautheimer, 1956) that there is strong evidence here of an interchange of ideas between the two men. In 1435, the year in which *Della pittura* was written, a distinct change took place in Ghiberti's style, evident in some of the panels of the Doors of Paradise executed in that year. Probably the change was conditioned both by the art of ancient Rome—he became a noteworthy collector of antiquities in the late 1430s and 1440s and, with other enlightened artists like Brunelleschi, probably took a keen interest in Roman studies—and by the theories set forth in *Della pittura.* Ghiberti's exposure to the humanist thinking of Alberti may have taken place as early as 1429, the year in which he is believed to have traveled to Rome. The evidence points to a meeting of the two men some years before the writings of *Della pittura,* and the young Alberti was probably in Rome about 1429.

Ghiberti's literary work, the *Commentarii,* was an important result of his new humanist leanings. Accepting the humanist division of history in which antiquity and modern times are separated by the "Middle Ages," he treated ancient art in Book I and "modern" art in Book II. Although they fall short of their goal both in conception and scholarship, these two books evidence a genuine humanist aspiration. Book III, compiled in a fragmentary and disorganized state from works of various ancient and medieval authors, expounds those disciplines (aside from the major problems of craftsmanship and execution) necessary for the training of the sculptor, namely, a knowledge of optics, taken from Alhazen, Avicenna, Witelo (Erazm Ciolek), John Peckham, and Roger Bacon; a knowledge of anatomy, taken from Averroës; a system of human proportions, taken from Vitruvius; and a knowledge of history, taken from Pliny. In both historical and theoretical emphasis the *Commentarii* reveals a humanist point of view. Technical problems are only touched upon, while the more academic aspects of art are emphasized by stressing a humanistic education for the artist.

One of the most striking examples of an art which manifested the ideas of Alberti was that of Piero della Francesca. A direct contact between the two artists in Florence at the time of the appearance of *Della pittura* is highly probable, and a later one is nearly certain in connection with the decoration of the Tempio Malatestiano in Rimini. In his old age Piero wrote *De prospectiva pingendi,* a work based on Alberti which proposed a system of perspective for the use of painters, and *De quinque corporibus regularibus* (a neo-Pythagorean treatise based on the *Timaeus* and plagiarized in Luca Pacioli's *De divina proportione*) a further fusion of mathematics and art which develops the modes of Pythagorean speculation for the use of painters and architects.

In Piero's paintings Albertian concepts are realized not only in his compelling use of "historical" narrative but also in his serene and majestic figures, which embody principles of decorum and classical harmony advocated by Alberti. The historical qualities are present especially in the *Legend of the True Cross,* the latter, in the *Madonna of Mercy* and the *Resurrection* in Sansepolcro. The *Flagellation of Christ* in Urbino is an exquisitely calculated exercise in perspective and human proportion. Piero's attitude contrasted with the atmosphere of Florence in the period from about 1445 to 1465, marking a certain shift away from humanism. Led by the Dominican, St. Antoninus, the movement exercised a marked influence over a number of artists, including Donatello. But, toward the end of the century, some of the characteristics that Alberti had voiced were reasserted strongly in the work of Florentine painters, culminating in Botticelli's blending of medieval and classical grace. Botticelli and his atelier, the *accademia di scioperati,* represent a new type of artist who is both rational and passionate, intelligent and caustic, has literary pretensions and great sensibility, and manifests a definite independence of spirit. In keeping with the new status of these artists among the humanists, the humanist poet Ugolino Verino eulogized Botticelli as a new Apelles, the equal of the ancient artists.

Humanist Themes in Renaissance Art

The impact of humanism on Renaissance art can be traced not only in the style and attitude of Quattrocento artists but also in the choice and treatment of the themes which they developed. The new interest in man and the world in which he lived strongly affected the outlook of the Renaissance artist. Paralleling the humanists' composition of biographies of their contemporaries, portraiture became very popular in the 15th century, developing generally in two opposing trends. On the one hand, there was concentration on portraying the specific physical characteristics of the model; this tendency is exemplified by the work of Ghirlandajo, reproducing in precise detail and with great fidelity the individual peculiarities of the figure portrayed. Ghirlandajo filled his religious frescoes with accurately delineated portraits of contemporary personalities, thereby calling forth the sharp rebuke of Savonarola who fought against a development which seemed to him to place art in the service of vanity. The opposing trend placed less emphasis on physical, surface qualities and used the portrait to present man as an ideal type exemplifying certain human virtues. In the work of Michelangelo, for example, the model was only a point of departure for the final image and was completely transformed. In Raphael's work, the individual features of the model were preserved but were generalized and made universal, so as to emphasize more strongly the moral qualities.

Another humanist trend which influenced the content of Renaissance art was the new interpretation and interest in history first manifested in collections of *exempla* of great men, such as Boccaccio's *De casibus virorum illustrium* and the *Trionfi* of Petrarch, in which famous men were presented according to a moral and philosophical order which transcended a more objective historical order or evaluation. There was a resulting tendency to combine historic heroes of the secular life with saints and other figures revered by the Church. In 14th-century painting, figures from antiquity, viewed as national heroes, were given places of honor in civic buildings (as, for example, in the already mentioned Sala Virorum Illustrium in Padua), and often personified Christian virtues.

The popularity of the gallery of heroes died out in the course of the 14th century but revived in full force toward the middle of the 15th. Paolo Uccello, in the years 1445–48, adorned the walls of the Casa Vitaliani in Padua with monumental figures of celebrated men. In Florence in the 1450s, Andrea del Castagno painted a series of famous men and women, drawn from antiquity and the life of his own times in the Villa Pandolfini in Legnaia near Florence (now in the Uffizi, Florence). Uccello and Castagno each painted an equestrian portrait of a Florentine *condottiere* on the walls of the Cathedral of Florence, Uccello of Sir John Hawkwood and Castagno of Niccolò da Tolentino. In the Hall of the Collegio del Cambio in Perugia in 1500 Perugino painted a gallery of heroes derived from the works of Livy and Plutarch.

Together with the new interest in man expressed in humanist painting, there was a new delight in the visible world. Landscape painting was markedly affected by the humanist culture. In Florence especially, there was a vital interest in cosmic order, in the workings of nature. The Florentines, however, adopted neither the astrological landscape dominated by celestial symbols, common to the Ferrarese, nor the pure and luminous landscapes of the Venetians. Their brilliant innovation came in the development of portraiture with a landscape setting, in which nature functions as an expressive complement to the human form and its activities. The problem of landscape development was given special attention between 1470 and 1480 in the workshop of Verrocchio. His pupil Leonardo tried to recreate in his landscapes the cosmic life which envelops man and of which he is an integral part. But in landscape paintings, as in portraiture, there was an opposing trend. Botticelli, for example, was strongly antagonistic to Leonardo's view and developed in his work a symbolic, primarily decorative landscape, in which he did not attempt to express the order of nature and its relation to man directly but rather through the allegorical meaning of his mythological subjects.

Humanist influence is reflected in the architectural backgrounds of such artists as Piero, Mantegna, Filippino Lippi, and Jacopo Bellini, as well as in the work of the young Ghiberti. On the whole they reflect studies of the antique, as for example, Mantegna's frescoes in Mantua. The Renaissance was vitally interested in a passage from Vitruvius (Book V, chap. 6) which discusses the three types of stage scenery: tragic, comic, and satyric. This passage seems to have provided inspiration for such architectural paintings as the Urbino and Baltimore panels, often attributed to Luciano Laurana, and for illustrations in Serlio's architectural treatise and in the 16th-century editions of Vitruvius.

The tendency of Renaissance artists influenced by humanism to view man as the measure of all things is strongly illustrated in the architectural concepts which dominated in the late 15th century and into the 16th. In Alberti's *De re aedificatoria,* completed and dedicated to Nicholas V in 1452 but printed for the first time with a dedication to Lorenzo by Politian in 1485, a guiding principle was put forth which expressed the preoccupation of many Florentine artists with man's perfection. In Book IX, chapter 5, Alberti stated that the "beauty of all edifices arises principally from three things, namely the number, figure and collocation of several members." And further on ". . . for every Body consists of certain peculiar parts, of which if you take away any one, or lessen or enlarge it, or reverse it to an improper place; that which before gave the Beauty and Grace to the Body, will at once be lamed and spoiled." Alberti echoed Vitruvius' use of the human figure as a module for building and as a beautifully proportioned microcosm—this was the famous figure of a man superimposed on a circle and square which was reproduced by Leonardo, Dürer, Francesco di Giorgio, Fra Giovanni Giocondo, and Cesariano, as well as by other artists of the Renaissance. Michelangelo later developed a similar formula when he asserted that the members of architecture depend on the members of man and that a knowledge of anatomy was essential to the architect.

It was not by accident that the Renaissance theorists and architects constantly referred to Vitruvius and that particular chapter in his treatise devoted to the appearance of sacred buildings and the ratio and harmony of their parts. By deriving the proportions of a temple from those of the human figure, all worthy architecture from the time of Alberti to Palladio was thus endowed with the properties of a living organism. After his Vitruvian studies, a city plan by Francesco di Giorgio was composed in the form of a man, with a fortress at the head, a tower at each extremity, and a basilica at the chest.

For Francesco di Giorgio, using a concept rooted in Neoplatonic philosophy, the circle is the most perfect building form and hence, a symbol of God. Alberti, too, had implied a preference for the round form, ". . . for nature aspires to absolute perfection." His humanist conception of ecclesiastical architecture expressed in his treatise on architecture was based on the idea that the harmonious perfection of geometric forms represents an absolute value. In this Alberti was inspired by the centrally planned buildings of ancient Rome—in particular by the Pantheon, the classical temple par excellence for the Renaissance—which provided him with historical precedents for the reconstituted classical architectural style he sought for his own day.

One of the most important spokesmen for an architecture influenced by humanist and Neoplatonic conceptions was Giuliano da Sangallo, who worked in Florence for Lorenzo the Magnificent. S. Maria delle Carceri in Prato, begun in 1485, is an early example of a Renaissance church built on the centralized plan of a Greek cross. In Sangallo's humanist-inspired project for Lorenzo's villa at Poggio a Caiano, built about 1480–85, he attempted to create an ideal retreat in the midst of nature, a kind of *de re rustica* as envisioned by the humanists. His plan echoed Pliny the Younger's descriptions of the ancient villa, and its entire program, the frescoes, frieze, and other details, also follow suggestions by Politian.

The many examples of the incorporation of humanist thought in the arts illustrate the general acceptance of humanist ideas concerning civic life, antiquity, learning, morality, and history among the ruling families which patronized the Quattrocento artists. This was especially true of Florence, where humanism thrived. It is not surprising, therefore, that so many of the artists, who were in contact both with these humanist-oriented patrons and with the humanists themselves (employed by the same patrons), absorbed much of the humanist outlook. Their work undoubtedly reflected not only their own tastes and conceptions but those of their patrons as well. In Florence, certainly, the artists moved in an environment that was receptive to the tendencies they were seeking to realize in their work.

The Medici and Neoplatonism in Florence

The domination of Florentine political life by Cosimo de' Medici after 1434 assured the continuation and strengthening of the humanist tendencies that already were strong in Florence. Cosimo had a near monopoly of artistic patronage both in his commissions and in the influence he exercised over the selection of artists by churches and monasteries. Because of this and the tendency of his associates to follow his tastes in their choice of artists, the Medicean influence was an exceptionally concentrated one which continued under Piero and reached its climax with Lorenzo. It extended into those signorial states whose rulers hired themselves out to Florence as *condottieri*— the Malatesta of Rimini and Federigo da Montefeltro of Urbino. A comparable concentration of patronage with equivalent or greater resources was possible only in the papacy, a condition which was to exist in the next century under Julius II and Leo X. But Cosimo's own tastes and probably his political shrewdness as a dispenser of patronage kept him from exclusively favoring humanists or classical and humanistic tendencies in the arts. The employment and support of Brunelleschi, Donatello, Ghiberti, and Michelozzo were balanced by the favor shown Fra Angelico and, especially, Benozzo Gozzoli, who demonstrate by their work that everything delightful was not necessarily under humanist influence.

In the 1480s, under the aegis of Lorenzo the Magnificent, the earlier tendencies of Florentine humanism found their focus in the Neoplatonism of Marsilio Ficino. André Chastel (1959) has rightly emphasized the importance of Ficino's ideas to an understanding of certain tendencies in the humanism and in the art of his period and later. To the extent that Ficino showed the way to a new allegorical interpretation of the ancient gods, heroes, and symbols within a Christian context, his writings help explain some of those elements found both in the arts of his time and in the writing of late Quattrocento humanists. Such humanists as Landino and Politian (and many lesser figures) found in Ficino an attractive synthesis of Christianity and antiquity, of medieval scholasticism and the spirit of Plato's dialogues. In the arts, this synthesis is strikingly illustrated by late-15th- and 16th-century funerary monuments. In the Sassetti Chapel in Santa Trinita, for example, classical motifs adapted from antique cameos and panels and medallions from the Arch of Constantine are incorporated within a basically Christian program, in which Religion and Justice are represented in antique guise. On a sarcophagus by Benedetto da Maiano in the Strozzi Chapel in S. Maria Novella, antique masks and griffons relate the pagan world to the Christian mystery. Antique motifs are integrated, in the bronze tomb of Sixtus IV, in the Vatican Grottoes, which Antonio and Piero Pollaiuolo executed in 1484–93, within a basically scholastic Aristotelian program. But it is in Michelangelo's plan for the tomb of Julius II that the classical theme of the triumphal glorification of the hero, expressed here by a complex Neoplatonic interpretation of life and the soul, reaches its culmination in the Renaissance.

The mythological paintings of Sandro Botticelli are among those in which a humanist, and specifically a Neoplatonic, influence is most explicit. The suggestion that Botticelli depended directly upon the *Giostra* of Politian for inspiration in his *Birth of Venus* and *Primavera* is defended by Panofsky (1960) though questioned by Ernst Gombrich (1945). The latter has noted that Ficino was the humanist best known to Botticelli's patron, Lorenzo, when the *Primavera* was painted. The Neoplatonic interpretation of the classical gods was treated in correspondence between Ficino and Lorenzo, as well as extensively in Ficino's works. Thus, E. Wind (1958) has been able to interpret these mythologies in the light of Neoplatonic thought. The contrast between the heavenly and the earthly Venus in the two paintings, and the interrelation of *humanitas, caritas,* and *sapientia,* of *voluptas, castitas,* and *venustas,* are evidence of the use made of allegory to communicate esthetic, moral, philosophical, and religious ideas. These paintings have an obviously literary, narrative quality that betrays their humanistic rhetorical and moral intent. It has also been demonstrated that there is a common inspiration in Botticelli's Venus (which attempts to recapture the lost *Venus Anadyomene* of Apelles), in the poetic writings of Politian, and in Ficino's statements on love. Botticelli's *Pallas Subduing a Centaur,* celebrating Lorenzo's diplomacy in ending the War of the Pazzi Conspiracy, also has obvious Neoplatonic significance and must be understood as the triumph of wisdom—of the *studia humanitatis*—over the baser instincts; a reassertion of the civilizing role claimed for intelligence by the humanists and bearing the same meaning for Quattrocento Florence as the Parthenon sculptures of the Lapiths and Centaurs had for Periclean Athens. The *Calumny,* another painting meant to re-create an ancient work of art, follows explicitly a description by Lucian of Apelles' painting of the subject. Lucian's work had been translated into Latin early in the century by Guarino da Verona and into Italian about 1472 by Bartolomeo della Fonte, a Florentine humanist; as early as 1435 Alberti had recommended this subject to painters. The painting, which also has an allegorical, moral meaning, shows Truth as a figure closely resembling Botticelli's heavenly Venus and pointing to heaven. The ideas of Ficino, supporting the notion of a *theologia poetica* developed in Landino's *Commentary on the Divine Comedy,* thus found expression in an art that was more "humanistic" than philosophical.

It was a younger Florentine contemporary of Botticelli, however, who in his mythological paintings perhaps came closest to expressing the ideas of those humanists who were conscious of the historical role of their tradition. Piero di Cosimo in a series of paintings executed for the house of Francesco del Pugliese in the late 1480s (one on the primitive life and possibly a second on Vulcan), utilized passages in Vitruvius and Lucretius which proclaimed man's ability to rise beyond a primitive, animal existence through his innate industry and ingenuity. Cicero had transmitted the views of the Stoic Poseidonios on the role of human intelligence and industry and had emphasized a comparable role for the early invention of rhetoric. Plato, in his *Protagoras,* attributed to the Sophist a similar line of thought in his tale of Prometheus. Toward the middle of the 15th century, Giannozzo Manetti in his work *On the Dignity and Excellence of Man,* had said, "everything after that first new and rude creation of the world seems to have been discovered, made, and perfected by us out of a certain singular and special acuteness of the human mind." Piero returned to this theme in some of his other paintings.

Already in earlier Renaissance art theory, man had been associated with perfection—with simple geometric forms symbolizing a universal structure and embodying *symmetria* (the idea of rational proportions, as expressed by Landino in 1487, which forms the underlying harmonic form of all creation). In *Della pittura* Alberti had recalled the famous saying of Protagoras that "man is the measure of all things." This humanist concept was perpetuated in Neoplatonic doctrine and became central to artistic thought in the time of Lorenzo the Magnificent. With the firmer establishment of Florentine Neoplatonism after the 1480s, the inherent order in art became bound to a universal symbolism, a vision of the perfection of man. Manetti had also praised the human form: "Therefore in what other creature can the composition of the members, the conformation of the features, the figure, the outward appearance either be or be imagined to be more beautiful than in the case of man?"

These ideas of Alberti and Manetti were absorbed into the Florentine Neoplatonism of Ficino and Pico della Mirandola. If it is true, as Chastel suggests, that the artistic aspirations of Florentine humanism were realized in the Vatican works of Raphael and Michelangelo, it is Raphael's *School of Athens* and *Parnassus* and related paintings of the Stanza della Segnatura which, while utilizing Neoplatonic themes, made the fullest statement of the Albertian program for a rhetorical and humanistic art. The *School of Athens* is the embodiment of Neoplatonic Pythagorean theory, connecting ratio with musical consonances, an interpretation of the harmony of the universe taken from Plato's *Timaeus*. The Stanza della Segnatura is a manifestation of late-15th-century humanist thought and mirrors the work of Ficino in so far as it reshapes the teachings of scholasticism, providing a complete concordance of pagan antiquity, Christian spirituality, and Roman history.

But the idealization of man's godlike figure by Manetti, Alberti, and other humanist theorists, perhaps found its finest expression in Michelangelo's ceiling paintings in the Sistine Chapel and in his monumental sculpture. Rather than the more narrative, rhetorical, allegorical, and historical qualities which had been central to the outlook of earlier humanist artists, Michelangelo's work manifests the philosophical vision of Plato and the genuinely Christian-classical conception of art common to the thought of humanists influenced by Neoplatonism in the late Quattrocento. The program of the Medici tombs in Florence may be considered as an artistic parallel to Ficino's *Theologia Platonica* and *Consonantia Moses et Platonis*. It also represents in visual form some of the doctrines of Florentine Neoplatonism: the juxtaposition of the two roads leading to God, as formulated by Landino, the *vita activa* and the *vita contemplativa,* while the personifications of Day, Night, Twilight, and Dawn which surround them symbolize the powers intermediary between the terrestrial and translunary worlds.

A third High Renaissance, classical artist, whose life, artistic activity, and thoughts have occasioned much admiration for him as the representative "Renaissance man," Leonardo da Vinci also drew upon Neoplatonic thought. He particularly shared Ficino's high estimate of the faculty of vision, yet he was equally indebted to the mathematical, scientific works of such 14th-century Parisian and Oxford nominalists as Nicolas Oresme, Jean Buridan, Thomas Bradwardine and John Peckham. Actively concerned with questions of perspective, anatomy, and natural movements, and with achieving a more penetrating psychological image of man in his painting, he was nevertheless somewhat contemptuous of the literary, humanist conception of art. Where Alberti had offered the artist an opportunity to raise his profession from a mechanical to a liberal art by emphasizing the intellectual aspects of his work, Leonardo proudly assimiliated the mechnical, constructive activities of the painter to the intellectual. He stressed that the mechanical was also essential and common to all other professions and disciplines. In his *Paragone* he held painting to be the queen of sciences because it can reproduce everything as well as invent things which never existed, presenting a durable picture of everything as a whole and not in parts. The painter is superior to the poet because "the only function peculiar to the poet is to invent the words of people who speak . . . in other matters the painter surpasses him."

Italian Humanist Centers Outside Florence

Florence was not the only center of either humanism or art in the 15th century. Padua's tradition of humanism went back before the time of Petrarch, who gave his library to the city and spent his last years in the university there, and it continued through the school of Gasparino da Barzizza, the teacher of Vittorino da Feltre. Although Padua's artistic heritage included works of Guariento, the first Paduan follower of Giotto, Filippo Lippi's frescoes, Donatello's "Gattamelata" and his reliefs on the high altar in the Church of S. Antonio, its artistic atmosphere remained provincial until the time of Mantegna, since the city's reverence for the literature of antiquity was not reflected in its art. In the academy of Francesco Squarcione, who was the local pedagogue, antiquarian, and humanist, learning was acquired by means of the imitation of Greek and Roman works. It was in this milieu that the art of Mantegna was nurtured.

In the earlier works of Mantegna, such as the *St. Sebastian* in the Vienna Kunsthistorisches Museum, one finds an overwhelming interest in classical remains. This is also true of the frescoes executed for the Ovetari Chapel in the Paduan church of the Eremitani in the 1450s, where considerable erudition is displayed in the garb of the heroic Roman legionaries, as well as in the architectural enviornment. While the Eremitani *St. James before Herod* is humanist in the narrow sense, comparable to a painting correctly transcribed from a Latin text, the *St. James Led to Execution* is far more dramatic, almost conveying the effect of an antique frieze. Complete absorption of the spirit of humanism did not take place until Mantegna's later period, although his archaeological quotations are inextricably bound with an element of moral probity. Mantegna's appointment as official artist to the Gonzaga court of Mantua in 1459 marks him as the first painter of the Renaissance to be entirely in the service of a humanist prince. In this court, amid innumerable antiquities and in association with such renowned humanists as Vittorino da Feltre, Mantegna acted as an arbiter of taste. Aside from paintings and décor, he produced designs for architecture, festivals, and scenery for Latin plays. In the frescoes for the *Camera degli Sposi,* in which Mantegna painted the portraits of Lodovico Gonzaga and his family, the figures are thoroughly permeated with a humanist sentiment. An increased interest in individual characterization and in human relationships is evident in these figures. The ceiling with its overwhelming illusionism is influenced by the dream of Roman grandeur. Ancient Rome, however, is not re-created until the *Triumph of Caesar* paintings (ca. 1484–94), which were designed together with a lost allegorical *Triumphs of Petrarch,* both designated as theatrical decorations. Precedents existed, to be sure, such as the series of triumphs, drawn largely from the *Antiquities* of Josephus, executed by Altichiero and Avanzo in the great hall of the Palace of Verona, and certainly known to Mantegna. But in Mantegna's work there is reconstructed the triumphal procession *all'antica* so frequent in ancient Rome. For Mantegna, Roman grandeur was allied to Roman *gravitas,* Roman triumph to Roman justice. Pedantic and doctrinaire in his display of classical antiquity, a certain materiality dominates both Mantegna's architecture and his heroes. This reenactment of the glories of the classical world coincided with the view of antiquity as a golden age which could be made to serve as an exemplar to the contemporary world. Directly in the spirit of the accounts of Caesar's triumphs by Appian and Suetonius, a true character issues forth from these panels. In the *Triumph of Scipio,* Mantegna nearly approaches the form as well as the content of Roman reliefs. Here too, the marked austerity signifies a climax in the heroic vision of Mantegna's humanistic belief in man's creative powers. Mantegna's important mythological paintings for Isabella d'Este's *studiolo* in Mantua (now in the Louvre) painted at the end of the century, among others, depicted Homer's tale of the affair of Mars and Venus. In this painting, a decrease in the emphasis on ethical quality is accompanied by a corresponding increase in vitality and realism, so much so that this work has even been cited as a satire on the antique, thus heralding the work of Ariosto. Mantegna's allegory of Minerva Expelling the Vices from the Garden of Virtue, from the same series, apparently represents his patroness, Isabella, as the goddess of wisdom. Both paintings are in a lighthearted, mocking manner in accord with the program of Paride da Ceresara, the humanist adviser and friend of Isabella. In the late works, however, for example, the Brera *Lamentation,* Mantegna's humanistic vision seems transformed from one which was suffused with a Roman ethos to one impregnated with the pathos and mysticism of Christianity.

For the wealth of antiquities which populate Mantegna's paintings, he had but to cast his eyes to nearby Verona, the city of Catullus, and Mantua, the city of Vergil. Felice Feliciano, in fact, describes an oft-repeated archaeological excursion on Lake Garda first made in 1464 with Mantegna and others. Here, in this fusion of nature and antiquity, of the real and the artificial, humanists searched for visual evidence that life had once been lived on a heroic plane. Reminiscences of these expeditions are apparent in the epigraphs found in a number of Mantegna's paintings and also in the manuscript illuminations (ca. 1459) noted by Millard Meiss (1957) as coming from the workshop of Mantegna—Renaissance depictions of antiquity depicting Guarino presenting a copy of Strabo to Marcello and Marcello presenting it to René d'Anjou.

The absorption of humanist influences into painting was also manifested in Venice in some of the work of Gentile and Giovanni Bellini, close contemporaries and brothers-in-law of Mantegna. The spread of humanist influence to Venice coincided with the awakening of the Venetian world to letters and science toward the close of the 15th century.

Following the time of Lorenzo the Magnificent, the center of allegorical exegesis shifted from Florence to Venice. Giovanni Bellini, with much encouragement from the humanist poet Pietro Bembo, executed the *Feast of the Gods* (Washington, D.C., Nat. Gall.) for Isabella d'Este, apparently as a wedding gift to her brother Alfonso and Lucrezia Borgia. Besides Bembo's direct influence in the choice of this theme, Edgar Wind (1948) has suggested the added influence of Ovid's *Fasti,* the contemporary Aldine publication of the *Priapeia* (Giovanni had close connections with the humanists of the so-called Aldine Academy), and the *Hypnerotomachia Poliphili,* an illustrated antiquarian romance published in 1499.

The *Hypnerotomachia,* attributed to Fra Francesco Colonna, a learned antiquarian and friend of Crasso in Verona (who was involved with the disciplines of law and architecture), is one of the more fanciful products of north Italian humanism. Among its woodcuts is a depiction of a Temple of the Sun in the form of an enormous stepped pyramid surmounted by an obelisk, an example of the Egyptomania of the humanists, particularly after the appearance of Horapollo's *Hieroglyphica* in 1419. The interest in things Egyptian and their symbolism is found in paintings as well, for example, in Titian's *Allegory of Prudence* (London, F. Howard Coll.), which shows a tricephalous monster modeled upon the companion of the god Serapis as he appears in his sanctuary at Alexandria, and also in the *décor* made by Pinturicchio in the Borgia apartments in the Vatican Palace.

Although the impact of humanism in northeast Italy (including Venice, Padua, Vicenza, Verona, Mantua, and Ferrara) acted upon an art that was gayer, more sardonic and sensuous, and less morally earnest, lyrical, and metaphysical than that in Tuscany, Umbria, and Rome, this made it possible to reflect more genuinely the satirical, voluptuary, and playful veins of so much of Greek and Latin literature. The classical painting of the Renaissance in Venice reached a culmination in the work of such 16th-century painters as Titian, Giorgione, and Tintoretto. Titian's mythological paintings the *Feast of Venus,* the *Bacchus and Ariadne,* and the *Bacchanal,* commissioned for Alfonso d'Este in Ferrara, followed descriptions of ancient paintings in the *Imagines* of Philostratus the Elder. Venice, Vicenza, and other cities in northeast Italy were also the principal scenes of the building activity of Andrea da Padova, better known as Palladio.

Palladio's ideas of a "fugal" architecture embodied the notion of spatial harmonics mathematically comparable to musical harmonics and were derived, as has already been mentioned, from Plato's *Timaeus.* The *Timaeus* revealed the mysterious harmony of the universe which many humanists discovered through Ficino's commentaries, in which the mathematical importance of physical reality and the rapport of architecture with music and philosophy were given great consideration. To the Renaissance architects, musical intervals and linear perspective were subjected to a numerical ratio, and the harmonies implicit in painting and in music (in the proportions and chords) were later cited by Leonardo. In the biography of Brunelleschi traditionally attributed to Antonio Manetti, it is written that Brunelleschi, who studied the proportions of the ancients and who was in close contact with the leading humanists (as well as the cosmographer-mathematician Toscanelli), approached in his architecture that universal synthesis most in accord with music.

It was Alberti who told Matteo de' Pasti during the building of S. Francesco in Rimini that by altering the proportions of the pilasters "si discorda tutta quella musica." As Wittkower (1952) has emphasized, the work of Palladio was the culmination of a humanistic, Neo-Pythagorean trend in Renaissance architecture that went back to Brunelleschi and Alberti. In the academy of his patron, the renowned humanist G. Trissino, Palladio became associated with mid-16th century humanist circles. Palladio was both a humanist and a working architect; he was also the author of books on ancient monuments and on architecture, an illustrator of editions of Caesar and Polybius, and the designer of such exquisitely proportioned classical buildings as S. Giorgio Maggiore in Venice and the Teatro Olimpico in Vicenza.

Humanism flourished at princely courts throughout Italy. Enormous enthusiasm for antiquity was manifested by Alfonso V of Aragon, king of Naples, who built the monumental triumphal arch in the Castel Nuovo. In Milan the Sforzas were men of learning and patrons of art and literature. In Rimini, the humanistic leanings of Sigismondo Malatesta produced one of the great monuments of the early Italian Renaissance, the Tempio Malatestiano, the medieval church of S. Francesco transformed for Sigismondo by Alberti into a temple for the glorification of the Malatestas. In the niches of the church were to be placed the sarcophagi of the illustrious figures at the court of Rimini and the Malatesta dead. The glorification of human achievement has rarely been more dramatically expressed than it is on the exterior of this temple. By placing the sarcophagi and their Roman inscriptions beneath massive Roman arches, Alberti transformed the medieval walls into a mausoleum for famous men. Profane glorification and Christian devotion are magnificently epitomized in this funerary monument devoted to the immortality of the Malatestas. In its time, the temple was both praised and denounced. Valturius, military chronicler of Sigismondo, admired its splendid repertory of literary and artistic images, accessible only to the initiate. Pius II, in his *Commentaries,* decried the impiety of the work and found this use of religious architecture for personal glorification excessive and hostile to the Christian faith. In the interior, Agostino di Duccio, borrowing innumerable motifs from Donatello and from Greek reliefs, helped to further the idea of the sanctuary-mausoleum as a manifestation of the modern culture. On the Area degli Antenati, a tomb commemorating two Malatesta ancestors, he carved reliefs depicting the Temple of Minerva, symbolizing *probitas,* and the Chariot of Triumph, symoblizing *fortitudo.* The reliefs in the Chapel of the Planets were derived from a variety of sources—Neoplatonic, neo-Aristotelian, medieval, astrological, the texts of Macrobius, and Cicero's *Somnium Scipionis* (dream of Scipio on immortality)—in order to re-create the antique spirit.

The influence of humanism at the court of Urbino—intellectually closer to the spirit of Florence—was more clearly articulated and moralistically inclined. There was a remarkable gathering of artists at this center of mathematical and humanistic disciplines. Piero della Francesca wrote on artistic perspective, and Pacioli in 1509 published the *De quinque corporibus regularibus.* Under Federigo da Montefeltro, pupil of Vittorino da Feltre and a student of Aristotle and of ancient history, architecture was raised not only to the summit of the arts but to the very acme of intellectual activity, attracting the interest of the most advanced Florentine humanists. Alberti and Piero were frequently at the court in the 1460s, just at the time when an architecture in accord with the Pythagorean-Platonic harmonic elements of their theories was developed in the design for the palace courtyard. At the end of the 15th century, encouraged by Elisabetta Gonzaga and her husband, Guidobaldo da Montefeltro, new ideals of court life and Platonic humanism were elaborated by Bembo and Castiglione.

In the beginning of the 16th century, with the consolidation of papal power under Julius II, Rome, the Eternal City, became once more as in antiquity the center of authority and learning. Here, the symbols of a glorious past were ever present, and in such undertakings as the plan for the museum of antiquities in the Belvedere court of the Vatican Palace, antique exploration was actively encouraged, and Florentine culture erupted from its narrower confines to become one of the essential components of Roman humanism and art.

The vision of the new courtier, the graceful, melancholy gentleman for whom love and poetry were the only respectable occupations, was brilliantly expounded in Castiglione's *Il Cortegiano,* which represents in its ideal of human perfection, esthetic and moral, a secularization of the teachings of the Florentine Academy, a Neoplatonic ideal without the theology of Ficino. In painting, the perfect balance of mind and body, the grace said by Castiglione to be the "strength at the core of the character," is perhaps most completely expressed by the Roman works of Raphael. Raphael's ideal was derived not from visual experience but from a vision conceived in the mind. This he explained in a letter written to Castiglione in 1516 in which he discussed the painting of a beautiful woman in terms of the *idea* conceived as the intuition of a perfect image which cannot be acquired through experience. His portrait of Castiglione in the Louvre exquisitely depicts the type of individual, developed to the point of perfection, that represented for him the culture of the courts of Rome, Florence, and Urbino.

Humanism and Art Outside Italy

Although German humanism and art will not be treated in this article, some mention must be made of Albrecht Dürer, who together with Hans Holbein the Younger, brought a classical style into northern art. Dürer's conception of classical art was drawn from his knowledge of the work of the Italian Renaissance rather than from humanists who were his close friends in Nürnberg, men such as Willibald Pirckheimer. Dürer absorbed from another German humanist, Cornelius Agrippa, called "Agrippa of Nettesheim," Ficinian Neoplatonic ideas which he incorporated into his art, for example, in his engraving *Melancolia I.* Although he abandoned the Albertian attempt to find one ideal human beauty, Dürer also composed important treatises on perspective and on human proportion. Holbein, who was closely associated with Erasmus and his circle of humanist friends, painted many portraits of them.

In France, it was not until the 16th century that humanist influences appeared to any meaningful extent; under Francis I, artistic life was enlivened by the influx of Italian artists, notably Leonardo da Vinci. During the third decade of the 16th century, the French court became more and more suffused with Italian influences, and the period of transition began which was to transform Fontainebleau into a "second Rome" from about 1530 to 1570. This appellation was an allusion to the large collections of antiquities concentrated there, as well as to the great number of Italian artists who gathered at the court. Drawings by the great masters became familiar and were distributed through engravings by René Boyvin, Antonio Fantuzzi, the Master L.D., and Etienne Delaune, among others. Francis I, the *prince idéal* of the humanists, satisfied his passion for belles-lettres by his veneration of Guillaume Budé and by the foundation of the Collège de France. The classical period of the so-called "French Renaissance" was that of the 1530s and 1540s. In that period numerous antique bronzes arrived in Fontainebleau. There Francesco Primaticcio and Il Rosso were decorating the galleries; Serlio published his architectural treatise; Rabelais wrote his principal works; and Philibert Delorme, recently returned from Rome, was building royal châteaux. In evidence everywhere was the return to the antique: renewal of the cult of Diana; publication of Vitruvius in France in 1547 by Jean Martin, illustrated by Goujon; Goujon's Fontaine des Innocents (1547); the great number of books published by Geoffroy Tory, as well as the later publications of a *Metamorphoses d'Ovide figurée* (1557), *Songe de Poliphile* (1546; illustrations attributed to Goujon), and the *Traité de perspective* by Jean Cousin (1560). Pontus de Tyard's poems *Douze fables de fleurs ou fontaines* provided themes for paintings. The *Imagines* of Philostratus the Elder were reflected in the works of Blaise de Vigenère (1578) and Remi Belleau, and inspired artists and poets who dazzled the populace with their royal triumphal entries and fetes. Interpretations of poetic works may also be found in Niccolò dell'Abate's figure of the Nile emerging from the reeds, in the Gallery of Ulysses at Fontainebleau, and in the paintings of the Maître de Flore in the same gallery, where the personifications of Venus, cupids, and nymphs relate directly to passages in Blaise de Vigenère.

Personal glorification and the continuation of the heroic ideal is perhaps best demonstrated in the Francis I Gallery (1534–37) at Fontainebleau, executed by Il Rosso. Although Panofsky points out that there is no literary evidence concerning its iconographic program, visual analysis reveals the direct paraphrasing of Latin and Greek texts, as well as the presence of the Virtues and Vices analogous to those developed by the Scholastic philosophers. The program of the gallery is a detailed commentary on the life of Francis I and, in the words of the poet Ronsard, all the ". . . virtues of this King, demonstrated in war and peace, in life as well as death." Personifications of past heroes are evoked to represent the greatness of Francis I: *L'Ignorance chassé* recalls Caesar; in the *L'Unité de l'état,* Francis I is idealized as a Roman emperor in a setting *à l'antique;* the *Eléphant fleurdelysé* celebrates Francis I as a wise and virtuous ruler, extolled here as a "new Alexander."

Mythological subjects are numerous at Fontainebleau in the works of Primaticcio, Niccolò dell'Abate, and Luca Penni, for which countless engravings after Raphael, Giulio Romano, and Perino del Vaga supplied the models. Penni, who worked at Fontainebleau between 1537 and 1540, best illustrates the rapport of the Fontainebleau school with the culture of the Italian Renaissance as exemplified by Raphael and his school. Penni's mythological scenes, for example, those depicting the story of the Trojan horse, the story of Diana, the *Birth of Love,* or his more classically oriented *Triumph of Flora* (1560–65), are comparable to the flowery metaphors of contemporary court poets. That poets and artists based their works on similar antique sources may be seen in the use of Ovid's *Fasti* as inspiration both for Primaticcio's allegorical frescoes at Fontainebleau representing Hercules and Omphale, and for Ronsard's *Satyr,* published in 1569.

A Humanist's Image of Humanism:
The Inaugural Orations of
Bartolommeo della Fonte

Professor Kristeller in his 'Humanism and Scholasticism in the Italian Renaissance'[1] as well as in his lecture on 'The Humanist Movement' in *The Classics and Renaissance Thought*[2] emphasizes the professional nature of humanism, assigning to it the teaching of grammar, rhetoric, poetry, history, and moral philosophy at the universities of Italy under the designation of the *studia humanitatis*. While he would not, I am sure, deny the wide cultural significance of the writings and activities of the humanists within the Renaissance, he does take a more restricted view of them than those philosophers and commentators who look upon the Italian humanists as simply one phase of a broadly humanitarian philosophical and religious outlook stretching from the ancient world to modern times, be it Jacques Maritain or Corliss Lamont. And he also differs with those scholars who regard humanism as the representative philosophy of the Renaissance, making them share this distinction with the Aristotelian professors of logic and natural philosophy, with the Platonists (whom he does not consider to be essentially humanists), with the natural philosophers, and with certain other less easily classifiable thinkers. Apart from their tracts on moral philosophy and their speculations on the rôle of man in the universe, he does not regard the writings of the humanists as philosophical. 'Thus I should like to understand Renaissance humanism, at least in its origin and in its typical representatives, as a broad cultural and literary movement, which in its substance was not philosophical, but had important philosophical implications and consequences.'[3] While it would be fair to say that, in this country at least, Kristeller's point of view enjoys a fairly general acceptance, it is not completely immune to controversy, apparently because its factual emphasis on the scholarly and professional status of the humanists gives less scope to free-floating historical imaginations.

The following essay, written 1958–59, was read to the Columbia University Seminar on the Renaissance on May 5, 1959. The microfilms used were purchased by Professor Kristeller with the aid of the Columbia University Fund for Research in the Social Sciences and kindly loaned to me. I have omitted the appendices of texts and bibliographies of Fontius, which may be consulted in the original edition. It was first published in *Studies in the Renaissance* 7 (1960): 90–147.

It is within this context that the inaugural orations of Bartolommeo della Fonte become of some interest. Della Fonte (or Fontius), 1446–1513,[4] was a minor humanist and a professor of poetry and oratory at the University of Florence in 1481–1482 and 1482–1483 and again from 1484–1485 through 1487–1488.[5] His colleagues at the university (which since 1472 taught the humanistic studies exclusively, the other faculties having been located in Pisa) were Demetrius Chalcondylas, Cristoforo Landino, Angelo Poliziano, and Naldo de' Naldi. Whereas the stipends of the first three in 1485 were 200, 300, and 250 florins respectively, della Fonte received 60.[6] While this may have been a measure of his fame and his political connections (Bernardo Rucellai seems to have been his sponsor whereas the other enjoyed the favor of Lorenzo de' Medici),[7] his philological studies have been well regarded, particularly by his biographer, the late Concetto Marchesi,[8] who was himself a leading Italian classical scholar.

Following the venerable university traditions of the middle ages and the Renaissance,[9] della Fonte addressed the students, his colleagues and the *ufficiali* of the *studio* at the commencement of his course of lectures in a public oration. These orations, six in number and probably all that he delivered while at the *studium* at Florence prior to printing them, are printed in three incunabula: Hain 7227, 7228, 7229. Hain 7227, which I use, and of which there are copies at the Biblioteca Nazionale (Magl. M. 7, No. 31a, leaves d4 and d5 missing) and at the Biblioteca Riccardiana (#537) in Florence, is without place and date. Hain 7228 is from the press of San Jacopo at Ripoli without date; Hain 7229 is Florence, 1487 'per Ant. Franc. Venetum'.[10] The orations are included in a Wolfenbüttel manuscript (43 Aug. Fol.), which I also use. Fontius, if he did not actually copy it himself, as seems probable from the handwriting, apparently supervised its copying and presented it to Matthias Corvinus while preparing a catalogue of the king's library in 1489.[11] An edition of some of his works, Frankfort, 1621, is based on this manuscript; the contents are identical.

The first oration, delivered 7 November 1481[12] at the commencement of his course on the *Argonautica* of Valerius Flaccus and the *Orations* of Cicero, was entitled *Oratio in laudem oratoriae facultatis*. The second, delivered 6 November 1482[13] when his course was on Lucan's *Pharsalia* and Caesar's *De bello civili*, was an *Oratio in historiae laudationem*.

In November 1483 he left Florence for Rome, wishing to escape from a most uncomfortable situation caused by the hostility of Poliziano, his colleague. Although he received an appointment to teach eloquence at the University in Rome, he was even more miserable there and managed to arrange his recall to the university in Florence, again through the agency of Bernardo Rucellai, in time to resume his lectures in 1484.[14] Thus on 8 November 1484,[15] when the *Punica* of Silius was the subject of his course, he gave an *Oratio in bonas artis*. The fourth, of 4 November 1485,[16] before his course on the *Odes* of Horace, was *In laudem poetices facultatis.* On 7 November 1486[17] he delivered a fifth oration *De sapientia* preceding his lectures on the *Satires* of Horace. On 7 November 1487[18] he made his sixth and last oration *In satyrae et studiorum humanitatis laudationem* announcing his course on the *Satires* of Juvenal. Apart from the possibility that this lecture course was a direct and renewed challenge to Poliziano, who had lectured in 1485–1486 on Juvenal,[19] this oration is of especial interest for its vigorous defense of the superiority of the humanistic disciplines over the professions of law and medicine (now taught at Pisa but competing for funds from a common budget).

In fact, however, it is the exceptionally high degree of self-conscious-ness concerning his profession and his sensitivity to the criticism or the neglect of it that lends all six of these otherwise undistinguished rhetorical exercises their importance. Fontius was, to my mind, a careful and even gifted philologist, commentator, and critic of texts. He was relatively mediocre in other respects. We do not have very many of his writings outside of these orations, his letters, some poems, and some of his textual studies. Very few of the fairly lengthy list of his works placed at the beginning of the manuscript collection of his letters by his heir and execu-tor Francesco Pandolfini have been located.[20] The one moral treatise (*Do-natus sive De poenitentia,*[21] contained in both the incunabula referred to and the manuscript) is neither subtle, profound, nor imaginative. The inaugu-ral orations, themselves, reveal a tendency to stock formulations and clichés. It is my contention that for this very reason his ideas are more representative of the prevailing opinions of his circle of patrons, professors, and students than those of a more gifted writer or original thinker might be—such, for example, as his two colleagues Landino and Poliziano.[22] With this in mind, and without denying him a certain capacity of showing insights that are intrinsically interesting, I propose to run through these orations in pursuit of a humanist's image of humanism.

In the first oration in praise of oratorical ability, after the usual introductions where he alludes to his having been added to a faculty dis-tinguished by Landino and Poliziano, he speaks of the great gift to man-kind made by the inventors of speech and writing. 'Proceeding thence in time, he who was more potent both in mental capacity and in suavity of speech compelled men by the powers of eloquence to cultivate mutual confidence among themselves, to serve the ends of justice, to enter into matrimony, and to assemble together in one town.'[23] But these capacities in the hands of the rulers of cities remained rude and without skill through many ages until the invention of rhetoric by Corax of Syracuse and its transfer to Athens and all Greece by Gorgias of Leontini, a man of the greatest knowledge of all things. The Romans, too, preferred deed to speech ('arationibus magis quam orationibus') until after the conquest of

Carthage and Macedonia, when they took up Greek rhetoric and oratory. Eloquence began to flourish in an incredibly brief time.[24] 'But afterwards when both the liberty of the Greek cities had been destroyed and the Roman republic reduced to servitude, it was little by little dissipated. Thence followed the devastation of Italy, the frequent barbarian invasions and overturn of the Roman cities, so that eloquence was so hostilely abused that it lay hidden for many centuries in squalor and darkness. At length it was brought forth into the light again by the works of the most noble poet, Francesco Petrarca; yet it was in such a corrupt condition that it retained but few features of its old form. It was raised up from this condition by the munificence of Eugenius IV, Nicholas V, King Alfonso, and Cosimo de' Medici.'[25]

After this short sketch of the origins of eloquence and its historical vicissitudes, which in della Fonte's hands becomes even more of a humanistic cliché, and which he will repeat in reference to the other branches of humanistc learning in succeeding orations, we come to the praise of oratory. 'All other human values perish in the shortest time: such as wealth, honors, beauty, health, power. The oratorical arts alone are the most firm bulwarks of our life which do not yield to the powers of enemies nor become corrupt in a brief interval of time. For they are with us always in our domestic affairs as well as in our public activities and cannot be taken away from us by fire, by sword, or by any violence. From whence arise greater advantages in private and public affairs than from eloquence? Whence richer rewards for every use and dignity of life? What, moreoever, is more excellent or more divine than to hold the minds of men by eloquence, to assuage the enraged, to arouse the torpid, to lead from whence you wish, and again to drive them wherever you wish? What is so truly necessary as to be furnished with these arms by which you yourself are able to protect yourself and yours, to punish the wicked, to care for the good, to embellish the fatherland, and benefit all mankind? What, at length, is more delightful than to be daily admired by the many, not for the greatness of one's fortune, not for the power of high offices but for one's very own genius and gift of speech? Can such great pleasure ever be gained from enviable riches and dangerous power as from facility in speaking to men? Finally, though we may be superior to beasts in many things, in this one we are far more outstanding, that we both have the power of reason and openly show it when we discourse among ourselves and reveal our thought by speech. Therefore we can do nothing more humanly, nothing more rightly, nothing more admirably than to excel other men in that quality by which we are especially superior to the brutes.'[26]

While it may not be necessary to quote so much rhetoric in order to understand della Fonte's motive for praising the same, this passage does reveal one interesting feature of our humanist's conception of humanistic studies. Rhetoric is indeed a rival discipline to those of the other professions, but here it is claimed that through it one not only achieves the advantage of making oneself superior to other men but that in so doing one becomes more peculiarly human. The highest and most distinctive type of man was not the philosopher, not Socrates, but the rhetorician, Gorgias. Renaissance Italian humanism in della Fonte's version of it may not yield the broad and generic philosophy of man that has sometimes been attributed to it. Nevertheless, it is interesting that in his forthright praise of the rhetorical arts he should claim that man's place in the universe was most properly achieved by means of them.

He turns immediately to a defense of humanism against ecclesiastical critics. 'Nor indeed should the fact that certain semi-barbarians detest and damn them as though they were contrary to the Christian religion deter you from our common studies. For these men do not convict our humanity of perfidy but reveal their own ignorance. . . . If they could discern how much the Latin excels the barbarian, the learned man the uneducated and rude, certainly they would blush and would cultivate this refined humanity as though something divine.' The Apostle Paul, the Greek fathers Basil and John Chrysostom, the Latins Lactantius, Jerome, and Augustine are duly cited as men who excelled in integrity and Christian sanctity 'yet also stood out in the elegance of their speech and writing'.[27]

'And if any one should judge that eloquence was the less to be sought after for the reason that in this age in judicial causes no speech by an orator is employed, and if that custom has become obsolete because of the vices of the times, still knowledge of the oratical faculty should not for that reason come to an end, especially since we are unable to extol any other art or science either by speaking or writing without its aid.'[28] And if Celsus writes eloquently of medicine this should not be thought to be part of the healing art. If Vitruvius writes lucidly of architecture this is due to the principles of rhetoric, not to the science of building. Eloquence should therefore continue to be studied even though of little use in forensic causes so that 'either living in literary retirement or active in public affairs we may treat of things in any place or time copiously, ornately, and lucidly. And whereas eloquence, the mistress of the whole human race, is acquired not only by nature but by practice as well and by art and imitation and by knowledge of the very greatest things', it needs to be carefully and systematically studied.[29] The mastery of these arts must be sought for the sake of speaking effectively in public assemblies and meetings and for carrying out the functions of ambassadors of princes and cities. For these purposes the study of the *Orations* of Cicero is indeed most praiseworthy.[30] Turning in peroration to his students, he added: 'You, moreover, dearest youths, who by the knowledge of these roads can reach to the highest peaks of refined humanity, should eagerly strive for this with me.'[31]

In summary three tendencies appear in della Fonte's defense or praise of eloquence: first, these are frankly the rhetorical arts that he is praising, and there is no danger of confusing them with philosophy; secondly, he sees eloquence as high in the order of qualities that render men peculiarly human; thirdly, he is very sensitive to a need to justify or affirm the usefulness of eloquence in the personal, the professional, and the civic life of his students. Moreover, the example of the early fathers should reassure them that it need not be contrary to the Christian religion.

The following year in his *Oration in Praise of History* della Fonte turned to another large branch of the study of letters ('facultas et eruditio litterarum'), historical literature, by way of introducing his course of the year on Lucan's *Pharsalia* and Caesar's *Civil War*. The structure of this oration follows what seems to have been a standard pattern for him: after an opening salutation and praise of the learning and distinction of his audience, he gives a general praise of the value to mankind of history; this is followed by an historical sketch of the origins of historical writing among the Greeks, how it flourished among the Romans, declined with ancient culture, revived with Petrarca, was sustained by the generosity of rulers, is now endangered again; to this is added a new statement of the utility of studying history, leading to a final exhortation to his students to devote to the study of his course as much zeal as he will try to give to teaching it.[32]

History as a branch of literature or (as he has it in a later oration[33]) of rhetoric manages, nevertheless, in della Fonte's treatment to transcend the conventionalities of his oratorical form and occasion. It is, in his view, through the existence and subsequent study of historical writing that mankind extends the range of its experience and hence of its knowledge and understanding. 'Thus it is through history that we who are long separated from the age of our ancestors, by reading of their deeds seem both to have lived in those times and to have been present at those events. For whereas this knowledge gained from not only the prosperous but also the adverse affairs of others certainly confers understanding free from all dangers, we owe very much to those who in order to make us and our posterity participants in past events founded history. They confer by their industry and labor the greatest utility on the life of mortals because it is essential to teach what is to be sought and what avoided. For when we read of the deeds of our ancestors, whether right or wrong ones, and we ponder their intentions, vicissitudes, and consequences, we are taught what is especially expedient for us. Since those who are born wise value prudence as the experience of many things, frequently they who eagerly study history surpass their ancestors in wisdom and prudence. For just as much as a long duration of time encompasses more events than the age of a single man, so much more prudent must he be thought who not only attains a knowledge of his own people and age but through accurate reading comes to know all nations and times. Thus they gather the richest fruits for effective living, both the young men whom the reading of history renders equal to their elders in prudence, and those of mature age who besides learning from experience are made learned by the examples of the past as well.'[34]

Having thus presented history as the arm of prudence in the conquest of practical wisdom, as opposed to philosophy based on rational principles, he turns to a humanistic version of the history of history. Some ages abound in great historians, but others signally lack them. Where kings and cities, powerful in their works and empires, reward the deeds of great men by celebrating their memory, there history, as among the Greeks and Romans, flourishes. The beginnings of history among the Greeks were rude and unpolished, merely records of times, men, places, and deeds. Herodotus and Thucydides brought it to greatness by utilizing rhetorical skill in their writing.[35] Thus his measure is still the utilitarian one of effectiveness. Listing many names, he includes Polybius, who 'wrote down forty volumes most accurately and learnedly of which only five survive'.[36] Similarly among the Romans the first historians were merely annalists, while their many notable historical writers 'as they were posterior in age so they were prior in eloquence'.[37] Then comes the familiar story of the decline of history along with the other good arts with the overturn of Rome by the barbarians. So great was the ignorance of the *studia humanitatis* that no one could write elegant Latin even if he had wanted to. Petrarca brought about a restoration of Latin to elegance, but history could not be repaired by this means alone.[38]

'For it is not in history, as it happens in other learned disciplines, that consequences are gathered by reasoning from those elements which pre- ceded. . . . For history is fabricated not by rational principles but by speech applied to actions or events. And for preserving and saving these there are two special aids, memory and letters.'[39] Since the one is limited to a lifetime and the other disappeared with the 'Gothic tempest', history could not survive.[40] Still certain writers such as Eutropius and Orosius attempted to continue the tradition, 'from whom we draw as it were shadows rather than true things and absolute images. Nor were letters entirely exiled by others in succeeding times, so that in certain more protected places far from the flames of war some men of religion wrote chronicles. But these men preserved neither a certain sequence of events, nor a true order of times, nor one whole body of history, since with this one the head is found, with that one the upper arm, with another the thigh without discrimination. So much distortion and deformity of the monu- ments of history, by which the knowledge of past events is possessed, took place that some men, indeed good, but partially educated, heaped up into a vast rubbish pile whatever in passing occurred to them without any distinc- tion of things, speech, or times, as though a ruin of fallen buildings.'[41] He cites as examples of such medieval historians the numerous volumes of Vincent of the Dominicans (Vincent of Beauvais), his successor Giovanni Colonna, of the same order, author of a work on the history of the world not unjustly called *The Sea of History* because of its tumid turbulence, and finally, Martin of the same order (Martin of Poland), who attempted to write of the lives of the popes and the Roman rulers.[42]

Fortunately in recent times history, too, was rescued from this turmoil by the support given to learning by Eugenius IV, Nicholas V, King Alfonso, and Cosimo de' Medici.[43] 'As is known both from Plato and long experience, as princes are toward public affairs so is the rest of the city, and whatever change of custom appears in them, the same is diffused into all people. Whereas princes formerly were uneducated, therefore the others also were rude and untaught. So that if any men should apply themselves to our studies, no honor, no dignity, no reward was proposed for them, which before all are needed to inspire men to the right arts. For just as a temperate sky and mild breezes bring about smiling fields, so the humanity and beneficence of princes renders men more eager for studies. Therefore, after those most liberal men began to draw men of talent to themselves by granting them honors, held erect by the hope of reward and glory, many devoted themselves to the study of letters; and each one according to this talent either collected ancient authors, or translated Greek writers, or composed new works. Thus then along with certain other good arts history was aided by many learned men.'[44]

Flavio Biondo wrote of events from the decline of the Roman empire to our own times. Leonardo Bruni embellished the Gothic war and our own people with a greater voice, and Poggio following him wrote of the same Florentine history. Bartolommco Fazio and Platina elegantly explained the deeds of King Alfonso and of the Christian pontiffs and emperors respectively. But alas, once again since the death of these princes letters have declined. He implores his audience of most humane citizens and you prefects of this 'literary gymnasium' not to allow Florence to fall behind other cities which she long excelled, and especially they should give support to the study of history.[45]

'For history confers the greatest utility on all. It deters the wicked from crime by the fear of infamy, and it inspires the good to virtue by the desire for eternal praise; by reading it private men are rendered eager to imitate the examples of their ancestors in doing great things and show themselves worthy of the greatest empires. Kings and princes themselves are inspired to distinguished actions for the sake of acquiring immortal glory through historians.'[46] How much then do we owe to those who gave their energy to writing history so that the memory of past events might be transmitted to us and our posterity, and in the first place to Lucan in verse and to Caesar in prose.[47] 'But as I make an end of speaking I urge each of you who will be hearers of this civil history that, perceiving its utility and amplitude, you devote yourselves with entire souls to Lucan and Caesar, most elegant authors and, for acquiring eloquence and receiving knowledge of great things, most useful.'[48]

As our own appreciation of the importance of humanist historical writing is increasing,[49] it is interesting to find della Fonte making so much of history both for its value as a source of practical wisdom and for its value as a source of examples of distinguished and moral behavior. While it is quite clearly thought of as a branch of literature, good history writing is regarded as necessarily rhetorically effective because by this means it can best carry out its functions of adding the experience of the past to that of the present and of inspiring living men to good and great deeds by the example of the dead great. Whether humanists in general regarded their professional activities as important to the civil community, it is clear that della Fonte felt a strong need to justify the importance of his teaching to the city which employed him. While his own historical writing consists of the same type of annals[50] that he regarded as a primitive form of history, this oration represents, certainly, a contribution to the theory of history, anticipating to some extent the more developed *artes historiae* of the middle and late sixteenth century.[51] Renaissance humanism, which produced the important histories mentioned by della Fonte, was through this oration not lacking in a history of history, and one that has certain merits. While his treatment of classical history was mainly a recitation of names, while his list of medieval historians omits such notables as Matthew Paris and Otto of Freising, let alone Giovanni Villani, and while his humanistic distortions are quite evident, still this oration manages to see historical writing in a historical perspective and to present the rudiments, at least, of a conception of the nature of history.

I skip over Fontius' next oration, presumably delivered in the year 1484 after his return from Rome, because the summary nature of its contents, *On the Good Arts,* makes it more appropriate for later treatment. And, indeed, the very next oration, *In Praise of the Poetic Art,* which introduced his course on the *Odes* of Horace of the year 1485–1486, deals with the third great division of literature. Following Ficino and echoing Plato in the *Phaedrus,* Fontius regards poetry as produced by a 'divine madness'. 'But he who comes to the doorposts of the poets without the inspiration of the muses, thinking he can make himself a bard by technique and learning, is vain and puerile in his poetizing. For noble bards, who are very few, create poetry not by art nor by science but rather by the divine spirit. . . . For God alone excites the madness of the poet and uses him as though a minister and messenger of his oracles. Our ancestors, the wisest of men, have affirmed concerning these matters that the other disciplines of the good arts can be accomplished by exercises and precepts, but the poetic

is aroused by the powers of genius and inflamed by the divine spirit. . . .
And the poetic itself is honored and worshiped before other most righteous
arts because proceeding from divinity it lifts the outstanding poets to
heaven and renders them immortal. For even though the oratorical faculty
is thought to excel among all studies and liberal disciplines, still no one can
be found among the Greeks who does not revere Homer more than Demosthenes and make the fame of Euripides and Sophocles more than that of
Hyperides and Lysias.'[52]

'Among us also there are very many who admire Vergil more than
Cicero, and in ancient times no oration of Messala or Pollio was celebrated
as much as the *Medea* of Ovid or the *Thyestes* of Varro. And not unjustly. For
if certain excellent men so very eagerly enslave themselves to the study of
music, which is of the ears alone, how much more ought we to listen with
our entire mind to the songs of poets, the perfect music not of our ears alone
but of our souls as well, especially since with high delight we derive the
utmost utility from the most weighty opinions and the most holy precepts
of the poets.'[53]

Despite the divinely inspired nature of poetry it is its moral usefulness
and the information it supplies that give it value. Especially Vergil,
Horace, Persius, and Juvenal contribute to morality, also Plautus, Terence,
Tibullus, and Propertius. 'Besides, in how many places these very poets
treat most elegantly of virtues, vices, human affections, of lower and higher
things, of the creation and nature of all things.'[54] Poetry is gracious,
voluptuous, and pleasurable to youths, who, when they are drawn into its
sweet-sounding study, do not become involved in angry lawsuits, in ac-
cumulating money, serving the more powerful, or falling into evil ways.
All peoples, however barbarous and cruel, have honored poets. Rulers
especially have paid homage to poets, not only Roman emperors but in
recent times Frederick of Aragon to Dante, the Emperor Charles IV, Kings
John II of France and Robert of Sicily to Petrarca. Why should he com-
memorate the study and office of the poet by reason of its usefulness to
mankind when wild beasts, stones, and trees are charmed by its sound and
squalid Charon, rough Pluto, beastly Hecate, cruel Cerberus, and the
horrible furies were tamed by the melodies of Orpheus?[55]

Then to what appears to be an exclusively rhetorical treatment of the
third branch of letters he adds a peroration designed especially for the ears
of his Florentine audience: 'But if the divine poetic art is rarely and heavenly conceded as a gift of the gods to a few most purified and most excellent
geniuses, if its delight and pleasure dominates and rules the souls of mankind, if high utility conjoined with high knowledge of every great thing
prevails over every human convenience, if not only peoples and cities and
princes and inhabitants of heaven delight in it but wild and enraged beasts
venerate it, you also, men of Florence, always thought to be the most

humane of all, should undertake with high zeal and ardor to embrace and honor the poetic art lest alone of all you should seem to have neglected the sweetest muses, foster-daughters of this city. Thus our citizens should show honor to Dante and Petrarca in this city's own name, so that not for any other things so much as for the ingenious and admired poetic art of its bards this our flourishing city may be most celebrated and most commended in the future among all peoples and nations in all eternity.'[56]

The oration of the next year, 1486, and the fifth of the whole series, was an equally rhetorical encomium of *sapientia,* and itself an exercise in that fifth and more controversial of the *studia humanitatis,* moral philosophy. That della Fonte was consciously engaged in something like a programmatic consideration of all of the branches of humanistic study seems indicated by his opening. 'Since in my previous orations I have separately extolled the oratorical, the historical, and the poetic capacities, and indeed conjointly all the most right arts together, I have considered what on this day I might speak about that would not be alien to my office. . . . I speak then what most briefly I am able to say concerning wisdom, the understanding of all things which are most honorable and excellent by nature, by which alone men are truly wise and by heavenly inspiration understand themselves.'[57]

The fatherland of *sapientia,* that quality so much praised by the humanists[58] and essentially different from *scientia,* is not in any one city but is in whatever we discern through the eyes or contemplate with the soul; it is wherever eternal minds ('sempiternae mentes') may be brought to bear on the sublime heavens, the air, or our own humble affairs. The true fatherland of wisdom is in the mind of God Himself, the author and supreme maker of all. 'Surely wisdom itself is not of human origin but divine because nothing in God is not a participant in the divine condition.'[59] 'Because of divine wisdom God knows not only Himself but his reason and essence also and whether present, past, or future. These perpetual designs ('exemplaria') of things He holds in the divine mind and He places his very essence among the forms in the middle of the mind, and as if some most absolute artisan He perfects this most ornate world and whatever things are in it by an admirable process ('ratione'). From this essence both power and order and multitude and variety of all things emanate. Of these some are so separated from matter that they can only be known by the sharpness of the mind, some are so conjoined with matter that they are immediately perceived by sense itself, and many are partly separated and partly joined and so spaced from each other by degrees of perfection that now they are surpassed, now surpass. Wisdom itself with the divine mind perceives these so many, so various, so elegantly disposed and collocated natures and produces them by ineffable art and governs them when produced.'[60] 'But this provident capacity of generation ('generatrix') of all things, as if it were not sufficient to govern celestially, fallen to us by a magnificent gift of God, dwells in our minds also. . . . . Entering into docile souls and removing madness, fear, greed, lust, and ignorance, it imbued them for the first time with the best morals. Then it taught them how to manage private affairs. Afterwards having assembled men in one place it founded the city and furnished public life with constitutions, laws, courts, arts, and every method of living well. From this capacity the elements of literature, from it the songs of most sacred prophets, from it the faculty of persuading developed. This alone drove the human soul to the contemplation of the nature of things in that order in which the divine mind itself had procreated them from the beginning. . . . . O wisdom, to be admired and embraced by you most humane men, whose gifts and powers you may discern are so great that nothing is so high, so middling, so low that it did not with God produce and most wisely preserve them.'[61]

Turning from this encomium of the gifts of wisdom to human civilization and taking up the more immediate needs of the supposed wise, he added: 'But when you have examined the most noble fatherland and the immortal origin of wisdom, and when you know how much it avails in divine and human affairs, it remains, prefects of learning, that you do not neglect wisdom's professors who day and night watch over the education of this distinguished Florentine youth and the instruction of your own children and grandchildren. These professors you ought to treat with greater munificence so that you will give hope of honors and prizes to those also who have not yet ascended to this most illustrious place.'[62] For what greater things can be conferred than knowledge and wisdom? Wealth rests in the hands of fortune, not in our counsels; kingdoms and powers also are gifts of chance; magistracies and honors stick to us only if we have virtue and knowledge; beauty and strength are from nature and but brief and fragile; pleasures of the body are the desires of cattle, not of men. 'Although if we would seek a virtuous pleasure, immortal gods, how great sweetness, how great joy, how great pleasure always fills the soul of the contemplative. . . . Since divine wisdom alone excels, what richer thing should we seek, what more powerful, what more honorable, what more beautiful, what more pleasurable? Wisdom is not in the arrogance of fortune, as riches and honors and powers. Wisdom is not in the necessity of nature, as distinguished appearance and health. Wisdom is not in the dominion of another, as other mortal things, but located in our own free will. Wisdom inheres in the souls of those who prudently and bravely carry on life, and it renders them happy and most blest.'[63]

Bartolommeo's moral philosophy, as illustrated in the above oration, is in no way distinguished but fairly typical of the humanists' echoing of the Senecan, Ciceronian veneration of the 'wise' man or sage. But it is clear that he was not in any pure sense a Stoic, for he spoke in the Neoplatonic terms made fashionable in his time of the source and nature of wisdom. On the other hand, more like the humanist followers of Aristotle of the early and mid-fifteenth century, he strongly emphasized the service to mankind and civilization of this quality, which he presumes to be part of the humanist's stock in trade.[64] He was a protégé of the Aristotelian Donato Acciaiuoli, a correspondent of Ficino, a colleague of Landino. All in all, as a rhetorician and philologist he was nicely eclectic and not at all a strict adherent to any one philosophical school.

Returning now to the *Oration on the Good Arts* of 1484, 'good arts' may be taken to mean the 'liberal' arts generally, for he covers in this oration not only the humanistic studies of grammar, poetry, oratory, and history but also philosophy, of which the humanistic study of moral philosophy is only one part. Beginning with grammar, he declares it the royal road to all other arts and studies because it contains the foundations of an understanding of them. Referring to the rival university subjects, he asks: 'What do the faculties of the physicians, the jurisconsults, or the philosophers have in themselves that is distinguished, excellent, delightful unless they are embellished by this learned companion? It is indeed the peculiar and greatest praise of this art that without it the sublimer sciences cannot exist, but this is perfected in itself. . . . Moreover this profession of grammarian, which some disdain as trivial and weak, embraces far more within itself than appears from without, for it contains the science of speaking correctly, and knowledge of the poets and the historians, as well as the signification of words, and not without a consideration of philosophy in very many places in the poets.'[65] Thus it would seem as if grammar itself contained all of the branches of the *studia humanitatis;* and, as will emerge, Fontius does seem to blend these various branches, moving toward the modern discipline of literature, *studia litterarum.*

Moving on to poetry, he calls it as above a 'divine madness driving pure minds to transcribe the truth in sounding numbers by an appropriate image'.[66] It began with the Egyptians, Assyrians, and Greeks in the form of religious prophecy and prayer. 'For when the first men instructed in milder ways of living began to assemble in a community, some most excellent man considered that no humanity could endure very long without the influence of divine religion. And so having contemplated by his own immortal genius the admirable works of nature, he came to believe that there is some one ruler of this world whom he himself both worshiped and taught others to adore. Solemnly addressing Him not in the common and vulgar speech which he used to men, he prayed to the divine power in a certain metrical harmony. Afterward others who followed in all, as is the custom, not only sang in greatly increasing praise of the higher powers, but also responded in song to those consulting the gods and wrote poems concerning the inhabitants of heaven.'[67] Thus Job, Moses, and Jeremiah among the Hebrews, Orpheus in Thrace, Linus, Amphion, and Musaeus in Greece all flourished as distinguished theological poets. So all whom the divine madness inspires are called prophets. Afterwards Homer addressed poetry to men, but still also much to the gods. Then poets turned to kings, wars, fables, loves, and other themes. 'But although the creators of heroic and celestial matters must truly be called poets, nevertheless there is great utility and delight in poetry either for the sake of speaking elegantly or for blessedly and happily living.'[68]

Turning to the art of rhetoric he will say a few things: 'without this the other disciplines appear speechless and mute. For indeed I believe that there is no learning which shows more how much man excels the beasts and silent creatures than this by which we are able to speak aptly, distinctly, and ornately. . . . I say that he was an earthly god who first by composing a speech persuaded men who were themselves previously uncultured to cultivate justice, to serve piety, to retain fortitude, to guard modesty. It was undoubtedly a great thing and worthy of every kind of praise by suavity of speech to compel rustic and wild men who were superior in force and strength of body to give up the most violent custom and let themselves become the equals of inferiors. See how many seditions have been suppressed, how many conspiracies extinguished, how many hostile wars composed, how many wild tribes and nations pacified by the power of oratory.' Among others he cites as examples Pericles and the Athenians, Marcus Valerius and the seceding plebs, Cicero's prosecution of Catiline.[69]

In this oration history is again considered as one of the *studia humanitatis,* but this time, as was more usual with Roman, medieval, and humanist discussions of the arts,[70] Fontius considers history as a subdivision of rhetoric. 'From this [rhetoric] we may gain images of the bravest and best men expressed in letters ('litteris') by historians for the sake of imitation. For history is a large part of the art of rhetoric, and although it is not ordinarily expressed through the principles of the orators ('rhetors'), still it emanates from them in such a way, and so depends on them, that, lacking this art of speech itself, history would appear crude and feeble. For the historians take over from the teachings of the orators the method of combining words, the character of a speech flowing with a certain smoothness and equality, vigor and sharpness, the order of things and times, and the expectation of counsels and actions and events. . . . But having briefly explained these matters concerning rhetoric, we end with what is the ultimate of our exposition, philosophy, the great gift of the gods.'[71]

In discussing philosophy he is less rhetorical and more explicit in his definitions. Adapting Cicero's definition of wisdom to his own purposes, he calls philosophy 'the knowledge of human and divine things, and the constant investigation of natures by opinion and science'.[72] It is opinion when the matter hides in uncertainty and is defined by no firm reason, science when the matter is perceived by some certain reason. Moreover, philosophy is divided into three parts: rational, moral, and speculative. Rational philosophy is the power of seeking and defining and distinguishing the true from the false—in other words dialectic or logic, although Fontius does not so name it. Moral philosophy consists entirely in action ('tota in actione') and is in its turn divided into three parts. 'Personal ('propria') philosophy instructs man himself and teaches the morals of man in the best manner. Domestic philosophy disposes of the home and family. Civil philosophy moderates and rules the city.'[73] All moral philosophy is perfected by the four cardinal virtues. Prudence, the judge of generated and mutable things, is seated in supervision over mortal affairs. Included within it are reason, understanding, circumspection, providence, docility, and caution. Fortitude, placed between fear and audacity, generates magnanimity, confidence, endurance, and firmness. Temperance is certainly a mean between pleasures and sorrows; modesty, reverence, thrift, abstinence, shame, and respectability follow after it. Justice, indeed, is to render to each what is his due; from it come innocence, friendship, concord, piety, religion, and humanity. 'Subject to it is the profession of the jurisconsult which, embracing law and equity, and having become important and practised widely, affecting many, is held in high honor.'[74]

Speculative philosophy is also divided into three parts. 'Natural philosophy considers whatever things are almost immersed in matter such as the four elements and whatever bodies are made and composed from them. The art of medicine is subject to it; this faculty comprehends both the diseases and the knowledge of their hidden causes, then of symptoms and after this of natural actions, and finally it requires knowledge of the interior parts. This art, first invented by Apollo, then celebrated by his son Aesculapius, soon made illustrious by Podalirius and Machaon at the time of the Trojan War, and finally perfected by Hippocrates, had most distinguished professors among the Greeks and Latins as well as the barbarians. Supernatural philosophy, furthermore, considering substances separated from matter itself, is claimed by theology, by which we contemplate those things surpassing the visible such as the divine and celestial. Disciplinal philosophy concerns itself with what can be partly separated and partly not separated from matter. There are four parts of this: arithmetic, which originated with the Phoenicians, comprehends numbers; geometry, invented by the Egyptians, contains dimensions. And music having its beginning with the same Egyptians, whence Pythagoras assumed it, is a certain measuring of voice and sound with constancy of perfect modulation. Astrology, which was first founded by the Chaldaeans, then expounded by the Egyptians, embraces the heavens and the stars.'[75]

Plato first rendered these scattered parts of philosophy into one body and whole animals. 'For Zeno and all the Eleatic school studied rational

philosophy only. Lycurgus, indeed, and Pittacus and Periander and Solon
wrote concerning the government of communities of men. Moreover,
Thales and Anaximenes and Anaxagoras considered natural things. Then
Plato, born after all of these, a man outstanding by nature and truly
divinely sent, left no part of philosophy unperfected, but, diligently embracing all, neither lacked in necessary matters nor fell into the useless.
Indeed he, together with almost all Greek philosophers, received the foundations of the whole of philosophy from the Hebrews and transferred them
to the Greeks.' Passing from this tribute to the hero of Florentine Neoplatonism to the praise of philosophy in general, he adds: 'Philosophy,
moreover, as the master and leader of our life, keeps far from and excludes
ambition, avarice, lust, envy, and the other iniquities of souls. Philosophy,
having investigated the good arts and the sciences and virtues with the
greatest zeal and diligence, always rightly counsels human life. For it
invents the very laws and rights and teaches the good arts. It establishes the
discipline of right living. It inquires into all things above, below, first,
last, middle.'[76]

That della Fonte regards the moral and civil utility of philosophy as
one of the five studies of the humanist seems clear from this treatment,
which parallels what he had to say about *sapientia* in the oration previously
discussed. Summarizing what he had covered in this present oration he
again indicates history as subordinate to rhetoric, unlike his extensive and
careful treatment of history in the oration of 1482. 'I have shown, as far as
my mediocrity permits, what grammar, what poetry, what rhetoric, in
which is history, what philosophy as a whole, within which is the science of
law and of medicine, contains.'[77] Alongside of the humanist, such as
himself, who worked in the disciplines of grammar, poetry, and rhetoric
with its sub-branch of history, he recognized the legitimacy of law, medicine, and theology as professions or faculties growing out of philosophy,
and probably also of logic and mathematics, which he does not mention.
All these latter, however, are regarded as carrying on specialized functions
dictated by these divisions of philosophy. The humanist, too, carried on the
specialized function of moral philosopher, but this was really identical with
the broad moral and civic ends of philosophy which are also reserved for the
humanist.

This is borne out by his peroration addressed to 'You best youths,
most beloved of my soul, who follow after me, this year expounding Silius,
in undertaking your studies.' They have but two ways, one of vices below,
one of virtues above, the one easy at first but hard later, the other hard at
first but the fruits richer and pleasanter. 'Moreover nothing can lead you
more safely and expeditiously to that goal than that you have come to know
all, if you can, or at least some of those sciences which I have described. For
thus rejecting all inert leisure, greed, and lust, and arriving at the rich fruit

and maturity of life, you should hold fast to that method of living best which brings us the highest utility and perpetual dignity.'[78]

There seems thus to be involved in Bartolommeo's persistent defense of humanism in all its branches a tendency to uphold its general importance to the civic community and to the moral life of the individual. *Humanitas* could almost be made synonymous with *urbanitas* or *civilitas*. Each of the several *studia humanitatis* and all of them conjointly are presented as bringing into being a civilized community in place of a previously wild and rustic condition, and each in its own way contributes to the maintenance and preservation of the docility, concord, and humanity of that community, so that the 'good arts' or the liberal arts are in reality the arts of civilization. That many persons today continue to defend the importance of the 'humanities' and the liberal arts as the major educational means of maintaining the decencies and civilities of modern life in an age of specialization should perhaps be mentioned.

All this is a prelude to the final oration of della Fonte *On Satire and on the Studia Humanitatis*. Skipping over the first part on satire which defends its moral value and, despite its obscenities, its religious legitimacy by citing Lactantius, Jerome, and Augustine,[79] we come to the main part of his oration, which is by far the most spirited and extravagant statement of the values of humanism he made. He begins: 'There have never been any well constituted cities or nations which have not cultivated the liberal arts with high energy. For, as I skip the Egyptians, Assyrians, and Greeks who were distinguished in developing all studies, our Italians also and the Romans were great in no one thing more than in the most virtuous and most righteous arts. But afterwards, depraved in morals, sunk into ruin by ambition, luxury, greed, lust, all the good arts declined with the Roman empire. But at length Italy, escaping from the most cruel hordes of barbarians, partly in the free cities, partly also under princes, began to rule and govern itself; little by little the right arts which lay in ruin for many centuries raised themselves up. But the first to be taught by appointed masters and doctors were medicine, which pertains to the cure of bodies, and legal science, for carrying on lawsuits and legal causes. For the sake of religion and faith philosophy also was cultivated in sacred convents. Only oratory and poetry lay ruined in squalor and darkness almost nine hundred years until the times of Dante and Petrarca.'[80]

Dante by his *Divina commedia* equaled all earlier prophetic poets, and Petrarca excelled with his love poetry. But Petrarca made such an important beginning in 'this our humanity' that every humanist is in debt to him. Then these studies received the support of certain benign princes: Eugenius IV, Nicholas V, King Alfonso, and Cosimo de' Medici.[81] To these names used so repeatedly by della Fonte he now adds: 'Nor indeed should Pope Pius Piccolomini and Federigo of Urbino be defrauded of the praise due them as lovers of men of eloquence. But these illustrious lights of letters having been extinguished, that great ardor of the men of talent was partly burnt out. Although in this our flourishing city, as it began with the poet Dante, so also it has persevered to this day in cultivating our common studies. For after him Petrarca was very celebrated. To him succeeded Boccaccio, the ablest of all in his age. After him Coluccio Salutati had sufficient eloquence but much more learning and prudence. Thence Niccolo Niccoli, and if he wrote nothing, still a liberal and learned man he gave much help to many mortals for study and writing. Younger than these; Leonardo Bruni and Ambrogio [Traversari] the monk excelled in elegance and dignity of life. Afterward Carlo Marsuppini in public lectures and Poggio in openly and lucidly writing both flourished. Then Battista Alberti contributed certainly very much to our studies. Most recently Donato Acciaiuoli was distinguished both in speaking and writing. And indeed their modesty keeps me from mentioning certain living scholars. But they one day will be distinguished, nor will they be numbered among the least. Certainly these most educated and learned men have made this flowering fatherland illustrious through the entire world for the splendor of its name. For surely great and even greater utility and honor and glory than I am able to speak of redounds to the fatherland from eloquent men most excellent both in talent and learning. Therefore our ancestors, the wisest of mortals and most respectful toward these matters, founded this school of the good arts and elected annual officials from the priors and elders of the city so that with greater authority these our studies might be celebrated.'[82]

Such an illustrious example of of aid to men of letters from the past should, of course, be emulated, and it is again 'fitting that you . . . aid scholars of humanity'.[83] Alluding to his own rivalry with Poliziano, which he was to continue in the very course of lectures on Juvenal this oration introduced, he argued that such competition among men of learning should be encouraged and should not stand in the way of increased support of scholars. 'For if any one should think from the dissensions of points of view which always exist among the scholars of these arts that their wills also are in conflict, he makes a serious mistake. For I, as I have never been the enemy of any one, so also I have never thought any one considered me an enemy other than disagreeing in opinion and point of view. In this matter it is far more useful and glorious to have had conflicts than to have lacked all emulation.'[84] They are no greater in number than they have been for the past six years (since 1481 when he was added to the faculty), but they have not become any less learned through practice. 'Since we are indeed celebrated by great praises through all peoples and nations, and we Florentines are thought to be the most eloquent of all, you ought to increase this constant and eternal future fame by providing a larger number of professors as well as by giving hope of the greatest honors and rewards to the others.'[85]

The humanities should be given even greater support than the other faculties (in Pisa). 'Nor indeed should any of you think that greater concern should be had for other arts than eloquence. For the other professions have definite limits beyond which their professors cannot move. For physicians are concerned with what pertains to preserving and restoring health; jurisconsults with what pertains to composing controversies. But we, wandering through all, embrace the study of all things, times, places, and men. For if any one would assert that a knowledge of historians, poets, and orators is our concern, I would indeed admit that our profession is more thoroughly trained in the interpretation of these. But still in explaining these very writings there are by far more and more excellent things than men not learned in our fields may see. For whatever orators and poets write concerning heaven and the stars, concerning higher as well as lower matters, concerning virtues and vices, on governing cities, and a thousand other subjects of that sort, all that it is necessary for us to explain in weighty and most refined speech accommodated to the senses of the audience. This we are not able to do without great knowledge of all subjects of study. But since we have to explain whatever thing happens notably, prudently, and elegantly, with a certain charm of manner even, who would not place us ahead of the teachers of the other arts?'[86] And with a final plea to the university officials to grant further funds to the humanities for the glory of the city and out of respect to its tradition he closed his oration.

This rather extensive survey of the public statements of one of the lesser humanists on the scope and value of his profession demands that, however briefly, we state our conclusions. Without any question Professor Kristeller is right in emphasizing the primarily rhetorical character of humanism and the articulation of its ideas out of the basic five *studia humanitatis*. Although sometimes for Bartolommeo della Fonte grammar and eloquence seem to be two sides of a tent of literature ('litterae') beneath which dwell the sub-disciplines of oratory, poetry, history with moral philosophy involved in them all,[87] there is a clear relationship of his varying divisions to the conventional list of grammar, rhetoric, poetry, history, and moral philosophy. It is to be noted that in practice grammar and rhetoric were the forms in which the professor of the humanities (of 'eloquence' or of 'poetry and oratory') analyzed what may be designated as four large branches of literature as they were derived from and found in ancient literary models, namely, the oratorical writings of Cicero or Isocrates or Demosthenes, the poetry of Latin and Greek authors, the historical writing of classical authors, and finally the very frequent prose essay or dialogue of the ancient writers of which Cicero's *Tusculan Disputations*, or his *De finibus*, or Seneca's numerous moral essays are representative and to which was not infrequently added Aristotle's *Ethics* or *Politics* or *Economica* or his *Rhetoric* or his *Poetics*. It points to the beginning of what we call 'classics' as a discipline.

It is further notable how Fontius claims for the professor of eloquence the need to know and expound everything that comes up in literature and hence to be concerned with what might be termed 'general philosophy' as distinguished from the special technical branches subserving the professions or faculties of medicine, law, and theology. While this might exclude except in a general way logic, mathematics, and natural philosophy, it would certainly include, besides the ethics and political theory common to the humanist, at least excursions into metaphysics and theology, although the humanist would be apt to approach these in a superficial, peripheral, and eclectic way.

Finally, and perhaps this illuminates the preceding point, the strongly utilitarian cast of della Fonte's arguments must be noted. While it would be natural for him to point out the value to the community of the study of eloquence in the course of arguing for greater support for his subject by the authorities and the general public, the extent and consistency of his plea and notion of the 'communication arts' as the producers and maintainers of civilization and good citizens goes far beyond his rhetorical necessities. This would tend to link him with Hans Baron's and Eugenio Garin's emphasis[88] on the civic character of humanism. Would it, on the other hand, be too much to suggest, rather, that as a teacher of youth he conceived of the humanist's rôle in a fashion similar to the ancient sophists, of whom he names Gorgias[89] and praises him for the extent of his knowledge? In addition his conception of the origins of the humanistic disciplines and their rôle as creators of civilization is remarkably close to the point of view attributed by Plato to Protagoras,[90] as well as to Cicero's, although Fontius nowhere in these orations mentions either the dialogue or the man. Whether or not there is anything more than a similarity here, it does suggest that della Fonte's claims to a kind of rhetorical preëmption of philosophy in a broad literary, moral, and civic sense has behind it this very ancient tradition of the sophists' claim to a monopoly of wisdom in their own day.

NOTES

1. *Byzantion* XVII (1944–1945), 346–374; also *Studies in Renaissance Thought and Letters* (Roma, 1956), 553–583.
2. (Cambridge, Mass., 1955), pp. 3–23.
3. *Ibid.*, p. 22.

4. Concetto Marchesi, *Bartolommeo della Fonte* (*Bartholomaeus Fontius*), *contributo alla storia degli studi classici in Firenze nella seconda metà del quattrocento* (Catania, 1900), states, p. 10, that he was born in 1445 because in a letter of 1495 he speaks of its being his fiftieth year. Arnaldo della Torre, *Storia dell' Accademia platonica in Firenze* (Firenze, 1902), p. 422, n. 1, corrects this to 1446 on the basis that the letter in question was dated Florentine style and hence written in 1496. For further study of Fontius see now: S. Caroti and S. Zamponi, *Lo Scrittoio di Bartolomeo Fonzio* (Milan: Edizioni Il Polfilo, 1974).

5. Marchesi, pp. 55–56, 68–69, 72–73, holds that he was appointed in August 1481 after the death of Filelfo shortly after he had finally been called back to Florence to teach, that he was forced to leave in the fall of 1483 because of his quarrel with Poliziano, that, despite the statement of the *deliberazioni* of the university of 3 November 1484 reappointing him for this season, quoted by Marchesi in his notes (n. 1, p. 69), Fontius did not return until the following fall. The chronology I use is based on the manuscript dating of his inaugural orations, for which, and for the acts of the university officials given by Marchesi, see note 12 below.

6. Giovanni Prezziner, *Storia del publico studio . . . di Firenze* (Firenze, 1810), 1, 163, lists Chalcondylas, Landino, Poliziano, and Fonzio as the faculty in 1485 with the salaries given. He gives, pp. 164–165, the 1488 roll as the same with Naldo Naldi added and suggests, after a letter of Poliziano naming him a colleague (*Epist.*, v, iii), that Bartolommeo Scala also had been added.

7. Marchesi, p. 55.

8. Cf. Part II, 'Gli studi classici'.

9. The formal rather than rhetorical nature of the medieval introductions to not only the arts course but the entire curriculum is stressed by R. W. Hunt, 'The Introductions to the Artes in the Twelfth Century', *Studia Mediaevalia in honorem admodum reverendi patris Raymundi Josephi Martin* (Brussels, 1943), pp. 85–112, and by Edwin A. Quain, 'The Medieval Accessus ad Auctores', *Traditio* III (1945), 215–264. Some of the inaugural orations and inaugural poems of della Fonte's illustrious colleague Angelo Poliziano as well as the inaugural 'sermons' of della Fonte's contemporary, the professor of Greek letters at the University of Bologna, Antonio Urceo 'Codro', may be cited as other Renaissance examples. Isidoro del Lungo, *Florentia* (Firenze, 1897), pp. 176–182, reconstructs the lecture course and corresponding orations and *sylvae* of Poliziano. The orations may be found in *Tomus tertius operum Angeli Politiani* (Lugduni, 1537). The *sylvae* are reprinted by del Lungo in his *Prose volgari inedite e poesie latine e greche edite e inedite di Angelo Ambrogini Poliziano* (Firenze, 1867). Some but not all of Codrus' 'sermones' are published, out of proper order, in a volume containing a miscellaneous selection of his works, 'Impressum Bononiae per Ioanne Antonium Platonidem Benedectorum 1502'. Ezio Raimondi, *Codro e l'umanesimo a Bologna* (Bologna, 1950), pp. 147–150, establishes their correct order and dates them from internal evidence. Only in some of the fifteen orations published in 1502 is the subject of the lecture course indicated.

10. It is probable that all three incunabula were published in close association

early in 1488 (1487 Florentine style). Copinger (1, 218) indicates that Hain 7227 was 'Florent. S. J. de Ripolis', but erroneously dates it 1478. Since the final oration was delivered in November 1487 (see note 18 below), it seems unlikely that the series could have been put into print before the end of the year (modern style).

11. Professor Kristeller very kindly secured and allowed me to use a microfilm of this manuscript. Although it was copied later than the incunabula cited, Fontius probably made this copy himself or, at the very least, supervised its copying. A comparison with Florence, Bib. Lor. XXXIX, 36 (a manuscript of Valerius Flaccus' *Argonautica*, copied, according to Marchesi, p. 139, by Fontius for Francesco Sassetti) and with Florence, Bib. Ricc. 539 (autographic notes and excerpts by Fontius) indicates the same or an extremely similar formal book hand. In general, whether an autograph or not, the Wolfenbüttel manuscript is textually more accurate and freer of errors than the in- cunabulum. It also, as succeeding notes indicate, supplies information as to date and subject of the orations and lecture courses that the incunabulum omits and makes it possible to correct Marchesi in several respects.

12. Wolfenbüttelel Cod. 43 Aug. Fol. (hereafter cited as 43 Aug.), f. 139^r. I follow the datings given by the manuscript, since the incunabulum omits them. Marchesi, p. 56, relying on inductive evidence, dates the orations differently, crowding the first five orations into the three years 1481, 1482, and 1483, including two apiece in the last two. It is his hypothesis that Fontius left for Rome in the fall of 1483 but did not return until the fall of 1485 contrary to the archival evidence quoted in his own footnotes. It is also his hypothesis that no oration was delivered in the fall of 1485 in order not to offend Poliziano and that the sixth and last of the series came in 1486–1487 on the grounds of an internal reference to the granting of a tenth by Innocent VIII to clerics attending the university in 1487—an argument equally ap- plicable to the year 1487–1488 which the manuscript names (see note 18). It is not necessary to assume that Fontius remained in Rome until after the spring of 1485 simply because he wrote a latter from Rome describing an event which occurred at that time. He could have taught his course and then revisited Rome. The act of the university officials gave him a one-year ap- pointment in November 1484 and a new act of June 1485 gave him a two-year appointment beginning the following November: Archivio di Stato fioren- tino. *Deliberazioni circa lo Studio Fiorentino e Pisano dal 1484 al 1492* n. 416, f. 107. 'Dicta die 3 novembris 1484. Supradicti officiales studii servatis servan- dis conduxerunt Bartholomaeum Fontium ad lecturam poetice et oratorie in Studio florentino cum eo vel iis concurrentibus. Pro tempore unius anni init. die primo dicti mensis novembris cum salario alias predictos officiales in una vice vel pluribus declarando in dicto anno et cum honoribus emolumentis privilegiis et aliis secundum ord.—Approbata fuit per dominos et collegia die 17 decembris 1484' (Marchesi 69, n. 1). *Deliberazioni circa lo Studio Florentino* etc. f. 112^v. 'Die 23 Iunii 1485. Supradicti officiales studii florentini et pisarum servatis servandis conduxerunt ad legendum et docendum in studio florentino artem oratoriam et poeticam Bartholomaeum gianpieri fontium

cum eo vel iis concurrentibus. Pro tempore duorum annorum initiandorum die primo mensis novembris proxime futuri 1485, quorum ultimus est ad beneplactium dictorum officiales. Cum salario florenorum sexaginta etc.' (Marchesi 73, n. 1). For these reasons it seems safer to follow the datings given in a manuscript copied or supervised by its author and prepared for the library of Matthias Corvinus while he was preparing a catalogue of the same library for the same king. These datings, furthermore, give one oration at the beginning of each academic year that Fontius most probably taught at the university. The Florentine archives supply further evidence as to Fontius' appointments, in addition to that already cited (but misinterpreted) by Marchesi: Archivio di Stato, Firenze; Ufficiali dello Studio, 1484–1508 (shelf mark 1981), vol. 5, f. 124^v. 'Die 24 mensis Octobris 1487 (conduxerunt) Dominum Bartholomaeum Fontium ad legendum in studio Florentino artem poeticem et oratoriam facultatem. Pro tempore unius anni initiandi die primo mensis Novembris 1487, cum salario florenorum sexaginta. . . . Approbata fuit dictum conductum per dominos et collegia die 2 Novembris 1487.' The 'Rotulorum Designationes' also indicate, f. 211^v, for 1484–1485, 'Bartholomaeus Fontius Fl. 60 (107)' (referring back to the folium on which appointment is recorded, which is the same as cited by Marchesi above); f. 213^r for 1485–1486, 'Bartholomaeus Fontius Fl. 60 (112)'; f. 214^v for 1486–1487, 'Bartholomaeus Fontius Fl. 60 (112)'; f. 215^v for 1487–1488, 'Bartholomaeus Fontius Fl. 60 (124).' For 1488–1489 and succeeding years his name no longer appears. His salary payments are also listed, but because of the irregular and dilatory manner in which the commune paid its professors, little information is forthcoming as to the exact dates of his appointments. The total paid out between July 1485 and December 1488, however, adds up to four times the sixty florins annual salary for the four years of his teaching covered by these records, ff. 178^r–186^r.

13. 43 Aug., f. 145^r.
14. Marchesi, pp. 58–73 with corrections of note 12.
15. 43 Aug., f. 153^r. Indication of lecture subject on f. 159^v. Hain 7227 (hereafter cited as 7227) omits mention of this.
16. 43 Aug., f. 160^r.
17. 43 Aug., f. 165^r. Indication of lecture subject in opening of next oration, f. 169^r; also 7227, sig. d5^r.
18. 43 Aug., f. 169^r.
19. Del Lungo, op. cit., p. 179.
20. Florence, Biblioteca Nazionale Centrale, Cod. Palatino Capponi 109 (77), beginning on verso of 4th unnumbered sheet in front (transcribed in Appendix 1). Since the manuscript contains letters dated as late as 1513, the year of della Fonte's death, this list, made by Francesco Pandolfini, his heir and executor, may be considered fairly complete. However, it does not seem to mention his *Annales,* cited below in note 50. His letters have been edited by László Juhász, *Bartholomaeus Fontius, Epistolarum libri III* (Budapest, 1931). His poems have been edited by Joseph Fógel and László Juhász, *Bartholomaeus Fontius, Carmina* (Leipzig, 1932). See Appendix II for a listing of some of the works of Fontius known to exist in manuscript or printed edition.

21. 43 Aug., ff. 118^v–130^v, 7227 sigg. f2^r–f12^v.
22. For Poliziano's orations see above, note 9. Those published in the Lugduni, 1537 edition, however, seem to be more concerned with the specific text or author that was the subject of the coming course and less with the general nature of the *studia humanitatis* than in the case of Fontius.
23. Fontius echoes the ideas but not the language of Cicero, *De inventione* 1, ii, 2.43 Aug., ff. 140^v–141^r; 7227 sig. a3^v: 'Procedure deinde tempore, qui magis et animi ratione pollebat et suavi locutione, fidem inter se homines colere, iustitiam servare, matrimonia inire, seque in uan moenia cogere viribus eloquentiae compulit.'
24. 43 Aug., f. 141^r; 7227 sigg. a3^v–a4^r.
25. 43 Aug., f. 141; 7227 sig. a4: 'Sed ea postea et civitatibus graecis libertate sublata et romana republica in servitutem redacta paulatim obmutuit. Vastatione deinde Italiae consecuta et crebric barbarorum incursionibus, frequentique romanae urbis eversione, tantam calamitatem perpessa est, atque adeo hostiliter agitata, ut permulta saecula in squalore ac tenebris latitarit. Sed prodiit tandem in lucem Francisci Petrarchae nobilissimi vatis opera; tanto tamen situ adhuc confecta, ut veteris formae non multa lineamenta reciperet. Erexit deinde de Eugenii quarti et Niccoli quinti et Alphonsi regis et Cosmi Medicis munificentia. . .'
26. 43 Aug., ff. 141^v–142^v; 7227 sigg. a4^v–a5^r: 'Caetera brevi peritura sunt omnia; opes, honores, forma, valitudo, potentia. Sola oratoria studia sunt vitae nostrae munimenta firmissima, quae neque adversariorum viribus cedunt, neque brevi intervallo temporum corruunt. Sunt enim sive domi, sive foris semper nobiscum, nec igni, nec ferro, nec ulla a nobis violentia extorquentur. Unde vero maiora proveniunt privatis aut publicis rebus quam ex eloquentia commoda? Unde ampliora praemia ad omnem vitae usum et dignitatem? Quid porro excelsius est aut dignius quam eloquendo tenere hominum mentes, sedare incensas, inflamare extinctas, et unde velis deducere ac rursus quo velis impellere? Quid vero tam necessarium quam muniri his armis quibus ipse te tuosque tegere, improbos laedere, bonos tueri, patriam ornare, et omne genus humanum iuvare possis? Quid tandem suavius quam a multis quotidie recoli non pecuniae magnitudine, non superborum fascium potestate, sed suo ipsius proprio ingenii (7227 ingenio) et faciundae bono? Ulla ne tanta in invidiosis divitiis et periculosa potentia quanta in homine dicendi copiam consecuto esse unquam voluptas potest? Denique cum rebus plurimis superemur, hac una longe brutis praestamus: quod et animi rationem habemus et eam aperte ostendimus cum colloquimur inter nos et dicendo sensa nostra exprimus. Quare nihil humanius, nihil rectius, nihil laudabilius facere possumus quam ut ea in re caeteros homines excellamus in qua maxime beluas superamus.'
27. 43 Aug., ff. 142^v–143^r; 7227 sig. a5: 'Neque vero a communibus studiis vos deterreat quod semibarbari quidam ea detestantur et damnant tanquam Christianae religioni contraria. Nam hi nostram humanitatem perfidiae non coarguunt sed ignorantiam suam detegunt. . . . . Qui si tamen dignoscerent (7227 discernerent) quantum latinus barbaro, disertus inculto ac rudi

praestet, erubescerent sane ac tanquam divinum numen hanc exultam humanitatem incolerent. . . . dicendi quoque ac scribendi elegantia praestiterunt.'

28. Aug., f. 143ʳ; sig. a5ᵛ: 'Quod si quis eloquentiam propterea minus iudicat
expetendam, quod hoc tempore in iudiciis nulla vox oratoris adhibeatur, etsi
mos ille temporum vitiis obsolevit, non propterea tamen ab oratoriae facultatis
cognitione cessandum est, cum presertim nullam aliam artem atque scientiam
aut dicendo aut scribendo extollere sine huius praesidio valeamus.' Vittorio
Rossi, *Il quattrocento* (5th ed., Milano, 1953), p. 154, also states: 'L'oratoria
guidiziale era in balìa degli avvocati, e nei tribunali si soleva disputare,
piuttosto che per via di discorsi, a botta e risposta', referring (n. 57) to a
passage from P. P. Vergerio, *De ingenuis moribus* which speaks of the decline
not only of judicial, but of deliberative and demonstrative oratory as well.
Although there are some instances of trials at which humanists made orations,
Rossi's further remark that the humanists, taken with Cicero's famous judicial
orations, found a substitute in the invectives they addressed to each other is
well taken. Certainly it is the fact that Roman judicial procedure was not
prominent in his own day that Fontius here laments.

29. 43 Aug., f. 143; 7227 sig. a6ʳ: '. . . aut in ocio litterato viventes, aut
aliquod publicum munus gerentes, quocunque loco ac tempore de omni re
copiose, ornate, dilucide pertractemus. At quoniam totius humani generis
eloquentia moderatrix non solum natura sed usu quoque et arte et imitatione
ac maximarum rerum cognitione percipitur . . .'.

30. 43 Aug., f. 144ʳ, 7227 sig. a6ᵛ.

31. 43 Aug., f. 144ᵛ; 7227 sig. a7ʳ: 'Vos autem adolescentes charissimi iis
itineribus cognitis, quae ad summum politioris humanitatis fastigium possint
perducere, ad illud mecum studiose contendite.'

32. Although the question of form is of no concern to the purposes of this paper,
Fonzio's expanded rhetoric may be compared with the concise statements of
the medieval introductions to commentaries on classical authors: 'Vita auctoris, titulus operis, intentio scribentis, materia operis, utilitas, cui parti
philosophiae supponatur'—all succinctly put. Cf. Quain, *op. cit.,* and note 9
above.

33. *In bonas artis* of 1484. Cf. below p. 114 and notes 70, 71.

34. 43 Aug., f. 145ʳ; 7227 sigg. a7ᵛ–a8ʳ: 'Qua fit ut qui a maiorum nostrorum
aetate longe distemus, eorum facta legentes et temporibus illis vixisse et rebus
eisdem interfuisse videamur. Quae sane cognitio ex aliorum cum prosperis
tum adversis rebus percepta cum doctrinam habeat omnium periculorum
expertem, plurimum debemus iis qui ut nos posterosque nostros praeteri-
tarum rerum participes facerent, historiam condiderunt. Sua enim industria et
labore maximam utilitatem vitae mortalium afferentes quid sequi quid vitari
oporteat docuere. Nanque maiorum recte aut perperam facta cum legimus,
corumque consilia, varietates, eventus perpendimus, quid maxime nobis expe-
diat admonemur. Cum vero multarum rerum experientia prudentiam gigni
sapientes existiment, frequenter historiam lectitantes maiores natu consilio et
prudentia facile superant. Quanto enim plura exampla rerum longi diuturnitas
temporis, quam unius hominis aetas complectitur, tanto est prudentior cen-

sendus is qui non suae tantum gentis aetatisque, sed omnium nationum et temporum memoriam accurata lectione complectitur (7227 consequitur). Itaque ad bene degendam vitam uberrimos fructus capiunt, cum iuniores, quos rerum gestarum lectio senioribus aequat prudentiam, tum aetate maturi, quos praeter experientiam rerum exempla quoque praeteritorum erudiunt.'

35. 43 Aug., f. 146^r; 7227 sig. a8^r.
36. 43 Aug., f. 147^r; 7227 sig. b1^r: 'Polybius quadraginta volumina quorum quinque tantum supersunt accuratissime dissertissimeque descripsit.'
37. 43 Aug., f. 147^v; 7227 sig. b1^r: 'Quos omnes ut aetate posterior ita eloquentia prior est.'
38. 43 Aug., ff. 148^r–149^r; 7227 sig. b2^r. Incidentally Fontius uses language that is suggestive of an early version of the 'failure of nerve' theory of the decline of the ancient world. He says (148^r, b2^r): 'una cum caeteris disciplinis historiae nervi torpescere, debilitarique incepere . . . .'.
39. 43 Aug., f. 149^r; 7227 sigg. b2^v–b3^r: 'Non enim in historia perinde accidit atque in caeteris sapientiae disciplinis, in quibus consequentia ex his quae praecesserunt ratiocinando colliguntur. . . . Historia nanque non rationibus, sed rebus adhibita oratione conficitur. Cuius tuendae atque servandae duo sunt pracipua adminicula memoria ac litterae.'
40. 43 Aug., f. 149^r; 7227 sig. b3^r: 'gothica . . . tempestate'.
41. 43 Aug., f. 149^v; 7227 sig. b3: '. . . ex quibus umbras quasdam potius quam veras res et absolutas imagines haurimus. Neque vero caeteris quae successere temporibus usque adeo litterae exularunt, quin in quibusdam munitioribus locis religiosi aliqui viri procul a bellorum incendiis constituti chronica scripserint. Sed ii neque certam seriem rerum, neque verum ordinem temporum; neque integrum unum corpus historiae servaverunt, quando apud hunc caput, apud illum lacerti, apud alium humeri sine ullo delectu locati fuerint. Accessit ad hanc tantam iacturam et deformitatem monumentorum, quibus rerum gestarum cognitio haberetur, quod nonnulli boni quidem sed parum eruditi homines, quae passim occurrerant absque delectu aliquo rerum orationis et temporum veluti lapsorum aedificiorum ruinas in vastum quendam aggerem contulerunt.'
42. 43 Aug., ff. 149^v–150^r; 7227 sig. b3^v. Vincent of the Dominicans turned out to be the only Vincent of the five in J. Quetif et J. Echard, *Scriptores Ordinis Praedicatorum* (Paris, 1719–1721) who wrote a history, namely the well-known Vincent of Beauvais and his famous *Speculum historiale*. Giovanni Colonna, died 1290, wrote *Mare historiarum ab orbe condito ad sancti Galli regis Ludovici IX temporem inclusive libri VIII*. The Biblioteca Laurenziana in Florence has a manuscript of this work running to 245 folia: Cod. Aedil. 173. Martin, one of nine of that name in Quetif et Echard, is certainly Martinus Polonus, fl. 1278, who wrote *Chronica de constitutione Romae tam summorum pontificum quam imperatorum Romanorum ex multis chronicis compilata*.
43. 43 Aug., f. 150; 7227 sig. b4^r.
44. Aug., ff. 150^v–151^r; 7227 sig. b4^r: 'Est vero et Platone auctore et longa experientia cognitum ut quales principes in re publica fuerint, talis quoque sit reliqua civitas, et quaecunque commutatio morum in illis apparuerit, eadem

in omnem populum effundatur. Quoniam igitur ineruditi antea erant principes, caeteri quoque rudes erant atque indocti. Quod siqui forte se ad nostra studia conferebant, nullus honos, nulla dignitas, nullum praemium proponebatur. Quae res in primis homines excitare ad rectas artis consuevit. Nam sicuti caeli temperies et benignitas aeris gignit segetes laetiores, ita humanitas et beneficentia principum homines ad studia reddit alacriores. Ergo postquam illi liberalissimi viri caepere ad se honoribus et muneribus ingeniosos allicere, multi spe praemii gloriaeque erecti ad atdudia litterarum incumbebant; et pro sua quisque facultate aut vetera conquirebat, aut graeca transferebat, aut nova opera componebat. Itaque tunc a multis doctis viris cum aliae quaedam bonae artes, tum etiam historia est adiuta.'

45. 43 Aug., f. 151; 7227 sig. b4^v.
46. 43 Aug., ff. 151^v–152^r; 7227 sig. b5^r: 'Quae pares verbis res gestas referens omnem utilitatem complectitur. Nam et infamiae metu a scelere ac turpitudine vitae deterret improbos, et aeternae laudis cupiditate ad virtutem accendit probos. Eius enim lectione privati quidam viri maiorum exemplis ad res magnas exequendas ingentibus animis inflammati, sese dignos maximis imperiis praestiterunt. Ipse vero reges ac principes ob immortalem gloriam per historicos assequendam ad praeclara facinora sunt incensi.'
47. 43 Aug., f. 152^v; 7227 sig. b5^r.
48. 43 Aug., ff. 152^v–153^r; 7227 sig. b6^r: 'Sed ut finem dicendi faciam, quicunque hanc civilem historiam audituri estis, adhortor ut eius utilitate amplitudineque perspecta Lucano et Caesari auctoribus elegantissimis et ad eloquentiam consequendam et magnarum rerum scientiam percipiendam utilissimis, totis animis incumbatis . . . .'.
49. Cf. Wallace K. Ferguson, *The Renaissance in Historical Thought* (Cambridge, Mass., 1948), ch. 1; Hans Baron, 'Das Erwachen des historischen Denkens im Humanismus des Quattrocento', *Historische Zeitschrift* CXLVII (1932), 5–20; T. E. Mommsen, 'Petrarch's Conception of the Dark Ages', *Speculum* XVII (1942), 239 ff.; B. L. Ullman, 'Leonardo Bruni and Humanist Historiography', *Medievalia et Humanistica* IV (1946), 59 ff.
50. Possibly a historical work more worthy of the name, but unlocated, is his *Principiorum et temporum libri VIII*, listed among his works by Francesco Pandolfini. Cf. note 20 above and Appendix I. Giovanni Lami published his *Annals* as part of his catalogue of the Biblioteca Riccardiana from Cod. Ric. 1172: *Adnotationes in Livium et Iuvenalem et annales suorum temporum* (1448–1483), ff. 84^r–127^r; printed Io. Lami, *Catalogus Cod. manuscriptorum qui in Bibliotheca Riccardiana Florentina adservantur* (Liburni, 1756), 193–197. Cf. S. Morpurgo, *I manoscritti della R. Biblioteca Riccardiana di Firenze* (Roma, 1892), p. 219. Reprinted, G. C. Galletti, *Philippi Villani Liber de . . . famosis civibus . . . et de Florentinorum litteratura* (Florentiae, 1847), pp. 153–159.
51. Cf. Beatrice Reynolds' analysis of these later treatises in 'Shifting Currents in Historical Criticism', *Journal of the History of Ideas* XIV (1953), 471–492.
52. 43 Aug., ff. 161^r–162^r; 7227 sigg. c5^v–c6^v: 'Verum qui sine musarum numine ad poeticos postes venit, artificio et doctrina se vatem posse fieri putans, vana est eius poesis et puerilis. Nobiles enim vates, qui perpauci sunt,

non arte neque scientia sed divino spiritu potius praeclara poemata concinunt. . . . Deus etenim solus furorem poetis incutit ac tanquam administris et oraculorum suorum utitur nuntiis. Quibus de rebus maiores nostri sapientissimi viri confirmavere, caetera bonarum artium studia fieri exercitationibus et praeceptis, poetam vero ingenii viribus excitari et divino spiritu inflamari. . . . Ipsaque poetice prae caeteris rectissimis artibus honoratur et colitur, quod a divinitate procedens erigit in caelum immortalesque reddit praestantis vates. Nam ex omnibus studiis liberalibusque doctrinis tametsi facultas oratoria praestare putatur caeteris, nemo tamen apud graecos inventus est qui non magis Homerum quam Demosthenem coluerit, pluribusque Euripidis et Sophoclis quam Hiperidis et Lisiae famam fecerit.' Cf. Plato's *Phaedrus* 245A; Cicero, *Tusculan Disputations* I, xxvi, 64; Marsilio Ficino, *Theologica Platonica,* lib. xiii, cap. ii, 'De Poetis' (*Opera, Basel,* 1576, I, 287): '. . . non hominum inventa esse praeclara poemata, sed coelestia munera, cuius illud affert signum in Phaedro, quod nullus unquam licet diligentissimus, et omnibus artibus erudidus, excelluit in poesi, nisi ad haec accesserit ferventior illa animi concitatio quam sentimus quando est Deus in nobis, agitante calescimus illo. Impetus ille sacra semina mentis habet.'

53. 43 Aug., f. 162ʳ; 7227 sig. c6ᵛ: 'Apud nos quoque permulti sunt qui Vergilium magis quam Tullium admirantur, et antiquorum aevo nulla tantum Messalae aut Pollionis oratio quantum Ovidii Medea aut Thyestes Vari celebrabatur. Neque iniuria. Nam si musico studio, quod aurium solum est, excellentes quidam viri tam percupide serviere, quanto magis carmina poetarum non aurium tantum sed etiam animorum nostrorum perfectam musicem debemus tota mente percipere? cum praesertim ex gravissimis poetarum sententiis, praeceptique sanctissimis cum summa delectatione utilitatem quam maximam referamus?' Cf. Marsilio Ficino's *Epistola de divino furore* of 1 December 1457 (*Opera,* I, 614): 'Hanc Plato graviorem musicam poesimque nominat, efficassimam harmoniae coelestis imatricem, nam levior illa, de qua paulo ante mentionem fecimus, vocum duntaxat suavitate permulcet, poesis autem, quod divinae quoque harmoniae proprium est, vocum atque motuum numeris gravissimos quosdam, et ut Poeta diceret, delphicos sensus ardentius exprimit, quo fit, ut non solum auribus blandiatur, verum etiam suavissimum, et ambrosiae coelestis similimum menti pabulum afferat, ideoque ad divinitatem proprius accedere videatur.'

54. 43 Aug., f. 162; 7227 sigg. c6ᵛ–c7ʳ: 'Praeterea quot in locis de virtutibus, de vitiis, de humanis affectibus, de inferis, de superis, de rerum omnium creationibus, et naturis vates ipsi elegantissime tractaverunt.'

55. 43 Aug., ff. 162ᵛ–614ᵛ; 7227 sig. c7ʳ–c8ᵛ.

56. 43 Aug., ff. 164ᵛ–165ʳ; 7227 sig. c8ᵛ–d1ʳ: 'Verum si divina poetice raro caelitus paucis purgatissimis excelentissimisque ingeniis munere deorum concessa est. Si eius oblectatio et voluptas animis hominum dominatur et imperat. Si summa utilitas cum summa omnium magnarum rerum cognitione coniuncta omnem humanam commoditatem exuperat. Si non populi modo et urbes et principes et caelites eam diligunt, sed etiam ferae immites et furiae venerantur, Vos quoque Florentini viri omnium semper humanissimi habiti

summo studio et ardore animi ad poeticam complectandam honestandamque innitimini, ne soli ex omnibus neglexisse suavissimas musas huius urbis alumnas videamini. Quae ita Dantem, Petrarchamque cives nostros suo numine ornaverunt, nullis ut aliis tantum de rebus quantum eorum vatum ingeniis admirandisque poematis nostra haec florentissima civitas apud omnes gentes et nationes in omnem aeternitatem celebratissima sit commendatissimaque futura.'

57. 43 Aug., f. 165; 7227 sig. d1ᵛ: 'Superioribus meis orationibus cum seiunctim oratoriam facultatem, historiamque ac poeticen, coniunctim vero cunctas rectissimas artis concelebrarim, saepe mecum cogitavi, quid hodierna die ab officio meo non alienum possem referre. . . . Dicam enim et dicam quae brevissime potero de Sapientia rerum omnium intellectu, quae honoratissime ac praestantissime sunt natura, qua sola homines vere sapiunt et caelestia numina se percipiunt.'

58. Cf. Eugene F. Rice, Jr.'s recent book, *The Renaissance Idea of Wisdom* (Cambridge, Mass., 1958), especially chapters 2 and 3. Rice does not refer to this oration of della Fonte's but intends only to be representative.

59. 43 Aug., f. 166ʳ; 7227 sig. d2ʳ: '. . . ipsa profecto non humani est generis sed divini, quoniam nihil in deo est divinae conditionis non particeps.'

60. 43 Aug., ff. 166ʳ–167ʳ; 7227 sig. d2ᵛ–d3ʳ: 'Hanc propter non se tantum, sed rationem quoque suam deus, essentiamque intelligit neque secus quam presentia, praeterita, et futura cognoscit. Haec rerum perpetua exemplaria in divinam mentem coegit, seque ipsam inter formas, mentemque mediam collocavit, ac tanquam artifex quaedam absolutissima ornatissimum hunc mundum et quaecunque in eo sunt admirabili ratione perfecit. Ab hac essentia et potestas et ordo et multitudo et varietas rerum omnium emanavit. Quarum nonnullae sunt a materia ita disiunctae ut solo mentis acumine cognoscantur; quaedam ita coniunctae ut ipso statim sensu percipiantur; pleraeque ita partim semotae, partim connexae, atque ita gradibus inter se perfectionis distantes ut modo superentur modo exuperent (43 Aug. exuperentur). Has tam multas, tam varias, tam eleganter dispositas, collocatasque naturas ipsa sapientia cum divina mente percepit et ineffabili arte produxit, gubernatque productas.' This passage obviously reflects the influence of Marsilio Ficino's Neoplatonist philosophy, but Fontius, as will be seen, was more of an eclectic than a devotee of one view.

61. 43 Aug., f. 167; 7227 sig. d3: 'Verum haec provida rerum omnium generatrix quasi non satis esset gubernare caelestia, magnificentissimo dei munere ad nos delapsa, mentes quoque nostras incoluit. . . . Quae dociles ingressa animos furore, metu, cupiditate, libidine, ignorantiaque remota in primis moribus optimis eos imbuit. Deinde rem ipsam familiarem curare docuit. Postea in unum locum coactis hominibus civitatem constituit, remque publicam institutis, legibus, iudiciis, artibus, omnique bene vivendi ratione munivit. Ab hac litterarum erudimenta, ab hac vatum sanctissimorum carmina, ab hac facultas persuadendi emanavit. Haec sola humanum animum compulit ad rerum naturas eo ordine contemplandas quo cum mente divina eas ab initio procreaverat. . . . O admirandam et a vobis humanissimi viri complectendam

sapientiam, cuius tantas opes et vires cernitis, ut nihil tam sit summum, tam mediocre, tam infima, quod non illa cum deo produxerit et sapientissime conservaverit.'

62. 43 Aug., ff. 167ᵛ–168ʳ; 7227 sig. d3ᵛ: 'Caeterum quando nobilissimam patriam et immortale genus sapientiae prospexistis, quantumque in divinis humanisque rebus valeat cognovistis, reliquum est, litterarii praefecti, ut eius professores, qui pro hac egregia iuventute florentina erudienda, proque liberis et nepotibus vestris instituendis dies noctesque invigilant, non negligatis. Quos vel ex eo debetis pro vestra humanitate atque prudentia tractare munificentius ut illis etiam qui nondum hunc locum ornatissimum ascenderunt maiorem spem detis et honorum et praemiorum.'

63. 43 Aug., f. 168; 7227 sigg. d3ᵛ–d4ᵛ: 'Quanquam si honestam expetimus voluptas, quanta dii immortales suavitas, quantum gaudium, quanta iocunditas insidet semper animo contemplanti. . . . Quod cum divina sapientia sola praestet, quid divitius, quid potentius, quid honestius, quid formosius, quid voluptuosius ea quaerimus? Sapientia non in temeritate fortunae, ut opes et honores et potestates. Sapientia non in naturae necessitate, ut egregia forma et valitudo. Sapientia non in alieno dominio, ut mortalia caetera. Sed in nostra libera voluntate locata est. Sapientia quorum animis haeret, vita prudenter fortiterque peracta reddit eos felices et perbeatos.'

64. Cf. Rice's discussion of wisdom and the active life, *op. cit.,* pp. 43–49. Note echoes of Cicero's views in *De inventione* II, ii, 2 in this oration, particularly in the passage in note 61 above.

65. 43 Aug., f. 154; 7227 sig. b7: 'Quid vero praeclarum quid excellens, quid delectabile in se habet aut medicorum, aut iurisconsultorum, aut philosophorum facultas, nisi hac erudita comite exornetur? Est quidem huius artis peculiaris ac maxima laus quod sine hac scientiae sublimiores non possunt consistere, haec autem in se sola perficiatur. . . . Haec autem grammatices professio, quam non nulli ut ieiunam tenuemque fastidiunt, multo plus intra se quam foris ostendat complectitur. Nam et recte loquendi scientiam et poetarum et historiarum cognitionem et verborum interpretationem continet non sine philosophiae in plurimis poetarum locis inspectione.' This oration of Fontius', as well as the next one discussed, may be compared with earlier humanists' discussions of the superiority of one or another profession or discipline. Cf. especially Salutati's *Tractatus de nobilitate legum et medicinae,* ed. Eugenio Garin (Firenze, 1947), and the works discussed by Lynn Thorndike, 'Medicine Versus Law at Florence', ch. 11 of *Science and Thought in the Fifteenth Century* (New York, 1929), and by Eugenio Garin, *La disputa delle arti nel quattrocento* (Firenze, 1947). A contemporary humanist inaugural oration on this theme is Filippo Beroaldo senior, *Declamatio philosophi, medici, et oratoris* (*Opuscula varia,* Basel, 1513), which, like Fontius, favors the humanistic study. Codrus' 13th 'sermon' (*op. cit.,* sigg. Q2ᵛ ff.) is 'In laudem liberalium artium'. This and Fontius' oration may also be compared with medieval attempts to define and classify the liberal arts, reconciling the traditional *trivia* and *quadrivia* with the various faculties of the medieval universities. Fontius seems here to reclassify the arts so as to make them conform to the

studia humanitatis and also to subordinate medicine, law, and theology to the general heading of philosophy, which was in part one of the root humanistic studies. Cf. the diagram of his scheme in note 77 below. For medieval schema cf. Martin Grabmann, *Die Geschichte der Scholastischen Methode,* II (Berlin, 1957), ch. ii, 'Ungedruckte Wissenschafteinteilungen und Wissenschaftslehren' and the literature there cited.

66. 43 Aug., f. 154ᵛ; 7227 sig. b7ᵛ: 'divinus furor puras mentes ad verum sonantibus numeris describendum decoro figmento impelles'.

67. 43 Aug., f. 155; 7227 sig. b8: 'Nam cum primi homines mitiorem vitam edocti in unum cogere se coeperunt, vir quidam excellentissimus cogitavit nullam humanitatem sine divinae religionis affectu durare posse diutius. Itaque suo ingenio immortali admirabilia naturae opera contemplatus unum aliquem esse censuit mundi huius moderatorem, quem et ipse primus incoluit et caeteris adorandum instituit. Huic solennia vota persolvens non communi ac vulgata oratione, qua ad homines utebatur, sed numerosa quodam concentu divina numina precabatur. Caeteri postea subsecuti omnia (ut solet) in maius adaugentes non solum laudes superis cecinerunt, sed deos consulentibus etiam carmine responderunt, poemata quoque ad caelites pertinentia conscripserunt.'

68. 43 Aug., f. 155ᵛ; 7227 sig. b8ᵛ: 'Sed quamquam heroicarum rerum coelestiumque fictores vere tantum poetae dicendi sunt, omnium tamen utilitas et delectatio magna est, vel ad eleganter dicendum vel ad beate feliciterque vivendum.'

69. 43 Aug., f. 156; 7227 sig. c1: 'Nam equidem si existimo nullam esse doctrinam quae magis ostendat quantum homo bestiis et mutis animantibus praestet, quam haec, qua loqui apte, distincte, ornateque valemus. . . . Deus inquam in terris ille fuit qui primus composita oratione iustitiam colere, pietatem servare, fortitudinem retinere, pudicitiam custodire prioribus ipsis incultis hominibus persuasit. Magna nimirum res et omni laudum genere digna fuit agrestes et feros homines suavitate dicendi compellere ut qui superiores vi et robore corporis essent posthabita violentissima consuetudine se inferioribus adaequarent. Age vero quot seditiones compressae, quot coniurationes extinctae, quot hostilia bella composita, quot ferae gentes et nationes vi sunt orationis pacatae.' Cf. Cicero, *De inventione,* 1, ii, 3: 'Profecto nemo nisi gravi ac suavi commotus oratione, cum viribus plurimum posset, ad ius voluisset sine vi descendere, ut inter quos posset excellere, cum se pateretur aequari et sua voluntate a iucundissima consuetudines recederet quae praesertim iam naturae vim obtineret propter vetustatem.'

70. Cf. Beatrice Reynolds, *op. cit.,* pp. 473–478.

71. 43 Aug., f. 157ʳ; 7227 sigg. c1ᵛ–c2ʳ: 'Ab hac imagines fortissimorum atque optimorum virorum litteris per historicos eleganter expressas ad imitandum assumimus. Est enim historia magna pars facultatis rhetoricae, quae licet separatim non sit expressa rhetorum praeceptionibus, ita tamen ab eis emanat atque dependet, ut sine hac ipsa dicendi arte inculta et rudis et debilis videatur. Verborum enim contexendorum rationem, et genus orationis cum lenitate quadam aequali profluens, et concionum nervos atque acumen, et rerum

ac temporum ordinem, et consiliorum actorumque et eventuum expecta-
tionem ex oratoriis disciplinis sumunt historici. . . . Sed his breviter de rhetorice explicatis, quod est ultimam nostrae narrationis philosophiam donum
ingens deorum absolvamus.'

72. 43 Aug., f. 157; 7227 sig. c2^r: 'Est autem philosophia humanarum di-
vinarumque rerum cognitio, naturarumque inquisitio constans opinione atque
scientia.' Eugene Rice, *op. cit.,* especially p. 39 and n. 32, makes much of the
humanist variations on a Ciceronian theme in the definition of wisdom.
Fontius defines 'philosophy' in the same language, which suggests again that
his oration on wisdom, discussed above, was intended to cover another large
area of the humanist's disciplinary concern. See below in this present oration
how much of 'philosophy' he makes the concern of the humanist also. Cicero,
Tusc. Disp., IV, xxvii, 57: 'sapientiam esse rerum divinarum et humanarum
scientiam cognitionemque, quae cuiusque rei causa sit'.

73. 43 Aug., f. 157^v; 7227 sig. c2: 'Propria virum ipsum, moresque viri optime
instruit. Domestica domum familiamque disponit. Civilis civitatem moder-
atur ac regit.'

74. 43 Aug., ff. 157^v–158^r; 7227 sig. c2^v–c3^r: 'Huic subiacet iurisconsultorum
facultas, quae legum aequitatem complectens et magna existens et late patens
et ad multos pertinens summo in honore habetur.'

75. 43 Aug., f. 158; 7227 sig. c3: 'Naturalis quae immersa penitus in materia
sunt, ut quattuor rerum elementa, quaeque ex his corpora constant et compo-
nuntur considerat. Huic ars medicinae subest, quae abditarum et morbos
continentiam causarum notitiam, deinde evidentium, posthaec etiam naturalium actionum, novissime partium interiorum scientiam requiret. Quae
quidem facultas ab Apolline primum inventa, deinde ab eius filio Aesculapio
celebrata, mox a Podalirio et Machaone troiani belli temporibus illustrata, ab
Hippocrate demum perfecta apud Graecos, Latinosque ac barbaros clarissimos
habuit professores. Supernaturalis autem substantias ab ipsa materia separatas
considerans theologiam sibi vendicat, qua supergressi visibilia, de divinis et
caelestibus contemplamur. Disciplinalis vero his intendit, quae partim
seiungi partim etiam non disiungi a materia possunt. Cuius quattuor sunt
partes: Arithmetica, quae a Phoenicibus orta numeros comprehendit; Geo-
metria, quae ab Aegyptiis adinventa dimensiones continet; Musicamque ab
eisdem Aegyptiis, unde Pythagoras assumpsit, principium trahens est vocis ac
soni certa dimensio cum constantia perfectae modulationis; Astrologia, quae a
Chaldaeis primo comperta, deinde ab Aegyptiis edita caelum ac stellas
complectitur.'

76. 43 Aug., f. 159; 7227 sigg. c3^v–c4^r: 'Zeno enim et omnis Eleatica disciplina
rationali solummodo studuit. Lycurgus vero et Pittacus et Periander et Solon
de gubernandis hominum caetibus conscripserunt. Thales autem et Anaximenes atque Anaxagoras de naturalibus rebus considerarunt. Plato deinde
post hos omnes natus vir natura praestans et vere divinitus missus nullam
partem philosophiae imperfectam reliquit. Sed omnes diligenter complexus
nec in necessariis defuit, nec ad inutilia delapsus est. Ipse quidem caeterique
fere omnes graecorum philosophi ab Hebraeis fundamenta totius philosophiae

acceperunt, ad Graecosque transfuderunt. Philosophia autem vitae nostrae magistra et dux ambitionem, avaritiam, libidinem, invidiam, caeteraque animorum iniquinamenta longe fugat atque excludit. Philosophia bonas artis et scientias et virtutes summo studio et diligentia indagata humanae semper vitae recte consuluit. Ipsa enim leges ac iura invenit. Ipsa bonos mores edocuit. Ipsa rectam vivendi disciplinam instituit. Ipsa omnia, supera, infera, prima, ultima media inquisivit.'

77. 43 Aug., f. 159^v; 7227 sig. c4^r: 'Ostendi quantum mediocritas mea tulit, quid grammatice, quid poetice, quid rhetorice, in qua historia, quid philosophia tota, in qua iuris et medicinae scientia inest, in se contineat.' Della Fonte's division of the arts may be diagrammed as on the chart on p. 85. Cf. Grabmann's diagram of Radulfus de Longo Campo's division of the sciences, *op. cit.*, II, 52, note 1.

78. 43 Aug., ff. 159^v–160^r; 7227 sig. c4: 'Vos autem adolescentes optimi et animo meo charissimi, qui me Silium hoc anno interpretantem et vestris studiis incumbentem prosecuturi estis. . . . Nihil autem vos tutius atque expeditius ad eam potest perducere quam vel omnes si potestis, vel aliquam saltem earum scientiarum quas modo recensui cognovisse. Ita enim omni inerti ocio, cupiditate, libidineque reiecta ad bonam frugem et vitae maturitatem pervenientes, eam optime vivendi rationem tenebitis quae summam nobis utilitatem et perpetuam afferat dignitatem.' 7227 omits the phrase 'Silium hoc anno interpretantem et' which indicates the subject of his lectures for the year. Since Marchese, *op. cit.*, p. 56, used this incunabulum but not this manuscript, he lists this oration without a lecture subject and as has been seen, note 12 above, dates the oration as in 1482 rather than 1484, most probably an error, unless, of course, Fontius was inventing a subject and a date in committing the oration to this manuscript copy.

79. 43 Aug., ff. 169^r–172^v; 7227 sigg. d5^r–d7^v contain the section on satire.

80. 43 Aug., ff. 172^v–173^r; 7227 sig. d8^r: 'Nullae unquam bene institutae civitates ac nationes non summopere liberalia studia coluerunt. Nam ut ommitam aegyptios et assyrios graecosque omnium doctrinarum generibus claros, itali quoque nostri, romanique nulla re quondam fuere insignes magis quam honestissimis et rectissimis artibus. Sed posteaquam ambitione, luxuria, cupiditate, libidine moribus depravatis pessum iere, omnes quoque simul bonae artes cum romano imperio concidere. Verum italia tandem fugatis hostibus immanissimis barbaris, ex quo partim liberis civitatibus, partim etiam sub principibus regere ipsa se coepit ac moderari; paulatim se rectae artes, quae permulta saecula iacuerant, erexcrunt. Sed in primis quae ad curationem corporum pertiet medicina, et ad lites et causa iuris scientia conductis magistris ac doctoribus legi ceptae. Religionis quoque ac fidei causa philosophia omnis in sacris conventibus culta est. Solae quidem oratoriae et poetice annos circiter (7227 circa) noningentos ad Dantis et Petrarchae tempora in squalore et tenebris iacuerunt.'

81. 43 Aug., f. 173; 7227 sig. d8.

82. 43 Aug., ff. 173^v–174^r; 7227 sigg. d8^v–c1^r: 'Neque vero Pius picolomineus pontifex et federicus urbinas merita laude fraudari debent eloquentium homi-

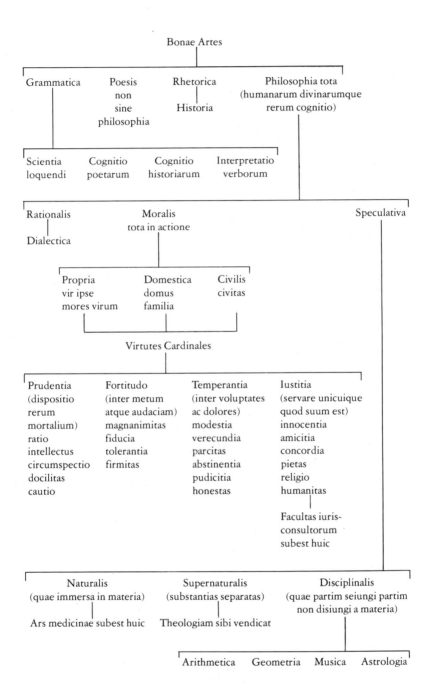

Bonae Artes

Grammatica   Poesis   Rhetorica   Philosophia tota
          non   (humanarum divinarumque
          sine   Historia   rerum cognitio)
        philosophia

Scientia   Cognitio   Cognitio   Interpretatio
loquendi   poetarum   historiarum verborum

Rationalis   Moralis   Speculativa
              tota in actione

Dialectica

      Propria   Domestica   Civilis
      vir ipse   domus   civitas
      mores virum familia

Virtutes Cardinales

Prudentia   Fortitudo   Temperantia   Iustitia
(dispositio   (inter metum (inter voluptates (servare unicuique
rerum   atque audaciam) ac dolores)   quod suum est)
mortalium)   magnanimitas modestia   innocentia
ratio   fiducia   verecundia   amicitia
intellectus   tolerantia   parcitas   concordia
circumspectio firmitas   abstinentia   pietas
docilitas   pudicitia   religio
cautio   honestas   humanitas

                                Facultas iuris-
                                consultorum
                                subest huic

     Naturalis   Supernaturalis   Disciplinalis
(quae immersa in materia) (substantias separatas) (quae partim seiungi partim
                                        non disiungi a materia)
Ars medicinae subest huic Theologiam sibi vendicat

          Arithmetica   Geometria   Musica   Astrologia

num amatores. Sed extinctis his clarissimis litteratorum luminibus ardor ille ingeniorum magna ex parte consumptus est. Quanquam in hac nostra florentissima civitate ut a Dante poeta coepit, ita quoque ad hanc diem perseveratum est in studiis communibus excolendis. Nam post eum Petrarcha fuit percelebris. Cui successit Boccaccius aetatis suae facundissimus omnium. Post quem Coluccius Salutatus eloquentiae satis habuit, sed plus multo doctrinae atque prudentiae. Nicholaus deindi Nicoli etsi nihil scripsit, liberalis tamen et doctus vir multis mortalibus ad studia et litteras opem tulit. His natu minores Leonardus Brunus et Ambrosius monachus elegantia et vitae dignitate praestitere. Carolus postea Martiopinus publice profitendo et Poggius aperte dilucideque scribendo floruerunt. Baptista subinde Albertus plurimum certe contulit nostris studiis. Novissime Donatus Acciaiolus cum orando, tum scribendo insignis fuit. Quosdam vero viventium non patitur me referre eorum pudor. Sed clari olim erunt, neque in postremis numerabuntur. Hi sane doctissimi ac disertissimi homines hanc florentem patriam per omnem terrarum orbem fulgore sui nominis illustrarunt. Magna enim profecto atque adeo maior, quam dici queat utilitas et honestas et gloria ab eloquentibus viris et ingenio, doctrinaque excellentibus redundat in patriam. Quare maiores nostri mortales sapientissimi et erga hanc rem perpientissimi hoc bonarum artium gymnasium posuerunt et officiales annuos e primoribus urbis ac senioribus elegerunt, ut maiore auctoritate studia haec nostra celebrarentur.'

83. 43 Aug., f. 174^v; 7227 sig. e1^v: 'decet vos . . . adiuvare studiosos humanitatis'.

84. 43 Aug., ff. 174^v–175^r; 7227 sigg. e1^v–e2^r: 'Nam siquis ex opinionum dissensionibus, quae semper erunt inter earundem artium studiosos, existimat voluntates quoque eorum adversas esse, vehementer errat. Ego enim, ut nemini unquam sum adversatus, ita quoque nunquam putavi adversarium quempiam me habere praeterquam in referenda opinione atque sententia. Qua quidem in re et utilius multo fuit et gloriosius contendisse quam omino aemulis caruisse.'

85. 43 Aug., f. 175^r; 7227 sig. e2^r: 'Cum vero per omnes gentes ac nationes magnis praeconiis celebremur, censeamurque Florentini eloquentissimi omnium, debetis hanc constantem et futuram famam vel maiore numero augere atque aliis spem praebere maximorum honorum et praemiorum.'

86. 43 Aug., f. 175; 7227 sig. e2: 'Neque vero quisquam vestrum existimet maiorem curam habendam esse artium reliquarum quam eloquentiae. Nam caeterae facultates certos limites habent, quos ultra earum professores non spatiantur. Quae enim ad conservandam aut restituendam pertinent sanitatem procurant medici. Consulti iuris, quae ad controversias componendas. At nos per omnia evagantes omnium rerum scientiam temporum, locorum, hominumque complectimur. Nam siquis erit qui asserat ad nos spectare historiarum ac poetarum et oratorum cognitionem, fatebor equidem in his magis assidue versari nostram interpretandi professionem. Sed tamen in his ipsis explicandis multo plura et excellentiora sunt quam videant homines nostrarum artium imperiti. Quotiens enim de caelo ac stellis, de superis atque inferis, de virtutibus ac vitiis, de moderandis urbibus, deque mille id genus

caeteris scribunt oratores ac poetae, totiens, nos oportet oratione gravi et perpolita et audientium senibus accommodata ea exponere. Quae facere non valemus sine multa omnium doctrinarum cognitione. Verum quaecunque res inciderit, cum a nobis sit explicanda memoriter et prudenter et eleganter cum quadam actionis etiam venustate, quis non aliarum artium nos doctoribus anteferat?' Cf. note 65 above.

87. Cf. above p. 57 and 43 Aug., f. 145^r; 7227 sig. a7^r: 'Magnos inter fruct-us . . . quos affert humano generi facultas et eruditio litterarum, illum vel maximum censeo quod earum ope gestarum rerum memoria conservatur.' Cf. also above p. 62 and note 57, p. 64 and note 65, p. 70 and note 86 for instances where Fontius groups oratory, history, and poetry together, with moral philosophy pervading all three and as a separate branch of letters.

88. Fontius' civic-mindedness would not be an unexpected tendency in a pupil and protégé of Donato Acciaiuoli. On Baron see *The Crisis of the Early Renaissance* (Princeton, 1955), passim, as well as his many earlier articles on this theme. For Garin's view, *L'umanesimo italiano: filosofia e vita civile nel Rinascimento* (Bari, 1952) is most representative.

89. See above p. 54 and note 24.

90. Plato, *Protagoras* 320c ff. On the relation of humanism to sophism, cf. Werner Jaeger, *Paideia* (2nd ed., tr. Highet, New York, 1945), 1, 297, 300–303, 312–313. Professor Kristeller also points to the connection with the sophists and cites Jaeger in his *Classics and Renaissance Thought,* pp. 11–12 and note 9.

Humanism and Poetry:
The Quattrocento Poetics of
Bartolommeo della Fonte

I

Some time between the summer of 1490 and the spring of 1492 the late fifteenth-century humanist Bartolommeo della Fonte (or, as he is frequently called, Fontius) wrote his *De poetice ad Laurentium Medicem libri III*. In 1960, as an appendix to my study of the inaugural orations of Fontius, I published the list of his works compiled by his student Francesco Pandolfini shortly after the death of Fontius in 1513.[1] To this I added a list of all the locations of these works, both manuscript and printed, that I could discover, including some not listed by Pandolfini. Shortly thereafter (in January 1961) I received a note from Professor E. H. Gombrich, director of the Warburg Institute, telling me that he had seen a manuscript of one of the unlocated items on the Pandolfini list (my number 33), namely Fontius' *Poetics*. Since he did not send me the location of the manuscript and spoke of writing a note about it some time, I did not pursue the matter. However, in the spring of 1964, alerted by my study, a former student of Professor P. O. Kristeller, Professor Giuseppe Velli of the Italian Department of Smith College, also discovered the location of this hitherto unknown manuscript and passed the information on to me through Professor Kristeller. The latter kindly obtained a microfilm[2] for my use, and Professor Gombrich has graciously consented to my going ahead and editing this work.[3]

I would not want to claim that the *Poetics* of Fontius is a major contribution in the history of literary criticism. But I have reason to believe that this is a very interesting and historically significant work, even if it cannot be compared to the *Poetics* of Aristotle or the *Ars poetica* of Horace, or in refinement of literary judgement to that of some of the humanist literary critics of the next century. Any claim as to the *quality* of the work is a value judgement that is inextricably involved with historical and literary-aesthetic evaluations of the entire field of Italian Renaissance literary criticism, on

This article is reprinted from *Studies in the Renaissance* 13 (1966): 40–122. The title has been altered from the original "The Unknown Quattrocento Poetics of B. d. F." The text of Fontius's poetics, and my analysis of his handwriting, have been omitted here and may be consulted by scholars in the original edition.

which there are many new studies,[4] as well as some older ones,[5] of varying value. I do not have the extensive knowledge of this field that is necessary for such a value-judgment. But the historical importance of this work rests on the fact that Fontius' *Poetics* is a *Quattrocento* poetics. Although there were important discussions of poetry by contemporary and greater humanists, particularly by Landino,[6] Poliziano,[7] and Pontano,[8] as Fontius himself says in his preface to Lorenzo de' Medici,[9] he has 'undertaken to write a *Poetics,* a subject on which Horace, alone of the Latins,[10] wrote certain precepts'. Presumably this work of Fontius is the first formal poetics written in the Renaissance[11]—at least it is as far as his knowledge and mine go.

This work is a dialogue in three books, in the Ciceronian manner. Fontius himself does most of the speaking. A young friend, 'Paulus Ghiaccetus Tertius',[12] furnishes objections for refutation. A still younger friend, Francesco Pandolfini, the same pupil and protegé mentioned above, takes the role of the dutiful student and would-be poet seeking information and promising to heed the injunctions of his master. The manuscript, MS. Latin 7879 of the Bibliothèque Nationale in Paris,[13] runs to fifty smallish folios. The text begins on folio 2^r and ends on 50^r. Dedicated to Lorenzo de' Medici, the title page bears the Medici crest, which indicates that it is a dedication copy. It is also an autograph, since the handwriting is identical with that of the Munich Macrobius copied and signed by 'Barptolemæus fontius' (Clm. 15738).[14]

The *terminus ante quem* is 8 April 1492, the death date of Lorenzo, but the work must have been written enough earlier for Fontius to have prepared and delivered his dedication copy. The *terminus post quem* is more difficult to establish. A reference on folio 42^r to Phocylides as a lyric poet 'quem nos olim tibi Francisce misimus' is vague in the term *olim,* but can be brought up to 14 August 1485 when Fontius wrote a letter[15] to Pierfilippo Pandolfini, father of Francesco, informing him that he had just made this translation and dedicated it to his son. This work, which must be Pseudo-Phocylides, has not been located. On folio 40^r there is a reference to another lost work, Fontius' commentary on the *Argonautica* of Valerius Flaccus.[16] According to Concetto Marchesi, Fontius' biographer, this commentary had an important influence on some of the early printed editions of Valerius.[17] In 1481–1482 Fontius had lectured on the *Argonautica* at the studio in Florence.[18] Here he says of it 'Argonautica cuius nuper interpretati sumus'.[19] *Nuper* is equally vague, but the work was not yet completed when on 30 January 1489 he wrote to King Matthias Corvinus sending him certain of his opuscula. Fontius promises that 'in a fairly short time our major volumes on Valerius Flaccus, dedicated to your name and worthier of your eminence, will follow'.[20] Later that year he went to Buda to organize the king's library and returned to supervise the copying of manuscripts for the library. When he again writes to the king on 16

September 1489[21] telling of the list of books to be included in the library, he makes no mention of this promised work, so that it may possibly have been delivered in person to the king during the year. At any rate it has disappeared, and the *Poetics* must have been written after January 1489. But we can come closer. The setting used by Fontius for his dialogue is the village of Ghiacceto where he was staying at his nephew's *pieve* beginning some time after 30 May and before 21 July 1490.[22] Although the dialogue is probably imaginary, he would most likely have had to stay in Ghiacceto, where he did in fact meet frequently with the other participants who stayed at the Ghiacceto villa in nearby Pelago,[23] before he could imagine the locale for his dialogue. Thus the *Poetics* most probably was written between the summer of 1490 and the spring of 1492. Therefore this work of Fontius precedes Marco Girolamo Vida's *De arte poetica* of 1527, generally thought to be the first of the Renaissance poetics, by at least thirty-five years. It also was written at least seven years before Giorgio Valla published his translation of Aristotle's *Poetics* in 1499. Fontius was without 'benefit of Aristotle'.

I once claimed that Fontius was an exceptionally good representative of the norms of *Quattrocento* humanism, since he was industrious, not very imaginative, and given to repetition of the standard school platitudes of humanistic circles.[24] Perhaps such a view is unfair to this man, for at least he seems to have been able to pull these commonplaces together into a coherent and revealing pattern. It may well be that his *Poetics* also will be thought to have this same synthesizing and summarizing character. For although it is possible to establish and even document his sources and precedents to an unusual degree (but not entirely), thus affirming his unoriginality and dependence, he nevertheless puts the elements that he utilizes together in an over-all representative way that demonstrates how humanism led logically to the conception and composition of poetics. It is also possible in his case to interpret his surviving writings—particularly his commentaries on ancient poets, his inaugural orations where he deals with the nature of poetry and its relation to other humanist *studia,* and his notebook compilations from ancient authors,[25] of which an exceptional number are extant—as a gradual preparation for this work on poetics.

One of the more interesting items in his notebooks is entitled: 'Collected under Cristoforo Landino publicly lecturing in Florence in the year 1464. Many items are what he himself did not say, but I collected from Tortelli.'[26] It turns out to be his student notes on Landino's exposition of Horace, *Ars poetica,* supplemented from Giovanni Tortelli's *Orthographia.*[27] Landino's commentary on Horace was first published in 1482.[28] Manuscript versions are undoubtedly earlier, but Fontius took these notes eighteen years prior to the publication when he was himself only eighteen, and he clearly dealt freely with Landino's ideas as he heard them, combining

them with Tortelli's. It is not surprising that there are considerable variations, particularly in the lines selected by Landino for comment in the
printed commentary, although a certain recognizable trace of these early
notes can be found. The notes reflect Fontius' own interest. The insertions
from Tortelli show that already at eighteen Fontius was developing ideas of
his own and not literally following his mentor Landino. Moreover, some of
what he draws from Tortelli shows up later in the *Poetics,* as will be seen.
There are references in these notes to ideas of Landino having been taken
from Porphyrion, and a comparison of the two commentaries does show
some dependence, but whether Fontius or Landino made the identification
explicit cannot be determined. In his printed commentary Landino refers
occasionally to Acron.[29]

What is of greater interest is the fact that Fontius made extensive
notes, labeled 'explanatio Acronis super Horatii Flacii poetria',[30] in a notebook that contains other items datable to 1467 and 1468, but not necessarily dating this item. Moreover, he possessed a copy, made by a contemporary and very possibly his friend Pietro Cennini, of Porphyrion's
commentary on Horace.[31] This contains numerous marginal comments in
Fontius' hand. Typically these notes, besides headlining items of interest to
Fontius, contain further citations of names or definitions supplied by Porphyrion. At *A.P.* 128, a crucial passage of ambiguous meaning in
Horace—'Difficile est proprie communia dicere': 'It is hard to treat in your
own way what is common'—Porphyrion comments: 'in aliud catholicum et
quasi interrogans, at enim inquiunt difficile est communes res propriis
explicare verbis.' Fontius writes in the margin in Greek, .ὸ. καθολικὸσ.
οὖ *universalis.*[32] At the very beginning Porphyrion comments, 'in quem
librum congessit precepta neopholomi de arte poetica, non quidem omnia
sed eminentissima'. Fontius writes in the margin, 'Neoptolemus de arte
poetica scripsit'.[33] C. O. Brink, who follows out this frequently ignored
cue from Porphyrion, has recently argued very cogently[34] that Horace,
indeed, incorporated an underlying structure based on Neoptolemus of
Parium in his *Ars,* and that Neoptolemus was an Alexandrian Peripatetic
who in turn based his *Ars poetica* on Aristotle—book III of the *Rhetoric,* the
Poetics, and the lost *De poetis.*

The possible transformations of meaning involved in such a two-
phased derivation become crucial in the above-mentioned line 128, and
119 as well—'Aut famam sequere aut sibi convenientia finge' ('Either
follow tradition or invent what is self-consistent'). Brink shows how much
hangs on the possible meanings of *communia* in 128 and of *publica* in line
131—'publica materies privati iuris erit' ('in ground open to all you will
win private rights'.) He believes that there are echoes of Aristotle's καθόλου here, that the more craft-minded Alexandrian critic, and the Roman poet after him, urge the would-be poet to follow the safer path of

tradition rather than inventing originally.[35] But in making the 'common' one's own the original Aristotelian problem from the *Poetics,* chapter 9, of reflecting universal truths or experiences poetically in concrete and particular episodes survives. *Publica,* on the other hand, refers to the traditional mythological themes which the Horatian poet may follow provided he does not become a slavish imitator. Fontius, besides recognizing that *communia* might mean *universalis,* an echo of Greek doctrine reflected in Porphyrion's use of *catholicus,* supplies in his earlier notes on Landino's lectures an interesting gloss on the meanings of *communia* and *publica:* 'Differe [sic] autem hoc teste Cicerone inter publica et commune quod publicum dicit id quod est commune omnibus in aliquo loco habitantibus ut theatrum, vie, platee et his similia. Communia autem sunt ea quae sunt omnibus quocunque loco sint communia ut hiems, aestas et omnia his similia.'[36] Landino in his later printed commentary simply interprets *communia* as unclaimed literary territory, or where the poet must invent for himself, while *publica* are 'ea quae ab aliis quoque scripta sunt'.[37] Thus Fontius in his early notes, whether he is following Landino or supplying his own interpretation, interprets *communia* as closer in meaning to *universalis* than Landino does later. Similarly in his marginalia in his copy of Porphyrion Fontius approaches closer to grasping a possibly original Aristotelian meaning that is echoed in Horace without any apparent knowledge of Aristotle.

Horace's *Ars* proceeds to explain how if one does attempt to win private rights on public ground, he should not be a slavish imitator and so follow the example of the cyclical poet. This corresponds to Aristotle's dictum in chapter 9 'that one must not aim at a rigid adherence to the traditional stories on which tragedies are based'. In this same chapter 9 there is also Aristotle's differentiation of the poet's function (in Latin *officium*) from that of the historian with his famous comment that poetry is more philosophical than history (because dealing with universals). The tradition in Horace and his commentators is to eschew the philosophical difference between poetry and history but to reintroduce the comparison in rhetorical terms, namely proper order. In Horace's words, lines 148–149, 'semper ad eventum festinat et in medias res non secus ac notas auditorem rapit' ('Ever he hastens to the issue and hurries his hearer into the story's midst, as if already known'.) All this is part of the need to introduce variety and originality into a borrowed theme. In Fontius' notes to Landino's lectures he writes at this same point where Landino comments on line 146, 'Nec reditum Diomedis': 'Demonstrat nos debere ita incipere aliquam rem ut observemus etiam quae traduntur ab oratoribus ut nihil quod supra vires sit capiamus prosequitur etiam etates quam varie sunt et varios mores . . . Adiungit etiam multa alia quae melius in textu apparebunt.' Apparently Fontius was sharper here than Landino, for he also writes in the margin 'De officio poete lege retro art. 4'.[38] Above in these manuscript notes at folio 64^r, which Fontius has also numbered '4', is Landino's comment on *Ars poetica* line 42 dealing with *dispositio* or 'order': 'Quod apud oratores esset vitiosissimus apud poetas autem in summa laude est.' Fontius was aware, in other words, that lines 146 ff. also dealt with order. Moreover at this point in these notes he writes in the margin, 'Hic dicit Tortellius in ortographia in dictione Aeneas 46.[39] Officium poete et historici.' Then he continues, 'Nam vitans Homerus in poemate historicorum similitudinem, quibus lex est ab exordio rerum incipere et continuam narrationem ad finem usque perducere, ipse poetic disciplina de rerum medio cepit, et ad id initium post-modum reversus est. Itaque ulyxis errorem non incepit a troiano littore decribere, sed quum primum navigantem eum ex insula calypsonis faceret, ex sua persona poeta ipse ad Phaeacas perduxit et illic in Alcinoi regis convivio narravit Ulyxes quemadmodum de Troia ad Calypsonem usque pervenit.' The passage continues showing how Vergil followed Homer's example in also introducing a narration from the historical beginning only in the middle of the poem at Dido's banquet. But Fontius' supplementing of Landino with Tortelli is not what he thought at this point, because the passage is taken almost word for word from Macrobius' *Saturnalia,* book 5, chapter 2.[40] Later Fontius copied an ornate manuscript of Macrobius for his Hungarian friend, Petrus Garasda,[41] and so he eventually had to be familiar with the original of this passage. What is even more interesting, he incorporated it in his own *Poetics.*[42]

Landino in his printed commentary to this same line 42 again made it a distinction between the orator's order and the poet's rather than the historian's and the poet's. Natural order was proper to orators whose audience was unlearned and where 'omnia perspicua in narrando esse oportet. . . . Artificiosus autem maxime est poetarum nam ad poetas legendos et doctiores et ociores accedimus, et si quid semel lectum non intelligatur, eundem locum saepius repetere licet. Quapropter isti artificio utuntur ordine, ut apud Vergilium videmus. Qui a septimo errorem Aeneae anno Aeneida incipit. Mox apud Didonem quae de excidio Troiano et variis navigationibus omiserat, suo ordine narrat . . .'[43] The exemplum was ancient and common, but Fontius saw the distinction as one between history and poetry for reasons of style; Landino as one between oratory and poetry for reasons of audience. Fontius seems to have been closer to Horace, as will be seen below.[44] It is interesting that in these early notes and in his glosses to Porphyrion he seems to reveal a more independent approach to Horace than his mentor, and one that in his own *Poetics* will make use of these early studies to achieve an exceptionally sound grasp of Horatian principles.

Fontius was not only familiar with Horace and his commentators, ancient and Renaissance, but made his own compilations of literary ideas and devices, geographic and mythological facts, ancient customs and practices. His notebooks show an amazing range of archaeological and philological curiosity.[45] He had a firm knowledge of the Latin poets and of the usual rhetorical treatises of Cicero and Quintilian. In addition he combed such writers as Strabo, Ptolemy, Diodorus Siculus, Dionysius of Halicarnassus.[46] More important, perhaps, in leading him to the formulation of a poetics was the fact that he, like so many other humanists, wrote commentaries on ancient poets. His first was a commentary on Persius.[47] This was written before 1477, when the first edition was printed. In the new literal (rather than allegorical) mode of explanation, the commentary is full of documented historical and geographical and archaeological explanations of Persius' references and allusions. It also analyzes the meaning of his statements, bringing forward comparative data from other Latin poets. It is particularly concerned with exploring the nature of satiric poetry, and begins with a historical explanation of this genre. Although he does discuss the various metres and their appropriateness, it is essentially philological criticism rather than interpretation in a wider aesthetic sense.[48] Nevertheless it is of interest as the first of two commentaries on satirical poets. His commentary on Juvenal survives in a single manuscript in contrast to the many manuscript and printed versions of the commentary on Persius.[49] He discussed satiric verse at least three times: in his introduction to his commentary on Persius, in an inaugural oration, and in the *Poetics*.[50] As will be seen immediately, he lectured on the *Satires* of Horace as well as on Juvenal.

It is impossible to speak of these scholarly studies of classical poets apart from his career as a professor of poetry and oratory at the studio in Florence between 1481 and 1488.[51] In 1481–1482 he lectured on the *Argonautica* of Valerius Flaccus. Reference was made above to his lost commentary on the *Argonautica,* and it was suggested that the eight books might have been delivered to Matthias Corvinus on Fontius' visit to Buda in 1489.[52] Unfortunately it has not turned up among the scattered manuscripts of the royal library. It was the custom at the university for a professor of the humanities—poetry and oratory—to give each year one lecture series on a poet and another on an orator or historian. Valerius Flaccus was accompanied by the *Orations* of Cicero. In 1482–1483 the subjects were Lucan's *Pharsalia* and Caesar's *De bello civili.* Fontius left Florence to teach at Rome in 1483 but was back at Florence in 1484. From then on he gave only one lecture series annually, apparently having been rehired on a reduced basis. There had been trouble with a more brilliant rival, Poliziano. In 1484–1485 the subject was the *Punica* of Silius; in 1485–1486 the *Odes* of Horace; in 1487–1488 the *Satires* of Juvenal.

In addition to his collections of notes and his various compilations, his written commentaries, his lectures on classical poets, Fontius also made some poetic translations from the Greek. His translation of Pseudo-Phocylides,[53] already mentioned, is lost. His translation of the *Argonauticon* of

Apollonius Rhodius,[54] however, exists in a Riccardiana manuscript. It is prefaced by a discussion of the *Genus Apollonii poetae Argonauticorum,* the *Argumentum,* and *Aliter Apollonii vita.*[55]

It seems to have been an important question in the history of literary criticism whether a given critic was a scholar-critic or a poet-critic— Aristotle or Horace.[56] Fontius' criticism was certainly the former, but the distinction is perhaps only relatively valid. It is particularly questionable in the Renaissance where so many scholars were also poets and in some instances gifted ones. The examples of Landino and Poliziano are sufficient. Fontius, too, wrote both Latin and Italian verse. He left two books of Latin verse—no. 36, *Elegiarum libri duo,* in the Pandolfini list.[57] Only one book has been found and published by Fógel and Juhász.[58] There are scattered additional poems listed by Kristeller in his review.[59] As to the quality, Kristeller wrote: 'Nearly all the poems are distinguished by an exquisite elegance which is the more admirable in that Fontius does not limit himself to the easier forms of the elegy, epigram and the eclogue but attempts in several instances the more difficult metres of the Sapphic and Asclepiadic strophes. . . . As models the poet expressly names Catullus, Propertius and Tibullus.'[60] The Pandolfini list also includes no. 40, *Sonnettorum et cantionum poema, Librii iiij (Lingua rustica composita).*[61] Little more than one book of these vernacular poems has been located and only a total of thirteen have been printed.[62] His own interest in Italian poetry was manifested in some remarks on Florentine neglect of Dante and Petrarch in his oration on poetry, to be discussed shortly.[63] I also edited a little dialogue called *Pelago* or *De locis triumphorum Petrarchae,*[64] written in Italian, as an appendix to my previous Fontius study; it is strictly historical and geographical. One cannot resolve the question whether Fontius was a scholar-critic or a poet-critic. The interesting question is whether his critical notions and approaches had any influence on his composition, but there is no evidence that they did except in the obvious way of providing classical models for imitation. This is a problem that badly needs invesigtation, especially in the case of the greater poet-critics of the late fifteenth and sixteenth centuries. O. B. Hardison's *The Enduring Monument* is notable among recent studies of Renaissance literary criticism in dealing with the practical use of theory by poets.[65]

Bartolommeo della Fonte's most significant preparation for writing a poetics lay in his inaugural orations. On 8 November 1484 he delivered his *Oratio in bonas artis* in the course of which he devoted slightly over two pages to the poetic art, labeled in the margin *De poetice.*[66] Next, before beginning his course of lectures on the *Odes* of Horace on 4 November 1485, he was prompted by the fact that 'Quintus Horatius Flaccus was both a supreme lyric poet and a satiric bard, and the one of all the Latins who wrote a book on *Poetics*' to give an inaugural oration on the poetic faculty. This ran to nine and a half pages.[67] Two years later on 7 November 1487 he introduced his lectures on Juvenal, noted above, with an oration in praise of satire and the *studia humanitatis*. The first seven pages were devoted to satiric poetry and poets.[68] Many of the ideas and a good deal of the language in which they were expressed are echoed in his *Poetics*. Whole phrases are taken over, but others are considerably modified. He exercised the privilege of quoting himself freely but not minutely. In these orations he had to make general statements about poetry (as well as about the other humanistic studies there treated).[69] Commentaries on the poets, the most usual humanist way of discussing poetry, tend to be fragmentary, following lines and sections of poems. Even commentaries on Horace's *Ars poetica,* such as Landino's, consist of scattered comments, except for very brief prefatory remarks. The inaugural oration gave an opportunity for a much fuller treatment, and certainly seems to have suggested in Fontius' case the expansion of a general treatment of poetry into a *Poetics*. But even though Fontius' *Poetics* is comparatively short, it was necessary to expand the roughly eighteen pages devoted to poetry in the orations to the fifty folios or ninety-seven pages of the *Poetics*. Since the manuscript pages are slightly smaller, the *Poetics* was roughly five times as long as his previous general comments on poetry, but much essential basic thinking about the art of poetry had obviously received a first testing in these orations.

Fontius was not the only humanist professor who dealt with poetry in his inaugural orations. Best known are Poliziano's *Sylvae,* or poetic prefaces, which deal with Homer, Hesiod, and Vergil, and finally, in the *Nutricia,* give a poetic sketch of the history of poetry.[70] Poliziano, however, did not compose a poetics. Other examples exist.[71] Landino apparently did not deliver such an oration on the general nature of poetry, although when he lectured on Petrarch's *Sonnets,* he introduced them with an oration praising Latin eloquence. 'È necessario essere Latino chi vuole essere buono Toscano.'[72] Apparently the strength of his commitment to the Latin rhetorical tradition carried over even into his attitude toward the great *volgare* lyricist. It has also, apparently, carried too much influence with historians of Renaissance literary theory as they regard the strength of humanist commitment to rhetoric in the *Quattrocento* as a force that prevented a general treatment of poetics. Fontius, however, wrote one, and it looks as though his programmatic treatment of the *studia humanitatis* in his orations, in which he systematically laid out the nature and present status of the oratorical faculty, history, the good arts all together, wisdom, satire required him also to include one on the poetic faculty.[73] And this led logically to writing a *Poetics*.

August Buck in what is otherwise one of the more thoughtful treatments of Renaissance literary theory was possibly misled by Landino when he claimed that a poetics in the *Quattrocento* would have been incongruous

with the nature of humanism.[74] 'During the first two centuries of humanism, from the time of Petrarch up to the end of the *Quattrocento,* rhetoric
had pushed the normative poetic into the background. The humanistic
author (*Dichter*) appeared as "poeta-rhetor", and when he defended poetry
with the help of the theological poetic, he thereby likewise had the humanistic studies in mind, that is, thus, the expansion of eloquence. In rhetoric,
and not in poetic, rules for artistic composition were sought.[75]
. . . Neither Pontano[76] nor any other humanist of the fifteenth century
attempted to work out a systematic poetics, since not even the need for
it was present.' The case of Fontius, however, indicates how the attempt
to define and differentiate the *studia humanitatis* led directly to an awareness
of the need for defining the nature of poetry (in his oration) and then on to
writing a *Poetics* itself, without the stimulus of any apparent knowledge of
Aristotle. In other words, the emergence of Renaissance poetics was not a
consequence of a weakening of humanism but rather of its chronic
preoccupations.

Let us now see more specifically how Fontius conceived of a *poetics.*

II

Fontius divided his dialogue into three books along logical lines. Book I
may be roughly entitled 'De dignitate poetices et poetarum'—the traditional defense of poetry and the poet but with certain particular qualities.
Book II he called 'De poeticis officiis'—the poetic functions, that which is
required in a poem. Book III is devoted to 'De varietatibus poematum' and
'Qui poetae in suo quisque genere floruerunt'—the nature of the genres and
the history of the leading poets in each.[77] It is evident that each of these
books had its precedents: Petrarch, Boccaccio, and Salutati most effectively
offering models for the defense of poetry; Horace's *Ars,* Servius, and Macrobius serving as chief sources for book II; and a variety of ancient writers
including Quintilian, Diomedes, Eusebius as well as Horace were utilized
for book III, but Tortelli's *Orthographia,* the *Suidas,* and most definitely
Fontius' wide-ranging study of classical writers were also drawn upon.
Originality was not Fontius' strong point as far as either the language or the
ideas of his dialogue go; his originality must be sought in a new combination of old themes and in the nuances of his emphases.

He begins his argument in book I with a declaration of the divine
origin of the poetic faculty and the divinity of the poet; afflated with a
celestial numen, he is divinely inspired.[78] The notion of the divine inspiration of the poet is supposedly of Platonic origin,[79] although early Greek
poets, especially Homer and Hesiod, attribute their art to the muses and
other divine beings. Fontius, who was a correspondent and in some degree
an associate of Marsilio Ficino, was certainly aware of the Platonic character

of this position. In fact, surprisingly enough he does not use this topos in the *Poetics,* although in his oration on the poetic faculty of 1485 he echoed the passage of the *Phaedrus* (245A) where entrance to the house of the poet is denied to one equipped only with technique and learning, and he also echoed Ficino's comparison of the songs of the poet and music in his *Epistola de divino furore.*[80] However, a distinction must be drawn between the much more elaborate Renaissance Platonist theories of divine inspiration based directly on Platonic texts and emanating from Ficino and his circle, and a more diffuse and persistent late antique, patristic, medieval, and early Renaissance tradition of the divine inspiration of the poet. E. R. Curtius has made this tradition familiar as a central theme of his *European Literature and the Latin Middle Ages.*[81] Ficino's discussion in his *Theologia Platonica,* lib. xiii, cap. ii, 'De poetis',[82] and Landino's exposition of divine inspiration and *furor poeticus,* citing the *Phaedrus* and *Ion,* in the prologue to his commentary on Dante,[83] are examples of the explicit Renaissance Platonist approach. Fontius seems to belong to the less explicit, more traditional version in his *Poetics,* closer to those of Mussato, Petrarch, Boccaccio, and Salutati.[84]

The genre of the defense of poetry as divinely inspired is actually an *omnium gatherum* of traditions and assertions reaching back as far as the Homer exegesis of the sixth century B.C., and including a much misinterpreted statement of Aristotle that the early Greek poets were theologians—meaning speculators concerning the nature of the universe. It includes not only the claim that moral philosophy, knowledge of history, knowledge of nature, and knowledge of divine matters are imparted allegorically by poets, but also the constant reference to certain writers of the Old Testament as poets. Moses, David, Solomon, Isaiah, Jeremiah, and Job are especially mentioned as divinely inspired Biblical poets in order to justify calling all poets divine—a doctrine that Curtius has labeled 'Biblical poetics'.[85] By writing obscurely, in allegory, in uncommon speech, poets simultaneously enhanced their authority with the uncomprehending masses and provided a delightful intellectual challenge to the learned. So the tradition ran.

Fontius' exordium is of this eclectic character. The poet, he held, was divinely inspired, but at the same time he explains his knowledge of divinity as based on observation and speculation. For Fontius the poet is a theologian both in Aristotle's and in the Platonist sense. A man of genius in primeval times, seeing the sublimity of the heavens, the course of the sun, moon, planets, stars, and other heavenly bodies, began to marvel at the works of nature. 'Thence, indeed, after long examination, seeing the certain movements of the orbs and the certain order, he thought there is some one governor of the universe by whose command all is ruled.' Beginning to worship Him, and teaching others that He was to be propitiated with offerings, the poet thought it proper to praise Him not in vulgar speech but rather by studied and rhythmic sounds. Such was the origin of poetry in songs and hymns of praise to the higher beings. 'And that they might gain greater authority with the masses they hid the high mysteries of divinity in poetic images.' The oracles of Apollo, the predictions of the sybils, and the dicta of the great prophets were delivered in verse. These *prisci poetae* wrote about God, the origins of all things, higher and lower beings, customs, laws, the immortality of souls, and whatever 'high and eternal thing can be understood by the soul and thought'.[86] In this context of divine subjects not only tragedy and epic, but lyric, elegy, and comedy took their origin from sacred rites of one or another of the gods, our Latin satiric poetry included.[87]

He proceeds from the origin of the poetic faculty to praise of the poet as the most ancient and erudite of all writers, and the dearest to the gods. Again learning, for Fontius, must be added to inspiration. Even a mediocre poet must know all antiquity, be copious in ornamenting and illuminating by style, know all the other arts and all philosophy. Poets are praised by all nations, but only a few are worthy of the name. Finally he offers his definition, which is the traditional one of the defense of poetry with Neo-platonic overtones: 'Poetic is diffused from the mind of God into the pure and purged minds of good men for the sake of revealing and brightening by decorous fables the divine, the human, the past, the present, the future. Poets, indeed, who are great and honorable and good and surely excellent men, remarkably formed by nature, instructed and perfected by art, practice, and knowledge of all things, are high prophets and theologians.'[88]

He next makes use of the dialogue form to have Paulus present the traditional list of accusations against poetry and the poet, which he will then refute and thus establish the dignity of the poet. The first poets were not great men but rude and ignorant, gifted only by nature for pleasing with charming song. As in the other arts they only little by little became cultivated and obtained some repute. Therefore they were not prophets or theologians and conferred little of value upon mankind but pleasure to the ears. Poets were not the most ancient writers; medicine and law are much older than Homer, the source of all poetry. Moreover, these professions are more sublime and honorable, and more useful. Elaborate lies and fictions should not be praised but rather simple, honest speech. Knowledge of antiquity would have been preserved by annalists and historians without the poets. Poets should not be praised for the virtues of the other arts but only for their own. They are ingenious men, not inept by nature for singing, and by practice and study they seem not unlearned in cultivated speech and various matters.[89]

The nature of this list of charges introduces an interesting aspect of the debate concerning poetry. The defense of poetry was usually considered to be a necessary justification of the poet and classical scholar against the criticism that the poets were pagan and incited to immorality. But Fontius omits these charges at this time (he will bring them forward later). Curtius asserts that the fourteenth-century humanist defenses of poetry by Mussato, Petrarch, Boccaccio, and Salutati were mainly to meet the attacks of puritanical religious critics.[90] However, Petrarch's chief defense of poetry is in his *Invective against a Certain Physician*,[91] and Boccaccio spends considerable effort in book XIV of the *De genealogia deorum*[92] in refuting the argument of the greater worth of the jurist. Salutati, to be sure, defends poetry as containing theological and moral wisdom and the study of ancient poets as legitimized by the allegorical method;[93] he also answers the attacks of Giovanni Dominici's *Lucula noctis* against the *studia humanitatis* in general by arguing their value for what he calls the *studia divinitatis*.[94] But Salutati also wrote a treatise on the relative *Nobility of Law and Medicine*,[95] in which in preferring law he associates it with the moral ends of the humanities. This is one of a number of humanist treatises discussed by Garin in *La disputa delle arti nel Quattrocento*.[96] Fontius here confronts the poet with the physician and the lawyer, but notably also with the historian and the orator separated out from the *studia humanitatis* in general. In other words there is a relationship between the genre of the defense of poetry and that of the dispute over the relative merits of the learned professions. Fontius first argues the relative merit of the profession of poet—the *dignitas poetae*—only to return afterward to the traditional theological and moral objections to poetry which he has Paulus bring forward.

This first set of objections to poetry also involves the problem of the place of poetry among the arts and sciences.[97] The scholastic attack on poetry, which is reflected in the polemic between Mussato and Fra Giovannino,[98] reduced poetry to a preparatory art for philosophy or to a methodological science. Salutati called poetry a *scientia sermocinalis* and was at great pains to find its relation to the *trivium* and *quadrivium* (which, unlike the *studia humanitatis,* did not include poetry). These, he considered, were presupposed by poetry, which added 'a delight of transformation and song'; 'poetic perfects all at once and moves the imaginative treasury of perceived matters, the memory, and leads it to action . . . , adding beyond this a sweetness of admirable harmony.' The poet is a *vir optimus* (compared to Cicero's orator, a *vir bonus*), whose office is to profit by delighting and to delight by profiting through praise and blame, by means of figured and metrical speech, especially moving and exciting the fantasy.[99] Salutati thus seeks to lift poetry above the liberal arts, including rhetoric, but at the same time considers it essentially the same as rhetoric but employing other technical means. He gives it a position in relation to the arts analogous to the position of theology in scholasticism.[100] Similarly Cristoforo Landino, Fontius' teacher and older colleague, located poetry above the liberal arts:

poetry 'is not one of those arts which our ancestors called liberal because they were more excellent than the rest . . . but it is a certain diviner thing which, completing all the others, is confined by certain metres and progresses by certain feet, and is distinguished by various lights and flowers . . .'[101] Landino, as will be seen, despite his Neoplatonism, like Salutati had a specifically rhetorical conception of poetry. Fontius had in his earlier oration on the good arts given poetry a parallel position to the other humanistic studies.[102] The extent to which he continues this and also manages to distinguish poetry from oratory will become apparent.

His replies to the objections are neatly headlined by marginal rubrics. Under 'the great genius of the poets' he answers the argument that the first poets were not great men since they simply sang by nature without art.[103] He admits that the first inventors of any art are not as polished as later practitioners who are aided and taught by imitation of their elders. But the first inventors must have been talented and distinguished men who stood out among their contemporaries if not in comparison to their successors. Just as agriculture has improved since the gods first taught it to men, so the arts of painting, modeling, navigating, and building have advanced from rude beginnings to the climax we see today. Although the first inventors were rude, still they were men of great genius, and this is true also of the poets.[104]

On 'the learning of the poets' he claims that the ancient poets were not only prophets and theologians because they were inspired by celestial fury but excelled in the other 'most humane arts'. His proof is the example of Moses, who led the Hebrews from Egypt, gave them laws and wrote the *Pentateuch,* of Solomon, David, Jeremiah, Job, and, among the students of the muses, Amphion, Musaeus, Linus, and Orpheus. 'In these men there was the highest virtue and singular knowledge and authority so amplified by the highest science and virtue that to this day their memory is held in gratitude in all lands.'[105]

As for 'the utility of poetry', poets have taught men to live together in justice, to love their parents in piety, to worship the heavenly beings in the right way, to bear adversity with fortitude. They have revealed the nature of the other-worlds, where sinners go, where the blameless, the eternal causes, the immortality of souls, and what road is opened to heaven by virtue. Here again he stresses the moral benefits to mankind in bringing it to civilized life, frequently attributed to the orator, along with the poet's more usual gift of religious knowledge and practice.[106]

More original, and characteristic of Fontius' philological leanings, is his factual discussion of 'the antiquity of poetic'. For he recognizes that the other humanities—history, rhetoric, philosophy—evolved out of poetry in antiquity.[107] 'For in the time of Homer, whom you have adduced, there were not yet any historians, rhetors, or philosophers in Greece. For history took its start from Cadmus of Miletus and Pherecydes, rhetoric from Tisias and Corax, philosophy from the poets themselves who were thought to be sages before the name of philosophy was born. And poets flourished for many ages before Homer.' There would be no memory of early antiquity without the poets. The same arguments apply to medicine and law. Even if medicine is thought to begin with Paeon and Machaon or their parent Aesculapius in the Trojan War, Orpheus lived in the same age, and Amphion and Linus were earlier, and before them other poets may be supposed. Law is most recent of all, dating back to the Twelve Tables engraved by the decemvirs.[108]

He moves directly into the debate over the relative status of the professions, asserting that 'poetry is more excellent than medicine and civil law'. 'It is no wonder you think medicine and law are sublimer than poetry when the crowd judges all by profit and not by its nature. Thus if you would say that poetry is the least venal art, I would not disagree that law and the cure of bodies are the most venal of all. But do you place the dignity of the liberal disciplines in profit? By this reasoning commerce will by far excel civil law and the medical faculty, since from it very often greater riches and wealth are gained.' Curing bodies has much that is distasteful; law is more fastidious. 'Nevertheless, it is nourished by quarrels and pastured in controversies and fears lest concord prevail among men.' Although it is pursued by distinguished men, it is not comparable to poetic. Philosophy is preferable to civil law because of the range of its subject matter. Moral philosophy is a part of philosophy only, and of this justice is a particle. Law derives its name from this and pertains solely to justice. Poetry, however, is concerned with the entirety of philosophy— God, the heavens and stars, the elements, the origins of things, virtues and vices—and all these things before there was any philosophy. Jurists, when they leave the forum and tribunal, have nothing to do with these things.[109]

Fontius is dependent in this brief treatment of poet versus doctor and lawyer on the livelier and lengthier chapter IV of book XIV of Boccaccio's *De genealogia deorum* where the poet's poverty and the lawyer's greed, the poet's breadth and the lawyer's limits are set forth. Petrarch's *Invective* is also echoed.[110]

Turning to 'the images of the poets', Fontius refutes the charge that poetry is fabulous and intricate rather than pure and simple. He uses the stock arguments. Since Christ and the prophets used parables, why should not poets? Aesop with his fables was more effective than all the philosophers in leading men to avoid dangers and acquire prudence. Examples of the value of fables in Roman history are recounted. If images and fables simplify truth, they apparently also complicate it, for he adds that poets are unjustly damned because of the inability of the ignorant to penetrate their veil of figuration to the hidden truth. This is the usual argument justifying an allegorical interpretation of the poets (as in the case of Boccaccio and Salutati),[111] but Fontius does not bring up allegory. As a matter of fact one of the interesting things about his treatment is the absence of emphasis on allegory. He argued instead for the need of great erudition in order to read the poets properly, certainly the philologist's and the humanist's approach. 'Therefore, it is not for all to perceive the mind of poets. Unless one approaches them closely, one certainly will not understand their meaning. Do you think that without perfect knowledge of the language which he is using, without education in all actions, history, mythology, geography, without the study of philosophy, and besides all this without a certain sharpness of mind and capacity for judgement it is possible to examine the inner meaning and quintessence of a poet?"[112] The kind of poetic interpretation he has in mind is well illustrated by his own commentaries on Persius and on the *Triumphs* of Petrarch, where linguistic meanings, historical, geographical, and mythological data are carefully supplied and weighed.

However, something of the nature of allegory remains in the example of learned poetic criticism he offers—applied to Homer, Vergil, and Dante. Yet there is an element of sound insight as well. 'What is there in all the liberal disciplines which is not gathered from Homer? What is poetry other than a certain paradigm of human life proposed to all for imitation?' The *Iliad,* however, he sees as revealing what is to be avoided. The stupidity of kings and populace are seen as Nestor and Antenor labor in vain to compose the quarrels of Agamemnon and Achilles, of the Greeks and the Trojans. 'And thus by sedition, anger, lust, wickedness all mingled the crimes of the princes fall on the people. In contrast, in the *Odyssey* Homer proposes Odysseus as an example of virtue and wisdom for us. . . . Moreover, Vergil has proposed for us in the *Aeneid* almost the same thing which Homer did, but by a different method. For he first shows the lusts and temptations of human life and later the strength of counsel and fortitude.' Dante also with great erudition and elegance revealed heaven, hell, earth, and purgatory for the contemplation of man, a picture woven of 'innumeris fictionibus'. Fontius' approach remains fundamentally moral and educational—didactic, as Hardison calls it.[113] But the lessons of poetry can only be read with thorough study. 'Do not, therefore, ascribe to vice what is made by study; rather you should urge talented men that great judgement should be acquired for interpreting all writers so that they can dig out the meaning of the poets, so that what is described by the poets with highest artifice is at length sought out with great industry and labor, and once discovered is the more valued.'[114]

This finishes his first defense of the dignity of the poet. His young friend Paolo da Ghiacceto is brought back to the attack with the more conventional charges of the immorality, irreligion, and paganism of the poets. Moreover, they live in the country far from courts and forums and are of no use to any one.[115] Fontius' reply to the first charge is that certainly some poets are depraved in their morals but he does not count them among the good poets. All disciplines have their evil individuals and none should be condemned for them. All arts should be honored for the utility and ease they confer on mankind, but poetry also confers an admirable pleasure. 'Who is so wild and rustic that he would not prefer and love that beyond the others?' Moreover, poetry and oratory, hardly dissimilar in many ways, also hold the ears and minds of men by the sweetness of their speech. 'Nevertheless, no one would deny that he is more affected and enflamed by poetry than by prose.'[116]

He continues to defend the moral value of poets by referring to their great contributions to civilization both in founding cities and saving peoples from defeat—Solon and Tyrtaeus. And he lists rulers who have favored poets. He then turns to the charge that poets are not friends to God.

'You have specially said that they are not friends of our God. I indeed believe that God is unique and one only, and He is the best and eternal. The pagan poets never thought otherwise. Moreover, besides Him, whose son the Gentiles call Jove, we Christ, the Asiatics and Libyans Mahomet, and other peoples by other names, there were and today are and always will be among mortals other minor deities, called heroes or saints; this I do not doubt. And I affirm that good poets are acceptable to this highest God, the ruler of the universe, the genitor of other gods and men, and to the other minor gods also, according to the variety of places, times and religions.'[117]

Although this statement is apparently a development out of the older humanist and contemporary Neoplatonic tendency to find elements of Christian truth concealed and partially recognized in the pagan religions, it is certainly a very forthright version of the position. Even within these traditions it would seem to be rather extreme to assert that Christ, Jove, and Mahomet differed only in name. Although there is evidence of Fontius' clear preference for classical over religious sources, there is also much evidence of his own personal piety.[118]

He follows up this statement by listing ancient poets and the gods to whom they were favorites. And as to Christ and His saints, 'Dante and Petrarch were, I think, completely acceptable.' Though Dante died in exile, he was dear to many cities. It cannot be argued that Ovid and Juvenal died in exile because of any obscenity in their poems; rather it was a question of personal offense to Augustus in one case, and an attack on tyranny in the other. As a last resort he turns to Biblical poetics to argue that the Biblical writers were close to God.[119]

As to the charge that poets flee the cities he replies that by retreating to the country poets can devote themselves to contemplation and thought about divine affairs, and so produce what benefits all ages and is pleasing to

God and His saints. 'If divine poetic is near to them, if lovable poets are inspired by divine power, what do I care if they are less pleasing to certain ignorant theologians?'[120]

The praise of solitude has a special place in humanist defenses of poetry, and we must comment on it briefly. Petrarch's treatise on *The Life of Solitude*[121] is the most famous elaboration of this theme, but it is matched by a vigorous defense of the solitude of the poet in the fourth book of his *Invective against a Certain Physician*. The third book contains the bulk of his argument on behalf of the poet.[122] Boccaccio devoted chapter XI of his own defense of poetry in book XIV of the *De genealogia deorum* to justifying the poet's preference for solitude.[123] There are in the course of the *Quattrocento* scattered humanist encomia of the *vita solitaria* and the *vita contemplativa*.[124] Scholarly emphasis recently has stressed the importance of the *vita activa* as a humanist theme.[125] Landino balanced the two outlooks against each other in the first book of his *Camaldulensian Disputations,* but rather favored the contemplative. It is in the third book that he presents his allegorical commentary on Vergil.[126]

Fontius himself had frequently stressed the value of the *studia humanitatis* to the civic community. All the defenders of poetry among the humanists also argue the usefulness of the poet to mankind, not only for the wisdom and knowledge he contributed but as founder of civilized life, as Fontius was immediately to claim in his peroration.[127] But poetry written in solitude was held to contribute to the eternal values of mankind and was not contaminated with the pursuit of power or gain. I would like to suggest that the defense of the solitary life by humanists should be viewed as related to the defense of poetry and its claim to parity, among the humanities, with oratory, which was more usually associated with civic goals. The solitary life was not antagonistic to the active life, nor was its defense opposed to civic humanism. Rather they were complementary themes within humanism as a whole.[128]

III

If the priority of Fontius' *Poetics* is to be upheld, and if this work is to be regarded as a poetics in anything more than its title, the claim must rest on what he does in his second book, which he refers to as *De poeticis officiis*. For, dependent as he is on Horace's *Ars poetica,* he does not merely write a commentary, as Landino does, but sets forth, however inadequately or unsatisfactorily from later critical points of view, his own *Ars*. And to my limited knowledge, superficial as it is, it shares this quality with many of the sixteenth-century poetics that have attracted the interest of historians, and it suffers, essentially, from no more limitations than they do. Besides Horace, he makes explicit use of the late antique Vergil criticism of Servius and Macrobius, who were in their own ways also dependent on Horace. In addition I have spoken of his dependence on Landino's early lectures on Horace and presumably on Landino's published commentary, his study of Acron and Porphyrion, his familiarity with humanist compilations such as Tortelli's *Orthographia* (which he does not hesitate to criticize in his own commentary on Persius).[129] By the time he wrote his *Poetics* he was a relatively knowledgeable scholar in his own right, familiar in detail with the Latin poets and some of the Greek, very much aware of their statements about other poets as well as of the full range of statements from available non-poetic classical writers. As his notebooks testify, and as his commentaries evidence, he had made thorough and telling use of these sources, although as subject to error as any. All these elements in his background equipped him more empirically than theoretically for writing a poetics. As should be expected, then, in an industrious and methodical but not very brilliant man, his ideas are knowledgeable and professional but also very traditional.[130]

Yet not entirely unoriginal: a conventional treatment, influenced by the Ciceronian rhetorical views prevailing among the humanists, would open with the usual categories of invention, disposition, and elocution.[131] Fontius certainly is familiar with this division and finds it difficult to think in other terms. Nevertheless he begins his discussion, not with invention, but with a topic drawn from Horace, lines 38–41, which is in the view of some interpreters the real beginning of the *Ars,* after a prefatory section on overall unity and propriety in a poem.[132] Horace writes: 'Sumite materiam vestris, qui scribitis, aequam viribus et versate diu, quid ferre recusent, quid valeant humeri' ('Take a subject, writers, equal to your strength, and ponder long what your shoulders refuse and what they are able to bear'.) The first office of the poet, says Fontius, 'is to estimate his own talent accurately, and he should know especially for what he is most fit in describing.' Clearly echoing Horace's language, he concludes, 'Quisquis enim saepe ac diu meditatus, quantum studio et natura valuerit, materiam sibi aequam et onus non exuperans vires desumpserit, ad exitum poema multa cum laude perduxerit.'[133]

Invention is taken up by Horace, not before disposition and diction but later at line 118, contrary to the interpreters who assume that he follows the Ciceronian formula. Actually he very briefly discusses disposition after this preliminary statement on the need for the poet to fit his capacities to this subjects, in lines 42–45. This is the only place he speaks specifically of order, although, as will be seen, he returns to it later in his section on content as an aspect of poetic originality, impact, and inner consistency. Here he merely says, 'Of order, this, if I mistake not, will be the excellence and charm that the author of the long promised poem shall say at the moment what at that moment should be said, reserving and

omitting much for the present, loving this point, scorning that.'[134] Significantly it is really the problem of opportuneness—εὐκαιρία—an aspect of
propriety that is emphasized and not the rhetorical theory of the proper
ordering of the parts of an oration.[135] Fontius follows Horace in his sequence as well as idea, and here introduces the distinction between poetic
and historical or rhetorical disposition and develops it along the line that
Horace later takes in stressing how to be original in the use of traditional
contents, lines 136–152. 'The second, not much less prior task', says
Fontius, 'will be so to distribute and divide the invented and undertaken
content that the poem begins not in the order serving the rhetor or the
historian, nor from the beginning of events; nor does it maintain the same
course in the remainder, subtracting much from the truth, adding much,
something here, something there, never really departing from what was
proposed but moving around it.'[136] Horace put it at line 148, 'Ever he
hastens to the issue, and hurries his hearer into the story's midst, as if
already known; . . . and so skillfully does he invent, so closely does he
blend facts and fiction, that the middle is not discordant with the beginning, nor the end with the middle.'[137] The occasion for Horace's remarks is
the need for imagination in dealing with a traditional myth and he has just
rejected the literal historical procedure of the 'cyclic writer'. Fontius does
not pick up this example but turns instead, in order to illustrate the
difference between poetic and historical order, to the same passage from
Macrobius (*Saturnalia*, V, 2) that he had quoted many years earlier from
Tortelli. Homer began the *Odyssey* in the middle and has Odysseus later tell
his story at the banquet of the Phaeacians. 'Following him, Vergil conducted the sailing Aeneas not from the Trojan destruction but from Sicily
into Libya, where at the banquet of Dido he recounts the disaster of his
fatherland and his own wanderings.'[138]

Horace deals next with diction or style in a relatively brief[139] section
of his poem, lines 46–118. He divides his discussion into sections on the
use of old and new words, on the appropriateness of metres and language in
relation to the subject, and on the need to have emotionally appropriate
language in relation to the character of the person speaking in order by
imitation to reproduce the corresponding affections in the reader ('si vis me
flere, dolendum est primum ipsi tibi').[140] Fontius condenses these notions
into his own next paragraph on the third task of the poet, which is to
ornament the invented and distributed content by an apt and appropriate
series of words according to the quality of the matter and the dignity of the
persons and things. First comes the needed correspondence of exalted language to exalted statuses, of the humble to the humble. Then the use of
appropriate speech by each kind of person. Next the question of old and
new and borrowed words is discussed with reference to the good example of
Vergil. Finally all the emotions are to be aroused by means of place, age,

cause, mode, matter, example, fortune, and other conditions of this sort.[141]

The fourth topic taken up by Fontius occurs late in Horace, lines 408–452, his final theme, 'whether a praiseworthy poem be due to nature or to art', together with the value of working for polish and seeking the criticism of friends.[142] Fontius follows the same line. Poems come from a gift of nature, from nature and art, and from art alone. Although the heroic poet is most truly one, and we can't all equal Vergil or Homer, still 'what at first seems scarcely possible, little by little by practice, study, and eagerness of mind becomes easy'. Paraphrasing but differing with Horace, 377–378, 'if a poem in aught falls short of the top, it falls to the bottom',[143] Fontius holds, 'Although whoever departs a little from the summit tends toward the bottom, and no mediocrity among poets is conceded as in other arts, nevertheless in approaching the summit one excels another to some extent. For the greatest of Greek poets—who would deny it?—is Homer. But Hesiod also was not low. Vergil is the prince of the Latins, but yet Ovid is not at the bottom.' Any one not of the highest poetic genius may withdraw from heroic verse and devote himself to lesser genres. 'In these also those who are not widely aided by talent and nature, still by art and study may obtain a distinguished name. As Ovid reports, among the Greeks Callimachus, who availed less by genius, excelled by art. And among our own Horace achieved by learning and practice what had been given to him less by nature.' Thus Fontius, like Horace,[144] stressed the value of study, erudition, and refinement in becoming a poet, despite his earlier insistence on divine inspiration. Perhaps poets could not count on it so much in his day. Finally, echoing Horace, lines 385–390 and 438–452, Fontius urges the aspiring poet to seek the criticism of friends.[145]

The next question is, at last, invention proper. He is concerned with the qualities of propriety, coherence, and unity in the entire poem and the limits of poetic license in the invention of subject matters. Here again he follows and shows a sound understanding of Horace.[146] While the poet should be coerced by no limits within a poem, and should wander about freely and safely, and much is permitted to him to create according to his fancy, 'because whoever does not do so will in no way be a good poet', all of this is permitted on condition that he does not confound, exceed, or join together things contrary to nature. Here is an echo of the opening passage of Horace, lines 1–37, but 'invention' involves much more. 'What does not serve propriety, what exceeds nature, what is not even allowed to allegory are to be eliminated. For just as paintings which have nothing similar to the truth do not merit approval, so poetic creations having no probable reasons will not be approved without offense to the reader.' The impossible and the fabulous must be attributed to gods.[147]

Fontius goes from the question of poetic freedom and verisimilitude of invention, which is a diffuse but central position of Horace, to the problem of poetic invention as distinguished from the historical. Since Horace's chief focus in his own discussion of invention was on drama,[148] and this has not yet become a very pressing question to the humanist critic, Fontius, like many sixteenth-century critics, turns to Vergil and epic. Digressions are common and permissible in poetry, but they must not be whimsical, like the 'painter in Horace' (*A.P.,* 12–21) who, asked to paint a ship-wrecked man, wished to paint a cypress. Poets should preserve a coherence of time and place and persist from beginning to end according to the way they proposed. 'Meanwhile it sometimes happens that poets write something contrary to all historical truth. When this happens it should be depicted most accurately of all so that it will appear to be done for just and necessary causes.' There follows the example of Dido. Vergil 'was not unaware that this most modest woman had not yet been born at the time of Aeneas' wanderings, but he falsified this so that he would not have to pass over an opportunity for celebrating Aeneas.' Because Greek cities were flourishing in Italy, the shores of Africa, inhabited by barbarians, were a better place to lead Aeneas. He next was able to show the moral strength of Aeneas when, warned by Mercury, he resists the allurements of Dido and once again pursues his fate in Italy. Vergil was thus able to celebrate in Aeneas the founder of the Julian *gens* and the ancestor of Augustus Caesar. 'Last of all he contrived it that the cause of the discords between Romans and Carthaginians would seem most just if it drew its origin from those who founded so great an empire.' 'You see, therefore, by what methods, contrary to the faith of history, against all truth, poets are sometimes permitted to lie. But he who does carry through everything so that the end corresponds to the beginning and the middle to both will have abused the office of lying.'[149]

His final remark is adapted from Horace, lines 125–127, 'If it is an untried theme you entrust to the stage, and if you boldly fashion a fresh character, have it kept to the end even as it came forth at the first, and have it self-consistent.'[150] The context of Horace's lines is the question whether to follow tradition or invent what is self-consistent. Fontius applies the value of self-consistency not to new invention but to the problem of how in a convincing and useful way to invent episodes that are not historically accurate—which is his way of adapting and following Horace. But his whole example with its fourfold interpretation of the purpose of Vergil is taken from chapter XIII of book XIV of Boccaccio's *De genealogia deorum,* 'Poets are not Liars'. That poets dealt in falsehoods was a common charge, stemming from moral and religious scruple, that had to be met in the defenses of poetry. The usual reply was that the poet veiled the truth in allegory and thus he either made it more palatable or revealed it in its true depth. Boccaccio's treatment is intended to show the usual fourfold interpretation, traditional to the middle ages: the literal or historical sense, the second or moral sense, 'concealed within the poetic veil, was to show with what passions human frailty is infested'. The third and fourth should have been the anagogic and tropological in Biblical exegesis, but Boccaccio gives them as Fontius also did, and both explanations are taken directly from Servius' *Commentary on Vergil's Aeneid* (introductory remarks—*intentio auctoris,* and ad IV, 628 and VI, 752).[151]

Boccaccio had introduced his remarks on Vergil's first purpose in lying by referring to Lucan as a metrical historian rather than a poet. Fontius seized upon this connection to compare the poet's invention with the historian's accuracy. In arguing the Horatian demand for self-consistency in content and plot, Fontius opposed the historically false to the historically true, whereas Horace compared invented and traditional plots. Thus it is possible to see how a humanist follows an earlier humanist source, based on a late classical commentator, but transforms the interpretation to correspond with his own appreciation of historical accuracy and with his perception of the more formal and aesthetic considerations in Horace. The whole treatment is placed in a new and strictly humanist context of striving for clear distinctions between the different modes of discourse embodied in the *studia humanitatis.*

Fontius apparently comes next to the question of the ends of poetry, based on Horace, lines 333–346, 'Poets aim to profit or delight. . . . He has won every point who blends the useful and the pleasing.'[152] But Fontius turns this immediately into a consideration of variety and balance both in style and content. This also is Horace's emphasis—aesthetic effectiveness and hence success. 'It is appropriate for the writer scrupulously to avoid two opposite faults: he should not simply describe the useful or the voluptuous only. For in serious matters the affections should very often be stirred by novelties, jokes, and the unexpected, and in light subjects they should at times be exalted by some weightiness of sentiment or example. For to persist to the end in the same tenor bores the reader and brings contempt on the writer.' Thus Horace lightens the tone of his satires with a certain playfulness, and Propertius especially pleases in his trifles when he scatters golden sentiments and venerable examples. 'For if any one at the same time thus mixes the pleasurable and the useful so that he at once delights and profits, he at length is read, loved, imitated, and pursued with great praise.'[153]

The aims of the poet in Fontius, as in Horace, are clearly not only the ethical or philosophical ones of profiting and pleasing but literary ones as well—with whatever inconsistency this suggests with the humanist's defense of the poet. He will not finally or for long stay away from his moral and philosophical justification, but right here it is subordinated to aesthetic purposes. The same paragraph continues with a discussion of the famous distinction of high, low, and middle styles which found its first extant expression in the *Rhetorica ad Herennium* but is possibly of Peripatetic origin.[154] Fontius follows *Ad Herennium* in stating the problem very formally and in not stressing the moral and social distinctions frequently associated with different styles since Aristotle. He agrees rather with Horace in requiring congruence and the introduction of complementary and balancing qualities. Although Horace does not name the three styles, he is very sensitive to the varieties and proprieties of style: 'Let each style keep the becoming place allotted to it. Yet at times even Comedy raises her voice.'[155] Fontius is further dependent on the *Ad Herennium* in the following passage: 'But whereas a writer who departs little from these often falls further into the contrary, let him beware lest while following a serious and sublime figure he become tumid, turgid, and redundant, or that a low style does not become silly, arid, and bloodless, or a middle style dissolute, languid, and dull.' This, of course, is also Horace's 'brevis esse laboro, obscurus fio' (lines 25–26), where, counseling variety, he warns against the monstrously inept.

Fontius, having comprehended this subtle artistry of the Augustan poet, next supplies illustrations of the accommodation of style to subject borrowed from Quintilian.[156] 'The good poet ought meanwhile to use all these figures of speech according to the quality of the subjects and the persons. We perceive that Homer did this when he gave that low kind of speaking along with heartiness to Menelaus, and, drawing language sweeter than honey from the mouth of Nestor, gave him the middle style. Placing Odysseus on high he conceded copiousness and magnitude and a certain fervor of speech to him like a winter storm.'[157]

These exempla parallel Horace's own in lines 120–124, and Fontius shifts to Horace's context—the need for self-consistency from beginning to end in invented subjects. Fontius moves right into the succeeding passage where Horace contrasts the 'cyclic writer's' slavish imitation with Homer's opening lines in the *Odyssey* (lines 136–142). Fontius shows originality by supplying Vergil's 'Arma virumque cano' instead. He adds other warnings about faulty beginnings, suggesting that the opening is no place to insert flattery, which should not be obvious but follow Vergil's example in praising the family line of Augustus through the device of the shield of Vulcan inserted in the middle of the work. The object, which is also Horace's, is to attain propriety and coherence in order, style, and content, and in this context it is imitation of traditional themes.

Fontius moves right into this question of imitation here—*imitatio* of classical models—and he advocates excelling a classical model in imitation. Thus Vergil excelled Theocritus in the *Bucolics,* Hesiod in the *Georgics,* and Homer in the *Aeneid.* This idea is taken from Macrobius' *Saturnalia,*[158] and so the problem of imitation gets a little complicated with Vergil's models, and Vergil as a model, and Macrobius. But like Horace ('Difficile est proprie communia dicere', line 128) Fontius is anxious to achieve originality and independence even in imitation. 'But in imitating, the most exact judgement is essential, since even in the greatest poets some faults are found [Horace's 'bonus dormitat Homerus', line 359], and the bad is more easily perceived than the good, which is especially likely to happen to those who without penetrating deeply within a poem snatch all at random without any discrimination. Therefore whoever imitates should fully know what it is and why it is imitable and strive to turn it into something better.'[159]

He comes penultimately to the crucial question of the relationship of poetry to philosophy in a passage that shows how impossible it is to separate philosophy from a morally conceived rhetoric in the Horatian or in the humanist tradition. 'Moreover, in addition, he should use similes, comparisons, examples of the elders, rites of tribes and peoples, prophecies, monsters, portents, divine powers, revolutions, the unheard of, the unexpected, jokes, serious matter, ridicule, wit, fables, pity, indignation, praise, blame, affections, and finally everything in its proper place. For whoever now soothes, now torments, partly relaxes, partly coerces, sometimes delights, sometimes terrifies, occasionally diverts, occasionally instructs the mind of the reader fully carries out the poetic function. The study of philosophy will especially aid in this.' The object is to play upon the thoughts and feelings of the listener with the devices of the poet—the old notion of *psychagogia*. The question is whether this is strictly speaking rhetoric, since it does not have specific ends of action. But it is modeled on Horace, lines 309–322: 'Of good writing the source and fount is wisdom. Your matter the Socratic pages can set forth, and when matter is in hand words will not be loath to follow.'[160] And Fontius follows with a knowledge, a content, of human action, copied almost literally from Horace: 'qui didicit patriae quid debeat et quid amicis' etc.[161] Fontius: 'Nam qui didicit qualis esse in deos, in patriam, in parentes' etc. 'He who has learned how we ought to act toward the gods, the fatherland, parents, spouses, children, relatives, friends, citizens, acquaintances, strangers; what is the duty of a senator, a judge, an emperor, a soldier, a city dweller, a rustic; what is fitting for a boy, an old man, a husband, a wife; what are the customs of the French, the Germans, the Greeks, the Italians, and the other peoples will easily arouse any emotion.'[162]

Horace in the passage Fontius was imitating adds: 'I would advise the learned imitator to look to life and manners for a model and draw from thence living words.'[163] Imitation here is *mimesis* in the Aristotelian sense, and what is to be imitated is the universal characteristics and customs of mankind. It is this that relates poetry to philosophy, and it is also what gives it a moral purpose. When Horace spoke of imitation as copying back at line 128—'Difficile est proprie communia dicere'—this may have been, suggests C. O. Brink,[164] an echo of Aristotle' notion of *mimesis—communia* reflecting the *universal* or καθόλου rather than the *traditional,* filtered through Neoptolemus, whose *ars poetica* Horace was using for structural underpinning of his own. Fontius, it will be recalled, in his marginalia to Porphyrion, who claimed Horace followed Neoptolemus, wrote in Greek and Latin at this passage .ὁ. καθολικὸσ. οὖ *universalis,* and in his notes on Landino's lectures on Horace quoted Cicero on the difference between *publica* and *communia.*[165] In his *Poetics,* Fontius, as has been seen,[166] settled for relating the Horatian use of *communia* to the context of literary imitation rather than *mimesis* of life. But it is interesting and important to note that the tradition of *mimesis* persisted through antiquity and reasserts itself in the Renaissance even though it had lost contact with its Platonic and Aristotelian roots. It persisted through the literary-poetic tradition, of which Horace was a part, as well as the rhetorical tradition, thanks to Cicero's insistence on the necessity of a philosophical base for oratory. It returned openly to the literary discussions of the sixteenth century[167] but in the fifteenth century had to distinguish itself from *imitatio* of classical models[168] as imitation of 'nature'. Fontius, by a careful reading of Horace, seem also to have moved in this direction. On the other hand, with respect to the visual arts, Panofsky has acutely observed that imitation of the classics was considered to be imitation of nature since they had already grasped nature best.[169]

The significance of the possibility that Aristotle is the remote source of Horace, as well as of the rather blind groping for the meaning of *communia* in Horace by Fontius, and of Horace's own very evident ambiguity and apparent ignorance of the original Aristotelian meanings of the ideas that suit him in Neoptolemus, lies in the question it raises concerning a favorite theme of recent interpreters of Renaissance poetic. Weinberg may be taken as typical, although actually he is more extreme than Spingarn, Baldwin, Clark, or Hardison. The humanists were primarily rhetoricians, and therefore they were capable only of a rhetorical conception of poetry, and freely imposed the rules of rhetoric, borrowed chiefly from Cicero, on poetry. Horace was of no help, because they read him in a Ciceronian way, and besides he was himself essentially rhetorical in his view of poetry. In Weinberg's words, 'The fact that, in Horace's theory, the internal characteristics of the poem are determined largely, if not exclusively, by the external demands of the audience brings his theory very close to specifically rhetorical approaches.'[170] While this is undoubtedly true to some degree, it is possible to question whether it is true to the extent Weinberg claims and as crucially. Very much of Horace's emphasis is also on internal coherence and the structural qualities of the poem, on propriety, not as what the public decently might expect, but as a congruence of style, structure, and content which will *ipso facto* have an impact on its readers. He is by no means unconcerned with the reputation of the poet, but he also does have an autonomous conception of the poetic art, conscientiously and assiduously to be pursued.[171]

Weinberg continues, in obvious reference to his views of Aristotle: 'In theories of this kind, the determining factor in the production of the work is not an internal principle of structural perfection, bur rather an acceptance of the assumption that all those elements are included in the work that will be susceptible of producing the desired effect upon the audience.'[172] But while there also seems to be in Horace 'an internal principle of structural perfection', it may well be asked whether there is not in Aristotle the assumption that elements are included 'susceptible of producing' a 'desired effect upon the audience'—namely pity and fear. The notion of 'catharsis', however, although scantily expounded in Aristotle, is admittedly totally absent from Horace and the Horatians.[173] In other words, there seems to be a false antithesis, or at least an exaggerated one, here.

Brink certainly seems to interpret Horace along different lines from Weinberg, and in addition insists at several points on the importance of distinguishing between rhetoric with its rules and necessities and the application of certain rhetorical principles to poetry.[174] The division of *res, ordo, facundia* (or *inventio, dispositio, elocutio*) without doubt is in Horace's *Ars* in a deliberately, but not entirely, unsystematic way, and with *ordo* played down in favor of overall unity and coherence. They are also present in Aristotle's *Rhetoric,* and, although they are not the fundamental principle of its organization, they are all three discussed in the *Poetics.*[175] Their presence in a discussion of poetry does not, therefore, *ipso facto,* reduce poetics to something indistinguishable from rhetoric.[176]

I am making this point, not because any or all of these issues can be resolved, but only because studies of Renaissance poetic criticism have tended to be too negative toward the value of the Horatian (and of the humanist?) influence and correspondingly oversanguine about the good influence of Aristotle's *Poetics* after it first began to have an impact in the 1530s. Moreover, it is difficult to see how this claim can be very effectively made when the same scholars complain loudly about how poorly Aristotle was understood even when he was interpreted, and how eager *Cinquecento* writers were to confuse his ideas with Horace's.[177] Marvin Herrick's study of *The Fusion of Horatian and Aristotelian Criticism*[178] is salutary in this regard.

To return to Fontius and his own clearly very Horatian position, in the final section of book II he shows himself eager to distinguish between the orator and the poet and to elevate the latter. 'Moreover, the end and intention of the poet ought not to be passed over in silence. And if I should say it was by speaking well to be of profit and pleasure to all mortals, I should not be in error. For there is high utility in singing of many and great affairs. There is great pleasure, moreover, in concealing in various wrappings and in clarifying by diverse lights. Wherefore, as the matter of the bard is far more excellent and outstanding than that of the orator, which you were easily able to see by yesterday's oration, so also the end is much more laudable and better.'[179] This claim of Fontius, which I believe corresponds also to his analysis of the nature of poetic practice in this book, stands in contrast to the statement of Landino as he begins his commentary on Horace, a statement of the similarity of techniques and the inferiority of the poet that has been much quoted to justify an interpretation of humanist poetic theory as rhetorical. '*Humano capite cervicem pictor equinam:* whereas in writing poetry invention, disposition, and style are first to be investigated, immediately at the beginning Horace states what applies to invention and disposition. For these are prior in time to style. Moreover the precepts of style are almost identical with the orator's and he can easily borrow these from rhetors. For the poet, as I also see pleases Cicero, is close to the orator, being a little more limited by metres than the orator, but freer in the use of words, the companion in many kinds of ornamentation, and almost the equal.'[180]

Although we shall consider in a minute whether Fontius really escapes this charge of viewing poetry essentially as rhetoric, his desire to separate the poet from the orator and establish the former's superiority is unusual among humanists and partly accounts for his composition of a *Poetics*. For this reason I shall quote his encomium of the poet as against the orator at greater length.

'Moreover, I foresee how great a quarrel I will incite over these matters with the orators, because I dare to put the poets ahead of them. Besides, orators, even the greatest of them, as far as their own office is of concern, ought to speak only about civil justice and the useful and virtuous [honesto], which happens either in deliberations or in demonstration of praise or blame. For whatever else they speak about will be totally the province of the other arts. Indeed, the greatest subjects of all and especially appropriate for poets, on God, on the creation of all things, on the lower and higher worlds, on the truly good and right, and on other matters of this kind should come neither in the senate, nor before the people, nor in forum or tribunal. In what does all the force and dignity and capacity of the poets consist? I omit what Democritus, what Plato, what Aristotle, the most excellent of all philosophers, felt about the divine fury of poets, about their great genius exceeding all humanity, about their singular and infinite knowledge of things. I pass over how much Cicero, also, the prince of orators, conceded to them in the defense of Archias.[181] Let them mention one orator, I ask, whom they would make equal to the poet Moses, either in knowledge of incomprehensible things, or admirable wisdom, or amplitude of actions, or fame, or glory, or eternity. Whom will they compare to the

bard Amphion, who by wisdom and song called the woodland men to a
milder culture, who founded laws and customs and the famous Theban
city? What shall I say of David, what of his son, Solomon, both of whom
were very great poets and most splendid and wise kings? And, as I pass by
such greatness and splendor of actions, if you will turn to the qualities of
learning and wisdom, will you make Demosthenes the equal of Solon, the
wisest poet? In him, good God how much gravity, how much fortitude of
mind, how much constancy! He guided the city as long as he was able; he
gave laws to the willing citizens; occupied with public affairs, he spontaneously left and wandered over the globe for the sake of acquiring all the
disciplines worthy of a free man. Finally what should I say of Homer and
Vergil whom I would oppose to all orators in amplitude of genius and
knowledge?'[182]

This comparison, which continues through another paragraph to
claim the distinction of rarity for poets, is his peroration to this book, and
he certainly speaks of poets rhetorically here. But must his analysis of poetic
in this book also be considered a reduction of poetry to oratory? Basically
only if the same conclusion must be drawn about Horace. Fontius' categories and artistic values are Horace's, although they are drawn freely and
imaginatively out of the *Ars* and presented in combination with other
values and out of Horace's own contexts. Primarily he sought congruence
and inner consistency of language, content, structure, and the capacity of
the poet. He urged a balancing off of opposite qualities, much as Horace
seems to have done, for instance variety within consistency—a tendency,
incidentally, which Brink attributes to Peripatetic influence.[183] He saw the
importance of vividness and of engrossing the reader by involving him in
the middle of things. Art must be and can be added to native talent, and a
poem must profit by delighting.

These are the old Horatian platitudes, but I believe they were taken
seriously. Certainly Fontius insists on the instructiveness of poetry and the
high moral and religious themes it should seek to purvey. And everywhere
is that much maligned quality of propriety—τό πρέπον[184] (whether of
Stoic or Peripatetic provenance in Horace). Propriety is not simply a matter
of adherence to the taste of the audience in order not to offend; it is always
explicated also as a matter of the internal congruities in the poem. The fact
that ancient and Renaissance poetics[185] seek the quality of propriety in
terms of a harmonizing of content, style, and structure has seemed regrettable to some modern critics who, perhaps with greater acumen, insist that
these qualities cannot be separated out or even talked about separately in a
well-wrought poem.[186] But this unity of form and content is a complicated
matter, and certainly Horace and Fontius and many other Horatian critics,
and most of the Aristotelian ones in the Renaissance,[187] essentially sought
the same end results. It is a tribute to Horace that he so successfully buried

the analytical structure of poetic within his *Ars*[188]—something which a prose dialogue cannot do. But if a poem can be analyzed into content, structure, and language and the degree to which these elements harmonize, it is not rhetorical just because rhetoric uses the same categories. The problem in a poem and in poetic analysis is different from oratory and rhetorical analysis, whether or not the poet or the critic realizes it. It is to the credit of Fontius that he did realize it to an amazing extent for his time and tradition, although very imperfectly, and he sought to emphasize the difference. Landino, who may well have been a superior critic, and Poliziano, who certainly was, allowed the distinction to remain blurred.[189] But it is out of the effort to differentiate properly between the *studia humanitatis* that humanism that was rhetorically oriented in its beginnings (though founded by a great poet) moved toward the definition and composition of a poetic. A similar separation of history from rhetoric was taking place in the same decades, and Fontius played a rôle in both processes.[190]

IV

Fontius' third book turns to 'the varieties of poems and what poets flourished in each of the genres'. This book revives an old tradition going back to the Alexandrian critics, who first classified poetry into genres and designated leading poets in each.[191] The two most important sources for its transmission to the Renaissance, which Fontius duly utilizes, were the tenth book of Quintilian[192] and book III of Diomedes, *De arte grammatica,* 'De poematibus'. According to Keil, Diomedes based this section of his work on Suetonius' *Lives of the Poets* as well as on Varro.[193] It consists of a classification of the poetic genres, definitions of each, and a mention of representative poets. Fontius, as will be seen, quotes liberally from his section on Roman drama, showing the correspondence of Roman and Greek forms. However, Fontius seems to have collected his other information independently of Diomedes. Diomedes himself quotes liberally from Horace's *Ars,* which is also an obvious source for Fontius. Apparently this work of Diomedes, a fourth-century grammarian, circulated in the early middle ages up through the Carolingian period, and it was incorporated word for word in Rabanus Maurus, *Libri duo de arte grammatica.*[194] Keil used three ninth-century manuscripts for his edition, and remarked that of all the others none seemed to be earlier than the fifteenth century. However, according to Sabbadini,[195] Nicholas of Cusa located a manuscript of Diomedes before 1437. This is now in the British Museum, Harleianus 2773, labeled as twelfth-century. This date needs to be rechecked. At least, the manuscript tradition after the Carolingian classical revival was a thin one. The fifteenth century, according to Keil,[196] copied Diomedes at least five times. Tortelli quotes Ennius in a passage to be found only in Diomedes as early as 1449.[197] There is at least one manuscript of Diomedes in Florence, so that Fontius could possibly have had direct access to a text, or he could have quoted from another humanist source such as Tortelli. He does not mention him or any of his sources. Besides Diomedes, Quintilian, and Horace, he makes liberal use of Eusebius-Jerome, *Chronicon,*[198] for datings, also picking up additional names from it, some of them scarcely known.

With all his dependence on these standard classical and humanist sources, it must also be recognized that he was widely read in classical literature and familiar with the many allusions to and individual mentions of obscure writers. Moreover, there is evidence that he made use of such Greek sources as Pseudo-Plutarch, *De musica* and Pausanias.[199] The *Suidas* lexicon was also available to him. Moreover, at least five years earlier, Poliziano had written his *Nutricia,*[200] one of his *Sylvae* or poetic introductions to his lectures at the studio. Besides putting forth a contemporary Neoplatonic view of poetry as divinely inspired, this poetic oration runs with gusto through the history of poetry. Thus Fontius had the work of his rival as a model, but in this third book he puts the stamp of his own sober and diligent scholarship, his concern for clear definitions and distinctions, his interest in historical sequences upon his treatment of the history of poetry. Although there is a family resemblance between his classifications and Poliziano's, due to the fact that they both depend on the same literary sources, there are interesting differences, and although the lists of poets also overlap, they too are not identical. Poliziano's is a parade of names and legends not unlike the processions of Petrarch's *Triumphs,* whereas Fontius has given us a cool and systematic account of the genres and their practitioners in as near to chronologial order as he is able, and with Greek tradition carefully separated from and compared to Latin. Poliziano makes his groupings according to theme and pays little attention to time, place, or metrical form. He ends briefly with Dante, Petrarch, and Boccaccio, and lengthily with an encomium of Lorenzo de' Medici as Maecenas and poet.[201] Fontius includes Dante and Petrarch within their proper genres. Poliziano has given a fine poetic vision of a tradition, Fontius a useful embryonic treatise on the history of poetry.

It will be recognized that the question of the nature of the poetic genres is a relative one.[202] Each particular schema seems to depend on some incomplete criterion, involving both form and content. Fontius begins with the one used by Diomedes,[203] dividing poetry into three kinds according to who does the speaking: 'the common, in which both the poet and his characters speak', 'the narrative, in which only the poet speaks', 'the active, in which only the characters presented speak'.[204] This (originally Aristotelian) basis of division immediately breaks down when the appropriate subject matter for each is added. 'In the common gods, kings, brave deeds, and lesser things also are described. In narrative whatever subjects pertain to philosophy and any other instruction are presented. In the active what is acted on the stage is the content.' He passes immediately to an announcement of his procedure which introduces the further criteria of metres and of content from a different point of view. This confusion was traditional, and to Fontius, who had the humanist's urge to classification, quite acceptable. He will deal first with 'heroic poems, then with lyrics and iambics as well as elegiacs, finally with writers of dramas in which the tragic, the comic, the satiric, and the mimic are numbered, and we will report concerning their poems and their beginnings in order.'[205]

Essentially Fontius had an empirical attitude toward these categories, because as he proceeds to deal with each he is concerned mainly to describe its historical origin or the basis for the use of the name given it. For instance, the heroic poem was so called because with Homer poets stopped singing of gods only and included the deeds of heroes and brave men. It was called *epos* by the Greeks because all was pursued in a constant tenor. But it was sometimes called Pythian because the oracles of Pythian Apollo were issued by his daughter, Phemonoe, in that kind of song, i.e., hexameters.[206] His procedure is to speak first of the legendary poets—the *prisci vates*[207]—and then in historical order of the leading Greek and Roman writers within the genre. Thus he passes from Amphion, Linus, Musaeus, and Orpheus to Homer, Hesiod, Tyrtaeus, Antimachus, Panyasis, Apollonius Rhodius, Aratus, and Theocritus among the Greeks, to Ennius, Lucretius, Varro Atacinus, Vergil, Macer, Ovid, Manlius (i.e., Manilius), Lucan, Saleius Bassus, Cornelius Severus, Rabirius, Pedo, Silius, Valerius Flaccus, Papirius Statius, and Claudianus among the Romans.[208] Wherever he can, which means wherever there is a reference in Eusebius-Jerome or in a historical work that he knows, he give the *floruit,* and he makes short critical characterizations, usually quoting standard opinion but sometimes reflecting his own judgement, of each.

His procedure is the same for lyric, iambic, and elegy. He seems to have compiled his list of poets from many sources, since it is more complete than Horace, Quintilian, or Diomedes.[209] But he is obviously influenced in his comments and choice of facts by all three. He picks up some, but not all, of his additional names from Eusebius-Jerome, making it obvious by repeating them literally.[210] Tyrtaeus was classified as an epic poet because of Horace's lines 402–403,[211] which he quotes. His lyric poets also are preceded by the early theological and legendary poets: Amphion, Linus, and Orpheus, but not Musaeus. In his place comes Thamyras. He relates the story about this less frequently mentioned figure that when he had taught music and preferred himself to the muses they took away his lyre and his sight.[212] Fontius could have taken this from a somewhat wordier entry in Tortelli's *Orthographia,*[213] or from Homer or Ovid and Propertius,

Tortelli's own sources, whom Fontius knew well. Fontius also introduces Biblical poets as *prisci vates* whenever he can. 'But also the sacred laws and hymns of the Hebrews are expressed in hendecasyllabics, Sapphics, and Pindarics.'[214] 'After Orpheus' he lists among the Greeks, and in historical order as he knows it: Alcman, Terpander, Sappho, Alcaeus, Stesichorus, Simonides, Phocylides (whom he claimed to have translated), Ibycus, Anacreon, Pindar, Corinna, Bacchylides, Telesilla, Praxilla, Cleobulina, and Erinna. Among the Latins, none before Catullus, then Horace, Caesius Bassus, Dante, and Petrarch[215]—the shortness of the Latin list contrasting with the length of the Greek list.

Among these Greek lyric poets the case of Corinna is interesting. She is not mentioned by Eusebius, Quintilian, Diomedes, or Tortelli. She is in *Suidas,*[216] but the information does not correspond to what Fontius says of her. 'But also Corinna flourished in the same age as Pindar; either because of the beauty of her form or the grace of the Aeolic tongue, which she preferred to Theban Doric, she was the victor when she contended with Pindar at Thebes.' Corinna is little known among the ancients. The three principal mentions of her are by Plutarch, Aelian, and Pausanias.[217] Only Pausanias' corresponds to Fontius' account. This seems to be his source. Greek manuscripts of Pausanias were in Italy in the fifteenth century, and probably even in Florence, judging by the existence of Cod. Laur. 56, 10 and 56, 11.[218] But there is also an ambiguous reference to Corinna in Propertius,[219] certainly known to Fontius. However, it does not correspond as closely as Pausanias. Moreover, Pausanias seems the more plausible in the light of the fact that he is one of the few sources for Sacadas of Argos, mentioned almost immediately by Fontius as an inventor of elegiac.

Fontius lists but few iambic writers among either Greeks or Latins: Archilochus and Hipponax; Bibaculus, Catullus, and Horace. Elegiac writers are similarly limited. His account of the origin of elegiac is curious. Some say King Midas invented it; others say Etheocles of Naxos or of Eretria, or Sacadas of Argos. Sacadas is in Pausanias,[220] as was just indicated, as well as in Pseudo-Plutarch, *De musica,*[221] an elegant source for a humanist interested in early poetic origins and mentioned by Landino,[222] but apparently not utilized by Poliziano for his very extensive list of *prisci vates* (which include sibyls and muses).[223] Midas and Etheocles are also obscure. The tale of Midas comes from the *Suidas* lexicon and Etheocles is apparently Theocles, the leader of the Boeotian colonists of Naxos, mentioned as the inventor of elegy in the *Etymologicon magnum,* a compendium in Greek available to Fontius.[224] Fontius considers Job Idumeus an elegiac poet. Among the Greeks there were Callimachus, Mimnermus, Euphorion, and Philetas; among the Latins Gallus, Ovid, Tibullus, and Propertius.[225]

His treatment of drama is more elaborate because it has so many subdivisions and he wanted to correlate the Greek forms with the Latin.

Here he seems to borrow several short definitions from Diomedes, but extends them with other matter picked up elsewhere. For example, he takes from Diomedes: 'Tragedy, moreover, is a representation of heroic fortune in adversity'; but then he adds, possibly in his own words, or in an excerpt from another source: 'First derived from praise of Father Liber, little by little extended to expressing the disasters of great kings and leaders, useful indeed for teaching all by the example of another.'[226] But the approach is conventional and easy to come by. Tragedy was more ancient than Phrynicus and Thespis. Aeschylus, Sophocles, and Euripides were the leading tragedians.

On the differences of tragedy and comedy he quotes Diomedes more liberally. He reports Cratinus, Plato, and Crates as early comic writers flourishing around the eighty-first Olympiad—a reference from Eusebius that can seem a little confusing.[227] Not much later come Aristophanes and Eupolis. Menander and Philemon represent new comedy. He speaks of satiric plays, which apparently were the satyr plays, and mentions Demetrius of Tarsus and Menippus as authors.[228]

Latin drama confronts the would-be historian of literature with a complexity of names and types. Fontius relies heavily on Diomedes here, and so explains what *praetexta, tabernaria, atellana, planipedia, togata,* and *palliata* are, and to what Greek types they correspond.[229] But with Roman satire he takes off on his own once more. It may be recalled that a large part of one of his inaugural orations had been devoted to satire. Although there is an early type of Roman religious poetry sometimes called satire, he will be concerned with the better known nondramatic variety of satiric verse. Roman satire is a poetic genre highly apt for castigating, speaking ill, and blaming. It is called satire only because of its similarity to the bitter reproaches which the petulant and lascivious satyrs utter in the Greek satyr plays. In Roman satire Lucilius Aurunca, Horace, Persius, and Jùvenal flourished. 'In resemblance to this satire and to old comedy our Dante composed his great poem with marvelous art, praising the good, condemning the evil to the underworld and eternal punishment.'[230] An old confusion of ideas about poetic forms seems to persist.

With a brief summary, he comes to the end of his dialogue. He has shown that poetic is divine and poets divinely inspired, that they comprehend heaven, earth, hell, gods, heroes, kings, wars, and whatever is great, that they are the authors of customs, laws, religions, and cities, that they are the most learned and excellent of all writers in the liberal arts (book I). He has narrated how 'the future poet' should approach the composition of a poem, and with what qualities and what devices, and what vices he should avoid (book II). He has demonstrated what the poetic genres are and has enumerated the heroic, lyric, iambic, elegiac, tragic, comic, satiric, and mimic poets to be assigned to each genre 'according to my recollection'.[231] In very summary fashion this is his conception of a *Poetics*. 'If I have expounded all effectively and in keeping with the dignity of the subject, I have indeed spoken as I ought. If less than this, certainly as I am able. You, however, should consider, not from this which I have related as much as from what I have omitted, that poetic is by far the greatest of all the arts.'

In similar fashion I may claim to have justified, not so much the high quality of Fontius' literary ideas and criticism, but how, historically, in his instance, as a telling representative case-history, the *studia humanitatis* evolved to the composition of a formal *Poetics*.

NOTES

1. 'A Humanist's Image of Humanism: the Inaugural Orations of Bartolommeo della Fonte', *Studies in the Renaissance* VII (1960), 90–125; appendix I, 'The Works of Bartolommeo della Fonte from Forence, Biblioteca Nazionale, Cod. Palatino Capponi 77', pp. 126–127; appendix II, 'Manuscripts and Editions of Located Works of Bartolommeo della Fonte', pp. 127–132. Hereafter cited as '*Fontius* 1960'. See this volume, previous essay. For his mss, editions and handwriting, see Caroti and Zamponi, sup. cit., in previous essay, n. 4.
2. Purchased with the aid of, and with thanks to, the Columbus University Council for Research in the Social Sciences.
3. I am grateful to all three scholars for this small act of international and intercollegiate coöperation. I only hope not to justify Professor Gombrich's fears that it "would hardly warrant publication in full since, like Shakespeare's Hamlet, 'it consists almost entirely of quotations'". I am indebted also to Professor James Hutton for supplying many references that I could not locate and for other suggestions.
4. In 1961 a long-awaited major work appeared: Professor Bernard Weinberg of the University of Chicago's *A History of Literary Criticism in the Italian Renaissance* (Chicago, 1961). Although it deals with 'literature' only as poetry and covers only the *Cinquecento* and the very end of the *Quattrocento*, this work is an indispensable manual because of the thoroughness of its coverage. This work is monumental in its scope but monolithic in maintaining its author's point of view, which is that of the so-called 'Chicago school' of Aristotelianism, fully and effectively expounded in its application to literature in *Critics and Criticism, Ancient and Modern*, ed. R. S. Crane (Chicago, 1952). Another notable work appeared the very next year, Professor Baxter Hathaway of Cornell University's *The Age of Criticism: the Late Renaissance in Italy* (Ithaca, 1962). More accurately titled, Professor Hathaway's book explores in depth a number of critical issues in sixteenth-century criticism and is particularly generous in acknowledging the validity and importance of the contributions

of that age even when they do not coincide with modern or ancient critical canons. Hard on its heels came Professor O. B. Hardison, Jr., of the University of North Carolina's *The Enduring Monument, a Study of the Idea of Praise in Renaissance Literary Theory and Practice* (Chapel Hill, 1962). Professor Hardison contributes a valuable survey of the types of literary theory prevailing in the Renaissance, including the *Trecento* and *Quattrocento,* but perhaps more importantly, analyzes the interplay of epideictic literary theory and poetic composition in sixteenth-century European literature.

5. The following are standard and well-known: Joel E. Spingarn, *A History of Literary Criticism in the Renaissance* (New York, 1899; enlarged Italian ed., Bari, 1905); Karl Vossler, *Poetische Theorien in der italienischen Frührenaissance* (Berlin, 1900, *Litterarhistorische Forschungen,* Heft XII); Orazio Bacci, *La critica letteraria (dall' antichità classica al rinascimento)* (Milano, 1910, *Storia dei generi letterari italiani* 8); Ciro Trabalza, *La critica letteraria nel rinascimento (secoli XV–XVI–XVII)* (Milano, 1915, *Storia dei generi letterari italiani* 9); Giuseppe Toffanin, *La fine dell'umanesimo* (Torino, 1920); Donald L. Clark, *Rhetoric and Poetry in the Renaissance, a Study of Rhetorical Terms in English Renaissance Literary Criticism* (New York, 1922); Charles S. Baldwin, *Renaissance Literary Theory and Practice,* ed. Donald L. Clark (New York, 1939). Of exceptional value in this study are: Marvin T. Herrick, *The Fusion of Horatian and Aristotelian Criticism, 1531–1555* (Urbana, Ill., 1946, *Illinois Stud. in Language & Literature* XXXII: I) and August Buck, *Italienische Dichtungslehren vom Mittelalter bis zum Ausgang der Renaissance* (Tübingen, 1952, *Beihefte zur Zeitschrift für romanische Philologic,* Heft 94). Francesco Tateo, *'Retorica' e 'poetica' fra medioevo e rinascimento* (Bari, 1960) considers chiefly the *Trecento* and the *Cinquecento.*

6. Cristoforo Landino presented his general ideas on poetry in at least three publications which repeat each other with minor variations: the introductory pages to book III of his *Disputationes Camaldulenses,* Cod. Laur. 53, 28, ff. 90^r–98^r (I also use Hain 9851, Florence, ca. 1480, sigg. fiii^r–fvi^v); his introduction to his commentary on the *Divine Comedy,* first published in Florence, 1481 (I use *Dante con l'espositioni di Cristoforo Landino,* Venice, 1578, 'Discorso del Landino che cosa sia poesia et poeta, et della origine sua divina et antichissima', unnumbered), his most extensive statement; his commentary on Horace, first published in 1482, Florence, A. Miscomini (I use Harvard Inc. 4917 B, *Horatii opera cum commentariis Acronis . . . ,* Venice, 1490, ff. 145–161).

7. His most important statement is in his *Sylva,* 'Nutricia', in Angelo Poliziano, *Le selve e La strega, prolusioni nello Studio Fiorentino (1482–1492)* per cura di Isidoro del Lungo (Florence, 1925), pp. 113–181, 'Absoluta est in Faesulano VIII idus octobris MCCCCLXXXVI.'

8. *Ioannis Ioviani Pontani Dialogus qui Actius inscribitur* (Giovanni Pontano, *I dialoghi* a cura di Carmelo Previtera, Florence, 1943, pp. 127–239).

9. F. 2^r of the text edited below. References to the text will simply give the folio numbers of the original manuscript with no other indication.

10. Fontius, of course, is speaking of ancient Latin authors, but he does not seem

to know of certain medieval treatises published or discussed by Edmond Faral, *Les Arts poétiques du XIIe et du XIIIe siècle* (Paris, 1924, *Bibl. de l'École des hautes études,* fasc. 238; reprinted, 1958). These include Matthieu de Vendôme, *Ars versificatoria;* Geoffroi de Vinsauf, *Poetria nova;* Gervais of Melkley, *Ars versificatoria;* John of Garland, *Poetria.* In C. S. Baldwin's judgement (*Medieval Rhetoric and Poetic,* New York, 1928, p. 195), 'their aim was not to organize the study of poetic, but to cover its elements by as many exercises as possible. Imitative writing of Latin verse, long part of the study of *grammatica,* has been combined with the theory of *rhetorica* through exercises in figures, and with its practice through exercises in *dictamen.* Doubtless the resulting aggregation was called *poetria* both because the exercises were still connected with the traditional *praelectio* and were oftenest in verse, and because, whether in verse or *dictamen,* they were focused on that heightening by ornament and by dilation which was conventionally regarded as poetic.'

11. As my discussion below will bring out, I believe this is the first Renaissance poetics in content as well as title. Previous humanist writing on poetry dealt with it in the fragmentary form of commentaries, or defended its dignity and distinguished it from other arts, or sketched its past. However inadequately, Fontius seems to have given the first general discussion of poetry as an art (in book II, cf. below).

12. 'Paulus Ghiaccetus Tertius', i.e., Paolo Cattani da Ghiacceto (or Diacceto as it is spelled today), a grandson of the Florentine statesman of the same name whose life Fontius wrote. (Cf. Wolfenbüttel Cod. 43 Aug. Fol., ff. 131^r–139^r.) The Cattani family had a villa in the village of Pelago nearby but took its name from Ghiacceto, where Fontius was living in the summer of 1490. Paolo da Ghiacetto III was an interlocutor in Fontius' dialogue *Pelago* or *Ragionamento sopra alchuni luoghi de' Triumphi del Petrarcha* (*Fontius* 1960, p. 135). The first Paolo da Ghiacceto was an ancestor of the statesman.

13. Cf. *Catalogus codicum manuscriptorum Bibliothecae Regiae* (Paris, 1744), IV, 409. Its provenance is indicated as the DuFresne collection. Leopold Deslisle, *Le Cabinet des manuscrits de la Bibliothèque impérale* (Paris, 1868–1881), I, 269–270, discusses the collection of Raphaël Trichet du Fresne, purchased by Colbert.

14. Cf. *Catalogus codicum latinorum Bibliothecae Regiae Monacensis* (Munich, 1878), tom. II, pars III, p. 200; f. 1, *Macrobii Theodosii Saturnaliorum libri VII;* f. 157, *Macrobii Ambrosii in somnium Scipionis libri II;* f. 233^v, at end, 'Barptolemaeus Fontius exscripsit Florentiae'. Cf. p. 44 above. Cf. also Guglielmo Fraknói, Giuseppe Fógel, Paolo Galyás, Edit Hoffmann, *Biblioteca Corvina, la biblioteca di Mattia Corvino re d'Ungheria,* tr. Luigi Zambra (Budapest, 1927), p. 105, n. 169.

15. Bartholomaeus Fontius, *Epistolarum libri III,* ed. Ladislaus Juhász (Budapest, 1931), lib. II, ep. 8, p. 33.

16. For these two lost works see *Fontius* 1960, p. 127, no. 38 (Phocylides) and p. 126, no. 2 (Valerius Flaccus).

17. Concetto Marchesi, *Bartolomeo della Fonte* (Catania, 1900), pp. 136–141, VI, 'Valerio Flacco'.

18. *Fontius* 1960, p. 94 and n. 12.
19. Text, F. 40ʳ.
20. Lib. II, ep. 11 (ed. Juhász, p. 36): 'quem non longo post tempore subsequentur maiora nostra in Valerium Flaccum nomini tuo dedicata volumina et tua celsitudine digniora'.
21. Lib. II, ep. 12.
22. On 30 May he was in Pelago, presumably staying at the Ghiacceto family villa, as his translation of Demosthenes' oration *De mala legatione* states at the end (Florence, Bib. Naz. Cod. Palatino Capponi 77, f. 71ʳ, 'Pelagi iii Cal. Junia 1490 Copiato dallo originale di mano delfontio adi 10 digennaio 1513 per me Francesco baroncini et finito detto di'). Lib. II, ep. 16 (ed. Juhász, p. 39) is inscribed Giacetti, 'XII Cal. Augusti 1490'.
23. This villa was the setting for his dialogue commentary on Petrarch's *Trionfi;* cf. text edited in *Fontius* 1960, pp. 134–147, f. 3ᵛ, 'con Pagolo da Ghiacceto nella sua villa di Pelago'.
24. *Fontius* 1960, pp. 94–95.
25. *Ibid.*, pp. 131–132, 'Additional Works of Fontius (E)'. Cf. now P. O. Kristeller, *Iter Italicum,* 1 (London and Leiden, 1963), 184–208, partial descriptions of Florence, Biblioteca Riccardiana codices 62, 151, 152, 153, 154, 421, 646, 673, 837, 851, 904, 907. Cf. Marchesi, *op. cit.,* parte 2a, 1, 'Gli excerpta', pp. 101–107. These descriptions supplement and overlap each other but are still not complete. See now (1983) Caroti and Zamponi.
26. Riccardiana, Cod. 646, ff. 61ʳ–84ᵛ. F. 61ʳ, 'Collecta sub Christophoro Landino publice legenti Florentie anno MCCCCᵒ supra quartum et sexagesimum. Multa sunt quae ipse non dixit; sed ego ex Tortellio vero collegi.'
27. Giovanni Tortelli of Arezzo (1400–1466), Vatican librarian under Nicholas V; his *Commentaria grammatica de orthographia dictionum e Graecis tractarum,* first editions, Rome and Venice, 1471, was generally known as *Orthographia.* Fontius used a manuscript in 1464. Citations will be from the Venice, 1495 edition. Among other things, this book contains an alphabetical biographical dictionary of Greek authors with excerpts from classical, mostly Latin, authors.
28. *Op. cit.* in n. 6.
29. E.g.·f. 147ᵛ of edition cited (Venice, 1490).
30. Riccardiana, Cod. 152, reported by Marchesi, *op. cit.,* p. 103. Kristeller, *op. cit.,* p. 188, does not include this item in his description of the manuscript but supplies the dates given for other material. I have not examined this item.
31. Riccardiana, Cod. 628. It is listed by Kristeller, *op. cit.,* p. 178, among his 'Excerpts' from the inventory as 'Horace. Owned by Barth. Fontius.' It turned out to be Porphyrion. I have not seen Ric. 700, also listed in 'Excerpts' as Horace owned by Fontius (Kristeller, p. 179). Cod. 628 has a humanist Italic hand, not of Fontius, but very close to that of Cennini in Cod. Laur. 53, 28. Comparison was based on microfilms and on B. L. Ullman, *The Origin and Development of Humanistic Script* (Rome, 1960), plate 70. I reserve judgement on the identification as in this particular style of

writing extraordinary uniformity can be achieved by different scribes. There are sufficient differences from the characteristic letter formations of Fontius to make it certainly not his, although the marginalia, in his cursive, definitely are his. The commentary on the *Ars poetica* runs from f. 105^r to f. 116^r.

32. F. 109^v.
33. F. 105^r. I use the Loeb Classical Library edition of Horace.
34. C. O. Brink, *Horace on Poetry: Prolegomena to the Literary Epistles* (Cambridge, 1963). Cf. part II, 'The Tradition of Literary Criticism and the "Ars Poetica'", pp. 43–150.
35. *Ibid.,* pp. 103–108.
36. Cod. Ric. 646, f. 81^r. Cicero, *De officiis,* I, 52 is not it but close.
37. *Op. cit.,* f. 151^v.
38. Cod. Ric. 646, f. 82^r.
39. *Ibid.,* f. 64^r.
40. *Ambrosii Theodosii Macrobii Saturnalia.* Apparatu critico instruxit . . . Jacobus Willis (Leipzig, 1963, Teubner), V, 2, 9–11.
41. *Vide supra,* n. 14.
42. Ff. 22^v–23^r. See p. 107.
43. *Op. cit.,* f. 147^r.
44. Pp. 114–115.
45. Cf. Marchesi, *op. cit.,* pp. 101–106. These 'excerpta' have not yet been systematically studied. His own interests ranged from the naturalistic in his first edition of Celsus and in Cod. Riccardianus 151 and 154, the archaeological in his collection of inscriptions (*Fontius* 1960, p. 131, B [the Ashmole MS. is now Oxford, Bodleian Lat. Misc. d 85]), his letter on ancient weights and measures (lib. III, ep. 7), to his lexicographic studies (cf. Marchesi, pp. 107–112). Also see Caroti and Zamponi.
46. Cf. the list of authors selected by Kristeller in his description of Fontius' excerpts, above n. 25.
47. Manuscripts and editions listed *Fontius* 1960, p. 120, appendix II, (I). Cf. D. Robathan and F. E. Cranz, *Persius, Catalogus translationum et commentariorum, Medieval and Renaissance Latin Translations and Commentaries,* ed. F. E. Cranz, Vol. 3 (Washington, 1976), 265–67.
48. Wolfenbüttel Cod. 43 Aug. Fol., ff. 15^v–17^v, Prohemium on satire. The commentary opens with an analysis of the appropriateness of iambic metre for invective and satire (ff. 19^r seq.). Cf. Marchesi, *op. cit.,* pp. 113–121.
49. Cod. Riccardianus 1172, ff. 11^r–35^r. Cf. Eva Sandford's discussion of this commentary in her article on the Juvenal tradition, *Catalogus translationum et commentariorum, Medieval and Renaissance Latin Translations and Commentaries,* ed. P. O. Kristeller, I (Washington, 1960), 227–229. Miss Sandford also refers to Fontius' independent selections and comments on Juvenal in Cod. Ric. 153, ff. 135–139, 'Ad Juvenalem quaedam adnotationes'.
50. See n. 48; p. 121; text ff. 47^v–49^v.
51. Details in Marchesi, pp. 49–63, corrected by *Fontius* 1960, pp. 91–94 and n. 12.
52. Above pp. 89–90 and nn. 16–21.

53. Above, p. 89 and n. 15.
54. Cod. Ricc. 539, 170 folios; cf. Marchesi, pp. 166–167; described by Kristeller, *Iter,* I, 193.
55. Ff. 1ʳ–3ʳ.
56. Cf. Brink's trenchant remarks, *op. cit.,* pp. 153–154.
57. *Fontius* 1960, pp. 127, 129–130.
58. *Carmina,* ed. Jos. Fógel and Lad. Juhász (Leipzig, 1932).
59. P. O. Kristeller, *Studies in Renaissance Thought and Letters* (Rome, 1956), pp. 381–382.
60. *Ibid.*
61. *Fontius* 1960, p. 127.
62. *Ibid.,* p. 130.
63. Below and *Fontius* 1960, pp. 107–108.
64. *Fontius* 1960, appendix IV, pp. 134–147.
65. Cited above. Cf. especially his fine discussion of the interplay of theory and practice in chapter IV, 'Varieties of Elegy', pp. 123–162, where he shows how the frequently despised epideictic theory of poetry is manifested in some of the most beautiful poems of the Renaissance.
66. These orations are all discussed in *Fontius* 1960, pp. 105–108, 112–113, 120. Although these orations first appeared in an earlier incunabulum, Hain 7227, the best text is Wolfenbüttel, 43 Aug. Fol., which in 1960 I suggested was his autographic presentation copy for Matthias Corvinus, king of Hungary. There is no longer any question in my mind that it is an autograph, as comparison with Clm. 15738 (cf. n. 14 above) makes clear. This is also the view of Edit Hoffmann in Fraknói et al., *op. cit.,* p. 106, n. 170. The discussion *De poetice* in his *Oratio in bonas artis* appears on ff. 154ᵛ–156ʳ of this manuscript.
67. Wolfenbüttel, 43 Aug. Fol., ff. 160ʳ–165ʳ; quotation f. 160.
68. *Ibid.,* ff. 169ʳ–172ʳ.
69. *Fontius* 1960, oratory, pp. 95–99; history, pp. 99–105; moral philosophy in the oration on wisdom, pp. 108–111; grammar, as one of the liberal arts, p. 112. Further indication of how his, and similar humanist, attempts to define and distinguish the humanities led to the development of autonomous notions of them is found in his letter to Bernardo Rucellai of 1 March 1513, lib. III, ep. 11 (ed. Juhász, pp. 60–64).
70. See above, n. 7. Other orations of Poliziano in *Tomus tertius operum Angeli Politiani* (Lyons, 1537).
71. The *sermones* of Antonio Urceo ('Codrus') are inaugural lectures published without title at Bologna, 1502. Some of Filippo Beroaldo the elder's *Orationes* were printed at Bologna, 1492. His *Orationes et opuscula* (Basel, 1513) has an 'oratio habita in enarratione epistolarum Ciceronis . . . continens laudem poetices' (ff. viiᵛ–ixᵛ).
72. 'Orazione facta per Cristoforo Landino da Pratovecchio quando cominciò a leggere in Studio i sonetti di M. Francesco Petrarca', in *Miscellanea di cose inedite et rare,* ed. F. Corazzini (Florence, 1853), p. 131.
73. See note 67.

74. *Op. cit.,* pp. 143–144.
75. Cf. Landino's declaration of the applicability of rhetorical principles to poetry at the beginning of his commentary on Horace, *Ars poetica,* f. 145. Quoted below p. 115 and n. 180.
76. Pontano's *Actius* is definitely not a poetics, but it engages in the kind of discussion of the stylistic differences and similarities of poetry, oratory, and historical writing that was bound to lead to more precise definitions of each, and autonomous concepts. Cf. Felix Gilbert, *Machiavelli and Guicciardini, Politics and History in the Sixteenth Century* (Princeton, 1964), chapter 5, 'The Theory and Practice of History in the Fifteenth Century' for a discussion of the growing clarity about the nature of history that emerged from humanistic discussions. Gilbert points to the lack of a classical model of historical theory such as Aristotle's *Poetics* to guide the historical speculation of the humanists (p. 105) and therefore stresses historical experience itself as leading to a new, autonomous conception of history (Guicciardini's) in the sixteenth century. He gives credit to humanist thought, however, in contributing to the new view (pp. 297–300). Gilbert stresses the *practice* rather than the *theory* of historical writing. There are, however, classical models of historical theory which acquired influence and authority in the sixteenth century, just as the *Poetics* did. These were the comments of Polybius in book XII of his *Histories;* Dionysius of Halicarnassus, *Letter to Pompey,* and the Pseudo-Dionysian *Art of Rhetoric;* Lucian of Samosata, *How to Write History.* The interest in and imitation of these works in the mid- and late-sixteenth century are discussed by Beatrice Reynolds, 'Shifting Currents in Historical Criticism', *Jour. of the History of Ideas* XIV (1953), 471–492, and pointedly, in a more recent study, by George H. Nadel, 'Philosophy of History before Historicism', *History and Theory* III (1964), 291–315, esp. pp. 292–309. The statements of Livy, Cicero, and Quintilian were of more influence on fifteenth- and early sixteenth-century humanism, and perhaps have some analogy to the currency of Horace's *Ars poetica* at the same time. At any rate greater refinement of differentiation between rhetoric, history, and poetry seems to have been a development of the late fifteenth century out of humanism.
77. Lib. I, ff. 4^r–22^r; lib. II, ff. 22^r–37^r; lib. III, ff. 37^v–50^r.
78. F. 4.
79. *Ion,* 533d–535a and 535e–536d; *Phaedrus,* 245a.
80. *Fontius* 1960, pp. 105–106 and esp. nn. 52 and 53.
81. Tr. Willard Trask (New York, 1953). Cf. pp. 214–227, 'Poetry and Theology', pp. 474–475, Excursus VIII, 'The Poet's Divine Frenzy'.
82. Quoted in *Fontius* 1960, n. 52 and n. 53 (*Epistola de divino furore*).
83. Landino cites *Ion* and *Phaedrus* here as well as in his similar statements in introducing book III of the *Disputationes Camaldulenses* and his commentary on Horace's *Ars poetica.* See above, n. 6.
84. For Mussato see Curtius, *op. cit.,* pp. 215–221; for Petrarch, *Invective contra medicum,* a cura di Pier Giorgio Ricci (Roma, 1950), Liber tertius, esp. p. 71, lines, 448–462, and *Epistolae familiares,* lib. X, ep. 4; Boccaccio, *De*

genealogia deorum, book XIV, chap. VIII, bk. XV, ch. VIII (Eng. tr. of books XIV and XV by Charles G. Osgood, *Boccaccio on Poetry,* Princeton, 1930); Coluccio Salutati, *De laboribus Herculis,* ed. B. L. Ullman (Zurich, 1951), lib. I, caps. ii, ix.

85. *Op. cit.,* pp. 40–41, and pp. 446–462, Excursus VI, 'Early Christian and Medieval Literary Studies'.
86. F. 4. The combination of the concept of 'Biblical poetics' with the notion of the legendary pre-Homeric Greek poets who were divinely inspired and founded the worship of the gods has certain analogies to the Renaissance Neoplatonic notion of *prisci theologi* put forth by Ficino and Pico. Neoplatonism undoubtedly gave an impetus to the spread of these ideas, but actually the notion goes back to Augustine, *De civitate Dei,* lib. XVII, capp. xiv, xxxvii. It is not unlikely that Augustine's statements contributed to Ficino's adapation of *prisci poetae* to *prisci theologi.* The subject needs investigation. Cf. Poliziano's *Nutricia,* lines 218–345, for a very extensive development of the list of *prisci poetae,* drawn from Pseudo-Plutarch, *De musica* and Pausanias, as well as commoner sources. For the probability that Fontius also used these writers, see p. 120 and nn. 218–222. Landino refers to the *De musica* in his introduction to his commentary on Dante.
87. F. 5.
88. Ff. 5ᵛ–6ᵛ.
89. Ff. 6ᵛ–7ᵛ.
90. *Op. cit.,* pp. 226–227.
91. *Op. cit.,* esp. lib. III.
92. *Op. cit.,* book XIV, ch. IV.
93. *Op. cit.,* esp. bks. I and II.
94. *Epistolario di Coluccio Salutati,* ed. F. Novati (Rome, 1891–1911), IV, 205 ff. Cf. B. L. Ullman, *The Humanism of Coluccio Salutati* (Rome, 1963), pp. 63–70.
95. *De nobilitate legum et medicinae,* ed. E. Garin (Florence, 1947).
96. Florence, 1947.
97. Cf. Weinberg, *op. cit.,* ch. I, 'The Classification of Poetics among the Sciences'. Hardison, *op. cit.,* also considers this question in his first chapter, 'The Classification of Systems of Criticism' covering poetry as philosophy, poetry as theology, as grammar, as part of logic, as a branch of moral philosophy.
98. Cf. Curtius, *op. cit.,* pp. 215–221.
99. *De laboribus Herculis,* lib. I, cap. iii, 'Quod poetica sit ars et que sit eius materia, et quod ex omnibus artibus sit composita, et quod ab ipsa natura profecta sit' (ed. Ullman, I, 17); cap. iv, 'Quod poetica ex trivio atque quadrivio perficiatur et ipsam solam posse quicquid efficit trivium explicare' (I, 21); passages quoted: 'delectationem commutationis et carminis (I, 22); 'poetica simul omnia perficit et imaginativam thesaurumque perceptarum rerum, memoriam, movet et reducit in actum . . . addendo super hoc dulcedinem admirabilis armonie' (I, 22–23). On the poet as *vir optimus,* caps. xii, xiii.

100. Curtius, *op. cit.*, pp. 2221–225 discusses scholastic classifications of poetry where poetry is 'infima inter omnes doctrinas'. Poetry in the humanist defenses is elevated above the liberal arts to a position analogous to theology among the scholastics. In fact, they argue that poetry contains theology hidden within its figures.

101. Cod. Laur. 53, 28, f. 90^v: 'non esse illam unam ex iis artibus quas nostri maiores, quoniam reliquis excellentiores sunt, liberales appellarunt, in quarum una altera ve siqui floruerunt in maximo sunt semper pretio habiti. Sed est res quaedam divinior, quae universas illas complectens certis quibusdam numeris astricta, certis quibusdam pedibus progrediens, variisque luminibus ac floribus distincta.'

102. *Fontius* 1960, pp. 111–120 and n. 77.

103. F. 7^v.

104. Ff. 7^v–8^r.

105. Ff. 8^v–9^r.

106. F. 9.

107. Fontius seems to anticipate, in historical soundness, the views of such classical scholars as Werner Jaeger, *Paideia* (2d ed., New York, 1943), and Bruno Snell, *The Discovery of the Mind* (New York, 1960).

108. Ff. 9^v–10^r.

109. Ff. 10^r–11^r.

110. Both works cited above.

111. Boccaccio, *op. cit.*, bk. XIV, chs. IX, X, XII, echoed by Fontius; Salutati, *De laboribus Herculis*, lib. II, cap. ii.

112. Ff. 11^r–12^r.

113. Ff. 12^r–13^r; cf. Jaeger, *op. cit.*, I, chs. 1, 2, on Homer as paradigm.

114. F. 13^v.

115. Ff. 13^v–14^v.

116. Ff. 14^v–16^r.

117. Ff. 16^r–17^r, then f. 17 for passage quoted.

118. Cf. Marchesi, *op. cit.*, parte IIa, XI, *Studi sacri*.

119. Ff. 17^v–18^v.

120. Ff. 18^v–20^r.

121. *De vita solitaria*, pp. 286–591 (with Italian translation) in Francesco Petrarca, *Prose*, a cura di G. Martellotti, P. G. Ricci, E. Carrara, E. Bianchi (Milano-Napoli, 1955).

122. *Op. cit.*

123. *Op. cit.*

124. Cf. the treatises of Poggio, Fazio, Platina, and Filelfo analyzed in my *Adversity's Noblemen* (2d ed., New York, 1965), esp. in chs. III and IV. For another statement of Fontius see his letter to Pietro Cennini of 26 August 1472, lib. I, ep. 18 (ed. Juhász), pp. 15–18. Neoplatonists favored contemplation.

125. Eugenio Garin, *L'umanesimo italiano, filosofia e vita civile nel Rinascimento* (Bari, 1952); Hans Baron, *The Crisis of the Early Italian Renaissance* (Princeton, 1955).

126. Landino basically favored contemplation, perhaps because of its central importance to the Ficinian Neoplatonic circle.

127. Ff. 20ʳ–21ʳ.

128. Lorenzo Valla at the end of his dialogue *De vero falsoque bono, libri tres* (Bibl. Vat., Cod. Ottobon. lat. 2075, f. 236ʳ) has Guarinus compare the Epicurean views of Vegius and the Christian Epicureanism of Raudensis in terms of this topos of the 'civic' orator and the 'sylvan' poet: 'Sed ut proprie utriusque differentiam signem afferam genus similitudinis humile quidem, sed tamen non absurdum, et ut reor novum et inusitatum. Maphaeus et Antonius de laudibus voluptatis uterque pro se suavissime quasi cantare visi sunt. Sed Maphaeus hirundini Antonius Philomenae magis comparandus. Cur hos viros potissimum istis avibus comparo? Scitis poetas finxisse has aves sorores fuisse Pandionis regis filias; credo quod videbantur in cantandae pene germanae; et in his significasse oratoriam atque poeticam, quae prope sorores sunt, atque ut hanc similitudinem ita illam discrepantiam notasse, quod in altera inest mira libido tecta et urbes incolendi, in altera vero arbusta et silvas; voluisseque hirundinem similem esse urbanae eloquentiae quae intra parietes in curia in subselliis exercetur; Philomenam quam lusciniam dicimus eloquentiae ne morali sed poetarum qui silvas et solitudines consectantur et loca non ab hominibus celebrata sed a musis amant. Ita quantum luscinia in cantando hirundini praestat vocalitate, vi, suavitate, varietate, tantum poetae vocem ipsorum oratoribus caeterisque praestare voluerunt.' Valla, however, used this comparison to state the superiority of one oration to another, and not that of a poet to an orator.

129. Wolfenbüttel Cod. 43 Aug. Fol., f. 19ᵛ. Fontius follows the authority of Herodotus and Strabo which he considers superior to that of Servius, Tortelli's source.

130. Although I have stressed this point before, above, p. 90, and *Fontius* 1960, p. 95, I do not minimize the value of his sound scholarship as a basis for originality.

131. See p. 115 and n. 180 for Landino's application of these categories to poetry in his commentary on Horace's *Ars poetica*.

132. Brink, *op. cit.*, pp. 11–12, differs with Norden's view that lines 1–38 deal with invention. Brink (p. 12) states: 'Matter, arrangement, and style are the subjects of this introductory section, but only inasmuch as they are affected by the principles of unity and wholeness. . . . Unity and wholeness, or the appropriateness of each part of a poem to each other part, are among the principles underlying the technical disquisition that is to follow; so most appositely, Horace places them at the beginning.'

133. F. 22ᵛ.

134. 'Ordinis haec virtus erit et venus, aut ego fallor, | ut iam nunc dicat iam nunc debentia dici, | pleraque differat et praesens in tempus omittat, | hoc amet, hoc spernat promissi carminis auctor' (*A.P.*, 42–45). I use the text in the Loeb Classical Library, edited with an English translation by H. Rushton Fairclough, *Horace, Satires, Epistles and Ars Poetica* (London and New York, 1929). The English translations are Fairclough's with my own corrections whenever he seems unduly free in rendering Horace's meaning.

135. Brink (pp. 228–229) argues that *decorum*, or appropriateness, is the second most important element of the poem, following the division into style (and arrangement) and content, and that it 'serves to join the two once again'. '*Decorum*, or appropriateness, is the common term of reference between style and content, style and emotion, and style and character.' Εὐχαιρία is a term translated by Cicero, *De officiis*, lib. I, 40, as 'occasio', another sense of 'appropriateness'. Brink does not agree that *decorum*, τὸ πρέπον, in Horace derives from Panaetius *via* Cicero. Referring (p. 30, no. 4) to G. C. Fiske and Mary A. Grant, Cicero's *De oratore* and Horace's *Ars poetica* (Madison, 1929, *Univ. of Wisconsin Stud.* XXVII,) Brink says, 'There are many undoubted likenesses between the writings of Horace and Cicero. . . . But so far as the structure of the *Ars* is concerned the likenesses are insignificant. The two scholars were careful not to define too closely Horace's assumed degree of reliance on Cicero. . . . They also tend to ignore the marked differences between rhetorical theory on the one hand and rhetoric applied to poetic criticism on the other. Since rhetoric is concerned in both instances the basic similarity may deceive the unwary.' On the untenability of the argument for Panaetius' influence, he states (p. 136) that scholars have asserted 'the pervasive presence of Panaetius and his theory of "appropriateness", or τὸ πρέπον; but other men than Panaetius, above all Aristotle, had debated this topic. Specific resemblances with Panaetius' theories are lacking. What resemblances can be claimed are of a general kind: talk of the obligations that are laid on a citizen or a member of a profession.' Brink's position only partially rests on the validity of his proof of Neoptolemus' peripateticism, which, of course, antedates Panaetius.
136. F. 23^r.
137. *A.P.*, 148–153: 'semper ad eventum festinat et in medias res | non secus ac notas auditorem rapit, . . . | atque ita mentitur, sic veris falsa remiscet, | primo ne medium, medio ne discrepet imum.'
138. See above p. 93 and n. 40; f. 23^v.
139. Cf. Brink, *op. cit.*, pp. 10–11, 13, 253.
140. *A.P.*, 102–103.
141. Ff. 23^v–24^v.
142. *A.P.*, 408, 'Natura fieret laudabile carmen an arte'.
143. 'Si paulum summo decessit, vergit ad imum.'
144. F. 25^v; ff. 25^v–26^r; for Horace's emphasis on craftsmanship, cf. Brink, *op. cit.*, pp. 255–256.
145. Ff. 26^v–27^r.
146. Cf. Brink, *op. cit.*, pp. 254–255 and *passim*. Fontius' own language, 'Considerabunt totius summam poematis' (f. 27^r), suggests Aristotle's *synola*. Cf. n. 186.
147. F. 27.
148. *A.P.*, 153–284. Cf. Herrick, *op. cit.*, chap. VI, 'Epic Poetry vs. Tragedy'.
149. Ff. 28^r–29^v.
150. 'Si quid inexpertum scaenae committis et audes | personam formare novam, servetur ad imum, | qualis ab incepto processerit, et sibi constet.'

151. *Servii Grammatici qui feruntur in Vergilii carmina commentarii,* ed. Georg Thilo and Hermann Hagen (Hildesheim, 1961), I, 4, 'intentio Vergilii haec est, Homerum imitari et Augustum laudare a parentibus; namque est filius Atiae, quae nata est de Iulia, sorore Caesaris, Iulius autem Caesar ab Iulo Aeneae originem ducit, ut confirmat ipse Vergilius a magno demissum nomen Iulo'; I, 573–574; II, 106–107.

152. *A.P.,* 333, 343: 'Aut prodesse volunt aut delectare poetae . . . omne tulit punctum qui miscuit utile dulci'.

153. Ff. 29ᵛ–30ʳ.

154. Fontius, f. 30ᵛ, after *Ad Herennium* IV, viii–ix (11–14). Harry Caplan in his notes on this passage (Cambridge, 1954, Loeb Classical Libr., pp. 252–253) gives the ancient references and suggests Theophrastus as a possible source. Cf. *Poetics* 1448b–1449a for Aristotle's differentiation of styles, not yet three.

155. Horace's discussion is *A.P.,* 73–98 (lines quoted, 93–94). Fontius, f. 30ᵛ, following *Ad Herenniun,* IV, x–xi (15–16).

156. *Institutio oratoria,* XII, x, 63–65.

157. Ff. 30ᵛ–31ʳ.

158. *Saturnalia, op. cit.,* V, 2, 4–5.

159. Ff. 31ʳ–32ᵛ.

160. *A.P.,* 309–311, 'scribendi recte sapere est et principium et fons. | rem tibi Socraticae poterunt ostendere chartae, | verbaque provisam rem non invita sequentur.'

161. *A.P.,* 312.

162. Ff. 32ᵛ–33ʳ.

163. *A.P.,* 317–318, 'respicere exemplar vitae morumque iubebo | doctum imitatorem et vivas hinc ducere voces.'

164. Brink, *op. cit.,* pp. 103–109.

165. See above, pp. 91–92 and notes 32, 33, 36, 37.

166. See n. 159.

167. Cf. Baxter Hathaway, *The Age of Criticism,* part I, 'Poetry as Imitation'. Richard McKeon, 'Literary Criticism and the Concept of Imitation in Antiquity', *Critics and Criticism, Ancient and Modern* (Chicago, 1952), pp. 176–231, is very disparaging of post-Aristotelian doctrines of imitation.

168. August Buck, *op. cit.,* pp. 54–67, discusses humanist rhetorical theories of imitation from Petrarch to Poliziano—imitation of literary models, not *mimesis.* I have not been able to use H. Gmelin, *Das Prinzip der Imitatio in den romanischen Literaturen der Renaissance* (Erlangen, 1932). Fontius in the letter to Bernardo Rucellai cited above, n. 69, moves from a concern lest too close adherence to the rules of an art stifle originality to an advocacy of imitation of the greatest representatives of poetry, rhetoric, and history: Vergil, Cicero, and Livy. See now (1983): Thomas M. Greene, *The Light in Troy: Imitation and Discovery in Renaissance Poetry* (New Haven, 1982).

169. Erwin Panofsky, *Renaissance and Renascences in Western Art* (Uppsala, 1960), pp. 29–30.

170. Weinberg, *op. cit.,* I, 71. Similar statements are easy to locate in Spingarn,

Baldwin, and Clark, all cited above. Only Hardison, though emphasizing a rhetorical conception of Renaissance poetics, is free from the expressionist prejudice and capable of recognizing the 'aesthetic' values of 'didactic art'. His closing words (p. 194) are: 'At heart all poetry is praise and celebration. This is the truth asserted by the theory of praise. Although we need not subscribe to it, it is neither perverse nor simple-minded. Certainly it must be kept continually in mind by those who would read and understand the literature of the European Renaissance.'

171. Brink, *op. cit.*, p. 225, says, to my mind with more balance, as his considered judgement: 'Four articles of Horace's poetic faith are now seen to be present not only in the smaller writings but in the *Ars* as well: the conviction that artistry is at the root of the art of poetry; the conviction that poetry aims at the "whole man", not only at "aesthetic man", and therefore has a function in society; the conviction that some kinds of verse can fulfil this function better than others; and finally the conviction that the Greek temperament, or else their sense of values, was more apt to generate that kind of poetry than the Roman.'

172. *Op. cit.*, pp. 71–72. Weinberg does add, however, that 'If Horace's thesis is a rhetorical one, it is incomplete rhetoric . . .', because it leaves out the element of the character of the orator or poet. Yet *A.P.*, 102–103, 'si vis me flere dolendum est primum ipsi tibi', imply at least an element of emotional projection on the part of the poet. And this does not type poetry as rhetoric but would seem to be a necessary ingredient of all art, even abstract and especially expressionist.

173. Brink (pp. 123–126) is dubious of the arguments of Norden and Rostagni that there is carry-over of *catharsis* into the moral goals of the poet in Horace.

174. *Ibid.*, pp. 79–84, 99–102, and *passim*.

175. The six elements listed at 1450a, spectacle, character, fable, diction, melody, and thought as parts of a tragedy, partially correspond to diction, arrangement, and content. Diction and melody come very close to Aristotle's own treatment of diction in *Rhetoric*, III, chapters 1–12; character, fable, and thought are parts of content or invention; arrangement is treated by Aristotle in close connection with fable or plot in the *Poetics*, rather than separately, as in *Rhetoric*, III, chapters 13–19. As for epic, Aristotle discusses content or plot in chapter 23 and the beginning of chapter 24; arrangement again is subordinate but part of plot; diction is discussed in the middle of chapter 24 and the last part of chapter 25. If, as Brink has argued, Horace reflects Aristotle's *Rhetoric, Poetics,* and *De poetis* filtered through Neoptolemus, the playing down of arrangement in both writers is more than an interesting coincidence.

176. Perhaps a more significant issue in antiquity and the Renaissance than the extent to which poetry could be analyzed into the same elements as rhetoric and still remain distinct was the relative merit of the large poem, epic and drama, and the more intimate lyric, elegy, iambic. Both Aristotle and Horace favored the large work, and drama over the epic. The humanists tended to admire Virgil, and had the example of Dante before them, but

they themselves wrote, for the most part, small poems. There is, perhaps, more of a temptation to make an elegy approach a short oration in technique, since the content might be similar. A long poem could become a verse treatise, but why does Lucretius escape the charge?

177. Weinberg, *op. cit.*, I, 154–155, writes, 'These same modes and habits were responsible for the fact that, throughout all this extensive comparison and equation of the *Poetics* and the *Ars Poetica*, there was no slightest intimation of the true state of affairs with respect of these two texts: the fact that they address themselves to essentially different problems, that they use widely different methods, and that they produce statements of a completely different nature about poetry. For theorists of this period, only the accidental—and sometimes the forced—resemblances between the two were discovered; their real opposition was not even suspected. So it was that Horace could be said to be an imitator of Aristotle, that many lines of his text could be identified with Aristotle, and at the same time the whole of the text could be read much as it had been before Aristotle had been brought into the discussion.'

178. Cited above, n. 5.

179. F. 33.

180. *Op. cit.*, f. 145, '*Humano capite cervicem pictor equinam.* Quoniam in poemate scribendo inventio dispositioque atque elocutio in primis investiganda est, statim a principio quae ad inventionem dispositionemque spectant exequitur. Nam haec tempore priora quam elocutio sunt. Praeterea elocutionis praecepta communia pene cum oratore habet poeta, et a rhetoribus facile illa mutuari potest. Est enim, ut Ciceroni quoque placere video, finitimus oratori poeta numeris astrictior paulo, verborum autem licentia liberior, multis vero ornandi generibus socius, ac pene par.' The last sentence is a direct quotation of Cicero, *De oratore*, I, XVI (70).

181. *Pro Archia poeta*, viii, 18–19.

182. Ff. 33ᵛ–35ʳ.

183. Cf. Brink, *op. cit.*, part II, 'The Tradition of Literary Criticism and the "Ars Poetica'", chapters 2, 3, *passim*.

184. *Ibid.*, pp. 228–230.

185. *Ibid.*, p. 235. The need for a principle of harmonization found expression in the ideals both of unity and decorum, and the need would persist so long as a poem was viewed objectively as analyzable into elements. *Decorum* does not seem to have attracted much interest among historians of Renaissance criticism, who favor the Aristotelian concepts of universality, imitation, and purgation. But the persistence of Horatian influence within the Aristotelian criticism suggests the need for some attention to this quality as a virtue rather than a vice.

186. R. S. Crane in his 'Introduction' to *Critics and Criticism, Ancient and Modern*, p. 17, finds this quality in Aristotle but considers it central to the viewpoint of what he calls 'the Chicago School'. 'It is the merit of Aristotle, uniquely among systematic critics, that he grasped the distinctive nature of literary works as *synola*, or concrete artistic wholes. . . . The Aristotle they have

reconstructed is not, it will easily be seen, the Aristotle of the Renaissance and neoclassical commentators or any of the more recent Aristotles of such interpreters as Butcher, Bywater, Murray, Lane Cooper, or Francis Fergusson. It may not, indeed, except in a general way, be Aristotle at all! They think it is . . .'

187. Cf. Weinberg, *op. cit.*, chapters 9–13, on 'The Tradition of Aristotle's *Poetics*', where *decorum* constantly comes up. There are forty-five index entries to *decorum* in this section and only eighteen to 'unity'.

188. Brink more than matches his scholarly reconstructions and analysis of rules and principles with his concern for Horace's qualities as a poet and their influence on his literary criticism. See especially his last chapter, 'Poetic Patterns in the "Ars Poetica" ': 'The poem shows that Horace did not want to give prominence to the headings of a textbook' (p. 245).

189. It is clear in Landino's case, as the quotation on p. 115 indicates. Poliziano was a superb critic and philologist, but his best statement on poetry is his poem about poetry which says nothing about its nature except to repeat the commonplaces of numinous inspiration and the *prisci poetae*, however uncommon the manner.

190. Cf. Gilbert's discussion in his *Machiavelli and Guicciardini*, cited above, n. 75, and his references to Fontius' oration on history, pp. 207–208.

191. Cf. Curtius, *op. cit.*, chap. 14, 'Classicism, I. Genres and Catalogues of Authors', pp. 246–251.

192. *Institutio oratoria*, lib. X, cap. I, 46–72, 85–100.

193. Heinrich Keil, *Grammatici Latini*, vol. I (Leipzig, 1857). Diomedes' text is pp. 297–529; 'De poematibus', pp. 482–492; on Diomedes' sources see p. liv. Both Suetonius' and Varro's works on the poets are lost.

194. Keil, p. xxxii.

195. R. Sabbadini, *Le scoperte dei codici latini e greci nei secoli XIV e XV*, I (Florence, 1905), 127 and n. 27; Keil, p. xxxii.

196. *Ibid.*, p. xxxiii.

197. Sabbadini, *loc. cit.* The Florence MS. is Cod. Laur. Aedilium 168, fols. 126–159ᵛ; cf. A. M. Bandini, *Bibliotheca Leopoldina Laurentiana; seu catalogus manuscriptorum* I (Florence, 1791), cols. 477–480.

198. *Eusebii Pamphilii Chronici canones, Latine vertit, adauxit, ad sua tempora produxit S. Eusebius Hieronymus*, ed. John Knight Fotheringham (London, 1923).

199. See p. 120 and nn. 217, 218, 220, 221.

200. *Op. cit.*, p. 181, 8 October 1486.

201. Lines 720–727, Dante, Petrarch, Boccaccio; lines 728–775, Lorenzo de' Medici; lines 776–790, Piero.

202. Curtius, *op. cit.*, p. 248, on difference of ancient and modern classifications.

203. However, the order is different. Diomedes, *op. cit.*, p. 482: 'Poematos genera sunt tria. aut enim activum est vel imitativum. quod Graeci dramaticon vel mimeticon, aut enarrativum vel enuntiativum, quod Graeci exegeticon vel apangelticon dicunt, aut commune vel mixtum, quod Graeci κοινόν vel μικτόν appellant.'

204. Fontius, f. 37ᵛ.

205. Ff. 37ᵛ–38ʳ.
206. F. 38.
207. See above pp. 98–99 and n. 86. Fontius' sources for the *prisci* are multiple. He could have drawn on Tortelli, *op. cit.,* for instance, Amphion, sig. eiiiʳ; Linus, sig. oviᵛ; Musaeus, sig. qiʳ; Orpheus, sig. qviiᵛ. But Fontius also has additional or different comments.
208. Fontius, ff. 38ᵛ–40ᵛ. Quintilian names Homer, Hesiod, Antimachus, Panyasis, Apollonius, Aratus, Theocritus but would exclude Pisandros, Nicander, Euphorion, and Tyrtaeus (the latter included by Horace). Fontius is identical, except for Tyrtaeus, whom he includes on Horace's authority. See Quintilian, X, I, 46–56, for the Greeks; his Latins (85–90) are Vergil, Macer, Lucretius, Varro Atacinus, Ennius, Ovid, Cornelius Severus, Serranus, Valerius Flaccus, Saleius Bassus, Rabirius, Pedo, and Lucan. Fontius includes all but Serranus and adds Manilius, Silius, Statius, and, after Quintilian, Claudianus. Quintilian orders his list according to importance as well as chronology; Fontius sticks to historical order in so far as he knows it.
209. Quintilian, 61–63, lists only Pindar, Stesichorus, Alcaeus, and Simonides, but alludes to the 'nine', again in order of value. Of Latin lyric poets, he names only Horace and Caesius Bassius. Catullus is mentioned for his iambics (96). Quintilian mentions as elegists only Callimachus and Philetas (59–60). Fontius adding Mimnermus and Euphorion. They agree on the Latins (93). Quintilian recommends only Archilochus 'of the three writers of iambics approved by the judgment of Aristarchus'. Fontius adds Hipponax. Neither mentions Semonides of Amorgos (59). They agree on the Latins (96). The order of treatment is different as well as the emphasis. In Diomedes' case lyric poets are not mentioned; only elegy, iambus, and satire correspond to Fontius, Diomedes adds epodes and bucolics, which Fontius omits. Diomedes in general names very few examples, being more interested in defining genres.
210. Wherever he can he supplies a terse characterization of each name. To this he adds from Eusebius-Jerome the Olympiad, contemporary rulers, or events, and most importantly tries to use this source to establish chronological order. He includes five lyric poets (see note 215) solely from the *Chronicon* (pp. 194, 203).
211. Fontius, f. 39ʳ: 'Quem Horatius *mares animos in Martia bella versibus exacuisse* commemorat' (*A.P.,* 403–404, in italics).
212. Ff. 40ᵛ–41ʳ.
213. Sig. giiʳ.
214. F. 41ʳ.
215. Ff. 41ᵛ–43ʳ. He seems to know Bacchylides, Telesilla, Praxilla, Cleobulina, and Erinna only from Eusebius-Jerome, although Bacchylides was one of the 'nine', and Porphyrion in his commentary on Horace, owned by Fontius, had compared an ode of Horace to one of Bacchylides (ad Hor. *Carm.* I, 15). Phocylides, whom he claimed to have translated (i.e., pseudo-Phocylides), survives only in fragments in readily accessible sources such as Clement of Alexandria, Plutarch's *Moralia,* Aristotle's *Ethics* and *Politics.* (Cf. J. M.

Edmonds, ed. *Elegy and Iambus,* Cambridge and London, 1944, *Loeb Classical Libr.,* I, 168–181.) Comparison with Poliziano's *Nutricia* shows the latter citing the 'nine' lyric poets beginning with Pindar and ending with Sappho, with no attempt at historical order (vv. 558–630), then adding nine more names of women lyric poets derived from the *Greek Anthology,* I, lxvii, 8 (vv. 631–636), making Sappho the tenth woman poet (vv. 637–639). But one of the nine is a misreading of the Greek adverb ἀγαχλὲα as a proper name. (Cf. Del Lungo's notes, p. 167.) The remaining eight are Praxilla, Nossis, Myrtis, Anite, Myro, Erinna, Telesilla, and Corinna. For his seventeen names, Fontius has sixteen—adding Terpander, Phocylides, and Cleobulina, omitting Mossis, Myrtis, Anite, and Myro (and, of course, Agaclea). The contrast between a poetic and an historical approach is evident in these two contemporary scholars, whose temperamental incompatibility and hostility is consistent.

216. *Suidae lexicon Graece et Latine,* ed. Gottfried Bernhardy (Halle & Braunschweig, 1852–1853), tom. II, pars prior, p. 344.

217. F. 42^v. Cf. D. L. Page, *Corinna* (London, 1953, Supplementary Paper no. 6 of the Society for the Promotion of Hellenic Studies), pp. 72–73; *Lyra Graeca,* ed. and tr. J. M. Edmonds (London and New York, 1927, Loeb Classical Library), III, 6–9. Cf. Pausanias, *Description of Greece,* ed. and tr. W. H. S. Jones (London and Cambridge, 1918–1935, Loeb Classical Library), IV, 264–267, IX, xxii, 3. Only Pausanias mentions her use of Aeolic and her beauty.

218. A. M. Bandini, *Catalogus codicum manuscriptorum Bibliothecae Mediсae Laurentianae varia continens opera Graecorum patrum* (Florence, 1768; repr. Leipzig, 1961), II, col. 306. Bandini judges both MSS. as XV saec.

219. *Lyra Graeca,* III, 10–11.

220. Fontius, ff. 43^r–44^r; Pausanias, II, xxiii, 8, 9; IV, xxviii, 7; VI, xiv, 9, 10; IX, xxx, 2; X, vii, 4, 5.

221. François Lasserre, *Plutarche de la musique, texte, traduction, commentaire, précédés d'une étude sur l'éducation musicale dans la Grèce antique* (Olten and Lausanne, 1954), pp. 114–116, 136–137.

222. Landino, introductory discourses to his commentary on Dante (see n.6), 'Che l'origine de' poeti sia antica' (pages un-numbered, 2d col. of his 2d page): 'Nè m'affaticherò al presente investigare, quello che veggiamo da Plutarco con diligentia esser cerco, nel suo libro de Musica: Chi primo fusse, appresso de' Greci inventore di versi . . .'

223. However, Pausanias is a major source for Poliziano. Cf. *Le selve e La strega,* pp. 130–139, Del Lungo's notes, *passim.*

224. *Suidae lexicon,* s.v. 'elegos'; *Etymologicon magnum seu verius lexicon,* ed. Thomas Gaisford (Oxford, 1848; reprinted Amsterdam, 1962), p. 327, s.v. 'Elegainein'.

225. Ff. 43^v–44^v.

226. Ff. 44^v–45^r. Cf. Diomedes, p. 482, line 26; p. 487, line 11.

227. Diomedes, p. 448, lines 13–16; Eusebius-Jerome, p. 193, 26, 81st Olympiad, 'Cratinus et Plato comoediarum'; p. 194, 14, 82d Olympiad, 'Crates

comicus'; p. 196, 3, 85th Olympiad, 'Aristofanes clarus habetur'; p. 197, 5–6, 88th Olympiad, 'Eupolis et Aristofanes scriptores comoediarum agnoscuntur'. A Plato and a Crates did write comedies.

228. Fontius, ff. 45^r–46^r.

229. Ff. 46^r–48^r. Fontius quotes Diomedes without acknowledgement as follows: p. 489, line 23 through p. 490, line 7; p. 490, lines 10–20; for Diomedes, line 20, where Keil reads 'In Atellana Oscae personae' Fontius has 'In Atellana oscenae personae'. There are other variations.

230. Ff. 48^r–49^r; Dante, f. 49^r; he loosely quotes Diomedes, p. 485, lines 32–36.

231. His peroration, ff. 49^v–50^r.

Humanism and Science:
Humanist Critiques of Natural Philosophy

The following paper considers some of the ways Renaissance humanists thought about science. It is not an attempt to survey the attitudes of all the major Italian humanists toward the science of their own day, though ideally, and given a lengthier format, it would be desirable to do that. Rather it looks in a concentrated way at statements concerning natural philosophy by three early Italian humanists who were especially formative in shaping a Renaissance cultural consciousness—Petrarch, Salutati, and Lorenzo Valla. Since humanist culture was pluralistic, internally controversial, and continually evolving, such a treatment is clearly inadequate, but it is offered in the hope that it will be suggestive, at least in a preliminary way, of the nature and the dimensions of the problem. Although it will attempt to avoid the thorny historical question of whether the "modern" science of the seventeenth century was more indebted to its humanist or scholastic predecessors, if indeed it was indebted to either, it will argue, however, that such humanist critiques of Aristotelian and scholastic natural philosophy, in combination with humanistic literary and linguistic theory, contributed certainly one important element in the cultural environment of the Galileian scientific "revolution." This element, perhaps itself controversial in the degree to which it entered into the thinking and consciousness of seventeenth-century scientists, and certainly something that needs a more up-to-date consideration than it has been given since the days of Ernst Cassirer and E. A. Burtt, was a widespread acceptance that human knowledge of the natural world, as well as of divine and human affairs, was subjective, culturally and historically relative, and essentially literary and linguistic in its formulations.[1]

By ancient and Renaissance definitions it would seem to have been

An Italian translation of this article (with an additional section on the historiography of Renaissance science) was presented as a Relazione to the Ninth Congresso dell'Associazione Internazionale per gli Studi di Lingua e Letteratura Italiano in Palermo in April 1976 on the topic "Letteratura e Scienza." It was published in the *Atti* of the Congresso as "L'Umanesimo italiano e la scienza" (Palermo: Manfredi Editore, 1979), 49–80. I am grateful to the Center for Medieval and Renaissance Studies of the University of California, Los Angeles, for the support and fruitful conversations that stimulated the writing of this preliminary consideration in the winter quarter, 1976, where it was first presented.

hard to unify literature and science. Yet Lucretius and Empedocles were frequently offered as evidence, not of the validity of the scientific content of their poems, but of the legitimacy of poetry which dealt with scientific or philosophical subjects. Insofar as literature could be considered didactic, as it most emphatically was held to be, its role was to teach as well as to delight and persuade. From the Renaissance humanist's point of view, poetry, rhetoric, history, and moral philosophy were all branches of literature. Although the first three, as well as producing original works, developed their own methodologies, grammar—the first of the *studia humanitatis*—was exclusively methodological and underlying the other four. But these humanistic studies should all have content, as well as style or form; it was, therefore, the obligation of the humanistic writer and scholar to have an extensive knowledge of all matters, which added up to the traditional definition of *sapientia—scientia omnium rerum divinarum et humanarum*. This included nature and geography as well as the divine and human realms, but it was clearly a literary knowledge (and an historical one) based on texts, and it did not need to rest on experience or theory.[2]

Humanists recognized that their classification of the arts was different from that of the scholastics because the latter elevated dialectical theology, natural philosophy, and the professional subject matters of law and medicine above the liberal arts. If there was a hierarchy of the arts for the humanists, poetry, and especially theological poetry—*theologia poetica* replacing the scholastic *theologia dialectica*—would be at the top. But basically, humanists tended to see all topics and arts equally as branches of literature, and they deplored the separation and splintering of the form and content of learning which they detected in the scholastic elevation of professional studies above the liberal arts. They endorsed broad conceptions of the arts as loosely unified and mutually supporting and overlapping, and saw but limited intellectual legitimacy in the applied studies of professional specialization. The ideally educated man, as the ideally equipped scholar and teacher, should be well rounded.[3]

While I am in fundamental agreement with Paul Oskar Kristeller's salutary efforts to establish a clear distinction between humanism and the scholastic disciplines and educational programs (which, as he points out, grew contemporaneously in Italy), one can also recognize the universalizing tendency of the humanists to claim all disciplines as their own, or to structure their interrelations in such a way that they would fall under the *studia humanitatis*. Kristeller stresses, as do I, that rhetoric and poetic were regarded as the major divisions of literature, to which the humanists—in accord with ancient tradition—annexed history and moral philosophy as sub-branches of letters.[4] But in their reaching out to claim and reclaim the other disciplines that had developed as part of the scholastic organization of learning in the late twelfth and thirteenth centuries in northern Europe, humanists invaded the field of theology and religious writing, as has been shown in recent years,[5] and the field of the dialectic as Cesare Vasoli has made clear.[6] This would leave, of the traditional branches of philosophy both ancient and scholastic, natural philosophy, or science. It will be my effort to show that at least some of the humanists in attacking and criticizing natural philosophy also attempted to undermine its theoretical or its epistemological bases and to claim the residue as part of the humanities.

The problem of the relations of humanism and science in the Middle Ages and the Renaissance is inescapably subordinate to the problem of the relation of religion and science. One may best illustrate this by reference to Dante, whose *Commedia* is regarded from our own historical perspective as one of the most pure and perfect examples of a literary work which projects a vision derived from science. But one may also see that in this work his religious and theological vision of the other world is supported by careful exposition of Greek astronomy, cosmology, meteorology, physics, and psychology as it was mediated to him through scholastic natural philosophy. For Dante, moral and religious failure and the difference between the more perfect (Adam, Christ, the Virgin) and the less perfect human derived from the imperfection of nature. As the light of St. Thomas tells him in *Paradiso* XIII (11. 52–81), there is slippage when the material wax is stamped with the ideal form and thus things will vary: *ma la natura la da sempre scema, similemente operando all'artista c'ha l'abito dell'arte e man che trema.* (76–78) Nature in its operations is here likened to a workman, it is true, but this is merely a simile. Dante wishes his readers to accept his conception that a true fusion or synthesis of science and theology, of natural law and divine purpose, exists.

For his Renaissance admirers, however, and they did not all agree, Dante's work was seen as more properly the assertion of a rival poetic theology having greater legitimacy than the natural theology of scholasticism we are sure he drew upon. Moreover, fourteenth-century humanists in Italy, in unacknowledged agreement with the Ockhamist scholastics of the North, undermined Dante's assumption of the identity of science and theology.[7]

In order to understand the fundamental shift in thinking about the relationship of God, man, and nature that occurred among the Italian humanists it is necessary to glance in a summary way at the new nominalist outlook, both for the striking parallels that will emerge and for the uniqueness of the humanist positions.[8] Nominalist theology no longer considers it legitimate to construct analogies between divine matters and nature, as it is known from human science. Its model for the relation of the divine and the human becomes law and the human polity as authenticated by the scriptural notion of Covenant. Strict application of dialectic breaks down the notion that universals have substance. Universals (class concepts) are useful and necessary intellectual implements of a hypothetical, not a metaphysical science. There can be no *analogia entis* where there is no *ens* other than the individual thing. *Notitia intuitiva* and conceptual realism assure knowledge of particulars which can conveniently be seen as the individual members of hypothetical genuses conceptually necessary to handle the empirically observed similarities of particulars. But only individuals and not the genuses are real.

Moreover, a metaphysical construction is regarded theologically as too confining to divine freedom, to God's will. Whatever the divinely created universe *seems* to be, one cannot insist that man can know it as rational by anything more than human standards, nor can this humanly invented rationality coerce divinity. The dialectic of *potentia absoluta Dei* and *potentia ordinata* was crucial to nominalist reasoning but needs to be properly understood. The distinction was a twelfth-century, not an Ockhamist, invention and was employed by Aquinas and others in the thirteenth century. But as Ockham, D'Ailly, Biel, and other nominalists use it, it is a thought-device which does not, as once was argued, expose this world to miracle and abritrary divine intervention (both of which, however, could occur). *Potentia absoluta Dei* represents, rather, the hypothetical total freedom of God to will and create as many and whatever sorts of worlds He wills, subject only to the law of contradiction. It does not suggest that God had in fact exercised this freedom or that men had any evidence that he had done so or that they necessarily could have such evidence. Rather the hypothetical possibility opened by *potentia absoluta* rendered the creation and the economy of salvation of the existing world, whether known by science or revelation, contingent. It could have been different. It is as it is out of no natural necessity but only because God so willed it to be. It is thus a sacred historical, a convenantal, not a natural existence.

God deals with men, therefore, through His revelation both in the Old and New Testaments which must have historical verity, and through His providential guidance of the Church. God also deals with men through nature, but this is not a fixed, rationally necessary and metaphysical nature but a hidden actual one that is as it is because it was so created, and which can be known and understood by men only within the limits of their own capacities and certainly in terms and categories invented by men except when these are decreed or directly revealed by God. But what order men discover in the natural world is order in their human terms and not necessarily identical to God's. Man's knowledge of nature is positivistic and statistical, but also regular, reliable, valid, and sacred. Just as man's salvation must be viewed in terms of divine promises and God's covenant with man, so the bounties and menaces of nature must be accepted as providential though they sometimes seem irrational or incomprehensible. Nature may have an order of man's discovering, but it is a contingent, probable, and not a necessary order. Nominalist theology, then, moved toward Biblical exegesis and inculcation of trust. It offered its greatest assurance in the *facere quod in se est* doctrine that God expected from man an effort to uphold his part of the bargain, but God would not withold His grace when man did his very best. Human capacity for goodness might be feeble at best, but man could trust in God and play the game as he understood it and obey the rules.

Nominalist science found its greatest achievements in the work of the Merton College *Calculatores* and in the impetus theory of Buridan and Oresme at Paris, though neither group could be strictly considered followers of Ockham, whose writings they knew. It is difficult to determine how much nominalist theology and logic influenced their science. One cannot, however, exclude the Duhem thesis of the anticipation of "inertia" by "impetus" altogether even though the latter theory retained the necessity of a mover, for its influence may have been indirect or dialectical, not a straight-line one, a loosening of the previous mental set and the introduction of probabilities for certainties. The natural-philosophical orientation of nominalism remained basically Aristotelian, as Moody and others suggest, but moved in a strongly empirical and positivistic direction in its criticisms of Aristotle—still a far cry from the rational necessitarianism of Galileo's new mathematical vision.[9]

However, my purpose in this paper is not to explore the connections of fourteenth-century and seventeenth-century science but to look at the relations of Italian humanists to both. As will be seen, the connection of humanism both to nominalist and Galileian science is problematical, but differently so in each instance. Humanists were very critical of their scholastic rivals' natural philosophy but in important respects seem to have taken over elements of the internal scholastic criticism of metaphysics and Aristotelianism. There is, however, no convincing evidence of their direct knowledge of nominalist writings such as Ockham's. There is also a good possibility that they developed their own "nominalism" on the basis of their linguistic and philological studies and under the influence of ancient studies of rhetoric and literature, especially Quintilian's.

On the other hand, the humanists made even less direct contributions to later science than the nominalists (with the possible exception of L. B. Alberti). By means of the new humanist vision of man's world and works as historical, relativistic, subjective in conceptions and modes of expression, however, they may well have made an even greater contribution to the general philosophical assumptions about human knowledge of nature present in the late Renaissance. These assumptions, as I will suggest, underlay scientific progress in the age of Galileo, making "modern" science hypothetical in its conclusions and requiring the invention of new methods of establishing the certitude of its knowledge—"mental experiment," mathematical and quantificational statement, and experimental discovery and verification.

We limit our account of the humanists to the three early but influential figures mentioned above whose ideas furnished the basic groundwork. Petrarch belittles in very strong terms the possible capacity of men to understand nature. He sees arrant pretension and downright heresy in many of his contemporary natural philosophers. He rejects scholastic natural philosophy as hopelessly entangled in the elementary discipline of dialectic in which old men engage in childish games with no relationship to reality. He despises the uselessness of natural philosophy and the study of Aristotle as preparation for the practice of medicine, because the doctors, in fact, learn no effective ways of curing the sick from their studies and resort to consolation and psychological counseling. They encroach on the realm of the rhetorician and moral philosopher, of the humanist, and seek to make up for their failure as practitioners of the mechanical art of administering to the body by usurping the humanist's liberal arts whereby he may rightfully cure souls.[10]

There is much personal spleen and rivalry in Petrarch's comments on doctors, and we should see his own humanism as evolving toward a composition of literary remedies for the psychic ills of the earthly sojourner. How else explain the popularity of his famous *De remediis utriusque fortunae*. It is a form of literary therapy of the word, more justified and successful in Petrarch's eyes than the physical therapy of the doctors.[11] True enough, Galileo's Paduan Aristotelians of the sixteenth century were serious theoreticians, committed to a total conception of the physical cosmos and to a methodology that could not work for his ends.[12] But there is much in Petrarch's charge that the subordination of scholastic science to a faltering physical therapy as part of the medical course contributed to its irrelevance as well as its persistence. We can perhaps suggest that the cosmic, astrological medicine that was practiced in the Renaissance ensured the survival of the Aristotelian-Ptolemaic world view, rather than, as frequently argued, the reverse.

Petrarch railed against the teachings of the eternity of the world, or the subordination of the individual soul to a world soul, or the infinity of worlds of the Epicureans. But he affirms, as evidence of divine providence, the rational and mechanical character of the universe as he finds Cicero relating it in the *De natura deorum*.[13] This is the view of the Greek Stoics, principally of Posidonius, reported by Cicero through the speech of "Balbus." The Stoic rational and purposive universe seems there to be a projection of human inventiveness and mechanical skill onto the cosmos which possesses these qualities, too, because nature necessarily is superior to human art. For Petrarch, who is not entirely oblivious to human inventiveness, this is an example of the wisdom of St. Paul (Rom. 1:20): "God has made it manifest unto them. For the invisible things of Him since the creation of the world are understood and clearly seen by the things that are made."[14] Petrarch is glad if Cicero or the Stoics, or even the Aristotelians, develop theories about nature that seem to confirm the teachings of Genesis concerning the creation of the world for the benefit of man. He sums up "Balbus'" arguments for the providential character of the world beautifully in a short paragraph. "And all this he does merely to lead us to this conclusion: whatever we behold with our eyes or perceive with our intellect is made by God and for the well-being of man and governed by divine providence and counsel."[15]

But at least twice he makes it clear that he sees an unbridgeable gap between such knowledge of nature, even of the huge cosmos of stars and planets, and knowledge of God and God's purposes—once in his *De otio religioso* and once here in the *De sui ipsius et multorum ignorantia.*

> The relation of one day or of one hour to a thousand years or to a thousand times a thousand years is similar to that between one small drop that has fallen as rain and the entire ocean and all the seas. The drop is enormously small, it is true, but a comparison is possible, and there is even some kind of proportion. The relation that holds between many thousand years—as many as you like, until the number no longer has a name—and eternity is absolutely null. In the first case there is a number great beyond all measure on one side and a number small beyond all measure on the other. However both are certainly finite. In the other case there is an infinite number here and a finite one there, which however great must not be judged small but null in comparison to it.[16]

So also man's moral and salvational status is incomparable and null in comparison to God on Whose infinite mercy he must lean in faith.

Whatever the natural world may be, whether as Aristotle or the nominalists viewed it, for Petrarch it is a separate and humanly ordered world unrelated to the absolute divine one. However anthropocentric and teleological Petrarch is, he can believe in God's purposiveness ultimately only on the basis of revelation and faith, not science or human analogues. His rejection of Aristotelianism is for its ineffectiveness, rhetorically and poetically, in inducing faith rather than for any specific shortcomings in its natural philosophy, but this renders its natural philosophy but one among the many that men have invented and will invent. Moreover, it is useless for the practice of medicine. But fearing its support of heretical views, he also cuts its fundamental anthropomorphic teleology off from God. The divine world and the natural world cannot be grasped in the same concept or spoken of with the same language.

Language, however, can be addressed to fellow men to aid them in finding some rationality in their daily lives, whatever their status or fortune. After all, the alter ego of Petrarch and interlocutor of the *De remediis* is *Ratio*. Reason can lift from sorrow and despair and can relieve from pride and fatuous hope. Artful use of language can help man to "will the good," which is better than to know the truth which no man can know. Reason and speech, on the model of Cicero and Seneca, can lead to a more ordered understanding of life and the world and a more ordered course of existence in the here and now. A more rational existence is above and better than despair and can open man to the reception of grace which would otherwise be most certainly excluded. But even so, the coming of grace remains a mystery totally in the hands of God. Man cannot change the nature of the world or the nature of man. He can change his understanding of the world and of himself; he can even in the light of such insights change his will and his course of life. But he cannot go beyond the realm of such subjectivity.[17]

Petrarch was not so much an influence for the Renaissance as a paradigm. His own conception of *imitatio* was that a modern should deepen his own insights through the inspiration of ancient works such as he sought to do in an imaginary dialogue with his heroes. Aristotle, he told his critics, was only a man. So, for Petrarch, were Cicero, Varro, Seneca, and the other classical authors to whom he addressed letters. It was a token of the potency of his own life and writings that his humanist successors did not always become cultistic imitators but instead carried his insights farther, knowing they had surpassed him, criticized him, but saw him as a pioneer.[18]

Directly linked to Petrarch in his basic thinking was his most potent follower, the Florentine chancellor, Coluccio Salutati. Salutati has been viewed mainly from the perspective of his transmission and implantation of humanist ideas into the Florentine political and social environment, undoubtedly a work of extraordinary historical significance. But Salutati, the man of action, grasped the need for this new culture to come to terms with contemporary late medieval theology, natural philosophy, and literature. In this he attained a practical success and an explicitness in an endeavor already begun by Boccaccio. Between his effective influence in the appointment of Manuel Chrysoloras to teach Greek at Florence—with the ensuing massive acquisition of Greek culture, science, and mathematics not already acquired in the scholastic reception—and his death-year polemic with Giovanni Dominici, in which he asserted and defended the necessary connection of *studia humanitatis* and *studia divinitatis*,[19] Salutati wrote the *De laboribus herculis*, his *De fato et fortuna* and *De nobilitate legum et medicinae*. All three works were substantial and cogent efforts to grapple with the relationship of humanism to traditional learning, to show the way to integration of the new and the old, and simultaneously to undermine the older mentality in a number of crucial areas. These works deserve far more study than they have received if we wish to understand the historical dynamic of the Italian Renaissance and the cultural revolution it produced.[20]

Salutati's salient position was a radical voluntarism which, when applied to the works of the intellect, led him to an almost equally radical nominalism and empiricism. Out of it came a deeply subjective conception of human life and culture but yet preserving the external structure of the traditional positions. A man who was clearly and deeply reverend and conservative, the very solidity of his personal qualities gave a strength and persuasiveness to his views which infected the whole succeeding generation of humanists who stemmed from the Florentine ambient. One might well argue that if the decades 1390 to 1410 were ones of crisis and the turning point of the Renaissance (*pace* Hans Baron), this was manifested and brought about by the literary efforts of Coluccio and his colleagues in a far deeper and lasting sense than by the resistance to the military threat of Giangaleazzo Visconti. Perhaps a different meaning can be given to the latter's famous saying that one letter of Coluccio was worth a thousand horse!

Salutati, in his amazingly perceptive treatise *On the Nobility of Law and Medicine,* juxtaposes not only the two professions in typical humanist *Disputa-delle-arti* fashion, but does so to science and action as well. He puts forth a whole new conception of the relationship of human culture and its knowledge of nature through science.[21] He sees the will and intellect as two sides of the rational self, yet the will is clearly in command. When something is thought by the intellect it is in order to instruct and inform the will so that it can then decide and act. But the self is not a passive recipient of sensual clues translated into ideas; "the first action [of the mind] does not even reach the intellect without the consent or the command of the will. Indeed the natural desire of knowing [Aristotle's] is not the intellect's but the will's, which precedes every intellection and act of the intellect not only in nature but by reason of time."[22] Nothing moves in the soul unless the will commands, "whose force, indeed, is so great and its hegemony over the other powers of the soul so large that, even though the instruments of the senses receive the images of sensible things, the effect of such reception scarcely proceeds farther without the commands of the will." For this reason, "very often we do not see the largest movement of things and the greatest sensible events."[23]

His "nominalism" directly follows from this voluntarism. He would abolish the distinction of earlier scholasticism and Aristotle which held that the certainty and nobility of knowledge varied with the nature of the objects of knowledge, according to whether they are contingent, relatively stable, or eternal and unchanging. "I, indeed," he says, "do not at all see the rationale of that kind of distinction, because to divide the act of knowing (*scire*) or science (*scientia*), which is certainly a *habitus* of the knower, according to the nature of the things which are known and over which science has command, does not seem rational; for knowing or science is not a passion of *habitus* or an operation of the thing known but only of the intellect of the person comprehending who is the subject of such a *habitus*."[24] He sharply separates knowledge of universals, including genera and species, from knowledge of individual things which are corruptible and contingent. Nor does he deny the possibility of constructing hypothetical classes and universals in order to save the phenomena, and, indeed, describes at length how *astrologi* assume the existence of ninth and tenth spheres beyond the visible eighth sphere of the fixed stars in order to account for the contrary motions and different speeds of revolution of the inferior orbs. He prefaced this by saying, "For what are perceived to exist naturally and according to absolute truth, whether they are known to exist by us from written or oral testimony, if they are corporeal things, we would hold that they exist by belief and opinion; if they are incorporeal, the charm of rational persuasion can be added to these [i.e., to belief and opinion]. Even if they are eternal things, certitude cannot be had."[25] Elsewhere in attempting to explain the nature of poetry he speaks of men knowing the qualities of God only from His effects, and thus being led to describe Him in terms of man, the most sublime thing man knows. But we also do this with other unknown beings, describing self-subsisting souls as "shades." "From this, although it is self-evident, it is clear that not only when we speak of God but also when we talk about incorporeal beings, we speak of them improperly and according to the outer shell, and what we say is false."[26] But if it is poetry, it contains the hidden truth within. Knowledge thus comes to be seen as attained by exegesis, and indeed, at one point he showed himself ready to introduce an arbitrary interpretation of scripture to make it support his argument. Divine and natural reality does indeed exist, but human conceptions, powerfully directed by the will, can truly be arbitrary.[27]

Of interest and importance is his treatment of the problem of contingency. The world of things, as man and the physician encounters it, is questionably contingent, a position which aligns him with those fourteenth-century scholastics who sought to affirm the contingency of the creation. But Salutati wishes to find a reconciliation of man's free will with divine providence, and of the contingency of things with laws of nature.[28] The will, "is, indeed, free, and liberty is inserted into it in such a way that if you take away liberty, the will would entirely not exist." Yet the will is subject to the necessity of its own nature; it is subject to the necessity of the first cause, God; "It is hence naturally necessary and inevitable to the will that it act freely . . . It has the necessity always to follow the first cause, yet freely and according to the exigency of its own nature. Our will is also subject to the necessity of the end, that is of the act which we intend to do." Similarly all objects encountered are at the same time contingent and subject to natural necessity. "For although fire ignites tinder naturally, yet it is contingent for this fire to ignite that tinder; it is also contingent that this is done in this place and time.[29]

Salutati's position, in effect, by seeing and consciously acknowledging the subjective and anthropomorphic character of all thinking and its subordination to human ends, resembles that of the nominalists, for it undermined belief in the natural necessity of a world order which concealed its anthropomorphic character, such as that of Aristotle. Yet Salutati felt the need to posit a world order beyond the contingent and subjectively perceived phenomenal world, however unknowable it might be. This position of double consciousness[30] arose from the theological imperative to save divine omnipotence from coercion by natural necessity, thus stressing divine will, and out of the direct historical experience of voluntaristic operationalism.

Possibly even more important as a cultural preparation for future science of a new type was his crucial argument for the nobility of law as being greater than medicine. Medicine dealt in an uncertain and fumbling way with the contingent physical data of the body which could not be demonstrated to have any consistent connection with underlying physical principles, since they too were extrapolated to save the phenomena. Law, on the other hand, consisted of the varied application of a fundamental, internally grasped principle of equity. The latter may be likened to a "mental experiment" that had an inherent necessity in its three rules: that one should do to others what one wished to be done to oneself; that one should not do to others what one did not want done to oneself; that what one wished to do to others should apply to oneself.

> And whereas what are found in us come from these high equities, as has been demonstrated, they have certain principles such as are not to be found in external things but which are inserted naturally in our minds in such great certitude that they cannot be unknown to us, and it is not necessary that we seek them externally, because, as you see, we have them intrinsically.

Moreover, though their promulgation varies in custom and practice from place to place, the same underlying reason prevails in them, else they are not laws.[31] The historical relativism combined with an innate, universal principle of equity of this observation was, of course, matched by the historical relativism with which the humanists learned to regard the history of language and literature. The differences of Greek, Latin, and the *volgare* were explored, recognizing the periodicity of styles and their cultural relevance, while at the same time, universal principles of language were sought. Salutati's declaration may be regarded as paradigmatic of this whole humanistic development that reordered the relationship of universal principle and concrete occurrence in the literary and historical worlds and recognized the literary conception of the fiction as a thought-experiment which sought to find a universal meaning concealed in the concrete fictional narrative. Can we not argue that this cultural transformation introduced with the humanist movement was, if not itself a preparation for a new kind of inductive-hypothetical thinking that entered into the new science, at least a very striking parallel and environing development?

If Lorenzo Valla's application of the methodological principle of historicity to the language of the Donation of Constantine was but one spectacular illustration of the new insights that humanist methodology made possible, his linguistic and philosophical critique of Aristotelian physics and metaphysics is of more specific relevance to the problem of literature and science in the Renaissance. Valla's nominalism was both literal and radical. Knowledge was conceived as arising out of the collective subjectivity of human discourse.

> There is no investigation of truth before a controversy concerning the matter is born. Hence truth is knowledge of the matter of controversy, falsity, indeed, lack of knowledge of the same thing; both are a kind of prudence or imprudence, wisdom or folly. Or we say truth is, on the one hand, knowledge of the mind concerning some matter; on the other hand, it is the signification of speech derived from the knowledge of the mind.[32]

This passage is taken from his first, still unpublished version of the *Disputationes dialecticae,* his *Repastinatio philosophiae et dialecticae* (Cod. Urb. lat. 1207)[33] in which he makes far more extensive and significant comment on the natural world than in the published versions. Truth and knowledge are, then, what an individual thinks they are, or what a segment of humanity agrees that they are. Since this can be known only through language and debate, oral and written (or, as in the case of animals, gestural), truth can best be discovered by linguistic and literary analysis, history, and criticism. Truth, in other words, is not that which is but what it is named or called, what speech about it signifies. It is meaning. Thus he regards faith and hope as intellectual virtues similar to science, wisdom, and truth, whereas charity is a true virtue because it is affect. For Valla all such intellectual qualities or faculties are subordinate to true virtue or vice which is affect or will, reducible to charity and fortitude, virtue, or vice according to its object and its strength or weakness. Virtue is man's affective power in a sense similar to Machiavelli's usage of *virtù.* "For to know or be wise about or understand is nothing except to believe and feel concerning things as they are held to be, and this is called truth."[34]

The human pursuit of pleasure or beatitude is all-powerful and all-determining. Intellectual culture and science are instruments by means of which the organism seeks to achieve these affective goals. Science itself is not what is demonstrated to be true but what (on the basis of any *accepted* proof) is held to be true. Hence the study of science should be the study of the literature of science and its history. It is the study of the dialogue of scientists between themselves and with others. Truth comes wrapped in language. It cannot, in fact, be separated from language. Man's pursuit of fulfillment is itself mediated by the specific structures of the languages he uses and by the languages arising out of his various cultures as he utilizes them: his historical time, his region, his traditions and institutions, his education, his particular experience.[35]

Valla believes that since the Advent of Christ, beatitude, not pleasure, is the true goal of human striving (although beatitude is itself a structurally and qualitatively superior kind of pleasure, being divine and eternal). But beatitude is also the true goal because we have had its truth revealed by the divine Word spoken by Christ and known in the literature of the Bible. It is for this reason that Valla becomes the founder of Biblical humanism, seeking to refine theological truth by strict linguistic and literary analysis of the scriptural text. Valla's acceptance of the truth of the scriptures is for him a matter of faith (as for all medieval and Renaissance Christians). But faith for him, as we have seen, is not significantly different from science.[36] Both are intellectual virtues.

Christians have inherited from antiquity the tools of literary expression, interpretation, and analysis embodied in the writings of Cicero and, above all, of Quintilian. They have also inherited ancient philosophy now adapted and transformed into scholastic Aristotelianism. Valla sees Boethius as the father of scholasticism. Scholasticism he sees as the perversion of Christian truth by subordinating it to ancient philosophies, especially those of the Stoics and Aristotle. Epicureanism has only the advantage that its incompatibility with Christianity is patent. It is also more honest and corresponds to the truly animal character of human existence as long as man is without knowledge of and faith in his immortality and possibility of salvation. The other two philosophies are to be repudiated because they seek to impose a rationalist illusion on human thought and behavior. Such are the thoughts of Valla in his *De vero bono* (first entitled *De voluptate*). But his *Dialecticae* were meant to be a companion piece to the former. The first version of the *Dialecticae,* completed in 1439, was contemporary with the later versions of *De vero bono*.[37]

The *Dialecticae* demonstrate that however dominant Valla's religious motivations were in shaping his thought, he did not turn away from their implications for understanding the natural world. A very large part of Book I deals, of course, with theological and moral questions such as God, the Trinity, the Procession of the Holy Spirit, the trinitarian human soul and man's virtues, and I have discussed these elsewhere. But a considerable section of Book I also consists of a survey of the kinds of classifications and thoughts concerning "nature" that could be drawn from human usage in speaking of them—his humanist methodology. The whole treatment of the book is set within the frame of a criticism of Aristotle. Here he eliminates all transcendentals except *res,* thing, that which is. He does not deny that the world exists, in other words, but it is *res* and comprehensible only through *verba.*[38] In the *De vero bono* he had made it quite clear that he believed the world was created for the sake of man, but this was admittedly the sense his Christian faith had to give it. He also said, "Nature has offered to mortals very many goods; it is our responsibility to know how to make good use of them."[39] *Res* as he uses it here in the *Dialecticae* is more neutral and unteleological. It is posited axiomatically.

Perhaps more important than his stark nominalism is his reduction of Aristotle's ten categories or predicaments to three: substance, quality, and action. Valla's reduction of the categories to these three predicaments which correspond to the structure of language—noun, verb, and adjectival or adverbial qualifier—is truly profound and far-reaching. The three, which are analytical abstractions never encountered separately are confronted together as "consubstantials," as Valla prefers to call them. They are formed into a consubstantial like a simple declarative sentence bundling together substance, quality, and action, which can then be analytically distinguished just as a sentence can be grammatically analyzed into the principle parts of speech and syntax. A recent paper by Amos Funkenstein stresses Descartes' nominalism and his reduction of substances into the three: God, souls, and matter or "extension." Valla also divides substances into three: spirits, bodies, and the composite embodied spirits. (Actually they are the same three, though divided differently.) Spirits are either creating or created, that is God or souls (disembodied, i.e., angels and demons, or embodied, as men and animals). But for Valla they are encountered as "consubstantials" with qualities and actions.[40]

Perhaps the significance of Valla's classification, like Descartes', lies in its simplicity, because, as both thinkers intended, it sweeps away a whole elaborate metaphysical apparatus of imposed structures in thinking about the universe. Descartes was post-Galileian and himself an important contributor to the scientific revolution. Valla hoped that he could bring about a religious and an intellectual revolution. What Valla had to say about "spirit," therefore, and particularly human spirit, was probably far more important in the intellectual history of the Renaissance than the few scraps he found to say about "body." (As indicated, I have discussed the former elsewhere).[41] But even in what he does have to say about "body" there are salutary suggestions of a different mental frame such as would at least release the possibility of a new conception of scientific thinking even if it does so dialectically and does not in any sense directly anticipate it.

"Body" is viewed heuristically and subjectively as whatever comes into contact with sense, or some sense, or can be touched. It can be classified into genera and species, but these are derived from human vocabulary and linguistic traditions rather than rational analysis or experiment. There are two kinds of body, vegetable and "invegetable." Valla describes "vegetable" first, further subdividing it according to common linguistic practice into legumes, fruits, various kinds of trees, etc. For the "invegetable" he resorts to the traditional four elements. He offers a subdivision of stone and mineral for earth, listing them in terms of human experience with the arts, building, and industry. Water, air, and fire, however, are skipped over except for the following skeptical declaration:

> But they seem to dream or wish to glory in things that, although fallacious, are yet marvellous. I do not concede the existence of the spheres, nor of elements of fire, nor of the five zones of the earth, nor that the sea is higher not only than the mountains but not even than the shores, nor that the earth is spherical (*globosa*), nor that air is changed into water and fire, nor again fire into air, nor other things of this sort which seem to me to approach closely the insanity of the astrologers concerning fortune and the lives of men.

It is interesting to note that, besides some theories that are certainly true (the sphericity of the earth), he particularly doubts what was at the heart of the Aristotelian conception of cosmological and terrestrial dynamics, the constant transformation of the elements into each other brought about by the annual cycle of the sun.[42]

Of even greater interest are parts of his ensuing discussion of "qualities." For Valla "quality" is far more important than "substance," the latter, of course, being central to Aristotle's conception of reality. Valla proposes that the limitations imposed by Aristotelians on defining predicaments and individual qualities because they are known *per se* is ridiculous because a real knowledge of a thing (not a tautological statement) can only be gained from a description of its qualities and actions. This is better provided by "interpretation"—a literary method—than by "definition."

Res, or a thing in general, "ought not to be defined but its existence noted since it is distinguished from nothing else. But whatever cannot be defined, certainly can be expounded by interpretation, as every *res* is completed by its signification, such as is also the condition of individuals."[43] He is, of course, reaffirming the emphasis of Quintilian and other literary and rhetorical theorists on answering the question *Qualis sit* rather than *Quid sit,* both of which follow after the primary *An sit* which applies to things in general or *res.* And in so continuing the ancient and medieval discussions of the *status controversiae* Valla favors the investigation of quality and action through interpretation which is literary rather than of substance (not detachable from quality and action) by definition which is dialectical and philosophical.[44] Qualities may be known either directly by the senses or by judgment of the soul from their actions, meaning here human actions rather than Aristotle's movements. Passing over these internal judgements rather summarily, he offers a fairly long discussion of qualities known by the senses, and these are of special importance in revealing his conceptions of nature.[45]

First, under "The Object of Sight," he primarily discusses "quantity" which he had taken away from Aristotle's listing of it as a special category and placed under "quality." But to make "quantity" truly qualitative means knowing accurately what is being determined, and there is no accuracy of language in calling a quantity large or small, very large or very small. Thus, he argues, we know quantity only when it is translated into number.

> Therefore, if to an inquiry concerning quantity it is necessary to reply through number, and number itself contains not only length, breadth, and depth, but also roundness, squareness, angularity, and other similar things, it is no wonder that *quotitas* contains *quantitas* rather than *quantitas quotitas,* just as the genus contains the species. For we do not measure number by quantity but quantity by number.

He thus illustrates how literary interpretation can approach the necessity for mathematics in its desire for precision. This suggests one reason for the extensive humanist interest in and support for a mathematical Renaissance and mathematical progress.[46]

A similar discussion of point, line, and surface ensues in which Valla arrives at a notion of space as quantitative but comprehended by the dimensionless abstractions of geometry. He regards it, however, more from the perspective of the practical construction of figures with pen or pencil rather than theoretically. The mark of the pen occupies no space, but, "we see space only by means of this line which is extended from one place where it begins to another place where it ends, although it is not so much space (we see) but a figure surrounding and signifying space."[47] Here he is remarkably similar to the usage of Leon Battista Alberti in *De pictura* who speaks of point and line as a *signum* which, though it cannot be divided, serves to systematize space.[48] Valla, however, wishes to use this argument against Aristotle who, according to him, unnecessarily claims the materiality of the point against Plato's abstract and theoretical use of geometric figures in describing the physical world. "But what does he gain," asks Valla, "by saying a point is an indivisible quantity if it is no quantity at all? Or if it is a quantity, why cannot it be divided, if it can be seen and conceived (*cogitari*), when certain tiny insects (*bestiolae*) which can scarcely be seen themselves have a thousand members?"[49] In pursuance of his argument that quantity is a quality within his classification of predicaments he argues further that the extension of points into lines, lines into surfaces and surfaces into solids, indeed, forms a body but that this is a substance rather than a variety of quality, for a body possesses quantity as one of its qualities, or it is compacted as a "consubstantial" of substance and quality.[50]

His discussion of motion is also of a certain interest because he wishes to refute Aristotle's designation of six types of movement and reduce it simply to change of place. Motion is not a quality but an action containing qualities in itself. These can be such as "frequency, force, brevity, persistence, retardation, slowness, distance, alternity, interval and similar qualities." He does not mention velocity or acceleration. Nor does he mention such theories as impetus or offer any explanation of what moves an object. Motion is simply an existence defined as the action of change of place of a body, observable by sight and touch, and characterized by a variety of qualities. Obviously it has nothing to do with the Galileian concept of inertia or with Aristotle's theory of projectile motion, or with impetus. But his treatment is another example of his philological positivism that cuts away the metaphysical basis of Aristotelian physics. Motion is not generation, corruption, increase, diminution or alteration but only the action of change of place with its attendant possible qualities.[51]

Time also receives an extended discussion. As Cicero says, it is difficult to define. Certain thinkers call it the motion of the heavens, others the number of movement, neither of which pleases him.

> For time can exist without the movement of the heavens, and if there were no heaven, and even if nothing moved. For there is no less time in the stability of the earth than in the movement of the heavens. Certainly chaos, if there ever was such, did not see the heavens moved, and it had a certain time. . . . Neither will time be the measure of motion because it also can exist without motion, especially since we know of movement by sight and touch, but we do not judge of time by these senses. Certainly time is not accelerated in rapid movement or retarded in slow. What therefore is time? It is not a substance or consubstance because it is neither body nor soul. It is not a quality because it does not inhere in anything but without intermission runs on. . . . Will it therefore be action? But the action of what thing?— the action of all things, at least, which are perceptible to our senses, but it is known through the soul not by the senses. . . . Thus time comes from existing and is, as I might thus say, in being, which in my judgment properly is essence according to action, not quality, . . .

Though time may be an inseparable part of existence, it is perceived subjectively, however, and, though we can speak of past and future, "it is hardly doubtful that time is only the present, just as the life of animals, just as all life. . . . But when we embrace the past and future in thought we make three species of time, just as most do, past, future, present." Time has many qualities but most of these are invented by men, qualities such as: "opportunity, inopportuneness, seasonableness, unseasonableness, maturity, immaturity, brevity, length, closeness, duration and the like. All such qualities would cease if we only considered present time and its instant. For those are not natural qualities but are invented by men and attributed to time, although there are parts and members of time such as age of life, century, age of history, lustrum, year, month, day, hour, minute and also week."[52]

If I have presented certain notions of Valla rather lengthily for a short paper, it has only been because I wished to use him as a paradigm of the relationship of humanism and science during the Renaissance, and this could be done only by presenting his thought in some detail. Valla can be seen as paradigmatic, first of all, because he illustrates more effectively than any other of the humanists the approach to a theory of literature and language—to a literary and linguistic science if you will—that their intensive study of ancient letters and rhetorical and poetic theory stimulated. The Renaissance period witnessed a closer approximation to a sophisticated, learned, and sharply analytical literary theory than any time since antiquity, and very possibly one that went beyond the ancients. Valla can also be seen as paradigmatic in the ways in which he, as also a number of other humanists before and after him (including, as we have seen, Petrarch and Salutati) along with such nominalists as Ockham, contributed to the breakdown of the ontological conception of the universe accepted from Aristotle by many medieval natural philosophers. He thus anticipated certain features of the philosophy and methodology of seventeenth-century science, though certainly not its specific content and procedures.

In substituting signification for universal being by means of his cultural and historical and linguistic relativism, Valla asserted the primacy of the subjective, of the humanly invented, of the conventional, of the culturally determined elements of existence over those of so-called nature. Culture, history, literature, language, affect, imagination, convention, and invention became for him (as they had also been in the process of becoming for Petrarch and Salutati and other early humanists) the primary qualities of existence (always excepting the divine realities entertained by faith which through the creation and providence held the ultimate priority). The human mind painted its qualities onto the external world; it was not a *tabula rasa* painted by sense perception of externals.[53] Mankind's changing ideas concerning the exterior world were seen as themselves secondary and dependent on religious conceptions and culture and, as thus, also relative and hypothetical and reflective of the constantly evolving world of history and culture.[54]

Perhaps before a Galileo could by mathematical reasoning, mental experiments, and experimental verification reestablish a sense of certitude concerning a new set of primary qualities in nature (the procedures recognized by us as those of modern science), it was necessary for this humanistic attitude so sharply exemplified in Valla to emerge in Renaissance and early modern culture. Perhaps it was necessary for the Aristotelian and other Hellenic conceptions of the universe as metaphysical and necessitarian (which had been broadly accepted into medieval natural philosophy though subjected to criticism on theological, logical, and physical grounds by the nominalists) to be subjected also to this humanist criticism on religious, psychological, and philological grounds before a hypothetical and operational conception of science could be developed.

At any rate it is interesting that Galileo, who, it has now been convincingly shown, was quite aware of fourteenth-century and earlier scholastic mathematical and physical developments and was, at least in his early career, influenced by them,[55] was also in many respects familiar with humanistic culture. Among other humanistic writings he discussed the dimensions of the Inferno as set forth by Dante and commented on the poetry of Tasso. But to my mind the most convincing indication of his grasp of the humanist notion of the relativity of thought and expression was his mastery of the dialogue form in arguing on behalf of his most important scientific positions.[56] His distinction between primary and secondary qualities is well known and important, as is the famous passage in *Il Saggiatore* where Galileo affirms the primacy of his new metaphysic of bodies moving in uniformly extended but measurable space and time in abstraction from all the actual qualities and conditions empirically encountered in the material world and grasped such as Valla did as "consubstantials." Dismissing all that was known by sensation and experience as "secondary," Galileo says:

> having now seen how many affections, that are thought to be qualities located in external objects, have truly no other existence but in us, and outside of us are nothing other than names, I say that I am quite inclined to believe that heat is of this character, and that the matter which produces heat in us and makes us feel it, which we call by the general name of fire, is a multitude of the smallest little bodies, shaped in such and such a way, moved with such and such a velocity. . . . [57]

Paradoxically, should we not recall that nearly two centuries earlier Valla had written that qualities are names of things known by the senses (or recognized by the soul from self-experience) which are part of a hypothesized universal underlying the appearance of things that exists as a compaction of the three predicaments of "substance," "quality," and "action"? Only for Valla the names and qualities known and experienced by man are primary, not secondary as Galileo and his successors would have them. And Valla is not at all concerned to move toward the discovery of a method to establish the nature and certitude of his hypothesized universe, a method (or methods) which we call natural science. But should not cultural historians and historians of science entertain and examine the possibility that conjectures and literary-theoretical constructions of humanists such as Valla's also contributed importantly to bringing about the kind of alterations in the general thought structure which facilitated the invention of science?[58]

NOTES

1. The paper is based on a *Relazione* prepared for the Ninth Congresso of the Associazione internazionale per gli studi di lingua e letteratura italiana on the general theme of "I Rapporti tra Letteratura e Scienza nella Storia della Cultura Italiana" meeting in Sicily in April 1976. Although my credentials are neither literary nor "science-historical," I believe my studies of Italian humanism and my projected examination of the place of humanism in sixteenth-century Italian intellectual history suggest the validity of raising once again the issues dealt with by Cassirer and Burtt (not to mention Koyré). There seems to be at least some consensus among historians of science that the definitions of Platonism by Burtt and Koyré are too imprecise to make them very useful. However, the scene is dominated by Platonism in the guise of "Hermeticism" as projected by the followers of Frances Yates, and the controversy over Duhem's thesis rages on spurred by the researches of A. C. Crombie and William A. Wallace, not to mention Freudian and psychohistorical studies of the reception of Copernicanism and the religion of Sir Isaac Newton. Such fascination with externalist and environmentalist considerations of the "scientific revolution" suggests that an introduction of possible humanist influence into the situation may not muddy the waters in any more perceptible way. Cassirer's very elaborate discussion is that of his chapter on "The Subject-Object Problem in the Philosophy of the Renaissance" in his *The Individual and the Cosmos in Renaissance Philosophy* (Eng. trans. by Mario Domandi, Oxford, 1963, original German version, Leipzig and Berlin, 1927). E. A. Burtt, *The Metaphysical Foundations of Modern Science* (New York, 1925, rev. ed. 1932).
2. Cf. Eugene F. Rice, Jr., *The Renaissance Idea of Wisdom* (Cambridge, Mass., 1958) and my "A Humanist's Image of Humanism: the Inaugural Orations of Bartolommeo della Fonte," *Studies in the Renaissance* 7 (1960), 90–125, es-

pecially Fontius's oration on *sapientia,* 108–11, his discussion of "philosophy" in his oration *In bonas artis,* 115–18, and the diagram of his classification of the arts in note 77.

3. The point was made by Fontius, ibid., and was still being made in 1559 by Carlo Sigonio in his oration *De laudibus studiorum humanitatis* (in *Orationes septem Caroli Sigonii,* Venice, 1560), and by Paolo Beni, a colleague of Galileo, in his inaugural oration of 1600 on the occasion of his appointment as professor of humanities at Padua: *Pro studiis humanitatis* (Padua, 1600).

4. Cf. Kristeller's classic essay, "Humanism and Scholasticism in the Italian Renaissance," first published in *Byzantion XVII* (1944–45) and reprinted in various places, perhaps most conveniently in his *Renaissance Thought, The Classical, Scholastic and Humanistic Strains* (New York, 1961), 92–119. Cf. my essay in note 2 above.

5. I have attempted to show this in my *In Our Image and Likeness, Humanity and Divinity in Italian Humanist Thought* (2 vols., London and Chicago, 1970), hereafter cited as *IOIAL.* Cf. especially part IV. Kristeller has stated his views on this question in a short piece, "The Role of Religion in Renaissance Humanism and Platonism," *The Pursuit of Holiness in Late Medieval and Renaissance Religion,* ed. C. Trinkaus with H. A. Oberman (Leiden, 1974), 367–70.

6. Cesare Vasoli, *La dialettica e la retorica dell'Umanesimo, "Invenzione" e "Metodo" nella cultura del XV e XVI secolo* (Milan, 1968). Cf. also: Quirinus Breen, "The Terms 'Loci Communes' and 'Loci' in Melanchthon," *Christianity and Humanism, Studies in the History of Ideas* (Grand Rapids, Mich., 1968), 93–105; Walter J. Ong, S. J., *Ramus, Method and the Decay of Dialogue* (Cambridge, Mass., 1958); Neal W. Gilbert, *Renaissance Concepts of Method* (New York, 1960); Angelo Crescini, *Le origini del metodo analitico, il Cinquecento* (Udine, 1965, Publicazioni dell'Università degli studi di Trieste, Istituto di filosofia), and his *Il problema metodologica alle origini della scienza moderna* (Roma, 1976); Lisa Jardine, *Francis Bacon, Discovery and the Art of Discourse* (Cambridge, 1974). I should like to make it clear that, while the humanist effort to "take over" dialectic as a branch of rhetoric had an important influence on pre- and post-Galilean methodological discussions, this present paper is about something else, more metaphysical perhaps.

7. Cf. André Chastel, *Arte e umanesimo a Firenze al tempo di Lorenzo il Magnifico* (Turin, 1964), 113–35; and Eugenio Garin, "Dante nel Rinascimento," *Rinascimento* (seconda serie) 7 (1967), 3–25, Eng. trans. in *The Three Crowns of Florence,* ed. David Thompson and Alan Nagel (New York, 1972), ix–xxxiv.

8. Despite the many fine studies of nominalism or "Ockhamism" in the last forty years, the subject has not attained the consensus that some of its proponents have hoped. I have found William J. Courtenay, "Nominalism and Late Medieval Religion," *The Pursuit of Holiness* sup. cit., 26–66 and Steven Ozment, "Mysticism, Nominalism and Dissent," Ibid., 67–92 clarifying, and Heiko A. Oberman's classic *The Harvest of Medieval Theology* essential, and my remarks on nominalist theology are based on them. For the "covenantal" aspects of nominalist theology see Courtenay, "Covenant and Causality in Pierre D'Ailly," *Speculum* XLVI (1971), 94–119. Part of the difficulty in

achieving consensus is that "nominalism" was not a broad late medieval culture but a movement with only partial agreement between those individuals nominally adhering to the party of "nominales." At the same time they share certain characteristics with other contemporaries. Part of the difficulty is also due to the study of "nominalist" theology, logic, and natural philosophy separately and frequently by quite different scholars. See note 9 for the problem of natural philosophy, the study of which is possibly even more fragmented than that of theology where at least the Oberman school takes some common positions which I find convincing.

9. The modern understanding of Ockham's philosophy owes much to Philotheus Boehner whose writings and translations have been widely circulated. Cf. his *Collected Articles on Ockham,* ed. E. M. Buytaert, (St. Bonaventure, N.Y., 1956), and his *William of Ockham, Philosophical Writings, A Selection* (Edinburgh and London, 1957, repr. Indianapolis: Library of Liberal Arts 193, 1964). The contributions of the late Ernest Moody to the study of late medieval logic and science and their relation to the Galileian "revolution" have also been notable. See now his *Studies in Medieval Philosophy, Science and Logic, Collected Papers 1933–69* (Publications of the Center for Medieval and Renaissance Studies of UCLA, No. 7, Berkeley, 1975). The following judgment of 1966 is penetrating: "As Aristotle's substance-property physics is related to Newtonian particle-mechanics, so Aristotle's logic of terms, built around the categorical proposition of subject-predicate form, is related to modern quantificational logic. In both areas the work of the fourteenth-century scholastics was that of revealing the inadequacy of the Aristotelian form of analysis, of suggesting in an ad hoc manner ways in which these limitations could be overcome, while failing to generalize them into new foundations, and, in effect, drawing the curtain on a tradition that had outlived its usefulness for science without taking the further step of replacing that tradition with a new and more adequate framework." Ibid., 389. The actual historical influence of medieval science on Galileo has been much discussed. Cf. especially Anneliese Maier, *Die Vorläufer Galileis im 14.Jahrhundert* (Rome, 1949) and *Zwei Grundprobleme der scholastischen Naturphilosophie* (Rome, 1951); William A. Wallace, "Galileo and the Thomists," in *St. Thomas Aquinas 1274–1974 Commemorative Studies* (Toronto, Pontifical Institute of Mediaeval Studies, 1974); Stillman Drake, "Galileo's New Science of Motion," in M. L. Righini Bonelli and William R. Shea, eds., *Reason, Experiment and Mysticism in the Scientific Revolution* (New York, 1975), 131–56; A. C. Crombie, "Sources of Galileo's Early Natural Philosophy," in ibid., 157–75. Two other recent attempts to "settle" the questions of late medieval science are: J. E. Murdoch and E. D. Sylla eds., *The Cultural Context of Medieval Learning* (Dordrecht, 1975), and Edward Grant, *Physical Science in the Middle Ages* (New York, 1971); ch. 3, ch. 6, and bibliographical essay are useful and clarifying. Of particular value for my own paper because he emphasizes the dialectical necessity of an inner weakening and criticism of an older world view in order for a newer one to emerge historically is Amos Funkenstein's "The Dialectical Preparation for Scientific Revolutions, On the Role of Hypothetical Reason-

ing in the Emergence of Copernican Astronomy and Galileian Mechanics," in *The Copernican Achievement,* ed. Robert Westman (Los Angeles, 1975), 165–203.

10. Petrarch's classic discussion is in his *Invective contra medicum, Testo latino e Volgarizzamento di ser Domenico Silvestri,* ed. P. G. Ricci (Rome, 1950). But Petrarch does not fear to reiterate this argument against the well-wishing advice of his physician-friend, the famous Paduan, Giovanni de' Dondi (or Giovani dell'Orlogio) Cf. *Epistolae recum senilium,* Lib. XII, 1 and 2, *Opera omnia* (Basel, 1581), 897–903 and 903–14. On dialectic cf. *Rer. fam.,* I, 12 (Rossi I, 51–52).

11. Petrarch's defense and exposition of the "therapy of the word" is best found in *De remediis,* II, 114, "De totius corporis dolore." He says: "Verba corporibus non medentur, fateor, nisi forsitan incantationes et anilia carmina fidei aliquid merentur; at medentur morbis animorum, quorum profecto sanitas corporeum dolorem, aut extingit, aut mitigat." etc. *Op. om.,* 201, Cf. for the ancient theory of verbal therapy, Pedro Lain Entralgo, *La curacion por la palabra en la antiguedad clasica* (Madrid, 1958), Eng. Trans. (New Haven, 1970).

12. Cf. Charles B. Schmitt's definitive discussion, "Experience and Experiment: A Comparison of Zabarella's View with Galileo's in *De Motu,*" *Studies in the Renaissance* 16 (1969), 80–138, espec. 123–28.

13. Cf. *Le Traite De sui ipsius et multorum ignorantia publie . . . par* L. M. Capelli (Paris, 1906), 44–52; Eng. trans. by Hans Nachod in Cassirer, Kristeller and Randall, eds., *The Renaissance Philosophy of* Man (Chicago, 1948), 79–86 (hereafter Nachod).

14. Cit. Capelli, 50; Nachod, 85.

15. Capelli, 52; Nachod, 86, ". . . semper una sit conclusio: omnia quecumque cernimus oculis vel percipimus intellectu, pro salute hominum et divinitus facta esse et divina providentia ac consilio gubernari."

16. Capelli, 64: Nachod, 99–100: "Unius enim diei, vel unius hore, ad mille annos sive ad mille milia annorum, sicut unius exigue stille levi imbre delapse ad omnem Occeanum, Cuntaque maria per quam minima quidem, aliqua tamen est comparatio et nonnulla proportio. At multorum, et quotcumque colueris millium annorum usquedum numero nomen desit, ad eternitatem ipsam prorsus nulla. Illa enim supra modum, hinc maxima et hinc parva, utrinque certe finita sunt. Hec autem contra, hinc infinita hinc finita, licet maxima, que illis admota, non exigua existimanda esse, sed nulla, . . ." Cf. Augustine, *De civ. Dei,* xii, 13., *IOIAL* 36, 338 n. 78.

17. Cf. *IOIAL,* ch. 1, espec. 47–50.

18. I mean, of course, a Petrarchan "paradigm," not that of Thomas Kuhn, although Jerrold Seigel has suggested the applicability of Kuhn's theory of scientific revolution to Petrarchan humanism. I have suggested in a paper on "Petrarch and Classical Philosophy," chapter 1 of *The Poet as Philosopher, Petrarch and the Formation of Renaissance Consciousness* (New Haven: Yale University Press, 1979), that Petrarch's conception of *imitatio* involved playing at the role of one's exemplar.

19. Cf. *IOIAL,* 560–62 and 809–10 for passages cited.

20. I have discussed these works in *IOIAL* ch. 2 but have certainly not said the last word on them. *Spero di non.* Much of what follows depends on my previous study of Salutati, but I believe I do move into new territory also here.

21. I cite Coluccio Salutati, *De nobilitate legum et medicinae* ed. Eugenio Garin (Edizione nazionale dei classici del pensiero italiano) (Florence, 1947) with Italian translation.

22. Ibid., 192, ". . . etiam ad intellectum non perveniat actus primus sine consensu vel imperio voluntatis. Naturale quidem sciendi desiderium non est intellectus sed voluntatis, quod omnem intellectum ac intellectus actum, non natura solum, sed ratione remporis antecedit. . . ." Cf. *IOIAL,* 64, 349 n. 37.

23. Ibid., 184, ". . . cuius quidem tanta vis est tantusque super alias anime potentias principatus, quod etiam licet sensuum instrumenta recipiunt sensibilium species, talis receptionis effectus sine voluntatis iussibus ulterius vix procedat! . . . etiam maximos rerum motus maximaque sensibilia sepissime non videmus." Cf. *IOIAL,* 67, 350 n. 46.

24. Ibid., 40, "Ego vero distinctionis huiusmodi rationem omnino non video, quoniam dividere scire sive scientiam, que quidem habitus est scientis, penes rationem rerum que sciuntur et super quas scientia cadit, michi rationabile non videtur; quoniam scire vel scientia nec passio est, nec habitus, nec operatio rei que scitur, sed solummodo comprehendentis intellectus qui talis habitus subiectum." Cf. *IOIAL,* 66, 349 n. 43.

25. Ibid., 126 and 128, "Nam naturaliter et secundum absolutissimam veritatem, que quidem esse scripto vel auditu percipimus, credulitate necnon et opinatione quod sint tenemus, si corporalia fuerint; quibus, si fuerint incorporalia, etiam potest rationabilis persuasionis accedere blandimentum. Certitudo vero, etiam si eterna sint, haberi non potest."

26. *Epistolario di Coluccio Salutati,* ed. F. Novati (Rome, 1891–1911), IV, 176–78, "Quibus, licet per se pateat, clarum est non solum cum de Deo loquimur, sed etiam cum de incorporeis sermo fiat, non improprie loqui eaque secundum corticem esse falsa." Cf. *IOIAL,* 62–63, 349 n. 32.

27. Cf. *IOIAL,* 669 and 854 n. 75 citing *De seculo et religione,* ed. B. L. Ullman (Florence, 1957), 141, ". . . cum maxime lata via expositoribus pateat . . ."

28. Cf. my discussion of his *De fato, fortuna et casu, IOIAL* 76–102, 353–62 nn. 60–126.

29. *IOIAL* 86–87, 357 nn. 92 and 94. Bibl. Vatic. Codd. Urb. lat. 201, f. 21r–v, Vat. lat. 2928, ff. 11r–12r: "Libera quidem est voluntas et adeo sibi libertas inserta est quod si libertatem abstuleris voluntas omnino non sit. . . . Naturale igitur necessarium et inevitabili voluntati est quod agat libere et cum ipsa non sit prima causa sed secunda, est de sui natura qua secunda est; necessarium habet sequi primam causam semper tamen libere et secundum exigentiam sue nature. Subiicitur etiam nostra voluntas necessitati finis, hoc est actus quem intendimus agere." (Urb. lat. 201, f. 21v, Vat. lat. 2928, f. 12r). "Nam quamvis ignis formitem urat naturaliter contingens tamen est hunc ignem fomitem illum exurere, contingens est etiam quod id fiat hoc loco vel tempore." (Urb. lat. 201, f. 21r, Vat. lat. 2928, 11r–v).

30. See *The Poet as Philosopher*, op. cit., chapter 2, "Petrarch and the Tradition of a Double-Consciousness."

31. *De nobilitate*, op. cit., 124, "Et quoniam ab illis summis equitatibus veniunt que in nobis reperientur, ut demonstratum est, habent quidem principia, que non in rebus extra, sed in nobis sunt, insertaque naturaliter in mentibus nostris tali certitudine sunt, quod nobis non possunt esse non nota, et quod ea non est necessarium ut queramus extrinsecus, quoniam, sicut vides, intrinsecus habeamus."

32. Bibl. Vatic. Cod. Urb. Lat. 1207, f. 51r, "Nec ante veri inquisitio quam rei controversia nascitur. Itaque veritas est notitia rei controversiae, falsitas vero eiusdem inscitia, quae est speties prudentiae aut imprudentiae seu sapientiae aut insipientiae. Seu dicamus veritas est tum notitia animi de aliqua re, tum orationis ex notitia animi profecta significatio." Cf. *IOIAL*, 152, 381 n. 117.

33. Since Urb. lat. 1207 is a late 15c. ms., Valla's first version of the *Dialecticae* continued to circulate after his revised versions. There is also another exemplar, Perugia, Bibl. della Badia di San Pietro, cod. 53. Valla's second version is that published in his *Opera omnia*, I, (ed. Garin) and in the other early printed editions. The third version is Valencia, Bibl. Capitolare, cod. 69 and Bibl. Vatic., Cod Ottob. lat. 2075, ff. 1–124v. Cf. Gianni Zippel, "Note sulle redazione della "Dialectica" di Lorenzo Valla," *Archivio storico per le Province Parmensi*, IV serie, 9 (1957), 301–14. Zippel's promised edition has now appeared (Padua: Antenore, 1982).

34. Urb. lat. 1207, f. 74v. "Nihil est enim scire et sapere et intelligere, nisi credere ac sentire de rebus ita ut sese habent, et haec vocatur veritas." Cf. *IOIAL*, 162, 385 n. 142.

35. Cf. Salvatore I. Camporeale' study of Valla's language theory developed in dependence on Quintilian in his *Lorenzo Valla. Umanesimo e teologia*, (Florence, 1972), 173–208. Dialectic cannot depart from *usitatissima loquendi consuetudine; sermo popularis atque eruditorum* should be the *magister loquendi* for logic. Cf. also his *Da Lorenzo Valla a Tommaso Moro* in *Memorie Domenicane*, n.s. 4 (1973), 53–55; and cf. my own analysis in *IOIAL*, 150–53. Note also Valla's discussion of the language of invention in the autograph ms. of his *Gesta Ferdinandi Regis Aragonum*, described and analyzed by O. Besomi, "Dai 'Gesta Ferdinandi Regis Aragonum' al 'De Orthographia' del Tortelli," *Italia Medioevale e Umanistica* 9 (1966), 75–121.

36. Cf. *IOIAL*, 572–76.

37. Cf. *IOIAL*, 103–50 for my extended analysis of *De vero bono*.

38. *IOIAL*, 151, 380 nn. 109, 110; Urb. lat. 1207, ff. 44r–48r.

39. Cf. *IOIAL*, 141, 377 n. 92, Urb. lat. 1207, 222r–v; *IOIAL*, 113, 366 n. 29, Urb. lat., 153r, "Natura mortalibus quam plurima bona proposuit. Nostra est illis bene uti scire." Actually Valla's position here is multifaceted and quite complicated. God pursues man with His benefits, and man should not be ashamed to take pleasure in those of this world. But also, driven by the passionate desire for beatitude, the man who has grace can and must spurn the things of this world. Valla's teleology is either subjectively generated by experience or is a matter of faith. Ultimately, I believe, he considers the world and its purpose to be that which men conceive it to be.

40. *IOIAL,* 151–54, 380–81 nn. 107–22, Urb. lat. 1207, 42v–67v. Cf. Amos Funkenstein, "Descartes, Eternal Truths, and the Divine Omnipotence," *Studies in History, Philosophy and Science* 6 (1975): 185–89.

41. *IOIAL,* 155–64, 381–7 nn. 123–47 covering Urb. lat. 1207, 67r–76v.

42. *IOIAL,* 164, 387 nn. 148, 149, Urb. lat. 1207, 76v–78r: "De corpore." Passage quoted 78r: "Sed somniare mihi videntur aut in rebus etsi fallacibus tamen admirabilibus velle gloriari. Ego nec speras, nec igneum elementum, nec quinque terrae zonas, nec marem altius non modo montibus sed ne litoribus quidem, nec terram globosam concesserim, nec aerem in aquam ignemque converti, nec rursus ignem in aerem, nec caetera huiusmodi quae proxime mihi videntur accedere ad insaniam astrologorum de fortuna et vita hominum . . ." He is obviously discussing Aristotle, *De generatione* II from Valla's extended discussion in the printed version, *Opera omnia* (Basel, 1540), I, xi, 670–72.

43. Urb. lat. 1207, 59v–60r: "Res autem ipsa diffiniri non debet, sed nota esse quia a nullo alio distinguitur. Caeterum quicquid non potest diffiniri, certe potest interpretationi exponi, ut res omnia significatione complectitur, qualis est etiam conditio individuorum."

44. Cf. Wesley Trimpi's careful analysis of the nature and development of these literary-rhetorical ideas in "The Quality of Fiction: The Rhetorical Transmission of Literary Theory," *Traditio XXX* (1974): 1–118, and espec. 9–23, "Fiction and the *Status qualitatis*" and "*Stasis* and the Apprehension of Quality."

45. Qualities are discussed Urb. lat. 1207, 78r–86r.

46. Urb. lat. 1207, 80v, "De objecto visus," "Quare si ad interrogationem per quantus necesse est respondere per numerum, et numerum ipse continet non modo longitudinem, latitudinem, profunditatem, [80r] sed etiam rotunditatem, quadritatem, angularitatem caeteraque similia, nimirum quotitas continebit quantitatem, non quantitas quotitatem tanquam genus spetiem. Quantitate enim non metium numerum sed numero quantitatem." For humanist contributions to the mathematical Renaissance, see Paul Lawrence Rose, *The Italian Renaissance of Mathematics, Studies on Humanists and Mathematicians from Petrarch to Galileo* (Geneva, 1976).

47. Urb. lat. 1207, ff. 81v–82v. 82r: "Nec in ea colorem aut latitudinem sed spacium modo quo quid protenditur a loco uno incipit ad locum ubi desinit respicimus, licet non tam spatium sit quam figura complectens ac signans spacium."

48. Leon Battista Alberti, *On Painting and Sculpture, The Latin Texts of De Pictura and De Statua,* edited with translations, introduction and notes by Cecil Grayson (London, 1972), 36: Liber I, 2, "Itaque principio novisse oportet punctum esse signum, ut ita loquar, quod minime queat in partes dividi. Signum hoc loco appello quicquid in superficie ita insit ut possit oculo conspici. Quae vero intuitum non recipiunt, ea nemo ad pictorem nihil pertinere negabit." Cf. Joan Gadol, *Leon Battista Alberti, Universal Man of the Early Renaissance,* (Chicago, 1969), 37–44, 66–69, and the important recent study of Samuel Y. Edgerton, Jr., *The Renaissance Rediscovery of Linear Perspective,*

(New York: Basic Books, 1975) who discusses Alberti's use of the term *signum* and its problems, 80–82 nn. 1–10. Edgerton does not interpret Alberti as having a subjective epistemology similar to Valla's but considers this rather a concession to the practical needs of the artist. I discuss Alberti's use of Protagoras' "Man is the scale and measure of all things" statement in the same treatise I, 18 (Grayson, 52, 53), as an indication of a position that perception is of qualities, similar to Valla's in "Protagoras in the Renaissance," *Philosophy and Humanism, Renaissance Studies in Honor of Paul Oskar Kristeller,* ed. Edward P. Mahoney (New York 1976), 182–84. Also see the following essay in this volume.

49. Urb. lat. 1207, 82r, "Verum quid attinebat dicere punctura esse quantitatem indivisibilem si nulla quantitas est? aut si quantitas est, cur dividi non possit si videri et cogitari potest? quom bestiolae quaedam quarum vix capax est visus mille ipse habeant membra."

50. Urb. lat. 1207, 82r–v.

51. Urb. lat. 1207, 86r–v. Cit. 86r: ". . . nec qualitas est sed actio qualitatem in se continens: crebritatem, vehementiam, brevitatem, assiduitatem, tarditatem, lentitatem, longitudinem, alternitatem, intervallum et similia."

52. Urb. lat. 1207, 87r–88v. Cit. 87r: "Nam tempus et citra motum caeli esse potest, et si caelum non esset, et si nihil etiam moveretur. Neque enim minus in terrae stabilitate quam in motu caeli tempus est. Certe chaos illud si unquam fuit nec caelum moveri vidit et tempus aliquid habuit." 87v: "Nec mensura motus erit tempus quod etiam praeter motum esse potest, praesertim quod motum visu tactuque cognoscimus quibus sensibus de temporibus non iudicamus. Quippe in celeri motu non acceleratur tempus, neque in lento retardatur. Quid igitur erit tempus? non substantia aut consubstantia quia nec anima nec corpus. Non qualitas quia non inheret, sed sine intermissione transcurrit . . . Erit ergo actio? Cuius autem rei actio? omnium rerum nostris saltem sensibus perceptibilium, sed quae animo non sensibus cognoscitur. . . . Ita tempus ex existendo et est sic dicam essendo quid meo iudicio proprie essentia est, pro actione inquam [88r] non pro qualitate ut festinantia pro festinatione." "Estque haud dubie tantum presens sicut ipsa animalis vita sicut omnis vita. . . . Caeterum quum praeteritum ac futurum cogitatione complectemur faciamus tres speties sicut plerique fecerant, praeteritum, futurum, praesens." "Temporis qualitates praeter has tres sunt opportunitas, importunitas, tempestivitas, intempestivitas, maturitas, inmaturitas, brevitas, longitudo, propinquitas, longinquitas et similia. Quae qualitates cessarent omnes si quidum presens tempus et eius tantummodo punctum consyderemus. Nam illa non sint naturalia sed ab hominibus inventa et tempori attribuita, licet sint temporis partes et membra: aevum, seculum, aetas, lustrum, annus, mensis, dies, hora, momentum, etiam ebdomada . . ."

53. Urb. lat. 1207, 76r–v, "Neque vero concesserim animam hominis velut tabulam rasam esse, in qua nihil pictum sit, sed pingi possit. . . . anima alitur discendo et ea quae percipit in se recondit, suoque calore ac sua luce transfigurat ut ipsa potius pingat alia quam pingatur ab aliis." Cf. *IOIAL,* 163–4, 386 nn. 145, 146, 147 for full passage and discussion.

54. Juan Luis Vives, the Spanish humanist and friend of Erasmus, deeply influenced by Valla, illustrates how this relativism concerning human knowledge grew from philological efforts at deeper understanding: ". . . inscii temporum et rerum gestarum non considerant, quae sunt in quoque scriptore consideranda, quibus temporibus vixerit, cuius opinionis de rebus, cuius sectae, qua autoritate, quomodo scripserit, qua dicendi sit usus ratione, qua lingua; sentiat omnia, quae scribit, ita esse, an varias inducat personas, et qua potissimum significet mentem animi sui, quo loco dicat, quo tempore, apud quos, joco, an serio; nam sunt haec omnia spectanda, ut eliciatur, quae sit cuiusque mens.", *De causis corruptarum artium*, p. 36 of *De disciplinis libri* XII (Lyons, 1551), cit. Crescini, *Le origini del metodo analitico,* op. cit., 89 n. 52.

55. Cf. articles of Drake, Crombie, and Wallace cited in n. 9, and Moody, op. cit., "Galileo and His Precursors," 393–408.

56. Antonio Favoro and Isidoro del Lungo, eds. *Le opere di Galileo Galilei,* vol. IX, Scritti Letterari (Edizione nazionale, Firenze, 1899). A careful study of the way Galileo uses his dialogues to confront whole mental sets is badly needed. William R. Shea, *Galileo's Intellectual Revolution* (London, 1972) makes an excellent start despite too sharp a confrontation of what he considers religious and rationalist viewpoints.

57. Favoro, vol. VI (1896), 347–52 for entire discussion, passage cited 350, lines 22–29: ". . . avendo già veduto come molte affezzioni, che sono reputate qualità residenti ne'soggetti esterni, non ànno veramente altra essistenza che in noi, e fuor di noi non sono altro che nomi, dico che inclino assai a credere che il calore sia di questo genere, e che quelle materie che in noi producano e fanno sentire il caldo, le quali noi chiamano con nome generale *fuoco,* siano una moltetudine di corpicelli minimi, in tal e tal modo figurati, mossi con tanta e tanta velocità . . ." This passage is cited and discussed by E. A. Burtt, op. cit., 73–80. An English translation is in Stillman Drake, *Discoveries and Opinions of Galileo* (New York, 1957). (Translation here is my own.) I would not want it thought that I merely follow Burtt or Drake in their emphases. I have always thought that this discussion by Galileo and his concept of primary and secondary qualities brought out an essential dimension of Galileo's philosophy of science, that the pursuit of mathematical precision and certitude was for him the counterpart of a deep awareness of the subjectivity of human experience and culture.

58. There is much further work to be done before the thesis set forth experimentally in this paper can be substantiated (or demolished). The question of Valla's actual influence immediately occurs. Whereas in religious thought and Biblical scholarship this was potent both positively on figures such as Erasmus and negatively in the Catholic hostility shown his writings in the sixteenth century, he had perhaps a more lasting influence in the development of philological study through his *Elegantiae Linguae Latinae* which was widely published and adopted as university texts. His *Dialecticae* was also influential but its influence has mainly been considered in the area of dialectic treated in his second and third books. There are natural philosophical passages in many of the works on dialectic which need to be considered and a surprising number

of humanist writings in natural philosophy by such figures as Pontano, Poliziano, Ermolao Barbaro, Giorgio Valla, Giovanni Pico della Mirandola, Celio Calcagnini, and others. Humanists of the late sixteenth century in particular need to be studied also for such writings, figures about whom we know much less than the earlier ones. The study of humanist influence on mathematical developments with direct links to Copernicus and Galileo has begun by Rose in the work cited above. The influence and importance of humanist art theory, particularly Alberti's but also of others, is arousing the interest of historians of science. One might mention Thomas B. Settle's "Ostilio Ricci, a Bridge between Alberti and Galileo," *Actes du XIIe Congres International d'Histoire des Sciences* (Paris, 1968–71), III B, 121–26. The relationship of humanism to the perplexing question of science and Hermeticism must be looked into, and finally the possible humanist quality of Galileo's own culture and circle and that of other scientific figures of his age must be investigated. The subject of the origins of modern science is obviously highly problematical and controversial in present scholarship, and perhaps the intrusion of an outsider from a related field will not contribute an excessive increase in the confusion now prevalent.

Humanism and Greek Sophism:
Protagoras in the Renaissance

This study is an attempt to determine the way in which several Renaissance thinkers regarded the thought of Protagoras, probably the most important and possibly the greatest of the Greek sophists. Although knowledge of Protagoras was clearly not very widespread in the Renaissance among either humanists or philosophers, no attempt will be made to survey the extent of his familiarity. Rather discussion will concentrate on a few fairly well known mentions or discussions of this thinker. Because both Renaissance knowledge of Protagoras and contemporary knowledge and understanding of him rest on such slender foundations, the value of this study will be somewhat factitious. The topic acquires its importance not so much from any demonstrable strength of influence or depth of understanding of Protagoras in the Renaissance but rather from our contemporary historical sense of a similarity between the Greek sophist movement and the Italian Renaissance humanist and Platonist movements. It is the consensus of a number of both ancient and Renaissance historians that even if there was no connection between the two, there ought to have been. [1]

The men of the Renaissance, however, viewed their past in their own ways. Humanists viewed western intellectual history in keeping with their notions of the need for a revival of Roman moral, rhetorical and historical thought. Following Cicero, they recognized that there were Greek precedents for this which they thought to be Socrates, Plato and subsequently the Stoics and the fourth century rhetorical schools. They had a mixed attitude toward Aristotle due to his dominant influence among contemporary scholastic theologians and natural philosophers. But all this could be very confused. Petrarch, for instance, did not distinguish between Socrates and Isocrates. A more accurate knowledge of antiquity grew only gradually.

We, meaning at least some twentieth-century historians, view their past differently and place great stress on the Greek sophists as the original

    This article originally appeared in the festschrift for Paul Oskar Kristeller contributed by his Columbia University colleagues, students, and seminar associates: *Philosophy and Humanism, Renaissance Studies in Honor of Paul Oskar Kristeller,* ed. Edward P. Mahoney (Leiden: E. J. Brill, 1976). It was written in 1971 for this volume and read to the Comparative Studies Colloquium of the University of Michigan History Department in 1972 and to Professor Arnaldo Momigliano's historiography seminar at the Warburg Institute in 1973.

founders of the type of intellectual movement with which we identify the Italian humanists, and we regard the sophists as having at least exercised an indirect influence on the humanists through Cicero and the Roman rhetorical tradition. As far as the Renaissance Platonists are concerned, they, following the tradition, reputation and direct statements concerning the sophists in the texts available to them, regarded them as diametrically opposed to Socrates and Plato and as the corrupt purveyors of a pseudo-knowledge or falsehood, or certainly no more than amoral orators. By and large the humanists also followed this tradition, occasionally acknowledging the ancestral importance of such rhetoricians as Tisias and Gorgias. We, on the other hand, are aware that this traditional view of the sophists has been subjected to significant revision in the modern study of Greek thought. It is now necessary to recognize that the sophists, still controversially, doubtfully, and variously interpreted, have been given a massive importance in the history of Greek and western thought by scholars such as Jaeger, Untersteiner, Guthrie and many others. Moreover, it is now generally acknowledged that many of the sophists were genuinely philosophical and not only opportunistically rhetorical as they were thought to be as recently as by Heinrich Gomperz (1912).[2]

Unquestionably Protagoras is now considered as the most formative and influential of these sophists, though the importance of Gorgias also must be recognized. Therefore the following question is raised in this paper: if Protagoras is thought by contemporary scholars to be in so many respects similar to the humanists and affiliated thinkers of the Renaissance in outlook and in the range of his intellectual and educational interests, what then did these thinkers of the Renaissance in fact know of Protagoras and how did they interpret his thought?

Although, as we have indicated, our study will be based on a few fairly well known references to Protagoras, it is not intended to claim that there were no others. We do not for instance look at the Aristotelian tradition where Aristotle's references to Protagoras in the *Metaphysics* could have been an occasion for comment. We shall be concerned with discussions of Protagoras as illustrations of the process by which knowledge and understanding of Greek thought grew or failed to grow in the Renaissance, and we shall be even more concerned with the extent to which these Renaissance thinkers identified with or rejected the ideas of this Greek thinker whom we are inclined to regard as their ancestor and as a man whose ideas of education, ethics and the origins of human culture, as we have been able to identify them principally from Plato's *Protagoras,* were in many features similar to those of the humanists.

The early Italian humanists, strongly Christian in their religious and moral concerns, admired Socrates and Plato, whose works they knew only from the *Timaeus,* the *Meno* and the *Phaedo.* They thought of the Platonic and Stoic traditions as ones with which, though pagan, they might identify themselves in opposition to scholastic Aristotelianism. They also considered themselves specifically as Ciceronian, but Platonic and Stoic also through the eyes of Cicero, as it were. Sophist and sophism, on the other hand, were terms of opprobrium for them, and they frequently characterized the nominalist scholastics of the fourteenth century as purveyors of *ventosa sophistica*—"windy sophistic."[3] Their growing preoccupation with a humanly centered theology, philosophy and ethics led them to admire Socrates as the first Greek thinker to turn philosophy to the study of man and to consider him, not the sophists, as their principal Greek predecessor in accord with what Cicero so frequently asserted concerning his own intellectual antecedents.

Perhaps if they had also possessed Cicero's lost translation of Plato's *Protagoras,* they would have had a different notion of at least this sophist. Protagoras and other sophists were not completely unknown in the Middle Ages and early Renaissance, as they are mentioned and quoted in such Latin writings as those of Cicero, Seneca and Aulus Gellius, and in works of Aristotle that were translated early.[4] Nor were the humanists averse to utilizing ideas and topics drawn from them, as may be illustrated by Petrarch's repetition of the story of the Choice of Hercules told by Prodicus but known through Cicero's citation of Xenophon.[5] But this knowledge was anecdotal, fragmentary and generally critical. Plato's *Protagoras* was first translated again by Marsilio Ficino as part of the *Opera platonis* ca. 1466–68 and began to circulate in printed editions beginning in the 1480's,[6] so that its influence was necessarily a late one, long after the humanists' notions of their movement and its past had been variously formulated. Protagoras' myth,[7] as attributed to him and related by Plato in the dialogue, strongly supports the notion of rhetoric and ethical education as critical in ensuring a civil order of "reverence and justice," and it corresponds to a fundamental conception of the humanists concerning their own moral and educational role in society. The humanists took over this conception from Cicero, particularly his declaration at the beginning of his *De inventione* that orators through their art of rhetoric brought civilization to mankind. But Cicero's view may be traced back through whatever number of intermediaries to Plato's *Protagoras,* which he had indeed also translated.

Moreover, another aspect of Protagoras' thought that might have been supposed to have had a sympathetic reception among the humanists was his dictum that "Man is the measure of all things." Surely an appealing statement for the Renaissance, a more comprehending discussion of its meaning might have occurred if Plato's *Theatetus* had been translated earlier than Ficino's version, also of 1466–68.[8] However, as we shall see, the saying was known and not entirely ignored, though suprisingly infrequent in mention, because of the several references to it and to Protagoras' position concerning it in Aristotle's *Metaphysics*.[9] Although Ambrogio Traversari translated Diogenes Laertius' *Lives of the Philosophers* in the 1430's, and this contained an important sketch of Protagoras' career and a number of anecdotes, it provides very scanty information concerning his ideas. Sextus Empiricus' more elaborate interpretation of Protagoras' dictum seems also not to have been of any influence, since, prior to Giovanni Francesco Pico della Mirandola, Sextus was apparently not studied, despite the existence of a few manuscripts of the Greek text and a Latin translation.[10]

Another problem was that Protagoras was frequently confused with Pythagoras, an easy orthographical error, though some modern scholars do indeed relate his thinking to the Pythagorean school, and there remains the mystery of Protagoras' choice of the word *metron*—"measure"—whatever its and his authentic meaning, which could also serve to associate him with Pythagoras. Petrarch, for example, quotes a genuine fragment out of Seneca, that "you can dispute about everything with equally convincing arguments on both sides, even about the problem of whether everything is disputable on both sides," and attributes it to Pythagoras. However, the context is interesting as he also finds it appropriate to quote the Socratic dictum, "this one thing I know, that I know nothing," and Gorgias and Hippias in the same passage in support of his own skeptical stance of pious ignorance in his *De ignorantia*.[11] Petrarch was reflecting the influence of Cicero's probabilism and semi-skepticism of the *Academica* here, which have some genuine dependence on sophist as well as Socratic doubt. Thus without true historical awareness Petrarch was betraying the existence of certain common positions in sophists, Socratics, Ciceronians, and himself as humanist.

Leon Battista Alberti was one of the few thinkers of the Renaissance to use Protagoras' "Man the measure" dictum. Appropriately he employs it on one occasion in the midst of a discussion of the dignity of man which occurs in book two of the *Libri della famiglia*. The date is a little uncertain because Alberti made a first draft in 1433–34 but apparently inserted supporting classical quotations over the next few years.[12] It is also quite clear that Alberti attributed no special significance to the passage in this usage, nor for that matter to the other classical quotations included along with it. He wishes to stress the greatness of man's powers and his active employment of them, and chides Epicurus for conceiving of gods as passive, for how can man who should imitate God imitate nothing? Rather, as Anaxagoras said, God created man to contemplate the heavens and the works of God, which is confirmed by man's erect posture. Chrysippus and the Stoics attest that man was made to observe and manage things; everything was created to serve man, while man was intended to preserve human society. It is at this point that he states, "Protagoras, another ancient philosopher, seems to some interpreters to have said essentially the same when he declared that man is the mode and measure (*modo e misura*) of all things." Next he mentions Plato's letter to Archytas of Tarentum to the effect that men were born to serve their fellows. Finally, he draws a conclusion that is of great interest in revealing Alberti's own conception of man but which patently lacks precise relationship to the positions of the ancient thinkers he cited in support of it. "It would take a long time to pursue all the sayings of the ancient philosophers in this matter, and very much longer to add the many statements of our own theologians. For the moment these have occurred to me, according to which, as you see, all of them admire, not leisure and passivity in man, but operation and activity."[13] Nonetheless it is of more than passing interest that Protagoras' famous saying, whatever its original meaning, was drawn into use by Alberti in support or embellishment of his own discussion of man.

Alberti, in the same years, made another passing use of Protagoras' dictum in his *De pictura* (*Della pittura*), apparently composed in Latin in 1435 and translated into a volgare version in 1436.[14] There, in book one, Alberti is stressing the importance of the proportionality of the objects of a painting to each other and suggests that the human figures in it present the best criterion or scale of comparison.

> Comparison is made with things most immediately known. As man is the best known of all things to man, perhaps Protagoras, in saying that man is the scale and measure of all things, meant that accidents in all things are duly compared to and known by the accidents in man. All of which should persuade us that, however small you paint the objects in a painting, they will seem large or small according to the size of any man in the picture.[15]

Clearly this use of Protagoras also is shaped to fit Alberti's own conceptions, as scholars have indicated. But perhaps a little greater subtlety is in order. Alberti declares that man is the most noticed thing in the painting to us. Though obviously he is utilizing the externally depicted figure of a man as an objective measure in the painting, and is not asserting the subjective criterion of judging the "nature" of things which is most generally considered to have been Protagoras' meaning, nonetheless Alberti is alluding to the subjective experience that, for an individual viewing a painting, man will be the most noticed thing in it. The human figure is not just a convenient measuring rod for the painter to get his dimensions into accurate scale, but the space will be subjectively viewed and measured by the human observer in accord with the proportionality of all objects and relationships to the man in it with whose presence and artistically depicted situation the observer will subjectively identify. Not exactly Protagoras, but not as totally opposed to Protagoras' clearly anthropocentric conceptions as at first it might seem.

Moreover, another feature of Alberti's statement is curiously related to the thought of Protagoras insofar as we can know it. He speaks of "the accidents of things" being made known by comparison with "the accidents of man." Again, it is the observer who subjectively becomes acquainted with, not the reality or essence, but the imitated image of an object in its accidentality of size, shape, color etc. by comparison to the imitated image, not of the reality or essence, but of the "accidents" of the man in the painting. Alberti could not have known Plato's *Theatetus,* yet what is discussed in that dialogue is Protagoras' position that a man judges the accidental qualities of things by his sense perceptions, which in turn are determined by the accidentality of the condition of the particular individual—the sick man judging something as cold which the healthy man judges as warm. Although Protagoras, in Plato's exposition, is talking not about an imitative representation of this situation but of the actually mimetic or subjectively perceptual character of knowledge, it is still of interest that Alberti attributes to Protagoras a meaning that in some ways approaches the one he seems to have had, at least as Plato depicted it in his dialogue. But this interpretation, for which Alberti had no basis in any of the texts then available to him, can thus derive from no direct historical knowledge of Protagoras' thought. It may thus rather derive from Alberti's own insights in discussing the art of painting, particularly that an imitation of a reality can only be produced by a manipulation of an imitation of its accidents. In thinking about the artist and the viewer in a new way, Alberti, as certain scholars have pointed out,[16] resorted to the analogy of the rhetorical relationship between orator and audience, the conception of which in its Latin sources derived from the Greek rhetorical tradition in which Protagoras had an important formative role. But Alberti in his interest in visual perspective became involved, through his analogy of orator and painter, in some of the philosophical problems arising out of the situation of an orator using words to communicate meanings by manipulating the responses in the mind of the reader. Alberti related these problems more specifically to the perspectival and optical problems of the painter which could be solved only by arranging or manipulating the representations of the accidents of the things depicted through perspective, proportionality, light, shade and color in order to control the response of the viewer. Protagoras' apodictic statement, though isolated and truncated, was in fact a philosophical assertion, the relevance of which to his own problems Alberti grasped even to the extent of reading into it greater meaning than the language itself contains. Moreover, the anthropocentric character of Alberti's conception of the artistic act is also evident in the manner in which he utilized Protagoras.

A more strictly rhetorical usage of Protagoras occurred shortly after Alberti's two references of the late 1430's, and though less intrinsically interesting, it comes from the hand of a humanist who was deeply concerned with the theoretical aspects of rhetoric, namely Lorenzo Valla. Moreover it is to be found in the first version of his important philosophical and methodological work, his *Disputationes dialecticae* of 1438/9,[17] and it was repeated in all subsequent redactions without apparent modification. In book three, which in general attempts to demonstrate the rhetorical nature of the syllogism and other dialectical figures, Valla takes up the problem of the "conversion" or *antistrophon,* in which an opponent who has been impaled on the horns of a dilemma reverses the figure and re-impales the initial proponent. Valla presents his main example in a long direct quotation from Aulus Gellius which recounts an episode, also presented in more abbreviated form by Diogenes Laertius, in which Protagoras agrees to teach the young man Euathius the art of argumentation. It is agreed that as part of his fee Euathius will give Protagoras what he is owed when he wins his first court case. Euathius delays taking a case presumably to avoid the payment. Finally Protagoras brings suit charging willful refusal to pay. He declares that if Protagoras wins his case he will have to be paid, but if he loses the case, Euathius will have won and also must pay. Euathius replies that if Protagoras wins the case, Euathius will have lost and will not have to pay, and if Euathius wins he will not have to pay. The jurors, confronted with this do not know what to decide and delay the trial to avoid an impossible decision. Valla, after giving a further example from Lactantius, presents his own solutions, addressing the court as though he were Protagoras and showing how he should win. Valla's actual concern was not with Protagoras but with Aulus Gellius' fallacious handling of the dialectical problem presented. However, the example does present another reminiscence of Protagoras within the context of a rhetorical-dialectical problem with which he apparently was authentically concerned in his career and writings, however little of his methodological treatises have survived. Valla, however, reveals no awareness of Protagoras' historical importance as the most theoretically oriented of the fifth-century sophists—in his systematization of rhetoric, his epistemology, and his theory of the origins of human culture.

Cardinal Nicholas of Cusa makes important references to Protagoras in his *De beryllo* of 1458 (some manuscripts and early editions confusing him with Pythagoras, as is also true with Alberti's texts).[18] These seem to have developed out of his earlier concern with numbering, measuring and weighing, activities in which the mind of man approached, by assimilation, the nature of the divine intellect. Toward the beginning of book one of his *De sapientia* (written in 1450), the Idiot says, "Since I have said to you that wisdom shouts in the piazzas and its cry is to dwell in the highest places, I will try to show this to you; and first I would like you to say what you see going on here in the market." The Orator replies, "I see over here money being counted, in another corner wares being weighed, in the opposite one oil and other things being measured." To which the Idiot comments, "These are the works of that reason by which men surpass beasts, for the brutes cannot number, weigh and measure; now consider, Orator, and tell me through what, in what, and from what this is done."[19] This, of course, is to assert that counting, weighing and measuring is the measure of man rather than that man is the measure of all things. And the effort of the dialogue is to argue that all these human activities derive from the divine exemplar. "Thus infinite wisdom is simplicity gathering into itself all forms, and it is the most adequate measure of all."[20] Thus, as Plato in the *Laws,* Cusanus declares that "God is the measure of all things."[21] For Plato, it was important to assert this in opposition to Protagoras' dictum. For Cusanus, on the other hand, we know that God is the measure by the similitude of man being the measure of all things—a subtle and crucial difference.

Nicholas does not weaken his stress on measuring as the characteristic human activity. In the first chapter of *De mente* the Idiot says, "I think that no one is or was perfectly a man who did not form some concept of the mind; indeed, I hold and I conjecture that the mind is the measure and limit of all things; in truth, it is called *mens* from *mensurans*."[22] And in chapter nine he is asked, "why, since as you say, Idiot, that it is called mind from measure, is the mind carried so avidly to measuring things?" "So that it may attain the measure of itself . . . ," he replies. In this pursuit of itself as a live measure in measuring other things the human mind also assimilates itself to their modes of being. "For it conforms itself to possibility as it measures all in their possible ways; thus [it conforms] to absolute necessity as it measures all in unity and simplicity as though God; to necessity in [created] complexity as it measures all in its characteristic mode of being; and to determinate possibility as it measures all things accordingly as they exist. It also measures symbolically by means of comparison, as when it uses number and geometric figures, and it transforms itself according to the likeness of such things. Hence, to those subtly perceiving, the mind is the live and unrestricted likeness of the infinite Equality."[23] This means that by its characteristic mode of being, that of measuring, the human mind manifests its likeness to the divine mind, which is the second member of the Trinity, the Word, or, as Cusanus also calls it, Equality.

Needless to say that this is a far cry from what Protagoras is alleged to have meant by anybody, and so far he has not been mentioned. But it presents the necessary context of Cusanus' own thinking within which it can be understood why he became excited about the Protagorean saying and defended it in *De beryllo*. The *beryllus*, of course, is a lens and the dialogue is built around this metaphor of a measuring device. Near the beginning, in enumerating the premisses of his argument, he comes to the third: "In the third place, note the saying of Protagoras: man is the measure of all things." Then follows a statement which we shall quote, followed by the fourth premiss in which he refers to Hermes Trismegistus because the two statements together make so clear his own use of the metaphor of measuring.

> For with sense man measures sensible things, with intellect intelligible things, and he attains to what are beyond the intelligible in excess; and he does this according to our premisses, for while he knows that the cognoscitive soul is the end of knowable things, he knows from the sensitive power that sensible things ought thus to be just as they can be sensed, concerning intelligibles, thus as they can be understood, concerning those which exceed moreover, thus as they exceed. Hence man finds in himself as if in a measuring reason everything that has been created.

The next premiss adds an essential clarification of this assertion of the measuring mind as a microcosm of the created world:

> Hermes Trismegistus said man is a second god. For just as God is the creator of real entities and natural forms, so man is the creator of rational entities and artificial forms which are nothing but likenesses of his own intellect, just as creatures are the likenesses of the divine intellect. Therefore man has an intellect which is in the likeness of the divine intellect in creating.

It is therefore by creating images and likenesses in the image and likeness of the divine intellect that the human intellect gathers into itself the created world. The mind is simultaneously the image of God and the image of the world.

In this famous statement Cusanus is also saying that God creates realities but man creates works of art. Moreover the realities are images of the divine intellect, which is clearly conventional Neoplatonic doctrine. But Cusanus is extending this theory to assert that man both makes images of his own ideas when he creates things and acts, and that he learns to know the realities which God has created only as images and likenesses the knowledge of which man can gain by measuring them. Man can know God as well as sensible and intelligible realities only through measuring images. Hence, as we shall see, he is led to show a more sympathetic understanding of Protagoras' position in the disputes of both Plato and Aristotle against him—that man knows realities only as his own senses reveal them to him.

But to make Cusanus' position clear, we must complete the quotation of this fourth premise:

> Hence [man] creates likenesses of the likenesses of the divine intellect. Just as there are extrinsic likenesses, namely artificial figures, so there are intrinsic likenesses, namely natural forms. In this way man measures his own intellect through the power of his own works. And from this he measures the divine intellect, just as truth is measured through an image; and this is enigmatic knowledge.[24]

Man sees divinity through a glass, darkly, but he also sees earthly realities, which are likenesses of divinity, through the images of his own measuring.

Therefore at the end of *De beryllo,* which is the lens of man's mind which by measuring discovers the unseen truth of the divine glory, he says:

> One thing remains, that we see how man is the measure of things. Aristotle said that Protagoras had said nothing profound in this. Nevertheless it seems to me that he held to something of great soundness. And first I consider that Aristotle rightly said in the beginning of the *Metaphysics* how all men by nature desired to know, and he declared this [desire] to be in the sense of sight, which man does not have for the sake of actions only but because we delight in it because of knowledge as it manifests many different things to us. If therefore man has sense and reason that he may use them not only for conserving life in this life but so that he might know, then sensible things must exist in order to nourish man in a double way, namely, that he might live and that he might know. Moreover it is more important and more noble to know because it has a higher and incorruptible end.[25]

In this statement Cusanus stresses the value of a knowledge of objects which comes through the senses. And he dwells, like Alberti, whose conception of Protagoras so much resembles that of Nicholas, on this *più grassa Minerva,*[26] finding in the very variety, contradictoriness and changeability of the sensual world the manifestation of the divine Creator. By contrast, for Plato and Aristotle, not this subjective experience but the objective knowledge was what mattered (though Cusanus' idea is certainly Platonist). Obviously, however, Protagoras as we are able to know him did not, like Cusanus, have such a religious end in his outlook. Taking into account the controversially different ways he is interpreted, certainly one side of Protagoras' quarrel with both Plato and Aristotle (or rather their quarrel with him) was his emphasis that judgement takes place through the sensation of constantly changing appearance. Cusanus shows here a delight in the sensuous world for which he found support even in the meagre knowledge he had of Protagoras and of Aristotle's criticism of the contradictoriness of his doctrine.

Indeed Cusanus embraces the very contradictoriness of the experience of the world as necessary to its cognition and to apprehension of divinity itself:

> For sensible things are the books of the senses in which the intention of the divine intellect is described in sensible figures, and the intention is the manifestation of God the Creator Himself. Wherefore, if you wonder concerning anything, why is it this way or that, or is constituted this way or that way, there is one reply: because the divine intellect wished to manifest itself to sensible cognition so that it might be known sensibly. For example, why is there so much contrariety in the sensible world? You would say for this reason, because opposites placed next to each other illuminate more, and the one knowledge is of both. So small is sensory cognition that, without the presence of contrariety, it would not apprehend differences. For this reason every sense wants contrary objects that it might discern better; therefore what is required for this is in the objects. For thus it is you progress through touch, taste, smell, sight and hearing. And consider carefully how each sense has a power of knowing, and you will find every object in the sensible world ordered for the service of learning. So the contrariety of primary objects serves tactile learning, that of colors the eyes, and so for all. In all these so varied objects there is an admirable revelation of the divine intellect. [27]

We need not carry this discussion of Cusanus' use of Protagoras further, though he has more to say. What is important to observe is not only that he used Protagoras within the confines of his own intellectual and philosophical system, which was vastly alien to Protagoras, but that he was able to discern the one element in the extremely fragmentary bit of Protagoras' thought known to him that he could exploit and fit to these purposes, namely Protagoras' measuring of the sensible world through individual sensations. This served Cusanus' ambitious and paradoxical goal of showing man that he could even find God manifested in the world of sensible attributes by using his own senses as measuring devices. Although Causanus' dialectic of otherness (derived from the Pseudo-Dionysius and Proclus) must seem undeniably appropriate to anyone versed in the Platonist and Neoplatonist traditions, it also leads him to a kind of sacred sensuousness to match his "learned ignorance." It is essential not to overlook the sincerity of his strategy of achieving theocentrism through anthropocentrism, nor, on the other hand, his truly late medieval delight in sensible objects. [28]

Another great Renaissance Platonist, who had better reason to know Protagoras since he had translated all of Plato's dialogues, including the *Protagoras* and the *Theatetus,* by 1468, namely Marsilio Ficino, found less reason to admire him. At least his casual comments are in a matter of course very negative. He refers, for instance, to thinkers who denied the existence of God, such as Diagoras, or who doubted whether one could prove the existence of God or not, such as Protagoras, but always in a glancing and hostile allusion.[29] He refers, of course, to the well-known fragment, also well-known in the Middle Ages and the Renaissance because it is cited several times in the writings of Cicero.

A more central and important mention of Protagoras has to do with the question of sense-knowledge. In book eleven, chapter six of his *Theologia platonica* Ficino set forth his proofs that the soul is immortal through its capacity to know eternal truths. Asserting that, "there is no truth in sensible things," he asks, "but why not in the soul?", and continues, "perhaps there is truth in the soul, but not, as Protagoras and Epicurus believed, in that part of the soul which is the sense, because it looks outside itself and is compelled to feel with a certain passion and is deluded by the frequent clouds of sensible things."[30] His knowledge of the *Theatetus* is echoed here.

The problem of sense-knowledge, as we saw in Cusanus, was, of course, connected with the Protagorean dictum that man is the measure of all things. Ficino alludes to the saying more than once, usually to dismiss it in an offhand way, as, unlike Cusanus, he considered it totally opposed and alien to his own philosophy. However, Plato's *Theatetus* was constructed around Socrates' exposition and refutation of Protagoras' sensualistic epistemology. Ficino wrote a short commentary on this dialogue, probably in the 1460's.[31] He seems, however, to have made it more an epitome than a commentary, for he follows the argument very closely, introducing little of his own except historical allusions to other thinkers who espoused similar doctrines and references to other Platonic dialogues where similar sophist arguments are refuted, and he does not take any special notice of the section of the dialogue generally designated today as "The Apology of Protagoras." It would seem as if Ficino considered the Protagorean theory of knowledge so palpably false that he had no need to discuss it other than to bring out Socrates' arguments.[32] He also alludes to the Protagorean position, that the opinion of anyone, based on sensation, is as true as that of anyone else, in his commentary on the *Philebus* and also in his commentary on the *Cratylus*. In the latter instance and at the beginning of the commentary on the *Theatetus* he places Protagoras among thinkers such as Heraclitus who regarded all reality as a constantly changing flow. In his commentary on the *Laws*, when he comes to Plato's declaration that God, not man, is the measure of all things, Ficino says, "By these words Plato seems to confute Protagoras, saying man is the measure of things, whose error is subtly refuted in the book *De scientia* (i.e. the *Theatetus*)."[33]

One might expect that a philosopher as deeply influenced by a direct knowledge of Plato as Ficino was, the first Latin to be so since antiquity, would have at some point in the elaboration of his own thinking to reckon with the problems that Protagoras raised. As I have indicated elsewhere, it was important to him to refute the epistemologies of nominalism, which were in some ways a late medieval counterpart to that of Protagoras. Ficino, as a matter of fact, refers to the capacity of the human soul to count and measure in book six of the *Theologia platonica*. In general this was an aspect of Platonism which was not particularly important to Ficino in contrast to Nicholas of Cusa who, as we have seen, turned the measuring capacity of man both toward the world and toward man into a sign of man's similitude to God. Cusanus also stressed sense-knowledge as a part of measuring. Ficino, however, speaks of man's capacity to number and measure as a proof that the soul is not corporeal since number is an image of unity which is incorporeal while everything corporeal is multiple. Measuring and number-ing, therefore, are non-sensory capacities and activities of the human soul and can for Ficino have little to do with Protagoras' sense-knowledge. Ficino introduces them as a contrast to the illusory knowledge of the boy who sees his image in a well and thinks it is himself.[34] Yet something of the dialectical interplay of sense-knowledge of a world in constant flux which is not knowledge but opinion, and the unchanging intellectual knowledge of eternity, which was so important to Plato and in his own way to Cusanus, and which kept Plato at least constantly presenting the ideas of Protagoras in his dialogues, penetrated also into Ficino here. But remark-ably little of it was related by him to Protagoras. In this particular discus-sion he does not mention him once.

On the other hand, it seems characteristic of Ficino that he refers several times to man's innate knowledge of God as stated in the *Protagoras* and makes a more elaborate comment on it in his commentary on the same dialogue. Although the idea is presented by Protagoras as part of his myth depicting the condition of man, Ficino ordinarily refers to it as a statement made by Plato and wishes to refute what he alleges are Protagoras' argu-ments against it. As we shall see his whole treatment is very ambiguous. For instance in book fourteen, chapter ten of the *Theologia* he wishes to answer an objection of "the followers of Lucretius" to his own claim that the knowledge of God, innate in man, was his most characteristic and distinguishing quality. It is objected that such knowledge was inculcated by early political leaders for political purposes. "Not at all," said Ficino:

It is impossible to say how rapidly human discoveries are changed, even true ones, let alone the false and simulated ones. All human customs change in a short time into opposite customs. Also the laws are opposite in different peoples at the same time, and what some consider wicked others think virtuous. Moreover, what is more ancient than religion? And what more glorious? But the founders of the laws certainly did not invent religion for the sake of coercing the people. For religion flourished in the world before there were cities and homes, and the scattered primitive men worshipped God, and those lawgivers themselves feared the divinities. Indeed Plato confirms this in his *Protagoras,* saying that men, even before they assembled or spoke or practiced any arts, from their beginning out of a natural knowledge worshipped God and erected altars and shrines. Moreover, at some point men would have rejected the yoke of religion, so hard it is and contrary to so many goods of life, had it been false and not founded on the stability of truth.

Of course, it was Protagoras who put forth the idea in his speech in the dialogue. But Ficino turns immediately to argue against Protagoras, as though he had said the opposite.

But perchance Protagoras might say religion is not natural but seems so because we drink it in at a tender age. We reply as follows to Protagoras: he learned from infancy to speak and drink, still speech and drink are natural. Everywhere and always men speak and drink because it is natural. But in some times and places they speak and drink in a different manner because the order of action is established by opinion rather than by nature. Similarly God is worshipped among all peoples in all ages because it is natural, although not by the same sacraments and rites. Speech because it is natural attains its end, which is the wish to communicate one to another. Drink also attains its end, which is to restore the body. I do not see why religion is not possessed from birth for its end. Its end is to enjoy God, its wish to enjoy Him forever.[35]

Possibly Ficino makes Protagoras the opponent of the position he took in the dialogue, because he questions his sincerity. Modern scholars have also questioned his sincerity because the notion of both an innate knowledge of God and of virtues seems to contradict other positions Protagoras seems to maintain.[36] Ficino may be considered then the first scholar to resolve the Protagoras question this way.

A little earlier in the *Theologia platonica,* book fourteen, chapter eight, Ficino refers to the same passage of the *Protagoras* in discussing man's similarity to God in that he worships himself. In doing so he actually also worships God because he heeds the voice of conscience which is the face of God in his soul.

They also think it wicked to dishonor the august majesty of their own mind by vile thoughts and sordid earthly cares, as though it were a divine statue. Indeed this natural notion generates shame and modesty in mankind so that we venerate not only the presence of other men as though they were divine but also the conscience of our own mind, as Pythagoras teaches, as though it were the face of God, which eagerly stimulates repentance of misdeeds in us even if we do not fear the punishment, and delights us with the memory of good deeds, as if the celestial soul would always shrink from the earthly blemish of sins. . . . Plato in his *Protagoras* especially considers it to be a sign of our divinity that we alone, as if participants in the divine lot on account of a certain kinship with God, know God and desire Him as our Creator, invoke and love Him as our Father, venerate Him as a King, fear Him as a Lord.[37]

Ficino repeats this passage word for word in chapter two of his *De Christiana religione*.[38] It obviously was a central idea to him. Yet it is specifically this notion of the innate sense of reverence and justice that Plato attributes to Protagoras in his dialogue.

Ficino, it would seem, was of two minds about Protagoras. He found it difficult to grant to him an insight of which he approved. Yet despite attributing it to Plato instead of Protagoras, he really knew that it was not Plato but Protagoras who had spoken both of man's primeval worship of God and his innate moral sense. Ficino's commentary on the *Protagoras*,[39] written presumably in the 1460's, but possibly later, shows that he continues to be ambivalent. Yet at a certain point he feels compelled to give Protagoras some credit, which he later weakens. It occurs at the point where Protagoras agrees to present his ideas in a myth, which Ficino immediately takes to be a reference to what he called the *prisca theologia,* the prehistoric (as it were) possession of religious insights by poet-prophets who present their thoughts in the form of poetic myths. Protagoras' narrative of the gifts of Epimetheus, Prometheus and Zeus obviously appealed to Ficino. He says:

At this point Protagoras by long circumlocutions proves that virtue can be taught. In these narrations it should be noted that he refers to certain mysteries of the ancients (*priscorum*). It is quite legitimate, although he may be a sophist, to read some good in him, and though he speaks prolixly in Plato, to derive something useful.[40]

Ficino then proceeds, not so much to paraphrase as to interpret the passage allegorically, relating it to his own conception of the creation and development of human civilization. He makes it quite clear that he knows it was Protagoras who attributed the knowledge of divinity and worship to man before he possessed the arts or civil justice.

Indeed, because that divine gift revealed itself immediately on account of that very kinship with the higher beings, man worshipped God before he spoke or practiced any of the arts; certainly on account of its miraculous power he first lifted the divine gift into something divine before he extended it through human beings.

Ficino even finds a similarity to Christ and to the Genesis account of creation.

> Prometheus, afflicted with pain on account of that gift, signifies that our demonic overseer [Christ], in whom also there can be passions, was moved by a certain mercy toward us, considering us on account of that gift of reason itself, given, or rather excited by him to lead a so much more miserable life on earth than the beasts as it is more care-ridden and deplorable. Protagoras, having observed this, put Epimetheus so far as it concerned this condition ahead of Prometheus. This, moreover, seems to be in a certain way similar to that saying, "It repenteth me to have made man (Gen. 6:6)." Also it may be recalled that man, just as it is held here as well as in Moses, was created last and out of earth. Also here the world had its beginning as if in a Mosaic way. But we speak of these things in other places.[41]

Ficino continued to interpret Protagoras' speech, developing his ideas on the gifts of *aidos* and *dikê* (*pudor et iustitia* as he translates them), showing how the former is really *temperantia* and that Plato would add *prudentia* and, in time of war, *fortitudo,* thus getting the four cardinal virtues. Ficino shows a high esteem for this account of the ethical basis of *civilitas* which one must assume reflects his close association with the humanist tradition and humanist moralists.[42] Yet it is the Platonist translator of Plato who is first able to appreciate this account of the origins of civilization.

> We, moreover, hold concerning all which has hitherto been disputed that it reposes in the depths of the mind in that golden saying of the ancients. First of all God Himself provides and counsels in all ways everywhere for our life and safety. Then civil virtue is a divine gift by which the commonwealth will be rightly and happily governed, lest anyone should perchance trust in himself without divine grace. . . . Finally we may remember how necessary it is that inviolate justice be sent from heaven, if those voices of the ancients sound eagerly in our ears. At one time miserable mortals, before civility was delivered from heaven, could not live separately lest they be continually attacked by wild beasts, nor again in communities lest they mutually destroy each other. Thus safety, which all the arts at once could not grant to us, at last was granted by justice alone.

Ficino's interest in this version of divinely given virtues out of which civilized society originated but which needed to be sustained by education in the humanities and by the very processes of society itself was obviously strong, however grudging his willingness to recognize Protagoras' author-ship of it. He continues summarizing Protagoras' description of the role of the arts, but he clearly believes that the original gift of aptitude for justice, as a gift of grace, was more important than Protagoras' argument that virtues can be taught. He concludes by saying:

> After this Socrates, lest the sophist might be admired by the audience on account of certain good things he narrated, having taken them from others, by a certain ironic, urbane and artful method of argu-ment rendered him ridiculous to those who were present.[43]

Thus Ficino, as many scholars after him, saw a basic contradiction between the two positions of Protagoras presented in Plato's dialogue, namely that reverence and justice are divine gifts innate in mankind, and that they may be and need to be taught. He either attributed the first idea to Plato, toned down Protagoras' meaning, or interpreted him as having borrowed it from others. Protagoras' use of myth excited him because he could relate it to his own notion of *prisca theologia,* and Protagoras' concern with the moral basis of civilization received his approval however much he doubted his authorship. He was little interested in the man-the-measure question, accepting Plato's refutation of its sensualism of the *Theatetus,* whereas it was just this question that attracted Alberti and Cusanus.

Other references to and discussions of Protagoras in the Renaissance may well be turned up by further study. Within the frame of those we have examined there emerges an interesting but tentative conclusion. Interest in Protagoras on the part of the humanists and rhetorical theorists was small or anecdotal. Alberti, who was led to cite him because of his mathematical and artistic concerns, also did see the possible relationship of his man-the-measure dictum for discussing the nature and nobility of man. Protagoras does not seem to have interested other writers on the nature and dignity of man, though this must be subject to further study. Nor did he attract those concerned with the role of the humanities as the basis of civilization. It was the Platonists, Nicholas of Cusa and Marsilio Ficino, who dealt most centrally with his ideas, Ficino having the best knowledge of him and interpreting him negatively. Perhaps this is not surprising, since Pro-tagoras' thought has come down to us from antiquity primarily in philo-sophical sources and it was the ancient philosophers who seem to have discussed him more than the rhetoricians. As a Greek "humanist" Pro-tagoras seems to have made more of a stir within the confines of philosophy. Whatever his thought may have been, he was honored by having Democ-ritus, Plato and Aristotle as his critics.

Protagoras in the Renaissance seems to have been understood in the context of each commentator's own thought and concerns, rather than with true understanding and precision. But this too is not surprising in view of the fragmentary knowledge possessed of him. Nor did the Renaissance disagree concerning Protagoras more than modern scholarship does, nor did it misunderstand him any more inadequately. In fact, in certain ways what is even more surprising is how many of the modern issues concerning the meaning of Protagoras' thought are already recognizable in Renaissance discussions. What is very certain, however, is that the Renaissance did not discern in him its predecessor, however much we today are inclined to see a resemblance.

NOTES

1. The so-called "rehabilitation of the sophists" is an interesting chapter of recent intellectual history which cannot be surveyed here. Werner Jaeger's *Paideia: The Ideals of Greek Culture* (trans. Gilbert Highet, second English edition, New York, 1945, first German edition 1933, I, 286–331: "The Sophists: Their position in the history of culture, The origins of educational theory and the ideal of culture, Education and the political crisis") has had perhaps the greatest influence in suggesting the ancestral "humanist" character of the sophists, and Jaeger stresses the role of Protagoras among them. Although Jaeger regarded Socrates and Plato as the culmination of Greek Paideia, his stress on the moral and educational role of Protagoras has suggested his similarity to the Italian humanists. Two books of 1948 continued to emphasize the continuity of an educational-rhetorical tradition from the sophists to, and through the Middle Ages: H. I. Marrou, *Histoire de l'éducation dans l'antiquité* (Paris, 1948) and E. R. Curtius, *Europäische Literatur und lateinisches Mittelalter* (Bern, 1948). It was P. O. Kristeller who in his Martin Classical Lectures, published in 1955 as *The Classics and Renaissance Thought* (Cambridge, Mass.; repr. New York, 1961 in *Renaissance Thought: The Classic, Scholastic and Humanist Strains*), led scholars to a more explicit interest in the possible sophistic origins of Renaissance humanism, though the Roman rhetorical tradition was always seen as the immediate model. My essay of 1960 on Bartolommeo della Fonte's inaugural orations ended on this note: "A Humanist's Image of Humanism: the Inaugural Orations of Bartolommeo della Fonte," *Studies in the Renaissance* 7 (1960), 125. J. E. Seigel's *Rhetoric and Philosophy in Renaissance Humanism* (Princeton, 1968) attempts to follow Kristeller's conceptions closely and suggests Cicero as the model of Renaissance humanists combining rhetoric and philosophy, Gorgias and sophist rhetoric as a model for "anti-philosophical" humanists such as Lorenzo Valla. Protagoras receives no mention. Heinrich Gomperz, *Sophistik und Rhetorik* (Leipzig and Berlin, 1912), had stressed a similar dissidence between Greek sophists and philosophers, and characterized the former, including Protagoras, as strictly rhetorical in their positions. Meanwhile Mario Unter-

steiner's *I sofisti* (Turin, 1949, Eng. trans. by Kathleen Freeman, Oxford, 1954) attempted a major reassessment of the importance of the sophists, especially Protagoras and Gorgias whose philosophical importance he sought to vindicate. Antonio Capizzi devoted an entire volume to a markedly extended edition and translation of the testimonies and fragments of Protagoras, to a philological analysis of key terms critical of Untersteiner in some respects, and to his own interpretation of Progatoras' place in the history of philosophical thought: *Protagora. Le testimonianze e i frammenti. Edizione riveduta e ampliata con uno studio sulla vita, le opere, il pensiero e la fortuna* (Florence, 1955). Also Rodolfo Mondolfo in his *La comprensione del soggetto umano nell' antichità classica* (Florence, 1958, Ital. trans. from original Spanish edition of Buenos Aires, 1955) gives major play to the role of Protagoras and the sophists in the development of an ancient activistic and subjective concept of man that was revived in the Renaissance. Of predictable future significance is W. K. C. Guthrie's third volume of his *A History of Greek Philosophy: The Fifth Century Enlightenment* (Cambridge, 1969) which devotes the first three hundred and nineteen pages to the sophists and gives particular emphasis to the "humanist" character of Protagoras' thought. Nancy Struever in her *The Language of History in the Renaissance: Rhetoric and Historical Consciousness in Florentine Humanism* (Princeton, 1970) is very much influenced by Untersteiner and other recent studies of the sophists and constantly makes comparisons between the qualities of Italian humanist ideas and those of the Greek sophists. Her study makes essentially external comparisons between the two groups whereas I attempt an "internal" comparison in this article by looking at how Protagoras was interpreted in the Renaissance. The above account is very inadequate, particularly on recent studies of the sophists, and conveys little idea of the revisionistic character of these discussions. My allusions to Protagoras will inevitably reflect some of these new conceptions, but I gratefully avoid setting forth a synthesis of my own since my concern is with Renaissance views of him.

2. In his *Sophistik und Rhetorik* (Leipzig and Berlin, 1912). See n. 1.
3. E. G. Salutati, *De fato et fortuna,* Cod. Urb. Lat. 201, f. 21 and f. 23ᵛ; cf. Trinkaus, *In Our Image and Likeness,* I (Chicago, 1970), 86–7, 357, n. 91.
4. Capizzi's (431–4) much more extensive assemblage of ancient references to Protagoras are conveniently indexed.
5. T. E. Mommsen, "Petrarch and the story of the Choice of Hercules," in *Medieval and Renaissance Studies* (Ithaca, 1959), 175–96.
6. P. O. Kristeller, *Supplementum Ficinianum* (Florence, 1937), I, cil–cl, lx–lxi.
7. Plato, *Protagoras,* 320b–322b.
8. See n. 6.
9. *Metaph.*: 1007b18–23, 1009a6–13, 1009b1–6, 1047a4–7, 1053a35–36, 1062b12–13. Cf. Capizzi's index and passages.
10. R. H. Popkin, *The History of Scepticism from Erasmus to Descartes* (New York, 1964, repr. 1968 ed. used here), 17, n. 3 citing mss. supplied by P. O. Kristeller: Marc. lat. X 267 (3460) and Vat. lat. 2990, ff. 266–381ᵛ; cf. Kristeller, *Iter Italicum,* II (London and Leiden, 1967), 252 and 358. C. B.

Schmitt, *Gianfrancesco Pico della Mirandola* (The Hague, 1967), 49–54 and *passim*.

11. L. M. Capelli, *Petrarque: Le traité De suis ipsius et multorum ignorantia* (Paris, 1906), 89; cf. Cassirer, Kristeller and Randall eds., *The Renaissance Philosophy of Man* (Chicago, 1948), 125–6.

12. Cf. L. B. Alberti, *Opere volgari,* ed. Cecil Grayson, I (Bari, 1960), 379; L. B. Alberti, *The Family in Renaissance Florence, I libri della famiglia,* Eng. trans. by Renée N. Watkins (Columbia, S. C., 1969), 2.

13. Grayson ed., 131–2; Watkins trans., 133–4. The translation is my own, slightly more literal than Watkins'.

14. Cf. Leon Battista Alberti, *On Painting and Sculpture, The Latin Texts of 'De Pictura' and 'De Statua,'* edited with translations, introduction and notes by Cecil Grayson (London, 1972), 3.

15. *Ibid.,* p. 53 Grayson's translation; pp. 52, 54 for Alberti's original Latin version. For Alberti's subsequent Italian version, cf. *Della Pittura,* ed. Luigi Mallé (Florence, 1950), 69–70.

16. Rensselaer W. Lee, "Ut pictura poesis; Humanistic Theory of Painting," *Art Bulletin* 22 (1940), 197–269, esp. 201, 219; J. R. Spencer, "Ut rhetorica pictura," *Journal of the Warburg and Courtauld Institutes* 20 (1957), 26–44; esp. 31–2, 36–44.

17. Urb. lat. 1207, ff. 151ᵛ–158ᵛ; *Opera omnia* (Basel, 1540) 744–5, Lib. III, cap. xiii, "De dilemmate antistrephonteque sive conversione." Cf. Aulus Gellius, *Noctes Atticae,* V, 10.

18. Nicholas of Cusa, *Opera omnia* (Heidelberg edition indicated below as H), vol. XI, *De beryllo,* ed. L. Baur (Leipzig, 1940), 6, 13ff.; 20, 5ff.; 48, 14ff.; 51, 6. *Opera omnia* (Strassbourg, 1488 edition, reissued, ed. Paul Wilpert, Berlin, 1967 indicated below as S r) II, p. 711, 6; pp. 717–8, 24; pp. 734–5, 65, 66; p. 736, 69. Giovanni Santinello. *Leon Battista Alberti, una visione estetica del mondo e della vita* (Florence, 1962), 287, n. 44 alludes to the mixture of usage of "Pythagoras" and "Protagoras" both by Alberti and Cusanus and shows that Cusanus at least understood it was properly "Protagoras." Cf. also Luis Martinez-Gomez, "El hombre 'Mensura rerum' en Nicolàs de Cusa," *Pensamiento* (Madrid) 21 (1965), 41–63, of which there is a resumé in *Nicolò Cusano agli inizi del mondo moderno: Atti del Congresso internazionale in occasione del V centenario della morte di Niccolò Cusano, Bressanone, 6–10 settembre 1964* (Florence, 1970), 339–45.

19. *Idiota de sapientia* (Heidelburg edition, ed. L. Baur, Leipzig, 1937), V, p. 6, lines 5–13 (Strassbourg reprint), I, 217: "Quoniam tibi dixi . . . etc."

20. H: V, p. 20, lines 16–18; S r: I, 224: "Sic infinita sapientia est simplicitas omnes formas complicans et omnium adaequatissima mensura. . . ."

21. 716c–d.

22. H: V, 48, lines 17–20; S r: I, 238: "Puto neminem esse . . . etc."

23. H : V, 89, lines 8–11: S r: I, 262: "Philosophus. Admiror, cum mens . . . etc." H: V, 90, lines 3–10; S r: I, 262: "Conformat enim se . . . etc."

24. H: XI, 6f.,; S r: II, 711, 6, 7: "Tercio notabis dictum protagore: hominem

esse rerum mensuram. Nam cum sensu mensurat sensibilia, cum intellectu intelligibilia, et quae sunt supra intelligibilia in excessu attingit, et hoc facit ex premissis, nam dum scit animam cognoscitivam esse finem cognoscibilium: scit ex potentia sensitiva sensibilia sic esse debere: sicut sentiri possunt, ita de intelligibilibus ut intelligi possunt, excedentia autem ita ut excedant. Unde in se homo repperit quasi in ratione mensurante omnia creata."

"Quarto adverte. Hermetem trismegistum dicere hominem esse secundum deum. Nam sicut deus est creator entium realium et naturalium formarum, ita homo rationalium entium et formalium artificialium quae non sunt nisi sui intellectus similitudines, sicut creaturae dei divini intellectus similitudiness, ideo homo habet intellectum qui est similitudo divine intellectus in creando. Hinc creat similitudines similitudinum divini intellectus: sicut sunt extrinsecae artificiales figurae, similitudines intrinsecae naturales formae, unde mensurat suum intellectum per potentiam operum suorum, et ex hoc mensurat divinum intellectum, sicut veritas mensuratur per imaginem, et hec est enigmatica scientia."

25. H: XI, 48f. S r: II, 734: "Restat adhuc unum ut videamus quomodo homo est mensura rerum, aristoteles dicit prothagoram in hoc nihil profundi dixisse, mihi tamen magna valde dixisse videtur, et primo considero recte aristotelem in principio metaphisice dixisse: quomodo omnes homines natura scire desiderant, et declarat hoc in sensu visus quem homo non habet propter operari tantum, sed diligimus ipsum propter cognoscere, quia multas nobis differentias manifestat. Si igitur sensum et rationem habet homo non solum ut illis utatur pro hac vita conservanda: sed ut cognoscat tunc sensibilia ipsum hominem pascere habent dupliciter: scilicet ut vivat et cognoscat. Est autem principalius cognoscere et nobilius: quia habet altiorem et incorruptibilem finem."

26. Alberti, *Della pittura* (*op. cit.*), 55. He wishes to be regarded not as a mathematician measuring abstract forms but as a painter placing things to be seen, and: ". . . per questo useremo quanto dicono più grassa Minerva. . . ." Giovanni Santinello argues the interrelatedness of the thought of Alberti and Cusanus in his appendix, "Nicolò Cusano e Leon Battista Alberti: Pensieri sul bello e sull'arte," 265–96, reprinted from *Nicolò da Cusa, Relazioni tenute al convegno interuniversitario di Bressanone nel 1960* (Florence, 1960), 147–83.

27. H: XI, 49, 8.; S r: 735, 66: "Sensibilia enim sunt sensuum libri in quibus est intentio divini intellectus in sensibilibus figuris descripta, et est intentio: ipsius dei creatoris manifestatio. Si igitur dubitas de quacunque re cur hoc sic vel sic sit vel sic sic se habeat: est una responsio, quia sensitive cognitioni se divinus intellectus manifestare voluit ut sensitive cognoscetur, puta cur in sensibili mundo est tanta contrarietas, dices ideo quia opposita iuxta se posita magis elucescunt, et una est utrius que scientia: adeo parva est cognitio sensitiva quod sine contrarietate differentias non apprehenderet, quare omnis sensus vult obiecta contraria ut melius discernat, ideo que ad hoc requiruntur sunt in obiectis. Sic enim si pergis per tactum: gustum: olfactum: visum: et auditum. Et attente consideras quam quisque sensus habeat cognoscendi virtutem tu reperies omnia obiecta in mundo sensibili et ad servitium cognosci-

tive ordinata. Sic contrarietas primarum qualitatum servit tactive; colorum oculis: et ita de omnibus. In omnibus his adeo variis admirabilis est ostensio divini intellectus."

28. In this, despite the sparseness of the texts, Cusanus made a brilliant use of Protagoras as the dialectical counter-part of Parmenides, whom he knew of through Proclus' commentary on Plato's *Parmenides,* the latter, affirming being as unity and identity, the former speaking for the Parmenidean realm of Non-being with its multiplicity, contradiction and otherness. Some modern students, interestingly, also interpret Protagoras as deliberately affirming the opposite realm to Parmenides' Being and see his thought as formed in reaction to the Pythagorean-Parmenidean tradition rather than simply being an outgrowth of the Heraclitean one as Plato seems to have supposed. Cf. especially Untersteiner, pp. 45 ff. and p. 50, n. 18 where he discusses earlier literature. Cf. also Italo Lana, *Protagora* (Turin, 1950), 80–83.

29. E. g. *Commentarium in Philebum,* cap. xxv, *Opera omnia* (Basel, 1572, repr. Turin, 1959), 1231; *In Convivium platonis,* Orat. III, cap. v, *Opera,* 1333.

30. *Theologia platonica,* ed. R. Marcel (Paris, 1964), II, 140: "Non est igitur in rebus sensibilibus . . . etc."

31. *Opera,* 1274–81. Cf. Kristeller, *Supplementum,* I, cxvi.

32. It is of some interest, however, that Ficino [p. 1279: "Hinc Theatetus, scientiam esse veram opinionem . . . etc."] seems to assign Protagoras' position that knowledge is true opinion to the realm of the orator and of public affairs, rather than science.

33. Cf. *Opera,* 1235 (*Philebus*), 1275 (*Theatatus*), 1311 (*Cratylus*), and 1499–1500 (*Laws*): "Quippe quum Deus omnium sit mensura, praecipue nobis, qui videlicet eatenus vel prosequi, vel fugere debemus singula, quatenus divinae menti voluntatique vel consonare, vel dissonare censentur. Hinc illud in Platonis epistola: Sapienti quidem viro lex Deus est, insipienti vero libido. Ambiguus vero hic legitur textus: alibi enim legitur ut traduxi. Quibus verbis Plato videtur Protagoram confutare, dicentem rerum mensuram hominem esse. Cuius error in libro de Scientia (i.e. *Theatetus*) subtiliter confutatur."

34. *Theologia platonica* (ed. Marcel), Lib. VI, cap. 2, vol. I, pp. 227–8. On Ficino's rejection of nominalism cf. *In Our Image and Likeness* (Chicago, 1970), 466–7.

35. *Theologia,* vol. II, 289–90: "Dici enim non potest . . . etc." to ". . . suum votum perpetuo frui."

36. For discussions of this controversy cf. Capizzi (255–62), who rejects Protagorean authorship, and Guthrie (III, 63–5, 265–6, 268–9), who accepts Protagoras as author and points to the statement on innate knowledge of divinity as the sticking-point of the controversy.

37. *Theologia,* II, 274: "Augustam quoque suae mentis maiestatem . . . etc." to ". . . timemus ut dominum "

38. *Opera,* 2.

39. *Opera,* 1196–1200. It is possible and likely that this epitome was written before 1469 along with his translations, in accord with Kristeller, *Supplementum,* I, cxvi. The content, however, particularly the reference to *prisca the-*

ologia, suggests it could have been written after 1474, the date of the completion of the *Theologia platonica* and the composition of *De Christiana religione.* It was obviously written before 1484 when it was first published with the *Opera platonis.*

40. *Opera,* 1297–8: "Ad haec Protagoras longis probat ambagibus doceri posse virtutem. In quibus notanda quaedam priscorum refert mysteria. Decet quamvis Sophista sit, nonnulla etiam legisse bona, et cum prolixe loquatur apud Platonem, utilia quaedam adducere."

41. *Opera,* 1298: "Quoniam vero divinum . . . etc." to ". . . mundum initium habuisse." Ficino goes on to develop his interpretation of the myth of Prometheus in a significant way, as has been noted by Olga Raggio, "The Myth of Prometheus, Its Survival and Metamorphoses up to the Eighteenth Century," *Journal of the Warburg and Courtauld Institutes* 21 (1958), 54, n. 56. Perhaps insufficient attention has been given to Protagoras' role, as depicted by Plato, in providing here a basic western myth of civilization. Ficino, though citing also Plato's *Philebus* and his *Timaeus,* basically follows Protagoras' version that Prometheus could give the intellect and technical arts but not *civilis virtus* which had to come from Zeus through Hermes. "Iuppiter igitur per Mercurium, id est, per angelum divinae voluntatis interpretem, civilis scientiae leges, id est, voluntatis suae decreta ad humanae societatis generisque salutem spectantia mentibus nostris inscribit . . . Unde intimus in nobis praesidet iudex inextinguibile rationis lumen, rectum veri falsique et boni malique examen, inevitabilis conscientiae stimulus."

42. *Opera,* 1298. Cf. also for Ficino's sense of the civic role of humanism the passage on same page beginning: "Cum vero ostenderit hactenus civilem virtutem . . . etc." to ". . . sed arbitrio, et exercitatione proveniant."

43. *Opera,* 1299: "Nos autem omnibus . . . etc." to ". . . feliciter gubernaturum." and "Denique quam necessaria . . . etc." to ". . . illum praesentibus deridendum."

PART TWO

Renaissance and Reformation

Humanist Treatises on the
Status of the Religious

Due attention has long been given to *philosophia moralis,* claimed as the fifth *studia humanitatis* by Italian humanists from the early fifteenth century, and as such a subject properly theirs. Scholars have been interested in "The Moral Thought of Renaissance Humanism"[1] (as Professor Kristeller entitled his recent survey) primarily for the special attitudes of humanists toward 'man',[2] toward 'nobility',[3] toward 'wisdom',[4] toward 'happiness',[5] toward 'civic'[6] activity and good citizenship. They have paid attention to attempts the humanists made to reconcile ancient philosophies with Christianity, principally those stemming from Florentine Neoplatonism. They have emphasized the scholarly activities of the humanists in editing and translating patristic writing—Latin and especially Greek. Less interest seems to have been shown in those humanist treatises that dealt directly with traditional medieval problems of ecclesiastical morality or with questions of Christian religious thought—not to call it 'theology'—or in the devotional writings and lay sermons of the humanists. In saying this, I am not forgetting the many contributions such as Garin's short but penetrating surveys (published in 1948 and in 1952 and reprinted in 1961 in *La Cultura filosofica del rinascimento italiano*[7]), or Kristeller's judicious summary in the fourth lecture of his *Classics and Renaissance Thought.*[8] Nor am I unfamiliar with the sweeping interpretation of humanism as essentially a chapter in the history of Christianity made by Toffanin and his followers. The contributions of Angeleri, Buck, and Seidelmayer are also of importance.[9]

The present paper is an attempt to discuss in greater detail than is usual the content of three of the more important humanist treatises in this area. The particular treatises were selected because they can supply (as it turns out) three different answers to the question of how the humanists viewed the position of special sanctity or meritoriousness granted emphatically and traditionally to the members of religious orders during the middle ages. These three authors—Francesco Petrarca, Coluccio Salutati, and Lorenzo Valla—were, moreover, certainly among the more important

This article, which first appeared in *Studies in the Renaissance* 11 (1964):7–45, led directly to the conception of my book, *In Our Image and Likeness,* and introduced my ideas concerning the religiosity and lay religious emphases of the humanists.

and influential—I hesitate to add representative—humanists. But whatever the impact of their authors, these treatises do illustrate how much the question of the value of their kind of secular existence and scholarly activities in comparison to the life of the religious, so generally granted superior value, was a matter of persistent concern to the humanists. As will also become evident, they illustrate the variety of ways in which the life and status of the regular clergy could be viewed by humanists with, at the same time, perfect consistency with their humanistic or classical allegiances.

One rightly starts with the *De otio religioso* of Petrarch.[10] In many respects this work is extremely traditional in its view of the status of the regular clergy. It does not in any way suggest that the monastic life was defective or inferior or even simply of equal value to life in the world. The status of the monk is regarded as both easier than that of the layman, because its objectives were more clear and it was more sheltered, and at the same time more strenuous, since the 'retirement of the religious' was a withdrawal from the world in order to do battle. Petrarch several times called the monks *militia Christi,* a notion that might be contrasted with Erasmus' criticism of monastic formalism in his *Enchiridion militis Christiani* written for a definitely secular Christian knight.

As in so many of Petrarch's writings, his meanings and intentions are revealed in his comments on his own relationship to the situation. This treatise was intended as a 'thank-you-note' to the Carthusian monks of Montrieux (Provence) with whom he stayed in January 1347 on a visit to his brother Gherardo, a member of this house.[11] Because at that time he had hurriedly passed over what this visit was to mean to him, he hoped to pay the tongue's debt with his fingers, if not more graciously, at least more durably. And to avoid the disease common to preachers of being both loquacious and deaf, he proposed so to modify his style that it would be a sermon to his present self and a letter to the absent monks, 'although, as I will confess it, in the most and greater part I am present'.[12] Thus, as in his *Secret,*[13] he again sets forth an ideal to which he subscribes but to which in his own life he does not or cannot conform. 'Listen', he tells them, 'rather to what I am saying than examine how I am living'.[14]

Although there is no evidence that he was ordained as a priest, Petrarch enjoyed the living of a number of benefices granted to him as a kind of ecclesiastical patronage of his literary career. But he never actively filled the priestly office. As Wilkins has shown,[15] in most respects he thought and acted as a layman. In this treatise, however, he took the opportunity afforded to preach, not so much to himself, as he proposed, but to the Carthusian brothers he addressed. Passing quickly from the troubles and perils of life in this world, introduced by citation of the penitential Psalm xlvi, he dwelt at first upon the theme *Vacate,* rest ye, retire, withdraw, urged on the brothers as having for its goal, not war, but eternal peace.

Unlike the Aristotelian teaching that one labors for the sake of rest, here one rests for the sake of rest.[16] 'Among others labor is sought for the sake of labor, among you quiet for the sake of quiet.'[17] He develops this opening theme rhetorically with many urgings and warnings against the temptations of life.[18] 'Love not the world and those things which are in it, for all is lust of the flesh, lust of the eyes, and worldly ambition; therefore Augustine [cf. *Confessions*, bk. 10] warns and informs us of these; but there are infinite other sayings of this kind for the counsel and consolation of souls.'[19] He repeats a great many of these. Then he turns to the traditional list of admonitions drawn from so many medieval pastoral works such as Gregory I's *Book of Pastoral Care*: let it be said to the greedy; let it be said to the lustful . . . ; let it be said to the melancholy . . . ; etc. 'Let it be said to the penitent, "Joy will be in heaven over one sinner doing penance' ",[20] and many more. Each of the individual counsels appropriate to the particular sin or sinner is drawn from the Scriptures. He advises the brothers to avoid all danger and not to test their own powers of resistance, for they are arts of the adversary. One step follows the other upward or downward; in this he follows St. Benedict and St. Bernard. 'Have your profession before your eyes, keep your vow, fulfill the rule; if you do this easily, it is sufficient.'[21] Each brother should know and beware of his own special weakness. 'Anger tortured this one, lust this, pride elevated another, *accidia* depressed that one.' Just because you are in the camp of Christ and under the best leader, do not think you are safe. Avoid especially the three great enemies: the snares of the world, the enticement of the flesh, the artifices of demons. Thus for twelve long pages in Rotondi's edition he has clung to the traditional hortatory formulae.[22]

Reference to the enemies of the monks leads to their war with Satan and the need not to flee from the victor to the vanquished. Here the humanist and historian of the illustrious men of Rome can add something special. 'We read in secular histories', Petrarch says, 'of the mockery of Labienus, who leaving the victorious Caesar crossed over to Pompey. . . . How much more justly should he be laughed at who, deserting Christ the most victorious king, flees to'[23] Satan? Then pointing out that military commanders try their troops in battle in order to know their qualities, so our Commander also tries us, although He knows us, that we may come to know ourselves and not, blind and ungrateful, attribute to ourselves powers that are His. To support this thought he quotes Cicero, 'O immortal gods, for I attribute to you what are yours. . . .' This gave him the opportunity to insert in a long parenthesis one of his apologies for Cicero's use of the plural 'gods' and a statement of his admiration and hope for Cicero, despite his paganism, because 'he had taught how the invisible things of God are seen through those which are made'.[24]

He then requotes the Ciceronian passage in a paraphrase after quoting a passage on the dangers of servitude to demons in St. Augustine's *De vera religione,* a work which Petrarch had been constantly citing, though following only somewhat freely. ('Et Augustinus in eo libro quem sepe hodie in testimonium arcesso—loquenti enim de otio religioso, quid opportunius quam *Vere religionis* liber astipuletur?')[25] Cicero can offer great consolation in keeping up the struggle against the powers of darkness.[26] And the great insecurity of life came not only from the threat of spiritual powers but from unforeseen calamities and the unexpected deaths of temporal existence. Therefore, he urges the brothers to constant vigilance, to avoid the enjoyment of peace, to 'choose war, not indeed for its own sake but for Christ's glory and eternal peace' (this time agreeing with the Aristotelian saying he earlier spurned). And he urges them to this by 'an example drawn from the gentiles' where not only Cato but Appius Claudius and Quintus Metellus warned lest 'security, *otium,* and quiet overturn what fear, *negotium,* and trouble kept in full vigor'.[27]

Next the enemies are dealt with, and this leads him away from the traditional temptations of the world, the flesh, and the demons to the realm of faith and doctrine. Men do not worship ivory, wood, or golden images of God.

> Nevertheless, in our own age, we see so many believe in them, that . . . the gold and silver gods, whom ancient kings, instructed by the words of holy priests, tore down out of reverence to Christ, are eagerly renovated today in injury to Christ by our kings and prelates. If indeed this is so, although they do not worship silver and gold as gods, . . . nevertheless, gold and silver are cultivated with as much reverence as Christ Himself is not, and often the live God is despised out of admiration for inanimate metals.

And it is no better to succumb to the madness of worshipping Hercules the furious, the homicide Mars, the adulterer Jove, or the thief Mercury.[28] A careful reader of the writings of their worshippers can discover for himself what the greatest prophets and the *Institutes* of Lactantius[29] tell us, that these gods are demons. Nor should we listen to those who have no faith in Christ and still expect a future Messiah. The destruction of Jerusalem, described by Josephus, should convince us of the justice of God's punishment of the Jews for the impiety and lack of gratitude.

> Enough on the Jews. What more? should we listen to the dolorous fables of Mahomet, or the quarrels and inscrutable ambiguities of the philosophers, or the poison of the insolent Averroes, . . . or, perchance, the sacrileges of Fotinus, the trifles of the Manicheans, or the blasphemies of Arius? And if all those things are far away from wholesome hearts, if neither the most miserable error of the pagans,

the obstinate blindness of the Jews, the hateful madness of the Saracens, the windy sophisms of the false philosophers, nor the devious and exotic dogmas of the heretics touch or delight souls or offer scarcely any hope, what should we regard, what do, what port should we seek in the shipwreck of this life except Christ in Whom all cast the anchor of their hope.[30]

And thus the monks are exhorted to renewed faith in the infinite mercy of God Who sent Christ His Son to dwell among us.

This leads to the discussion of the Advent, predicted both by Isaiah and the Erythraean sybil. Both Lactantius and Augustine testified to the agreement of the Biblical prophecies and the sybilline. And the great age of the sybils—dating back to the time of Romulus and to even before the Trojan Wars—cannot be doubted.[31] Then citing the well-known passages from Vergil—*Eclogue* vi, 6, 7 and *Aeneid* vi, 798–800—he added:

This, indeed, religious and pious reader, although spoken of Caesar, rather concerned the Celestial Emperor, whose advent was preceded by signs in all the world. Hearing these, the poet, not aspiring higher, applied them to the advent of the Roman emperor, than whom he knew none greater; if the true light had flooded his eyes, no doubt he would have applied them to the other. Now indeed to us, thanks to Him who even so undeservedly loved us, all these things are clear without any external witnesses, and the rays of divine light so overflow the eyes of the faithful that there is no blind man who does not see in his mind the sun of justice, Christ, and although by truth itself, it has been most truthfully said: 'Blessed are the eyes which see what you see.'[32]

Those who knew Christ in the flesh are next compared with the subsequent generations who must know Him by faith, and he gratefully follows the books of St. Augustine, 'that standard-bearer of the City of God', in refuting the doubters and the enemies of the faith.[33] Thus in his own day rustics are seen firmer in faith than the apostle St. Thomas and not demanding to see the nail holes and the wound. And on the other hand, considering the condition of mankind, it is a blessing that 'although the Son of God punishes as a judge he also shows mercy like a father'.

Behold our weakness is before our eyes always and we do nothing which does not warn us of the human condition and misery. Some have written whole books and others fine treatises concerning this. Pliny in the seventh of his *Natural History* briefly touched on this but in excellent syle and a florid richness of sentences. And Augustine dealt more widely with it in the *City of God*. Concerning it Cicero above all filled the book of his consolation. There was also some impulse in me to say something about this.[34]

From all this faith lifts us. 'Therefore rejoice, human nature, from the extremes of misery made happier than you could become by [your own] nature alone.'[35]

In this Petrarch subscribes to the Christian-Augustinian view of history as occurring within the context of divine providence and the salvation of mankind in the fulness of time. How does this view relate to the new secular conception of the succession of antiquity, dark ages, and modern times, which the late Professor Mommsen found adumbrated in Petrarch's *De viris illustribus?*[36] That Petrarch was himself aware of this question is shown by the fact that in continuing the passage just quoted he makes use of the occasion to differentiate between the kind of knowledge that antiquity affords and what can come only from Christian faith.

> Heed this, O men of literary talent, listen, Plato, Aristotle, Pythagoras; not that ridiculous circuit of souls and vain metempsychosis, but rather the secret of true salvation is hidden here.

Varro, Cicero, Demosthenes, Vergil, and Homer are also thus addressed.

> You have left us much concerning clouds, rain-storms, lightning, winds, ice, snow, tempests, hail, much on the nature of animals, the power of herbs, the qualities of things, much, finally, concerning the heaving of the sea, the quaking of the earth, the motions of the heavens and the stars, sharply disputed and subtly treated. But in what ways heaven may be joined and united with earth, this alone of all you did not see. . . . Between heaven and earth, certainly the distance, I confess, is great but finite, between God and man infinite. . . . Certainly it is well known that in some of your books God is preached and His Word, and much about the highest point of faith and the coeternal persons of Father and Son, which is in agreement with the evangelical Scriptures, according to Augustine, namely, that, 'In the beginning was the Word, and the Word was with God, and the Word was God.' And that all was done through Him, and without Him nothing was done. But how that Word became flesh, how joined to the earth it dwelt in us, this the learned Plato did not know, as Jerome said, of this the eloquent Demosthenes was ignorant.

The real point of difference was over the incarnation. Plato is alleged to have said, 'No God is mingled with men', but Seneca spoke better who said, 'God comes to men, no mind is good without God'. But neither knew that the one true conjunction of divinity and humanity was the incarnation.[37]

After a brief discussion on the exact nature of the incarnation and a warning against the possibilities of heresy latent in a faulty understanding of it,[38] Petrarch returns to addressing the monks. Ending his digressions concerning the enemies within the world, he now warns them against the enemies within their walls. There is the danger of diffidence and of their resolution breaking down over particular arguments. He discusses how these should be met.[39] It is important to have models for behavior, and as Jerome said, every group has its own sort of princes.

> The Romans may imitate as leaders the Camilluses, the Fabriciuses, the Reguluses, the Scipios. Philosophers may propose to themselves Pythagoras, Socrates, Plato, and Aristotle. Poets may emulate Homer, Vergil, Menander, Terence; historians Thucydides, Sallust, Herodotus, Livy; orators Lysias, the Gracchi, Demosthenes, Tully. And now we come to our own: the bishops and priests may have as an example the apostles and men of apostolic times. . . . We, moreover, have provided as our princes Paul, Antony, Julian, Hilary, Macarius, and, as we return to the truth of the Scriptures, our prince is Elijah, is Elisha, our leaders the sons of the prophets! Thus, brothers, those who were Jerome's leaders are your leaders; further we have Jerome, himself, and Augustine and Gregory, and all those anywhere who for love of Christ, by leading a solitary and eremitical life have been known to have been distinguished by religious leisure.

Significant in these lists is the fact that the monastic heroes, both his own and those taken from Jerome, were all patristic or Biblical rather than the well-known medieval founders of monastic orders and the medieval saints. The monastic heroes are derived from antiquity just as those of the generals, philosophers, poets, historians, and orators were. However, he does refer to the fact that he discusses others in *De vita solitaria*,[40] and later in book II he makes a reference to the example of St. Francis' struggle against *voluptas*.[41] With five more pages of exhortation to the monks to follow these leaders and to have faith and not to need the evidence of miracles, the first book ends.[42]

We must even more hurriedly pass through Petrarch's second book. He first presents his version of the miseries and evils of worldly life and of contempt for the world. He dwells on the downfall of all past human greatness.[43] Where is Babylon? All is change and decay. 'As it may be said with Heraclitus, we enter the same and a different city at the same time. Into the same city twice we enter and do not enter.'[44] 'O mournful and unhappy transformation, all into worms and into serpents, all at length fell into nothingness.'[45] It is salutary to watch funerals and to open recent graves with rotting corpses. He takes full advantage of an opportunity to quote Cicero, Seneca, and other ancients on the miseries of life and evils of

sensuality. He carefully avoids quoting any of his numerous medieval predecessors on this theme—as if he wished deliberately to show the value of the
classics for such strictly religious rhetoric.[46]

The late Professor Mommsen in another brilliant study showed how
Petrarch was the first to restate the ancient choice between paths of virtue
and vice as illustrated by Prodicus's story of Hercules at the parting of the
ways (transmitted by Xenophon and quoted by Cicero, Petrarch's source).
Professor Mommsen points out that this passage was unique and that
elsewhere Petrarch considered virtue as coming from divine grace rather
than within man's choice.[47] This is true of this treatise also, for here he
argues that all paths to happiness are false except trust in the strong right
arm of God. '"Blessed are all who trust in Him." Indeed true confidence
does not arise except from virtue. . . . And by knowing that "the salvation
of man is vain, in God we shall do virtue, and he will reduce our enemies to
nothing"; this is our salvation, our virtue, this our security, this our unique
remedy against the anger of God—to retire, to hope, to fear, to pray "lest
in His fury he condemn us, lest His anger accuse us"'.[48]

For present purposes this most limited exposition must suffice. Petrarch here views the monastic life not so much as separated from the life of
the worldly but as the safer and more fully religious way. He apparently felt
no friction between his own way and that of the monks, only admiration
and a few regrets. His treatment is fundamentally hortatory and rhetorical,
perhaps showing that the classicist's rhetoric could outdo the medieval
preacher's though Petrarch also uses much of the latter. It is in his second
book, which I have treated so lightly, that the classical models for bewail-
ing the mutability and fragility of human affairs—the life outside the
monastery in the world—show their mettle. Yet even in book I, where the
state of life and the conflicts within the monastery walls are the main stress
of his sermonizing, he falls back mainly on the classical Christians for
support—on Augustine, Lactantius, and Jerome. Moreover, he shows little
sense of any distinction between asserting the truth of the Christian vision
on the basis of faith and revelation and exhorting the monks to stand firm
in their religion. To be religious seems to mean quite simply to be a
religious; this appears to be in this treatise as true for Petrarch as it was a
commonplace of the medieval outlook.

On the other hand, Petrarch's concern for a release from the respon-
sibilities and distractions of worldly existence for the sake of peace of soul
and literary productivity, as set forth in *De vita solitaria,* is well known. In
De otio religioso Petrarch called *De vita solitaria* cognate in purpose[49] though
there is no direct allusion to an *otium literatum.* It should not be forgotten,
however, that he writes his treatise from without the walls and from
without the order, if not as a layman technically (since he was a non-serving
member of the secular clergy), at least in the spirit of a layman. And it

would thus seem that he accomplished what he set out to do, to write a sermon to himself, so that he could well be religious without being a religious. If this distinction between having faith and leading the life of a member of the regular clergy tends to be blurred, it could mean either that only the professional 'religious' was a true Christian and man of the faith or, on the other hand, that the layman could be just as much a man of faith except more exposed to the world's dangers and distractions. This would seem to be implied in Petrarch's attitude expressed in this treatise, and it would mean that the privileged and special position of sanctity and merit granted to the religious in medieval Catholicism was being diluted and that the difference between layman and regular clergy was becoming one of degree, or lesser degree. It did not occur to Petrarch to allude to the special sanctity and greater merit of the religious because he was not prepared in any sense to attack or to ridicule them (as later humanists were to do), but by the very fact of not alluding to this or affirming their special status except in admiring the comparative safety and serenity of their conditions of life he was contributing to an eventual challenge to the notion that the professional religious were inherently more meritorious or more pious than lay Christians.

Another important humanist treatise on the life of the regular clergy was Salutati's *De seculo et religione*.[50] This is a lengthier and more systematic treatise, one that was more traditional than Petrarch's in its explicit exposition and acceptance of the *doctrine* of the higher degree of sanctity and merit in the life of the religious. Book I of thirty-seven chapters runs to eighty-seven pages in Ullman's edition and deals with the dangers of secular life. Book II of fifteen chapters runs to seventy-nine pages and stresses the advantages of the religious. Much of it seems, as Ullman at one time apparently felt,[51] conventional and rhetorical, a good example of how a humanist could turn his talents to any mode of eloquence with relative indifference to the subject matter or the point of view. Salutati was so important and influential a figure in firmly establishing the new humanistic disciplines in Florence that historians seem to demand that his ideas conform to those of some of his famous protegés, or at least show more apparent consistency.[52] Where they do not, sometimes an effort is made to discount or explain away those that do not fit. Even though this work was relatively early (Ullman dates it c. 1381), let us bear in mind the precedent of Petrarch's contradictory writings and not be too hasty to give Salutati a split personality or to disbelieve his sincerity when inconsistency is encountered. It is not exclusively medieval to be religious, and Salutati's religious notions may well be regarded as perfectly consonant with his humanism. His ideas from work to work and even within the confines of a single work may very well also be inconsistent. This is not a completely unheard of occurrence in the history of thought. On the other hand, the fact that a man is a humanist, i.e., a rhetorician, doesn't necessarily mean that he is not serious about the ideas he presents, although, of course, on occasions he may not be.

Let us look first at some of what may be called the humanistic sides of this work. Referring to his citations of Cicero, Vergil, Juvenal, Sallust, Livy, Aristotle, Homer, and Propertius, Ullman states, 'Etsi vestigia litterarum renascentium in hoc opera pauca sunt, non tamen plane desunt.' And since, he says, except for Papias medieval writers are cited 'fere nunquam', besides Augustine the fathers are 'vix' cited, Ullman adds, 'Hoc ergo sensu opus Colucii inter opera humanistica poni potest.'[53] In fact, Walafrid Strabo is cited indirectly, Thomas Aquinas is paraphrased without acknowledgement, and other medieval writers are cited; Gregory the Great, Justin, and Jerome are further fathers cited; Macrobius, Servius, Isidore of Seville, and Boethius are late classical, early medieval figures cited more than once; Balbus, Florus, Horace, Lucan, Ovid, Persius, Pliny, and Valerius Maximus are additional Roman writers cited, the last one four times.[54] Of course, classical citations, as such, do not make a Renaissance humanist, as they were about as common in the middle ages. Moreover, Salutati, like Petrarch, antedated the great additions to the works of Latin writers and the translations from the Greek which came predominantly in the *Quattrocento*. Furthermore, the bulk of his references in this work are overwhelmingly scriptural. It is rather the kind of use made of classical references that distinguished the Renaissance humanist from his medieval predecessor.

What has puzzled Ullman and others about this work is that, while written by a successful worldly man of letters who had already attained fame and influence in civic affairs through his position as the first humanist chancellor of the Florentine state, this treatise was, nevertheless, so outspoken in its condemnation of secular life. Apart from the very effective eloquence employed to deter Niccolò da Uzzano, recently entered into the Camaldulensian Cloister of S. Maria degli Angeli, from regretting his decision (and to benefit other readers also to whom Coluccio alludes), it is possible to find a clear and consistent position toward the secular world in this treatise.

Chapter 35 of book 1 is titled 'That the world is the minister of necessities'.[55] It is well known that both St. Augustine and St. Thomas Aquinas found a place for this world in their writings (although in crucially different ways), and it would be no shock doctrinally to find amidst all the other sharply negative chapters on the world in Salutati's treatise, which by their titles as well as their contents are outspokenly condemnatory of secular life, a recognition of the importance, notwithstanding, of worldly civilization for the sustenance of life, but subordinated to the higher religious function of the church, namely, the salvation of souls. Salutati, however, does not confirm this expectation. Instead he surprises us in this chapter by making use of one of the classical conceptions of the early life of mankind to strengthen the devotion and resolve of his friend Niccolò to lead a severely ascetic existence within his cell. 'Indeed the world provides things necessary to us, necessary certainly for passing through this corruptible life.'[56] The conception is Augustinian and not neo-Aristotelian, clearly. But Coluccio is unwilling to permit even the degree of worldliness Augustine had allowed in book XIX of the *City of God* (well-known and heavily cited here by Salutati). His limits are more drastic. Consulting the barest necessity of nature, he would permit only that and nothing of civilization. 'For nature desires hunger to be repressed, thirst extinguished, rain and cold repelled, the force of winds and heat to be driven off. Anything beyond this is from evil.'[57]

He then adds a remarkable passage which utilizes for his own purposes the ancient conception of a harsh primitive life (to be distinguished, as Lovejoy and Boas have shown,[58] from the other classical conception of a soft primitivism in a golden age). It is, of course, the moral purity and simplicity of the primitive life that should induce the modern man, who cannot go back to the primitive age, to seek the equivalent in the monastery.

> How easy it is to satisfy these necessities the first age teaches, which, as is read, satisfied hunger with acorns, conquered thirst from brooks, drove off cold with skins, avoided rain, wind and heat through caves and grottoes. This is that most innocent age which the poets, extolling in many praises, called golden, then Saturnine. O happy acorns, O health-giving rivers. The poisons of delicate food did not then excite lust by their heat; nor did languid drunkenness insanely tempt the brain; there was no arguing with neighbors over boundaries or over government. All things were in common. Grass provided beds, caves homes, not guarded, not closed, but open to all. Hidden then, indeed not yet invented, were those two quarrelsome words which disturb the peace of mortals, and which bar to men the road to heaven, which are inciters of avarice and authors of contentions, namely, 'meum' and 'tuum'. . . . But now we are so worldly and given to delights that, in comparing that age to our customs, indeed, not customs but abuses and crimes, we think it fabulous and not historical, and we say it is impossible for the fragile life of our own times to return to that harshness. I admit it is more fragile because more vicious, and as the fomenter of vices more pleasure-loving. Certainly it seems impossible to return to the frugality and mutuality (*communionem*) of early times.[59]

The classical sources of this notion are plural. Juvenal, Vergil, and

Boethius[60] are either echoed or quoted directly in this passage. Perhaps it is better not to try to designate Salutati's point of view as Stoic or as that of any of the other possible classical schools. As will be seen, it is consistent with another argument later in this treatise in book II. This conception of the primitive austerity bears, perhaps, the same relationship to his specific views on the life of the religious as Petrarch's praise of the life of solitude bore to his admiration of monastic retirement—except that Salutati makes the connection much more explicit. Indeed he continues in a most interesting way. He does not agree that men of his day are too delicate to withstand the rigors of a primitive life. Men can submit to monastic discipline.

> Take away greed, wretched man, depose riches, renounce the world, lead your life according to the precepts, attempt to fulfill the counsels, subdue your will to the divine will, . . . begin to love God, hate the world, love poverty, hate riches. You cannot leave these things unless you hate them, you cannot go over to the others unless you love them. Do not accuse our age of weakness. Our body is potent to undergo all hardships. I do not refer you to Daniel and his companions turning to a diet of herbs from the delights of the royal table. I do not propose to you as the greatest example that precursor of the Lord among men born to women; nor the anchorites of whose miracles we read in the *Vita patrum;* nor the hermits even of our times; nor the monks, many of whom we see choose poverty, love fasting, flee all pleasure. For I know that when I mention these the lover of the world will reply that they both now can and then were able to do this only while filled with the grace of the Holy Spirit, and that the spirit inspires when, where and how it wills, and that this does not depend on our own free will.[61]

Therefore, he proposes two natural examples drawn from contemporary secular life: the harsh existence of the Carinthian mountaineers, compelled to live in this severe way, and the despicable condition of sailors on the ships sailing out into the Atlantic to England, an adventure undertaken for the smallest of rewards.[62] 'Indeed we are able to abandon the world and subjugate our bodies to that extreme necessity of nature.'[63]

Another classical *topos* used by Salutati in this work also has to do with the admirable nature of abstinence. Chapter 9 of book II deals with 'The Vow of Poverty'.[64] Among other observations on the evil of wealth, he remarks in a vein similar to the one discussed above, 'Nor do we wretched mortals think it contrary to nature that through avarice we appropriate those things created for the use of all to the dominion of our own property, and although they ought to serve our life we make them instruments of our crimes, pleasures and other wickedness.' Worldly goods, he states, fall into the Stoic class of *media* or indifferent things, 'and thus are only good if we use them well, for they are bad for those using them poorly'.[65] After further condemnation of riches, citing Jesus, Paul, and Ecclesiastes, he turns to a consideration of the lesson of history.

> If we would recall that altogether there were and there are two cities destined for mortals, one spiritual which we call 'of God' and the other, indeed, carnal which we may call 'of the world'; and if to one or the other of them we commit our loves and the goal of our actions; it will occur to us that each city was established by paupers and ruined and corrupted by the rich. And first, if you will, we will examine what authors this mundane city had. Although I easily could, I do not wish to discuss all kingdoms but I shall investigate that one which was greatest and strongest of all and which still retains the principate, at least in name, specifically that of the Romans.[66]

Salutati then devotes the next four pages (in Ullman's edition) to a review of Roman history, utilizing Florus' epitome, Pliny, Juvenal, Eutropius, Cicero, but mainly Livy, Valerius Maximus, and Sallust as his sources. Here is the standard classical view of the poor, moral, and abstemious early Romans, who brought about the rise of Rome to world dominion only to encounter its downfall after the age of Scipio and Cato in the hands of men of great wealth.[67]

> What more [can be said] when the books of all the historians are full of the poverty, moderation and abstinence of the Romans? These paupers founded so great an empire that, as a noble and truly great historian [Sallust] said, 'afterward, when riches began to be honored, and glory, empire and power followed them, virtue began to fade, poverty to be held shameful,' rich successors brought it to ruin. . . . For the Republic of the Romans, which the pauper Romulus founded and the poorest princes raised to such greatness that its empire was bounded by the ocean and its glory, indeed, by the stars, and from the rising to the setting of the sun all, tamed by arms, obeyed only them, this the rich men, cruel Sulla, ferocious Cinna and ambitious Marius shook to its foundations, and the even richer men Crassus, Pompey the Great, and Gaius Caesar the son of Lucius utterly destroyed. Thus in the memory of these events, as in a kind of mirror, mankind can see that for establishing, increasing and conserving this earthly city, poor men excel rich.[68]

There has recently been a flurry of interest on the part of historians in the possible political influence of Florence's humanist chancellors. It is worth noting that Salutati wrote these lines in 1381 during the rule of the *popolo minuto,* after the rise of the Ciompi, and prior to the overthrow of this regime by the oligarchy in the very next year. Perhaps his views do have some contemporary significance, but perhaps more reflective than deter-

minative. It should also interest Hans Baron that these republican sentiments were uttered in the middle of such a 'medieval' book as *De seculo,* and
a considerable time before Salutati wrote his *De tyranno,* the pro-imperial-
ist, 'medieval' sentiments of which Baron finds so hard to explain.[69]

Our interest in this chapter does not stop with Salutati's essay on the
public benefits of poverty in the 'city of the world'. He deals in parallel
fashion with the experience of the Catholic Church as the 'City of God'.
'Moreover, what may I say of that city which looks toward heavenly Jerusalem?'[70] Was not Christ, its founder, a pauper who said when he entered
Jerusalem, 'Foxes have holes and the birds of the air have nests, but the Son
of Man has nowhere to lay his head'?[71] What of Cephas, what of Paul, what
of Peter, what of Ananias and Saphyra?

> Thus it is manifest that all those first founders of the heavenly city and
> the Catholic Church in the renewal of time either were paupers or sold
> all that they had and chose voluntary poverty by sharing in com-
> mon. . . . These poor and humble men, by infinite martyrdoms
> through two hundred and thirty and more years, from Nero, the first
> persecutor of Christians, to the emperors Diocletian and Maximus
> [*sic*], in whose time the tenth plague of persecution boiled up, found-
> ed the Catholic Church. After Constantine, who did not endow so
> much as enrich the Church and hand to it the proud ornaments of the
> imperial height (as may be said with everybody's permission), these
> our prelates, in whom just as in the case of those other leaders of the
> earthly kingdom first the love of money and then of empire increased,
> after they had likewise dined on honey and oil, become bejewelled
> with gold and silver, dressed in linen and damask robes of many
> colors, become excessively elegant, and proceeded to rule—these pre-
> lates rendered that glorious city abominable. Now (what is most to be
> lamented) although they see the Christian faith, once diffused
> throughout the world, has lost so many lands to the Saracenic abom-
> ination, although they see the old schism of the *Graeculi* separate so
> many peoples, so many cities and so many once opulent kingdoms
> from the unity of Holy Mother Church, just as if it were too large a
> mass and there were too great a multitude of faithful, by electing two
> supreme pontiffs at various times (if they can still be called elections
> which hatred or ambition or the other turbid passions of human minds
> extort and which are not celebrated in zeal of faith and for the building
> of celestial Jerusalem), they have created the most pernicious schism.
> Thus, just as those princes and founders of both cities, while they
> loved poverty, in laying the foundations of those two cities not only
> perfected them into a huge work of the greatest size but enlarged them
> by miraculous increases with labor and blood, so these rich men, with

wealth corrupting minds and good customs, destroyed almost all with their glorious wealth of all things. This being so, unless we rejoice in being fools, if we wish to serve the heavenly or earthly city, if we wish to show ourselves useful to both or either one, who does not see that riches, which so corrupt and defile their possessors, ought to be cast away?[72]

Notable here is the direct undiscriminating parallelism between the two cities and the equality of their corruption and the absence of any clearly stated subordination of the one to the other. Adhering to the monastic vow of poverty apparently offers the only substitute for a return to the pristine days of the Roman republic or the early centuries of the apostolic church.

It is apparent that Salutati managed to combine a classical Roman interpretation of history with the Augustinian-Christian conception of the two cities, and to utilize this, in addition, to express his views of the contemporary state of the church as well as to confirm his monastic reader in his vow of poverty. A further application of a humanistic interest to a Christian religious practice may be seen in chapter 11 of book 11, *De oratione,* 'On Prayer'.[73] This is the longest chapter in the book, nineteen pages when most chapters run to two or three pages in Ullman's edition. It is a humanist discussion of the rhetoric of sacred discourse—the Christian addressing himself to his God. First of all, the proper psychological attitude must be present in the person praying; therefore a discussion of the three theological virtues and the four cardinal virtues ensues. Many interesting topics are taken up in connection with these. Under charity he takes up the question of what is legitimate self-love as the measure of our love for our neighbor and inveighs against love of our bodies from which all the civilized arts, which he lengthily enumerates, flow.[74] He feels called upon to explain away the Old Testament injunctions to destroy one's enemies and offers his own principles of exegesis; 'whatever sprinkling of maledictions is found within the oracle of the Holy Scriptures certainly ought to be referred to the rule of true charity or the divine justice by some mystery of exposition, or it should be expounded in such a way in the light of a higher sense that love of God and of neighbor are in no way contradicted, since a specially wide way is open to expositors . . .'[75] His discussion of prudence leads to a direct assertion of rhetorical principles;[76] justice involves him in a discussion of free will and divine providence, since it is unjust to pray for what has not already been provided for by God.[77] The relationship of oral spoken prayer to inner spiritual meditation is considered. Although true prayer is of the heart and not of the mouth, vocal prayer should not be neglected. Through it we serve God in body as well as spirit, and a sluggish spirit can be aroused by voices.[78]

In considering prayer Salutati required the presence of the separate virtues, theological and moral. In the previous chapter 10, 'On the Vow of Obedience',[79] he had included an astounding passage on the motivations of virtue. The reference to Professor Mommsen's paper on Petrarch and the choice of Hercules will be recalled.[80] In the *De otio religioso* Petrarch did not manifest the new classical conception of virtue as the choice of a path in life but made virtue depend, traditionally, on divine grace. Mommsen's discussion was an elaboration and correction of an earlier paper by Erwin Panofsky,[81] who had credited Salutati with the first nonmedieval account of virtue in his *De laboribus Herculis*[82] and in the letter to Giovanni da Siena on which it was based.[83] Salutati, in these later pieces, had not endorsed the pagan conception but had only stated it. In the passage that follows from the *De seculo et religione*, ii, 10 he sharply attacks what he takes to be the pagan approach to virtue as both desirable for its own sake and for the enjoyment of a clear conscience. By the way he begins, he seems to want to be taken quite seriously.

> I don't know if I speak truly, still most devoutly I dare to assert that all those who do something virtuous in any way other than in obedience to divine majesty not only do not acquire merit but act badly. And all those who, for example, do frequent acts of fortitude or temperance only for the reason that they might be brave or temperate (and not merely that they might seem so)—all such not only are wise after the flesh but also do not differ from the philosophers of the Gentiles. (For I omit the Romans who sought mundane glory for themselves as the end of all their [virtuous] actions). Do not those philosophers who wish virtue to be the goal of all goods (which was especially the opinion of the Stoics; I dismiss the others of vainer opinions), contenting themselves with themselves, as they say, require nothing further from their actions except the secret of consciences and that they can become virtuous and enjoy the acquisition of virtue? In what way would we say a Christian differs from these pagans who, forgetting the command of God and losing the *habitus* of this virtue [of obedience], acts not that he might please or obey God but only that he might do some good!? Certainly, securely I will say that he is so much the worse if he has been established in grace by the regeneration of baptism and taught the truth in the Gospel, and yet neither does as he ought nor practices virtues themselves in the proper way. Indeed, he tries against reason, to joy in virtues, and by joying in them he is more truly said to abuse them.

Even grace is not a sufficient cause of virtue. As he stresses here and in the next chapter (already discussed), it should be one's free will to fulfill the eternal commands of God in voluntary devotion—a thoroughly Augustinian position. 'Let us therefore not know earthly things, but, since we are forced by the necessity of nature to nothing, let us faithfully obey God, to whom we have promised faith, in the liberty conceded to us in our will.'[84]

Based on similar reasoning is Salutati's affirmation in chapter 6 that superior merits are due those who live bound by vows—the technical criterion of the religious.[85] Instead of totally rejecting the secular way of life, or blurring the differences between it and the religious (as Petrarch seemed at times to do), Salutati reverts to the conception common in medieval moral theology of a spiritual hierarchy leading upward from ordinary lay Christians, through the secular clergy, to the religious, with each status differing in the corresponding degree of its religious perfection and therefore meriting higher or lower rewards. The reason for the highest merits being conferred on the religious is stated by Salutati as follows:

> For you upon entering religion, have dedicated yourself, your will and your work to God. . . . This is truly a *holocaust,* that is, a total consumption and burning up in which all that we are and can be we commit to God and leave nothing in our own power. This they do not do who without the vow offer only works. And on this account it is not right that they should merit as much in the benefits of God as those who are indebted by vows. For who merits more of grace, he who would give only the fruits of the tree to a superior in such a way that he is held to give them only as much as he pleases, or he who gives both tree and fruit under such conditions that after the gift he is unable to revoke it? No one would doubt that he who gives more merits more. . . .[86] Moreover, whoever does good out of free will, as happens in one free of a vow, does a single good; but whoever vows and also does good while he obligates himself by a vow, deserves and does a good. In making a vow, even though he creates a debt, nevertheless he does good. For they should not be heard who madly attempt to assert that goods which are done without a vow are greater than those we do out of obedience to a vow, adducing that we are more obligated to the one giving by free will than to one paying a debt (as if because by vowing one is made a debtor he does not proceed from free will), and that we owe nothing to someone freely promising something because he promised. . . . Certainly they err. For in far greater charity, which is the end of the precept, it is vowed and perfected than if we simply offer something.[87]

As can be seen from this passage, Salutati preserves and defends the basic medieval conception of the superior perfection of the life of the professional religious, that is, those who by vowing or professing constituted the professional.

This notion of degrees of perfection, together with its essential counterpart—the notion of the total sacrifice of the individual's will to the divine will (we should become 'non actores sed sola instrumenta')[88]—must already in his time have encountered criticism of the sort we shall shortly consider in Lorenzo Valla (below), judging by his reference to 'those who madly attempt to assert'.

How central these ideas were to his conception of the relationship of the laity, the clergy, and the religious may be seen in their exposition in his closing exhortation:

> When we were born in succession to the first parents, to whom we all are heirs and sons, we were born vessels of wrath. And soon by the establishment of Holy Mother Church, through the purification of baptism, we are renewed in grace. Indeed, the first and true religion, in which receiving the signature of Christianity one renounces the devil and his works, is our faith, and if properly observed is indeed fully the way of perfection to God. Yet by perverse custom it is so mixed with temporal affairs that, unless the mercy of God overcomes our injustice, although many are called, few will attain to the benefits of election. Perfection, however, is fuller when by daily service of divine majesty, though still in abundance of things, we bind ourselves outside the world through the clerical order. Indeed the fullest perfection in this life is when we not only follow God, shunning the devil, when we not only give ourselves in service of God, relinquishing the world (for a cleric ought not to involve himself in secular affairs), but also when we offer ourselves to God through a vow of chastity, obedience and poverty, and consecrate ourselves as a true holocaust on the altar of religion. Thus not improperly it can be said, as I indicated above, that to all Christians sowing in good soil a thirty-fold fruit is reserved, to clerics a sixty-fold, to the religious, indeed, a hundred-fold.[89]

Although this discussion of the treatise will end on this very traditional and, doctrinally, completely orthodox note, it should not be forgotten that in my selective analysis he was shown to be effectively humanist in the service he was able to render his argument on behalf of the monastic life through the new disciplines and points of view. These were his discussion of the classical legend of the hard primitive life of the golden age as an inducement to monastic asceticism, his adoption of the classical Roman interpretation of history attributing Roman greatness to poverty and the parallel lesson of the decline of the church through affluence, his interest in the rhetorical and moral philosophical nature of prayer. Although he showed little restraint in his graphic depiction of the dangers and temptations and evil consequences of secular life in his highly rhetorical first book, it is quite clear that he did not reject his own status of a layman. This is no inconsistency brought about by a purely rhetorical endorsement of the religious life on behalf of his friend Niccolò da Uzzano, as Ullman and Garin have suggested. The layman, according to his very explicit argument, could lead a moral and religious life, but one of lesser perfection and merit than the cleric's, and still less than that of the religious. There was no contradiction in Salutati's mind between humanism and his inherited religious faith and practices (called his 'medievalism' by von Martin and by Ullman); nor was there any inconsistency in being a lay Christian and regarding the status of the religious as spiritually superior. As he said in his reply to Giovanni Dominici:

> connexa sunt humanitatis studia; connexa sunt et studia divinitatis, ut unius rei sine alia vera completaque scientia non possit haberi.[90]

Salutati's two most famous protegés, Leonardo Bruni and Poggio Bracciolini, both wrote works that in a less direct way than the ones we are considering here dealt with the religious orders. Each of these works, Bruni's *Oratio in hypocritas*[91] of 1417 and Poggio's *Dialogus contra hypocritas*[92] of 1447–1448, was primarily rhetorical in character, expressing a sharp hostility principally to the friars, admitting that their impugning of the motives of the religious did not apply to all, conceding that hypocrisy was also present among the laity.[93] They are of far more social than doctrinal importance, since neither one of them so much as considers the question of the validity of the status of the religious either to affirm it or to question it. Bruni's oration is short, compact, rhetorically effective and ends with an affirmation of the importance of conscience as a monitor of religious and moral integrity.

> For indeed the good man is joyful and gay from good conscience of his deeds and from good hope which no fear of punishments disturbs. On the other hand their misdeeds burn the hypocrites and may be observed as furies before their eyes. For it is necessary for them, although they are evil, to think sometimes about themselves and their errors. For each man is constituted as a right and perpetual judge of himself and his actions. This is certainly a most sure and true judgement which can not be deceived or seduced or circumvented in any way. For it is not believed because of witnesses, nor is the accused censured by means of documents, nor is he defended by a patron through favor or eloquence. This judge knows all, was present at every crime, and one is not judged once only but often and frequently. The condemnation of this internal judge forces tears from you and compels you to weep among sacred things. But believe me, . . . this is a game and a joke compared with that eternal and ineffable judgement of God which awaits you after death.[94]

It is difficult to consider these works as having very much theoretical or doctrinal importance, although they certainly reveal the growth of hostility toward the clergy in some humanist circles. At any rate they do not contribute to the problem of this paper.[95]

When in c. 1441, sixty years later than Salutati's treatise, Lorenzo Valla wrote his dialogue on *The Profession of the Religious (De professione religiosorum)*[96], it was as if he wished to reply directly to his predecessor, so opposite is it in viewpoint. A more likely target, however, was such a work as San Bernardino's *De Christiana religione*[97] or Girolamo Aliotti d'Arezzo's *De felici statu religionis monasticae.*[98] The participants in the dialogue are simply 'Frater' and 'Lorenzo'. This is not a subtle or cautious work, but bold and outspoken in challenging the fundamental doctrinal basis of the privileged position of the religious. He starts right in as follows: 'I ask before all . . . why . . . you will receive greater remuneration from God. . . . When the layman and the religious differ and depart from each other in no quality of mind or body, and to both all things are equal which happen extrinsically to men, and both are engaged in the same actions of life, is nevertheless greater remuneration owed by God to him who has professed that sect which you call "religion" and hence call yourselves "religious" than to him who has professed no sect, neither yours nor the monks'?'[99] Valla's attack is partly philological, questioning the propriety of the language, but this rests on the more fundamental questioning of the religious assumption. He proceeds to defend his use of the word 'sect' rather than 'religious order, which the friar had protested against. 'Still I prefer to call this, about which you wonder, a sect rather than a religion, not only for reasons of style but also out of necessity. For since I do not think as much ought to be attributed to this your life as you attribute, it seems too much that you impose on it such a sacred and venerable name as "religion". Otherwise there is no reason why we should be arguing. For if you alone are "religious", it must be conceded that you are the best of all men. That this, as I believe, is not so, I am about to dispute.'[100] He goes on to suggest that the differences between various religious orders are comparable to the difference between philosophical sects.

Valla anticipates the Reformation position here, which denied any special status or vocation to the clergy or to the members of religious orders, considering each Christian equal in status as far as externals were concerned. Valla resumed his argument by asking whether a priest or a pope was 'religious' or whether none other than the friar could be. This position was not so much arrogant with respect to members of religious orders as contemptuous of other persons. 'For what greater praise can be given me than to be called "religious" and what greater vituperation than to be called "irreligious"? For what else is it to be religious than to be a Christian? . . . Religion is the same thing as faith, and "religious" the same as "faithful", faithful, I say, not as though dead without works, but with works in the way in which one can be called a true Christian.'[101] Refusing to acknowledge the traditional degrees of perfection distinguishing the different stages of holiness, Valla proceeds to argue that if the friar's position is accepted, all others must be condemned as not religious. 'And so since you would make you only religious who have professed, and you would deny that others are truly religious, what else do you admit but that you alone are Christians, you alone good, you alone pure and sinless; moreover the others you would damn, despise, hurl into Tartarus. . . . Since this is so I do not act ungenerously toward you if I hesitate to call you "religious" when many others also, who have not professed that sect or rule, ought to be called "religious" since they lead most saintly lives, and many of your brothers ought not to be called "religious" because they live most iniquitously.'[102]

After further argument on this proposition that the religious and the lay Christians can be equal in magnitude of virtue but unequal in kind, the question is raised: granting that some Christians live subject to rules and vows, why should they acquire greater merit with God for this? The friar gives the following reasons: first, they promise and always observe poverty, chastity, and obedience. Secondly, they are in this way restricted more than other men. Thirdly, if they lapse they will suffer greater punishment. Thus they should receive a greater reward if they keep their rule. In reply Valla engages in a dialectical disputation attempting to turn the Friars' words back on themselves. These claims seem to mean that the greatest of our virtues can be increased by taking a vow and for this reason our reward should be greater. But is not a man who is exposed to the greater danger and overcomes it deserving of the greater reward? And should not the man who lives in a more tranquil and sheltered situation and fails to do his duty receive a greater punishment? When he gets the friar to admit this, he says that the first is the situation of the lay Christian in the world, who, exposed to greater peril, merits more for his goodness, while the second, the taker of vows, should be more severely punished for his lapses. The friar protests: 'You drive me almost to insanity with your words; you weaken our virtues, you almost take away our rewards, you increase our vices, you multiply our penalties, religions and all religious, truly as you have said, you hurl into the mire.'[103]

The argument turns to whether a vow has any merit in it *per se.* 'Again, Valla, the humanist, indulges in an extended discussion of the meanings of words. 'Vow' means both prayerful wish and devout promise. How does *votum* differ from *sponsio* (pledge) or *iusiurandum* (oath)? After a lengthy analysis of their meanings, Valla concedes that 'you do make an oath or promise, but I do not concede the vow'.[104] If a pledge to observe poverty, chastity, and obedience is valid, what need is there for an oath? If it is invalid, you have promised nothing. The friar replies that a pledge is valid, but an oath makes it more valid. Valla asks how health can be healthier, the full fuller, the perfect more perfect. His argument comes down to claiming that an oath does not make a virtuous life any more virtuous, that the real test for divine mercy is the inner attitude and not the outer form. 'Profession is not a *votum* but a *devotio*. For it is to devote, *devovere,* to speak briefly, as *dicare* or *dedicare*.'[105]

Turning to the contents of the vow, obedience, poverty, and chastity, Lorenzo concedes that they confer merit but apart from profession. But, he adds, 'These are not necessary to every one.'[106] On the specific pledge of obedience to superiors Valla asks why, if with baptism one promises God future obedience to his commandments, need one pledge obedience to men? How can you give what you already have given? The friar replies: 'I do not retract my pledge, nor do I give to a man what I have given to God, nor do I promise to God what I previously promised. But in those things in which I have a choice while serving God such as in dressing, eating, going, acting, lying, sleeping, remaining awake, and finally speaking, the liberty of doing these things, and as I said, the choice, I hand over to another.'[107] Valla questions the validity of thus trying to have another ruler besides Christ. He cites Hebrews xi. 37–38 depicting the sacrifices of the faithful to show that the religious cannot be compared 'to those retaining their own liberty' in degree of sanctity.[108] What then of kings, pontiffs, and other rulers, must they be bound to obedience? To the friar's statement that rulers are granted merit if they rule well, we, if we obey well, Valla asks:

> Is there thus no middle ground so that we only either have servants or serve? . . . Not all are lords and not all are servants, and not all are teachers and not all are disciples; they do not obtain a lesser degree of merit who are in the middle. And, as desirable as it is to belong to the status of prelates and preceptors, just as miserable is it to be in the number of subjects and disciples. Certainly this is of far less dignity than to be, as I have said, in the middle and for one to be able to be without a lord and to live and know without a master. I do not venture to say that it is a sign of an abject and ignorant soul to commit oneself to the charge of a tutor in the manner of a boy and to the care of a preceptor. But if he is able to admonish, teach and rule others, why does he subject himself especially to others who, as frequently happens, are ignorant and unworthy. . . . A greater reward is given to those who rule well than to those who obey well . . . thus your pledge of obedience is a kind of servitude. . . . While I would prefer to be the master rather than a servant of others, I certainly prefer to be master of myself.[109]

With this affirmation of individualism applied to the monastic vow of obedience, Valla concludes his attack on it by saying, 'To obey the rule is to obey God, not man, which we also do. Nor can another rule be held better than the one handed down by Christ and the apostles.'[110]

Thus in this discussion, too, Valla takes a position that is firmly opposed to a basic medieval Catholic conception, namely, that of the authority that inheres in sacerdotal and abbatial office. Obedience had a place only between the Christian and God, without the intervention of man, except in a tutorial relation. Obviously this attack on the moral and juridical aspects of the religious life involved more than a simple question of the superior merit a monk might gain by adherence to his vow of obedience, and it contrasts notably with the passage cited above from Salutati which found virtue solely in submission to divine command.

In discussing the vow of poverty Valla made an equally fundamental attack on another favored medieval value, though a value that could also be cherished from a Renaissance humanist point of view, as the case of Salutati's discussion of the primitive life and Roman virtue shows. Nor does Valla launch into the kind of satiric invective so easy to indulge in at that time and best illustrated by Poggio's *Contra hypocritas* and his *De avaritia*, showing the great wealth of the religious. Rather he questioned the whole notion of poverty as being in any way valuable except as a token of humility. Is it poverty to live as you do lacking nothing essential, not even wine? You are poor men in desire, but your virtue is no greater than that of others who have not professed poverty. Is it necessary to embrace poverty if I can live innocently with wealth? The poor in spirit, not in goods, are praised, and the rich are disapproved only in spirit. 'What do you ask? If you and I differ not at all in living temperately and frugally, how can it be that you are a pauper and I a rich man . . . ?' The friar suggests that he might sell all and give it to the poor. Valla replies: 'should I also sell all my books and distribute the proceeds? Is it the precept for the apostles and for those to whom it was granted to reply to princes to be without books, without learning, without premeditation? Codices are necessary to me and also not a little money with which I may buy many codices and other needs of life. For what would be more perverse than to give your possessions to beggars and become a beggar afterward yourself? . . . So it is sufficient if I do not revel and delight in riches and renounce them not in fact but in spirit.' The friar answers: 'Then you concede that we are like the apostles who renounce riches in spirit and so in fact.' To which Lorenzo: 'Nothing less. I said money is necessary to me to buy codices. You, if you do otherwise and hand it to paupers, are stupid and do not love yourself as your neighbor.'[111] The monks and friars deserve little for their poverty because they are relieved of destitution and care. 'You give up the hope of acquisition but also the solicitude. You will not have better things but will not suffer worse things either.' I hope to please God as readily as you do but without renunciation. 'Non exterior homo sed interior placet Deo.'[112] If he lavished all his wealth on the poor, he would lack necessities and be unable to defend religion. He might become impious and unable to care for an old or sick parent or wife and child. [113] There are Aristotelian and Ciceronian (rather than Epicurean) overtones in this emphasis on the need for wealth to do good deeds. But the more fundamental argument of Valla against the ideal of poverty was that it should be a spiritual attitude, not a literal act.

On the vow of continence he seems to turn as much on the priest as on the regular clergy. And again his is an argument for the acceptance of a moderated sensual life as well as against the notion that sexual abstinence by itself is of any value. 'It is much better to be safe in the middle than on high with danger of ruin. O that bishops, presbyters, deacons were husbands of one wife and not rather, forgive the saying, lovers of more than one whore. . . . Yet priests will not merit on account of chastity more than I will merit. For in this respect women would be in a worse condition since they cannot be priests, and yet with God there is neither Greek nor barbarian, master nor slave, neither male nor female. . . .'[114]

The general conclusion of his dialogue is that submission to a rule, the religious life, is motivated by fear rather than love, and hence is an inferior kind of Christianity to his own lay existence. It is not that individual monks and friars are evil or hypocrites, though he concedes many are, but that the whole basis of considering their life more perfect in sanctity is a false one.

You obey: I assume the care of others. You live poor and continent; I lead a life equal to yours. You have bound yourself for keeping this, I have not thought that servitude necessary. You do rightly by necessity, I by choice; you out of fear of God, I out of love; perfect charity drives away fear. If you had not feared that otherwise you could not please God, certainly you never would have bound yourself. For what else induced you to make your profession . . . except that no cause should deflect you from the worship of God through free will. Thus you see hardly anyone entertaining your company unless wicked, criminal, poor, destitute and who otherwise despairs of serving either God or his own body well. . . . And so all the way of the vow, all imposition of a fast, all oath and finally all law (your profession is a certain law) was invented on account of fear, that is, as I speak more openly, on account of bad people. . . . Did not Paul say, The Law is imposed on account of transgression? . . . Thus I don't know what else you can ask of God except the fruit of obedience, poverty and continence. But you are not content with this and demand that you be placed above others on account of danger. But if you consider the danger of punishment among you, consider in my case the danger of sinning more easily, who am bound by no anchor of fear. This makes the same act of virtue greater in me than in you. [115]

He apparently is ready to broaden his attack to include the secular clergy as well as the religious.

> Therefore let us make both you and us equal in the manner of Paul, who of those eating and not eating said, 'each observes in his own sense,' and conclude: Thus profession does not render men better, such as deaconhood, priesthood, episcopacy and papacy. You are not better because you have been consecrated a deacon or priest, but you wished to be consecrated that you might become better; nor because you have sworn do you for that reason merit much, but you have sworn that you might merit much; nor are you good because penalties have been proposed for you, for you are able to be evil, but in order that you may be good you undergo the danger of punishment.[116]

Various holy men have not been inferior for not having professed religion or been a bishop or priest. He is aware of how meritorious the founders of convents have been, although their followers depart from goodness. He offers, finally, as evidence that he is not the enemy of the friars a peroration of praise, which is in some ways even less than faint.[117]

There is no doubt in my mind that Valla moved far in this treatise toward a repudiation of the entire medieval conception of a sacerdotal hierarchy and a special profession of those leading a more perfectly religious life—the religious. And the basis of his attack was evangelical and primarily Pauline. It was more than a defense of the religiosity of the laity; it was a reassertion of the universality and multiplicity and equality of the ways to salvation open to all who are Christian in spirit. It was built on a more literal and historical interpretation of Paul's attack on the special sanctity of adherence to the Hebrew law.

This treatise, first edited by Vahlen on the basis of a unique manuscript (Bib. Vat. Cod. Urb. Lat. 595), was not published in his *Opera omnia* and was probably hardly known at all in the sixteenth century. If it had achieved a wider circulation it would undoubtedly have been given a strongly favorable reception by the reformers, more so than that which his much more ambiguous *De libero arbitrio* received.[118] Perhaps, if it had then been known, we would be calling Valla a 'Pre-reformer' today. However, it is quite clear that he had no intention of attacking the historical authority of the church, even though in his *Apology*[119] he does not retract the ideas expressed in this treatise but reaffirms them. Undoubtedly he could not have recognized the significance and the interpretation I have just given to this treatise, since it requires historical hindsight to do so. It would be unhistorical, then, to claim him and his thought as part of the Reformation, since no man then knew it was to occur within eighty years. Yet the resemblance of his ideas to those of the reformers is none the less striking.

A more relevant question is the relation of these ideas to his humanism. My analysis of Petrarch and Salutati has made clear that there is no single necessary one, because they took such opposite positions. To my mind the connection in all three lies in the effort to define the relation of the lay Christian to the professional religious. The humanists' claim to the field of moral philosophy could not be isolated from religion, so that they became lay preachers and religious counselors as well. Such were Petrarch and Salutati. Valla seems to have drawn a logical conclusion from this situation—two generations ahead of the Erasmian Christian humanists,[120] and no less emphatically.

NOTES

1. Pp. 289–335 in *Chapters in Western Civilization* (3d ed., New York, 1961). Apart from this reference and those given in footnotes 2–6 I shall make no attempt to list any more of the enormous literature on humanist moral philosophy.
2. Giovanni Gentile, 'Il concetto dell'uomo nel Rinascimento', in *Il pensiero italiano del Rinascimento* (Firenze, 1940), pp. 47–113.
3. Cf. Aldo Vallone, *Cortesia e nobiltà nel Rinascimento* (Asti, 1955).
4. Eugene F. Rice, Jr. *The Renaissance Idea of Wisdom* (Cambridge, Mass., 1958).
5. Cf. my *Adversity's Noblemen: the Italian Humanists on Happiness* (New York, 1940; rev. ed., New York, 1965).
6. Hans Baron, *The Crisis of the Early Italian Renaissance: Civic Humanism and Republican Liberty in an Age of Classicism and Tyranny* (Princeton, 1955); Eugenio Garin, *L'umanesimo italiano; filosofia e vita civile nel Rinascimento* (Bari, 1952).
7. 'Desideri di riforma nell'oratoria del Quattrocento', *Contributi alla storia del concilio di Trento e della controriforma* (Florence, 1948, *Quaderni di 'Belfagor'* I), and pp. 166–182 of *La cultura filosofica del Rinascimento italiano* (Florence, 1961); 'Problemi di religione e filosofia nella cultura fiorentina del Quattrocento', pp. 70–82 in *Mélanges Renaudet (Bibliothèque d'Humanisme et Renaissance* XIV, 1952) and pp. 127–142 of *La cultura filosofica*. See below notes 72, 95, 114 for a discussion of the relationship of Garin's discussion to the present one.
8. Cambridge, Mass., 1955, 'Paganism and Christianity', pp. 70–91 (reprinted in his *Renaissance Thought,* New York, 1961, pp. 70–91). In connection with the religious thought and activity of the humanists another notable paper of Kristeller's should be mentioned: 'Lay Religious Traditions and Florentine Platonism', *Studies in Renaissance Thought and Letters* (Rome, 1956), pp. 99–122.
9. Giuseppe Toffanin, *Storia dell'umanesimo* (enlarged ed., Bologna, 1950); C. Angeleri, *Il Problema religioso del Rinascimento* (Florence, 1952, a bibliogra-

phy); A. Buck, 'Das Problem des christlichen Humanismus in der italienschen Renaissance', *Sodalitas Erasmiana I, Il valore universale dell'umanesimo* (Napoli, 1950), pp. 181–192; M. Seidelmayer, 'Religiös-ethische Probleme des italienischen Humanismus', *Germanisch-Romanische Monatsschrift* xxxix (1958), 105–126.

10. *De otio religioso*, not *De otio religiosorum*, as G. Rotondi effectively argues in his 'Le Due redazioni del *De otio* del Petrarca' *Aevum* ix (1935), 27–77; cf. pp. 32–33. Guido Martellotti carried to completion Rotondi's edition, *Il 'De otio religioso' di Francesco Petrarca* (Città del Vaticano, 1958, *Studi e Testi* 195). This edition, hereafter cited as 'Rotondi', while not definitive, is a vast improvement over the text of the Basel, 1581 *Opera omnia*, with which I first struggled. Martellotti, in his introduction, pp. x–xv, convincingly shows how defective and full of lacunae and corruptions the old printed editions are (and this corresponds to my more limited experience), so that they must now be regarded not as a first redaction but as poor and incomplete versions of the text edited by Rotondi. The latter is essentially that of Bibl. Vat. Cod. Urb. Lat. 333. The necessary study of the manuscript tradition, and particularly of those manuscripts which diverged and apparently form the basis of the old printed editions, remains to be made.

11. E. H. R. Tatham, *Francesco Petrarca, the First Modern Man of Letters* (London, 1926), ii, 395–444; E. H. Wilkins, *Studies in the Life and Works of Petrarch* (Cambridge, Mass., 1955), p. 13; the same, *Life of Petrarch* (Chicago, 1961), pp. 58–59. Martellotti, *op. cit.*, pp. xii–xiv, shows that Petrarch was still revising the work in 1357, but not after 1360.

12. Rotondi, p. 2: '. . . quamvis, ut quod est fatear, maiore et meliore mei parte sim presens.'

13. *De secreto conflictu curarum mearum*, pp. 22–215 (with Italian translation), in Francesco Petrarca, *Prose*, a cura di G. Martellotti, P. G. Ricci, E. Carrara, E. Bianchi, (Milan-Naples, 1955, La Letteratura Italiana Storia e Testi 7). Cf. p. 214: 'Adero michi ipse quantum potero, et sparsa anime fragmenta recolligam, moraborque mecum sedulo. Sane nunc, dum loquimur, multa me magnaque, quamvis adhuc mortalia, negotia expectant.' And p. 192: 'deque aliis scribens, tui ipsius oblivisceris.' Cf. my discussion of the *Secretum* in 'Petrarch's Views on the Individual and his Society', *Osiris* xi (1954), 168–198, especially pp. 181–182.

14. Rotondi, p. 15: '. . . potius auditura quid loquar, quam inspectura quid vivam.' Cf. also the remarkable autobiographical statement on pp. 103–105, where he describes his own belated study and love of the Scriptures under the stimulus of Augustine's *Confessions:* 'Accessit oportuna necessitas divinas laudes atque officium quotidianum, quod male distuleram, celebrandi, quam ob causam psalterium ipsum daviticum sepe percurrere sum coactus, e quibus fontibus haurire studui non unde disertior fierem, sed melior, si possem, neque unde evaderem disputator maior, sed peccator minor. Has ergo Scripturas, quas ego advena necdum notas odore illectus adamavi, sero licet, vos velut indigene et in his a principio enutriti amate, colite, veneramini, frequentate; nunquam de manibus vestris, si possibile sit, certe de mentibus vestris, nunquam excidant.'

15. 'Petrarch's Ecclesiastical Career', *Studies in the Life and Works of Petrarch,* Chap. 1. Wilkins states (p. 3): '. . . and he decided very naturally to enter the clerical profession. He must, then, have taken the tonsure. There is no evidence, however, that he took even the minor orders; theoretically only one who had taken those orders could hold benefices, but in Petrarch's time this requirement was not enforced. He certainly never took the major orders. No one of the benefices he received involved the cure of souls.' The passage quoted in the previous footnote, however, does suggest that he at least participated in divine services, whether or not he was fully ordained as a priest and thus able to say masses.

16. Rotondi, p. 2; *Psalms* xlvi. 10 (Vulg. xlv. 10).

17. *Ibid.,* p. 4: 'labore labor apud ceteros; apud vos autem quiete quies queritur.'

18. *Ibid.,* pp. 4–10.

19. *Ibid.,* pp. 9–10: "'. . . Nolite diligere mundum, neque ea que in mundo sunt, quia omne quod in mundo est concupiscentia carnis est et concupiscentia oculorum et ambitio seculi." [Augustine, *De vera religione* 4.] Horum ergo commeminit nosque commonuit Augustinus, sed infinita sunt alia id genus ad consolationem animarum et consilium dicta.'

20. *Ibid.,* p. 13: 'Dicitur penitenti: "Ita gaudium erit in celo super uno peccatore penitentiam agente . . .'" (Luke xv. 7; Gregory, *Libri regulae pastoralis,* especially iii.)

21. *Ibid.,* p. 14: 'Habetote ante oculos vestros professionem vestram: votum servate, implete regulam; id si lete facitis satis est.' (Benedict, *Regula monachorum,* cap. 7; Bernard of Clairvaux, *De gradibus humilitatis,* cap. 3–6, 9.)

22. *Ibid.,* p. 14: '. . . hunc ira torquebat, hunc libido, hunc superbia extollebat, hunc deprimebat accidia . . .'

23. *Ibid.,* pp. 16–17: 'In secularibus historiis irrisum legimus Labienum quod, relicto Cesare victore, ad Pompeium transiverit. . . quanto iustius irridendus qui Cristo victoriosissimo rege deserto ad illum [Sathanem] confugit . . .'

24. *Ibid.,* pp. 17–18, "'O dii . . . immortales, vobis enim tribuam que vestra sunt." . . . qua "invisibilia Dei per ea que facta sunt intellecta conspiciuntur" . . . didicisset.' (Cicero, *Pro Sulla* 40; *Romans* i. 20.) This brief discussion of the value of Cicero for Christian religious exhortation is repeated on Lactantius' authority later on (p. 86) and at much greater length in Petrarch's *De sui ipsius et multorum ignorantia* (*Opera onmia,* Basel, 1581, pp. 1035–1059; cf. Nachod's translation in Cassirer, Kristeller and Randall, *The Renaissance Philosophy of Man,* Chicago, 1948, pp. 79–91).

25. Rotondi, pp. 18–19; Augustine, *De vera religione,* iii.

26. *Ibid.,* p. 19: 'Hec ciceroniana, pro re paucissimis immutatis, in usus nostros sic vertere libuit, ut anime salutem et de invisibili hoste victoriam a Deo recognoscere tali etiam teste discamus.'

27. *Ibid.,* p. 20: 'optate bellum, non quidem pro se, sed propter Cristi gloriam et eternam pacem.' '. . . quas metus et negotium et labor in suo vigore tenuerunt, everterunt securitas, otium et quies. . . .'

28. *Ibid.,* pp. 21–22: 'Nostra tamen etate tam multos eis credere cernimus etiam

ex nostris, ut pudor et stupor occupet cogitantem aureos et argenteos deos, quos prisci reges sanctorum pontificum verbis instructi propter Cristi reverentiam delevere, ad Cristi iniuriam certatim a nostris hodie regibus ac pontificibus renovari. Si bene est quoniam argentum et aurum non ut deos colunt . . . colitur tamen argentum et aurum tanto cultu quanto nec Cristus ipse colitur et sepe vivus Deus inanimati metalli desiderio atque admiratione contemnitur. . . .'

29. Lactantius, *Divinae institutiones,* II, 18; also *Epitome,* 28.

30. Rotondi, p. 24: 'Et de Iudeis quidem hactenus. Quid deinceps? An dolosas Maometi fabulas, an philosophorum dissonas et inextricabiles ambages ac temerarii virus Averrois . . . an forte potius de illo vel sacrilegia Photini, vel Manichei nugas, vel Arii blasphemias audiamus? Que si omnia procul absunt a pectoribus sanis, si neque miserabilis paganorum error, neque cervicosa et obstinata Iudeorum cecitas, neque odibilis Saracenorum furor, neque fallacium philosophorum ventosa sophismata, neque hereticorum devia atque exotica dogmata tangunt animos aut delectant, aut nullam penitus spem salutis ostendunt, quid circumspicimus, quid agimus, aut quem inter huius vite naufragia portum petimus, nisi Cristum in quo quisquis spei sue anchoram iecit. . . .'

31. *Ibid.,* pp. 27–28: *Isaiah* vii. 14; Augustine, *De civitate Dei,* XVIII, 23, Lactantius, *Divinae institutiones,* IV, 18. Petrarch takes his reference to Lactantius from this chapter where Augustine claims to have recollected the scattered sayings of the sibyl from Lactantius. Petrarch also repeats Augustine on the great age of the Erythraean sibyl.

32. *Ibid.,* p. 29: 'Que quidem religiosus et pius lector, quamvis de Cesare dicta, ad celestem potius trahet imperatorem, cuius in adventum toto orbe signa precesserant, que audiens poeta neque altius aspirans ad imperatoris Romani, quo nil maius noverat, reflexit adventum, cuius si vera lux oculis affulsisset hauddubie ad alium reflexisset. Nobis vero iam, gratias illi qui usque adeo immeritos nos dilexit, hec omnia sine ullis externis testibus clara sunt et ita se oculis fidelium divine lucis radii infundunt, ut nemo tam cecus sit qui non "iustitie solem" Cristum mente perspiciat; et quamvis ab ipsa veritate verissimum dictum sit "Beati oculi qui vident que vos videtis'" (*Luke* x.23).

33. *Ibid.,* p. 31: 'illum signiferum *Civitatis Dei.'* Petrarch paraphrases *De civitate Dei,* XVIII, 51–54, in this section.

34. *Ibid.,* p. 38: '. . . quamvis enim [Dei filius] ut iudex puniat miseretur ut pater . . . En fragilitas nostra ante oculos nostros semper; nichil agimus quod non nos humane conditionis admoneat atque miserie, de qua quidem integros ediderunt libros, tractatus alii eximios, de qua Plinius Secundus VII *Naturalis historie* breviter attigit, sed stilo excellenti ac florida ubertate sententiarum, de qua et Augustinus latius agit libro *Civitatis Dei,* unde Cicero ante omnes librum sue *Consolationis* adimpleverat, de qua michi quoque nonnunquam fuit impetus loqui aliquid. . . .' Cf. Pliny VII, 6 ff.; Augustine, *De civitate Dei,* XXII, 22, 23; Cicero's *De consolatione,* a lost work, was known to Petrarch through quotations in Cicero's *Tusculanae disputationes.* Petrarch's own 'something' may refer to this work, pp. 34–37, to his *Secretum,* written four or five years earlier, to his *De remediis utriusque fortunae.*

35. *Ibid.*, p. 39: 'Gaude igitur, humana natura, de extremis miseriis facta felicior quam toto capere possis ingenio.'
36. Theodor E. Mommsen, 'Petrarch's Conception of the "Dark Ages" ', in his *Medieval and Renaissance Studies* (Ithaca, 1959), pp. 106–129, originally in *Speculum* XVII (1942), 226–242.
37. Rotondi, pp. 39–40: 'Intendite, queso, huc ingenia literata, audite Plato, Aristotiles, Pithagoras: non hic ridiculus ille circuitus animarum et vana metempsicosis, sed maius quoddam vere salutis archanum latet. . . . Multa de nubibus, de imbribus, de fulminibus, de ventis, de glacie, de nive, de tempestate, de grandine, multa de animalium naturis, de potentiis herbarum, de qualitatibus rerum, multa denique de tumore pelagi, de tremore terrarum, de motu celi ac stellarum disputata acriter et tractata subtiliter reliquistis, at quibus modis terre celum iungeretur atque uniretur unum hoc ex omnibus non vidistis. . . . Inter celum nempe et terram distantia ingens, fateor, sed finita est, inter Deum vero et hominem infinita. . . . In quibusdam sane codicibus vestris predicari Deum et eius Verbum et multa, que circa summum fidei verticem et coeternam Patri Filii personam evangelicis apicibus conveniant Augustino testante notum est, quod scilicet "in principio erat Verbum et Verbum erat apud Deum et Deus erat Verbum", quodque "omnia per ipsum facta sunt et sine ipso factum est nichil", at qualiter "Verbum" illud "caro factum sit", qualiter terre iunctum "habitarit in nobis" "hoc doctus Plato nescivit", ut ait Ieronimus, "hoc Demosthenes eloquens ignoravit" . . . "nullus Deus miscetur hominibus". . . . "Deus ad homines veniet, nulla sine Deo mens bona est".' Cf. Augustine, *De civitate Dei*, x, 29; *John* i. 1, 3, 14; Jerome, *Epist.* LIII, 4; Seneca, *Epist.* LXXIII, 16.
38. *Ibid.*, pp. 41–42.
39. *Ibid.*, pp. 43–47.
40. *Ibid.*, p. 48: " '. . . romani principes imitentur Camillos, Fabritios, Regulos, Scipiones; philosophi proponant sibi Pithagoram, Socratem, Platonem, Aristotilem; poete emulentur Homerum, Vergilium, Menandrum, Terrentium; historici Tuchididem, Salustium, Herodotum, Livium; oratores Lisiam, Graccos, Demosthenem, Tullium et, ut ad nostra veniamus, epyscopi et presbyteri habeant in exemplum apostolos et apostolicos viros . . . Nos autem habemus propositi nostri principes Paulum, Antonium, Iulianum, Hilarionem, Macharium et ut ad veritatem Scripturarum redeamus noster princeps Helias, noster Heliseus, nostri duces filii prophetarum"; equidem, fratres, hi sunt vestri duces, qui Ieronimi duces erant. Insuper et ipse Ieronimus et Augustinus et Gregorius et omnino quisquis aliquando hactenus pro Cristi amore solitariam atque heremeticam agens vitam religioso otio claruisse noscitur' (Jerome, *Epist.* LVII, 5, which Petrarch liberally quotes). Petrarch adds (pp. 48–49): 'Non est animus nominatim hic reliquos attingere, quorum nomina satis in secundum *Solitarie vite* partem congessisse videor.' Cf. *De vita solitaria*, II, iv–ix, in *Prose*, pp. 430–482.
41. *Ibid.*, p. 74.
42. *Ibid.*, pp. 49–54.
43. *Ibid.*, pp. 55–58.

44. *Ibid.,* p. 60: '. . . eandem simulque aliam civitatem ingressos, ut dicatis cum Heraclito: in eandem civitatem bis intramus et non intramus.'

45. *Ibid.,* p. 63: 'O flebilis et infelix transmutatio! Omnia in vermes inque serpentes, omnia tandem in nichilum abiere.'

46. *Ibid.,* pp. 63–76. But cf. p. 65 for mention of St. Bernard, p. 74 for St. Francis.

47. Theodor E. Mommsen, 'Petrarch and the Story of the Choice of Hercules', *Medieval and Renaissance Studies* (n. 36), pp. 175–196; originally in *Jour. of the Warburg & Courtauld Inst.* XVI (1953), 175–196. Cf. in this connection p. 192 (*J.W.C.I.* p. 189).

48. *Ibid.,* pp. 77–78, "'. . . beati omnes qui confidunt in eo". Vera quidem confidentia nisi de virtute non nascitur. . . .et scientes quia "vana salus hominis; in Deo faciemus virtutem et ipse ad nichilum deducet inimicos nostros". Hec est, non alia, salus nostra; hec nostra virtus, hec nostra securitas, hoc remedium unicum contra iram Domini: vacare, timere, sperare et orare "ne in furore suo arguat nos neque in ira sua corripiat nos.'" (*Psalms* ii, 13, cvii. 13–14, vi. 2.)

49. *Op.cit.,* 286–591. Cf. Jacob Zeitlin's excellent introduction to his English translation (Urbana, 1924). Cf. my 'Petrarch's Views' etc. (cited n. 13), pp. 183–196. Petrarch considered the works as paralleling each other. Cf. Rotondi, p. 6: 'Sileo que sequuntur, nam et ea me scripsisse recolo in eo libro, quem huic et materia et stilo valde cognatum *De solitaria vita* nuper edidi, qui hunc ut tempore, sic serie rerum preit, et omnia ad unum tendunt, ad notam scilicet mortalis insanie magis labore gaudentis quam laboris fructu.'

50. *Colucii Salutati De seculo et religione* ex codicibus manuscriptis primum edidit B. L. Ullman (Florence, 1957, Nuova Collezione di Testi Umanistici Inediti o Rari XII). Citations will refer to this as 'Ullman edition'.

51. *Ibid., Praefatio,* p. vi: 'Liber ergo Colucii non est speculum mentis auctoris sed demonstrat eius facultatem disputandi et scientiam divinarum scripturarum. Si res postulasset, contra vitam monasticam perinde disputare potuisset.' This statement provoked me to question whether 'Colucius homo esse mediaevalis, ut ita dicam, non modernus videtur' (p. v) in a review, *Renaissance News* XI (1958), 216–218. Whereupon Giuseppe Toffanin took up the question of a possible conflict of medievalism and humanism in Salutati in a short article (*Rinascimento* IX, 1958, 3–10; reprinted in his *Ultimi saggi,* Bologna, 1960, pp. 149–157). 'Per Coluccio Salutati'. Toffanin chided Ullman for regarding this work as in any way exceptional. It was not rhetorical but a sincere facing of the relationship between a medieval outlook and the Stoic ethic of Cicero. In *Rivista critica di storia della filosofia* XV (1960), 73–82, 'A proposito di Coluccio Salutati', Eugenio Garin emphasized the rhetorical character of this treatise in support of Ullman. Ullman has now replied in *The Humanism of Coluccio Salutati* (Padova, 1963). Although he reaffirms his feeling that the work is rhetorical, that Salutati also argued against another friend entering a monastery, and feels 'in almost complete accord' with Garin, he makes the following statement (p. 28): 'Perhaps what I have just said is sufficient to remove the misunderstanding of

my brief and possibly ambiguous remarks in the introduction of my edition of the *De seculo et religione*. I certainly had no thought of questioning Coluccio's sincerity. He believed that a man should hold to his monastic vows, therefore he brought every argument and every rhetorical device to bear on his Camaldolese friend.' On the previous page he had said, in reference to Alfred von Martin's *Mittelalterliche Welt-und Lebensanschauung im Spiegel der Schriften Coluccio Salutatis* (Munich, 1913), 'Martin's thesis has been seized upon by those who do not believe in a Renaissance. . . . Coluccio in particular was a humanist in a state of evolution, with many medieval traits clinging to him. Martin goes too far in thinking that Coluccio believed all he said, that he favored monasticism under any circumstances. Coluccio was sincere in urging it upon the monk. . . . He accepted the institution of monasticism but did not himself become a monk.' He would have been just as sincere if called upon to argue against entering a monastery. Although in a footnote I cannot discuss in detail my reactions to Ullman's statements here and elsewhere in this book, I need to say, as I hope my analysis of this work of Salutati will make clear, that there is a compatibility between such a so-called 'medieval' point of view as a defense of monasticism and 'humanism'. Moreover, Salutati's very acceptance of the 'medieval' notion of the relation of lay, secular-clerical, and religious states was not in the least inconsistent with his remaining a layman and feeling himself a good Christian and admirer of monasticism.

52. The previous footnote touches on this question. The political inconsistency of Salutati's *De tyranno* with the views of Bruni has especially bothered Hans Baron, *The Crisis of the Early Italian Renaissance,* chap. 7. The methodological misconception which insists that historical developments must be consistent to be meaningful cannot be discussed here.

53. Ullman edition, 'Praefatio', p. vi.

54. Cf. Ullman's 'Index Auctorum et Nominum' and page references given. Of course, in this, as in other works, Salutati frequently makes use of a medieval work without naming it. Cf. Toffanin, *op. cit.,* pp. 156–157; also Walter Rüegg, 'Entstehung, Quellen und Ziel von Salutatis "De Fato et Fortuna"', *Rinascimento* V (1954), 11–17.

55. Ullman edition, p. 80, 'Quod mundus sit ministrator necessariorum'.

56. *Ibid.:* 'Ministrat equidem necessaria nobis mundus, necessaria quippe ad vitam hanc corruptibilem transigendam.'

57. *Ibid.:* '. . . famen enim reprimi, sitim extingui, imbres et frigora pelli, ventorumque et estuum vim arceri natura desiderat. Quicquid ultra est a malo est.'

58. *A Doctumentary History of Primitivism and Related Ideas,* eds. A. O. Lovejoy, G. Chinard, G. Boas, R. S. Crane (Baltimore, 1935), 1, 9–11.

59. Ullman edition, pp. 80–81: 'Quam facile vero his necessitatibus satisfiat, docuit etas prima, que famem, ut legitur, glande replevit, sitim compressit undis, frigora depulit pellibus, imbres, ventos, et estus antris ac specubus evitavit. Hec est illa innocentissima etas quam poete multis laudibus extollentes tum auream, tum Saturniam vocaverunt. O felices glandes! O

saluberrima flumina! Non excitavit tunc estuantium ciborum virus suo calore libidinem; non tentavit cerebrum insanie simillima marcens ebrietas; non fuit cum proximo de finibus controversia, non de regno. Omnia communia erant. Thoros herba, domos antra non custodita, non clausa, sed cunctis patula ministrabant. Sublata tunc erant, imo nondum reperta, illa duo litigiosa vocabula que mortalium pacem turbant queve claudunt hominibus viam in celum, que sunt avaricie fomites et contentionum autores, scilicet "meum" et "tuum". . . . Sed adeo mundo et deliciis dati sumus quod illa nostris moribus, imo non moribus sed abusibus ac flagitiis, comparantes fabulosa, non hystorica, reputemus, dicimusque fragiliorem fore temporis nostri etatem ut ad asperitatem illam impossibile sit redire. Fragilior autem est, fateor, quia vitiosior et, quod vitiorum fomes est, quia delicatior. Impossibilis profecto videtur reditus ad frugalitatem et prisci temporis communionem. . . .'

60. Juvenal, vi, 1 seqq.; Vergil, *Eclogues* 4, 6, 9, etc.; Boethius, *Consolatio,* ii, 5, 23–24, 25–26.

61. Ullman edition, pp. 81–82: 'Tolle cupidinem, miser homo, depone divitias, abrenuntia mundo, duc vitam tuam sub preceptis, coneris adimplere consilia, subde voluntatem tuam voluntati divine, . . . incipe diligere deum, odire mundum, amare paupertatem, horrere divitias. Non potes hec relinquere nisi odio habeas; non potes ad illa transire ni diligas. Nec iam etatis nostre fragilitatem accuses. Potens est enim corpus nostrum per omnes incommoditates transire. Non referam tibi Danielem et socios in legumina regie mense delicias commutantes. Non proponam tibi in exemplum maximum illum inter natos mulierum domini precursorem; non anachoritas, de quibus mirabilia legimus in vita patrum, non heremitas etiam nostri temporis; non cenobitas, quorum multos videmus eligere paupertatem, amare ieiunia, et omnem fugere voluptatem. Scio enim quod, cum istos obiecero, respondebit amator mundi illos spiritus sancti gratia suffultos hec facere nunc posse et hactenus potuisse, et spiritum spirare quando, quantum, et ubi vult hocque a nostre voluntatis arbitrio non pendere.'

62. *Ibid.,* pp. 82–82.

63. *Ibid.,* p. 83: 'Mundum quidem reliquere possumus et deo servientes ad extremam illam necessitatem nature nostra corpora subiugare.'

64. *Ibid.,* pp. 121–131, 'De voto paupertatis'.

65. *Ibid.,* p. 123: 'Nec cogitamus miseri mortales contra naturam esse quod illas ad usum omnium procreatas per avariciam in nostre proprietatis dominium vendicemus, cumque vite nostre debeant deservire, facimus illas nobis flagitiorum, voluptatum, et cunctorum scelerum instrumenta. . . . et ita tantum bona si illis utamur bene. Nam male utentibus mala sunt.'

66. *Ibid.,* pp. 124–125: 'Quod si cogitaremus duas omnino fuisse et esse debitas mortalibus civitates, unam spiritualem quam dei dicimus, alteram vero carnalem quam mundi possumus appellare, et ad alterutram ipsarum affectus nostros et finem nostrorum operum statueremus, occurreret nobis utramque civitatem a pauperibus institutam, a divitibus vero dirutam et corruptam. Et prius, si placet, de hac mundana civitate quos autores habuerit speculemur.

Nolo, licet facile possem per cuncta regna discurrere, sed illud quod omnium maximum et fortissimum fuit et quod adhuc saltem nominis obtinet principatum, Romanorum videlicet, perquiramus.'

67. *Ibid.*, pp. 125–128. Cf. Ullman's footnotes for Salutati's classical sources.

68. *Ibid.*, pp. 127–128: 'Quid plura, cum pleni sint omnium hystoriarum libri de paupertate, moderatione, et abstinentia Romanorum? Hi paupers tantum imperium fundaverunt quod, "postea quam", ut nobilis et veritate insignis hystoricus ait, "divitie honori esse ceperunt et eas gloria, imperium, et potentia sequebatur, hebescere virtus, paupertas probro haberi cepit", successores divites everterunt. . . . Rem enim publicam Romanorum, quam pauper fundavit Romulus et pauperrimi principes ad tantam magnitudinem evexerunt ut imperium occeano, astris vero gloriam terminaret et eis ad occasum ab ortu solis omnia domita armis parerent, divites, L. Silla crudelis, Cinna ferox, ambitiosusque Marius, labefactaverunt, et ditiores, M. Crassus, Gn. Pompeius Magnus, ac Gaius Cesar, Lucii Cesaris filius, funditus destruxerunt. Ut in hac rerum gestarum memoria quasi quodam in speculo videre possit mortalium genus ad hanc terrenam civitatem instituendam, augendam, atque conservandum paupers divitibus prestitisse.'

69. Vide supra note 52. Hans Baron referred to the passage discussed without connecting it to the Florentine political situation in his earlier article: 'Franciscan Poverty and Civic Wealth as Factors in the Rise of Humanistic Thought', *Speculum* XIII (1938), 16–17. However, Marvin B. Becker specifically connects this passage and the one cited below in note 72 with the doctrines of the *Fraticelli* and their active role in the uprising of the Ciompi: 'Florentine Politics and the Diffusion of Heresy in the Trecento: a Socioeconomic Inquiry', *Speculum* XXXIV (1959), 74–75, note 88.

70. Ullman edition, p. 128: 'Quid autem de illa civitate que ad supernam spectat Ierusalem dicam?'

71. *Ibid.*, pp. 128–129; *Matthew* viii. 20.

72. *Ibid.*, pp. 129–131: 'Ut manifeste cunctis appareat illos primos in renovatione temporum celestis civitatis et ecclesie catholice fundatores aut pauperes extitisse aut venditis omnibus que habebant et in communi collatis paupertatem voluntariam elegisse. . . . Hi pauperes et humiles infinitis martiriis per ducentos treginta et amplius annos ab Nerone, primo Christianorum persecutore, usque in Dyoclitianum et Maximum imperatores, quorum tempore decima plaga Christiane persecutionis efferbuit, ecclesiam catholicam fundaverunt. Quam post Constantinum, qui non dotavit sed ditavit ecclesiam et superba sibi tradidit imperialis apicis ornamenta (pace cunctorum dictum sit), hi nostri presules, quibus sicut aliis illis ducibus terrene civitatis primo pecunie, deinde imperii cupido crevit, postquam simulam, mel, et oleum comederunt et ornati sunt auro et argento et vestiti sunt bysso et pollimito et multicoloribus et decori facti sunt vehementer nimis et demum profecerunt in regnum, illam civitatem gloriosam abominabilem reddiderunt. Nunc, quod summe deflendum est, cum videant Christianam fidem olim toto orbe diffusam abominatione Saracenica tot terrarum spacia perdidisse, cum videant antiquum Greculorum scisma tot populos, tot

urbes, totque quondam opulentissima regna ab unitate sancte matris ecclesie separasse, quasi adhuc nimia moles esset nimiaque fidelium multitudo, duos summos pontifices variis temporibus eligendo, si tamen electiones censende sunt quas vel odium vel ambitio vel alie mentium humanarum turbide passiones extorquent, non que in zelo fidei et in edificationem celestis Ierusalem celebrantur, scisma perniciosissimum pepererunt. Ut, sicut illi utriusque civitatis principes et autores, dum paupertatem dilexerunt, nedum fundamenta duarum illarum urbium iacientes in ingens maxime molis opificium profecerunt sed incrementis mirabilibus inter labores et sanguinem aucti sunt, ita isti divites corrumpente pecunia mentes et bonos mores pene cuncta cum sua gloriosa rerum omnium opulentia destruxerunt. Que cum ita sint, nisi desipere gaudeamus, si celestis vel terrene civitati servire, si nos utrique vel alterutri volumus utiles exhibere, quis non videt dimittendas esse divitias, que suos adeo corrumpant et attaminent possessores?'

Garin ('Desideri di riforma', cited in n. 7, p. 169) singled out this passage from Salutati in order to associate him with later humanist diatribes against the corruption of the clergy. But, curiously, he combined the phrase 'vestiti sunt bysso' cited just above with a phrase from book 1, chap. 21 (Ullman edition, p. 46), 'non religiosus sed potius Ciprica mulier videatur', and then quotes at length from this earlier passage, which satirizes the vanity of a friar and the false arts of his preaching to prove 'Quod mundus sit spectaculum delictorum'. Apart from his taking this passage out of its own context, it is interesting that Garin's concern with Salutati is confined to seeking evidence of anti-clericalism rather than examining Salutati's position on the status of the regular clergy.

73. *Ibid.*, pp. 137–156.
74. *Ibid.*, pp. 138–140.
75. *Ibid.*, p. 141: '. . . quicquid execrationis sparsum inter divinarum scripturarum oracula reperitur aliquo sane expositionis misterio ad vere caritatis regulam aut divine iusticie desiderium referri debeat vel alicuius altioris sensus lumine sit taliter exponendum quod caritati dei et proximi nullatenus contradicat, cum maxime lata via expositoribus pateat . . .' .
76. *Ibid.*, pp. 145–149. His discussion here includes a short exposition of the Lord's Prayer.
77. *Ibid.*, pp. 149–152.
78. *Ibid.*, pp. 154–155.
79. *Ibid.*, pp. 131–137, 'De obedientie voto'.
80. Cf. supra note 47.
81. *Hercules am Scheidewege und andere antike Bildstoffe in der neueren Kunst* (Leipzig and Berlin, 1930, *Studien der Bibliothek Warburg* XVIII), p. 155.
82. *Coluccio Salutati De laboribus Herculis,* edidit B. L. Ullman (Zurich, 1951, *Thesaurus Mundi*).
83. Printed by Ullman in *De laboribus Herculis,* pp. 585–635.
84. Ullman edition, pp. 134–135: 'Nescio si verum dicam, devotissime tamen ausim asserere cunctos qui citra divine maiestatis obedientiam virtuosum aliquid operantur, nedum non mereri sed improbe facere, et omnes qui agunt

verbi gratia frequentes actus fortitudinis vel temperantie ob hoc solum, ut fortes vel temperati sint, non etiam ut videantur, nedum carnaliter sapere sed etiam a gentilium philosophis non differre. Omittamus enim Romanos, qui cunctarum actionum suarum finem sibi mundanam gloriam proponebant. Nonne illi philosophi qui terminum bonorum omnium virtutem, ut ceteros vanioris sententie dimittam, esse volebant, que maxime Stoycorum opinio fuit, se ipsis, ut aiebant, contenti nichil ulterius de suis actionibus requirebant nisi conscientie secretum et ut virtuosi possent evadere secumque de virtutum acquistione gaudere? Quid igitur ab istis differre dixerimus Christianum qui dei iubentis oblitus et huius virtutis habitum derelinquens, non ut deo placeat vel obediat, sed solum ut bonum aliquod faciat operatur? Certe secure dixerim tanto deteriorem quanto constitutus per baptismi regenerationem in gratia et in evangelio veritatem edoctus nec sic agit ut debet nec ipsis virtutibus utitur ut deceret, imo virtutibus contra rationem nititur frui, quibus sic fruendo verius dicatur abuti. Non igitur terrena sapiamus sed, cum ad nichil cogamur necessitate nature, deo, cui fidem promisimus in libertate nobis de nostra voluntate concessa, fideliter pareamus.

Toffanin ('Per Coluccio Salutati', *Ultimi saggi,* pp. 155–157), I discovered subsequently to writing this paper, selected this exact quotation to show, through the addition of one more sentence—'Pareamus quidem alacriter et in caritate, sine qua, sicut sentit apostolus, cuncta virtutis operatio nichil est'—Salutati's agreement with Bonaventura and his opposition to Cicero's view of virtue as an end in itself. Toffanin cites Bonaventura's *Hexameron,* '. . . virtutes informes et nudae sunt philosophorum, vestitae autem sunt nostrae . . .' . I am inclined to think that Salutati's stress, here, is on obedience, rather than on charity and grace. Either stress, however, is clearly antagonistic to the pagan view of virtue which Mommsen and Panofsky see emerging in the Renaissance around the story of the choice of Hercules. However, I would be less secure now (1983) in calling his statement "Augustinian"!

85. Ullman edition, pp. 109–114, 'Semper habenda professionis sue memoria et quod maius sit meritum religiosorum quam eorum qui citra voti vinculum operantur.'
86. *Ibid.,* p. III: 'Tu enim te ipsum, voluntatem et opera tua deo religionem ingrediens dedicasti. . . . Hoc est vere holocaustum, id est totum exustum et incensum, in quo totum quod sumus et possumus deo committimus, et nichil in nostra relinquimus potestate. Hoc non faciunt qui sine voto solum operas offerunt, et ob id apud dei benignitatem non est dignum ipsos tantundem quantum votis obnoxios promereri. Quis enim plus gratie meretur, an qui solum fructus arboris sic superiori donaret quod ad illorum prestationem nisi quantum sibi placuerit non teneatur, an qui et arborem donat et fructus tali condicione quod etiam post donationem nequeat revocare? Nemini dubium illum qui plus donaverit plus mereri . . .' . Cf. *Eadmeri Monachi [Cantuariensis] Liber de sancti Anselmi similtudinibus* (Migne, P. L., tom. 159), cap LXXXIV, 'Similitudo inter monachum et arborem', col. 656: 'Cujus igitur horum obsequium domino illi magis videtur acceptum? An

illius, qui, quando quantumque voluerit, dat ei de fructu propriae arboris, vel illius qui arborem et fructum totaliter offert? Imo magis illius qui arborem totam dat ei cum fructu.' This may not have been Salutati's source, but it unquestionably was a medieval commonplace.

87. Ullman edition, p. 112: 'Etenim qui bonum libera voluntate facit, sicut evenit in solutis a voto, unicum bonum facit; qui vero vovet et facit, dum voto se obligat, meretur et bonum facit. Dum autem vota reddit, licet faciat debitum, nichilominus bonum facit. Non enim audiendi sunt qui delirantes conantur asserere bona que sine voto fiunt his que ex obedientia voti facimus esse maiora, adducentes quod plus obligamur libera voluntate donanti quam debitum persolventi, quasi quod vovens debitor factus sit, non ex libera processerit voluntate, et quod aliquid libere promittenti nichil eo quod promiserit debeamus. . . . Errant hi profecto. Nam longe maiore caritate, que finis est precepti, vovetur atque perficitur quam si simpliciter aliquid prebeamus.'

88. *Ibid.,* p. 113.

89. *Ibid.,* p. 163: 'Quando nascimur successione primi parentis, cuius omnes heredes sumus et filii, nascimur ire vasa moxque institutione sancte matris, ecclesie, per baptismi lavacrum renovamur in gratia. Prima quidem et vera religio, in qua diabolo et suisque pompis caratherem Christianitatis accipiens abrenuntiat, fides est nostra, plene quidem, si rite servetur, via perfectionis ad deum, adeo tamen perversa consuetudine temporalibus permixta negociis quod, nisi dei benignitas superet iniusticiam nostram, licet multi vocentur, pauci tamen sunt ad electionis beneficium perventuri. Plenior autem est quando quotidianis divine maiestatis servitiis, in copia tamen rerum nos extra seculum per clericatus ordinem obligamus. Plenissima vero perfectio est in via cum non solum deum sequimur diabolum fugientes, non solum in dei servitio famulamur relinquentes mundum (non enim debet clericus secularibus se negociis permiscere), sed etiam nos ipsos per castitatis, obedientie, et paupertatis votum deo offerimus et verum holocaustum in religionis altario consecramus, ut non incongrue dici possit, quod et superius attigi, omnibus Christianis tanquam in terram bonam seminantibus trigesimum fructum, clericis sexagesimum, religiosis vero centesimum reservari.'

90. *Epistolario di Coluccio Salutati,* ed. F. Novati (Rome, 1891–1911), iv, 216. Excerpt in Garin, *Il Pensiero pedagogico dello umanesimo* (Florence, 1958), p. 60.

91. Florence, Biblioteca Medicea-Laurenziana, Pl. 52, Cod. 3, ff. 25–30.

92. Edited and translated into Italian by Giulio Vallese (Naples, 1946), on the basis of *Poggii Florentini dialogus, et Leonardi Aretini oratio adversus hypocrisim* ad fidem MSS edita et emendata a Hieronymo Sincero Lotharingo, Lugduni, MDCLXXIX. This edition was reprinted in 1691 and 1699. The text is printed by Vallese pp. 79–112.

93. Bruni, *op. cit.,* f. 28ᵛ: 'Nec ego solum de religiosis verum etiam de secularibus loquor. Nam in utroque genere haec infanda reperitur pestis.'

94. *Ibid.,* f. 30: 'Nam bonus quidem vir letus et alacris est, ex recte factorum conscientia et ex bona spe, quam nulla penarum formido conturbat. Hypo-

critas autem sua urunt facinora et quasi furiae ante oculos observantur. Necesse est enim illos quamvis sint improbi interdum de se ac de suis erratis cogitare. Est enim unusquisque recte ac perperam factorum iudex sibi ipsi constitutus. Hoc est certissimum profecto ac verax iudicium quod neque falli neque seduci neque circumveniri ullo modo potest. Non enim testibus creditur, neque tabulis arguitus reus, non a patrono per gratiam vel eloquentiam defenditur. Omnia scit iudex, omnibus interfuit, nec semel tantum quis sed saepe frequenterque iudicatur. Huius interni iudicis condemnatio, lacrimas illas tibi excutit et inter sacra plorare compellit. Sed crede mihi, . . . hic ludus et iocus est, ad sempiternum illud ineffabilemque dei iudicium, quod te post mortem expectat.'

95. Garin, 'Desideri di riforma' (n. 7), pp. 170–173, uses these two works along with other humanist diatribes against the corruption of the clergy, regular or secular, as part of his argument that there was a continuing humanist reform movement within the confines of Catholicism, culminating in Savonarola and Gianfrancesco Pico, which sought a purification of customs and a deepening spirituality. As should be clear, my concern here is not with humanist denunciation of clerical abuses but with their basic notions of the status and relations of laity, clergy, and religious.

96. Edited from an apparently unique manuscript, Biblioteca Apostolica Vaticana, Cod. Urb. Lat. 595, fols. 1^r–25^r, by M. J. Vahlen, *Sitzungberichte der kaiserlichen Akademie der Wissenchaften,* Phil.-Hist. Klasse, Bd. 62 (Vienna, 1869), pp. 99–134. Now photographically reprinted in Laurentius Valla, *Opera omnia* (Turin, 1962), Tomus alter, pp. 287–322. Cf. also Vahlen's *Laurentii Vallae Opuscula tria,* Bd. 61, pp. 9–15 (Turin *Opera,* pp. 135–141), 50–66 (176–192). The date is controversial. Vahlen limits it to after 1438 and before 1442, Giorgio Radetti, in a recent review of the calculations of Vahlen, Mancini, and Sabbadini concludes that it must be 1442. Cf. his introduction, pp. xxvii–xxix, to Lorenzo Valla, *Scritti filosofici e religiosi* (Florence, 1953).

97. *Quadragesimale de Christiana religione,* Sermo XVI, *De sacra religione,* art. III, cap. III: 'Tertia ratio est quia homo in religione premiatur copiosius, et maxime propter tria': '. . . ratio triplex est: primo, ratione praeceptorum; secundo, ratione consiliorum; tertio, ratione votorum' (*Opera omnia,* Firenze-Quaracchi, 1950, 1, 189 ff.).

98. In Hieronymus Aliottus, *Epistolae et opuscula* (Arezzo, 1769). Aliotti (Agliotti, or Jeronimo Aretino) was an interlocutor in Poggio's *Dialogus adversus hypocrisim* (n. 92).

99. *Op. cit.,* p. 103: 'Quaero ante omnia, . . . numquid id, . . . plus te a deo remunerationis assecuturum, eam vim habeat, quod cum duo inter se nihil mentium corporumque qualitate differant assintque utrique paria omnia quae extrinsecus hominibus accidunt et in eisdem ambo actionibus vitae versentur, plus tamen remunerationis a deo debeatur huic qui professus est istam sectam, quam religionem et inde vos religiosos appellatis, quam illi non professo aliquam sectam nec vestram nec monachorum . . .'

100. *Ibid.,* p. 104: 'Tamen hoc de quo miraris quod sectam malui dicere quam

religionem, non modo venustatis a me habita est ratio sed etiam necessitatis. Cum enim ego non tantum isti vestrae vitae tribuendum putem, quantum vos tribuitis, nimium visum est, vos huic rei tam sacrum venerandumque nomen imponere. Aliter non est causa, cur disputemus. Namque si vos soli religiosi estis, concedendum erit, optimos eosdem omnium hominum esse. Quod ita non est, ut sentio, de quo disputaturus sum.'

101. *Ibid.*, p. 105: 'Qua in re non tam arrogantes de vobis quam contumeliosi in ceteros videmini. Quae enim mihi laus contingere uberior potest aut e contrario maior vituperatio quam vel religiosum esse vel irreligiosum? Nam quid est aliud esse religiosum quam esse christianum et quidem vere christianum? . . . ut idem sit religio quod fides et religiosus quod fidelis, fidelis, inquam, non tamquam mortuus sine operibus sed cum operibus et qualis dici possit vere chistianus.' Cf. James i. 26–27.

102. *Ibid.*, p. 106: 'Itaque cum vos religiosos tantum modo facitis, qui professi estis, ceteros vero religiosos negatis, quid aliud quam vos solos christianos, vos solos bonos, vos solos mundos immaculatosque fatemini, alios autem damnatis, contemnitis, in tartarum abiicitis? . . . Quae cum ita sint, non feci illiberaliter in vos, quod religiosos appellare dubitarim, cum et multi aliorum, qui istam sive sectam sive regulam professi non sunt, religiosi vocari debeant, quia sanctissime vivunt, et multi vestrorum vocari non debeant, qui coinquinatissme.'

103. *Ibid.*, pp. 106–111; p. 111: 'Ad insaniam paene me redigis verbis, virtutes nostras extenuas, remunerationes prope aufers, vitia auges, poenas multiplicas, religiones ac religiosos omnes vere ut dixisti in lutum praecipites agis.'

Liber de sancti Anselmi Similitudinibus (n. 86), cap. LXXXI–LXXXII, may be compared with the interchange in Valla reported here; cols. 653–654: 'Sed dicet aliquis: Melius esset ut Deo sine professione serviret spontaneus quam in monasterio professione se alligans servire cogeretur invitus. Hic autem est respondendum quia tanta distantia est inter illum qui non vult facere Deo promissionem serviendi sibi, et eum qui libenter eam facit, quanta inter homines duos qui ambo ex debito debent servire domino uni. . . . Sic autem et Deus inter professum monachum et nolentem profiteri judicat, si eos contra eum pecasse poeniteat. Non solum autem professum mitius judicat non professo, sed etiam quolibet laico adhuc in saeculo constituto. Licet enim uterque idem peccatum committat, tamen si toto ex corde monachum poeniteat deliquisse, eumque ordinem, cui se subdidit, ferventi amore custodiat, majorem quam laicus misericordiam consequetur, quantumlibet ille poeniteat saecularibus adhuc detentus. Si vero poenitere noluerit, majori quam laicus damnationi subjacebit.'

San Bernardino, *op. cit.* (n. 97), p. 191, may also be compared: 'Ex iam dictis patere potest quod qui facit aliquid sine voto, dat ei solum quod facit propter eius amorem. Qui enim non solum facit, sed etiam vovet, non tantum dat ei quod facit, sed etiam potentiam qua illud facit; facit enim se non posse quin faciat quod prius non facere licite poterat. . . .

'Et his tribus rationibus clarescere potest quod qui ex voto aliquid operatur, plus Deo donat, plura bona multiplicat atque firmius in bono opere se confirmat, ceteris paribus plus meretur, et sic per consequens in caelesti gloria copiosius praemiatur. . . . Haec autem dixisse velim de Religione et religiosis servantibus professionem suam, non autem de dissolutis et sceleratis.'

104. *Op.cit.*, pp. 113–115; p. 115: 'Quod vos facitis, iusiurandum sive promissionem esse concedo, votum non concedo.'

105. *Ibid.*, pp. 116–118; p. 118: 'Non est professio votum sed devotio. Est enim devovere, ut brevissime dixerim, quasi dicare aut dedicare.'

106. *Ibid.*, p. 119: 'Verum non omnibus ista necessaria sunt.'

107. *Ibid.*, p. 121: 'Non retracto ego sponsionem meam, nec homini do, quod deo dederam, nec iterum deo promitto, quod ante promiseram. Sed in quibuscumque etiam deo serviens arbitrium habebam, ut vestiendi, vescendi, eundi, agendi, cubandi, dormiendi, vigilandi, postremo loquendi, horum omnium libertatem et ut dixi arbitrium a me in alterum transcribo . . .'

108. *Ibid.*, p. 121: 'illis, libertatem suam retinentibus'.

109. *Ibid.*, pp. 122–123: 'Ergo nihil est medium, nisi ut aut servos habeamus aut servitia simus . . . ? Non sunt omnes domini nec omnes servi, non omnes praeceptores nec omnes discipuli: nec minorem gradum o[b]tinent qui in medio sunt. Atque ut optabile est assequi statum praelatorum praeceptorumque, ita miserum in numero subditorum discipulorumque esse, certe longe hoc minoris dignitatis quam ut dixi in medio esse et per te posse sine domino et sine magistro vivere et scire. Non ausim dicere, abiecti indoctique animi signum et sibi ipsi diffidentis, in morem pueri tutoris se praesidio ac praeceptoris tutelaeque committere. Nam si idoneus est, ut alios admoneat, doceat, regat, quid ita se aliis subiicit, praesertim, ut frequenter evenit, imperitis et indignis . . . maius praemium deberi iis qui optime praesunt, quam qui optime obediunt. . . . Itaque genus servitutis est vestra ista obedientiae sponsio. . . . Ego tamen dominum me aliorum malim esse quam servum aut certe dominum mei.'

110. *Ibid.*, p. 123: 'Parere regulae est deo parere, non homini, quod et nos facimus, neque alia melior tradi regula potest quam est tradita a Christo atque apostolis.'

111. *Ibid.*, p. 124: 'Quid quaeris? Si nihil in vivendo temperate atque frugaliter ego et tu discrepamus, qui tandem fieri potest ut tu pauper sis, ego dives . . . ? . . . Etiamne libros vendam et erogabo? Apostolis praeceptum est hoc et illis quibus sine libris, sine studio, sine praemeditatione tributum erat ut principibus responderent? Mihi vero codices necessarii sunt et pecuniae eaeque non paucae, unde codices plurimos et cetera vitae praesidia coemam. Nam quid perversius quam tua mendicis dare ut postea ipse mendices. . . . Itaque satis est, si opibus non fruar, non oblecter, eisque non re sed animo renuntiem. . . . Nihil minus. Dixi mihi necessarias esse pecunias ut coemam codices. Tu si aliter facis tradisque illas pauperibus, stultus sis, qui non te ut proximum amas.'

112. *Ibid.*, p. 125: '. . . deponis spem acquirendi, sed et sollicitudinem, non es habiturus meliora, sed nec peiora passurus.'

113. *Ibid.*, p. 126.

114. *Ibid.*, p. 127: '. . . praestatque multo tutos esse in medio quam in summo cum ruinae periculo. Utinam, utinam episcopi, presbyteri, diacones essent unius uxoris viri et non potius, venia sit dicto, non unius scorti amatores. . . . Non tamen plus sacerdos ob continentiam quam ego merebitur. Nam hoc modo peiore essent condicione feminae, quae nequeunt esse sacerdotes, cum tamen apud deum non sit neque graecus neque barbarus, neque dominus neque servus, neque masculus neque femina.' (Galatians iii, 28.)

Garin, 'Desideri di riforma' (n. 7), pp. 172, 173, uses this work of Valla to emphasize his criticism of the corruption of the clergy, quoting the passage—'Utinam, utinam' etc.—just cited and the one on p. 125—'non exterior homo sed interior placet deo'. It should be clear, here also, that Valla goes beyond corruption to question the basic validity of the status of the religious. The latter is my chief concern in this paper.

115. *Op. cit.*, pp. 130–132: 'Tu obedisti, ego curam aliorum gessi, tu pauperem egisti et continentem, ego parem tibi vitam egi; tu ad haec custodienda te alligasti, ego mihi istam necessariam servitutem non putavi; tu necessitate recte egisti, ego voluntate, tu timore dei, ego amore: perfecta caritas foras mittit timorem. Si non timuisses te aliter non posse deo placere, profecto numquam te alligasses. Nam quid aliud ad promittendum vos induxit . . . nisi ut nulla vos a cultu dei per libertatem arbitrii causa reflecteret. Ideoque non videas fere quempiam ad vestrum consortium se conferre, nisi sceleratum, nefarium, inopem, destitutum et qui aliter vel deo vel corpori suo bene servire posse desperet. . . . Etenim omnis ratio voti, omnis indictio ieiunii, omne iusiurandum, omnis denique lex, est autem professio lex quaedam, propter metum inventa est, id est ut apertius loquar, propter malos. . . . Nonne inquit Paulus: *lex propter transgressionem posita est* [Romans xiii. 4] . . . Itaque non intelligo, quid aliud a deo possitis exigere, nisi fructum obedientiae, paupertatis, continentiae. At vos hoc non contenti ceteris anteferri postulatis periculi gratia. Quodsi in te periculum poenae consideras, considera et in me periculum peccandi facilius, qui nulla timoris ancora sum alligatus: quod facit eandem virtutis actionem in me quam in te esse maiorem.'

116. *Ibid.*, p. 132–133: 'Ideoque et vos et nos, more Pauli, qui de manducantibus et non manducantibus inquit, *unusquisque in suo sensu abundet* [Romans xiv. 3, 5], faciamus pares concludamusque, ita professionem homines non reddere meliores, ut diaconium, ut presbyterium, ut episcopatus, ac papatus. Nec quia diaconio aut sacerdotio initiati, iccirco meliores estis, sed iccirco initiari voluistis, ut meliores essetis: nec quia iurastis, iccirco multum meremini, sed iccirco iurastis, ut multum mereremini: nec quia poena proponitur vobis, iccirco boni estis, potestis namque esse mali, sed ut boni essetis, periculum poenae subistis.'

117. *Ibid.*, pp. 133–134. That the peroration was faint praise and meant to be is witnessed by the friar's reply: '. . . perorationeum tamen tuam non probo, quae non tam laudum fraternarum, quam timoris tui testimonium fuit. Cum enim proprium esset institutae orationis in vituperatione fratrum finem face-

re, ut copiosissime poteras, tu tamen, ne odium tibi illorum concitares, in laudatione facere maluisti.'

118. Cf. my introduction to the English translation of *De libero arbitrio* in Cassirer, Kristeller and Randall, *The Renaissance Philosophy of Man,* p. 153.

119. The relevant portion of the *Apology* is printed by Vahlen (pp. 135–138). Cf. also Radetti's translation, *op. cit.,* pp. 447–450.

120. Erasmus wrote his *Enchiridion militis Christiani* in 1501 and first published it at Louvain, 1503, roughly sixty years after the date of Valla's treatise. Although the religious spirit may be judged similar, Erasmus' comment on monasticism—which gained a place for this book on the index—was a more cautious one, 'Monasticism is not piety but a way of living, either useful or useless in proportion to one's moral and physical disposition' (Raymond Himelick's translation, Bloomington, Ind., 1963). *Desid. Erasmi Roterodami Opera omnia* V (Louvain, 1704), col. 65: 'Monachatus non est pietas, sed vitæ genus pro suo cuique corporis ingeniique habitu, vel utile, vel inutile. Ad quod equidem ut te non adhortor, ita ne dehortor quidem.' Cf. E. Reusch, *Die Indices Librorum Prohibitorum des sechzehnten Jahrhunderts* (Tübingen, 1886, photo-reprint Nieukoop, 1961), pp. 83, 100, 156, 185, 221, 477 etc. for condemnations of the work in various sixteenth century *indices*. Presumably ignorance of Valla's work in the sixteenth century accounts both for its absence from the *indices* and from praise by reformers.

The Religious Thought of the
Italian Humanists: Anticipation
of the Reformers or Autonomy?

For the intellectual historian who has ventured into the study of the history of religious ideas there is the awareness that he has but traced the course of a single thread or two within the seamless garment of history. And yet he cannot entirely refrain from looking at the results of his researches in their general historical bearing. So it is with the history of the religious thought of the Renaissance and the Reformation that there is an obligation bearing on the historian of Italian humanist religious writing to consider its relationship both to the wider context of its own epoch and to that of the subsequent, possibly more dramatic, Reform. Each of these two critical phases in the formation of the modern world has been given distinctive, highly differentiated characters by some at least of its historians, and these periods have sometimes been seen as representing even opposite values to our contemporaries. Yet each of them, however interpreted, has been re-garded well-nigh universally as revolutionary in its breaking of continuity with past tradition and in its introduction of viable new approaches to man's material and spiritual life. This essay will, then, venture anew with full awareness of complexity and necessary tentativeness into the historical problems of the relationships of Italian humanist religious thought with late medieval scholastic theology and with (necessarily but a few) ideas of the Reformers, weighing but not finally answering the delicate question of dependence, independence and interdependence.

Moreover, it plunges into the context of an almost chaotic variety of historical interpretations of the broadest range of evidence and human activities with its thin line of *Ideengeschichte*. For the more these epochs are studied the more different aspects of each are singled out as granting to it what historians insist must be its "revolutionary" essence. Changes in the

This paper, the first written after publication of *In Our Image and Likeness* (1970), was a cautious attempt to explore the book's implications for the historical relationship between Renaissance and Reformation. Its thinking led directly to the author's participation in the planning and organization of the University of Michigan Conference on Late Medieval and Renaissance Religion. It was published among the papers of the conference in *The Pursuit of Holiness in Late Medieval and Renaissance Religion*, ed. C. Trinkaus and H. A. Oberman (Leiden: E. J. Brill, 1974), 339–66.

economic structure, in political ideas and behavior, in legal institutions, in family life, in moral attitudes, in education and higher culture, in philosophy and science, in the relationships of church and state, in methods of warfare, in constitutions, in attitudes toward past historical periods and tradition, in religiosity, in theology, in ecclesiology, in the functioning of ecclesiastics, in church finance, in the conception and usage of the sacraments, in church governance, in the attitude toward Scriptures and Tradition, in the final authority in religious matters, in epistemology or metaphysics, in the need for grace for insight or justification, in the role of works, in the status of man as conceived in relation to God—all of these changes and many others are singled out as the one critical element that either produced the revolutionary character of the period or was its chief consequence. While all these separate aspects of these periods may be supposed to constitute the strands from which a seamless garment is woven, to the working historian they too often rather seem but the scattered fragments of colored glass from a broken mosaic that it is his task to cement together once again and so reconstruct the splendid whole of history.

In our particular instance we have set out to show (what I cannot think should have been anything but obvious) that the humanists of the Italian Renaissance, as men living in a strongly (if not deeply) religious era, were themselves heavily concerned in their writings with religious questions, and made from their own standpoint and through their own humanistic intellectual disciplines some important contributions to the history of Christian thought.[1] But such has been the historiography of the Renaissance since the time of Voltaire (and indeed since the time of Erasmus, Luther and Bellarmine) that this period came to be looked upon as the tragic interval when Christian Europeans lost their bearings and flirted with sensualism and the alluring doctrines of a pagan Epicureanism. Or, on the other hand, the Renaissance has been interpreted as chiefly responsible for the ensuing blasphemies of the Reformation, or as the inevitable consequence of a medieval Catholicism that departed from its evangelical origins and blended far too promiscuously with the secular world. Or, from a nonreligious perspective, the Renaissance has been hailed, and is still hailed, as the harbinger of the Enlightenment, of the repudiation of the ecclesiastical domination of secular life characteristic of medieval society, as the first feeble expression of, if not an atheistic or agnostic view of the cosmos, a blithely irreligious outlook, as the first phase of modern secular culture and of a bourgeois civic community where ethics and politics had become fully secularized and human energies turned toward the practical solution of purely earthly problems. Thus a combination of secular and religious historiography manages to dispense with both the Renaissance and the Reformation (Catholic or Protestant) as mutually alternative aberrations or interruptions in the smooth and continuing flow of the course of European history (with the alternative period functioning as the glorious seed time for the revolutionizing of the modern world).[2]

But assuming the continuing historical existence and relevance of the Catholic and Protestant Reformations, is it possible to read the Renaissance out of European history as either mere decadent continuation of the medieval past or as abortive and unnecessary revolutionary caesura? Is it possible to look at the art of the Italian Renaissance without observing the overwhelmingly religious and Christian character of its subjects? For even where classical subjects come to be depicted, it has been made amply clear how Christian was their allegorical meaning. It is true that the Church was the great patron of the arts as their principal consumer and thus dictated this subject-matter, yet often enough the patrons of ecclesiastical art were also laymen. It is also true, whether with clerical or lay patronage, that Christian theme is often unfolded against a richly sensuous background of colors and forms sometimes revealing artists' and patrons' delight in the lush or the lovely of this world (and the next), sometimes manifesting almost photographically the lavishness of the contemporary scene and its material life. A celestial vision of both worlds may indeed have displaced the agony and the asceticism, but the Christian conceptualization cannot be denied.[3]

Patrons of the arts and of letters, ecclesiastical or secular, were unquestionably men who regarded themselves as religious and Christian, however much the secular ruler or patrician may have engaged in the wordly arts of commerce, politics and war. How then could they be regarded as a social or institutional source for the development of a non-religious outlook? Indeed it would seem that one of the vast and crucial phenomena of this period was the blending of the religious and the secular such as is increasingly coming to interest at least some historians of the arts, culture and society. But for evidence of the conscious recognition or pursuit of a new conception of religion more satisfyingly blending the human and the divine, should one not look at the men of letters and the philosophers (as well as to the direct manifestations in behavior)? For new ideas or new structuring of old ideas would seem to find expression from men of ideas however much their social environments may be thought to engender the conditions that provoke new thinking. And one should look, perhaps, at new types of thinkers, uncommitted by institutional and professional connections to established ways of thought and expression. Such at least are some of the assumptions we must make in seeking for the general historical significance of Italian humanist religious thought and for its relations with other contemporary intellectual and practical movements and with preceding and succeeding phases of culture. And we must, as we have been striving to do, stress continuity and change simultaneously.[4]

Humanism, as an efflorescence of the rhetorical tradition, was medieval as well as Renaissance, as we well know from Alcuin's influence at the court of Charlemagne, or from the potency (however disputed) of John of Salisbury and his school in twelfth-century Chartres. Yet mid-fourteenth-century Petrarchan humanism was new for its time, building out of the isolated fragments of a rhetorical and classical revival of the late thirteenth century, especially from Dante's circle presided over by Brunetto Latini, from the Paduan cenacolo of Albertino Mussato and others, from Arezzo, and even from Bologna of the great university where Dante's Giovanni del Vergilio taught.

In the dark shadows and nauseating fumes of the depths of the *Inferno,* Dante presents his picture of the disastrous sins and crimes that were characteristic of his day. And it was, indeed, these new modes of social behavior, sins according to Dante's perspective, perhaps secularism according to a later conception, that lay the basis for the great moral, religious and philosophical crisis of the early and middle Trecento. For these souls of the *Inferno* were Dante's fellow Italians and Florentines. And Dante had to look nostalgically backward a good century to find many who were suitable for Paradise. The world of the early fourteenth century did not fit easily into the older Christian vision, though the earlier medieval past also had its share of spectacular sinners.

One must be aware of movements and counter-movements, currents and cross-currents, deeply shadowed relief and delicate nuance in history. And the fourteenth century manifested all of these: from the serene joy of a Giotto fresco or the *Fioretti* of San Francesco to the gloomy *Speculum humanae vitae* and the death frescoes of the Campo Santo. Nonetheless by mid-century, domestic disasters such as harvest failures, bankruptcies and revolutions, national tragedies such as the slaughter of the flower of French chivalry in the opening battles of the Hundred Years War, the ominous symbolism of the kidnapping at Anagni and the quartering of the Roman papacy at Avignon, were crowned by the Black Death with its bitter harvest of corpses and deserted towns and villages.

Much has been written on the melancholy and despair which followed in the wake of the Black Death, of its impact on literature and the arts, of its stimulation of widespread penitential movements, including the spectacular processions of flagellants. In very fact the most profound transformation and uprooting of medieval institutions and modes of behavior and perception, of affectivity and thought, were already occurring. It is too complicated to weigh here whether these drastic external events, and prime among them the epidemics of bubonic plague which crossed Europe only to return again and again for the next half-century and more, were the sole causes of the profound changes that were to come, or whether they only hastened them on. Yet even earlier there had begun a religious crisis of even more profound and lasting dimensions than these political and demographic crises, one that did not find its resolution for more than two hundred years. When it did (and such as it did in the Reformations), it left Europe divided into warring sects not hesitating to smite, stab, burn, slay in behalf of creed and dogma. Thus it is our perception that the complex question of the inter-relations of late Middle Ages, Renaissance and Reformations finds a unity in the common condition of response to a great and enduring crisis.[5]

This spiritual crisis which in the fourteenth century succeeded to the momentary and fragile thirteenth-century sense of triumph witnessed on the popular level a host of religious movements seeking a revival of piety, a return to the ideal of the Apostolic Life, a preparation for the coming of the Third Age of monkly brotherhood, or, if it so turned out, Armageddon. The serenity of Giotto and the optimism of the early decades proved to be not its major but its minor key, and the depths of anxiety and despair were everywhere to be seen. The degradation and corruption of ecclesiastical institutions were only too evident.

The religious and spiritual crisis also had its intellectual side, and Renaissance humanism together with Ockhamism, the *via moderna,* were manifestations of it.[6] While my chief concern is with humanism, it is necessary to comment first on the historical role of the Ockhamist movement in order to clarify and understand that of the humanists. The process by which the medieval world-view (if it can be argued that there was a single one) broke down was long and complex. Fourteenth-century Ockhamism and Petrarchan humanism were two parallel modes of asserting a repudiation of preceding thirteenth-century scholastic efforts to forge a unity between revelation and reason, to build an ever more refined Aristotelian metaphysical structure out into the non-perceptual space of faith and theology. In this repudiation Ockhamism made its major impact in the two principal problem areas where inherited Christian theology was being challenged by historical events, namely the theoretical and the moral.

When in the twelfth and thirteenth centuries a conception of a rationally comprehensible, naturally determined universe, drawn from secular (i.e. Greco-Arabic) science, was projected against the prevailing anthropomorphic, mythopoeic Biblical version of the creation, somehow these two views of the universe had to be reconciled, or one of them vindicated against the other. The growth of secular natural philosophy at the arts faculties of the universities, first the northern and then more and more importantly the Italian, meant indeed that from the beginnings of scholastic thought there were those who saw no possibility of a theoretical reconciliation but at best separate and parallel realms entertained by reason and faith. The growth of Ockhamism and the *via moderna* in this context meant, on the other hand, that an even more critical and direct assault on the stronghold of thirteenth-century scholastic theology (already challenged by natural philosophy) was taking place. [7]

The older theology was undermined by the Ockhamists' twin denials that perception and comprehension of earthly things could validly be extrapolated into a theology, and that the all-powerful God of the Christian faith could be constricted by the requirements of a logically rational metaphysical system. In place of rational theology, the Ockhamist sought a direct, intuitive approach to God in a renewed theology of revelation and faith, if not a down-right fideism. The contemporary spread of fourteenth-century mysticism indicates that simultaneously a more direct approach to the Deity was being sought in many quarters. Such are the intellectual and theoretical dimensions of the great Renaissance-Reformation religious crisis, and this was not resolved, if it was then resolved, until the age of Galileo and Newton. [8]

However, it was the religious and moral aspects of this crisis that were of significance for understanding the humanists' role. The same awakening and expansion of European societies which brought Greek science, logic and metaphysics to the Latin West in translations of Arabic and Byzantine manuscript texts had generated the proto-modern worlds of the medieval commune and the Renaissance city-state, of the industrial towns and the international commercial and financial community, of rural crisis and agricultural expansion, of the national monarchies and the territorial princely states. New, demanding, activist, ambitious modes of experience and behavior drew many sectors of the European populace into its networks. It was not simply an early phase of a bourgeois revolution; it was much more complexly an enormous quickening of the tempo of life, an outpouring of human energy from an expanding population that bore its fruits not only in the new centers of material wealth and new types of economic, political and ecclesiastical activity in the greatest variety, but also in new kinds of misery, suffering, inner tensions, competitiveness, warfare and domestic violence. The responses of the men of the eleventh, twelfth and thirteenth centuries to their rapidly changing conditions of life were magnificent in their efforts to create effective new modes of order—the consolidation of the Church through the centralizing Hildebrandine reforms and the creation of the papal and episcopal bureaucracies and an ecclesiastical judicial system, the new urban and feudal types of political organization, the revival and institution of a secular juridical system based on Roman law, the evolution of the university as the training ground for these new professions. Yet both the elements of disorder and anarchic conflict on the one hand, and those of order, organization, professionalization, on the other, transformed and challenged the traditional religious experience and conceptions of an acceptable moral life.

In breaking down the thirteenth century's theological and philosophical syntheses, the Ockhamists were equally concerned with the seeming untenability of a moral theology that rationalized the good civic life, set forth in Aristotle's *Ethics,* as the secular equivalent of Christian charity. Almost more critical than the problem of epistemology (the knowledge of God, the relationship of faith and intellect) in the Ockhamist school was the problem of the relationship of free will and grace, analyzed by theologians in incredible complexity, and leading frequently to a dual system where the good citizen freely and deliberately acted in the world with restraint and responsibility according to natural moral canons but found himself entirely dependent on supernatural grace for his salvation as a justified Christian.

At the same time it was averred that by God's ordered power His covenant with believers meant that He would not withold his grace from those who had done their voluntary best to live virtuously, according to the principle *facere quod in se est.* This combination of a theology of grace and a voluntarist ethics would appear simultaneously among the humanists.

Although there were many other motives for the revival of the rhetorical tradition and classicism in the Italian humanist movement, certainly the Petrarchan pattern also needs to be understood in the context of the same religious and moral crisis that in the north had given birth in those very years to Ockhamism. Humanism, the classical-Christian rhetorical tradition, did not require, nor did it develop a systematic philosophy or a theology. A number of individual humanists, however, did develop philosophical and religious positions of their own and made greater contributions to the history of late medieval religion than has sometimes been thought. Thus, though any systematic comparison of two philosophical or theological systems, nominalist and humanist, is out of the question (because of the unsystematic character of most humanist religious writings, at least), still there are some striking parallels between the theoretical postulates of the rhetorical tradition (where, as in the case of Salutati or Valla, they are formulated) and those of nominalism. The anti-metaphysical stance, the tendency toward epistemological probabilism as far as universals are concerned, the preoccupation with the relation between word and thing, with signs, language and reality are common to both, as well as a direct factual concern with human motivation and action. Where the two traditions differed was essentially in the more practical, action-oriented character of humanist writing, which contrasted with the theoretical interests of the scholastics of the *via moderna,* in the usual humanist avoidance of any systematic analysis of epistemological issues, though not of the structure of speech and language. The humanists who talked about the Ockhamists were, by and large, from Petrarch on, contemptuous of the endless intricacy and the *ventosa sophistica* of these *Brittani* and "prattling dialecticians". But both movements shared, perhaps unknown to themselves, a common repudiation of those thirteenth-century scholastic systems that sought an accommodation with Aristotle. As Petrarch's invective *De sui ipsius et multorum ignorantia* shows so clearly, he was even more opposed to the Aristotelian natural philosophy of his own day, which seemed to abandon concern with faith and any effort toward a Christian life. The early humanists tended to confuse the intellectualistic arguments of the Ockhamists with those of the natural philosophers and the physicians in a broad condemnation of the irrelevance of all scholastic philosophy. Petrarch did not take into account the quasi-fideism and the anti-intellectualist voluntarism of the nominalists, so similar to his own.[9]

He had a greater sympathy and bond with those clerical intellectuals of the fourteenth century who attempted to revive the theology of St. Augustine. Critical in Petrarch's image of the saint was the latter's conflict between his experience of a quest for happiness and his intellectual position of Christianized Neoplatonism.

While it is necessary to reject the thesis that Petrarch and Salutati were influenced by the order of Augustinian Hermits in any formal way, it is also true that they found a close spiritual kinship with the ideas of such Augustinians as Dionigi of Borgo San Sepolcro and Luigi Marsili. Moreover, the ideas of such a major figure in the order as Gregory of Rimini have a striking parallel to those of some of the early humanists. Gregory, who is usually counted as belonging in some respects to the nominalist school, turned to man's internal subjective experiences as a reality-basis on which a Christian theology could be constructed, and in this deliberately imitated the alleged founder of his order. As is well known, Petrarch constructed his *Secretum* around just such a self-analysis of his inner experiences in his search for an existentially authentic religious vision that might overpower the distracting and fragmenting allure of secular motives. He replaced the Ockhamists' logical analysis with psychological analysis.[10]

When we look more closely at Petrarch's surprizingly developed religious philosophy, we discover, what our knowledge of him could predict, that he is exclusively concerned with the subjectivity of belief and the sense of salvation, with how the individual regards himself in this life in relation to the divine promises. Men everywhere are overcome with despair. Even in the Carthusian monastery where his brother Gherardo was a monk, he feels that the brothers' most dangerous enemy is their despair of justification. But was it not also within the fold of the Augustinian Hermits that Brother Martin Luther first experienced his sense of despair and of divine hatred that led him to his subjective theology of *sola fide?* Let us look at a few passages from Petrarch's treatise addressed to the Carthusian Brothers, his *De otio religioso.*[11] I do not know if one can ever answer the question posed in our title—anticipation or autonomy?—but the amazing closeness of Petrarch's religiosity to Luther's will permit us to face it in all its sharpness.

As in Luther's case, despair stems from man's consciousness of his weakness and his sins. Mankind's enemy would not dare to assert that anything is beyond God's power, as he would then lose all credence. Instead he insinuates that while God can do all and wishes to give all goods to mankind, it is man himself who is unfit and unworthy to receive such gifts, and many begin to meditate as follows:

> God indeed is the best; but I am the worst; what proportion is there in such great contrariety? I know . . . how far envy is removed from That Best One, and on the contrary I know how tightly iniquity is bound to me . . . I. confess the mercy of God is infinite, but I profess that I am not fit for it, and as much as it is greater, so much narrower is my mind, filled with vices. Nothing is impossible to God; in me there is a total impossibility of rising, buried as I am in such a great heap of sins. He is potent to save: I am unable to be saved. For however great the clemency of God, certainly it does not exclude justice, and mercy as immense as you wish must be reduced to the measure of my miseries. . . [12]

It is this sense of the nothingness of man's efforts at sanctity that seems to have pervaded the later Middle Ages, and it underlay one of the central doctrines of the Ockhamist school, the emphasis on God's absolute power. His *potentia absoluta* could not be related in any rational way to human insights and experiences; only faith in His promises could reassure. So, too, Petrarch finds the doctrine of the infinitude of God's power so overshadows man that it renders hope that man can win salvation through his own powers and merits utterly ridiculous. At the same time, it produces the great assurance that despite enormous distance between the divine and the human, God will save man. Thus he counsels that divine omnipotence should be measured psychologically, not rationally:

> These thoughts and others of the same sort which enter souls, when they bring them a salutary fear and dispel torpor, are to be considered as a sort of silent counsel of angels loving us; yet when they take away all hope and trust, they are to be avoided as hostile errors and dangerous roads to ruin. For where do they lead the soul which follows them except to desperation, the worst of all evils? But nothing should terrify us, since the divine power is not limited by any conditions of nature, nor does it employ the force of its own action only toward those things which are properly disposed, but brings order to those which are indisposed. The mercy of God by far transcends human misery and justice . . . . . . Anyone who considers that He will not show mercy to someone who wishes forgiveness, or that He is only able to show mercy in proportion to man's sin, thinks badly about

God and has a poor opinion concerning His power and mercy, since the sin of a man, however great it is, is certainly finite, the goodness of God infinite, His power infinite. . . . We seem worthy of punishment, unworthy of mercy, and in both we are not mistaken: for it is our part to be afflicted, His to be merciful. And it is a worthy thing for His dignity to swallow up our lack of dignity, which certainly could not happen if the sin of man could impede the mercy of God. [13]

Finally, passing over a long discussion of the dynamics of faith, we come upon a statement which is appositely close to Luther's doctrine. After quoting St. Paul, Romans vii:22–23, "For I delight in the law of God after the inward man: but I see another law in my members warring against the law in my mind, and bringing me into captivity to the law of sin which is in my members." Petrarch asks:

Who indeed does not fear what he sees the Apostle fearing? Or who in such great danger would hope for any other gift except that according to the apostolic counsel "by walking in the spirit he should not fulfill the lust of his flesh?" And since this, as I have said, without God granting, cannot be done, he should say with the same Apostle, mourning and fearing, "O, wretched man that I am, who shall deliver me from the body of this death?"; and resuming hope solely through the mercy of God he should reply to himself, "I thank God through Jesus Christ our Lord"; to that One who alone is able to succor in this internal and domestic battle it must be cried out; He must be humbly beseeched that He should liberate us from the body of this death, *whence the merit of man does not liberate but the grace of God alone* [unde meritum hominis non liberat, sed gratia Dei solius], to Whom nothing, I do not say is impossible, but not even difficult. [14]

Petrarch, of course, was putting forth the doctrine of *sola gratia,* not *sola fide.* But the anticipation of the latter is clear enough, and there is much in Petrarch's psychological emphasis on the necessity of faith in the soul of the Christian that can link his position with Luther's. With respect to those scholars and commentators on Luther who stress the uniqueness of his theological position, and its insight, one may point to the great closeness of inner religious dynamics of the two positions. Yet at the same time one may raise the question whether it was, after all, theology which brought about the Reformation. After all this statement of Petrarch's and so many similar ones that do indeed anticipate Luther, did not by themselves bring about the ecclesiastical separation of Christendom into new schisms and churches. Perhaps the basic differences between the two men lay in their historical circumstances and roles. It is clear in this instance that the Reformation, however much European history may have been leading up to it in the preceding two centuries, was not a matter of the history of ideas alone but involved the whole concatenation of events culminating in the successful break from Rome, "successful" in that Luther's break became a historical break, and Luther's heresy became a new orthodoxy, whatever one may think of more recent oecumenical views that the heresy was not a heresy, the break not an intended break, and that canonically the schism is capable of repair.[15] The rejection of the externals of religion, both sacramental and ecclesiological, remained only an implied one for Petrarch who never questioned either the sanctity of the sacraments, the validity of monasticism, or the authority of popes and bishops, however, severely he criticized the abuses and corruption of the Avignonese curia. The crucial difference lay in the degree of finality about these questions, and Petrarch, however much he seems to anticipate Luther theologically, must be seen as playing a role that was autonomous to the development of the religious thought of the humanists in Italy (and his other readers) where the ideas had their chief consequences.

Fittingly, we are also able to make a comparison between Petrarch and Calvin. Much as Petrarch the humanist admired Cicero, Seneca and Horace for their literary gifts and for their powers of persuasion, which men of his time should emulate in calling men back to virtue, he also severely criticized their conceptions of the relationship of human virtue to divine power. There is an implied Pelagianism in the rhetorical notion that man can call man to virtue, as there was equally in the Thomist notion of the approximation of Aristotelian civic virtue to the golden rule, and as there was in the Ockhamist notion of man's freedom to be virtuous in humanly conceived terms, though dependent on grace for justification (which was presumed not to be witheld from the man who had done his very best to fulfill the divine commandments: *facere quod in se est*). Petrarch follows the same path as the nominalists, for he sharply criticizes the claim of the honored pagans that virtue is a sufficient goal for man.

> Thus when the illustrious pagan philosophers refer everything to virtue, the philosopher of Christ (*Cristi philosophus*) refers virtue itself to the author of virtue, God, and by using virtue enjoys God, nor ever stops with his mind before he has reached him. For thus he will hear a certain great philosopher of Christ saying, "Thou hast established us for thy sake, and thus our heart is restless until it rests in Thee."[16]

Not only is virtue not the goal for the "philosopher of Christ" (Erasmus was not the first by any means to use this phrase), but virtue itself depends on divine grace. Petrarch then quotes Horace: "It is enough to pray God who gives and takes away that He should give life and wealth: I will myself bring peace to my soul," and Cicero: "Then death is waited in most serenity when a man is able to console himself with his own praises [for his virtues] while life is declining." Jean Calvin in the final edition of the *Institutes* similarly discusses the ancients' claim to virtue as within the power of man:

> Moreover some of them have advanced to such a degree of presumption as to boast that we are indebted to the gods for our life, but for a virtuous and religious one to ourselves; whence also that assertion of Cicero, in the person of Cotta, that, since every man acquires virtue for himself, none of the wise men have ever thanked God for it. "For," he says, "we are praised for virtue, and in virtue we glory; which would not be the case, if it were a gift of God, and did not originate from ourselves." And a little after: "This is the judgement of all men, that fortune must be asked of God, but that wisdom must be derived from ourselves."[17]

Petrarch replied to this classical argument that man's virtue, which the pagan attributes to himself, is not his at all but is directly a gift of God.

> What thence besides sin remains which, since it is voluntary nor derived from anywhere else than from the soul itself, certainly is established as the sole property of man? Therefore there is no matter of consolation or glory for him from what is in the power of others; in what is in his own power, moreover, there is much matter of shame and fear; no one is such a slave of sin that he does not know this.[18]

One may recall at this point that Calvin, though carefully reserving to the eternal decree of divine predestination man's spiritual powers: to be virtuous, to become justified, to inherit eternal life, nevertheless grants a very full range of secular capacities to man, himself, and especially praises the ancients who had first developed them—the lawyers, natural philosophers, rhetoricians and logicians, physicians and mathematicians.

> We shall not be able even to read the writings of the ancients on these subjects without great admiration: we shall admire them, because we shall be constrained to acknowledge them to be truly excellent.[19]

Yet, Calvin argues, the Fathers of the Church, particularly the Greeks, extolled human powers too greatly for fear both that they would

> incur the derision of the philosophers . . . ; and, in the next place might administer to the flesh, of itself naturally too torpid to all that is good, a fresh occasion for slothfulness.[20]

Petrarch, it is well known, was much concerned with *accidia,* his own and others'. *Accidia* was his version of the old sin of sloth or indolence. Moreover, as we have seen, the state of despair, which led to distrust in God's mercy, was the true form of this very sloth.[21]

In his most popular Latin prose work, *De remediis utriusque fortunae,* Petrarch inaugurated the discussions in the Renaissance of that most central of humanist concerns[22]: the nature, powers and condition of man. And Calvin, in the very chapter of the *Institutes* from which we have been quoting, sets forth his interpretation of this very same theme. "Man, in His Present State, Despoiled of Freedom of Will, and Subjected to a Miserable Slavery" is his translated title. Calvin wishes to make clear within the terms of his theology what may properly be said on the dual themes of the dignity of man and the misery of the human condition, and he takes it as an occasion to criticize his predecessors, both Christian theologians and pagan philosophers. And he wishes to set forth his doctrine in such terms that it will avoid the twin dangers of man's falling into slothfulness through excessive discouragement concerning his powers, or of his arrogating to himself, through excessive pride in his capacities, the honor which right-fully belongs to God. His purpose is not only expository but rhetorical as well,

> for man, being taught that he has nothing good left in his possession, and being surrounded on every side with the most miserable necessity, should, nevertheless, be instructed to aspire to the good of which he is destitute, and to the liberty of which he is deprived; and he should be roused from indolence with more earnestness than if he were supposed to be possessed of the greatest strength.[23]

Interestingly, the entire point of Petrarch's treatise was to supply an encyclopedia of remedies, not for the accidents of fortune, but for their psychological impact on men. Indeed, Book I is intended to reduce the false state of elation induced by favorable events by stressing in situation after situation the false picture of man's truly miserable condition that the fortunate man entertains in order to induce him to regain his sobriety. Book II supplied the remedies for bad fortune, in similar fashion consoling against the state of melancholy that unfavorable events, both major and trivial, bring about. It is in chapter 93 that he addresses the general state of despair produced by thought of the misery of the human condition—*accidia* again. And here Petrarch sets forth what was to be the first of the Renaissance treatises on the dignity and excellence of man. Commencing with man's creation in the image and likeness of God, passing through the capacities of mind and soul, human inventions, the bounties of nature, man's superiority to animals through his creativity, Petrarch comes climactically to man's salvation and deification through the Incarnation:

> Add the immortality of the soul and the road to heaven and for a small price an inestimable reward, and what I knowingly delayed until the end is so great that I would not understand them through my own

powers unless I had learned through the teaching of faith: the hope of resurrection, and that this very body after death will be reassumed, indeed agile, and shining and inviolable with much glory in resurrection, And what surpasses all dignity, not only human but angelic, humanity itself is so conjoined to divinity that He who was God is become man, and likewise one in number He begins to be God and man, perfectly containing two natures in himself, so that He makes man God, having been made out of ineffable God, and His humility is the highest happiness and glory of man . . . Does the human condition not seem to you much ennobled in this one person? And does his misery not seem much purified? But what, I pray, can man, I do not say hope, but choose, but think that is higher than that he should become God? Behold, now he is God.[24]

And Petrarch completes his exposition with a refutation of the main defects of man as alleged by Innocent III in his famous *De miseria humanae conditionis*.

It is significant that Calvin also sees the importance of right doctrine for its consolatory and encouraging effects (though also regarding it as unassailably true, of course). He, too, deals at length with the question of man's creation in the image and likeness of God in *Institutes* II, xv. Let me quote but one passage, holding traditionally that the term "image" applies to man's soul:

> For although the glory of God is displayed in [man's] external form, yet there is no doubt that the proper seat of his image is in the soul. I admit that external form, as it distinguishes us from the brutes, also exalts us more nearly to God: nor will I too vehemently contend with anyone who would understand by the image of God that
>
> > ". . . while the mute creation downward bend
> > Their sight, and to their earthly mother tend,
> > Man looks aloft, and with erected eyes
> > Beholds his own hereditary skies",

a passage from Ovid's *Metamorphoses* frequently quoted in works on the dignity of man. Calvin resumes:

> Though the soul, therefore, is not the whole man, yet there is no absurdity in calling man the image of God with relation to the soul; although I retain the principle just laid down, that the image of God includes all the excellence in which the nature of man surpasses all the other species of animals. This term, therefore, denotes the integrity which Adam possessed, when he was endued with a right understanding, when he had affections regulated by reason, and all his senses

governed in proper order, and when, in the excellency of his nature, he truly resembled the excellence of his Creator. And though the principal seat of the Divine image was in the mind and heart or in the soul and its faculties, yet there was no part of man, not even the body, which was not adorned with some rays of its glory.[25]

Calvin, of course, regarded the Fall of man and the Incarnation as integral parts of this theology and hastens to add:

There is no doubt that Adam, when he fell from his dignity, was by this defection alienated from God. Wherefore, although we allow that the Divine image was not utterly annihilated and effaced in him, yet it was so corrupted that whatever remains is but horrible deformity. And therefore the beginning of our recovery and salvation is the restoration which we obtain through Christ who on this account is called the second Adam because he restores us to true and perfect integrity.[26]

Calvin's theology of God and man is intricate, and I do not intend to discuss it further here, except to point to one other interesting parallel to Petrarch. In the very next chapter, having set forth the original dignity and excellence of man, Calvin wishes to deal with "God's Preservation and Support of the World by His Power and His Government of Every Part of It by His Providence."[27] Here he seeks to do two things: vindicate God's *potentia absoluta* by showing that God can and does operate outside the laws of nature, thus giving a sense of the personal providence of God toward individuals. And, as a corollary of this, he wishes to refute the notion of fortune as something separate from divine providence. His purpose is to overcome the sense of helplessness and despair that either an over-deterministic naturalism or a too accidental, fortune-ridden view of the external world will induce in man. The similarity of the purposes to those of Petrarch, both in Petrarch's opposition to the Aristotelian natural philosophers and in his efforts to refute and undermine the conception of fortune, is striking.

And so we must raise again the question of the relationship of Petrarchan humanism to the Reformation. And again my historian's judgement intervenes. Petrarch was the poet and rhetorician writing two centuries earlier, and however much he needed to enter into theological questions in his concern with the psychological state of his contemporaries and their need for renewed self-confidence and faith, he did not evolve an elaborate theology, nor did he contemplate reform of sacraments or church. Calvin, though his *Institutes* (as Quirinus Breen has cogently argued)[28] were written in a rhetorical and humanistic style and intention, did certainly have the goal of root and branch reformation. All that Petrarch wished and hoped for was renewal, quickening, renovation and revival within the existing structure. There is an implied criticism of the clergy in that he, a semi-layman, should endeavor to undertake this renewal, but it was never more than an implication, and Petrarch remained on the best of terms with numerous clerical friends. What his religious writings helped to bring about was a consciousness of the need for an extra-institutional, personal renewal of religion. It was also his purpose to bring about a revival of classical letters and of Roman civic virtue. His *Viri illustres* are grave, noble models of lay moral responsibility. Making it quite clear that he understood their limitations because they were pre-Christians, he had no more trouble reconciling their moralism with his theology of grace than did Dante.

Petrarch's own most illustrious follower, Coluccio Salutati, made three major contributions to humanist religious and moral thought in his treatises: *De seculo et religione, De laboribus Herculis* and *De fato et fortuna*.[29] Particularly this last work is relevant to our discussion, for he sought to make the connections between divine providence, grace and free will, between natural order, chance, and fortune systematically clear where Petrarch had established their relations more by implication and juxtaposition and taken many positions in such a loose way as to be charged with inconsistency. Salutati was a graver, more responsible, but less gifted and spontaneous man. If any of the humanists may be said to have resembled the classical model of a Ciceronian statesman, surely it was he. Doctrinally he perhaps came closer to achieving in this treatise the position which Calvin sought to uphold. Man should trust and rely absolutely on the divine providence and foresight which utilized the natural order discovered by the philosophers only as means to God's ends. Simultaneously man should accept on faith that he has free will and strive to fulfill the divine commands. God in his power could upset natural orders at any instant and produce the seeming accident of change; He could turn man's will to nought by his intervention through fortune. Like Calvin, Salutati was deeply influenced by the Stoic conceptions of a rationally provident deity and universe and of an innate sense of political and moral order in mankind. But also like Calvin, he viewed man's powers and nature's orders as circumscribed and limited by the *potentia absoluta* of the omnipotent God. He was concerned, moreover, in detail with the central problems of fourteenth-century nominalist theology, those concerning grace, free will and contingency, and addressed himself to them in an effort to revindicate the providence of God toward particulars and the viability of a theology that sought to establish credible connections between the insights of faith and the experience of men. As Calvin did after him, he referred to the theories of the Ockhamist school as windy sophistry (*ventosa sophistica*), yet he derived many of his philosophical positions from the nominalists. Following the precedent of both Scotus and Ockham he asserted the primacy of the will and urged upon his contemporaries that they had the inner strength of will to conform to right reason if they submitted to the divine commands and patiently waited the dispensations of His providence, whether for seeming good or ill. Men were justified through divine grace and providence, but sinned and were damned of their own will with merely divine prescience. In either case men were fully responsible for their actions and the consequences in a state of coefficiency with providence.[30]

Yet Salutati, despite the similarity of some (but decidedly not all) of his theological positions to Calvin's, despite also some difficult moments in his career when he was compelled to criticize and oppose the papacy for its worldliness, for the schism, for its anti-Florentine political actions, was in no sense a reformer. His very piety and gravity led him constantly to orthodoxy and conservation. He retained the central medieval conception of the higher sanctity and greater merits of those who bound themselves by vows. He believed merits and sins begot greater rewards or punishments, though not salvation or damnation. Yet he anticipated many aspects of the Reform in both his theology and his emphasis on a lay piety (which did not contradict his doctrinally conservative view of the monastic life). He was a man purely of his age, therefore, responding thoughtfully and appropriately to its immediate religious problems, which indeed did also anticipate many of the problems of the Reformation era. Judging by his attitude toward the great schism, however, it would seem as unthinkable for him as it was for Erasmus to countenance any destruction of the unity of Christendom.

One must, moreover, speak briefly of Salutati's humanism in relation to the organized religious culture of his day. Severely criticized by the Dominican, Beato Giovanni Dominici, for both his interpretations of classical poetry in a Christian sense through allegory and for his more Franciscan stress on the primacy of the will, we have in Salutati's reply a humanist manifesto of the value of the *studia humanitatis* both for the necessary training of the clergy and for the advancement of Christian learning and faith in the *studia divinitatis*. He himself had carried out the programmatic items of his manifesto in many important ways so that it is possible to conclude that he not only contributed a *theologia poetica,* finding Christian religious insights concealed by allegory in the pagan myths of Hercules and other figures, but that he also was an outstanding practitioner of what Petrarch and the humanist movement in general sought to achieve in its religious concerns, namely something that might well be called *theologia rhetorica*. Though I have not found a contemporary use of the term, it does seem appropriate for the humanists' conception of putting all the language arts and sciences—the secular study of the world—at the service of the propagation of the Divine Word, which is often enough repeated by them and manifested in their religious writings. Moreover the German Cardinal, Nicholas of Cusa, who was closely associated with many Italian humanists, did indeed give this concept of the nature and task of theology his blessing, calling it in his *Idiota: theologia sermocinalis*. And Salutati as a matter of fact spoke of his own discipline as *scientia sermocinalis* or *philosophia sermocinalis*.[31]

Although one cannot in a brief essay give more than a fragmentary notion of the extent and character of Italian humanist religious thought, it seems impossible to skip over Lorenzo Valla and Giannozzo Manetti. Of all the humanists who in any way are thought to have anticipated Reformation thought Valla is certainly the best known, especially for his *De . . . donatione Constantini declamatio,* his *Adnotationes in Novum Testamentum* (now attracting scholars with the recognition of a manuscript of the version Erasmus edited, and the edition of an earlier version by Perosa), and his *De libero arbitrio dialogus.* I shall not specifically discuss these works nor his *De professione religiosorum dialogus,* seemingly unknown to the Reformers though anticipating in some ways their desanctification of the monastic life, nor his *De mysterio Eucharistiae sermo,*[32] notable for its nominalist interpretation of the sacrament. Possibly the most original mind of the Italian Renaissance, Valla simultaneously assumed the most thorough-going rhetorical stance in rejection of both ancient and medieval metaphysical philosophy and developed the most intellectually consistent vision of God and man. Basing himself on his analysis of language as the empirical reflection of human experience, he combined his own version of a nominalism with a linguistic positivism when it came to the Scriptures and the knowledge of the divine. But more than that, he asserted by a philological critique of ancient and humanist ethics a naturalistic view of human nature built around the will as an elementary reaching out of the organism toward gratification in pleasure, love, or divine fruition. It is not only that his so-called Christian-Epicureanism anticipates that of Erasmus, but that he was able to develop a unifying insight into the thought of St. Augustine that reduced it to a harmony with classical Platonic eros-philosophy, hedonism, eudemonism and a Pan-Epicureanism. His thought presents the paradox of a rejection of classical philosophy and ethics and an affirmation of Christianity through a Biblical literalism which at the same time by the character of his vision of human psychology and of man's concept of the divine managed to reunite the entire range of Christian and classical ethics and theology. Thus charity and fortitude become one, and self-sacrificing and self-gratifying love, both springing from the same basic drive, develop into the one or the other according to both the depth of vision and the magnanimity or strength of soul of the individual. Radical in the fullest meaning of the term, Valla's anthropology was beyond the capacity of his time to comprehend. He has been too superficially accepted as a forerunner of the Reformation by Protestant scholars and, in the past, too superficially rejected as an enemy of the Church by Catholics, some of whom are today rushing to claim him. To him, of all the humanists, the term "autonomy" belongs. For though he had an enormous influence that can only partly be documented on subsequent humanist thought, Italian and northern, as well as in a fragmentary way on Protestant, Catholic and Radical Reform ideas, he best represents the humanly-centered conception of the role of the scholar and thinker as the analyst of the word, both human and divine, that was the hallmark of Italian religious thought.[33]

Giannozzo Manetti, in many respects also a pioneer in the development of Biblical scholarship, remained apparently unknown to the Reform period and certainly unappreciated. I shall not discuss this aspect of his work, except to point out that he was the first humanist to master Hebrew and to make a new Latin translation of the Hebrew Psalter, that he also made his own translation of the Greek New Testament and discussed in a cautious way the problem of scriptural and philosophical translation, rejecting the freer more rhetorical canons of earlier humanist translations for a stricter more literal method in the name of scholarly precision and theological truth. Moreover, he embarked on a new mode of interpreting Old Testament and New Testament history, seeing the Old Testament not simply as the prefiguration of the New but as the historical record of the religious history of the Hebrews and of the Jews, distinguishing between them as separate and different stages of religious development of God's people.[34]

The work of Manetti which was best known was, of course, his treatise on the *Dignity and Excellence of Man,* for which we are still awaiting a modern edition, not to mention an English translation. Going far beyond his predecessors, in many ways akin to if not influenced by Valla, Manetti more than any other of the humanists built his vision of man around the critical Genesis passage 1:26, "And God said, 'Let us make man in our image, after our likeness.'" Due to his excellent library of Latin, Greek and Hebrew philosophical and religious works, which today forms the nucleus of the Vatican Fondo Ebraico and a large part of its Fondo Palatino Graeco and Latino, Manetti was able to draw on a wide range of both patristic and classical sources for his combination of the patristic vision of man as the divine image and the probably Posidonian synthesis of Stoicism and Platonism, which as Cicero reports it in Book II of *De natura deorum* is the most laudatory classical discussion of man surviving. Certainly Manetti's views of man, though stated cautiously and with intended orthodoxy, and in large part through excerpts, were in content bold and far-reaching. Certainly he was far more extravagant in his picture of man's reaching toward divinity through his earthly actions than either Luther or Calvin could tolerate. God honored man in making him the most beautiful, the most creative, the most wise, the most opulent and the most potent of all His creatures. Moreover he is less concerned to stress the Incarnation as the correction and restoration of man after the Fall than to suggest that it was meant to complement man's great gifts received through his creation in the divine image, for God would have sent his Son incarnate in a human person even if man had not sinned in order to shower further glory upon him. Certainly in this aspect of his theological vision Manetti represented an autonomous Renaissance position even though the theme of the dignity of man remained important in the ideas of Catholic and Protestant thinkers of the Reformation period.[35]

Ideas such as Manetti's exercised an influence through their transformation into the more systematic philosophical ones of Ficino, Pico and other Platonists of the late Quattrocento and the Cinquecento. Their philosophies are generally well known and their connections with northern Reformation thought have been discussed by others such as Eugene Rice,[36] Sears Jayne[37] and Lewis Spitz.[38] More systematically than their humanist predecessors, and more explicitly, they linked together the qualities of divinity with the achievements and aspirations of humanity, which were regarded as tokens or signs of man's immortal destiny. They have been hailed by Frances Yates as the initiators of a new vision of man as a *magus,* controlling, manipulating, creating with the materials of nature, like God the Creator. But they were shown the way to these aspirations by Manetti and other humanists. Their theological positions were complex but not always as unorthodox as they have been charged. Their classical-Christian synthesis and their stress on the immortality of the soul had an influence at the Fifth Lateran Council through Luther's fellow Augustinian Hermit, the Cardinal Egidio da Viterbo.[39] But since the direction sought was a broadening and diffusing of the sources of doctrine, rather than a narrowing down and tightening, it was doomed to be rejected by Protestant and Catholic Reformer alike, though enjoying a vogue with some figures in both camps. In these days of reviving Oecumenism, it is perhaps arousing new interest.

We cannot conclude this discussion of the autonomous and the anticipatory aspects of Italian humanist religious thought without turning to a third option and a third religious movement, namely the enormously influential employment of humanism for religious ends by Erasmus and his followers. The influence of Valla and other Italians on Erasmus is well known-of, if not in detail and depth very well known. Nor is there agreement on the nature of Erasmus' religious thought, itself, which would be important for a valid comparison. I am not an Erasmus scholar, and must follow in the footsteps of my betters. With the recent work of Spitz[40] and Kohls[41] and others,[42] we know how complex and changing his theological ideas were. Even more recently Béné[43] has emphasized the deep influence of Augustine, especially his *De doctrina Christiana* on Erasmus, and this approach is congenial to the point of view I am about to put forth—but from the sidelines or from another battle-front as it were.

It seems to me that if the religious works of the Italian humanists may be characterized as efforts to develop a *theologia rhetorica,* even more should this conception apply to Erasmus. It must be remembered that humanists writing on religious subjects were trying to reach and influence a wide range of readers, lay and clerical. They conceived of their writings as literature (*bonae litterae*), not science (*scientia,* though there are exceptions), however much their writing sprang from doctrinal preconceptions. One can speak of their religiosity and their religions thought much more readily than of their theology, because it was rarely that systematic. They produced lay sermons, both formally and in the disguise of dialogues or treatises. Salutati's *De fato* and Valla's *Disputationes dialecticae* are exceptions in that they do attempt to deal with basic theological and philosophical questions systematically, but they are humanistic and not scholastic in form. The great influential works of Erasmus also turn out to be extended or collected lay sermons, significantly in print. Such were the *Colloquies,* and such was the *Enchiridion,* one of the main texts from which scholars have sought to extract his theological ideas. Erasmus is constantly attempting to influence the attitude and behavior of his reader. True enough this does represent a religious position, and it seems to me one that might also aptly be called a *theologia rhetorica.* We should remember, too, his great work of editing, translating and commenting on the Scriptures and the Fathers, in which he follows the precedents of Traversari, Manetti, Valla and other Italians. We perhaps have here a *theologia philologica.* Together the two terms may be said to comprise what Cusanus called *theologia sermocinalis,* although the broadened conception that humanists such as Valla had of rhetoric might justify *theologia rhetorica* as sufficiently inclusive. In respect to this conception of the role of religious thought and writing, which is to be sure not devoid of a specific theological content, it seems to me that Erasmus most perfectly fulfils the promises and programs of the religious thought and studies of the Italian humanists. It is a true case of anticipation here, and fruition as well. More than anyone he made actual what was their ideal.

In token, rather than proof of this, I would point to one of his last great works to be completed: the *Ecclesiastes sive Concionator Evangelicus,* otherwise known as the *De ratione concionandi.*[44] It bears the notion of a "churchman" rather than a "cleric," or better still a Christian orator, for the words *Ecclesiastes* in Greek and *Concionator* in Latin mean identically, from *ecclesia* and *conventio*—popular assembly—the haranguer or orator, the man who addresses the congregation. (The Latin verb *contio* is a contraction of *conventio.*) Erasmus' book is indeed a handbook for a Christian orator, inspired by, if not directly modelled on, such works as Cicero's *De oratore* or the *Institutio oratoria* of Quintilian, so critical in Valla's thinking. To quote

Erasmus' preface: "We divide the argument into four books. In the first we demonstrate the dignity of the office and in what virtues it is necessary for the *Ecclesiast* to be endowed. In the second and third we adapt the teachings of rhetoricians, dialecticians and theologians to the use of discourse (*conciontandi*). The fourth, as a kind of catalogue, groups together and shows to the *Ecclesiast* what principles or ideas he ought to look for and in what part of Scripture they may be found."[45]

Thus he has divided his work according to the traditional subjects of rhetoric, the character of the orator, the art and parts of the oration, and finally dialectic, used here in the new humanist and old Ciceronian sense of invention, the finding of the appropriate topics or *loci* for the most persuasive discourse. Any study of the book will show that, while it is full of doctrine that can be pulled forth from the interstices as it were and put together in some kind of scheme, it is in literal fact a study of sacred linguistics and rhetoric, and in a fully technical sense.

Can we now conclude, in what is a most fragmentary account of a vast and complex subject, that the religious thought of the Italian humanists, itself complex and various, was a series of limited responses to the profound crisis of Christianity that began in the early fourteenth century and ran at least to the late sixteenth century, only to find a regrettable and provisional solution by fission? As such it was bound to anticipate and even influence in some respects the religious ideas of the Reform, both Protestant, Catholic and Radical. Historically, however, it did not seek reform in the drastic ways that it came about but in a milder spiritual transformation and quickening. Can we consider that it had in its inherited rhetorical notions of discourse and verbal communication as central to human experience the ideal of developing and practicing a *theologia rhetorica*? This is a notion that we find best exemplified in the work of Erasmus, though there are also important elements of such an approach to religion in Luther, especially in Melanchthon, definitely in the ex-humanist Calvin, and most assuredly in Ignatius Loyola. Thus, as a normal part of the historical process, the humanists did anticipate the Reformers, but much more significant is their rather unsystematic elaboration of a characteristic and autonomous position of their own.

NOTES

1. This was, certainly, one major goal of, *In Our Image and Likeness: Humanity and Divinity in Italian Humanist Thought*, 2 vols. (London and Chicago, 1970), though I should not wish it to be judged as innovative as this sounds nor limited to this purpose. The ensuing paper is based heavily on this book but

seeks to explore an issue only peripherally touched upon in it. Future citations will be to IOIAL.

2. It would require a history of modern historiography to document this assertion properly, and Ferguson's well-known *The Renaissance in Historical Thought* (Cambridge, Mass., 1948), would merely begin it. The point is, however, to stress the mythological aspects of our *Renaissance-Begriffe*, which may well play an analogous role in our historical perceptions to that of Antiquity in the Renaissance, itself. Lewis W. Spitz is preparing the welcome companion-piece: *The Reformation in Historical Thought*.

3. The oft-mentioned vista of Renaissance Florence as a frontispiece for manuscripts of *De civitate Dei*, perhaps overlooks the irony that this view is simultaneously city of man and city of God. Cf. A. Chastel, *Art et humanisme à Florence au temps de Laurent le Magnifique* (Paris, 1959), 182 and n. 4.

4. As Professor Oberman has argued, thought also is history. However, I would certainly stress the importance of documenting and analyzing what Professor Trexler calls "religious behavior", whether popular, élitist, lay or clerical, illiterate or erudite, and I would certainly expect there to be important divergences. But in the final analysis, thinkers and writers remain members of their culture however much their critical and articulate self-consciousness seems to place them above or aside it. The "outsider" is always also "insider."

5. "Crisis" is admittedly a problematical term that can also exploit a dramatic pseudo-pathos. Yet if there has to be a turning-point in history it is perhaps better that it should be grasped in the perduring, chronic sense of two centuries or so rather than bursting out every three or four years. I am enough of a structuralist to believe that "secular" change is the historian's proper concern.

6. *Pace* the statements in *The Pursuit of Holiness* by Oberman, Courtenay and Kristeller on the use of nominalism, *via moderna*, Ockhamism. Since there is no agreement (nor perhaps should be), I use these terms interchangeably but not totally indiscriminatingly. *Via moderna* is the most generic, Ockhamism the most specific, nominalism possibly the most satisfactory.

7. These comments are my distillation of the literature discussed above by Courtenay and cited there. The last sentence here indicates that Professor Courtenay's salutary stress on the modifying tendencies of recent scholarship and on the links of fourteenth-century scholasticism with thirteenth still leaves the impression of a significant discontinuity, which now needs to be more carefully stated.

8. Despite Professor Oberman's emphasis on somewhat different elements I am gratified by the substantial agreement that seems to exist on the general "shape" of the history of the period—an agreement at which we arrived by quite independent routes.

9. There has, of course, been a stress on the humanists' attacks on scholasticism as directed against their contemporary nominalists and natural philosophers, particularly by Professor Kristeller in his classic "Humanism and Scholasticism in the Italian Renaissance" of 1944, reprinted most conveniently in his *Renaissance Thought* I (New York, 1961). His *Le Thomisme et la pensée italienne de la Renaissance* (Montréal and Paris, 1967), might also seem to indicate a

continuity with thirteenth century scholasticism. Moreover, such recent studies of Lorenzo Valla as Mario Fois, *Il pensiero cristiana di Lorenzo Valla nel quadro storico-culturale del suo ambiente* (Rome, 1969), 64–8; Giovanni di Napoli, *Lorenzo Valla, Filosofia e Religione nell' Umanesimo Italiano* (Rome, 1971), 25–77, 110–124 as well as Cesare Vasoli, *La dialettica e la retorica dell' Umanesimo: 'Invenzione' e 'Metodo' nella cultura del XV e XVI secolo* (Milan, 1968), tend to stress humanist criticisms of nominalism. However, as Kristeller knows, admiration for Aquinas was limited in numbers, and Valla's praise of him, as Di Napoli also is aware, was for his piety, not his theology. What seems to be true is that the humanists, especially Valla, were very critical of nominalist dialectic, and of Aristotelian metaphysical categories. They seem not to have been aware, or possibly to comprehend, that nominalist "Covenant" theology and the *potentia ordinata* demanded precisely the kind of textual-historical approach the humanists were themselves advocating. Salutati most definitely took the categories of his theological discussion from contemporary scholasticism and, while not agreeing with all of it, certainly coincided in viewpoint on a number of points. In Valla's case where scholastics made a strict separation of theology and philosophy, he could only approve, but where theology was 'contaminated' by dialectic and metaphysics, he would heartly disapprove. The most recent study of Valla seems to place its emphasis rightly on the revolutionary character of Valla's theological conceptions and methods, which were central to the development of the culture as a whole and not limited to humanists. In fact, Vallas greatest support came from figures such as Cusanus and Bessarion. Cf. Salvatore I. Camporeale, *Lorenzo Valla, Umanesimo e Teologia* (Florence, 1972).

10. U. Mariani, *Il Petrarca e gli Agostiniani* (Rome, 1946); IOIAL, chap. I; cf. H. A. Oberman, *The Harvest of Medieval Theology* (Cambridge, Mass., 1963), 57–98 and passim. G. Leff, *Gregory of Rimini* (Manchester, 1961).

11. Ed. G. Rotondi [Studi e Testi, 195] (Vatican City, 1958), cit. as Rotondi. References will be to Rotondi and IOIAL where the Latin is given in the notes.

12. Rotondi, 24–5; IOIAL 29, 334 n. 58.

13. Rotondi, 25; IOIAL, 30, 335, n. 63.

14. Rotondi, 66–7; IOIAL, 40–1, 340–1 n. 86.

15. Cf. Hubert Jedin, "Mutamenti della interpretazione cattolica della figura di Lutero e loro limiti," *Rivista di Storia della Chiesa in Italia,* 23 (1969), 361–77.

16. Rotondi, 92; IOIAL, 45, 342–3 n. 97; Aug. Conf., I, i.

17. Ioannis Calvini, *Institutio Religionis Christianae,* ed. Wilhelm Baum, Eduard Cunitz, Eduard Reuss, Vol. II (1559) ed.) (Brunswick, 1869), I. i, 3, col. 187, Quin etiam eo licentiae quidam eorum proruperunt, ut iactarint deorum quidem esse munus, quod vivimus; nostrum vero quod bene sancteque vivimus. Unde et illud Ciceronis in persona Cottae, quia sibi quisque virtutem acquirit, neminem ex sapientibus unquam de ea gratias Deo egisse. Propter virtutem enim laudamur, inquit, ut in virtute gloriamur. Quod non fieret si donum esset Dei, non a nobis. Ae paulo post: iudicium hoc omnium mor-

talium est, fortunam a Deo petendam, ab se ipso sumendam esse sapientiam. The English translations are John Allen's.

18. Rotondi, 100; IOIAL, 45, 343 n. 99.

19. *Institutiones,* ed. cit., II, ii, 15, col. 198, Imo ne sine ingenti quidem admiratione veterum scripta legere de his rebus poterimus; admirabimur autem, quia praeclara, ut sunt, cogemur agnoscere.

20. *Ibid.,* II, ii, 4, col. 188, Ex quibus veteres mihi videntur hoc consilio vires humanas sic extulisse, ne si impotentiam diserto essent confessi, primum philosophorum ipsorum cachinnos, quibuscum tunc certamen habebant, excuterent; deinde carni suapte sponte nimis ad bonum torpenti novam desidiae occasionem praeberent.

21. Cf. Siefgried Wenzel, "Petrarch's Accidia," *Studies in the Renaissance* VIII (1961), 36–48.

22. Cf. Klaus Heitmann, *Fortuna und Virtus, Eine Studie zu Petrarcas Lebensweischeit, Studi italiani,* I (Cologne-Graz), 1958. Citations will be to Bibl. Vatic., Cod. Urb. lat. 334.

23. *Institutiones,* ed. cit., II, ii, 1, Hominem arbitrii libertate nunc esse spoliatum et miseriae servituti addictum—title of Cap. II; Nam ubi omni rectitudine abdicatur homo, statim ex eo desidiae occasionem arripit; et quia nihil ad iustitiae studium valere per se dicitur, illud totum, quasi iam nihil ad se pertineat, susque deque habet. Rursum vel minutulum illi quidpiam arrogari non potest, quin et Deo praeripiatur suus honor, et ipse temeraria confidentia labefactetur. Ad hos ergo scopulos ne impingamus, tenendus hic cursus erit, ut homo nihil boni penes se reliquum sibi esse edoctus, et miserrima undique necessitate circumseptus, doceatur tamen ad bonum quo vacuus est, ad libertatem quo privatus est, aspirare, et acrius ab ignavia excidetur quam si summa virtute fingeretur instructus.

24. Urb. lat. 334, f. 230r; IOIAL, 190–1, 398 n. 9.

25. *Institutiones,* ed. cit., I, xv. 3, Quamvis enim in homine externo erfulgeat Dei gloria, propriam tamen imaginis sedem in anima esse dubium non est. Non infitior quidem, externam speciem, quatenus nos distinguit a brutis animalibus, ac separat, simul Deo propius adiungere. Ne vehementius contendam, si quis censeri velit sub imagine Sui, quod quum prona spectent animalia caetera terram, os homini sublime datum est, coelumque videre iussus, et erectos ad sidera tollero vultus [col. 136]. Quamvis ergo anima non sit homo, absurdum tamen non est, eum animae respectu vocari Dei imaginem: esti principium quod nuper posui retineo, patere Dei effigiem ad totam praestantiam, qua eminet hominis natura inter omnes animantium species. Proinde hac voce notatur integritas qua praeditus fuit Adam quum recta intelligentia polleret, affectus haberet compositos ad rationem, sensus omnes recto ordine temperatos, vereque eximiis dotibus opificis sui excellentiam referret. Ac quamvis primaria sedes divinae imaginis fuerit in mente et corde, vel in anima eiusque potentiis, nulla tamen pars fuit etiam usque ad corpus, in qua non scintillae aliquae micarent [cols. 137–8].

26. *Ibid.,* I, xv, 4 col. 138, Quin Adam, ubi excidit e gradu suo, hac defectione a Deo alienatus sit minime dubium est. Quare etsi demus, non prorsus ex-

inanitam ac deletam in eo fuisse Dei imaginem, sic tamen corrupta fuit, ut quidquid superest, horrenda sit deformitas. Ideoque recuperandae salutis nobis initium est in ea instauratione quam consequimur per Christum, qui etiam hac de causa vocatur secundus Adam, quia nos in veram et solidam integritatem restituit.

27. *Ibid.,* X, xvi col. 144, Deum sua virtute mundum a se conditum fovere ac tueri, et singulas eius partes sua providentia regere.

28. In his *Christianity and Humanism: Studies in the History of Ideas* (Grand Rapids, 1968), chap. 4, "John Calvin and the Rhetorical Tradition," 107–129.

29. Cf. IOIAL, chap. II.

30. *Ibid.,* 76–102.

31. For Salutati, *Ibid.,* 555–62. Cusanus—cf. *Texte seiner philosophischen Schriften,* ed. Petzelt (Stuttgart, 1949), 314–5, Unde haec est sermocinalis theologia, qui nitor te ad Deum per vim vocabuli ducere modo quo possum faciliori et veriori.

32. Cf. IOIAL, chap. III and 674–81, 633–8.

33. Cf. IOIAL, 160–70. For Catholic studies of Valla cf. Fois and Di Napoli sup. cit. Camporeale, sup. cit., though a Dominican, manages to avoid sectarian apologetics.

34. IOIAL, 571–601, 726–734.

35. *Ibid.,* 230–58. We have now (1983) *Ianotti Manetti De dignitate et excellentia hominis,* ed. Elizabeth R. Leonard (Padua: Antenore, 1975).

36. Eugene F. Rice, Jr., *The Renaissance Idea of Wisdom* (Cambridge, Mass., 1958); "The Humanist Idea of Christian Antiquity: LeFèvre d'Étaples and His Circle," *Studies in the Renaissance,* IX (1962), 126–60.

37. Sears Jayne, *John Colet and Marsilio Ficino* (London, 1963).

38. Lewis W. Spitz, *The Religious Renaissance of the German Humanists,* (Cambridge, Mass., 1963).

39. Cf. John W. O'Malley, *Giles of Viterbo on Church and Reform, A Study in Renaissance Thought* (Leiden, 1968).

40. Spitz, op. cit., chap. IX, "Erasmus, Philosopher of Christ," 197–236.

41. E. W. Kohls, *Die Theologie des Erasmus,* 2 Vols. (Basel, 1966).

42. e.g. E. V. Telle, *Érasme de Rotterdam et Le Septième Sacrement* (Geneva, 1954): W. P. Eckert, *Erasmus von Rotterdam Werk und Wirkung.* Vol. I, *Der humanistische Theologie* (Cologne, 1967).

43. Charles Béné, *Érasme et Saint Augustin, ou influence de Saint Augustin sur l'humanisme de Érasme* (Geneva, 1969). Now (1983) there are also the books of Marjorie O'Rourke Boyle on Erasmus's religious thought: *Erasmus on Language and Method in Theology* (Toronto, 1977); *Christening Pagan Mysteries* (Toronto, 1981); *Rhetoric and Reform* (Cambridge, Mass., 1983).

44. In *Opera omnia* (Leiden, 1704), Tom. V, cols. 767–1100.

45. *Ibid.,* cols. 767–8, Summam argumenti in quattuor libros digessimus. In primo demonstravimus muneris dignitatem, et quibus virtutibus oporteat esse praeditum Ecclesiasten. In secundo ac tertio quae sunt in praeceptionibus Rhetorum, Dialecticorum, ac Theologorum, ad usum concionandi accommodamus. Quartus velut elenchus commonstrat Ecclesiastae quas sententias ex quibus Scripturae locis petere debeat, quem tamen hactenus absolvimus, ut studioso lectori viam modo commonstraverimus, alioqui res erat nec unius nec exigui voluminis.

The Problem of Free Will in the
Renaissance and the Reformation

The question of free will is not simply one of granting the moral autonomy of individual men as against submitting them to the all-seeing care of divine providence. The prevalence in the last century of theories of organic evolution, of economic determinism, of unconscious motivation has made us see the problem today in a new and strictly secular light. It also suggests, perhaps, that the assertion of the primacy of the individual, if it actually was a characteristic of the Renaissance, was not necessarily the ultra-modern doctrine it has been thought. At any rate, the contemporary references should suggest that even during the transitional periods of the Renaissance and the Reformation the problem of free will could have had a wide cultural import.

The present paper will deal with material that is for the most part familiar. It will seek to indicate some of the relations of Renaissance, largely Italian humanist, thought on free will to the Reformation treatment of the problem. It will raise the question of whether both of these cultural movements, which seem to contrast in so many ways, do not in certain essentials grapple with the same cultural problem, whether both find themselves in opposition to traditional medieval modes of thought on similar grounds.

Stated in its broadest terms, the cultural problem of the Renaissance and Reformation, with which the question of free will was directly concerned, was the fact and the consequence of a divorce between ethics and economics, between the moral and the expedient, between the spiritual and the material. While one set of values and one set of rules and injunctions applied to the individual's pursuit of goodness and spiritual well-being, an

---

This paper, written in the mid- to late forties as an offshoot of my translation of Lorenzo Valla's *Dialogue on Free Will*, was first published in *Journal of the History of Ideas* 10 (1949):51–62. It has been reprinted in *Renaissance Essays From the Journal of the History of Ideas*, ed. P. O. Kristeller & P. P. Wiener (New York: Harper & Row, 1968), 187–98. The article has some personal interest in its indication of a relationship between late medieval nominalism, Renaissance humanism, and Reformation thought at a relatively early stage of my scholarly career. I would possibly state my arguments in a more subtle and nuanced way now, in keeping with the extensive scholarship in these areas since that time. But I do not find myself in fundamental disagreement with most of the assertions that follow.

entirely different set applied to his conduct of business, political relations and the daily routines of worldly life.

The problem was by no means a new one, but the striking difference between the periods of our interest and the one immediately preceding is that medieval thought on the question of the relation of individual well-being to the necessities of social life had by and large sought to unify, synthesize, or reconcile the two. The devices were many and varied. Perhaps the most characteristic principle of reconciliation was that of the double standard whereby one ethics and one life was required of the spiritually braver monks, and another set, equally efficacious for salvation, was applied to ordinary Christians through the penitential system with its flexibility and willingness to consider individual differences. This medieval tendency toward integration was also to be seen in the philosophic *summas,* both in the very notion that in one work the sum of all knowledge and insight on all spheres of life could be covered, and in their contents, which were frequently directly concerned with unification.

The basis for medieval efforts at unity and for the Renaissance-Reformation sense of cleavage was to be found in social history. Neither universalism nor the later disjunctive thinking were mere cultural patterns in themselves. Both were related to a reality in which the problems first asserted themselves. Medieval ways of thinking were part of the heritage of an agrarian, kinship society, and much of what came to be sanctified as morality by the Church was the pragmatic wisdom of this society. Another essential element was the static and hierarchical nature of feudalism, which made it an easy matter for thought to relate seeming differences into an organically integrated whole in which one part served another and was served by another and each contributed to the well-being of all in its functionally differentiated way.

A fission occurred when and as a new commercial society with its entirely different requirements and imperatives for survival and its new definition of success as competitive and accumulative grew up within the old society with its economic end of maintaining a man in the condition in which he was born. To be strictly historical it would be well to emphasize that this process was already under way in the twelfth century and therefore a good century before the monumental attempts to depict a unity and reconcile conflicting attitudes made by the great thirteenth century scholastics. From a social and economic point of view undoubtedly the Renaissance and its home, the mercantile city, must be dated from the twelfth century. Culturally, however, there was an intervening effort to reassert unity when the danger to it first threatened.

It is important to add that neither the Renaissance nor the Reformation should be regarded as examples of cultural lag, of clinging to outworn moralities in the face of new technical conditions. The disjunctive, each-against-all style of thinking that flourished was as true a depiction of the actual life situation created by the new social system as could be conceived. The highly competitive character of the new economic individualism and the simultaneous lack of control over the market on the part of the individual who had to depend on such general forces as the statistical aggregate of everyone's behavior were among the essential ingredients producing the double system of value.

Certainly, also, such pressure toward aggressive individualism accompanied by the fortuitous quality of the outcome would lead to speculation about free will and the opposing forces of Fortune, Fate, Providence and Predestination. While these remarks might thus set the stage for a discussion of cultural qualities in general, it should be clear how much they also may apply to thinking about free will. And it should be obvious that this was no subject of idle speculation but a question involving crucial problems of existence.

Thomas Aquinas' notions illustrate the effort to find a synthesis and thereby reinforce the Church's claim to universality. Essentially, his position was that individuals have freedom of moral choice without in any way detracting from God's omnipotence, because this circumstance is in accord with the good of the universe and with its structure of hierarchically descending powers by means of which God unfolds His nature. Nor is divine providence in any way a limitation of human freedom, because freedom of the will is in itself a participation in the providential government of the universe.

He says, "Now through being capable of providence, a man can direct and govern his own actions also. Therefore the rational creature participates in the divine providence not only in being governed but also in governing; for it governs itself in its own action, and also other things."[1]

Human freedom is conscious because it involves knowledge of means and ends. External frustrations and obstacles to the exercise of the will may be able to prevent human actions, but man retains the power to discriminate between good and evil among exterior things. The passions have a greater power to destroy human judgment and freedom of choice, but even here sometimes "the reason is not entirely engrossed by the passion," and man can will to move differently than the passion inclines him.[2]

Even in the case of action under the influence of such a powerful passion as fear stimulated by external or other danger, it need not be entirely involuntary, "in so far as, under the circumstances, it hinders a greater evil which was feared." Man is therefore thought of as capable of facing and meeting the exigencies of material life in a free and rational and moral way. Aquinas, furthermore, recognized that behavior under the influence of a passion such as fear, when it has no relation to a real danger, may be unfree; "it is involuntary . . . if such a fear were not threatening."[3]

Man was therefore capable of directing both his material and his moral life freely and rationally without being deterred by external fortune or by Grace.

Not all the succeeding scholastic writers followed Aquinas in defending the unity of experience. Especially the Nominalists began to express a theory of cleavage between an inner and an outer world in their writings. Beginning with William of Ockham, they broke decisively with the Thomistic position. On the one hand, Ockham argued that a truly charitable act had to be motivated in the most completely free, almost arbitrary manner, to have merit. Charity as the result of acquired *habitus* was neither free nor morally valuable. On the other hand, man's salvation did not depend on his merits but completely on God's absolutely free will. God could justify both those who merited salvation and those who did not; he could reprobate either.[4]

Since virtues and sins were determined not by the specific nature of the actions but by divine decree, social behavior was essentially amoral as far as its effectiveness in the world was concerned. "Hatred of God, stealing, adultery, and the like, of course, have sinful circumstances connected with them according to the generally accepted law, inasmuch as the person who performs them is obligated by divine precept to the contrary. As far as the absolute being of those acts is concerned, however, they may be performed by God without any sinful circumstances attached to them. They may even be meritoriously performed by man if they fall under divine precept, just as now their opposites, as a matter of fact, fall under the divine precept."[5]

The consequence of this position is to give man free will in the realm of secular life but in effect to deny the validity of freely willed morality for attaining salvation except when God happens to accept it as valid. Free will, however, is limited even in the natural world insofar as action is in conformity with any regularly recurring phenomena or natural forces. It can exist only where there is room for contingency. "Freedom is opposed to necessity in the same way as necessity is opposed to contingency. Thus freedom is some kind of indifference and contingency and is distinguished against the natural active principle. Nature and will are two principles with opposed modes of origination."[6]

In this way Ockham anticipated the humanists both in dissociating morality from natural life and in opposing free will to predestination in one sphere, to natural necessity in the other. Even more, it should be emphasized that he was not so much of a Pelagian as an anticipator of Luther. In fact, he held Thomas Aquinas, rather, to be Pelagian and attacked him for it.[7]

Humanist writers divide into several schools of thought, but all of them were characterized by a separation of the material and the moral. For some, freedom of will was possible in the world of material relations but not where spiritual well-being or salvation was concerned. For others man possessed spiritual freedom but no power over external events.

Hardly a century after Aquinas and not a generation after Ockham, Petrarch denied the possibility of finding any choices over the goods of fortune or of arriving at anything but moral ruin in urban occupations. The real question for him was whether man had sufficient freedom of the will to put aside the passionate attachments he makes to worldly fame, to the beauties of nature and art, the resentments at others' successes, the self-hatred that frustration in the competitive world bred. Could contemplation of human misery and death and the Christian teaching make one indifferent, as Augustine argued in *The Secret,* or was the involvement in the very pressure of life in the competitive world too habit-forming for one to overcome, as Petrarch feared? "I have not strength to resist that old bent for study altogether." "Want of will you call want of power. Well, so it must be, if it cannot be otherwise." God alone may lead one "safe and whole out of so many crooked ways," so that we may "hear the world grow still and silent, and the winds of adversity die away."[8]

Petrarch had many successors in this half-hearted, disbelieving Stoicism, particularly in the early Quattrocento.[9] Reason was still the key to freedom of will, but it retained no power to direct political and economic life, in which fortune held sway. Reason could overcome the passionate yearning for the goods of fortune and oppose fortune with virtue. But such perseverance was rare.

It was in the second half of the century that the great Neoplatonic exponents of rational freedom wrote. Marsilio Ficino and Pico della Mirandola in particular have seemed to express that high confidence in human capacity and almost worshipful reverence for the dignity of man with which we have usually sought to invest the Renaissance. From many directions in recent years there has come a recognition of the primarily religious nature of Neoplatonic thought, including that of the Renaissance. And while it is perfectly true that Ficino had an exalted view of man's God-like capacities and located man at the center of the chain of being where, as a microcosm, he contained within himself all qualities of the universe, high and low, the true use of philosophy he held to be the religious one of withdrawing the soul from worldly care toward the realization of the divine. He emphatically does not have the sense of domination and control over the universe and particularly the world of social and economic life or of physical nature that many scholars have sought to attribute to him.[10]

On the contrary, Ficino says, while our souls are dependent on God and His providence, "our body is attracted in a violent attack by the body of the world through the forces of fate . . . and the power of fate does not penetrate our mind if our mind has not previously immersed itself by its own will in the body subject to fate. So no one should trust his own intelligence and strength enough to hope he can wholly avoid the sicknesses of the body or the loss of things. Every soul should retire from the pestilence of the body and withdraw into the mind, for then fortune will spend its force in the body and not pass into the Soul. A wise man will not fight in vain against fate, but rather resist by fleeing. Misfortunes cannot be hunted down, but can only be fled from."[11]

Pico's eloquent praise of human powers has been cited so frequently as to be a commonplace. "O great and wonderful happiness of man. It is given to him to have that which he desires and to be that which he wills." While man is endowed with free will, the earthly things are to be spurned and through philosophy the knowledge of divine things is to be arrived at, and the internal discord of the soul overcome.[12] Here again, in the middle of the most extravagant notions of human greatness, is the dualism that withdraws man from the world and gives him rational freedom only in order to enable man to make the withdrawal.

It is the limited nature of the moral freedom taught in the Renaissance that seems to have been overlooked by certain contemporary philosophers and religious thinkers. And it is at this point that the relationship with Reformation thought can be established. A frequent interpretation, that of Reinhold Niebuhr in *The Nature and Destiny of Man,*[13] for example, has been to the effect that the greatest cultural contrast existed between the Reformation, on the one hand, and the Renaissance, on the other. The Renaissance, furthermore, was thought of as being the culmination and logical outcome of scholastic moral speculation, which in some respects it was.[14]

It was particularly the reformers' denial of free will and their deprecation of the rationality of human moral acts that has led to this view of contrast. The emphasis that has come out of the Renaissance writers so far cited might seem to justify this view, for all sought to affirm the rational freedom of man to achieve virtue or salvation. But if the comparison is placed in a wider context then similarities emerge.

Whereas medieval thought attributed to man the rational capacity both to lead a moral life in the ordinary secular pursuits of this world and to achieve salvation, both the humanists and the reformers denied that man could do both. The humanists took the first step and denied the possibility of subordinating economic to moral ends, but left man the necessary free will to flee contamination by the world and to gain salvation by his own powers, if he so chose. The reformers, particularly Luther, also denied that there was any possibility of morality in business or politics but took the further step of denying man the power of achieving either virtue or justification by his own free will.

Salvation came by faith or by election. And through faith man gained that inward Christian liberty which Luther praised. "It is more excellent than all other liberty which is external, as heaven is more excellent than earth."[15] It is, to be sure, an important step beyond the humanists' hard-won inner freedom, but still it is a step in the same direction. The important thing is that the conception and the end are the same: the impossibility of moral action in secular life, and the inner peace and freedom that comes with release from guilt about worldly cares.

On the other hand, it should not be thought that either the humanists or the reformers, even if they so intended had any appreciable effect in lessening their contemporaries' ever-growing absorption in material interests and in efforts to discover rationally controllable laws governing nature and history. It is a paradox that the limitation of free will both reinforced the amoralism and determinism of social and natural science and led to ultimately greater human powers of control over the external environment. Free will was thereby acquired in the very area in which it was most vigorously denied, but not for moral ends.

It may seem strange that in the discussion so far the only Italian Renaissance writers who wrote specifically on "Free Will" have not been mentioned. Both Lorenzo Valla and Pietro Pomponazzi furnish a sort of mathematician's check on the present thesis, for both took positions much more explicitly close to those of the Reformation.

Valla composed his *Dialogue on Free Will*[16] around 1440. In it he vigorously attacked the notion that philosophy and the use of reason could be the handmaiden of theology and denied that there was any way open to man for comprehending the contradiction of man's seeming possession of free will and God's powers exercised in "hardening" this man and "showing mercy" on that one.[17] While divine foreknowledge might not contradict human freedom, divine predestination seemed to. He classified all events into three categories: "natural phenomena always running the same course," "fortuitous things" which through having a kind of statistical predictability "follow a certain course of their own," and "affairs of the will".[18] The last left no loopholes for freedom, however, for just as God "created the wolf fierce, the hare timid, the lion brave, the ass stupid, the dog savage, the sheep mild, so he generated some men hard of heart, others soft, he generated one given to evil, the other to virtue, and further he gave a capacity of reform to one and made another incorrigible."[19] The individual's "inborn character"[20] will determine voluntary behavior. The crucial area for freedom of choice was also moral and religious for Valla. And here his position is very close to that of the reformers. "And if we entrust our life to friends, should we not dare to entrust it to Christ who for our salvation took on both the life of the flesh and the death of the cross? We don't know the cause of this matter; of what consequence is it? We stand by faith, not by the probability of reason."[21]

Valla's treatise seems not to have caused much of a stir among the Italian humanists. Even Pomponazzi, whose erudition and citations went to extremes, failed to mention it. The reformers and Erasmus in his conflict with Luther, however, recognized it for what it was. Erasmus, though disparaging, classed Valla with "Manichaeus" and Wyclif.[22] Luther in his reply to Erasmus, *The Enslaved Will*, remarked, "Indeed, for my part, one, Wyclif, and another, Lorenzo Valla, as well as Augustine, whom you (Erasmus) except, is my entire authority."[23] And in *The Table Talks*, Luther said, "Lorenzo Valla is the best Italian that I have seen or discovered. He disputes ably on free will. He sought simplicity in piety and letters at the same time. Erasmus seeks after him as much in letters as he condemns him in piety."[24] Referring to the distinction between foreknowledge and divine will, Calvin succinctly remarked, "But Valla, a man otherwise not much versed in theology, appears to me to have discovered superior acuteness and judiciousness by showing that this controversy is unnecessary, because both life and death are acts of God's will rather than of his foreknowledge."[25]

Modern judgments of this treatise of Valla have for the most part miscomprehended its meaning and failed to see its connection with the Reformation. Even Ernst Cassirer went so far as to say, "for the first time since the days of the ancients the problem of freedom was cited before a purely worldly forum, before the judgment chair of 'natural reason'."[26] Curiously, Leibniz, whose praise of Valla Cassirer cites, took this treatise and added to the principal device of the argument, a mythological analogy on the fate of Sextus Tarquinius,[27] in order to reach the rational reconciliation of human freedom and divine providence which Valla repudiated.[28] Leibniz actually took the position that modern interpretation has seemed to want to attribute to the Italian Renaissance in general and to Valla's treatise in particular.

Luciano Barozzi, writing in 1890, seems to have justly seen that Valla's methods of proof are more like modern positivist and statistical research and that, like modern positivist philosophers, Valla solved the problem of human liberty by a psychological determinism.[29]

Pomponazzi, even more explicitly than Valla, revealed the divorce between moral and religious goals on the one side, and scientific, secular ones on the other. Although the facts are certainly dubious and need a fresh examination, he has been given the reputation of a proponent of the Alexandrian school and of a restorer of a pure, pre-scholastic Aristotelianism. More significant, he accepted the crude pseudo-naturalistic doctrine of the astrological determination of human as well as natural events. There would seem to be little room for human freedom in the thought of such a man. Consequently it is consistent to find him ending his *Five Books on Fate, Free Will, Predestination and the Providence of God* with an assertion of the absolute incompatibility of theology and rational thought.[30]

Although he professes to stand by the teachings of the Church wherever they are in contradiction with the views of natural reason he is citing, the view that Pomponazzi was genuinely skeptical is not without some plausibility. The most satisfactory explanation of the problem of human freedom according to human wisdom was that of the Stoics. To them fate ruled all, and that explained why there were good men and bad men, sheep and wolves, poor and rich, and no discernible justice. It has always been thus, so it will always be. "Under the moon all is corruption." The earth is its dung heap. God has regard only for the totality of the species and the equilibrium of good and evil in the universe, which individuals cannot alter. But since human wisdom is erroneous, we must follow the teachings of the Church, which seek to reconcile human freedom and divine providence—something that can only be understood on faith.[31] Thus from the side of the secular, Aristotelian Renaissance the circle of relationship between religious denial of individual freedom and secular determinism is completed. Neither in morality, nor in social relations, nor in natural phenomena are rational insights open to man. There is only predestination and election or reprobation, worldly success or failure, approximate cause and observable effect. The proof of divine justice and wisdom lies in positive recognition, without interposition of reason, of the facts asserted by the Scriptures; moral righteousness becomes a matter of visible proofs in the individual's conduct; economic wisdom is judged alone by success or failure; nature is neither good nor bad but all determining.

NOTES

1. *Summa Contra Gentiles*, Lib. III, cap. 113. Translation by English Dominican Fathers.
2. *Summa Theologica*, I, II, 10, 3.
3. *Ibid.*, I, II, 6, 6.
4. *Tractatus de Praedestinatione et de Praescientia Dei et de Futuris Contingentibus*, Q. I, B; ed. Ph. Boehner, (*Franciscan Institute Publications* No. 2), St. Bonaventure, N.Y., 1945, p. 5. Cf. Paul Vignaux, *Justification et Prédestination au XIVe Siècle*, (*Bibliothèque de l'École des Hautes Études, Sciences Religieuses*, vol. 48), Paris, 1934, pp. 120–127.
5. *Super quattuor libros sententiarum subtilissimae quaestiones etc.*, Lib. II, Qu. 19, N., O.; as cited and translated by S. C. Tornay, *Ockham, Studies and Selections*, La Salle, Ill., 1938, pp. 180–181.
6. *Sent.* I, dist. 2, qu. 1, U., B., cf. Tornay, *op. cit.*, p. 175.
7. Vignaux, *op. cit.*, p. 133, n. 1, emphasizes his affinity to Luther.
8. *De secreto conflictu curarum mearum;* as translated by W. H. Draper, *Petrarch's Secret, or the Soul's Conflict with Passion*, London, 1911, p. 192.

9. E.g. Salutati, Giovanni Conversino, Poggio.
10. E.g., Anders Nygren, *Agape and Eros,* Part II, Vol. II, London, 1939, chap. 5, "The Renewal of the Eros Motif in the Renaissance." His many apt citations show the zeal of Ficino to approach and become like God, but none bear out his assertion that, "He sings the praise of *Man*—but be it noted, of empirical earthly man. For it is precisely as the earthly creature of sense that he is, that man is a microcosm." p. 456.
11. Cited from a letter to Cavalcanti (*Opera Omnia,* Basel, 1561, p. 633) by P. O. Kristeller, *The Philosophy of Marsilio Ficino,* New York, 1943, p. 298.
12. Giovanni Pico della Mirandola, *De Hominis Dignitate, Opera Omnia,* Basel, 158-38, p. 314 ff.
13. New York, 1941–1943.
14. Both Nygren and Niebuhr take this view, emphasizing that the Middle Ages synthesized classical paganism with Pauline Christianity and that the Renaissance purified and restored the former. The Reformation, on the other hand, was held to have renewed an original, un-Hellenized form of Christianity.
15. *Christian Liberty, Works,* Philadelphia, 1915, Vol. II, p. 343.
16. *De Libero Arbitrio,* ed. Maria Anfossi (*Opusculi Filosofici: Testi e Documenti Inediti o Rari Publicati da Giovanni Gentile,* VI), Florence, 1934.
17. *Ibid.,* p. 49.
18. *Ibid.,* pp. 23–24.
19. *Ibid.,* p. 37.
20. *Ibid.*
21. *Ibid.,* p. 50.
22. *De Libero Arbitrio Diatribe sive Collatio, Opera Omnia,* vol. 9, Leyden, 1706, col. 1218.
23. *De Servo Arbitrio,* ed. A Freitag (*Werke,* WA, Bd. 18, 1908), p. 640.
24. *Tischreden,* Bd. I, WA., 1912, #259.
25. *Institutes of the Christian Religion,* Eng. trans., Philadelphia, 1816 et seq., Bk. III, chap. 23, section 6.
26. *Individuum und Kosmos in der Philosophie der Renaissance, (Studien der Bibliothek Warburg,* X), Leipzig-Berlin, 1927, p. 82.
27. Valla, *Op. cit.,* pp. 31–38.
28. *Essais de theodicée sur la bonté de Dieu, la liberté de l'homme, et l'origine du mal,* Amsterdam, 1710. Ed. J. E. Erdmann, *Opera Philosophica . . . Omnia,* Berlin, 1839–40, §§413–417.
29. *Lorenzo Valla,* (R. Istituto di Studi Superiori . . . in Firenze, Sezione di Filosofia e Filologia, Publicazoni, 25), Florence, 1891, chap. 7, "La dottrina del Libero Arbitrio di Lorenzo Valla ed i moderni Positivisti."
30. *De Fato, Libero Arbitrio, Praedestinatione, et Providentia Dei Libri V,* Basel, 1567, Cf. Walter Betzendörfer *Die Lehre von der zweifachen Wahrheit bei Petrus Pomponatius,* Tübingen, 1919, pp. 84–6. This work of Pomponazzi deserves a more thorough analysis of its relation to medieval and Reformation thought on its subject.
31. Betzendörfer, *Ibid.;* Antonio Corsano, *Il Pensiero Religioso Italiano dall'Umanesimo al Giurisdizionalismo,* Bari, 1937, ch. 2, "Il Pensiero Religioso del

Pomponazzi," p. 92, n. 1, cites Pomponazzi, *Op. cit.,* p. 1012, "Sufficit enim quod in caelo non reperitur malitia. Infra autem globum lunae, cum omnia tendant ad interitum, fetida sunt et putentia. Veluti enim in animali aliquae partes sunt nobiles de necessitate et aliquae ignobiles, sic mundus est unum animale et de necessitate habet ista sublunaria tanquam stercora."

Erasmus, Augustine, and the Nominalists

In 1524/25 Erasmus and Luther engaged in their great exchange over free will which clearly revealed the depth of difference between these two reformers. But because of the ambiguity of Erasmus' position as a "reformer" with a small "r" in contrast to Luther's as a "Reformer" with a capital "R" much of the significance of this debate has been obscured. The issue of free will, which Erasmus raised in his *Diatribe on Free Will* and to which Luther replied in his lengthier treatise *On the Enslaved Will,* was indeed critical and central to the massive religious and cultural problems that were being worked out in the Protestant Reformation and the Catholic Counter-Reformation, and Erasmus early saw this, long before the Council of Trent and in the very years in which the Catholic Reform movement was gathering strength for its unsuccessful efforts of the thirties and early 'forties. But Erasmus had in mind a different outcome than either Luther or the Catholic Reformers envisioned and certainly one that was totally alien to the path of repression followed by Paul IV after he had taken command of the Catholic response and broken with his erst-while reforming colleagues. It was essential for Erasmus to differentiate his reformation from Luther's, which he accomplished by his diatribe, but in many respects Luther's crushing reply did more than affirm his own theology and showered Erasmus with ignominy and ridicule such as to render his position feeble indeed. Caught between the oncoming battle of giants, this lover of peace, but also a man deeply convinced of his own vision of Christianity as a religion of concord, elaborated and reiterated his positions but ceased to represent any threat of becoming a third force. [1]

For Erasmus was a humanist, and his religious reform program was a humanistic one which in many ways was lost sight of in the debate over free will. But for Erasmus a humanistic reform program was more than a method of combat and was in fact part of a deeply conceived theological and philosophical position. Essential to it was both the doctrine of free will and that of grace, but the position itself was a broader one and provided the matrix within which these specific theological points became critical. Gor-

---

This article on Erasmus's views of the free-will problem in comparison here with his interpretations of Augustine and the late scholastics on this question was published in *Archiv für Reformationsgeschichte* 67 (1976): 5–32. I consider it a more developed exposition of my conception of humanism and the free-will problem. It is more recent than the previous paper.

don Rupp has asked, "How seriously must we take Erasmus as a theologian?" in introducing the English translation of his *Diatribe*.[2] But this only reveals how easily Erasmus is misunderstood within our still conventional conceptions of what a theology is.

What this paper attempts to do is to present a close analysis of an important section of a too-neglected work of Erasmus, his *Hyperaspistes Diatribae adversus Servum Arbitrium Martini Lutheri*,[3] or "Hotly Defended Diatribes." It is the closing section of this work[4] which he had put together in great length and detail over the ensuing years. Perhaps he had a sense that its length and detail of Biblical commentary would prove burdensome to his readers, for he says, "Up to now we have replied, not without heavy tedium, to the Lutheran disputations, or brawls rather. Now we shall pull together a few things on the sum of the matter, and soon put an end to the volume."[5]

In order to unravel his meaning it will be necessary to go through this section of the *Hyperaspistes* in some detail, for Erasmus, as we know, is often oblique. But it does come together in the end. It purports to be a history of theological discussions of the free will-grace question, and of the varying meanings of the central terms—a comparison of the various positions in order to place himself and Luther in an historical context. But the very historical context he presents will turn out to be the heart of his theology, certainly of his conception of theology, and in this way he finally differentiates himself, not only from Luther, but from the entire tradition of the doctrinal and professional theologian. We have used the title: "Erasmus, Augustine, and the Nominalists" because he devotes much space to both, and in partial agreement and disagreement with both, in order to clarify his own position and put his quarrel with Luther in historical perspective. Although there will be many citations in which Erasmus refers to Luther, my concern will not be with Luther's hardly subtle yet definitely elusive position except through Erasmus' notion of it. Although Luther can also be designated as a "Biblical Humanist," and both Erasmus and Luther were in their own ways influenced by the great Italian Biblical humanist, Lorenzo Valla, it is unlikely that Erasmus understood Luther any better than Luther understood him. Here we shall only try to understand Erasmus, and it is possible that if Luther had understood him to be as we shall present him, he would have found him even more outrageous, or possibly he even did. Erasmus sticks to his position that his quarrel with Luther, as well as Luther's with the apologists of the Church and much of history of the free will controversy, boiled down to a quarrel over words. I wish to take him seriously in this, for we may well find the answer to Professor Rupp's question here. But though he begins with a brief argument concerning the traditions out of which the key words in the controversy came, and seeks to show that semantics lay at the base of the whole theological controversy, it is not here that the heart of his position may be found. He is more than, far more than, an etymologist and philologist dealing with theological texts, though, superbly, he also is both.

Liberum arbitrium came from the ancient schools of philosophy who attributed much to human reason, undoubtedly ignorant of grace. "The magnificence of the names (*to autexousion* Greek, *liberum arbitrium* Latin) did not correspond to the reality they explained," and neither can be found in the canonical books. Yet they have found respectability, "because these words, taken over from those who were close in time to the Apostles, or even saw them, have been received in such great consent of the ages by the foremost ecclesiastics even up to this day, without injury to grace." Indeed it would be foreign to Christian modesty "to make a tragedy of the fact." There are so many terms not found in the Scriptures which nonetheless have been accepted, words such as *homousion, perpetua virginitas, tres personae, una essentia.* On the other hand, the words *fate* and *necessity* have been rejected because they were hateful to the philosophers and are even more hateful to Christians because they are associated with Manichaeus who divided man into two opposing principles, one necessarily good and one necessarily evil.[6]

We make application of this to Luther, unfairly it has been argued because Luther recognized man's freedom in secular matters, but, as we shall see, Erasmus was aware of the distinction and thinking only of his theology. What he seems to have in mind is Luther's famous *simul iustus et peccator* doctrine which held that man remained a sinner even after he had been justified by faith. It may well be that this doctrine was at the heart of Luther's differences with his foes, Catholic and humanist alike, who felt that a necessitarian universe prevailed unless men contributed in some degree to their own salvation or perdition. At any rate, Erasmus says that Augustine also was accused of Manichaeism but was able to refute this charge, though he does not see how Luther can, "who makes the whole man, even according to his principal parts (i.e. mind, spirit and body), flesh, and Satan reigns in him even after the infusion of Spirit . . ."—the *simul iustus et peccator* doctrine. Moreover, if the term, "free will" is challenged as borrowed from philosophy, "fate" and "necessity," far worse, come from astrology.[7]

Turning directly to the "matter" (*res*) at issue, he begins his review of the history of theology on the questions of grace and free will. The *Orthodoxi* (the early Christian Fathers whom Erasmus knew through his editions of their works) attributed more to the powers of man than later theologians. Augustine was partially responsible for this departure from ancient orthodoxy in that he attributed faith and good will to man's natural powers before the rise of Pelagianism, but then he wrote hymns of damnation against them. As a result, "if anyone should consider how slender it is what this man and his follower Bernard (of Clairvaux)," and others, "left to free will, he would have to agree that free will had been asserted in name rather than proven in actuality."[8] Bernard, who also exemplified Augustine's views for him though he invented his own terms, splendidly defined *liberum arbitrium* as a habit of soul free with regard to itself, and *voluntas* as a rational motion presiding over both sense and appetite. Bernard distinguished three areas of human freedom, that of nature, council and fulfillment (*naturae, consilii, complaciti*) but in effect denied freedom to the last two, council meaning the assent of the will to a grace already given, and fulfillment man's final salvation. Only nature seemed free, but there, with Augustine agreeing, man was left solely with the power to will the this or the that but not good or evil. "It adds nothing more to the question," he says, "that certain theologians attribute free will to impious men and damned spirits since they are able to do this or that but not to act or will well."[9] Clearly Erasmus was aware of a natural operation of the will toward mundane matters, as was Luther, Augustine and Bernard as well, and that it was not at issue as far as man's relation to God was concerned. It is quite clear that Erasmus recognizes that the crux of the argument with these three stalwart defenders of grace had to do with man's spiritual, not his natural, freedom of will, though, as we shall see, Erasmus does hold that man possesses naturally the powers to intend the good and to make moral choices.

The point of this argument, however, is to show the essential rigidity of this kind of thinking in Luther and in his two predecessors, Bernard and Augustine. Yet later he will seek extenuations of Augustine's position in his many distinctions and see it as but verbally different from the scholastics including the nominalists.

All three also seem to imply that there is no significant difference between men and animals. "They also profess the following: Where there is no will, there is no sin or merit, nothing more than in brute animals in which there is only natural appetite since reason is lacking, without which there is no will. . . . But as they would have it, how little difference there is between the natural appetite which is common to us with the animals, and the kindred will so twisted toward evil that it can in no way be bent toward the good?"[10] Behind this assertion of their failure to distinguish man from the animals lies the question of original sin and of how much of man's divine image was lost with the Fall. Luther exaggerates original sin and man's consequential loss of his dignity so much that in rightly refuting the Pelagians he almost becomes a Manichaean. "For while he leaves no seed of virtue, nor any propensity to rectitude in human nature, which he makes totally flesh, that is impious affect, does he not so assert the evil nature of man that grace does not so much *recreate* a sick nature as *create* a new one?"[11]

Luther twists this transition from vice to piety which is called a *renascentia* in such a way that it seems to be a kind of "resurrection" from not-being to being, and from death to life, hardly recognizing that Paul was following the Hebrew practice of speaking in metaphors when he called the justified man "a new creature reborn in Christ." In the same manner we may speak of a man who is recalled from the depths of despair to good hope as "revivified," as also one whose behavior has drastically changed. There is a large difference between weakness (or sickness) and extinction, and Erasmus holds that through Adam's sin, "free will was wounded not extinguished, weakened not amputated, sickened not dead, dim-sighted not blind, bent low not overthrown . . ." The opposite, he claims, was constantly and strongly asserted by Luther who would, instead, deny that there is any free will at all. Thus for Erasmus, as we shall also see below, Luther's notion of the total destruction of the divine image in man after the Fall effectively denies man's dignity as well.[12]

Erasmus adds that the author of the pseudo-Augustinian *Hypognosticon* affirmed a weakened capability of good in the post-lapsarian soul but retained the name of free will and its rationality by which he meant the soul's knowledge of its situation, that what was first established as part of its nature can be repaired in nature. Moreover the ancients (*Veteres*) also agree that "once the will has been liberated by the Spirit, it cooperates with grace."[13] Erasmus' own position on free will is seen by him as in agreement with pre-Augustinian orthodoxy, but not because of the authority of antiquity but rather because he finds a congruity with the position he has independently developed on the basis of his own thinking. Perhaps we should suggest even now, as it begins to emerge, that Erasmus is very little concerned with the this or that of what is strict orthodox dogma but, historicistic in outlook, rather views all these positions, even Luther's, historically as part of a living, continuing tradition within which divergences occur in specific reaction to specific provocations, rarely departing irrevocably from the Christian fold.

At any rate these orthodox ancients, like himself, divide the process of justification into a beginning (*exordio*), increase (*incremento*) and consummation (*summa*), corresponding in fact to the three standard parts of an oration. As we shall soon see Erasmus thinks basically in terms of process, especially processes of transformation, and it would not be an accident if the "ancient orthodox" with their own rhetorical training should be found by Erasmus to think similarly to himself. But this tripartite division of the process of justification became in fact a standard part of the history of theology. For these ancients will plays no part in the first and last phases but only in the middle between grace dragging to justice and consummating to glory. "Here they attribute something to *liberum arbitrium* both for good and evil, namely that now, liberated by grace, the will cooperates with operating grace, or withdraws itself from it."[14] If the entire operation is ascribed to grace and, as they concede, man acts with active "justifying" or "operating" grace, and does no injury to grace, "why is it absurd if we, similarly, say that the *liberum arbitrium* of man aids operating grace?"[15]

How then can Augustine differ with this? The orthodox and the Pelagians accept this position, which Augustine does not, by saying that the good purpose of man is *aided* by grace rather than *given.* "And here (Augustine's) axiom is relevant: Multa Deus facit in homine bona, quae non facit homo; multa vero facit homo, quae non facit Deus. By these words he means that God makes good will in us without us. Likewise, so that he may explain the modes of this question, he makes a third grace, namely preparing grace, which he distinguishes from operating and cooperating. By this comment he would escape having to attribute anything to the will of man in receiving justifying grace."[16] With this we get to the nub of Erasmus' argument, that by inventing and changing words the effort is made, even by the venerated Church Father who had influenced him so much through his *De doctrina Christiana,* to get around what was otherwise conceded, namely that there is an innate urge to goodness in man, a *vis naturalis,* which was weakened, not destroyed, by the Fall. He permits himself here his usual irony even against the revered saint: "But if we concede that the grace of God is given to no one unless willing; and preparing grace is a gift of God; another preparing grace will be needed which prepares the prepared for it, and again one for this other, and likewise on to infinity until it is come to a gift of nature."[17]

As for the Pelagians, he feels some compunction to explain how they could share his views but does not yield much in his own position in face of the implied accusation. Again it is a controversy over words. "I do not know what the Pelagians thought. I go only by the words which Augustine cites from the books of Julian, which in my opinion, by an agreeable interpretation, can be held for authentic. A large part of this contention seems to be born from words rather than from the reality itself, and logomachies of this kind easily end in quarrels if anything of human contention is added."[18] With this Erasmus proceeds to unfold a complicated argument concerning the meaning of "merit," a key term in his contemporaneous debate. We shall find here that he aligns himself in certain critical aspects with the position of at least some of the late medieval scholastics generally known as "nominalists," although in the end he will want to differentiate his own position also from theirs.

However much at various times Erasmus railed at the scholastics because of their concern with mere words and their infinite distinctions,[19] we shall find that he is very concerned to make distinctions himself here concerning the usage of words in order to prove that debate over free will has been poisoned by looseness of language. But just because he seems to agree with both the Pelagians and the late medieval theologians who were frequently charged with Pelagianism in their own day and ever since should not lead us to forget that he is finding that his own interpretation can agree with their words but not necessarily with their philosophies or theologies. On the other hand, it should not surprise us that there could be something in common between the humanist in his concern with rhetoric and the careful interpretation of texts and the nominalists and their acceptance that they were living in a world contingently created and ordered in its specific qualities by the will of God, not in a naturally necessary metaphysical universe. For both, the careful scrutiny of language became essential, particularly the language of God's Word (*Verbum*) in the Scriptures—held by Erasmus to be preferably interpreted as God's Speech or Discourse (*Sermo*) as the more accurate but also theologically more sound translation of the Greek term *logos*.[20]

Just as a little earlier he had explained that Paul's statement that reborn man was a "nova creatura" was a rhetorical exaggeration deriving from Hebrew literary traditions, so here on the question of merits he follows the common humanist practice and takes human usage, not as the equivalent of theological truth, but as the index of what meaning can and cannot be derived from language. He plunges right in to one of Luther's most telling arguments: that the doctrine of merits implied that God sold His grace to man, that it was thus a commercial transaction in which man by his good works sought a just reward for his labors and so expected grace, or bought it through the purchase of an Indulgence. Whatever the justice of Luther's attack on contemporary ecclesiastical practice, in reaction to which he at least partly developed his doctrine or had derived his theological insights, Erasmus does not go into it (though, as we know, he shared many of Luther's criticisms of their abuse). His critique of the misuse of the term "merit" applied equally to clerical practice and Protestant criticism. "When (the word) merit is spoken, it should not be immediately understood in such a way that it excludes grace, just as would be the case in the commercial transactions of men where, after a workman has received just compensation for his work, neither party owes the other thanks (*gratia*) . . . Such are the works and such are the merits which, as the Apostle Paul writes, fight with grace. But merit is spoken of in a certain [different] way because it excludes *indignitas* or lack of worth. The grace of God, more precious (than something human) is more to be embraced when it is offered and more to be served when given. Therefore, just as he is said to be unworthy of grace who either neglects the gift or does not serve it when it is possessed and abuses it, so he is in a certain way worthy (*dignus*) of the gift of God who when it is offered speedily accepts it and once received takes care with the greater precautions not to lose it."[21] Thus this distinction in the usage of merit between a situation of commercial exchange and one of

possessing the proper dignity or worth to merit a gift seems to him fundamental, and he proceeds to offer many examples of common human usage
to establish his point. When one sees not just the meaning of the word but
the different character of the applicable situations in this way, "it does not
bring it about that a benefit is converted into payment of a debt for a work
performed but rather that the benefit is not given either to those unwilling
to receive it, or to the ingrate, or to him who will badly use it. For it is to
be *conjectured* that among men he will not use something well who does not
accept it as he should. In the same way it should be *imagined* in the case of
the grace of God."[22]

The epistemological implication in this last statement is worth noting. From an analysis of linguistic usage revealing different types of common human situations in which the same word may be used, one can
conjecture concerning human motivation and then *imagine* by analogy concerning theological truth. As we shall stress later, this is clearly a rhetorical
conception of the relationship of language and truth.[23] He follows with an
exposition of several scriptural examples making the same point, particularly the parable of the master distributing talents which ends with the
passage: "To him who has will it be given, and he will abound, and indeed
from him who has not, it will be taken away even that which he has."[24]
Erasmus comments: "For he is said not to have who has in such a way that
he does not have a benefit, that is, who either ascribes it to his own merits,
or who does not use it as he needs to do."

This leads him directly to affirm the correspondence of his conception
to the late scholastic doctrine of *meritum congruum*. "Therefore what is here
called dignity (or worth) in receiving and using (grace) well, I believe the
theologians call *meritum congruum* (fitting merit). That word (merit), if
rightly understood, does not fight with the word for grace, . . . especially
if you refer to the promise of God. A promise is gratuitous and gratuitous is
whatever flows from this source, yet it would be incongruous that such
great grace be conferred on adversaries or increased for those badly using it.
Just as the merit which corresponds to payment is of a certain nature, so are
the works which correspond to debt, and they both fight directly with
grace."[25] There is possibly some confusion here on the part of Erasmus
between *meritum congruum* and *meritum de condigno*. According to Oberman
dignitas actus and *meritum de condigno* were both applied to acts made worthy
by the already present grace. But Erasmus' merit of worth rather than
reward seems, as he puts it, also to apply to those to whom God is about to
give grace. Therefore he is correct in saying it corresponds to *meritum de
congruo*.[26] Moreover merit through dignity or worth is closely linked to the
degree to which the image of God in man was preserved after the Fall which
shows his awareness and concern for the general conception of the dignity of
man, based originally on man's creation *ad imaginem Dei,* so strongly af-

firmed in the Renaissance. It does seem as though in the Reformation debates over freedom of the will, the humanist proponents of the dignity of man would tend to be found affirming at least the possibility of a restoration of the divine image in fallen man based on its vestigial presence in man after the Fall and before the infusion of grace. This would be Erasmus' merit of dignity or worth, corresponding to the nominalists' *meritum congruum.*

Having thus re-stated his own position in a way which corresponded to the Renaissance humanist context of his theology (but by no means was his position identical with that of each and every humanist, e.g. Lorenzo Valla's[27]), Erasmus turns to an even more specifically humanist conception of salvation as a process. There is no doubt that a stress on will and affect, as well as an insistence on the need for grace, went hand in hand in Renaissance humanist thought with a rhetorically necessary belief in the possibility of the transformation of men's ideas, feelings, convictions and wills by the resources of human culture, and most signally by rhetoric and poetry, the literary arts. At the same time recognition of the possibility of direct divine intervention to transform the individual's soul without such human means was retained. But this reliance on miracle, or on what some, at least, of the nominalists emphasized as the *potentia absoluta Dei,* was regarded not as occurring in the ordinary course of man's individual and collective history, the creation of what the nominalists called the *potentia ordinata Dei.* Instead it was seen as extraordinary. Many of the Italian humanists, without using those nominalistic terms, did in fact think within the structure of a dialectic of the two powers of God, the ordered and the absolute. God could act in an extraordinary way outside the laws of nature on the norms of history, but ordinarily He acted through His ordered, created means, including His Church and the natural powers and cultivated arts of men. Culture, in other words, was regarded as autonomously cooperating both with the powers of nature and with providence, though ultimately it too had to be regarded as an instrument of God. It is not surprising therefore that Erasmus next presents his conception of the gradual onset of grace and sees its stages as analogous to several examples of human and natural phenomena. Revealingly he stops in the middle to assert: "Always I except the *potentia absoluta* of God by which, suddenly, He makes those whom he wishes different. I speak of those things which He does for the most part (*plerunque*)." This is a clear use of a distinction made by certain of the nominalists (though, as Courtenay argues, not Ockham). More significant, however, for our argument is his mode of presentation.[28]

Just as in the first section of his summation Erasmus looked for the emergence of a balanced insight concerning free will and grace from the sacred and secular historical experience of mankind, so here he looks for the same process in the individual. Historically minded, he quite genuinely preferred what came out of the dialectic of discourse through the ages to the explosive and sudden reassertion of one of the extremes he saw in Luther—the discourse between ancient philosophies and early Christian theologians, Greek Fathers and Latins, the formation and taking of positions out of opposition first to Manichaeism and then to Pelagianism by Augustine, both heresies representing the possible extremes, the settling upon a more balanced view by medieval scholastics and the *recentiores,* culminating perhaps in his own humanistic and historical theology. And he seems here to affirm that in the case of individual conversion this too was a gradual, not a sudden or violent, process, as he read Luther's "either/or" of having or not having faith, and, as we shall see, he regarded Augustine's conversion also as a gradual transformation so reading the *Confessions,* rather than emphasizing the dramatic scene in the garden.

But his target is Augustine's later doctrines here, "who feared lest, because a man assents to preparing grace, he should seem to merit justifying grace," and, "that the beginning of grace might seem to arise from *liberum arbitrium,*"[29] if, as *Pelagians* argued, grace aided a man's good intentions. In Erasmus' view, Augustine would have had nothing to fear if he had properly distinguished the word "good," just as the words "merit" and "wages" had been distinguished. As there are many degrees of grace, so there are many degrees of goodness or justice, and a man's conversion and justification was ordinarily a gradual historical process. Augustine, himself, found many names of grace, distinguishing sufficient from proficient, operating from cooperating, driving from preparing. "Now there can be many degrees of preparing or driving grace, just as God by various means and little by little transforms a man, nor otherwise does nature little by little make a man or a physician little by little restores a man. Therefore as frequently a man assents to operating grace which confers justice, so the beginning of grace is not from man but from preparing or driving grace which precedes and through some occasion excites the man to a knowledge that he is displeased with himself and wishes to become better. And innumerable are the forms by which God does that: sometimes through a wife, a servant, or a faithful friend He calls to the husband, master or unfaithful friend; sometimes likewise He does it through a disease, or a bereavement, or another calamity; other times by the ministry of the Word; some He arouses by prodigies, or by ghosts, or in dreams; and often, as though from an ambush He hunts a man for salvation by means of those things which especially captivate him: such as the uxorious through a wife, or as He caught Saint Hubert in the hunt, or lovers of studies through literature; some He draws by the secret whistling of the Spirit. Good intent is not immediately called good in such a way that it renders a man blessed. For whoever truly has a good intention is just by grace, but here he is called 'good' because he accedes to some image of the good and recedes in some degree from evil."[30]

Erasmus adduces other lengthier examples. One that Augustine liked was the comparison of light and shadow which Erasmus illustrates by the experience of approaching Naples through a tunnel cut through a mountain (presumably a spur of Vesuvius). "That light by which you approach closer becomes larger and more evident until you most clearly discern every-thing." But this is not a good metaphor, for grace comes to us. "It would be more fitting if it were the light which mutually approached the one approaching closer to it, just as grace comes near to the one coming near."[31] He makes another striking comparison between "birth" and spir-itual "rebirth," that is he compares the process of justification known as *renascentia* to the natural growth process of an embryo. "What adheres to the womb is not immediately a man; a coagulate is little by little made by nature, and it grows in the manner of a plant or a fungus; then it feels also, and freed by the art of nature becomes a foetus; you see that it is an animal, but how long is the time before it unfolds itself as a rational soul; yet by these degrees, little by little, a perfect man is made; nor is that infused by which he becomes a man unless the matter has been previously prepared. Let us imagine, for the sake of teaching, that first there is the seminal fluid, soon the coagulate, then the plant, soon the animal, then a man, but a rude and imperfect one, at length a true man. Therefore, as we are born, so also are we 'reborn.'"[32]

As he made allowance also at this point for the sudden act of God's *potentia absoluta,* so a little earlier he repudiated the Stoic view which made all sins equal, teaching that man suddenly, without mediation, is either totally good or totally evil. Even if this were true according to some reasoning, yet it should be repudiated as contrary to common sense and from the custom of the Scriptures.[33] But at the same time, as he turns to the metaphor of medical cure, he seems to incorporate some Stoic notions, speaking of a *vis insita* which fights disease and without which the physician cannot effect a cure. Just "as there is a native power of vision in man" which he has in vain unless he is offered light, so the light offered does not help if he does not look or closes his eyes. "Thus also grace, little by little, arouses the befogged or sick nature until it comes to that gift by which we are rendered blessed as far as may be in this life. For he is blessed who free from sins is given justice. But as this is a goodness, indeed goodnesses, not properly so called, yet is a certain progress toward that sufficient grace which the *recentiores* call *gratum facientem,* so there are also degrees of justice through which a man, bit by bit, is made into true justice."[34] He grants what Augustine says, that good intention is not aided by grace but is given by grace. "Yet," he argues, "as there is in the nature of man a proclivity toward vices through which Satan perpetually solicits for sinning, so there is also present in man a natural appetite for virtue, though imperfect. The driving grace of God solicits it for justice, exciting what hides weakly in man. If anyone should call this instinct of nature for virtue and piety (*hunc naturae nisum ad virtutem ac pietatem*) 'good intention,' he would say, as I think, nothing absurd."[35] Thus he does hold to something of the Stoic vision of the innate seeds of justice in man, which can be aroused by grace. But weak as they are, they can be involved in a gradual process of unfolding and growth.

From this his next section on the virtue and wisdom of the pagans logically followed, for if certain seeds of virtue and piety remained after the Fall, the ancient pagans and pre-Christian Jews would, as men, have manifested them. "If anyone would say that in a man not yet reborn into the spirit there is no faith or knowledge of the things which pertain to piety, no good will, no justice, no virtue although imperfect, he should refer the matter to the paradoxes of the Stoics, since we read in the histories of the pagans examples of virtue of the sort which sometimes deservedly put us Christians to shame. In the books of the philosophers we find precepts of such a kind that, as some teach, they seem drawn from the volumes of the Prophets they so agree in doctrine. From these sources certain good works are born among them, which, I admit, are not meritorious and do not generate justifying faith, but still they render the soul more capable of grace."[36] The Jews also, by their religious insights, were rendered "more capable of receiving the Gospel." Erasmus finds that Paul, who took on the harder task of *erudiendi Gentes* (educating the pagans), thought that some Gentiles were more curable because they sinned more lightly, "that is, in them there were less perversity of soul, which also happened among the Jews. Their perversity, moreover, was not of nature but of free choice, for perversity is one thing, error is another, another to flee justice, another to be impious."[37] Luther, however, made the pagans equal to the malice of Satan by exaggerating their vitiated nature. Thus Erasmus stood fast by the spirit of his famous *Sancte Socrate ora pro nobis* in linking and insisting upon the potential goodness of the pagans as the equivalent of the vestiges of goodness in man that opened the possibility of the gift of grace.

But his most effective argument for recognizing the universal potential for salvation is the case of Saint Augustine, which Erasmus traces in his early years of paganism and heresy through the *Confessions*. Augustine was a good man, then, before his conversion. By his early works of moral goodness he prepared for his later grace, "or as the scholastics say, he merited by *meritum congruum*."[38] What is true for Augustine is true for many men, displeased with themselves and wishing to be given a better character. Erasmus has heard many whom he knew lacked a sincere faith and a spotless life saying, "Oh that God would give me faith." He would reply to them: "'It is not for you lightly to choose so great a gift of God but also to walk in it.' 'In what ways?' they ask. 'Open up the Holy books,' I say, 'go to sacred sermons, pray frequently, give money to the needy, commend your safety to pious men, draw a little away from your vices as far as you are able. Those things which are seated in you are of the present; God's grace is not of the future.' And I think that I have given pious council. Whoever wishes for himself to be given a good will, does not entirely lack one, and whoever desires the gift of faith does not entirely lack faith, but what he has imperfectly he wishes to perfect by divine aid."[39] This is Erasmus' equivalent of the late scholastic emphasis on the *facere quod in se est* principle, if a man does his very best, God will not withold his grace.

Erasmus' concern with the onset of grace and its relation to the natural powers of man for goodness at the beginning of a gradual process of justification was thus extended from the conversion of the individual to the providential history of mankind. Pre-Christian Jews and pagans were in some way also manifesting these same powers. But ultimately these powers came from God who created the world and mankind. It is no surprise, therefore, that he places great emphasis on a general grace in which all men share, as distinguished from the peculiar grace received by individuals. He believed that by confusing these two much of the debate over free will unnecessarily arose. Earlier, at the end of the section where he discussed salvation as ordinarily gradual, he wrote: "Now let us assume that movements of the soul of this sort, although imperfect without grace, flow forth from the very powers of nature. Is the grace of God imperilled by these? I do not think so. Who would think thus? Since whatever of good is left in us and all this which we are able to do or are is a gift of God. Therefore, from whatever source you begin the recess from vices and the progress toward virtue, it originates from grace not from us. Nor did this prevent Augustine from sometimes croaking, 'What do you have that you have not received, and if you have received it, why do you glory as if you had not received it?' It could likewise be croaked over glorying in wealth, beauty, strength, excellence of birth, glowing health, mental dexterity, success in business. Finally, if anyone despises womankind, pleased with himself that he is born a male, the same words could be directed to him: 'What do you have which you have not received?' Thus this saying of Paul does not exclude free will but represses the arrogance of a man not knowing that he, himself, exists by gift of God, whatever he is, if there is any good at all in him. . . . Even those things which we are able to do by our natural powers thus arise in us in such a way that yet they are from God from whom all things flow."[40]

Erasmus' penultimate section returns to an elucidation of his basic argument that the quarrel over free will is a quarrel over words that originated from the ill-chosen ones the early Fathers took over from the Gentiles. The section as a whole shows how in turn each of his basic representatives of theological history tended to over-emphasize one side of the question in order to combat an excess or danger it saw. Jerome quarrelled with Ctesiphon but later said the same thing himself. "The language is diverse but the meaning is the same." Therein lies the danger. "Ultimately, the treatment of this entire question of by what means the grace of God works in man has many recesses which it is not necessary curiously to explore. It is agreed that whatever is in us entirely derives from the liberality of God. But to define how He dispenses his munificence toward us, though it may be an act of pious speculation, I certainly do not think it is necessary. And yet in no question did Augustine more freely delight."[41] But, as he had shown, "the opinion of the scholastics, which seems to attribute more to free will among those not reprobate, does not differ so much from the opinion of Augustine, except that they vary in words rather than in substance." It all began with the Ancient Christians who showed no consistency in their own writings, frequently affirming the same position they had before attacked in an adversary, all because, "there are many species of justice, good will and faith," and, "these were not sufficiently distinguished by the Ancients. . . . Nevertheless none of them was so unjust to free will that he did not attribute something to it."[42]

He passes on to his critique of Augustine's ambiguity, to be followed by that of the Lutherans and finally the *Recentiores*. He tries to show by analysis of seven passages from Augustine that the saint, tacitly at least, recognized some powers of free will in man, and explicitly the power not to do good or to reject grace. Erasmus says, about this concession, "What moreover, is that, except that a man, through natural powers can bring it about, not that he may be blessed in the beyond, but that he is more prepared here for divine grace. Whoever through human reason knows many things and believes what are true concerning God, who imbibes a love of wisdom from the books of the philosophers, who, according to his own small measure, strives to attain the habit of virtue, is in some way more capable (of grace) than the cross soldier who, practised in profound ignorance of things and the greatest crimes, does not ever even think about God." But, for fear of going too far, Augustine attributes even the wish for grace to the aid of grace. One could also attribute man's power to do evil to necessity. "If one wished to be sophistical, it is not even true that free will suffices for evil, for it would not suffice if it should be wiped out by the general movement of the first cause." Therefore it must be admitted that *insit in homine nativa quaedam vis appetens honesti* (there is present in man a certain natural force seeking virtue). And Seneca was right in saying: "It is, moreover, a large part of goodness to wish to become good."[43] But Augustine insists on the contrary: "to desire the aid of grace is the beginning of grace." Erasmus comments that Augustine fears that "if we concede that even in wicked men there is some desire for grace from the very sense of nature, again the cause will be endangered that the beginning of grace should not be from free will. This must be vigorously abominated, except that whatever free will can do flows forth from the gift of God." Erasmus does not object if anyone wishes to add "peculiar grace" to the long list of graces by which men recede little by little from vicious habits and approach justice. "But to raise a tragedy from these minutiae I do not think is the part of Christian tranquillity; it is better to permit, as Paul held, each to abound in his own sense of the meaning."[44]

Augustine, then, in fighting the Pelagians, "by his zeal for grace attributed so little to free will that it was something in name but not in fact." Similarly Augustine held that unbaptized children would be burned by the eternal fires. "Later theologians moderated both of his views, attributing more to free will than he attributed, and distinguishing fitting merit (*meritum congruum*) from condign merit, acquired faith from infused faith, perfect will from imperfect." As to child-burning, Jean Gerson did not seem to despair if the piety of the parents sought the aid of God.[45]

He comes then to the Lutherans. "Now what to the theologians seems too little in the teachings of St. Augustine concerning free will, that to Luther seems too much. He brings in the language of necessity from which Augustine constantly abstained, and he does not even attribute to free will the power to subtract oneself from grace, which Augustine did not deny to it. But those who, indeed in piety of purpose but yet too incautiously, exaggerate the magnitude of grace in this as much as they can take away from the powers of nature. Likewise they seem to act as if, should they deny that any achieve salvation either in the Law of Moses or in the law of nature, they would in this raise higher the glory of the Advent of Christ against those who are accustomed to say, 'What new did Christ bring?' Meanwhile, they do not notice that that very way in which men were saved before the manifestation of the Gospel was received by gift of Christ who, according to His goodness, was lacking to none, although according to the dispensation of divine wisdom in the variety of times and persons He communicated Himself sometimes in one way and sometimes in others."[46] Their exaggeration, he grants, is more directed to the stupidity and malice of men into which they had thrown themselves of their own free will than to the vitiated nature resulting from Adam's sin. They should beware lest they fall into the ditch of the Manichaeans, from which they can progress to the pit of Hell. In thus attributing the entire salvation of man to grace, they ought to remember that the will of man, once it is liberated, acts simultaneously with agent grace and brings it about in so acting, not that grace is owed him, but that it is not withdrawn from him for indignity or lack of worth. They should also recall that it is in the power of man not to turn away from driving grace and that God esteems such a man worthy of richer grace, that it is in man's choice to persevere or cut himself off from grace. Then they would not believe in the absolute necessity of all.things. But they would also recall the gifts of nature are themselves by the gift of God, and there is nothing about which man can glory. Man, they should recall, is totally in the hands of God who can annihilate him if He wishes.

The more recent theologians (*recentiores*, which certainly includes the nominalists) come close to falling into the ditch of the Pelagians and should take care not to go further. They are reminded how horrible it is to God for men to strive by their own powers and to glory in themselves when no one should glory in the Lord. They should give thanks to God for the natural powers in which they excel, and if any are accepted by God for such works, it not out of justice but from His immense goodness which condescends to our imperfection. "Finally, they should remember that those powers of nature will justly be snatched away by God, if anyone abuses them or wishes to arrogate them to himself. Neither should they deceive themselves with the words of 'liberty,' 'merit,' 'worth,' 'condignity,' 'congruency,' and 'due,' since the whole affair is owed to the gratuitous kindness of God. But the more diligently they surround grace with these, so much the more are the powers in these given by God, the more eagerly they strive for pious works."[47]

Having thus sought to discover agreement with Augustine along the lines of moderation offered by later theologians, Erasmus, in turning to his contemporaries, early Lutherans and late medieval scholastics primarily of the nominalist camp, offers them exhortation rather than argument. Throughout he has insisted that a common sense view of the language used would reconcile the opposing positions, which themselves derived, not from any superior insight, revelation, or interpretive or dialectical acumen, but out of a certain zeal for leaning one way or another in order to avoid the one danger or the other.

He comes now to an ultimate statement of his own views in which the authentic character of his theology becomes clear. It is manifestly based on a rhetorical conception of knowledge as embodied in language, and of the Christian religion as the "speech" of God promulgated through divine *Sermo*. *Speech*, rather than *Verbum* or *Word*, was central to his conception of history and the human community as comprising, or as engaged in, a giant process of discourse through which men sought agreement with each other in the light of their mutually discrete interpretations of the divine discourse of the Scriptures. Erasmus does not say this here. Rather he manifests it (though he did say it quite explicitly elsewhere in his defense of his translation of the New Testament).[48] Let us listen, in part, to how he concludes. "Moreover, if there will be anyone to whom Augustine seems unjust to free will and the more recent seem to have given more than equitably, let him enter safely between the two ways, and let him believe also in those stages by which, as I have said, we are prepared for grace and that he will not lack peculiar grace, thus in accord with our own model in which in all things free will cooperates with grace and grace with free will. In sum, let us rather enter into this in such a manner that we may gain the grace of God, rather than that we should curiously dispute how grace works in us. For by too many subtle arguments of this sort we shall lose the grace of God, which we should seek by whatever ways grace works in us, especially since God, everywhere uninvestigable, works His power over created things by such various ways."[49]

In this spirit he recognizes the justice of the views of all sides. First, the proponents of grace who exaggerate it and weaken the powers of nature, "are moved by just causes." So also they who, "do not suffer anyone to be saved or die except from some kind of merits . . . are moved by no lighter reasons." "Although their views differ, yet, since they flow from the same fount of piety, it is fitting that they be interpreted agreeably, not railed at, but guided into concord." For they do agree on many items of faith: that man is mercifully saved, but no one is unjustly damned, and the grace of God is lacking to no one; that by the greatest energy a man should be shown what is seated in himself (*quod in ipso situm est*—again Erasmus' version of *facere quod in se est*); and that whatever of good there is in us is entirely to be ascribed to divine goodness.[50]

As for the Scriptures, though they seem to war with themselves, it is hardly a great business to bring them into harmony if we distinguish the meanings of words as he has shown, "and if we consider that God acts for various reasons in saving and damning men, nor does He immediately do for all what we read He has done for this one or that one for dispensation." Offering examples of such special acts of God toward individuals, he concludes, "These things which have particular causes it is not necessary to extend to a general doctrine." Certainly a philological and historical, rather than a metaphysical way to approach the interpretation of the Scriptures, this was perhaps characteristic of his humanism and the direct consequence of his extensive Biblical studies. Always the specific, never the general: Erasmus is almost historicistic, though sacred history would also be included in this approach. He applies the principle immediately to the current debates: "Again, if there are any whom God by sudden and violent movement ravishes to Himself, such as Paul, from these a universal dogma should not be established. He calls some out of profound ignorance, some from the deep swamp of crimes; others He allows as though to circle around the divine gift for a long time."[51]

How then should men discover God's message of salvation if a systematic theology cannot be constructed from the Scriptures? By engaging in discourse with each other in the manner in which God speaks to us: "Now if we are not able to follow entirely according to reason by what ways and by what stages He works in us, certainly we ought to speak in the manner of the Scriptures, in the manner of the Holy Fathers. Indeed, what does the Scripture say? It does not say all striving of man is inane, it infers nothing about how you should live, God either saves if He decides or loses if He so decrees, but this is how He speaks: 'Turn toward me and I will turn toward you' . . . 'Come to me all ye; Strive to enter through the narrow gate; Be ye sober and vigilant; Liars, change your heart; Give alms; Forgive and it will be forgiven you; Be a guardian to the orphan and help the needy.' By speeches of this sort let us mutually exhort each other to penance and mutual charity; putting aside all evil colloquies which corrupt good morals, brother should speak to brother; let us mutually love one another; let us mend into better that which we have ignorantly done in sin; let us approach the grace of God by pious works; especially let us accommodate both our writing and our speech to the necessity of our neighbor. For we should speak one way to the elated, the ferocious, the one pleased with himself and bearing an erect spine against the Lord; otherwise to those close to coward-ice and desperation. To the first we should offer the testimony of the Scriptures which teach how men can do nothing by their own powers and how much danger there is for a man to trust in his own talents. To the others we should offer the testimony which teaches how much a man can also excel by himself, if he wishes to strive to do so, and how the goodness of God is prepared by showing what is in himself."[52]

Clearly, Erasmus' theology is a pastoral and a rhetorical theology, not ignorant of the systematic, dialectical schools, nor entirely without a sub-stantive position. Ultimate theological truth is, however, limited to what can be *imagined* on the basis of human *conjecture* concerning custom and the meaning of the Scriptures, as we saw above.[53] Hence his need for reliance on the historically manifested "assent of the ages." Thus his position is one that, according to circumstances is left open to the assertions of either side of the disputes, and certainly here in the case of the powers of man for contributing to his salvation as over against his total dependence on divine grace, Erasmus, depending on the circumstances, will strongly support either one. The Scriptures, themselves, should be interpreted in this open-ended way, that of admonishing according to the need of the recipient in the long medieval-Renaissance tradition that reached back through Grego-ry the Great's *Book of Pastoral Care* to the homiletic writings of the Greek Fathers. Indeed, "the Scriptures," he says, "since now they compel these, now compel those, should be interpreted according to the quality of those to whom one speaks"[54]—a strictly pastoral and rhetorical principle. Other-wise, he says, they will seem to fight with themselves in many places, when nothing fights less than Scripture with Scripture.

Clearly also, Erasmus was striving for an open, as well as an irenic, Christianity in which all, except the fanatical extremes, could exist to-gether. We know that he lost this struggle, but we should also know that, although always loyal to the Catholic Church, he represented a position that was both critical and understanding of Catholic orthodoxy and, up to a point, Lutheranism. This is embodied in his final words: "As I make an end to this volume, I do not depreciate the judgment of the reader here, and I beg indulgence, just as Luther did. But whatever has been set forth by us I submit to the Catholic Church, prepared to be corrected if it departs from the truth. Now let Christ illuminate us all, one with Luther, that we may all with one mouth, the same mind and the same doctrine preach the common Lord of all, to Whom eternal glory. Amen."[55]

My own final word addressed to Professor Rupp's question cited above, "How seriously must we take Erasmus as a theologian?" is, "Very."

NOTES

1. It should be clear that Erasmus could not possibly conceive of himself as leading, or even participating in a "third church" or "third force," since his loyalty to the Church of tradition was a fundamental tenet of his religious philosophy (and not even "Nicodemism"). For a recent discussion of his position and contemporary Catholic musunderstandings of it, see H. A. Oberman with T. A. Brady, Jr., eds.: *Itinerarium Italicum: The Profile of the Italian Renaissance in the Mirror of its European Transformations* (Leiden, E. J. Brill, 1975), xxii–xxiii (H. A. Oberman), 64–84 (from M. P. Gilmore: "Italian Reactions to Erasmian Humanism"). See now M. O. Boyle's definitive study, *Rhetoric and Reform* (Cambridge, Mass.: Harvard Univ. Press, 1983).
2. "*Introduction, The Erasmian Enigma,*" *Luther, Erasmus: Free Will and Salvation, Erasmus, De Libero Arbitrio,* trans. and ed. by E. Gordon Rupp with A. N. Marlow (The Library of Christian Classics XVII), 8.
3. LB X (i.e. *Opera omnia* . . . , ed. J. Le Clerc, Leiden, 1706, T.X), cc 1249A–1536F. Cf. C. Augustijn: "*Hyperaspistes I:* La doctrine d'Erasme et de Luther sur la 'Claritas Scripture,'" *Colloquia Erasmiana Turonensia,* (Paris, 1972), 737–58, "il n'existe pas d'étude consacrée spécialement à cette ouvrage volumineux," 737. Cf., ibid., n. 3 for a list of studies.
4. Cc. 1521B–1536 F. First ed. of *Lib. II,* Sept. 1527 (Augustijn, 737).
5. 1521B, "Hactenus non sine gravi taedio Lutheranae disputationi vel rixae potius respondimus. Nunc de summa rei pauca perstringemus, ac mox finem imponemus volumini."
6. 1521B–D, "non perinde respondet magnificentia nominum ad rem quam declarant. . . . cum hae voces ab iis usurpatae sint, qui fuerunt proximi temporibus Apostolorum, aut ipsos etiam viderunt Apostolos, tantoque seculorum consensu in hunc usque diem ab Ecclesiae proceribus receptae sint, citra, gratiae injuriam, alienum sit a modestia Christiana, nunc super his movere tragoediam . . ."

7. 1521D–F, "qui totum hominem etiam juxta pracipuas illius partes facit carnem, et in hac regnantem Satanam, etiam post infusum Spiritum . . ."

8. 1522A, "Quod si quis expendat quam exile sit, quod hic vir, et hunc sequuti Bernardum . . . relinquunt libero arbitrio, fatebitur liberi arbitrii nomen assertum potius quam rem probatam."

9. 1522A–E, (E), "Nihilo magis ad rem facit, quod quidam impiis hominibus, ac damnatis Spiritibus hactenus tribuunt liberam voluntatem, ut possint hoc aut illud agere, non ut possint bene agere seu velle."

10. 1522F–1523A, "Fatentur et illud, Ubi non est voluntas, ibi non esse neque peccatum neque meritum, nihilo magis quam in brutis animantibus, in quibus tantum est appetius naturalis, eo quod absit ratio, sine qua nulla est voluntas . . . Verum haec utcunque habent, quantulum interest inter appetitum naturalem, qui nobis cum brutis communis est, et voluntatem omnibus agnatam, sic ad malum intortam, ut ad bonum nullo modo flecti possit?"

11. 1523B, "Dum enim nullum honesti semen, nec ullam ad recta propensionem relinquit humanae naturae, quam totam facit carnem, hoc est, affectum impium, nonne naturam hominis malam inducit, ut gratia non tam recreet naturam aegrotam, quam creet novam?"

12. 1523B–E, (D), "liberum arbitrium per peccatum vulneratum fuisse, non extinctum, debilitatum, non amputatum, morbidum, non mortuum, lusciosum, non caecum, incurvatum, non dejectum . . ."

13. 1523E, "Consentiunt et in hoc Veteres, quod fatentur humanam voluntatem, jam Spiritu liberatam, cooperari gratiae . . ."

14. 1523F, "ibi tribuunt aliquid libero arbitrio et in bonum et in malum, videlicet ut jam per gratiam liberatum gratia operanti cooperetur, et sese ab ea subtrahat."

15. 1524A, "quid absurdi sit, si dicamus similiter hominis liberum arbitrium adniti operanti gratiae?"

16. 1524B, "Et huc pertinet illud eiusdem axioma, *Multa Deus facit in homine bona, quae non facit homo: multa vero facit homo, quae non facit Deus:* quibus verbis hoc sentit, quod Deus bonam voluntatem facit in nobis sine nobis. Idem ut explicet quaestionum modos, facit tertiam gratiam nimirum praeparantem, quam distinguere videtur a gratia operante et cooperante. Hoc commento effugit, ne quid tribuat hominis arbitrio in recipienda gratia justificante." Cf. Augustine, *Contra duas epistolas Pelagianorum,* II, 8, 21 (Migne *PL,* 44, 586). The second *multa* in Augustine's maxim should be *nulla.* Erasmus errs in citation both in LB X and Basel: Froben, 1527, p. 540. Erasmus is referring to *De gratia et libero arbitrio,* caps. 32 and 33 for Augustine's discussion of preparing, operating and cooperating grace.

17. 1524B–C, "Verum si hoc concedimus, Dei gratiam nulli dari nisi volenti, et gratia praeparans Dei donum est, opus erit alia gratia praeparante, quae ad illum praeparet praeparatricem, et rursus ad hanc alia, atque item in infinitum, donec veniatur ad naturae donum.'

18. 1524C–D, "Quid senserint Pelagiani nescio, tantum ex verbis ago, quae ex libris Juliani refert Augustinus, quae mea sententia potuissent commoda interpretatione pro veris haberi, magnaque pars huius contentionis ex verbis

nasci videtur potius ex re ipsa, et huiusmodi λογομαχιας (logomachias) facile exeunt in rixam, si quid accesserit humanae contentionis."

19. For a recent review of Erasmus' comments on the scholastics as a whole, together with St. Thomas in particular, cf. J.-P. Massaut's salutary judgments in "Erasme et Saint Thomas," *Colloquia Erasmiana Turonensia,* op. cit., 581–611.

20. Cf. W. J. Courtenay: "Nominalism and Late Medieval Religion," in C. Trinkaus with H. A. Oberman, eds.; *The Pursuit of Holiness in Late Medieval and Renaissance Religion* (Leiden, 1974), 26–59 for a presentation of nominalism as a theology of "contingency" and "covenant." Cf. C. Trinkaus: "The Religious Thought of the Italian Humanists, and the Reformers: Anticipation or Autonomy?," ibid., 339–66, for a discussion of parallels of humanism and nominalism. Cf. the same: *In Our Image and Likeness: Humanity and Divinity in Italian Humanist Thought* (London and Chicago, 1970), ch. 3 passim.

21. 1524D–E, "Cum meritum dicitur, non statim intelligitur tale, ut excludat gratiam, quemadmodum in commerciis hominum, posteaquam artifex pro opera justam mercedem accepit, neuter alteri debet gratiam, . . . Talia sunt opera, taliaque merita, quae Paulus Apostolus scribit pugnare cum gratia. Sed meritum quoddam dicitur, quod excludit indignitatem. Gratia Dei quo res est pretiosior, hoc magis est amplectanda cum offertur, servandaque cum est oblata. Ut igitur indignus gratia dicitur, qui vel oblatam negligit, vel possessam non servat et abutitur, ita quodammodo dignus est dono Dei, qui cum offertur alacriter accipit, et acceptam summa solicitudine cavet ne perdat."

22. 1515B, "nec efficit, ut beneficium vertatur in mercedem operi debitam, sed ne beneficium detur vel nolenti, vel ingrato, vel male usuro. Nam apud homines conjectandum est eum non bene usurum, qui non sicut oportet accepti. Idem imaginandum est in gratia Dei."

23. Cf. p. 291. Cf. C. Augustijn, op. cit. for a discussion of the epistemological problem of interpreting the Scriptures in Luther as Erasmus sought to confute it in *Hyperaspistes I.*

24. Math 13:13, Luke 19:26.

25. LB X, 1525D–F, "Is enim non habere dicitur, qui sic habet, quasi non habeat beneficium, hoc est, qui vel suis meritis adscribit gratiam, vel secus utitur ea quam oportet. Quod igitur hic dignitas dicitur in bene accipiente et utente, hoc, opinor, Theologi vocant meritum *congruum:* ea vox si recte intelligitur, non pugnat cum vocabulo gratiae, . . . praesertim si referas ad Dei promissionem. Promissio gratuita est, et gratuitum est quicquid ex hoc fonte promanat, non tamen congruit, ut tanta gratia conferatur aversantibus aut male utentibus augeatur. Ut igitur est meritum, quod respondet mercedi, ita sunt opera, quae respondent debito, et ex diametro pugnant cum gratia."

26. Cf. Heiko A. Oberman: *The Harvest of Late Medieval Theology: Gabriel Biel and Late Medieval Nominalism* (Cambridge, Mass., 1963, repr. Grand Rapids, 1967), "A Nominalist Glossary," 471–2 and 466. The confusion lies in Erasmus' use of *dignitas* for the nominalist *meritum congruum* whereas the nominalists reserved *dignitas* for *meritum de condigno,* an act "performed in a state of grace and therefore worthy of divine acceptance" (471). It is notable that

Erasmus refers to the promise of God, on which the nominalists based their *facere quod in se est* doctrine by which they legitimated *meritum congruum*. Erasmus clearly differs in words but not in his meaning from the standard nominalist usage.

27. As is well known, Erasmus saw Valla's position on free will as closer to Luther's. Yet his dependence on Valla for the development of his own "Biblical humanism" was manifest, and Valla's influence on his epistemological and historical conceptions is perhaps just beginning to be understood. Cf. Salvatore I. Camporeale: *Da Lorenzo Valla a Tommaso Moro, Lo Statuto Umanistico della Teologia, Memorie Domenicane,* N.S. n. 4 (1973), 9–105 (this is in a volume subtitled: *Umanesimo e teologia tra '400 e '500*). Also see Camporeale's *Lorenzo Valla, Umanesimo e Teologia* (Florence, 1972).

28. LB X, 1527F, "Semper excipio Dei potentiam absolutam, qua subito facit alios quos vult. De iis, quae plerunque facit, loquor." This statement of Erasmus, who implies that Luther saw men saved exclusively by God's *potentia absoluta,* throws light on how contemporaries saw Luther's relationship to nominalism, a question much debated in recent scholarship. Cf. Steven Ozment's assemblage of articles on this question in *The Reformation in Medieval Perspective* (Chicago, 1971) and his "Mysticism, Nominalism and Dissent," in *The Pursuit of Holiness,* 67–92. Erasmus' reference to *potentia absoluta Dei* clearly aligns him with what William J. Courtenay, op. cit. 42–3 regards as a minor, not the dominant, position of the Nominalists. *Potentia absoluta,* according to Courtenay, meant for Ockham not the extraordinary or miraculous act of God outside of His established order of nature and history but the dialectical possibility of God's having acted differently than His actual creation, thus rendering it contingent rather than necessary, and historical and convenantal rather than 'natural.' Cf. 40–1 and citations from Ockham, Gregory of Rimini, Pierre D'Ailly and Gabriel Biel in note 1. However, Courtenay grants, 43, "there is some evidence that points" in the direction Francis Oakley argues for D'Ailly and Gregory, namely that *potentia absoluta Dei* was conceived as the extraordinary or the miraculous. References to Oakley in note 2. Also on this, cf. Oberman, op. cit. 37–8. Ozment in his cited article, 80–3, argues for "a presently active *potentia Dei absoluta*" as essential to late medieval doctrine. It is not my intent to pursue this question here but simply to note that Erasmus' usage of *potentia Dei absoluta* was not totally extraordinary. However I am grateful to Professor Courtenay for some pre-publication comments that have led me, hopefully, to a clarification of where Erasmus "understood" in relation to this question.

29. 1526D, "Submovimus igitur scrupulum, qui torquebat Augustinum sollicitum, ne quod homo gratiae praeparanti assentitur, videatur promereri gratiam justificantem. Submovendus est et alter, quo metuit, ne gratiae initium videatur a libero arbitrio proficisci."

30. 1526E–1527A, "Jam praeparantis sive pulsantis gratiae possunt esse plurimi gradus, sicut Deus variis modis ac paulatim transformat hominem, non aliter quam natura paulatim fingit hominem, aut Medicus paulatim restituit hominem. Quoties igitur homo assentitur gratiae operanti, quae confert justitiam,

initium gratiae non est ab homine, sed a gratia praeparante sive pulsante, quae praecessit, per occasionem excitans hominem ad eam cogitationem, ut sibi displiceat, optetque fieri melior. Innumerabiles autem formae sunt, quibus id agat Deus: Interdum per uxorem, servum, aut amicum fidelem vocat, maritum, herum et amicum infidelem; Interdum idem facit morbo, orbitate, aut alia quavis immissa calamitate, nonnunquam ministerio verbi; Nonnullos prodigiis aut spectris, aut insomniis (sic); Et saepe velut ex insidiis venatur hominem ad salutem per eas res quibus maxime capitur, velut uxorios per uxorem, et divum Hubertum cepit in venatu, et amantes studiorum per litteras; Nonnullos trahit secreto sibilo Spiritus. Nec statim bonum propositum sic dicitur bonum, ut reddat hominem beatum. Quisquis enim vere propositum bonum habet, is justum est per gratiam, sed hic bonum appellatur, quod accedit ad aliquam boni imaginem, et aliquo gradu recedit a malo."

31. 1527D, "Ea lux quo propius accedis, hoc fit major et evidentior, donec clarissime cernas omnia. Illud non congruit in hac similitudine, quod ad illam lucem nos accedimus, cum gratiae lumen magis accedat ad nos: quemadmodum Sol paulatim discutiens, noctis caliginem ad nos venit. Magis autem congrueret, si lumen esset, quod vicissim accederet ad propius accedentes: Sicuti gratia appropinquat appropinquanti."

32. 1527E–F, "Non statim est homo quod haesit in matrice, paulatim fingitur a natura coagulum, et augescit more plantarum et fungorum: deinde sentit etiam, tandem absolutus naturae artificio foetus prodit: animal esse vides, at quantum est temporis, priusquam sese explicet anima rationalis, sed tamen iis gradibus paulatim fit homo perfectus, nec infunderetur id per quod fit homo, nisi materia prius praeparata. Fingamus enim docendi gratia, primum esse liquorem seminalem, mox coagulum, deinde plantam, mox animal, deinde hominem, sed rudem et imperfectum, tandem vere hominem. Ut igitur nascimur sic renascimur."

33. 1527A–B, "Nisi forte nobis placet Stoicorum opinio, qui faciebant omnia peccata paria, docentes hominem repente, aut summe bonum est, aut summe malum. Quod etiamsi juxta rationem aliquam verum esset, tamen quoniam sermo abhorret a sensu communi, et a consuetudine sacrarum litterarum, repudiandus est." See now (1983) M. O. Boyle, "Stoic Luther," *Archiv für Reformationsgeschichte* 73 (1982), 69–93.

34. 1528A–B, "ita gratia naturam caligantem et aegrotantem paulatim excitat, donec veniat ad illud donum, quo beati reddimur in hac duntaxat vita. Beatus enim est quisquis liber a peccatis, donatus est justitia. Sed ut est bonitas, imo bonitates potius, non proprie dictae, sed tamen progressus quidam ad illam sufficientem gratiam, quam recentiores appellant gratum facientem: ita sunt et justitiarum gradus, per quos homo paulatim fingitur ad veram justitiam."

35. 1528D, "Verum ut inest homini naturae proclivitas ad vitia, per quam Satanas perpetuo sollicitat ad peccandum, ita inest in homine naturalis appetitus honesti, licet imperfectus. Hunc Dei gratia pulsans mille modis sollicitat ad justitiam, excitans quod in homine latebat invalidum. Hunc naturae nisum ad virtutem ac pietatem, si quis bonum propositum appellet, nihil, ut arbitror, absurdi dixerit."

36. 1529D–E, "Quod si quis dicat in homine nondum spiritu renato, nullam esse fidem aut cognitionem eorum quae pertinent ad pietatem, nullam bonam voluntatem, nullam justitiam, nulla virtutem, quamvis imperfectam, rem adfert omnibus Stoicorum paradoxis παραδοξοτεραν, cum in Ethnicorum Historiis legamus eiusmodi virtutum exempla, ut merito nos Christianos aliquoties pudefaciant, in Philosophorum libris eiusmodi reperiamus praecepta, ut quidam conentur docere, ea fuisse de Prophetarum hausta voluminibus, adeo consentiunt dogmata. Ex his fontibus nascebantur apud illos quaedam bona opera, quae fateor nec promerebantur, nec gignebant gratiam justificantem, sed tamen reddebant animam gratiae capaciorem, . . ."

37. 1530B–C, "His aliisque plurimis facti sunt capaciores Evangelii. At Paulum duriorem susceperat provinciam erudiendi Gentes, . . . Et tamen in his sanabiliores reperit, qui levius peccarant, hoc est, in quibus minus erat perversi animi, quod idem accidit in Judeis. Perversitas autem non naturae est, sed liberi arbitrii. Aliud enim est perversitas, aliud error: aliud vacare justitia, aliud esse impium."

38. 1531C, "sive, ut Scholastici loquuntur, merito congruo promeretur eam . . ." What Erasmus adds here is of interest in the context of his earlier criticisms of the scholastics and his obvious knowledge and sympathy for the doctrines of late medieval nominalism in this work (1531C–D): "Et si poterat Augustinus per vim liberi arbitrii audire concionantem Ambrosium, legere libros sacros, erogare stipem in pauperes, vacare precibus ac meditationibus, confabulari cum piis hominibus, eosque rogare ut Domino salutem ipsius suis precibus commendarent, quid est cur sic exsibiletur opinio Scholasticorum, quae tradit hominem per opera moraliter bona promereri de congruo gratiam justificantem?"

39. 1531D–E, "Quod de Augustino propositum est, idem dici potest de homine multis vitiis involuto; sed tamen sibi displicente optanteque mentem meliorem sibi dari. Sic enim audivi quosdam dicentes: Utinam Deus donaret mihi fidem . . . Quibus respondebam: Tuum est non leviter optare tantum Dei donum, sed etiam abire. Quibus inquiebant modis? Evolve, inquam, sacros Libros, adi sacras conciones, ora frequenter, eroga pecuniam in egenos, piis hominibus commenda salutem tuam, detrahe paulatim vitiis quod potes. Haec quae in te sita sunt praestanti, non defutura est Dei gratia: et arbitror me dedisse pium consilium. Qui optat sibi dari bonam voluntatem, non omnimo caret ea, et qui optat fidei donum, non prorsus caret fide, sed quod habet imperfectum, optat auxilio divino perfici."

40. 1528F–1529B, "Jam donemus huiusmodi motus animi, licet imperfectos sine gratia, ex ipsis scatere naturae viribus, num periclabitur Dei gratia? Non opinor. Qui sic? Quoniam hoc ipsum, quod in nobis relictum est boni, et totum hoc quod possumus aut sumus, Dei donum est. Undecunque igitur incipias recessum a vitiis ac progressum ad virtutem, a gratia est exordium non ex nobis. Nec obstat, quod nunquam non occinit Augustinus, 'Quid habes quod non accepisti, et si accepisti, quid gloriaris quasi non acceperis?' (I Corinth. 4:7, cf. Aug. *Epist.* 214, prefatory letter I to *De grat. et lib. arb.*, § 3.) Idem occini potest de divitiis, forma, viribus, generis claritate, prospera

valetudine, ingenii dexteritate, rerum successu glorianti. Denique si quis despiciat foeminam, sibi placens, quod mas natus sit, ei possent eadem verba ingeri, 'Quid habes quod non accepisti?' Hic igitur sermo Pauli non excludit liberum arbitrium, sed premit hominis arrogantiam, non agnoscentis se ex dono Dei esse, quicquid est, si quid omnio boni est. Idem docet II Corinth. 3:5 distinguens has voces *a nobis,* et *ex nobis.* 'Non sumus,' inquit, 'sufficientes cogitare aliquid a nobis quasi ex nobis, sed omnis sufficientia nostra ex Deo est.' Etiam illa, quae possumus naturae viribus, sic a nobis oriuntur, ut tamen ex Deo sint, a quo fonte promanant omnia."

41. 1532C, "Sermo diverus est, res eadem. Denique tota haec causa tractans quibus modis Dei gratia operetur in homine, multos habet recessus, quos curiosius excutere non est necesse. Constat quicquid in nobis est, id totum a Dei liberalitate proficisci. Caeterum quomodo dispenset suam in nobis munificentiam definire, ut sit piae speculationis, certe non arbirror esse necessarium. Et tamen in nullo genere materiarum libentius deliciatur Augustinus."

42. 1532C–F, "Ostendi Scholasticorum opinionem, quae inter non reprobatas plurimum tribuere videtur libero arbitrio, non ita multum dissidere ab opinione Augustini, nisi quod variant in vocabulis potius quam in re. . . . sint multae species justitiae, bonaeque voluntatis ac fidei, quoniam haec non satis evidenter distinguuntur a Veteribus, . . . Nullus tamen illorum tam iniquus fuit libero arbitrio, quin aliquid tribuerit."

43. 1533B–D, "Quod autem illud est, nisi quod per naturae vires homo potest assequi, non ut illico sit beatus, sed ut divinae gratiae sit praeparatior. Qui per rationem humanam multa intelligit, crediteque de Deo quae vera sunt, qui ex Philosophorum libris imbibit amorem sapientiae, qui pro modulo suo ad habitum virtutis enixus est, aliquanto capacior est crasso milite, qui in profunda rerum ignorantia maximisque sceleribus versatus, ne cogitavit quidem unquam de Deo. . . . Quod si libeat sophisticari, ne id quidem verum est, quod liberum arbitrium ad malum sufficit. Non enim sufficeret, si destitueretur generali motu primae causae. . . . igitur insit in homine native quaedam vis appetens honesti, . . . 'Est autem,' ut Seneca scribit, 'magna pars bonitatis, velle bonum fieri.' " Cf. Aug. *De correp. et grat.* 31; Seneca, *Ep. ad Luc.* 34,3.

44. 1534C–D, Aug. *De correp. et grat.,* 2: "Desidare auxilium gratiae, initium est gratiae." Erasmus: "Quod si concedimus in hominibus etiam scelerosis esse aliquod gratiae desiderium ex ipso naturae sensu, rursum causa periclitabitur, ne gratiae initium sit a libero arbitrio. Quod vehementer abominandum esset, nisi quicquid potest liberum arbitrium, ex Dei dono proflueret. . . . Caeterum ex his minutiis excitare tragoediam, non arbitror esse Christianae tranquillitatis, praestiterit fortassis permittere, ut juxta Paulum hactenus quisque in suo sensu abundet."

45. 1534D–E, "Augustinus adversus Pelagianos decertans, studio gratiae tam parum tribuit libero arbitrio, ut nomine tribuat aliquid verius quam re. . . . Utramque sententiam posteriores Theologi moderati sunt, aliquanto plus tribuentes libero arbitrio quam ille tribuebat, ac distinguentes meritum con-

gruum a merito condigno, fidem acquisitam a fide infusa, voluntatem perfectam ab imperfecta."

46. 1534E–F, "Jam quod Theologis in Augustini de libero arbitrio sententia visum est parum, id Luthero videtur nimium, qui necessitatis vocabulum invehit, unde constanter abstinuit Augustinus, ac ne illud quidem tribuit libero arbitrio posse se a gratia subtrahere, quod illi non negat Augustinus. At qui pio quidem animo, sed tamen incautiore, quo gratiae magnitudinem exaggerent, quicquid possunt, demunt naturae viribus, perinde mihi facere videntur, quasi si quis neget ullos salutem adeptos, vel in Lege Mosi, vel in lege naturae, quo magis attollat gloriam adventus Christi, adversus eos qui dicere solent, quid novi Christus attulit? Nec animadvertunt interim hoc ipsum, quo servabuntur homines ante proditum Evangelium, fuisse ex dono Christi, qui pro sua bonitate nulli deest. Quanquam pro divini dispensatione, pro temporum ac personarum varietate aliter atque aliter sese communicat."

47. 1535C–D, "Postremo meminerint etiam illas naturae vires a Deo juste eripi, si quis vel abutatur, vel sibi velit arrogare. Nec ipsos fallant libertatis, meriti, digni, condigni, congrui, debitique vocabulis, cum summa totius negotii debeatur gratuitae Dei benignitati, sed tanto diligentius ambiant gratiam, quanto plus virium in hoc a Deo datum arbitrantur, tantoque studiosius contendant ad opera pietatis."

48. Cf. the study of Erasmus' theology of *sermo* by Marjorie O'Rourke Boyle, *Erasmus on Language and Method in Theology* (Toronto: University of Toronto Press, 1977). I wish to express my debt to Dr. Boyle's stimulating and penetrating insights.

49. LB X, 1535D–E, "Porro si quis erit, cui et Augustinus videatur iniquior libero arbitrio, et recentiores plus aequo largi, inter utramque viam tuto incedat, credatque etiam in illis gradibus, quibus, ut dixi, praeparamur ad gratiam, non deesse gratiam peculiarem, sic ut pro modulo profectus nostri cuique in omnibus et liberum arbitrium gratiae, et gratia libero arbitrio cooperetur. In summa magis in hoc incumbamus, ut Dei gratiam adipiscamur, quam ut curiose disputemus quomodo gratia in nobis operetur. Nam huiusmodi nimium subtilibus logomachiis citius amiserimus Dei gratiam, quam assequamur quibus modis gratia operetur in nobis, praesertim cum Deus ubique impervestigabilis tam variis modis exserat vim suam in rebus conditis."

50. 1535E–F, "Jam ut fatear justis causis permotos, qui gratiae vim exaggerantes, naturae vires extenuarunt: ita non levioribus causis commoti sunt, qui non passi sunt quenquam servari aut interire, nisi ex qualibuscunque meritis: quorum sententias licet dissidentes, tamen quoniam ex eodem pietatis fonte manant, commode decet interpretari, non exagitare, et in concordiam redigere, vel in hoc interim concordes inter nos, in quo illi non discordant. Consentiunt enim in his, hominem misericorditer servari, neminem autem injuste damnari, nemini deesse gratiam Dei summa vi praestandum homini quod in ipso situm est: quicquid tamen in nobis est boni, totum divinae bonitati adscribendum."

51. 1536A–C, "et si perpendamus Deum variis rationibus agere in servandis ac

damnandis hominibus, nec statim hoc in omnibus facere, quod in hoc aut in illo pro dispensatione fecisse legitur. . . . Haec, quae peculiares habent causas, non oportet ad generalem pertrahere sententiam. Rursum si quos Deus subito violentoque motu rapuit ad se, veluti Paulum, ex his non est constituendum universale dogma. Alios vocat ex profunda ignorantia, gravique scelerum lerna: alios diu patitur veluti ambire divinum munus." On Erasmus' ideas of history in comparison to current Renaissance conceptions of secular history, cf. Peter Bietenholz' salutary study: *History and Biography in the Work of Erasmus of Rotterdam* (Geneva, 1966), especially section IX, 39–46. Bietenholz does not place much emphasis on Erasmus' sense of gradual historical and personal development, though he does stress his notion of time as *kairos* or timeliness, or occasion provided by God to which man may respond, and he does refer to his historical relativism in judging earlier Christian thinkers (31). As we have seen, Erasmus does believe in recess and progress and gradual transformation in a natural process under divine aegis as well as in the more dramatic and sudden interventions of providence. I believe, as should be apparent in this paper, that one can go farther than Bietenholz did in constructing Erasmus' sense of history from his central concern with free will, grace and salvation. I would support Myron P. Gilmore's view (*"Fides et Eruditio:* Erasmus and the Study of History," *Humanists and Jurists, Six Studies in the Renaissance,* Cambridge, Mass., 1963, 87–114) that Erasmus' historical consciousness was profound.

52. 1536C–E, "Quod si non possumus omnino ratione consequi quatenus, quibus modis, quibusque gradibus operetur in nobis, certe loquamur more Scripturarum, more sanctorum Patrum. Quid vero loquitur Scriptura? Non dicit, inanis est omnis conatus hominis, nihilo refert quomodo vivas, Deus aut servabit si statuit, aut perdet si decrevit, sed ita loquitur: 'Convertimini ad me, et ego convertar ad vos:' . . . 'Venite ad me omnes,' 'Contendite intrare per angustiam portam,' 'Sobrii estote et vigilate.' 'Praevaricatores redit ad cor.' 'Date eleemosynam.' 'Remittite et remittetur vobis,' 'Judicate pupilo,' 'Subvenite inopi.' Huiusmodi sermonibus nos invicem exhortemur ad poenitentiam et caritatem mutuam, omissis malis colloquis, quae corrumpant bonos mores: frater fratri dicat, Diligamus invicem, emendemus in melius quae ignoranter peccavimus, piis operibus ambiamus Domini gratiam; privatim autem accommodemus et scripturam et vocem nostram ad proximi necessitatem. Aliter enim loquendum elato, feroci, sibique placenti, et erectam cervicem gerenti adversus Deum: aliter pusillanimi et desperationi proximo. Illi proferamus testimonia Scriptuarum, quae docent quam homo nihil possit suis viribus, quantumque discrimen sit hominem suis fidere praesidiis. Alteri proferamus testimonia, quae docent quantum homo sibi quoque praestare possit, si velit adniti: quamque sit Dei parata benignitas praestanti quod in ipso est."

53. Cf. above, p. 281.

54. 1536E, "Scriptura vero, quoniam nunc hos compellat, nunc illos, juxta qualitatem eorum quibus loquitur, interpretanda est. Alioqui secum ipsa multis in locis pugnare videtur, cum nihil minus pugnet quam Scriptura cum Scriptura."

55. 1563E–F, "Ut finem voluminis faciam, non hic deprecabor lectoris iudicium, et exigam obsequium, quemadmodum fecit Lutherus, sed quicquid a nobis dissertum est, Ecclesiae Catholicae submitto, paratus corrigere, si quid excidit a veritate discrepans. Porro Christus illuminet nos omnes una cum Luthero, ut omnes uno ore, eadem mente, eademque sententia, praedicemus communem omnium Dominum cui gloria in aevum. Amen."

The Religious Foundations
of Luther's Social Views

This paper advances a twofold thesis:[1] that the key to Luther's apparently contradictory social philosophy lies in his religious dualism and that, although the social forces of his time may have affected his social outlook, it was through his religious teachings that these forces exerted their main influence.

Luther's religion appealed to the personal sense of isolation of the individual, to his feeling of "not counting," of not being needed in the "commercialized" system of providing salvation into which the medieval church seemed to be turning. In his *Treatise on Christian Liberty* (1520), one of his most influential works, he made clear his purely subjective position. Justification is by faith alone, and reliance on the external machinery of works or the sacraments does not bring salvation but is a barrier to it. Recognition of the historical and revealed truth of Christianity is not enough: the thing that matters is what this knowledge means personally to each individual, to you and me.

> I believe that it has now become clear that it is not enough nor is it Christian, to preach the works, life and words of Christ as historical facts, as if the knowledge of these would suffice for the conduct of life . . . Rather ought Christ to be preached to the end that faith in Him may be established, that He may not only be Christ, but be Christ for thee and for me, and that what is said of Him and what His name denotes may be effectual in us.[2]

In discussing the sacrament of communion in his *Treatise on the Blessed Sacrament,* he argued that belief in the transformation of the nature of the bread and the wine "profiteth us nothing in this sacrament: a change [in us] must occur and manifest itself through love."[3] On this basis he rejected the

---

This study of Luther's social philosophy as an expression of his religious vision was written in the forties and published in *Essays in Medieval Life and Thought,* ed. J. H. Mundy, R. W. Emery, and B. N. Nelson (New York: Columbia University Press, 1955), 71–87, a volume honoring Professor Austin P. Evans. If I were to rewrite it today (1983) I should certainly emphasize the correspondence of his social views to his famous declaration concerning the man who has been saved: *Simul justus et peccator.* A more recent interpretation of Luther is to be found in my essay in part three: "Luther's Hexameral Anthropology."

medieval doctrine that the validity of the sacraments and of works lay in their objective character without regard to the person performing them. For the impersonality of this position, he substituted his own subjective teaching.

> There are many who, regardless of this change of love and faith, rely upon the fact that the mass or the sacrament is, as they say, *opus gratum opere operato,* that is, a work which of itself pleases God, even though they who perform it do not please Him . . . Such fables please me not . . . For it was not instituted for its own sake that it might please God, but for our sake that we might use it rightly, exercise our faith by it, and by it become pleasing to God. If it is merely an *opus operatum,* it works only harm; it must become an *opus operantis.*[4]

To make it clear that the objective character of actions is meaningless for salvation, Luther pointed to the deceptiveness of external appearances.

> It is indeed true that in the sight of men a man is made good or evil by his works, but this being made good or evil is no more than that he who is good or evil is pointed out and known as such . . . But all this remains on the surface, and very many have been deceived by this outward appearance and have presumed to write and teach concerning good works by which he may be justified, without even mentioning faith . . . He, therefore, who does not wish to go astray with those blind men, must look beyond works; nay, turning his eye from works, he must look upon the person and ask how that is justified.[5]

The sensuous world could have little spiritual importance for men. Otherwise men would trust objective reality and lose the only truly valuable inner experience. The sacrament of the Mass was no more than a visible sign of spiritual fellowship with Christ and the saints, and it should not be regarded as establishing an objective fellowship. In fact, if the subjective sense of fellowship with Christ could be objectively demonstrated, "we should not be strengthened nor trained thereby to put our trust in the invisible and eternal things, or to desire them, but should much rather be trained to put our trust only in the temporal and visible things . . . we should thus be prevented from ever coming to Him."[6]

In recognizing only subjective religious experience as valid, Luther rejected the medieval effort to establish an objective structure linking God and man, eternity and time, the other world and this world, spirit and flesh. But he did not oppose institutionalized religion with otherworldliness *per se.* He rejected the monastic variety of otherworldliness, because it, too, sought to arrive at eternity through this-worldly practices, substituting tangible devices for the true, subjective, personal relation to eternity. Moreover, although the influence of Eckhardt and the Friends of God on

Luther is well known, no one may claim that personal mysticism (any more than asceticism) exhausts his position. For Luther did more than reject and condemn the externality and the mechanical, impersonal character of Catholicism as he saw it. He held an alternative social and ethical theory which sprang from his religious subjectivism and which, like it, was opposed to medieval theory.

Luther's support of the princes and of secular authority generally might be regarded as the expression of a trend toward greater political universality and away from the myriad local institutions, both secular and religious, of the Middle Ages. Luther, however, supported the state, not because it represented a more universal form of social organization than feudalism, but because he considered an objective and secular brotherhood to be unrealizeable. Like his emphasis on a subjective faith, the only universality he believed possible was spiritual and subjective. He objected strongly to any institution that claimed to realize social justice—even more if it pretended to brotherly love. He made this clear in his discussion of the confraternities or lay religious brotherhoods of the later Middle Ages—again contrasting the valid spiritual brotherhood with the invalid attempts to make brotherhood concrete and objective.

> Therefore for the right understanding and use of the brotherhoods, one must learn to distinguish rightly between brotherhoods. The first is the divine, the heavenly, the noblest . . . the fellowship of all saints . . . In this we are all brothers and sisters, so closely united that a closer relationship cannot be conceived, for here we have one baptism, one Christ, one sacrament, one food, one Gospel, one faith, one Spirit, one spiritual body, and each is a member of the other; no other brotherhood is so close . . . Organized brotherhoods have one roll, one mass, one kind of good works, one festival day, one treasury, and, as things are now, their common beer, common feast, and common debauch, but none of these binds men so closely together as to produce one spirit, for that is done by Christ's brotherhood alone.[7]

Luther's real grievance concerning attempts to realize a community through social organization, as in the case of these brotherhoods, was that they inevitably became self-centered and thus destroyed the Christian's capacity for genuine inner communion.

> For there they learn to seek their own good, to love themselves, to be faithful only to one another, to despise others, to think themselves better than others and presume to stand higher before God than others. And thus perishes the communion of saints, the Christian love, and the true brotherhood established in the holy sacrament. Thus a selfish love grows in them; that is, by these many external

work brotherhoods they oppose and destroy the one inner, spiritual, essential, common brotherhood of all saints.[8]

As a counterpart to the social and spiritual chaos he saw all about him, Luther developed a vision of a spiritual community dwelled in by faith and, although unattainable in objective reality, to be described in the concrete terms of an actual city.

> *Communicare* means to take part in this fellowship, or as we say, to go to the sacrament, because Christ and all saints are one spiritual body, just as the inhabitants of a city are one community and body, each citizen being a member of the other and member of the entire city. All the saints, therefore, are members of Christ and of the Church, which is a spiritual and eternal city of God.[9]

Luther projected into this conception the old, nostalgic ideal of the medieval town, where every citizen purportedly worked for the common welfare and shared in the public benefits and losses.

> To carry out our homely figure: it is like a city where every citizen shares with all the others the name, honor, freedom, trade, customs, usages, help, support, protection and the like, of that city, and on the other hand shares all the dangers of fire and flood, enemies and death, losses, imposts and the like. For he who would have part in the common profits must also share in the losses, and ever recompense love with love. Here we see that whoever wrongs a citizen wrongs the entire city and all the citizens; whoever benefits one deserves favor and thanks from all the others.[10]

However much Luther affirmed a subjective community of saints conceived in terms borrowed from history, he did not believe that any enduring mutuality or cooperation was possible in the world. In this he was unlike those medieval figures who believed that something of the inner Christian law of love should be discoverable in the natural community of men. As a remedy for the disunity and conflict he saw around him, Luther proposed a spiritual leveling whereby degrees of sanctity would be abolished and each individual's faith be made the test for his membership in a truly mutual Christian community of the spirit. But it was a test to be made by each person alone and no one could make it for him. "Who can receive or apply, in behalf of another, the promise of God, which demands the personal faith of every individual? . . . Where there is a divine promise everyone must stand upon his own feet."[11]

This egocentric conception was made necessary by Luther's dismissal of the ideal objective community, which hardly existed in his day. Rapacious economic acquisition and mutual social rivalry made a sham of the efforts to express through sacraments and through the various devotional orders and brotherhoods a communal or even a charitable relationship. At the same time, men were in great need of care and cooperation and fellowship. Luther, therefore, offered them a subjective feeling of community in Christ and with the saints. But this could only be realized by the individual who intensely felt a need for this, only by a miserable suffering individual. "Therefore, this holy sacrament is of little or no benefit to those who have no misfortune or anxiety or do not feel their adversity."[12]

A personal response to the disintegration of the medieval community inspired Luther to lead the Christian to a subjective faith in God and to a realization of a spiritual Christian fellowship. In this way, he helped the Christian to see the real, objective nature of the external social world. The Christian thereby becomes aware that genuine fellowship does not exist in the society of this world but at the same time feels a subjective fellowship with other Christians and with all men. He cannot live with men in actual social fellowship, but he can inwardly feel and express the same love for them that Christ feels toward him.

> Lo, thus from faith flow forth love and joy in the Lord, and from love a joyful, willing and free mind that serves one's neighbor willingly and takes no account of gratitude or ingratitude, of praise or blame, of gain or loss. For a man does not serve that he may put men under obligations . . . but most freely and willingly he spends himself and all that he has, whether he waste all on the thankless or whether he gain a reward.[13]

Community experienced subjectively meant for Luther religious individualism and indifference to the concrete effects of individual Christian action in the real world. The Christian acted out of the love of Christ with which he was overflowing, having acquired confidence and faith in the divine promise. Inwardly the faith is subjective; outwardly love merely manifests the inward faith that produces it. "A man willingly serves another without hope of reward, and for himself is satisfied with the fullness and wealth of his faith."[14]

Though the results of one's actions do not matter to the Christian, the actions themselves possess an objective nature. Although unmotivated by self-interest, the Christian's acts must be genuinely helpful to the needs of others—as a true expression of love. "And this is what makes it a Christian work to care for the body, that through its health and comfort we may be able to work to acquire and to lay by funds with which to aid those who are in need, that in this way the strong may serve the weaker."[15]

On the other hand, as we have seen, Luther did not believe that morality could be objective. He therefore repudiated the system of differentiating between the merits of actions according to external circumstances—a system that had made possible medieval moral casuistry. He also rejected the notion that particular orders or vocations were holier than others. Since good works were basically reflective of the inner faith of the Christian—"For the works are acceptable not for their own sake but because of the faith which alone is, works and lives in each and every work without distinction"[16]—the man of faith cannot help doing continuous good works by the mere fact of existing.

> Now since the being and nature of man cannot for an instant be without doing or not doing something, enduring, or running away from something (for, as we see, life never rests), let him who will be pious and filled with good works, begin and in all his life and works at all times exercise himself in this faith . . . In brief, nothing can be in or about us and nothing can happen to us but that it must be good and meritorious, if we believe (as we ought) that all things please God.[17]

And to the Christian all callings are equally meritorious, since through any of them he may manifest his love by serving the community. In this way Luther combined his subjective conception of faith with the objective demand for service to the community. This has led to the view that Luther was contradictory or, at least, ambivalent in his social views. But if it is considered that the traditionalistic demands for service to the community and for restriction of egoism had for him no objectively moral purposes but were guides as to how Christian love and faith would be manifested if they were sincere, the contradiction may be viewed as perfectly consistent with his religious dualism.

A possible explanation for this consistent inconsistency may lie in the way Luther carried his religious views over into secular matters. If a spiritualized religion of faith is put forth to relieve the emptiness of an institutionalized religion such as medieval Catholicism, it is also consistent or even necessary to view secular affairs as devoid of the spirit and true morality. By this token the business of this world may be—and, indeed, is—best conducted according to requirements short of religious perfection. Religion and morality, with their values of faith and community, should then be confined to their true inner subjective sphere, and secular matters should be judged objectively and pragmatically. Then the Christian could participate in the affairs of the world without taint, since, as far as religion is concerned, it was his faith and love that mattered. The worldly need not temper their actions by any moral constraints because there is no merit to be gained toward salvation by so doing; they could be guided solely by the need to protect their own interest from the rapaciousness of others. Religiously every man fulfilled his duties in his calling, and there was no need to sanction morally what obviously contradicted community welfare: for community could exist only in spirit and not in reality. Economically, the world could go its sinful way safe from the interference of religious zealots who might erroneously seek their salvation through its reform.

In place of what he took to be misguided attempts to make actual conditions conform to the Christian ideal (such as the Peasants' uprising), Luther offered a dual set of values whereby the old ideal of mutual love could be kept in the heart while the harsh conditions of reality were accepted and put up with as well as could be. The real social meaning of Lutheranism lies in its ethical sentimentalism (which gives the individual a sense of his own decency and nobility in the inmost recesses of his heart), combined with a shrewdness in external dealings which needs no justification because that is "the way things are."

This dualism of subjective attitude and social behavior was fully and explicitly advocated in his treatise *Secular Authority: to what Extent it Should be Obeyed* (1523). Like St. Augustine, Luther distinguished between the *civitas Dei* and the *civitas terrena.* He divided men into two groups: those of the fleshly city and those true believers in Christ who form in spirit a Utopia where everyone guards the interests of everyone else. "And if all the world were composed of real Christians . . . no prince, king, lord, sword or law would be needed."[18] But Luther did not advocate the establishment in history of such an anarchic Utopia of mutual sacrifice, because Christians of any kind are very rare, and even these are subject to human passions and are prone to serve themselves. On the other hand, his picture of the kingdom of the world shows even more emphatically how little his conception of a Christian community had to do with social reality, past or present. Worldly society was a pack of beasts that had to be ruled by the sword, and harshly, to prevent it from destroying itself. The real remedy for the ills of worldly society was not the establishment of a Christian community in this world but the political state. For St. Augustine the worldly society had been the natural consequence of the incomplete development of the men within it, but for Luther the state was divinely established above society for the specific purpose of directing and curbing men.

> Since few believe and still fewer live a Christian life, God has provided for non-Christians a different government outside the Christian estate and God's kingdom, and has subjected them to the sword, so that even though they would do so, they cannot practice their wickedness . . . Even so a wild savage beast is fastened with chains and bands, so that it cannot bite and tear as is its wont, although it would gladly do so . . . If it were not so, seeing that the whole world is evil and that among thousands there is scarcely one true Christian, men would devour one another, and no one could preserve wife and child, support himself and serve God; and thus the world would be reduced to chaos.[19]

To those who thought a genuine Christian community might be established he said, "Take heed and fill the world with real Christians before ruling it in a Christian and evangelical manner. This you will never accomplish; for the world and the masses are and always will be un-Christian, although they are all baptized and nominally Christian."[20] Thus, since the world cannot be reformed, the two kingdoms should coexist. Internally, Christ's rule gives to Christians the fellowship of saints; externally, secular rule maintains law and order.

> For this reason these two kingdoms must be sharply distinguished, and both be permitted to remain; the one to produce piety, the other to bring about external peace and prevent evil deeds; neither is sufficient in the world without the other . . . Where there is only secular rule or law, there, of necessity, is sheer hypocrisy, though the commandments be God's very own. Without the Holy Spirit in the heart no one becomes really pious, may he do as fine works as he will. Where, on the other hand, the spiritual government rules over the land and people, there evil is given free rein and the door is opened for every kind of knavery; for the natural world cannot receive or comprehend spiritual things.[21]

Thus Luther carried over into his views of the state the same dualism that characterized his religious outlook. What is important, however, is the implication he drew for Christian action. While the Christian could not gain salvation or merit from good works, he needed to perform them as an expression of the self-sacrificing love that he has received from God through faith. As far as his own interests are concerned, he should gladly yield them. But in loving his neighbor, he must take into consideration that the latter may not (probably will not) be a Christian. His neighbor must be benefited by the Christian's acts, not according to Christian criteria but according to his own secular ones. This requires the Christian to use force, defend property and other selfish interests, to participate fully in the affairs of the world according to their own sordid necessities.

> As concerns yourself, you would abide by the Gospel and govern yourself according to Christ's word, gladly turning the other cheek and letting the mantle go with the coat, when the matter concerned you and your cause. In this way, then, things are well-balanced, and you satisfy at the same time God's Kingdom inwardly and the kingdom of the world outwardly, at the same time suffer evil and injustice and yet punish evil and injustice, at the same time do not resist evil and yet resist it. For in the one case you consider yourself and what is yours, in the other you consider your neighbor and what is his. In what concerns you and yours, you govern yourself as a true Christian;

in what concerns others and belongs to them, you govern yourself according to love and suffer no injustice for your neighbor's sake; this the Gospel does not forbid but rather commands.[22]

This double standard of behavior for the Christian allowed Luther to advocate traditional Christian morality and at the same time to sanction and give decisive support, on moral grounds, to worldliness, both political and economic. It goes far in clarifying the seeming inconsistency of his views. He explicitly advocated inconsistency, based on a religious principle.

How far he was willing to go in sanctioning political worldliness may be seen in such statements as these:

> Although you do not need to have your enemy punished, your weak neighbor does. You should help him, that he may have peace and that his enemy may be curbed . . . you are under obligation to serve and further the sword by whatever means you can, with body, soul, honor, or goods. For it is nothing that you need, but something quite useful and profitable for the whole world and for your neighbor . . . The reason you should do this is, that in this case you would enter entirely into the service and work of others, which benefited neither yourself, nor your property, nor your character, but only your neighbor and others; and you would do it not to avenge yourself or to recompense evil for evil, but for the good of your neighbor and for the maintenance of the safety and peace of others.[23]

Luther, of course, thought that the inner moral realm could in this way be kept unmarred by the effects of the ruthless external behavior he sanctioned. One may justly ask whether that was really possible. Nevertheless, by the plausibility with which he taught his doctrine, he helped to insure the lasting success of such dualism as an historically significant attitude. Perhaps this influence was due to the coincidence of his double standard of inner feeling and outer behavior with the historical need for such a theory. Evil as the world and one's licit actions in the world were, they were also given moral sanction. Luther could not barefacedly teach that what one did had no relation to one's inner feelings; but by separating the two, while sanctioning worldly acts in the name of sacred duty to others, he achieved a workable adaptation of the stricken consciences of his contemporaries to the objectively un-Christian deeds they could not avoid performing in the age in which they lived.

Luther's well-known attacks on the practices of great merchants and moneylenders as well as his apparently "traditional" notions of trading at a just price and lending without interest create greater difficulties of explanation. How can such views be reconciled with the thesis of a double standard for inner feeling and outer action? Hypothetically, the same reasoning that clarifies his statements on secular authority might be applied. His position, however, as set forth in his two sermons *On Usury* of 1519 and 1525 and in his treatise *On Trading and Usury* of 1524,[24] is more ambiguous. Nevertheless, certain declarations indicate that a similar interpretation is relevant.

He carefully distinguished between the spiritual and material aspects of the conduct of everyday business. He concerned himself only with the spirit, the orientation of the will. "It is our purpose here to speak about the abuses and sins of the trade so far as they concern the conscience. The injury they work to the purse we leave to the care of princes."[25] This distinction itself is an innovation. Secular law and economics is one thing, morality another. His admonitions were thus specifically directed at Christians. Acting on the basis of love, a Christian merchant would seek to fill the needs of the community on an equitable basis. He would be more anxious to do his neighbor "no injury than to make large profits." But clearly this is a rare event. "But where are such merchants? How few merchants there would be and how trade would fall off, if they were to amend this evil rule and put things on a Christian basis."[26] He was just as emphatic here in believing that a literal application of Christian principles would be impossible. He counted on political authority to check the abuses of the profit motive rather than seeking to reform the world according to Christian views.

> The world needs a strict, hard, temporal government that will compel and restrain the wicked not to steal and rob and to return what they borrow, even though a Christian ought not to demand it, or even hope to get it back. This is necessary in order that the world may not become a desert, peace may not perish, and trade and society may not be utterly destroyed: all of which would happen if we were to rule the world according to the Gospel.[27]

The Christian, however, must be ready to risk losing his property or the money he has lent. Luther listed three ways of trading that could be considered wholly Christian—but these, it must be emphasized, were all considered to be ways in which the individual would manifest his faith and love through self-sacrificial acts and not as practical ways of conducting business. The first is to submit to extortion and add the cloak to the coat that is demanded; but, Luther added, if this were generally practiced there would be little trade, "because reason and human nature flee and avoid that sort of risk and damage above all else."[28] The second way is to give freely to all who are in need: this, too, would lessen trade, because one would worry less about "accumulations of property."[29] The third way is lending without interest, which would also lessen trade. Thus Luther required of the Christian what he fully recognized were "unnatural" acts of trusting everyone and taking all risks. But this is not a theory of economics but a counterpart of his conception of justification by faith which could not permit any vision of sure salvation through meritorious works.

> These three ways of dealing, then, are a masterly keeping of the commandments not to presume upon the future nor to put trust in any man or in self, but to depend solely on God. In this way everything is paid in cash and the word of James is applied 'If God will, so be it.' In this way we deal with people as with those who may fail and are unreliable; we give our money without profit and take the risk that what we lend may be lost.[30]

This view has its obvious secular counterpart: "In God we trust, all others cash."

It should be noted that Luther's assumptions about human nature are contrary to those usually associated with economic "traditionalism," which would seem to require some greater reliance on the ordinary goodness of mankind. With his fargoing skepticism on this score, Luther could not fail to be aware that such a rigorous standard of behavior was unlikely even among Christians. Some more tolerant and moderate attitude was necessary if the merchant was not to be driven away—and Luther had no intention of abolishing trade. He made, of course, the common distinction between the legitimacy of local traffic and the evil of foreign trade, but this could not solve his problem. For this reason he offered pragmatic advice on how a merchant might realize a profit equitably. Here the reliance on what was customary in the neighborhood, or the attempt to calculate profit as payment for time, labor, and risk of the merchant, indicates that his economic thinking was conservative. But as he well knew, apart from a harshly rigoristic approach to the situation, all trade was selfish in its motivations. Too strict a calculation of the risks to the conscience was foreign to his whole approach. The merchant was assured of his sympathy in this respect.

> I would not have anyone's conscience so perilously strained or so closely bound on this point as to insist that one must strike the right measure of profit to be the very *heller;* for it is not possible to get at the exact amount that you have earned with your trouble and labor. It is enough that with good conscience you seek to arrive at the exact amount, for it lies in the very nature of trade that the thing is impossible . . . If you therefore take a little too much profit unknowingly and unintentionally, let that go into your Lord's Prayer, where we say 'Forgive us our debts,' for no man's life is without sin. Besides, the time will come when you will get too little for your trouble; throw that in the scale to balance the times when you have

taken too much . . . It is not selfishness or greed that forces you to this mistake, but the very nature of your occupation.[31]

Morality in economic affairs thus remains subjective and a matter of intention; practice is governed by external circumstance. The considerable leeway here allows profits to come unintentionally and as part of unavoidable sin. Luther seems to be yielding to the inevitable temptation of his doctrine of subjective sin and virtue: that of letting the intention cover the deed, however contradictory the two may be. Such a double standard can facilitate a very large development of business, for whenever a sharp practice occurs, the businessman can fall back on the fact that he meant well. And the fluid, uncertain nature of the merchant's occupation, once it is recognized as essential to it, provides further excuses. Luther furnished the means for avoiding the bad conscience that would result from a literal application of moral absolutism. Trade itself, he argued, is a pragmatic affair of approximation; he was ready to make good conscience immune from the uncertainty of outer events.

Thus, Luther applied both relative and absolute standards. On the strict side, he required only Christians to live according to absolute moral standards. Taking these teachings literally, and so putting up with the harsh practices of their neighbors, was not so contrary to the actual circumstances of many persons. A good part of the population, in fact, had to endure the monopolistic squeeze of the big merchants, bankers, and moneylenders. Luther contributed a toleration of these activities in the name of Christian self-sacrifice. Indirectly, he weakened by this doctrine the resistance of the artisans, small traders, and peasants to the social changes that were worsening their condition.

Catholic teaching, through late medieval moral casuistry, had an effect of giving encouragement to a mercantile economy by means of a distinction between usury and income from investments.[32] The Catholic method was to weave in a host of circumstances to mitigate or explain away the immorality of the practice in question. As a consequence, a moral approval was sometimes given to what was in fact a ruthless struggle for the accumulation of wealth and power. Perhaps it made more sense to call a spade a spade, as Luther did, to emphasize the utterly un-Christian nature of the new social conditions. To the many contemporaries who heeded his call, this position must have been part of the reasons for their doing so. And his approach was, perhaps, more effective than the canonists' in encouraging the new social trends (although this was certainly far from his purpose)—by making them seem the inevitable way of the world which all Christians had to bear virtuously out of implicit trust in God and forgetfulness of self. Moreover, by a permissiveness of his own, and a subjective morality of intent, he also made it easier for merchants to practice their trade without it pricking their consciences too much.

Luther wrote so voluminously that it is impossible not to find him contradicting himself on innumerable occasions. But the real meaning of his thought is not to be tested by comparing his contradictory statements on details, taken by themselves, but by determining whether there is an inner consistency in his position as a whole. It has been seen that his position was built on a dual attitude toward the world: as he held in *Christian Liberty,* there is an "inner freedom" and an "outer bondage." In this period of history there was a widening separation between the inner feelings and ideals of men and the external political and economic conditions of their existence. Luther's theory of two contradictory spheres of existence, which all men had to recognize, corresponded to this reality. As changing historical conditions reshaped men's conceptions of life as a whole (and in Luther's day these were expressed in religious terms), their ideas concerning politics and economics necessarily changed also. The fact that Luther neither totally accepted nor completely rejected the new institutions does not make his position archaic. The historical period itself was contradictory, and he was closer to his time in affirming a dualism than in seeking a forced consistency.

NOTES

1. The following paper is deeply influenced by such earlier efforts to unravel Luther's social position as those of Max Weber, *The Protestant Ethic and the Spirit of Capitalism* (New York, 1930), Chap. III; Anders Nygren, *Agape and Eros* (2 vols. in 3; London, 1932–39), Part Two, Vol. II, Chap. VI; Ernst Troeltsch, *The Social Teaching of the Christian Churches* (2 vols.; New York, 1931), Vol. II, Chap. III, Section 2; Karl Holl, *Gesammelte Aufsätze zur Kirchengeschichte,* Vol. I: *Luther* (Tübingen, 1921), Chap. III; R. H. Tawney, *Religion and the Rise of Capitalism* (New York, 1926), Chap. II, Section 2; Erich Fromm, *Escape from Freedom* (New York, 1941), Chap. III, Part 2; Reinhold Niebuhr, *The Nature and Destiny of Man* (2 vols.; New York, 1945), Vol. II, Chap. VII, Section 2; Benjamin N. Nelson, *The Idea of Usury* (Princeton, 1949), Chap. II; and Roland Bainton, *Here I Stand* (New York, 1950), Chap. XIV. Without attempting to give a point-by-point comparison of my views with previous writings, I may suggest that I have found the discussions of Troeltsch and Nelson more cogent and closer to my own views because of their emphasis on the "modern-conservative" (rather than the "medieval") character of Luther's teachings. But I cannot, of course, hold anyone else responsible for my own possible misconceptions. The present essay is offered not because it is wholly original or definitive but because a fairly clear overall pattern in Luther's social thought seemed to emerge in the course of my study of his familiar works. The method used is to be described as an "ideal-type" of

the kind of reasoning that seems to underlay Luther's turnings from situation to situation. A more chronological and historical treatment would undoubtedly blur the lines of the present study, but if this paper's somewhat simplified results can sharpen the issues or stimulate further discussion, it will have served its purpose.

2. *Tractatus de libertate Christiana*, in *D. Martin Luthers Werke*, kritische Gesamtausgabe (as yet incomplete; 57 vols. in 67; Weimar, 1883–1947), VII, 39–73. This edition is hereafter cited as WA. The English translations are from H. E. Jacobs *et al.*, eds., *Works of Martin Luther* (6 vols.; Philadelphia, 1915–32), hereafter cited as *Works*. (I am indebted to the Muhlenberg Press for permission to quote from this.) Passage cited: WA, VII, 58–59; *Works*, II, 326–27.

3. *Eyn Sermon von den Hochwirdigen Sacrament des Heyligen Waren Leychnams Christi: Und von den Bruderschaften*, in WA, II, 742–58 (tr. in *Works*, II, 9–31). Passage cited: WA, II, 751, Section 19; *Works*, II, 22.

4. *Ibid.* (WA, II, 751, Section 20; *Works*, II, 22–23). The Latin in this passage was left thus untranslated by Luther. He is clearly trying to emphasize the difference between "a work performed for the sake of the result" and "a work performed for the sake of the doing"—the objective and the subjective viewpoints, respectively.

5. *Christian Liberty* (WA, VII, 62–63; *Works*, II, 332–33).

6. *Blessed Sacrament* (WA, II, 753, Section 21; *Works*, II, 24).

7. *Ibid.*, in the section *Concerning the Brotherhoods* (WA, II, 756, Section 4; *Works*, II, 29–30).

8. *Ibid.* (WA, II, 755, Section 3; *Works*, II, 28).

9. *Ibid.* (WA, II, 743, Section 4; *Works*, II, 10).

10. *Ibid.* (WA, II, 743, Section 5; *Works*, II, 11).

11. *De Captivitate Babylonica Ecclesiae*, in WA, VI, 484–573 (tr. in *Works*, II, 170–293). Passage cited: WA, VI, 521 ("*De sacramento panis*"); *Works*, II, 208–9.

12. *Blessed Sacrament* (WA, II, 746, Section 10; *Works*, II, 15).

13. *Christian Liberty* (WA, VII, 66; *Works*, II, 338).

14. *Ibid.* (WA, VII, 64; *Works*, II, 336).

15. *Ibid.* (WA, VII, 64; *Works*, II, 335).

16. *Von den guten Werken*, in WA, VI, 202–76 (tr. in *Works*, I, 184–285). Passage cited: WA, VI, 206–7, Section 5; *Works*, I, 190.

17. *Ibid.* (WA, VI, 212–13, Section 13; *Works*, I, 198–99).

18. *Von weltlicher Oberheit, wie weit man ihr Gehorsam schuldig sei*, in WA, XI, 245–80 (tr. *Works*, III, 228–73). Passage cited: WA, XI, 249–50, Section 3, *Works*, III, 234.

19. *Ibid.* (WA, XI, 251, Section 4; *Works*, III, 236).

20. *Ibid.* (WA, XI, 251, Section 4; *Works*, III, 237).

21. *Ibid.* (WA, XI, 252, Section 4; *Works*, III, 237–38).

22. *Ibid.* (WA, XI, 255, Section 6; *Works*, III, 241–42).

23. *Ibid.* (WA, XI, 254, Section 5; *Works*, III, 240–41).

24. *(Kleiner) Sermon von dem Wucher* (1519), in WA, VI, 1–8, and *Eyn Sermon von*

dem Wucher (1520), in WA, VI, 36–60 (tr. in *Works,* IV, 37–69). *Von Kaufshandlung and Wucher* (1524), in WA, XV, 293–313 (tr. in *Works,* IV, 12–36). As with other of Luther's later writings, I do not use his *An die Pfarrherrn, wider den Wucher zu predigen,* of 1540.

25. *Trading and Usury* (WA, XV, 294; *Works,* IV, 14).
26. *Ibid.* (WA, XV, 295; *Works,* IV, 15).
27. *Ibid.* (WA, XV, 302; *Works,* IV, 22).
28. *Ibid.* (WA, XV, 301; *Works,* IV, 21).
29. *Ibid.* (WA, XV, 301; *Works,* IV, 21).
30. *Ibid.* (WA, XV, 302; *Works,* IV, 22).
31. *Ibid.* (WA, XV, 297; *Works,* IV, 16–17). The most carefully worked out and thoughtful review of Luther's shifting positions on usury is Nelson, *The Idea of Usury;* cf. especially pp. 45–56.
32. I am primarily concerned with the psychological effects of late medieval casuistry. For a more precise discussion of canonist doctrine and legal techniques, cf. Benjamin N. Nelson, "The Usurer and the Merchant Prince," in *The Tasks of Economic History,* annual supplemental issue of *The Journal of Economic History,* VII (1947), 104–22.

Renaissance Problems in Calvin's Theology[1]

Professor Roy W. Battenhouse has recently presented us with a most stimulating and perceptive essay on "The Doctrine of Man in Calvin and in Renaissance Platonism."[2] In it he argued that the general mode of Calvin's thought about the states of man—innocent, fallen, and saved—conformed to the pattern of Renaissance neoplatonist ideas of the different levels of human existence. Although the specific conclusions and content of Calvin's thinking (e.g., predestination and the denial of free will) were on their face diametrically opposed to those of Pico dell Mirandola and Ficino,

> Calvin's rejection of humanism for theology, and of reason for revelation, seems to have been a rejection more often of conclusions than of basic definitions and assumptions. . . . Calvin's doctrine of man may have a subterranean dependence on the very Renaissance optimism and rationalism which Calvin sought to reprove and chasten.[3]

Although there may be certain emphases in Professor Battenhouse's arguments that might well be supplemented, the present paper is essentially an independent and parallel consideration of some of the concerns that Calvin shared with Renaissance writers, including some humanists. Its focus is on the way in which Calvin dealt with certain general problems of the relation of man and his world rather than on the extent to which he was or was not neoplatonic, stoic, humanist, or scholastic—to all of which schools he was in some ways indebted and from which he in other ways decisively differed.

The key question in the history of Christian ethics has been the relation of value to reality. To what extent could the Golden Rule, the injunction to "love thy neighbor as thyself," be realized, human nature being whatever it happened to be thought to be and the world whatever way it was conceived? Calvin's thinking on this question took place after two centuries of particularly agitated concern with the problem, and it was his conviction that through his theology he had resolved the moral crisis it

---

My interest in Calvin and Renaissance problems came out of the same discoveries and concerns ventured in "The Problem of Free Will in the Renaissance and the Reformation." Yet it is interesting to me to observe now in the early eighties how much I was concerned in the late forties and early fifties with an effort to systematize Renaissance thinking about the human condition. Only, if I were writing it now, I would probably title it "Calvin and Renaissance 'Anthropology'!" This article is reprinted from the first volume of *Studies in the Renaissance*, 1954, 59–80.

had presented. Some periods of time and some systems of Christian thought make rather bland assumptions about the ease with which a Christian can live according to his values. Not so the last two centuries of the Middle Ages. One of the Reformation's challenges to the authority of the Church was based on the fact that—despite the voices of gloomy prophets, skeptical critics, and ardent proponents of reform—the Church was committed as an institution to the premise that with its aid an individual could lead a Christian life, the consequence for many being either a resort to hypocrisy or descent to despair. With only a limited amount of exaggeration it could be said that Luther and Calvin in their separate ways sought to show how one could not lead a Christian life and still remain a Christian. Weber and Troeltsch, among many others, have made this clear.[4] Nevertheless, the immediate influence of each of the reformers was to stimulate a striking intensification of faith which had its counterpart in a reformed Catholicism.

How was this accomplished? In Luther's case there was an apparently simple separation of Christian faith from the unchristian works one was compelled to perform in the circumstances of the world. Without entering into his actually rather complicated position,[5] it may be said for purposes of comparison that Luther affirmed a subjective inner fulfillment of Christian values, coupled with a recognition of the objective necessity of conforming to the unchristian outward circumstances.

Calvin also started with a separation of subjective and objective elements. His method, however, was to demonstrate that despite contemporary pessimism, the objective nature of the material world, society, and man really did manifest the hand and purpose of God, and that it was the subjective corruption and debility of human perception, consequential to the Fall, that made things seem perverse and uncertain. Men tended to overestimate their own righteousness, taking their seemingly good motives at their face value and exaggerating their moral capacity because any notion that they were superior appealed to their vanity. Viewing affairs according to their own distorted perceptions, men could never see the true purpose and hand of God in the world, and so they failed to appreciate his wisdom and goodness even in the manifestations of disaster and evil in natural and human events.

Calvin seems to conceive of the human defect in essentially perceptual terms:

> Because from our natural proneness to hypocrisy, any vain appearance of righteousness abundantly contents us instead of the reality; and everything within and around us being exceedingly defiled, we are delighted with what is least so, as extremely pure, while we confine our reflections within the limits of human corruption. So the eye, accustomed to see nothing but black, judges that to be very white,

which is but whitish or perhaps brown. Indeed, the senses of our body
may assist us in discovering how grossly we err in estimating the
powers of the soul. For if at noon day we look either on the ground or
at any surrounding objects, we conclude our vision to be very strong
and piercing; but when we raise our eyes and steadily look at the sun,
they are at once dazzled and confounded with such a blaze of bright-
ness, and we are constrained to confess that our sight, so piercing in
viewing terrestrial things, when directed to the sun, is dimness itself.
Thus also it happens in consideration of our spiritual endowments.[6]

Professor Battenhouse has noted the similarity of passages such as this to
Plato's myth of the cave.[7] It might be said that while for Plato men sinned
out of ignorance, for Calvin men were ignorant out of sin.

Calvin, therefore, took it upon himself to show in the first book of the
Institutes the objective evidence of the rationality and order of nature and
society which indicate their divine origin and acceptability to man. At the
same time he felt compelled to indicate all the idolatrous and anthropomorphic and magical distortions of reality introduced by men into
their conception of it. In this respect he revealed a kinship, not only
between his theology and the ancient Greek quest for an underlying rationality, but also with the new scientific attitude that was taking shape in
his own time and reached a culmination in the seventeenth century.[8] Like
the new philosophy of science, his point of view was also a development out
of the fourteenth-century nominalist separation of subjective conceptions
from objective perceptions. Calvin's effort to eliminate religious subjectivism ran parallel to the later effort of Galileo to eliminate or control the
subjective factors distorting the observation of natural phenomena by distinguishing between primary and secondary qualities and correcting for the
error and bias of the observer.

It is interesting that Calvin believed that in this way not God but the
divine order might be discovered and that he rejected any tendency to
identify God and nature, such as Spinoza was to formulate.

> I confess, indeed, that the expression nature is God, may be used in a
> pious sense by a pious mind; but it is harsh and inconsistent with
> strict propriety of speech, nature being rather an order prescribed by
> God; it is dangerous in matters so momentous, and demanding pecu-
> liar caution, to confound the Deity with the inferior course of his
> works.[9]

Is it too much to compare this attitude to the general positivism of the
scientists concerning ultimate causality and their concentration on the
discovery of phenomenal regularities and orders?

At any rate there are many passages in this first book which seem to chastise men for failing to appreciate the grandeur of their world or even of their own natures, emphasizing, of course, that such a "Discovery of the World and of Man" should reflect glory on its Divine Maker and not on his miserable beneficiary.

> Of his wonderful wisdom, both heaven and earth contain innumerable proofs: not only those more abstruse things which are the subjects of astronomy, medicine, and the whole science of physics, but those which force themselves on the view of the most illiterate of mankind, so that they cannot open their eyes without being constrained to witness them. Adepts, indeed, in those liberal arts, or persons just initiated into them, are thereby enabled to proceed much further in investigating the secrets of the Divine Wisdom. Yet ignorance of those sciences prevents no man from such a survey of the workmanship of God, as is more than sufficient to excite his admiration of the Divine Architect. In disquisitions concerning the motions of the stars, in fixing their situations, measuring their distances, and distinguishing their peculiar properties, there is need of skill, exactness and industry; and the providence of God being more clearly revealed in these discoveries, the mind ought to rise to a sublimer elevation for the contemplation of his glory. But since the meanest and most illiterate of mankind, who are furnished with no other assistance than their own eyes, cannot be ignorant of the excellence of the divine skill, exhibiting itself in that endless, yet regular variety of the innumerable celestial host—it is evident that the Lord abundantly manifests his wisdom to every individual on earth. Thus it belongs to a man of pre-eminent ingenuity to examine with the critical exactness of Galen, the connection, the symmetry, the beauty and the use of the human body. But the composition of the human body is universally acknowledged to be so ingenious, as to render its maker the object of deserved admiration. And therefore some of the philosophers of antiquity have justly called man a microcosm, or world in miniature; because he is an eminent specimen of the power, goodness, and wisdom of God, and contains in him wonders enough to occupy the attention of our minds, if we are not indisposed to such a study. [10]

While a passage such as this can be regarded as similar in spirit to Book XXII, chap. 24 of St. Augustine's *De Civitate Dei,* or to Psalm 19 (to which Calvin makes reference in the preceding paragraph), there is also in it an element of special veneration of the more penetrating knowledge and appreciation of divine workmanship that is open to the scholar and man of science. And while he, indeed, refers to sentiments expressed in the books of Job and Isaiah, there is a distinctive quality in his grandiose imagination which visualizes God as an artist displaying his powers to a rapt human audience through the media of the elements. Thus he seems to have been in sympathy with the grandiloquent portrayal of the colossal power of natural forces that was part of sixteenth-century artistic sensibility. The following passage is patently not that of a Shakespeare, nor adequately descriptive of a Leonardo drawing, but it has an aesthetic quality related to their fascination with meteorological powers.

> Now what illustrious specimens of his power have we to arrest our attention! unless it be possible for us not to know what strength is required to sustain with his word this immense fabric of heaven and earth; now by his mere nod to shake the heaven with roaring peals of thunder, to consume whatever he choose with lightnings, and set the atmosphere on fire with the flame; now to disturb it with tempests in various forms, and immediately, if he please, to compose it all to instantaneous serenity; to restrain, suspended as it were in air, the sea, which seems by its elevation, to threaten the earth with continual devastation; now raising it in a tremendous manner, by the tumultuous violence of the winds, and now appeasing the waves to render it calm.[11]

In another passage Calvin bids man admire the handiwork of God in the beauty of the stellar order.

> Consider how great must have been the Artist who disposed the multitude of stars which adorn the heaven in such regular order that it is impossible to imagine anything more beautiful to behold; who fixed some in their stations so that they cannot be moved; who granted to others a freer course, but so that they never travel beyond their appointed limits; who so regulates the motions of all that they measure days and nights, months, years and seasons of the year, and also reduces the inequality of the days, which we constantly witness, to such a medium that it occasions no confusion. So also, when we observe his power in sustaining so great a mass, in governing the rapid revolutions of the celestial machine, and the like.[12]

While Calvin could stand in wonder at the power and beauty of the universe, he was primarily a theologian and a moralist, and he never lost sight of his major scheme of inducing men to submit themselves to the Divine Purpose rather than their own. And all these passages were intended to show that behind the disorderly appearance of natural and human events there lies a reality of order on a scale that is incomprehensible from the puny perspective of man. For example:

> When thick clouds obscure the heavens, and a violent tempest arises, because a gloomy mist is before our eyes, and thunder strikes our ears,

and terror stupefies all our faculties, all things seem to us to be blended in confusion; yet during the whole time the heavens remain in the same quiet serenity. So it must be concluded, that while the turbulent state of the world deprives us of our judgment, God, by the light of his own righteousness and wisdom, regulates all those commotions in the most exact order and directs them to their proper end. [13]

He was perhaps even more concerned to refute the false interpretation that men placed upon the chaotic character of historical events and personal destinies. Even when God seemed to be operating in an arbitrary and capricious way through fortune, order prevailed.

It must also be observed that, although the paternal favor and beneficence of God, or the severity of his justice, is frequently conspicuous in the whole course of his providence, yet sometimes the causes of events are concealed, so that a suspicion intrudes itself that the revolutions of human affairs are conducted by the blind impetuosity of fortune; or the flesh solicits us to murmur, as though God amused himself with tossing men about like tennis balls. [14]

I will return to this theme, for one of the main concerns of the Renaissance was with the nature of fortune and the individual's relationship to it. There were many conceptions of fortune, and Calvin is linked to this historical period by his general interest in this problem rather than by his particular position, which distinguishes him from other figures and movements.

A prior consideration is again epistemological. If, as he argued, human perception has been debilitated by inherited sin, and if the vanity of self-sufficiency has tempted men to make unwarranted inferences from the meager facts in their possession, how can they profess to know the truth, or how can they discover it for themselves? Only, said Calvin, through the *Scripture*.

For if we consider the mutability of the human mind—how easy its lapse into forgetfulness of God; how great its propensity for error of every kind; how violent its rage for the perpetual fabrication of new and false religions—it will be easy to perceive the necessity of heavenly doctrine being thus committed to writing, that it might not be lost in oblivion, or evaporate in error, or be corrupted by the presumption of men. [15]

It has frequently been remarked that the Bibliolatry of Protestantism corresponds to the humanists' adulation of the classical text. There was in Calvin such a veneration for ancient and written doctrine, but he was no idolater. He did not consistently hold to a literal interpretation of the Scripture. He was perhaps more interested in explication and meaning than moved by a desire for simplicity and philological purity such as animated the textual criticism of men like Erasmus and Valla. He considered it demeaning to God to take the tales and superstitions of the Bible at their face value.

> The Anthropomorphites also, who imagined God to be corporeal, because the Scripture frequently ascribes to him a mouth, eyes, hands and feet, are easily refuted. For who, even of the meanest capacity, understands not, that God lisps, as it were with us, just as nurses are accustomed to speak with children. Wherefore such forms of expression do not clearly explain the nature of God, but accommodate the knowledge of him to our narrow capacity. [16]

In keeping with such a principle of "accommodation," Calvin did interpret the Scripture in an extraordinarily critical and rational manner—where he chose to. [17] But it would be misleading to think of this, or him, as anything but religious. How was he or anyone else to know that his interpretations were the truth? Human vanity and stupidity could as easily misinterpret the Scripture as the evidence of God's works in nature. And what determined that men believed in the Scripture at all? In the final analysis, for Calvin truth was accessible only to those who had been illuminated by the Holy Spirit.

> Let it be considered then as an undeniable truth, that they who have been inwardly taught by the Spirit, feel an entire acquiescence in the Scripture, and that it is self-authenticated, carrying with it its own evidence, and ought not to be made the subject of demonstrations and arguments from reason; but it obtains the credit it deserves with us by the testimony of the Spirit. . . . Therefore, being illuminated by him, we now believe the divine original of the Scripture, not from our own judgment or that of others, but we esteem the certainty that we have received it from God's own mouth by the ministry of men to be superior to that of any human judgment, and equal to that of an intuitive perception of God himself in it. [18]

The fact that Calvin was so concerned with epistemological questions is interesting and significant. Ever since the work of the fourteenth-century nominalists, the question of the certainty of knowledge has become almost as important as the content of it. This concern was to remain a constant feature of the history of modern philosophy. Yet this skepticism was accompanied by an enormous increase in the amount and accuracy of human knowledge. To some it has seemed that the method of doubt was the cornerstone of science. Calvin and Calvinism never truly resolved this question, and it can be seen that it was fundamental to the whole structure of his thought. He asserted at the same time both a drastic devaluation of man's capacity to know and a great and complex doctrine about God, the world, and man. Reliance on the testimony of the Spirit did not overcome the contradiction. And, as is well known, the question of proof has haunted the subsequent history of Calvinism.

It is perhaps of greater relevance in this paper to deal now with the content of Calvin's position, leaving aside the problem of proof. Perhaps the major emphasis of his theology was not merely upon the benevolence, the omniscience, and the omnipotence of God, but also upon his omnioperative character, his constant supervision and control of all events, natural and historical and spiritual, and his wise and rational utilization of all men as instruments of his purpose. It is not enough to make God the Creator of the world, which then runs along according to its appointed laws.

> But faith ought to penetrate further. When it has learned that he is the Creator of all things, it should immediately conclude that he is also their perpetual governor and preserver; and that not by a certain universal motion, actuating the whole machine of the world, and all its respective parts, but by a particular providence sustaining, nourishing and providing for everything which he has made. [19]

In place of the traditional vision of a self-sufficient God, absorbed in self-contemplation, Calvin had a new image of the deity corresponding to the energetic man of affairs of the new economic and political order.

> God asserts his possession of omnipotence and claims our acknowledgment of this attribute; not such as is imagined by sophists, vain, idle and almost asleep, but vigilant, efficacious, operative, and engaged in continual action. [20]

The crucial question is how this view relates to human affairs in his thinking, for it involves both the seemingly accidental nature of historical events that plagued men of his time, which was talked of under the concept of fortune, and the question of the scope of human capacity and action in influencing human destiny or events in general, which was discussed as the problem of free will. It is on these issues that Calvin's relation to the Renaissance may be most clearly seen.

According to Calvin, while some had laid the outcome of human events to fortune, others held that God originally gave men an instinct or natural capacity for reason, and thenceforth men ran their own affairs. Although wishing to refute both views, Calvin conceded that events often seemed fortuitous and that human action "appears to proceed from voluntary inclination in the creature."[21] Particularly in the matter of social status, many "attribute it to human industry, or to fortune, that some men remain in obscurity, and others rise to honours"; nevertheless, in spite of appearances, "it is from the secret counsel of God, that some rise to promotion and others remain in contempt."[22]

Stated thus flatly, Calvin's position of predetermination by God as far as natural and historical events are concerned, predestination and election from eternity as far as salvation, would seem to end matters and stand in patent contradiction to the newer humanistic currents of thought.[23] Calvin, however, did not leave matters there where popular conceptions leave Calvinism. Instead he entered into particulars about the actual operation of his doctrine and contrived to leave the world looking not so very different from the way it appeared to his contemporaries but, to his view, making more sense.

In the first place, if God controlled the world in such minute detail that not a thing happens apart from his direction, it would seem as though human helplessness would be enormously increased. Calvin, however, was no friend of sloth and, admiring the industrious, wished no such consequence. To his mind it was not the fact of divine providence but man's uncertainty about the real state of affairs that paralyzed him. He was, therefore, careful to try to save and explain the phenomena of both free will and fortune, although denying the ultimate reality of those forces.

First he sought to show how fortune could properly be understood without men being reduced to inactivity by the seeming chaos of events.

> Yet since the dullness of our minds is very much below the sublimity of the divine providence, let us endeavor to assist them by a distinction. I say that notwithstanding the ordination of all things by a certain purpose and direction of God, yet to us they are fortuitous: not that we suppose fortune holds any domination over the world and mankind, and whirls all things about at random, for such folly ought to be far from the breast of a Christian; but because the order, reason, end and necessity of events are chiefly concealed in the purpose of God, and not comprehended by the mind of man, those things are in some measure fortuitous, which must certainly happen according to the divine will.[24]

Such doctrine did not need to discourage men. In fact they could now feel assured of wisdom and order behind the seeming work of fortune.

The appearance of free will also had to be recognized, because there was a grave danger that if all events were known to be divinely ordered, men would cease to act. This was not a mere juxtaposition of opposing concepts by Calvin, nor a mere pious admonition. For him free will was itself an instrument of providence. Doctrinally, his position was clear, detailed, and explicit. Many men argued as follows:

"If God has fixed the moment of our death, we cannot avoid it; therefore all caution against it will be but labor lost." Men, however, took certain precautions.

> And men in general exert all their faculties in devising and executing methods by which they may obtain the object of their desires. Now either all these things are vain remedies employed to correct the will of God, or life and death, health and disease, peace and war, and other things which, according to their desires and their aversions, men industriously study to obtain or avoid, are not determined by his certain decree. . . . In short they supersede all deliberations respecting futurity, as opposed to the providence of God, who without consulting men has decreed whatever he pleased. And what has already happened they impute to the divine providence in such a manner as to overlook the person who is known to have committed any particular act. Has an assassin murdered a worthy citizen? they say he has executed the counsel of God. . . . Thus by these persons all crimes are denominated virtues, because they are subservient to the ordination of God.[25]

Calvin here has anticipated the stock argument against his doctrine. But he is willing to give up neither divine providence nor human responsibility.

In opposition to this argument Calvin urged the greatest exercise of prudence and intelligence in the conduct of life as a duty in keeping with the very nature of providence. Here is how he reconciled his rationalism with his deprivation of men of the determination of their destinies:

> He who has fixed the limits of our life, has also entrusted us with the care of it; has furnished us with means and supplies for its preservation; has also made us provident of dangers; and that they may not oppress us unawares, has furnished us with cautions and remedies. Now it is evident what is our duty. If God has committed to us the preservation of our life, we should preserve it; if he offers supplies, we should use them; if he forewarns of dangers, we should not rush rashly into them; if he furnishes remedies, we ought not to neglect them.

Indeed, the measures men took were themselves part of providence, and it became their pious duty to God to exert themselves prudently.

> You conclude that it is unnecessary to guard against danger, because if it be not fatal, we shall escape it without caution; but on the contrary the Lord enjoins you to use caution, because he intends it not to be fatal to you. These madmen overlook what is obvious to every observer—that the arts of deliberation and caution in men proceed from the inspiration of God, and that they subserve the designs of his

providence in the preservation of their own lives; as on the contrary, by neglect and slothfulness, they procure for themselves the evils which he has appointed for them. For how does it happen that a prudent man, consulting his own welfare, averts from himself impending evils, and a fool is ruined by his inconsiderate temerity, unless folly and prudence are in both cases instruments of the divine dispensation? Therefore it has pleased God to conceal from us all future events that we may meet them as doubtful contingencies, and not fail to oppose to them the remedies with which we are provided, till they shall have been surmounted or shall have overcome all our diligence.[26]

While this point of view may not be entirely convincing to us, to Calvin it ended the old conflict between free will and fortune that had been so particularly on the minds of Renaissance writers (e.g., Machiavelli). Both were vindicated as part of the providence of God. Man was incited by this doctrine to oppose his free will (or virtù) to fortune as part of the divine work; and he was not to be discouraged when his efforts failed, as this was also part of the action of his busy God. Neither God nor man might anymore be slothful.

This was a new ideal of human status. God, in so far as he was conceived in the image of the elite of society, had been thought of as passively contemplative, enjoying his leisure, or as a military commander at the head of the hosts of the righteous, or in other roles. To Calvin, God was an artist, or an architect; but most characteristically for him, a busy God worked through busy men, who by their activity improved their position in the world as far as this corresponded to the divine project, and by this means furthered and cast glory upon that project.

Calvin did not feel that this point of view was contrary to human needs and feelings. Understanding that the course of human events, as well as of nature, was predetermined in accordance with divine wisdom and justice, men should derive certain advantages from this. In the first place they would attribute all prosperity to God and take it as a sign of divine benediction. Secondly, calamities, whether due to human or natural action, were also from God. Basically men would simultaneously make use of all human and material aids for their benefit that they were able to, and would take responsibility for their own crimes and failures.

He will rank it among the blessings of the Lord, not to be destitute of human aids which he may use for his own safety; he will neither be remiss in taking advice, therefore, nor negligent in imploring the help of those whom he perceives to be capable of affording him assistance; but considering all creatures that can in any respect be serviceable to him, as so many gifts from the Lord, he will use them as legitimate instruments of the divine providence. And as he is uncertain respecting the issue of his undertakings, except that he knows that the Lord will in all things provide for his good, he studiously aims at what, according to the best judgment he can form, will be for his advantage. Nor in conducting his deliberations, will he be carried away by his own opinion, but will recommend and resign himself to the wisdom of God, that he may be directed to the right end. But he will not place his confidence in external helps to such a degree as, if possessed of them, securely to rely on them, or if destitute of them, to tremble with despair.[27]

Trust in divine providence, instead of limiting man in his pursuit of worldly goals, should, according to Calvin, strengthen his confidence in his own powers, so long as he recognized that they came from the Lord. Man also should not be ashamed to seek his own advantage, as this was again in furtherance of the divine purpose. Fortune, good or bad, was no longer indifferent to the merits of the action—divinely viewed, of course—but the very consequence of them.

On the other hand, it should not be imagined that Calvin had a very rosy view of the external conditions of his time. In the face of the widespread misery and calamity, his doctrine, he claimed, also offered a valuable psychological reward.

Amidst these difficulties must not man be most miserable, who is half-dead while he lives, and is dispirited and alarmed as though he had a sword perpetually applied to his neck? . . . What can you imagine more calamitous than such a dread?[28]

This anxiety-ridden state of mind, arising out of the social and political disorders of his times—the wars, pestilences, civil disturbances, economic overturns, and social oppressions—could not be overcome by attributing these occurrences to fortune and seeking to defy it or to flee to the green hills. Calvin's doctrine alone might prevent demoralization.

On the contrary, when this light of divine providence has once shined on a pious man, he is relieved and delivered not only from extreme anxiety and dread with which he was previously oppressed, but also from all care. For, as he justly dreads fortune, so he ventures to commit himself to God. . . . How is it that their security remains unshaken, while the world appears to be revolving at random, but because they know that the Lord is universally operative, and confide in his operations as beneficial to them.

In short, "ignorance of providence is the greatest of miseries, but the knowledge of it is attended with the highest felicity."[29]

When Calvin turned from his vindication of the divine providence in Book I of the *Institutes* to his depiction of the state and nature of fallen man in Book II, he was notoriously contemptuous of man. Despite his deprecation, however, he did not deprive man of an ability to control human affairs and to direct the course of nature through science. He thought of man as deprived of free will and thoroughly corrupted morally by the Fall of Adam. But what is frequently overlooked is that he meant this lack of free will to apply primarily to man's ability to determine his spiritual condition. Man could not save himself no matter how hard he tried; and moral virtue carried with it no merit toward justification and salvation, since the latter were predestined from eternity. It is significant, however, that in fact Calvin recognized the capacities of man in secular and social matters, though he denied them in spiritual things. Such spiritual abilities as leading a happy life or loving one's neighbor were dissociated by Calvin from the more egoistic talents of the understanding and will.

Free will with regard to spiritual matters was totally annihilated by the Fall. Man was

> exiled from the kingdom of God in such a manner that all the affections relating to the happy life of the soul are also extinguished in him, till he recovers them by the grace of regeneration. Such are faith, love to God, charity towards our neighbors and an attachment to holiness and righteousness. All these things being restored by Christ, are esteemed adventitious and preternatural; and therefore we conclude that all have been lost.[30]

As for men's natural capacities, Calvin was able to have it two ways. On the one hand, they were debilitated and corrupted, thereby allowing him to account for human inadequacies and failures in the practical and speculative realms. At the same time, however, men retained some of their original powers, thereby showing his recognition of the obvious capacities of men. Calvin made it clear that he felt men did retain very great rational powers. He described the vanity of the intellect and its overcurious pursuit of the fruitless and the unimportant, its lack of judgment. Yet, he conceded, it was capable of making discoveries about inferior matters and even had some slight sense of superior things. To make his position clear he felt that

> it will be useful for us to propose the following distinction; that there is one understanding for terrestrial things, and another for celestial ones. . . . In the first class are included civil polity, domestic economy, all the mechanical arts and liberal sciences; in the second the knowledge of God and of the divine will and the rules for conformity to it in our lives.[31]

In what concerned the area of human affairs, Calvin found all men endowed with an "instinctive propensity to cherish and preserve" society, which took the form of a "perpetual consent of all nations, as well as all individuals, to the laws." Even criminals consented with their minds, although their passions were too powerful to restrain them; others who were critical of injustice in the laws recognized a higher law in equity. "Yet it is certainly true that some seeds of political order are sown in the minds of all." No doubt his early study of civil law and his youthful commentary on Seneca's *De Clementia*[32] had sown seeds of admiration for political justice in Calvin's mind.

In his admiration of man's mental and manual facilities, he rejected the Platonic theory of the recollection of ideas from a previous existence in favor of a theory of invention and intellectual progress.

> Scarcely an individual can be found whose sagacity does not assert itself in some particular art. Nor have they an energy and facility only in learning, but also in inventing something new in every art, or in amplifying and improving what they have learned from their predecessors.[33]

Because these capacities were unequally distributed to men, it was clear to Calvin that they were the gift of the Spirit both to mankind generally and to some individuals in more specific ways.

> But whereas some excel in penetration, others possess superior judgment, and others have a greater aptitude to learn this or that art; in this variety God displays his goodness toward us, that no one may arrogate to himself as his own what proceeds merely from divine liberality. . . . God inspires particular motions according to the vocation of each individual.[34]

The importance of Calvin's doctrine of vocation, beyond the fact that it gave a religious sanction to the existing division of labor, lies in the stress he placed upon the individual's duty to carry out his special abilities effectively. In this way each man would actually be working for the objective social interest and thus fulfilling a divine mandate. At the same time failure to use his abilities well would penalize the individual in regard to his own material existence—betokening God's punishment of his negligence.

In this way Calvin made an important distinction between the general work of the Spirit operating through all men for the objective furtherance of the divine scheme, and the special work of the Spirit in justifying certain men only for salvation. The doctrine of *vocation* applied to all men, because the rewards and penalties for successful or inadequate application of one's endowments by the Spirit were all of this world. The doctrine of *election* applied only to the "saints." These gifts of vocation were, nevertheless, an essential part of God's objective mandate and plan. As such they should not be spurned by the pious.

> Yet let us not forget that these are most excellent gifts of the Spirit, which for the common benefit of mankind he dispenses to whomsoever he pleases. . . . Nor is there any reason for inquiring what intercourse with the Spirit is enjoyed by the impious who are entirely alienated from God. For when the Spirit of God is said to dwell in the faithful only, that is to be understood of the Spirit of sanctification, by whom we are consecrated as temples to God himself. Yet it is equally by the energy of the same Spirit, that God replenishes, actuates, and quickens all creatures, and that according to the property of each species which he has given it by the law of creation. Now if it has pleased the Lord that we should be assisted in physics, logic, mathematics, and other arts and sciences, by the labor and ministry of the impious, let us make use of them; lest if we neglect to use the blessings therein freely offered to us by God, we suffer the just punishment of our negligence. But, lest anyone should suppose a man to be truly happy, when he is admitted to possess such powerful energies for discovering the truth relating to the elements of this world, it must likewise be added, that all the faculty of understanding, and the understanding which is the consequence of it, is in the sight of God, a fleeting and transitory thing, where there is not a solid foundation of truth.[35]

In this passage Calvin has expressed a very complicated attitude. He gives a support to worldliness which at the same time subordinates it to providence, and a subordination of worldliness to divine purposes which simultaneously appreciates the objective results of human activity and discounts its ultimate meaning. This ambivalent attitude corresponds very closely to the joyless pursuit of knowledge and material wealth which seemed to be incumbent on all men but yielded no deep satisfactions because of its perils, uncertainty, and, even more, lack of a clear relationship to human spiritual happiness. This was not the mood of much of the Renaissance, but it was the mood of a good many humanists and of other sensitive men of the time. And it was to this dour tone that Calvinism appealed.[36]

Calvin was, perhaps, correct in feeling that such a worldly activity could lead men away from their spiritual fulfillment, and in recognizing that it was at the same time not directly or necessarily opposed to man's highest potentialities. Such a divorce between spiritual development and economic or technical progress was a cultural condition that many writers had commented on since the early fourteenth century. Calvin theologized it into the objective work of the divine mandate. What it came to with him was a plea to accept the existing stage of human development as the final and inscrutable work of God.

By his theory of a twofold human understanding Calvin contributed to a process of externalization of human motives. This very simply means exactly what he was preaching—that man by his own efforts in science and material activities had some possibility of realizing limited worldly goals, but none at all of achieving moral and spiritual ends. Calvin was, of course, very critical of the debasement of man involved in this condition, but at the same time he could not help reinforcing it by regarding it as the just punishment of man's sins and by excluding the possibility of other conditions.

Calvin sought to restore an integrity between motivation and action. He was particularly acute in seeing that the existing separation between internal intentions and external actions was in many ways more apparent than real. But his acuteness of perception could not change the contradictions, so that he was driven to more radical conclusions about the moral capacities of human nature than those of most previous thinkers concerned with this problem. The latter, including many humanists, were content to recognize a separation between the subjective and objective spheres of life and tended to look either for an exclusively subjective fulfillment or for moral reform of the external sphere.

Calvin, in effect, restored a negative integrity by arguing that neither in action nor in motivation was man in effective control over himself. He was corrupt internally and externally, although capable in a spiritually neutral way externally. It is important to suggest that for many of his contemporaries this condition was a vivid part of their experience of life. If this was so, Calvin's denial of free will had a great deal more plausibility for these men than it does for our own more easily offended moral sensibilities.

Calvin went much further in his discussion of this question in the remaining part of Book II of the *Institutes,* where he took up the inner spiritual and psychological side of man in great detail, and in Book III, where he discoursed on how within the framework of his theology a Christian might piously conduct his life. Enough has been said, however, to indicate the essentials of his position on the nature and life of man.

In summary, Calvin was concerned with several closely connected questions that might be considered "Renaissance Problems," namely: (a) the epistemological question of the relation of subjective perception to objective truth, (b) the related question of man and the universe—*microcosmos* and *cosmos*—(c) the question of the fortuitous or providential character of events, and (d) the question of man's free will.

Professor Battenhouse has shown that Calvin in his notion of the original condition of man before the Fall derived his ideas from the Platonists' high estimates of the spiritual potentialities of human nature.[37] I have tried to show how even in his conception of fallen man Calvin also shared the high regard of the Renaissance for man's capacities in the practical and intellectual spheres. Where he differed from his contemporaries, and particularly from the humanists, was in completely abandoning any hope for the spiritual or moral regeneration of mankind by its own efforts, and in believing that the small minority of the Elect, alone, for some inscrutable reason of God's were decreed from eternity for justification. And they, too, for all that, were merely actors in a cosmic drama in the theater of the world. As Professor Battenhouse has pointed out,[38] this image also was shared with the neoplatonists, and it was constantly utilized by Shakespeare. But in all these others, and in most of the humanists, there was a concern for mere man, and a tragic sorrow at his plight that is hard to find in the more realistic, more logical, and harsher theology of Calvin.

NOTES

1. An early version of this paper was read before the New England Conference on Renaissance Studies, at Northampton, Mass., October 30–31, 1953.
2. *Journal of the History of Ideas,* IX (1948), 447–71.
3. *Ibid.,* 469–70. Of course, the writings of Pico and Ficino might well be considered as much theological as humanist.
4. Max Weber, *The Protestant Ethic and the Spirit of Capitalism,* tr. Talcott Parsons (London, 1930); Ernst Troeltsch, *The Social Teaching of the Christian Churches,* tr. Olive Wyon (London, 1931), II, 515–656. Cf., on the other hand, Reinhold Niebuhr's defense of Reformation theology against what he considered to be the falsely optimistic Medieval Catholic and Renaissance views of man, particularly his *The Nature and Destiny of Man* (New York, 1941 and 1943). I have emphasized a contrary view to that of Niebuhr in "The Problem of Free Will in the Renaissance and the Reformation," *Journal of the History of Ideas,* X (1949), 51–62.
5. For a more extended discussion see my essay, "The Religious Foundations of Luther's Social Views," in *Essays in Medieval Life and Thought. Presented in Honor of Austin Patterson Evans* (New York: Columbia University Press, 1954).
6. The present study is based on Calvin's final and definitive version of the *Institutio Christianae Religionis* published in 1559. I have used the edition of Wilhelm Baum, Eduard Cunitz and Eduard Reuss (Brunswick, 1869), Vol. II of which contains the 1559 version. References will be to book, chapter, and paragraph. Translations are from John Allen's version (6th American ed.; Philadelphia, 1932).
   "Quia enim ad hypocrisin natura propensi sumus omnes, ideo inanis quaedam iustitiae species pro iustitia ipsa nobis abunde satisfacit. Et quia nihil intra nos vel circum apparet quod non sit plurima obscoenitate in-

quinatum, quod paulo minus foedum est pro purissmo arridet, quamdiu
mentem nostram intra humanae pollutionis fines continuemus. Non secus
atque oculus, cui nihil alias obversatur nisi nigri coloris, candidissimum esse
iudicat, quod tamen subobscura est albedine, vel nonnulla etiam fuscedine
aspersum. Quin ex corporeo sensu propius adhuc discerne licet quantum in
aestimandis animae virtutibus hallucinemur. Nam si vel terram despicimus
medio die, vel intuemur quae aspectui nostro circumcirca patent, validissima
perspicacissimaque acie videmur nobis praediti; at ubi in solem suspicimus,
atque arrectis oculis contemplamur, vis illa quae egregie in terra valebat, tanto
fulgore protinus perstringitur et confunditur, ut fateri cogamur, illud
nostrum in considerandis terrenis acumen, ubi ad solem ventum est, meram
esse hebetudinem. Ita et in reputandis spiritualibus nostris bonis contingit";
I, i, 2.

7. *Op. cit.*, 462, in reference to *Inst.*, III, ii, 19.
8. Please note that I am not claiming any causal relationship between theology
and science but am only suggesting that there was a parallel epistemological
structure in them. In Calvin's case this was not merely a restatement of the
classical idealist point of view. The latter (e.g., Plato) regarded the dualism
between chaos and order as part of the metaphysical structure of the universe.
Calvin on the other hand regarded the anarchic elements of both nature and
human history as anarchic or chaotic only in appearance, but in reality a part
of a divinely determined order of events. His concern was epistemological. My
impression is that this holds true of the early modern philosophy of science as
well. However, Professor Robert K. Merton in his "Science and Technology
in the Seventeenth Century," *Osiris*, IV (1938), 360–632, has attempted to
demonstrate an intimate relationship between Calvinist ideas and scientific
theories in seventeenth-century English scientists.
9. "Fateor quidem pie hoc posse dici, modo a pio animo proficiscatur, naturam
esse Deum; sed quia dura est et impropria loquutio quum potius natura sit
ordo a Deo praescriptus, in rebus tanti ponderis, et quibus debetur singularis
religio, involvere confuse Deum cum inferiore operum suorum cursu, noxium
est"; I, v, 5.
10. "Mirificam eius sapientiam quae testentur, innumera sunt tum in coelo, tum
in terris documenta: non illa modo reconditiora, quibus propius observandis
astrologia, medicina, et tota physica scientia destinata est; sed quae rudissimi
cuiusque idiotae aspectui se ingerunt, ut aperiri oculi nequeant quin eorum
cogantur esse testes. Equidem qui liberales illas artes vel imbiberunt, vel
etiam degustarunt, earum subsidio adiuti longe altius provehuntur ad intro-
spicienda divinae sapientiae arcana; nemo tamen earum inscitia impeditur
quominus artificii satis superque pervideat in Dei operibus, unde in opificis
admirationem prorumpat. Nempe ad disquirendos astrorum motus, distri-
buendas sedes, metienda intervalla, proprietates notandas, arte ac exactiore
industria opus est; quibus perspectis, ut Dei providentia explicatius se profert,
ita in eius gloriam conspiciendam, animum par est aliquanto sublimius as-
surgere. Sed quum ne plebeii quidem et rudissimi, qui solo oculorum admin-
iculo instructi sunt, ignorare queant divinae artis excellentiam, ultro se in ista

innumerabili, et tamen adeo distincta et disposita coelestis militiae varietate exserentem, constat neminem esse cui non abunde sapientiam suam Dominus patefaciat. Similiter in humani corporis structura connexionem, symmetriam, pulchritudinem, usum, ea quam Galenus adhibet solertia pensiculare, eximii est acuminis, Sed omnium tamen confessione, prae se fert corpus humanum tam ingeniosam compositionem, ut ob eam merito admirabilis opifex iudicetur. Ac proinde quidam ex philosophis olim hominem non immerito vocarunt μιχρόχοσμον, quia rarum sit potentiae, bonitatis et sapientiae Dei specimen, satisque miraculorum in se contineat occupandis nostris mentibus, modo ne attendere pigeat"; I, v, 2–3.

11. "Iam potentia quam praeclaris speciminibus nos in considerationem sui rapit? nisi forte latere nos potest cuius sit virtutis, infinitam hanc coeli ac terrae molem suo verbo sustentare; solo nutu nunc fragore tonitruum coelum concutere, fulminibus quidlibet exurere, fulgetris aerem accendere; nunc variis tempestatum formis conturbare, eundem ipsum statim, ubi libuit, uno momento serenare; mare, quod assiduam terrae vastationem minari sua altitudine videtur, quasi in aere suspensum coercere; et nunc horrendum in modum tumultuoso ventorum impetu concitare, nunc sedatis undis, pacatum reddere"; I, v, 6. Calvin's French prose style has long been admired, but he was equally a master of a Latin style whose flavor Allen most ably captures in his translation. However much he may have been inspired by acknowledged Biblical models, this language is his own, and the imaginative quality is sixteenth century in its emphasis on a single purpose behind the shifting manifestations of meteorological power.

12. "Prioris exemplum est, dum reputamus quanti fuerit artificis, hanc stellarum multitudinem, quae in coelo est, tam disposita serie ordinare et aptare ut nihil excogitari possit aspectu speciosius; alias ita inserere et affigere suis stationibus ut moveri nequeant; aliis liberiorem cursum concedere, sed ita ut errando non ultra spatium vagentur; omnium motum ita temperare, ut dies et noctes, menses, annos et anni tempora metiatur; et hanc quoque, quam quotidie cernimus, inaequalitatem dierum ad tale temperamentum redigere ut nihil confusionis habeat. Sic quoque dum potentiam observamus, in sustinenda tanta mole, in tam celeri coelestis machinae volutatione gubernanda, et similibus"; I, xiv, 21.

13. "Quum coelum occupant densae nubes, exoriturque violenta tempestas, quia et tristis caligo oculis obiicitur, et tonitru aures percellit, et sensus omnes terrore obstupefiunt, videntur nobis omnia confundi et misceri; eadem interim semper manet in coelo quies et serenitas. Ita statuendum est, dum res in mundo turbulentae iudicium nobis eripiunt, Deum ex pura iustitiae et sapientiae suae luce hos ipsos motus optime composito ordine temperare ac dirigere in rectum finem"; I, xvii, 1.

14. "Iam et hoc addendum est, quamvis aut paternus Dei favor et beneficentia, aut iudicii severitas saepe in toto providentiae cursu reluceat, interdum tamen eorum quae accidunt occultas esse causas, ut obrepat cogitatio, caeco fortunae impetu volvi et rotari res humanas; vel ad obloquendum nos caro sollicitet, ac si Deus homines quasi pilas iactando, ludum exerceret"; I, xvii, 1.

15. "Nam si reputamus quam lubricus sit humanae mentis lapsus in Dei oblivionem, quanta in omne genus erroris proclivitas, quanta ad confingendas
identidem novas et fictitias religiones libido; perspicere licebit quam necessaria fuerit talis coelestis doctrinae consignatio, ne vel oblivione deperiret, vel
errore evanesceret, vel audacia hominum corrumperetur"; I, vi, 3.

16. "Anthropomorphitae etiam, qui Deum corporeum ex eo sunt imaginati quod
os, aures, oculos, manus et pedes scriptura illi saepe ascribit, facile refutantur.
Quis enim, vel parum ingeniosus, non intelligit Deum ita nobiscum, ceu
nutrices solent cum infantibus, quodammodo balbutire? Proinde tales loquendi formae non tam ad liquidum experimunt qualis sit Deus, quam eius
notitiam tenuitati nostrae accommodant"; I, xiii, 1. However, Quirinus
Breen (John Calvin: A Study in French Humanism [Grand Rapids, 1931], 154)
argues that he gave "unqualified approval" to the work of Erasmus and Valla
even after his preconversion humanist days.

17. Such a suggestion of a principle of interpretation based on the assumption of a
changing and evolving human culture and mentality and an eternal Divine
Truth, in which it is the purpose of God to reveal himself according to the
capacities of different ages to comprehend him, may well bear further investigation. It contrasts as much with the medieval "figural" mode of exegesis as
with humanist philology; cf. Erich Auerbach, "Figura," Archivum Romanicum,
XXII (1938), 436, and his Mimesis (Princeton, 1953), 73–76. Calvin throws
further light on his methods, showing that he adds to the notion of "prefiguration" that of "accommodation": "non propterea mutabilem iudicari
Deum debere quod diversis saeculis diversas formas accommodaverit, prout
cuique expedire noverat" (II, xi, especially 13 and 14). Within the framework
of a providential history of mankind, to which he obviously and tenaciously
holds, he has introduced a notion of the historical relativism of the divine
Word.

18. "Maneat ergo hoc fixum, quos spiritus sanctus intus docuit, solide acquiescere
in scriptura, et hanc quidem esse αὐτόπιστον, neque demonstrationi et
rationibus subiici eam fas esse; quam tamen meretur apud nos certitudinem,
spiritus testimonio consequi. . . . Illius ergo virtute illuminati, iam non aut
nostro, aut aliorum iudicio credimus, a Deo esse scripturam; sed supra humanum iudicium, certo certius constituimus (non secus ac si ipsius Dei
numen illic intuermur) hominum ministerio, ab ipissimo Dei ore ad nos
fluxisse"; I, vii, 5.

19. "At vero fides altius penetrare debet, nempe ut quem omnium creatorem esse
didicit, statim quoque perpetuum moderatorem et conservatorem esse colligat; neque id universali quadam motione tam orbis machinam quam singulas
eius partes agitando; sed singulari quadam providentia unumquodque eorum
quae condidit, ad minimum usque passerem, sustinendo, fovendo, curando";
I, xvi, 1.

20. "Et sane omnipotentiam sibi vendicat ac deferri a nobis vult Deus, non
qualem sophistae fingunt, inanem, otiosam et fere sopitam; sed vigilem,
efficacem, operosam, et quae in continuo actu versetur"; I, xvi, 3.

21. Ibid., I, xvi, 4.

22. ". . . industriae hominum vel fortunae adscribunt quod alii iacent in sordibus, alii ad honores emergunt . . . arcano eius consilio alios excellere, alios manere contemptibiles"; I, xvi, 6.

23. Of course it is an exaggeration to think of any one humanist point of view on such matters. Opinion ranged from Valla's inability to resolve the logical contradiction between predestination and free will, to the optimistic affirmations of moral freedom by Pico or Erasmus. There probably was a unity, however, on the desirability of free will, whatever difficulties seemed to confront it. Cf. my paper on "The Problem of Free Will," cited in n. 4, above.

24. "Quoniam tamen longe infra providentiae Dei altitudinem subsidit mentis nostrae tarditas, adhibenda est quae eam sublevet distinctio. Dicam igitur, utcunque ordinentur omnia Dei consilio certa dispensatione, nobis tamen esse fortuita. Non quod fortunam reputemus mundo ac hominibus dominari, temereque omnia sursum deorsum volutare (abesse enim a christiano pectore decet hanc vecordiam); sed quoniam eorum quae eveniunt, ordo, ratio, finis, necessitas, ut plurimum in Dei consilio latet, et humana opinione non apprehenditur, quasi fortuita sunt, quae certum est ex Dei voluntate provenire"; I, xvi, 9.

25. "Si mortis nostrae punctum signavit Dominus, effugere non licet: frustra igitur in cautionibus adhibendis laboratur. . . . omnes denique vias excogitant, et magna animi intentione excudunt, quibus id quod concupiscunt assequantur: aut haec omnia inania sunt remedia, quae captantur ad corrigendam Dei voluntatem, aut non certo eius decreto terminantur vita et mors, sanitas et morbus, pax et bellum, et alia quae homines, prout vel appetunt vel oderunt, ita sua industria vel obtinere vel refugere student. . . . In summa, omnia quae in posterum capiuntur consilia tollunt, perinde ac Dei providentiae adversa, quae, illis non advocatis, quid fieri vellet decrevit. Deinde quidquid iam accidit, ita providentiae Dei imputant, ut conniveant ad hominem, quem id ipsum designasse constet. Occidit sicarius probum civem? exsequutus est, inquiunt, consilium Dei. . . . Ita flagitia omnia virtutes vocant quia Dei ordinationi obsequantur"; I, xvii, 3.

26. "Namque is qui vitam nostram suis terminis limitavit, eius simul curam apud nos deposuit, eius conservandae rationibus subsidiisque instruxit, periculorum quoque praescios fecit, ne incautos opprimerent, cautiones ac remedias suggessit. Nunc perspicuum est quid sit nostri officii: nempe, si vitam nobis nostram tutandam commisit Dominus, ut eam tueamur, si subsidia offert, ut iis utamur; si pericula praemonstrat, ne temere irruamus; si remedia suppeditat, ne negligamus. . . . Tu cavendum non esse periculum colligis, quia, fatale quum non sit, simus etiam citra cautionem evasuri: Dominus autem ideo ut caveas iniungit, quia fatale tibi esse noluit. Non expendunt insani isti quod est sub oculis, consultandi cavendique artes inspiratas hominibus esse a Domino, quibus providentiae eius subserviant, in vitae propriae conservatione. Quemadmodum contra neglectu et socordia, quae illis iniunxit mala, sibi accersunt. Qui fit enim ut vir providus, dum sibi consulit, imminentibus etiam malis se explicet, stultus inconsulta temeritate pereat, nisi quod et

stultitia et prudentia divinae sunt dispensationis instrumenta in utramque partem? Ideo nos celare futura omnia voluit Deus, ut tanquam dubiis occurramus, neque desinamus parata remedia opponere, donec aut superata fuerint, aut omnem curam superaverint"; I, xvii, 4.

27. "Nam inter Domini benedictiones reponet, si non destituetur subsidiis humanis, quibus ad incolumitatem suam utatur; itaque nec in capiendis consiliis cessabit, nec torpebit in ope eorum imploranda, quibus suppetere conspiciet unde iuvetur; sed a Domino sibi in manum offerri reputans quaecunque commodare sibi aliquid possunt creaturae, ipsas, tanquam legitima divinae providentiae instrumenta, ad usum applicabit. Ac, quum incertus sit quem sint exitum habitura quae negotia aggreditur (nisi quod in omnibus Dominum suo bono prospecturum novit) ad id studio aspirabit quod sibi expedire ducet, quantum intelligentia menteque assequi potest. Neque tamen in capiendis consiliis proprio sensu feretur; sed Dei sapientiae se commendabit ac permittet, ut eius ductu in rectum scopum dirigatur. Caeterum non in externis subsidiis ita eius fiducia subnitetur, ut si adsint in iis secure acquiescat; si desint, perinde ac destitus trepidet"; I, xvii, 9.

28. "Inter has angustias annon oportet miserrimum esse hominem, utpote qui in vita semivivus anxium et languidum spiritum aegre trahat, non secus ac si imminentem perpetuo cervicibus gladium haberet? . . . Tali ergo trepidatione quid calamitosius fingas?" I, xvii, 10.

29. "At ubi lux illa divinae providentiae semel homini pio affulsit, iam non extrema modo, qua ante premebatur, anxietate et formidine, sed omni cura relevatur ac solvitur. Ut enim merito fortunam horret, ita secure Deo sese audet permittere. . . . Unde id quaeso habent, quod illis nunquam excutitur sua securitas, nisi quia, ubi temere mundus volutari in speciem videtur, Dominum ibique operari sciunt, cuius opus confidunt sibi fore salutare? . . . extremum esse omnium miseriarum, providentiae ignorationem; summam beatitudinem in eiusdem cognitione esse sitam"; I, xvii, 11.

30. "Unde sequitur, ita exsulare a regno Dei, ut quaecunque ad beatam animae vitam spectant, in eo exstincta sunt, donec per regenerationis gratiam ipsa recuperet. In his sunt, fides, amor Dei, caritas erga proximos, sanctitatis et iustitiae studium. Haec omnia quum nobis restituat Christus, adventitia censentur, et praeter naturam; ideoque fuisse abolita colligimus"; II, ii, 12.

31. ". . . distinctionem nobis proponere operae pretium est. Sit ergo haec distinctio, esse aliam quidem rerum terrenarum intelligentiam, aliam vero coelestium. . . . In priore genere sunt politia, oeconomia, artes omnes mechanicae, disciplinaeque liberales. In secundo, Dei ac divinae voluntatis cognitio, et vitae secundum eam formandae regula. . . . naturali quoque instinctu, ad fovendam conservandamque eam societatem propendet. . . . Hinc ille perpetuus tam gentium omnium, quam singulorum mortalium in leges consensus. . . . Manet tamen illud, inspersum esse universis semen aliquod ordinis politici"; II, ii, 13. I have included in this note the passages cited in my next paragraph also. Breen, *op. cit.*, 159–61, cited this and paragraphs 12 and 15 to demonstrate "The Precipitate of Humanism in Calvin the Reformer" (chap. 7); and François Wendel, *Calvin, Sources et Evolution de sa Pensée Religieuse*

(Paris, 1950), comments, p. 143, "L'humaniste que continuait à sommeiller en lui se réveille soudain a notre surprise" and, p. 155, in reference to the surviving "seeds" of justice, "Il y a là, n'en doutons pas, un souvenir très net de l'idée stoicienne d'une unité organique de la societé humaine." Cf. also Josef Bohatec, *Budé und Calvin* (Graz, 1950), 383–95. Calvin's clearest praise of the ancients is in II, ii, 15: "Imo ne sine ingenti quidem admiratione veterum scripta legere de his rebus poterimus; admirabimur autem, quia praeclara, ut sunt, cogemur agnoscere!"

32. Breen, *op. cit.*, chaps. 3, 4, 5; Wendel, *op. cit.*, 8–20; Bohatec, *op. cit.*, 439–64. See now (1983) the edition of this work by F. L. Battles and A. M. Hugo (Leiden: Brill, 1969).

33. "Nemo prope reperitur cuius in arte aliqua perspicientia non se exserat. Neque sola suppetit ad discendum energia et facilitas, sed ad excogitandum in unaquaque arte novum aliquid, vel amplificandum et expoliendum quod alio praeeunte didiceris"; II, ii, 14.

34. "Quod autem alii praestant acumine, alii iudicio superant, aliis mens agilior est ad hanc vel illam artem discendam, in hac varietate gratiam suam nobis commendat Deus, ne sibi quisquam velut proprium arroget, quod ex mera illius liberalitate fluit. . . . Adde quod singulares motus pro cuiusque vocatione Deus instillat"; II, ii, 17.

35. "Neque tamen interim obliviscamur haec praestantissima divini spiritus esse bona, quae in publicum generis humani bonum, quibus vult, dispensat. . . . Neque est cur roget quispiam, quidnam cum spiritu commercii impiis, qui sunt a Deo prorsus alieni? Nam quod dicitur spiritus Dei in solis fidelibus habitare, id intelligendum de spiritu sanctificationis, per quem Deo ipsi in templa consecramur. Neque tamen ideo minus replet, movet, vegetat omnia eiusdem spiritus virtute, idque secundum uniuscuiusque generis proprietatem, quam ei creationis lege attribuit. Quod si nos Dominus impiorum opera et ministerio, in physicis, dialecticis, mathematicis et reliquis id genus voluit adiutos, ea utamur; ne si Dei dona ultro in ipsis oblata negligamus, demus iustas ignaviae nostrae poenas. At vero, ne quis hominem valde beatum putet, quum sub elementis huius mundi tanta veritatis comprehendendae energia illi conceditur; simul addendum est, totam istam, et intelligendi vim, et intelligentiam quae inde consequitur, rem esse fluxam et evanidum coram Deo, ubi non subest solidum veritatis fundamentum"; II, ii, 16.

36. Breen makes much of the positive aspects of Calvin's doctrine of "common grace" as a bond linking him to the humanists (*op. cit.*, 159). He does, however, subject secular capacities to providence and makes it a pious duty to cultivate them. I have analyzed the prevalence of a pessimistic note in some of the humanists in my *Adversity's Noblemen* (New York, 1940) and have emphasized a similar concern about the relation of vocation to happiness in "Petrarch's Views of the Individual and His Society," *Osiris,* XI (1954), 168–98. Wendel indicates that one of Calvin's purposes in depicting the capacities and insights of the impious was to prove that men were without excuse for their sins, since they had a knowledge of good and evil (*op. cit.*, 155).

37. *Op. cit.*, 454–55.

38. *Ibid.*, 463–65.

PART THREE

Renaissance Philosophy of Man

The Renaissance Idea of the
Dignity of Man

The dignity of man attained its greatest prominence and was given its characteristic meaning in the Italian Renaissance. As an idea it is usually ill-defined and tends to express a complex of notions, classical and Christian, which writers of the period desired to assert. The word *dignitas* is a Latin rhetorical and political term indicating either the possession of high political or social rank or the moral qualities associated with it. It is used with great frequency by Cicero who begins to give it some of the connotations of general worthiness it acquired during the Renaissance. It is derived from the same root as *decus* and *decorum* (Sanskrit *dac-as*, "fame"). Cicero discusses dignity as the quality of masculine beauty as a subtopic to the fourth, but most emphasized, virtue to be sought by man, *decorum*, or propriety, which he derives from Panaetius' concept, *to prepon* (*De officiis*, I. 27, 36). In the course of this discussion Cicero applies the term "dignity" to the human race, as that quality which distinguishes it from animals (ibid., I. 30):

> But in every investigation into the nature of duty, it is vitally necessary for us to remember always how vastly superior is man's nature to that of cattle and other animals: their only thought is for bodily satisfactions. . . . Man's mind on the contrary, is developed by study and reflection. . . . From this we may learn that sensual pleasure is wholly unworthy of the *dignity of the human race* (emphasis added).

Passages such as this were well known to the Italian humanists, and following Cicero's precedent, they were able to identify the dignity of man with *humanitas* itself, the quality of being most truly human which was to be acquired through the study of the liberal arts—the *studia humanitatis*, from which they derived their name. The notion of the dignity of man is thus in its origins linked with the Petrarchan ideal of the *viri illustres* stressing high civic or military achievement to be attained through emulation of Roman heroes, i.e., with the pursuit of glory or fame.

This article was written for the *Dictionary of the History of Ideas*, vol. 4 (New York: Charles Scribner's Sons, 1973), 136–47. A summary of my previous studies on the Renaissance philosophy of man, it seemed a fitting introduction to the more exploratory papers which comprise part three.

Moreover, Renaissance humanists found in Cicero another even more precise depiction of the excellence of the human species, and this one also derived from Stoic-Middle Platonist Greek sources, most likely Posidonius. After discussing the rationality, design, and providential character of the cosmos as a whole and its inanimate and animate parts, the Stoic, "Balbus," presents his arguments "that the human race has been the especial beneficiary of the immortal gods" (*De natura deorum* II, 54–66). Man excels in the intricacy and functional aptness of his organs and physiology, in his erect posture from which he contemplates the heavens, in the acuteness of his senses, in his mind and intellect, in his gift of speech, in the pliancy and ingenuity of his hands with which he creates the works of civilization, has dominion over the earth, and sets about "the fashioning of another world, as it were, within the bounds and precincts of the one we have." And all of this is the outcome of a general providence with which divinity looks after the human race and of a special concern for individuals who are even assigned particular gods as their guardians.

This analysis of the excellence of man, as presented by Cicero, may be regarded as the most fully developed classical laudation of the dignity of man that has survived, and as representative of Greek rationalism and optimism at its peak. Whether it is a direct transposition of the ideas of Posidonius or a Ciceronian synthesis of other sources, it was to have a direct and powerful influence on Renaissance humanist treatises on the dignity of man. But long before this happened, in antiquity, this cluster of ideas was blended with biblical conceptions of the nature and role of man in the universe within the history of the Judeo-Christian tradition. From the combination of these two traditions the Renaissance idea of the dignity of man specifically developed.

The critical text was Genesis 1:26, "And God said, Let us make man in our image, after our likeness . . . ," supplemented by 1:28, "And God blessed them, and God said unto them, Be fruitful, and multiply, and replenish the earth, and subdue it: and have dominion over the fish of the sea, and the fowl of the air, and over every living thing that moveth upon the earth."

The critical exegesis was that of Philo Judaeus. His first-century Hellenistic Greek synthesis of the Old Testament and the current tendencies in classical thought blending Stoicism, Platonism, and Peripateticism seems indeed to have anticipated important elements of later pagan Neo-Platonism, and even certain aspects of the Hermetic myths of man and the creation. Unquestionably, and more importantly for our subject, it had a strong influence in shaping the analogous efforts of Alexandrian Christian thinkers of the second and third century to integrate acceptable elements of classical thought with their scriptural faith.

In his commentary on Genesis, *The Mosaic Creation Story* (*De opificio mundi*), Philo stresses that the divine image in man is the mind. Molded after the archetype of the Mind of the universe, the human mind is like a god in man. Man was created by God for the double purpose of utilizing the universe and contemplating its maker; therefore, it was necessary that the rest of the universe be already created and that man be made on the sixth day. God "desired that on coming into the world man might at once find both a banquet and a most sacred display. . . ." Since man's mind was created out of divine breath and man's body from clay, "man is the border-land between mortal and immortal nature . . . ," an idea repeated both by ancient and Renaissance Neo-Platonists.

The principal contributions of the Greek Fathers to the development of this theme were made by Clement of Alexandria and Origen in proximate dependence on Philo, and by Basil and Gregory of Nyssa in less direct dependence on him. Although important variations were present among them, all four were heavily influenced by Platonism. A central emphasis was on man's "similitude" to God, which in the Greek word of the Septuagint, *homoiosis,* connoted the dynamic process of becoming like God, or Platonic "assimilation." Man's creation in the divine "image" indicated his original state of perfection, whereas, after the Fall, man was involved, through the Incarnation, in a process of movement toward a restoration of the "image" in a heavenly state, finally fulfilling man's creation in the image and likeness of God. This process was a *mimesis* of God or of Christ. Regarding the soul as a "mirror," Gregory of Nyssa teaches that by "seeing" and "knowing" God in one's self, by assimilation, man becomes like God, *theopoiesis* or *theosis,* moving from *homoiosis* or *praxis* of virtue and purification to *theoria* or *gnosis* in an infinite mystical progression.

Gregory of Nyssa's most specific treatment of the status of man was his *De opificio hominis* (*On the Creation of Man*), extending his brother Basil's uncompleted commentary on the creation, his *Hexaemeron,* to the divine work of the sixth day. Gregory's treatise was translated into Latin in the late fifth century by Dionysius Exiguus and again by Scotus Erigena in the ninth, and thus was available in the Latin West as a model for successive schools of Christian Platonism.

Somewhat out of the main line of Greek development, but also influential in the West through eleventh- and twelfth-century translations by Alfanus and by Burgundio of Pisa, was the late fourth-century treatise of Nemesius of Emesa, *De natura hominis,* ordinarily confused by Latin copyists with the treatise of Gregory just mentioned. Man, in his own person, joins mortals with immortals, rational beings with irrational; as a microcosm (*mikros kosmos*) he reflects the whole creation; by divine providence all creatures have their being for him; for man's sake God became man so that man might reign on high being made in the image and likeness of God:

"how can we exaggerate the dignity of his place in the creation?" Echoing Sophocles' *Antigone,* Nemesius proclaims:

> Man crosses the mighty deep, contemplates the range of the heavens, notes the motion, position, and size of the stars, and reaps a harvest from both land and sea, learns all kinds of knowledge, gains skill in arts, pursues scientific inquiry. . . . He gives order to creation. Devils are subject to him. He explores the nature of every kind of being. He busies himself with the knowing of God and is God's house and temple (*De natura hominis,* trans. W. Telfer, Library of Christian Classics, Philadelphia [1955], IV, 254–55).

Stressing man's this-worldly role and powers, as well as his eschatological ends, drawing on a wider range of classical sources than Gregory, and certainly dependent on the Stoic tradition associated with Posidonius, and on Galen and the Peripatetics, Nemesius was a rich source of both classical and Christian ideas about the nature of man. His treatise was available and used by twelfth- and thirteenth-century theologians. In its emphasis on both the sacred and secular goals of man, it clearly anticipates the Renaissance conception of the dignity of man. It enjoyed sufficient prestige to be included in the library prepared for Federigo, Duke of Urbino (Bibliotheca Vaticana, Codex Urbinatus latinus 485), and among the Greek manuscripts assembled by Giannozzo Manetti (Palatinus graecus 385), himself a principal author of the genre among the Italian humanists. An even more popular and widely diffused Greek patristic work in Latin translation in the Western Middle Ages and Renaissance contained generous excerpts from that of Nemesius, John Damascene's *De orthodoxa fide.* Thus there was no lack of texts offering models of the Greek Fathers' synthesis of Platonic and Stoic conceptions of the key position of man in the universe with the biblical and Christian visions of man's dignity based on his Creation and on the Incarnation.

It was, however, the teachings of the Latin Fathers which, through the depth of their influence within the Western theological tradition and through the constant availability of texts, contributed in the most formative way to the development of the Renaissance idea of the dignity of man. The great and dominating figure was, of course, Augustine of Hippo. But prior to Saint Augustine significant differences from the strongly established Greek theological tradition became apparent in the works of Tertullian, Arnobius, Lactantius, and Ambrose. Greek patristic thought in its dependence on Platonism tended to regard the creation in emanationist terms, so that in a sense the presence of the divine image in man was an estrangement of the divine nature; the reformation of man toward his divine origins, after the Fall, through incarnational grace, was a return to an original perfection. Latin patristic thought placed greater stress on *creatio ex nihilo,* where even the unformed matter of corporeality and earth had a value in a divine order, and the justification of man through the atonement meant a *reformatio in meliore.* In place of a cyclical "renewal" ideology, the germs of a notion of eschatological and even historical progress were present. Perhaps these differences were due to the circumstances that Western theologians tended to be jurists and rhetoricians rather than philosophers, as such more influenced by Stoic notions of an immanent justice and order in human affairs, and more oriented toward "action" as a fulfillment of ideals rather than contemplation or mysticism as a release from and transcendence of material chaos. Even though strongly Platonist elements were present in Cicero's eclectic adaptation of Greek philosophy to rhetorical uses, it may well be argued that Western Church Fathers tended to be "Ciceronian" rather than "Platonist" in the classical influences operating upon them.

For Augustine the notion of man's creation in the "image" of God was far more crucial than his "similitude" to his Maker, which was a quality of an image. Whereas creation according to an "image" was a directly purposive act that established a specific relationship between creator and creature, "similitude" signified a formal relationship only, which of course could increase with a man's progress toward his ultimate fruition. Two works of Augustine were central in establishing the tradition of Western thought concerning the nature and dignity of man as a consequence of the character of his creation in the "image" of God. His *De Genesi ad litteram* is a carefully analytical exegetic work that provided answers for most of the thorny questions raised by the complicated language of Genesis as well as by the twofold account of man's creation. Subsequent medieval exegetes relied heavily upon it; it was a major authority for Peter Lombard's *Sententia,* for example. In his work Augustine interprets the use of the plural in "Let *us* make man in *our* image . . ." as indicating that the entire Trinity participated in man's creation, a thought that was seized upon later as further evidence of the great honor paid man by his Maker. The Fall was interpreted as seriously and severely corrupting the "image" of God in man but not entirely obliterating it, whereas man's similitude, which lay in his capacity to perform virtues, was entirely lost until restored by the divine grace of the Atonement.

A deeper and more significant influence came from Augustine's *De Trinitate,* a work which not only sought to establish the nature of the divine Trinity but also examined all of the creaturely trinities to be found in the *vestigia* of divinity immanent in the creation. Chief among these was the trinity in man. Augustine saw a correspondence between Father, Son, and Spirit and the divine mind or memory, the divine intellect, and the divine will or love. In the most particular sense man's possession of the image of

God meant that his soul also was triune in the simultaneous and inseparable possession of these three faculties.

Although man with his trinitarian soul was a spiritual being (as were also God and the angels), it is significant that Augustine gave full and equal value to the affects and passions of the will, along with memory and intellect. Intellect and will were regarded as equally imbued with goodness or subject to sin, depending on the direction of their exercise, good if directed toward divinity, the creative power of the universe, defective and thus evil if turned away. In this respect Augustine and the Western theological anthropology influenced by him were closer to the Latin rhetorical tradition than to Hellenistic intellectualism and mysticism. Moreover, though not denying the existence, need, and value of mysticism and contemplation, there is an inherent stress on dynamic action in which the human will acts co-efficiently with divine grace.

Augustine managed to avoid the opposite dangers of gnostic dualism and Pelagianism by this conception. Moreover, his view of the body and of matter accepts their full validity in their properly subordinated role within the totality of the divinely sanctified creation. Thus he regarded both an unformed spirit and body as present in the initial creation of man in God's image and likeness, which, possessing *rationes seminales,* are given their form in man's second creation out of clay and divine breath. It is in the discovery of the beauty of form and the vestiges of divinity even in corporeal things that man in his terrestrial existence is drawn toward the Creator, but for this he needs the illumination of grace. Thus while an authentic structure of Neo-Platonism is at the core of Augustine's thought, derived from the influence of Victorinus and Ambrose, and from his direct reading of the Platonists, this structure was significantly modified in a way that differed from the Christian Platonism of the Greek Fathers and which can be regarded as coming from his familiarity with the attitudes of Roman Stoicism embodied in the rhetorical tradition, above all those of Cicero.

Other classical ideas concerning the nature and cosmic role and destiny of man were transmitted to the Latin West (as well as to Byzantine East, medieval Judaism, and, soon, the Arab world). Works such as Boethius' *Consolation of Philosophy,* Macrobius' *Saturnalia,* and especially his *Commentary on the Dream of Scipio* (an excerpt from Cicero's *De republica*) were late classical compilations containing a mélange of ancient notions on creation, the eternity of the world, the place of man, his goals, and destiny that fed into and influenced medieval as well as Renaissance ideas. Strikingly important among these sources for future attempts to look at the dignity of man's creation, nature, redemption, and even deification were the legendary writings of Hermes Trismegistus, regarded as an Egyptian prophet-sage of equal sanctity with the sybils as early as Lactantius. These writings, dating from the first to the third centuries A.D., were broadly concerned with the role of man in the universe in relation to the Great God and to the lesser gods; mythological in mode of presentation, they purported to be early revelations of Hermes, a supposed contemporary of Moses.

The corpus in large extent survived in the Greek East. In the West a translation of a portion of it known as *Aesculapius* and attributed to Apuleius circulated as early as the time of Augustine who quotes it extensively in book eight of *The City of God*. A number of passages attributing divine powers and a destiny of deification to man were frequently cited by medieval discussants of the theme of the dignity of man as well as by such Renaissance luminaries as Ficino and Pico della Mirandola who begins his famous oration with the quotation "A great miracle, Aesculapius, is man."

Other later classical works and translations of a Neo-Platonic provenance also entered into the body of writings associated with discussions of our theme. A work attributed also to the same Apuleius, *On the God of Socrates,* and Chalcidius' partial translation and commentary on Plato's *Timaeus* were among the few available Platonic writings in the Latin West.

The problem of the theme of the dignity of man in the Latin Middle Ages is complex and by no means adequately investigated. Certain major tendencies or occasions for discussing it may be distinguished as well as certain chronological phases which did not necessarily influence succeeding ones in a developmental way. The first of four tendencies or occasions lay in the continuing efforts at exegesis of Genesis and the compilation of works entitled *Hexaemeron* or *On the Six Days' Work*. Here Augustine's interpretations from the *De Genesi ad litteram* were formative. Medieval hexameral literature is extensive and by no means sufficiently studied, though an obvious means of tracing the history of cosmological, physical, and anthropological ideas. One may mention Bede's, Abelard's, Thierry of Chartres', and Robert Grosseteste's versions, all of which were influential. Works of this nature were not confined to a single line of interpretation but reflected the controversies and movements of their particular ages.

A second type of speculation that gave rise to discussions of man's dignity and place in the cosmos were the efforts to construct a Platonic-Christian theology utilizing essentially Greek patristic and non-Christian Neo-Platonic sources rather than Augustine's precedents and version of Neo-Platonism. Unquestionably the most important figure among those engaged in efforts of this type was the ninth-century theologian Scotus Erigena. His own work *De divisione naturae* was an original Christian Platonist theology which placed man centrally in the cosmic hierarchy as a link between the spiritual and corporeal worlds. Moreover, he added to the sources of Christian Platonism available in the West by his translation of Gregory of Nyssa's *De opificio hominis* referred to above, and, most significantly, of the writings of the fifth-century Greek theologian who is known as (Pseudo-) Dionysius the Areopagite. These, with their emphasis on a celestial and an ecclesiastical hierarchy mirroring the former, on the epistemological difficulties of passing from the uncertainties of human knowledge of visibles to a knowledge of divine invisibles, had a wide and varied influence not only on the three major phases of a revival of Christian Platonism, the Carolingian, the Chartrain, and the Florentine, but also on the Christian Aristotelianism of the scholastic period. These latter thinkers found a certain parallel between the Christian Platonist hierarchical thinking of the Pseudo-Dionysius and the concern with hierarchy among the Arabic commentators, both the Neo-Platonic and their Aristotelian opponents. But in all these instances the question of the place of man in the chain of being became crucial.

Twelfth-Century Chartrain Platonism was indebted to Scotus Erigena both for his own writings and his translations. More important were the number of attempted new syntheses of Platonism and Christianity, returning again, on the model of the Greek Fathers, to the problem of man as an image of the divine engaged in a process of assimilation in the recovery of the lost glory of his creation and in a progress toward a new, higher sanctification through the Incarnation and the Atonement. Among the twelfth-century Platonists who discussed man as both a microcosm and a being able to ascend to the divine or descend to the brute were Bernard Silvester in his *Cosmographia*, Alain of Lille in his *De planctu naturae*, Thierry of Chartres in his *De sex dierum operibus*, William of Conches in his *Philosophia* and his commentaries on the *Timaeus* and on Boethius. Outside of the more strictly Neo-Platonic circles the theme of man's creation in the divine image and likeness, his fall and the recovery of the divine image through the incarnate Christ found expression in the writings of such diverse figures as Honorius of Autun, Peter Abelard, William of St. Thierry, Hugh of St. Victor, and most importantly Peter Lombard who attempts a systematization of earlier, chiefly Augustinian, Christian thought on the meaning and dignity of man's creation.

A third thematic direction became manifest in the late twelfth and early thirteenth centuries. As early as Lactantius' fourth-century laudation of man in his *Divine Institutes* and *God's Creation*, an opposing genre to the dignity of man, namely, the topic of "the misery of the human condition" was to be found in Arnobius' *Contra nationes*, and Lactantius' work seems to have been a direct refutation. In both Arnobius and Lactantius theme and counter-theme are arrayed against each other. When at the end of the twelfth century the deacon, Lotario de' Conti, the future Pope Innocent III, wrote his famous *De contemptu mundi, seu de miseria humanae conditionis libri tres*, he also promised, but failed, to write a companion treatise on the dignity of man. By this time these two themes had become recognized literary genres. Earlier in the century a Cistercian follower of Saint Bernard of Clairvaux, Alcherus of Clairvaux, had written a treatise, *De spiritu et anima,* and had entitled the thirty-fifth chapter, *De dignitate humanae conditionis;* the work as a whole was a miscellaneous compilation of quotations on the soul, and this chapter repeats the theme of the nobility of man's creation. The chapter in question itself closely paralleled a little work attributed to Ambrose (but more likely Alcuin's) of the same title.

A fourth aspect of the medieval consideration of the dignity of man comes with the development of scholasticism and the preponderant influence of Aristotelian and metaphysical modes of speculation in the thirteenth century. Even though there remain certain influences of the earlier Augustinian and Neo-Platonic interpretations, even though the same critical sources are known and quoted by the scholastics, a major new emphasis, even among the anti-Aristotelians, is placed on a more naturalistic treatment of the nature and powers of man, directly dependent upon Aristotle's *De anima.* Along with the formal consideration of the nature and powers of the different parts of the soul, there remains some concern with man's position in the universe, but this is regarded essentially in static, hieratic terms rather than as a dynamic, operative potential for restoration of the divine image, or for irremediable bestialization. While it would be ridiculous to argue that there was a decline in concern for the pastoral and homiletic role of theology in the cure of souls, the impetus toward discovering a philosophic, metaphysical, or scientific basis for the Christian vision of the world was so powerful as to all but overshadow the more traditional emphasis.

Typically the dignity of man was discussed in the many commentaries on the *Sentences* of Peter Lombard, not at Book I, Distinction II, Question VII, "In what way is the image of the Trinity in the soul?," the traditional Augustinian occasion for stressing man's dignity, but at Book II, Distinctions XVI and XVII, "On the creation of man," and "On the creation of the soul," where the question is typically raised of whether the dignity of man, or the image of God in man, is more excellent than in the angel. The answers vary with subtlety.

Thomas Aquinas may be cited as one out of many discussions:

> . . . properly and principally the image follows the intellectual nature; . . . where the intellectual nature is more perfect, there the image is more express, and thus, since the intellectual nature is of far greater dignity in angels than in man, . . . it is necessary that the image of God is more express in angels than in the soul. . . . The image of God is also assigned to man, but not so properly, with reference to certain subsequent properties, such as that man dominates the inferior creatures . . . and according to this and other conditions of this sort, nothing prevents man from being more in the image of

God than the angel. But this is relatively [*secundum quid*] and not absolutely because the judgment of similitude and diversity which is assumed from the essentials of a thing is much more firm (*Commentum in quattuor libros sententiarum*, Lib. II, D. XVI, Q. I, art. iii, Parma [1856], I, 526; passage translated by Charles Trinkaus).

Nominalist theology in the fourteenth and fifteenth centuries, in keeping with its premisses, was skeptical of such discussions. Gabriel Biel, for example, in his commentary on the *Sentences,* avers: "Properly speaking no creature is a vestige of the Trinity but only improperly, metaphorically, or by assumption because it accords with a corporeal vestige in many things."

While the theme of the dignity of man had a variegated history in classical and Christian antiquity and in the Latin Middle Ages, it had not been developed into either a clearly defined literary form or an internally consistent set of ideas.

There were, on the other hand, certain elements in the history and culture of the Renaissance which favored its development into a definitive literary and philosophical genre. One such element, certainly, was the humanist movement, which in its commitment to a revival of classical motifs in literature (rhetoric and poetry) and classical attitudes in history and moral philosophy was eager to demonstrate its equally strong conviction that antique rhetoric, poetry, history, and philosophy were not in conflict with Christianity but could actually strengthen religion. The available theme of the dignity of man, a genuine blend of classical and Christian ideas and topics in its inherited forms, fitted perfectly this requirement.

In the second place the very notion of "dignity" involved the question of relative status, as its medieval comparison of man and angel had shown; it thus fitted with equal ease into the spread of a rhetorical outlook through the influence of humanism in which the function of the arts is seen to be to praise or blame, the encomium and the diatribe, and to establish the place of the individual in the eyes of contemporaries, posterity, and ultimately eternity by this means.

In a moral order guided by rhetoric there is, moreover, an emphasis on individual achievement in action as well as on inner moral worth as manifested outwardly by virtue. Whether the so-called individualism of the Renaissance was the cause or the consequence of the rhetorical outlook, there can be no doubt of its existence, and this also, with its stress on freedom of choice, was to find appropriate expression in the theme of the dignity of man.

Finally, it may be argued, there was an inherent tension between the increasing secularism manifested in the expanding economic, political, and social activities of late medieval Europe and those elements of medieval Christianity which stressed asceticism, withdrawal, contemplation, poverty, humility, the anguish, misery, and worthlessness of *homo viator,* earthly man. There was no such tension between these new manifestations of the historical dynamism of human energy and the equally Christian vision of the dignity and excellence of man. This theme must therefore be considered as a deeply formative pattern of Renaissance thought and expression through its capacity to offer a resolution of this tension.

The Trecento Italian humanist and poet, Francesco Petrarca, was the first Renaissance figure to write on this theme, and his circumstances and motivation are revealing. He was perennially concerned with the troubled consciousness and consciences of his own age, its formlessness, its lack of depth of Christian commitment, its morally and spiritually ruinous materialism, its need for a sense of historical direction, its emotional volatility, its shallow and shortsighted vanity, and its intense personal and religious despair. More significantly, he also felt that he knew where the remedy lay, or at least the direction in which it could be sought.

A work of his old age, *On His Own Ignorance and that of Many Others,* was a diatribe against the preoccupation of the established intellectuals of his day with Aristotelian natural philosophy. He was not so much opposed to Aristotle as to the unrelatedness of his study to the moral and spiritual anguish of his contemporaries. By this he aligned himself against both the physicians and other lay intellectuals of the university arts faculties and against the scholastic theologians for this remoteness from the pastoral role of the clergy. He cast himself into the new role of a lay moral counselor to his contemporaries and called on others to adopt this role as well, offering as models Seneca, Cicero, Livy, Vergil, and Horace, who as Roman moral philosophers, rhetoricians, historians, and poets had cast themselves into similar roles. He sought to emulate the work of these figures in his own writings. His numerous letters to contemporaries are full of moral counsel. His major historical work *De viris illustribus* offered the lives of great Roman statesmen as examples of men of dignity to be emulated for their moral virtues by his contemporaries. His epic poem, *Africa,* was to offer Scipio Africanus as a new Roman-Italian culture-hero.

In turning to the pagan Romans as models of the utilization of culture for moral elevation, Petrarch had no confusion (despite many scholars' perplexity over his seeming ambiguity) about the fundamentally Christian character of his enterprise. Petrarch was deeply Christian and deeply religious. He was quite clear and quite aware that these classical authors were not. An even more compelling and admired mentor was Saint Augustine who had found for himself and offered to the world a way of reconciling the Christian revelation with those values of the ancients which were culturally, morally, and politically necessary for responsible life in the chaotic historical and natural world. In his *Secret Conflict of My Cares,* Petrarch portrays himself, for the benefit of his contemporaries, as experiencing a similar conflict to that resolved by Augustine in his *Confessions*. The resolution lay, he thought, in a religious renewal of faith and a trust in salvation by grace that could overcome the prevailing self-doubt and despair—and this should be combined with a secular renewal of self-confidence in man's ability to perform morally and socially worthy actions as exemplified by the sense of civic responsibility of the virtuous pagans. To stand firm and virtuous in the midst of the blows of Fortune was more than to achieve individual security or material success. It meant the restoration of man's inner spiritual dignity without which he would sink into and become part of the chaotic morass of sin and disorder that were the conditions of earthly existence. It meant the retention of a spiritual self-confidence that was identical with a confidence in the ever-available, divine mercy of the Creator. The great perils in the life of man, which endangered him in this world and the next, were the superficial elation of *superbia,* when by whatever accident Fortune favored him, and the ruinous desperation of *accidia* and *dolor,* when Fortune frowned. It was essential for man to know his true condition and his true worth.

Such were the motivations that led him to seize upon the fragmentary elements of the theme of the dignity of man that were present in the medieval and classical sources known to him and to give them a literary formulation that anticipated the Renaissance development of this theme in its central aspects if it did not necessarily serve as its specific model. Appropriately, his treatise on the dignity of man occurred as a chapter in his most popular work, *The Remedies of Both Kinds of Fortune* (II, 93, *De tristitia et miseria*).

Later humanist and Platonist discussions of the dignity of man were more extensive and elaborate, involving more complex theological and philosophical concepts. Through all their variations, however, the two basic arguments presented by Petrarch with rhetorical succinctness remained fundamentals. Theologically and philosophically, man's dignity derived from the character and purpose of his creation and the resulting position and role this gave man in the universe, from the freedom and the capacity to ascend toward the divine, conditions inherent in the image of God in which he was created and restored to man in the Incarnation. Historically and existentially, man's dignity derived from his individual and collective actions and creations in this world from which came his earthly fame and greatness, tokens of the individual's contributions to the high cultures and civilizations mankind invented and constructed.

The writings of two Italian humanists on the nature and powers of man and his goals and place in the universe were particularly critical in preparing the way for the further development and a more general acceptance and explicit expression of the theme of the dignity of man when it was resumed some eight decades after Petrarch in the mid-Quattrocento. Coluccio Salutati's *De fato et fortuna* of the 1390's sought a reconciliation of the Stoic philosophy of the relationship of the individual and "providence" with the contemporary Christian discussions of the theme. It was again the ideas of Augustine that gave him his cue. As did Petrarch and many other humanists, Salutati affirmed the primacy of the will, and found the basic creative force in the universe to be divine providence as the manifestation of divine will. Within it and in fulfillment of it human will acted creatively in organizing the affairs of men in this world, and by the very definition of will had to be free. Yet it was totally in harmony with divine providence. Through being voluntarily operative in the world, man expressed his condition of having been created in the image of God.

Man would seek worthy ends both for this life and the next and would manifest his active, providential, voluntarist nature as the image of God, but he would also accept the limitation of being God-like but not God, Himself. In the ultimate deification of heavenly fruition, however, he would attain the full realization of his dignity which he could only partially attain in this life in emulation of God and fulfillment of his role as an image of God.

Although, for both Petrarch and Salutati, salvation was a matter of supernatural grace whose actuality man should fully accept to avoid the catastrophe of despair and willful defection from his nature, men were susceptible to rhetorical inducements to rational behavior and could be moved to love and dignity by the incitements of their wills. For both humanists the Roman Stoicism of Cicero and Seneca had shown the way, though ignorance of Christ had left them blind to the true faith.

Lorenzo Valla, on the other hand, found in Augustine certain eudaimonistic elements which he transformed into a Christianized Epicureanism and into a rhetorical theology that was radically voluntaristic and even erotic in its basic conception of human nature. Man, in the image and likeness of God, was a trinitarian spirit or soul, a single substance with the three qualities of energy, intellect, emotion. Energy and emotion, weak or strong, guided the intellect in its determinations, used it as an instrument of their purposes, distorted it out of extremes of cowardice or rage. Thus man acted upon the world in pursuit of his pleasures, in fulfillment of the urges of his passions and his love. If he possessed faith and the hope of heavenly fulfillment, the divine pleasures of fruition and the love of God for the sake of the loving, not for His own sake, were his goals. If, as after the Fall, and before the Advent, man had no knowledge of the Christian promises, or other more powerful allures weakened or suppressed his faith in them, he became pleasure-seeking and utilitarian in his instrumental use of the things of this world for gratification. Valla was a striking apostle and advocate of the power of man, when armed with faith, to transcend all the basically animal-like qualities of his nature and to rise to the semi-divine.

He laid great stress upon action, passionate and providential, in which man not only emulated God but fulfilled his nature and dignity as the divine image and likeness.

The most precise and straightforward statement of these views of human nature is contained in the first book of Valla's *Dialectical Disputations* (in its first redaction called *Repastinatio dialecticae et philosophiae*). On the other hand, he defended Epicureanism obliquely in his *On True Good* (*De vero bono,* or *De voluptate* in its first version). In dialogue form he presents first a Stoic's complaint of the ills of life to be remedied by virtue, then an Epicurean's refutation of virtue as an end and his praise of pleasure, and finally a Christian's defense of heavenly pleasure as the true good of man. The first version was written by 1432 and the third and final one by 1442. In 1445 or 1446 Bartolomeo Facio wrote *On the Happiness of Life* (*De vitae felicitate*) as a hostile imitation of Valla, defending Stoicism and refuting Epicureanism but setting man's true good in a Christian-Stoic vision of true happiness as residing in the restoration of man's immortal soul to its heavenly place of origin after a life of virtuous restraint among the miseries of this life.

Discussions such as these of man's happiness and true good, as also those on free will and fate and fortune, were centrally concerned with the problem of the nature and status of man in the cosmos and in this life, and they led straight into the renewed treatment of the theme of the dignity of man. In 1447 the same Bartolomeo Facio was sent an outline of a treatise on the dignity of man composed by an Olivetan monk, Antonia da Barga (*Libellus de dignitate et excellentia humanae vitae*). Da Barga urged Facio to take this treatise and add the polish and elegance a humanist could give it, and thus produce the treatise on the dignity of man that Innocent III had promised and never completed. Facio did so, and his *On the Excellence of Man* (*De excellentia hominis*) appeared in 1448, dedicated to Pope Nicholas V, but making no mention of Antonio da Barga. Facio's treatise follows da Barga's quite closely, introducing, however, some amplifications and variants, some of which were borrowed from his own *De vitae felicitate*.

Facio's was promptly followed by Giannozzo Manetti's much more elaborate, erudite, and laudatory treatise, *On the Dignity and Excellence of Man* (*De dignitate et excellentia hominis libri IV*). Manetti was apparently prompted by King Alfonso of Naples to write the treatise because Facio had dedicated his to Pope Nicholas V, and it was completed by late 1452 or early the next year in the version in which we have received it in manuscript. However, the same Antonio da Barga mentions in another work of his of 1449 that Manetti had written a work *De dignitate hominis ad Anthonium Bargensem*. Thus da Barga, who was certainly a friend of Manetti, may also have urged him to write a now-lost earlier version.

Manetti retains all of the traditional religious arguments for man's dignity to which he adds any that he can draw from classical sources such as Cicero, *On the Nature of the Gods,* Aristotle's *De anima* and *Ethics.* Moreover, he makes a number of assertions that are quite clearly original. However, as in his other writings, he tries to mask his own originality behind lengthy citations. He also utilizes a far wider range of sources than he admits to or cites directly, sources which he possessed in his extensive library of Latin, Greek, and Hebrew philosophical, theological, and exegetical works which he read in all three languages. His background as a Florentine merchant, statesman, civic-humanist, pupil, and follower of Ambrogio Traversari (followed later after the composition of this work by his role as advisor to both Nicholas V and King Alfonso) undoubtedly helped to influence the much more appreciative view of man's this-worldly dignity and achievements which he incorporated into his theological conception of the dignity of man. There is no question that Manetti made explicit the new conception of man, which was already implicit in Petrarch, Salutati, and Valla and which was supportable from both Greek and Latin classical and patristic texts. Manetti, of course, sought to project a new Christian synthesis of these sources, and this determined the form of his work.

Manetti's was not a profound work, but it was an insistent and an impressive one for the completeness of its arguments on behalf of the dignity of man and for the fullness and almost lack of restraint in their assertion. It was significant also as indicating that the cultural environment, within which the Platonists' views of the dignity of man were shortly to follow, was already highly receptive to their ideas. Other important humanist defenses of human greatness and progress were also being produced, such as the Bolognese humanist Benedetto Morandi's defense of man against Giovanni Garzoni's repetition of the traditional view of human misery (in two works of 1468–70, *De humana felicitate* and *Secunda reluctatio contra calumniatorem naturae humanae*) of especial interest because of Morandi's clear projection of the doctrine of progress under human guidance. Another important defense of man came in the 1480's by Aurelio Brandolini, an Italian humanist at the court of Matthias Corvinus of Hungary (*Dialogus de humanae vitae conditione et toleranda corporis aegritudine*).

The theme of the dignity of man, which had thus been given a definite literary form by the Italian humanists, derived from and contained within itself two divergent theological and philosophical positions. Man's dignity lay in his creation in the image and likeness of God, which could be interpreted as meaning either that it was man's destiny to transcend the limitations of his image-likeness and to ascend to eventual deification by a progress toward perfect assimilation of image and model, or that man thought, felt, and acted in a godlike manner in his domination, utilization, guidance, and reconstruction of the world of sub-human nature. The first position was both Neo-Platonist and Greek patristic in its provenance, the second was more closely related to a loose syncretism of Stoicism and Middle Platonism best expressed in Roman rhetorical philosophizing but which also could find some confirmation in a literal interpretation of certain biblical passages.

The Italian humanist movement found it natural to juxtapose the two positions contained in the traditional treatments of the theme without necessarily providing any logical or systematic reconciliation, and in fact Augustine had wrought a theologically more integrated reconciliation of the transcendental and immanent elements in the theme which was a precedent and a model for the humanists. This humanist juxtaposition or merely rhetorical reconciliation was of great historical significance for it provided a system of thinking whereby sanction and justification could be offered to a life of activism and worldly achievement which was at the same time incorporated into traditional religious values and goals. The humanists, prompted by the needs of their contemporaries sought and devised a way to make the best of both worlds, as it were.

It was however, the revival of Platonism, which occurred in Florence in the '70's, '80's, and '90's of the Quattrocento and was widely disseminated from there, that provided a philosophical and systematic integration of these two motifs involved in the consideration of the dignity of man. The principal author of this new synthesis, which indeed pulled together disparate elements within the biblical-Christian tradition as well as within the classical tradition and then sought parallel elements in the two, was Marsilio Ficino. Ficino, who had been set to work as a young man translating the works of Plato by Cosimo de'Medici, did not by any means produce what modern philosophers could recognize as a pure and historically accurate interpretation of Plato in his own philosophical writings. He was, on the contrary, deeply affected by a number of influences operating upon him. One was the tradition of lay piety of which the humanist writings on the dignity of man had been a notable expression and within which Ficino, ordained as a priest in 1473, had always actively participated. Another was the humanist movement, itself, with its zeal for the recovery of classical texts and monuments to which Ficino's many important translations not only of the corpus of Plato but of the principal Neo-Platonic philosophers, the Hermetic *Poimandres,* the *Orphic Hymns,* and the *Chaldaic Oracles* made a major contribution. A third was the Western Latin theological tradition within which Augustine, of course, played a leading role as a model of a Christian Platonist, but which also influenced Ficino through his early scholastic training and subsequent studies, so that he was very well versed in the varying currents of Latin theology. Moreover, though the influence of Aristotle had been dominant in thirteenth-century scholastic theology and continued to be within the Thomist tradition, this was to a high degree permeated with the hierarchical ideas of the Christian Neo-Platonist, the

Pseudo-Dionysius, as well as by those of the Arabic commentators. It was not difficult to "Platonize" what was already so Neo-Platonic.

That these were the dominant movements shaping Ficino's thought is significant because from them the impulse toward a reconciliation of the transcendental and immanentist elements in the theme of the dignity of man could be found, especially in Augustine and the humanists. It is notable that, although he knew of them, Ficino seems not to have been especially influenced by the medieval Neo-Platonism of Chartres or of his near-contemporary Nicholas of Cusa, or by contemporary Byzantine Platonic doctrines such as Plethon's or Bessarion's. What he wrought was an original synthesis of Christianity and ancient Platonism and Neo-Platonism, but one that also definitely reflected the Augustinian departures from Greek patristic thought and the Renaissance humanists' stress on the validity and importance of the this-worldly dignity of man within the framework of his continuous pursuit and ultimate achievement of immortality and deification. But this was a fully articulated and unified philosophy rather than merely rhetorical juxtaposition as in the case of the humanists.

This position was manifested in two aspects of Ficino's thought. One was the stress on the role of reason in man, as a free faculty, not bound into any of the traditional Plotinian determinist systems projected by Ficino—providence to which man was tied by his highest faculty of the intelligence, fate operating through astral influences to which man was tied by his faculty of imagination, and nature which claimed man's senses and corporeality as a part. Thus while man was contained within himself and was dynamically linked to all parts of the universe, was its node and coupling, through reason and the cognate will man could freely favor and resist any of these levels of being. This meant that although man was part of and had a place in the universal hierarchy, he could also transcend it and escape from it and had a more dignified role than any other created being, approaching in freedom and creativity the state of divinity, itself.

The second aspect of Ficino's thought which manifested his position on the dignity of man was his stress on man's natural appetite for immortality and deification. This could be discovered in the character of man's thought and actions which Ficino analyzed systematically into twelve characteristics of God which man was driven by his will to make actual. In delineating man's pursuit of these divine qualities, however, he becomes certainly as eloquent as the humanists, if he does not surpass them, in his depictions of the glories of man's actions and ideas in all areas of this-worldly experience. While it is true that Ficino also emphasizes many magical and supernatural powers, with which he believes man is endowed, this is not at the expense of or in diminution of his deep appreciation of man's secular this-worldly achievements as signs of man's natural appetite to become God.

The entire striving in our soul is that it become God. Such striving is no less natural to men than the effort to flight is to birds. For it is always in men everywhere. Likewise it is not a contingent quality of some men but follows the nature itself of the species (*Theologica Platonica* XIV, 1; ed. Marcel, II, 247).

It may, thus, be argued that Ficino gave philosophical and theological form and system to central attitudes of the Renaissance humanist tradition, particularly to those associated with the theme of the dignity of man. It may also be argued that this emphasis, together with his pursuit of a universal theology and anthropology to be found in all human traditions and religions, pagan and Christian alike, constitute the central themes of his philosophy. Both these themes, the dignity of man in his pursuit of deification, and the universality of all human traditions in this pursuit, were also central to the development of Renaissance culture. Ficino and the Renaissance Platonists, in other words, do not represent a divergence from the major historical impulses of the Renaissance toward a contemplative otherworldliness, as it is frequently claimed, but complete an intellectual response to a basic need for a mode of reconciliation of the expanding secular goals and activities of the men of the period with their still fervently held religious piety and otherworldly ends, a need which found expression and partial fulfillment in the humanist treatises on the dignity of man which preceded and accompanied the Platonist movement.

The best known expression of the Renaissance theme of the dignity of man occurs in Giovanni Pico della Mirandola's *Oration* of 1486, introducing the theses he offered for debate. Although Ficino preceded him in projecting man's transcendence of the hierarchy by a multi-level freedom which determined its being by its operative choice (Ficino's *Theologia Platonica* was published 1482, probably composed by 1474), Pico gave the position a unique dramatic and rhetorical sharpness and clarity, and followed it up by an even wider-ranging pursuit of a universality of human striving for fulfillment in the historical, religious, magical, and intellectual traditions known to him. It is significant that the theme of the dignity of man had been carried since antiquity in the form of an exegesis of Genesis 1:26, for Pico's comments in his *Oration* are applied to Adam and the mode of God's creation of man, and he followed this in 1488–89 with his *Heptaplus*, which is an extension of the traditional *Hexaemeron*, or six days work, to the seventh which includes the divine and human sabbatical. Pico presents a Neo-Platonic cosmology and anthropology in this work, but one that was notably modified by his knowledge of the medieval Jewish magical tradition, itself, containing Neo-Platonic elements, the Cabala. To the three worlds of nature, the planets, and the intelligences, Pico adds the Cabalistic fourth world of man, which is outside the others, yet utilizes them, is their fulfillment. The deification and the dignity of man is central to each of the six days work of creation and is related in the sixth chapter to each of the seven books, for man was created on the sixth day. Thus Pico restores the theme of the dignity of man to the hexameral tradition but renews this exegetical tradition with new Cabalistic, Hermetic, Averroist, and Neo-Platonic ideas.

A final reference may be made to the work of the Augustinian preacher and theologian, Egidio da Viterbo (Giles of Viterbo), general of his order, of great influence in propagating Ficino's Christian Neo-Platonism at the courts of Julius II and Leo X and at the Lateran Council. His commentary on the *Sentences "ad mentem Platonis"* reverts to the scholastic argument as to whether the dignity of man exceeds that of the angel. Egidio without hesitation projects man's dignity as higher not only because of Christ's Incarnation as man, but because of the dynamic freedom of man's striving to become God, which contrasts with the static, hierarchical fixity of the angels' position.

The idea of the dignity of man did not cease to find exponents among both philosophers and writers in the sixteenth and seventeenth centuries in Italy and elsewhere. The influences of both Italian humanism and Florentine Platonism were too potent for these characteristic ideas and forms of discussion of man to be lost. However, its subsequent history is beyond the scope of this article. One observation only may be permitted. Histories of single ideas or clusters of ideas are difficult to delimit because they ordinarily embody entire complexes of notions that are subject to greatly varying interpretations in different philosophical and literary schools and currents. Though the dignity of man was not primarily an Aristotelian idea, it had its Aristotelian supporters, and even such an austere Stoic-Aristotelian as Pietro Pomponazzi felt compelled to polemicize against it. But ultimately more important than its involvement in the debates of Platonists and Aristotelians was to be the impact of the Protestant Reformation and Catholic Reform, on the one hand, and of the emergence of the new science, on the other. Both these sixteenth-century developments were drastically to alter the conception of man and his place in the universe and consequently the entire conception of the dignity of man, though the Renaissance concept of man itself had important implications for both these developments.

BIBLIOGRAPHY

Charles Trinkaus, *"In Our Image and Likeness": Humanity and Divinity in Italian Humanist Thought* (London and Chicago, 1970), for principal texts discussed and bibliography. See also the following works, and especially those by: Cassirer, Garin, Gentile, Javelet, Kristeller, Ladner, Di Napoli, Paparelli, and Yates. Javelet, Ladner (*Idea of Reform*), and Landmann have important bibliographies. Herschel Baker, *The Image of Man: A Study of Human Dignity in Classical Antiquity, the Middle Ages and the Renaissance* (Cambridge, Mass., 1947; reprint New York, 1961). Ernst Cassirer, *Individuum und Kosmos in der Philosophie der Renaissance* (Leipzig and Berlin, 1927; trans. New York, 1964); idem, "Giovanni Pico della Mirandola," *Journal of the History of Ideas,* 3 (1942), 123–44, 319–54; reprinted in P. O. Kristeller and P. P. Wiener, eds., *Renaissance Essays* (New York, 1968), 11–60. Ernst Cassirer, Paul Oskar Kristeller, John Herman Randall, Jr., eds., *The Renaissance Philosophy of Man* (Chicago, 1948). Y. M. J. Congar, "Le thème de Dieu-Créateur et les explications de l'Hexaméron dans la tradition chrétienne," in *L'homme devant Dieu: Mélanges offerts au Père Henri de Lubac* (Paris, 1963), pp. 189ff. B. Domanski, *Die Psychologie des Nemesius,* Baeumker Beiträge, III (Münster, 1900). Ludwig Edelstein, *The Idea of Progress in Classical Antiquity* (Baltimore, 1967); idem, "The Philosophical System of Posidonius," *American Journal of Philology,* 57 (1936), 286–325. A.-J. Festugière, *La révélation d'Hermès Trismégiste,* 4 vols. (Paris, 1950–54). Eugenio Garin, "La 'Dignitas Hominis' e la letteratura patristica," *La Rinascita,* I (1938), 102–46; idem, ed., *Testi umanistici sul "De anima"* (Padua, 1951); idem, *Giovanni Pico della Mirandola* (Florence, 1937). Giovanni Gentile, "Il concetto dell'uomo nel Rinascimento" (1916), reprinted in idem, *Il pensiero italiano del Rinascimento* (Florence, 1940), pp. 47–113. P. Gerlitz, "Der mystische Bildbegriff (εἰκών und imago) in der frühchristlichen Geistesgeschichte," *Zeitschrift für Religions- und Geistesgeschichte,* 15 (1963), 244ff. Karl Gronau, *Poseidonios und die judische-christliche Genesis-exegese* (Leipzig, 1914). J. Gross, *La divinisation du chrétien d'après les pères grecs* (Paris, 1938). Klaus Heitmann, *Fortuna und Virtus, Eine Studie zu Petrarcas Lebensweisheit* (Cologne and Graz, 1958). Werner Jaeger, *Nemesius von Emesa, Quellenforschung zum Neuplatonismus und seinen Anfängen bei Poseidonios* (Berlin, 1914). Robert Javelet, *Image et ressemblance au douzième siècle de saint Anselme à Alain de Lille,* 2 vols. (Strasbourg, 1967). J. Jervell, *Imago Dei: Genesis 1:26 f. im Spätjudentum, in der Gnosis und in den Paulinischen Briefen* (Göttingen, 1960). P. O. Kristeller, "Ficino and Pomponazzi on the Place of Man in the Universe," *Journal of the History of Ideas,* 5 (1944), 220–26, reprinted in *Studies in Renaissance Thought and Letters* (Rome, 1956), pp. 279–86; idem, "The Philosophy of Man in the Italian Renaissance," *Italica,* 24 (1947), 93–112, reprinted in *Studies in Renaissance Thought and Letters,* pp. 261–78; idem, *The Philosophy of Marsilio Ficino* (New York, 1943), Italian trans., *Il pensiero filosofico di Marsilio Ficino* (Florence, 1953). Gerhart B. Ladner, "The Concept of the Image in the Greek Fathers and the Byzantine Iconoclastic Controversy," *Dumbarton Oaks Papers,* 7 (1953), 1 ff.; idem, *Ad imaginem Dei: The Image of Man in Medieval Art* (Latrobe, Pa., 1965); idem, "*Homo Viator:* Medieval Ideas on Alienation and Order," *Speculum,* 42 (1967), 233–59; idem, *Idea of Reform* (Cambridge, Mass., 1959; rev. ed. New York, 1967), Chapters II, V; idem, "The Philosophical Anthropology of St. Gregory of Nyssa," *Dumbarton Oaks Papers,* 12 (1958). Michael Landmann, et al., *DE HOMINE, Der Mensch im Spiegel seines Gedanken* (Freiburg and Munich, 1962). R. Leys, *L'image de Dieu chez Saint Grégoire de Nysse*

(Brussels and Paris, 1951). R. A. Markus, " 'Imago' and 'Similitudo' in Augustine," *Revue des études augustiniennes,* 10 (1964), 125ff. F. Masai, *Pléthon et le platonisme de Mistra* (Paris, 1956). E. Massa, "L'anima e l'uomo in Egidio Viterbo e nelle fonte classiche e medievali," in *Testi umanistici sul 'De anima.'* H. Merki, ΟΜΟΙΩΣΙΣΘΕΩ: *Von der platonischen Angleichen an Gott zur Gottähnlichkeit bei Gregor von Nyssa,* Paradosis VII (Fribourg, Switzerland, 1952). Rodolfo Mondolfo, *La comprensione del soggetto umano nell'antichità classica* (Florence, 1958). J. T. Muckle, "The Doctrine of Gregory of Nyssa on Man as the Image of God," *Mediaeval Studies,* 7 (1945), 55–84. Giovanni di Napoli, " 'Contemptus Mundi' e 'Dignitas Hominis' nel Rinascimento," *Rivista di filosofia neoscolastica,* 48 (1956), 9–41; idem, *L'immortalità dell'anima nel Rinascimento* (Turin, 1963). Gioacchino Paparelli, *Feritas, Humanitas, Divinitas: Le componenti dell'Umanesimo* (Messina and Florence, 1960). F. E. Robbins, *The Hexaemeral Literature: A Study of Greek and Latin Commentaries on Genesis* (Chicago, 1912). A. Struker, *Die Gottesebenbildlichkeit des Menschen in der altchristlichen Literatur der ersten zwei Jahrhunderte* (Münster, 1913). J. E. Sullivan, *The Image of God: The Doctrine of St. Augustine and Its Influence* (Dubuque, Iowa, 1963). R. McL. Wilson, "The Early History of the Exegesis of Genesis 1:26," *Studia Patristica,* 1 (1957), 420ff. Frances Yates, *Giordano Bruno and the Hermetic Tradition* (London and Chicago, 1964; reprint New York, 1969).

Themes for a Renaissance Anthropology

Cultural anthropology, or the comparative study of the vast varieties of human cultures encountered in the new and old worlds since 1492, developed into a scientific discipline in the post-Darwinian late nineteenth century. But its scholarly origins can be traced back to the late Renaissance descriptions and speculations in Italy, France and elsewhere. Beginning in the fourteenth century there had been an efflorescence of writings on the nature and status of man as a divine creation and within the scale of being, loosely designated as 'the Renaissance philosophy of man'.[1] It is this Renaissance forerunner of the discipline of anthropology, particularly in its religious context, that will be the subject of this essay.

Renaissance conceptions of man derived from a number of intellectual traditions of which two were critical: the revived ancient conception of *humanitas* (or Greek *paideia*) which formed the core of the *studia humanitatis* and the humanist movement,[2] and the Christian medieval tradition of discussions of *conditio hominis* under the complementary titles of *De miseria humanae conditionis* and *De dignitate humanae conditionis*.[3] It was the combination of these two traditions—one classical, one Christian—which gave the characteristic form and content to Renaissance treatises on man and which differentiated the Renaissance philosophy of man from its predecessors. This in turn was closely linked with, if not a central ingredient of, a Renaissance *'theologia rhetorica'*.

Humanitas and Genus Humanus

By *paideia* or *humanitas* ancient Greeks and Romans meant what we today would regard as the 'culture' acquired by growing up in a particular society. However, they thought of these terms as referring to a generic human culture rather than their own peculiar one[4] and the education which in-

This paper was written for the Eugenio Garin festschrift, edited (without listing his name) by Tullio Gregory. The paper appeared as "Il pensiero antropologico-religioso nel Rinascimento" in *Il Rinascimento: Interpretazioni e Problemi* (Rome/Bari: Editori Laterza, 1979), 103–47. An English version of this volume, *The Renaissance: Essays in Interpretation* (London/New York: Methuen & Co., Ltd., 1982) includes "Themes for a Renaissance Anthropology," pp. 83–125. This article seeks to present a generalized interpretation of Renaissance philosophies of man, classified according to genres and analyzed by themes and positions. It was written at the American Academy in Rome, Spring 1977.

stilled *paideia* or *humanitas* was, again, *the* education and not simply their own. Moreover, they denied that what Asians and barbarians acquired through their own *mores* was culture. Rather, by taking over Greek or Roman ways, they believed that any people could acquire universal *paideia* or *humanitas*. We tend to find that ancient education was aristocratic or plutocratic and so regard it as offensive to our notion that culture and education should be universal. It was not so much that the ancients wished to confine culture to the upper classes, but that they believed its acquisition in some way differentiated and elevated its possessor over the mere practitioner of manual labour or the mechanical arts, even including those of painting, sculpture, architecture and musical performance. Culture was for most of its proponents and theorists in antiquity, and in the Renaissance as well, something that was superimposed on the natural characteristics of mankind. It was the product of nurture and convention rather than of nature, though some individuals were considered to be better endowed by nature with the gift of acquiring culture.

The assumption that men existing in their age might learn how to acquire the *humanitas* and culture which the ancients knew how to possess was basic to the Renaissance notions of the revival of antiquity, however specified. This meant that the contemporaries of the humanists who composed the *vulgus* were without culture. Indeed, the notion that the men of the Middle Ages were, if not barbarians, barbaric in their lack of culture, derives from the classical conception of *humanitas* which the humanists found in Cicero, Quintilian, Aulus Gellius and their other sources. Inherent in the humanists' admiration for *humanitas,* however, with its *Homo sum: nihil humani alienum mihi puto,*[5] and its universality, was a recognition that there was a difference between one way of speaking, feeling and thinking and its appropriateness to a given situation and another. The very ancient sophistic emphasis on the subjectivity and relativity of ideas and values, which despite his social rigidities was manifested even in Cicero (especially in the *Academica*), and even more in Quintilian with his reservation of the *status controversiae quale sit* to the orator, gave rise to a comparative and relativistic view of vocabulary, meaning, syntax, composition, style, even language as has recently been shown. There was not one point where culture was at its peak or a single classical moment. Time, place and circumstances determined the multiple particular qualities that were appropriate. *Propria* became more valid as a criterion than *vera* and recaptured some of the Gorgianic *kairos*. Not only did human culture come to be seen as variable and relative, but man himself began to be seen as infinitely plastic and socially adaptable.[6]

Listen to Pontano, in his *De sermone,* on how discourse manifests the social character of the virtues:

Just as reason, herself, is the guide and mistress for directing actions, so speech is the administrator of all those things which, conceived in the mind, and activated by thinking, are dragged forth into the public world, since, as it is said, we are born sociable and must live together. Wherever speech is greater and more frequent, there is a richer supply of all those things in which life is lacking (since need is given as a companion to all men at their birth). Through speech life itself is made far more adaptable as well as more capable both of acquiring virtues and of attaining happiness.[7]

Developing his conception of the virtues as the bonds of society directly out of his study of rhetoric, Pontano distinguished between two basic types of rhetoric. First there is the 'oratorical art' by which men may become civil leaders 'in the most populous cities and in the greatest enterprises'.[8] Here the traditional formal rhetorics—forensic, legislative and epideictic—come into use. There is also, however, a more general function of speech which in the daily discourse of life creates and manifests the variety and differences of individual and collective culture.

For we are not speaking at all about that part of rhetoric which is called the oratorical strength and skill or the rhetorical art, but only about that common speech by which men approach friends, and carry on their daily business in gatherings, conversations, family and civil meetings and customs. For this reason those who are engaged in such matters are commended according to a quite different criterion than those who are called orators.[9]

Thus Pontano asserted that culture is not only attained by cultivation of the high language arts among the élite of society, but is also made up of the daily intercourse of all men in their societies, thus rendering the meaning of culture closer to modern anthropological usage. He moved on to an exposition of the variety and diversity of the use of speech in different and among different peoples. At this point, in a lengthy but compelling and definitive passage, he established the principle of cultural relativism which so many humanists derived from their studies of history and language:

Nor indeed does nature depart from herself in this matter or from that variety and dissimilitude which are characteristic of her. Since the manner of speaking of some persons is severe and somewhat sad, of others joyful and gay; of one the talk is smooth and fancy, of another crude and harsh; also this one reveals in his speaking the customs of the city but that one those of the country, there is the type who would like to seem witty and affable and the contrasting kind who would be severe and rigid and the one who is especially truthful and hostile to all pretence, to whom no dissimulation or what is called 'irony' in

Greek is pleasing. Therefore the type of speech strongly seems to follow both the nature of the speaker and also his customs. Why is this? Because peoples and nations, either by their very nature or by established custom and usage, approve and hold in high value what others elsewhere disapprove, and some are more taciturn and others, on the contrary, more loquacious. Boastful speech delights the Spaniards, colourful and complicated language the Greeks; the talk of the Romans was grave, that of the Spartans brief and rough, the Athenians fulsome and stilted, the Carthaginians and Africans shrewd and sly, as was said of their nature. Thus it happens that one kind of colloquy is more highly approved in one place and less so in another. [10]

For Pontano social existence required two central virtues—urbanity and veracity. These were manifested by men's manners of speaking and, following Aristotle, he saw these as desirable means between extremes. Urbanity is what may be called 'an especially admirable solace and lightening of the cares and burdens of labours honourably undertaken'. Veracity is what may be called 'that which so characterizes man himself that through it human conciliation may be established, trust flourish in the city, our actions and transactions become linked together, and our promises and teachings observed'. [11]

Although Pontano formally followed Aristotle's relativistic moral casuistry, he was also indebted to the more morally neutral analysis of Cicero which placed the virtues in a graduated spectrum (as we know Lorenzo Valla also did in opposing the Aristotelian mean). But Pontano's own insights seem closer to the kind of personification of the political modes presented by Plato in the ninth book of the *Republic* (which Pontano was not likely to have been following). For he saw that certain characterological types emerge from the involvement of a man in the nexus of the possible moral-rhetorical relations available in society. Opposite to the man of veracity, or truth, himself a central and necessary character-type in Pontano's thinking, come all of the graphically portrayed types of deceivers such as the 'adulators, and those who make a merchandise out of words whenever they use pleasing and flattering speech'. [12] Also opposite to the urbane man, but from a different direction, is the quarrelsome and contentious man whom Pontano described as follows:

And as some use this gift of speech conceded by nature for reconciling friendships, for consoling and comforting others in their troubles, labours and griefs, others, the contentious, use or abuse it rather in the opposite way, arousing hatred and stirring up quarrels as well as sowing the seeds of discord. . . . They are certainly odious kinds of men, and very similar to flies, as they seem entirely born for uproar, annoyance, disquiet and for disturbance and weariness of life! [13]

Although his concern was with the accurate description and subtle definition of the terms used to denote such characters, it is clear that he saw the
various modes of using language arising out of the social experience of
mankind as crystallized in certain personal cultures or moral linguistic
structures. Individual styles of speaking correspond to specific ways of
relating to other persons. The array of combinations of *verba* and *res,* the
language and concepts, which these different but typical social experiences
and stances of human culture present, were understood and explained as
humanitas by Pontano—something a modern anthropologist might call
'culture' in our own very different modern sense.

But *humanitas* was also a specific virtue, and the *habitus* of the *vir
humanus.* Pontano discussed the differences between *comitas, popularitas* and
humanitas as variants of *urbanitas* or *facetitas.* These virtues comprise the
range and variety of attitudes and behaviour characteristic of men who seek
to enliven and console their fellows and bring them into pleasant and
enduring companionship. It is evident from Pontano's and other humanists'
usage of *humanitas* and *humanus* in their writings that the word often occurs
in the context of the quality or the mode of human relationships, so that the
notion of the 'humane' as an aspect of the 'human' was not totally excluded
from the Greek and Latin notions of *paideia* and *humanitas* as cultural or
educational concepts. This we will claim despite the frequent humanist
citation of Aulus Gellius' pronouncement that Latin *humanitas* does not
mean Greek *philanthropeia* but *paideia.* What Pontano at least meant by
humanus is shown in his description of a friend, the philosopher Giovanni
Pardo:

> He was humane toward every kind of human life and action . . . he
> did nothing proudly, nothing arrogantly; in his approach, his speech
> and his behaviour he presented himself as an equal to everyone; he
> took it badly when he saw anyone being insolent to another person;
> the accidents of friends and citizens weighed heavily upon him; he
> consoled the suffering, helping them as much as he was able, visiting
> them, assisting them, giving his direct help; he stood by anyone at
> any time as a gracious and affable companion. [14]

As to the general qualities of *humanitas* and *comitas,* which also are called
civilitas by some:

> *Humanity* differs from *comity* in several ways. For whoever is moved by
> other persons' injuries, inconveniences, captivity, grief, poverty, ban-
> ishment and other ills, him we call 'humane', yet not in any sense
> 'companionable'. . . . But there is in both qualities a certain kind of
> communality of living in deeds and transaction which we would like
> to call either 'facility' or 'tractability'. [15]

Humanitas might then be said to be a Renaissance cultural ideal which sought through the *studia humanitatis* to pursue those studies which might most contribute to human and civil well-being. But *humanitas* was also construed to be a broad but identifiable conception of man characterized by sympathetic concern for the well-being of other individual humans and for the general well-being of the civilization or culture which sustained men's common life. Both of these conceptions of *humanitas* were rooted in the ancient humanist myth of the origins of civilization through the language arts. It was put forth as such in Cicero's *De inventione,* or in Protagoras' tale in Plato's dialogue of the gifts of reverence, justice and the liberal arts given by Zeus to primitive man. Giannozzo Manetti, praising the language arts as evidence of the greatness of human inventiveness, gave his own version of this myth:

> For when primitive man and his ancient successors became aware that they could not live for themselves alone without some kind of mutual exchange and reciprocal influence, they invented a certain subtle and acute art of speaking so that, by using their tongues to shape words, they could make known to all those listening their hidden and intimate thoughts. After this, when by the passage of time men had multiplied in an amazing way and populated the different regions and provinces of the globe, it became necessary for script to be invented. . . . Hence such various kinds of languages, such various types of letters, are seen to have come into existence and spread. [16]

Thus the notion of the linguistic disciplines fulfilling essential moral and social functions for the common life of mankind was deeply embedded in *humanitas*—the root term and concept of humanism. Culture and moral responsibility were inseparably connected.

A different, but also paradigmatically humanist, view of the formation of human character and society may be found in the *Epistola: De nobilitate et distinctione humani generis* of Antonio de Ferrariis, Il Galateo, composed *c.* 1488. [17] Pontano considered Il Galateo to be his best example of the man of comity. According to Il Galateo, the Latins and Greeks had divided mankind into civilized cultures (their own) and all others, whom they had called by that fetid term, 'barbarians'. Il Galateo preferred to call the others *externi*. But these others also used contemptuous terms for foreigners. Some peoples divided men according to social status rather than ethnic culture, into nobles and commoners, but Il Galateo's own view, following Cicero and Plato, was to consider the *optimates* not as a social class but as a group distinguished by their *mores,* meaning that they possessed not just morally neutral and different customs but goodness, so that for him the distinction between the more civilized and morally superior and those who are barbarian or morally inferior occurs within one nation and not between various nations. Thus other peoples have, as equivalents of the Greek *philosophi* and the Latin *sapientes,*

> gymnosophists, magi, Chaldeans, priests, prophets. Among the Arabs also in more recent times many excellent men distinguished themselves in the studies of wisdom. We Christians have had at one time our own kind who followed after true wisdom and taught it to us—the Apostles and the Evangelists. [18]

Thus for him the true and essential distinction between men is based upon the principle by which men are separated from animals, namely mind and reason. Men, indeed, differ from each other so much and have such different customs that they even seem to differ in species: 'And the very name man is equivocal and is not given the same meaning by everyone, for instance in the case of man as depicted and true man.'[19] Differing from Pontano's structuring of the modes of human behaviour according to the necessities of the civic order and of private advantage, Il Galateo establishes a universal criterion according to a fixed hierarchy of being. He is, however, aware of a tension between these two ordering principles of human culture.

The more men prevail in the use of the mind, according to Il Galateo, the more they are participants of *verae humanitatis.* But some of the worst men possess family, wealth, fame, office, power, physical strength, beauty, agility, eloquence, the favour and grace of the people or the friendship of princes. Hence he divided all peoples into philosophers on the one hand and the plebeians or *vulgus* on the other; this division corresponding not to their external circumstances at all but only to their degree of education and moral goodness. He depicted these two kinds of men, portraying them as two mutually related types and reflecting in this the humanists' frequent insecurity and sense of moral superiority rather than Pontano's social functionalism. The *philosophus,* but not the *vir civilis* who seeks to please the *populus,* is the true aristocrat born only for himself and the immortal gods. The *philosophus,* in a conflation of Christian saint and Stoic sage, is totally honest, open, self-sacrificing and humble, whereas the men of the *vulgus* only pretend to serve the virtues and conceal their deep selfishness; 'they think it most beautiful to show off their wisdom, to display their most saintly customs, to conceal their crimes'.[20]

How do men fall into these two moral classes? Again, he suggests all customs are relative. What is fitting for one kind of man is not for another. Yet these two contrasting patterns emerge from *educatio* in our own modern sense of the word 'education'. Il Galateo offers a brilliant description here, not unlike the one Plato put into the mouth of Protagoras, of the way in which all aspects of upbringing are educational. 'Education is large and very potent in human affairs, and those first foods offered to tender souls are of great moment in all of life'.[21] Plato was thankful he was a Greek not because the Greeks were a superior race but because they had superior *mores et studia.* It is so easy for the young to admire the scurrilous and spurn the teachings of philosophers; just as patients resist the prescriptions of their doctors so they ignore the pleas, the praise and the blame of the philosophers, even though they are held to be *sapientes* by the *vulgus:*

> But since nothing is easier than to deceive onself and nothing more divine in life than to know oneself, since we are men, we are deceived many times, but never are we more proud and arrogant than when we correct and condemn the counsels and actions of those of whom we scarcely deserve to be students.[22]

Il Galateo was not a frustrated schoolmaster but a member of a distinguished noble family. What he projects in this *Epistola* had long been a humanist stereotype: the opposition of the scholar to the vulgar self-interest of the men of affairs and of the common people. It is a version of the discussions of true nobility that had evolved since Dante's *Convivio.*[23] In Galateo's version the humanist, himself, is given the blessing of having achieved true humanity. For it is really the humanist whom Galateo calls 'philosopher'—the teacher of youth by praise and blame and society's moral guardian.

Particularly significant was Galateo's linkage of learning with piety. Christ's life was not *civilis* but truly *philosophica.* The *docti* are the true Christians and those of the beatitude, 'Blessed are we when men revile us and when we are persecuted for the sake of righteousness'. Such are we, the *sapientes,* 'when the vilest plebeians judge us to be insane'. But the plebeians, 'conscious of their own stupidity and malice', speak as follows: 'They—the *sapientes*—are the ones we sometimes have held in contempt. . . . We, the irrational ones, thought their life insane and their end without honour. Lo how they are reckoned among the sons of God! . . . Therefore we have departed from the way of truth.' The barbarians are those leading a brutish life whatever their race, class or family. The nobles are the virtuous men even if of barbarian or servile origin. 'For who, unless he was ignorant of human affairs and of true nobility, would call Horace plebeian or ignoble?'[24] So also Vergil, Cicero, Demosthenes, Socrates, Aristotle, Plato, Theophrastus, Hippocrates and Homer were truly noble though of humble origin.

For Galateo, as for Petrarch, *otium* was a high value:

> How great and how blessed is the life of leisure whenever it is present to any degree, those who are not philosophers would not know. . . . Leisure among the wise is held to be blessed, but among the barbarians, that is among uneducated men and those of the lower

classes, as lazy idleness worthy of contempt and shame. Therefore only philosophers labour that they may rest and be at leisure, ordinary people, indeed, labour daily so that they may labour and suffer the more.[25]

There is in this position a summing-up of a major type of humanist thinking about man and his position in society—one which links classical learning and the type of the Roman sage with the holy man of Christianity. A new conception of lay piety, if not of lay sainthood, was quietly forged through this synthesis of Stoic sage and Christian martyr. In its stress on *otium* it contrasted with the attitude of an Alberti, a Valla, or a Manetti as described below—but not with their sense of moral righteousness and superiority. One should not, however, see this humanist concept of *otium* as totally one of withdrawal. Pontano speaks of the 'urbane' man as aware that

> just as idleness and all sorts of quiet are granted us for the sake of relaxing and so that the return to labours and affairs may not be sodden, for the same reasons jokes, sayings, wit, charm and humour are granted and not so that life, our thoughts and all our studies should be placed in them or so that we might appear to be wasting away in leisure and idleness.[26]

Conditio Hominis

Another Renaissance ideal, that of *operosità* (the opposite of *ozio* or leisure), found its roots more in the patristic exegesis of Genesis 1:26, where creative man is seen as made in the image of God the creator. Though Petrarch with his twofold *otia* (*religiosum* and *litterarium*) may seem to have founded the humanist myth of the Stoic-Christian sage, he managed to convert it into a more activist and creative notion of his own role as moral midwife, and in this he necessarily projected a different and more positive image of the condition of man. It is to this second Renaissance humanist myth of creative man, with its Christian roots (but also combined with Protagorean-Ciceronian conceptions) that we now turn. We shall reserve for a third section our discussion of some of the more radical religious and cultural implications that underlay the more diffuse treatments of *humanitas* and *conditio hominis*.

Viewing the literature on the *conditio hominis* theme from Petrarch to the late sixteenth-century defences of the humanities, one should first emphasize its rhetorical character. Although its substance was central to Renaissance thought and of great historical importance, its form and function was also characteristic. Petrarch's declarations on the misery of the human condition were meant to be monitory and those on the dignity of man consolatory. Despite the hazards arising from his constant revisions, a development may be traced from the self-expressive and self-analytical lyricism of the *Canzoniere* and the profound dramatization of his personal conflicts in the *Secretum,* to a more directly active and hortatory kind of writing in the *Invectivae* and the *De remediis* and the later versions of the *De viris illustribus*—not that Petrarch ever abandoned an earlier practice altogether or stopped attempting to modify it! What he comes to is rhetorical history, on the one hand, and what may be called *theologia rhetorica,* on the other. Although Petrarch's contribution to Renaissance historical consciousness is admittedly very important, only the latter will be treated here. If in the *De ignorantia* he embraced 'the words that move and sting' of Latin rhetoric, it was in the context of what he had called his *homiliae* in the *Contra medicum* or in the way we should characterize the speeches of *Ratio* in the *De remediis,* that is, as lay literary sermons. It is exactly in this that the humanists' revival of antiquity, and their response to contemporary moral, psychological and social conditions, intersect.[27]

The *De remediis* is a highly fragmented work, yet has an amazing range and sweep of content. Its two books are divided into 122 triumphs and 132 despairs. Some are grand and some petty, but they are not merely miscellaneous, for Petrarch follows certain conventional structures: a review of the course of life; a catalogue of goods and evils according to the standard Aristotelian categories of soul, body and externals; the various high and low social states; the rewards and punishments of political power and weakness; the satisfactions and annoyances of family and friends. Authenticity of reportage breaks through the conventionality of the categories. Though short and sometimes stereotypical, his qualitative familiarity with the life of his world is patent. It is indeed the actual conditions of men in his time that he is depicting, abstracted into his 254 commonplace situations of elation and sorrow. What he offers by way of counselling in the persona of *Ratio* is again the idealization of the reciprocal polarities of human existence (what I have elsewhere called a 'double-consciousness'). The wise man, who now need no longer be the sage but can be the ordinary man, should know that misery lurks behind every prosperous condition and this should temper his triumph; he also should know that, whatever his wretchedness, disappointments and suffering, as a man he occupies a place of great dignity and great future hope in the universe. The picture of the human world which emerges is not that of a capricious fortune or an accident-dominated scene, but of a structural duality or ambiguity in all of life's circumstances. The advice Petrarch offers is how to cope with the emotional hazards of life. It is the message of the possibility of attaining moral identity and autonomy, and a serenity and calm under all conditions. *Ratio* does not bring salvation, but it brings the sense of having a soul and being a person in the world that opens the possibility of faith and hope and to which there may come grace. But we shall discuss that later.

What Petrarch contributed to his readership, which extended through nearly four centuries, was a sense of dignity and sanity that was compatible with piety, and he did this for a period of history in which the struggle for power, wealth and prestige was becoming frantic, and the deprivations desperate. His consolatory-monitory rhetoric did nothing to sedate the harshness of events, but offered a pattern of rationality in personal attitude and behaviour that perhaps helped to preserve civilization, and gave a moral theodicy for religious faith in the midst of the horrors of the age which he, himself, had so well depicted.

Petrarch also contributed a specific pattern for the statement of the dignity of man which was repeated with variation and amplification in the ensuing treatises on this theme.[28] The pattern was traditional and medieval in part. The human species, created by plural act of the Trinity in its image, received a soul with memory, intellect and will mirroring the divine Trinity of Father, Son and Spirit, as in the Augustinian exegesis recapitulated by Peter Lombard. Man was placed over the other species and walked erect in token of his contemplation of the divine and his effort to regain his similitude to God through virtuousness. Through Christ's incarnation he could take pride in his potentiality for divinization and look forward to immortality. He was protected by guardian angels, and through his superior powers of intellect not only ruled the beasts but created civilization.

Petrarch's own statement, itself one of his lay sermons of the *De remediis,* did not have the 'free-standing' literary autonomy of later Renaissance treatises. It brought the Christian message from the over-refined abstractness and technical language of scholastic theology, found in the more ontologically oriented thirteenth century and in the more critical and dialectical fourteenth-century, to the level of the ordinary man. For him the dignity-of-man theme was complementary to that of human misery, and he seems to have been encouraged to project the former as a complement to the latter by a letter from a Grand Prior of the Carthusians (*Senili XVI. 9*). In this case, and in that of the first formal literary treatise on *The Excellence of Man* by Bartolomeo Fazio in 1447, monastic figures such as the Grand Prior and Antonio da Barga (once Prior of the Olivetan house of San Miniato in Florence), seem to have provided the incitement. It is also probable that Giannozzo Manetti's much expanded treatment of 1453 had an earlier version inspired by the same Antonio da Barga.[29] In all three instances Pope Innocent III's *De miseria humanae conditionis* was in the background. As the then Cardinal Deacon Lotario da Signa said to Peter, Bishop of the church of Porto and Santa Rufina:

> If indeed your paternity should urge it, Christ willing, I will describe the dignity of human nature; for just as through the one (the *De contemptu mundi*) the elated is humbled, so through the other (the *De dignitate humanae naturae*) the humble is exalted.[30]

Both Petrarch and Fazio professed to fulfil Lotario's unfulfilled offer. Manetti, on the other hand, polemicized directly against him. More importantly, both Petrarch's and Fazio's treatments of the dignity-of-man theme are bound together with the complementary *de miseria* one, and both are directed toward moral counselling and rhetorical efforts toward consolation and monition. The topical format of Petrarch's *De remediis* may be compared with that of Pope Innocent's famous work. The popularity of both throughout the late medieval and early modern period was enormous (judging by Maccarrone's listing of manuscripts and editions to 1600 for Lotario and Nicholas Mann's compilation of *De remediis* manuscripts, with Fiske's listing of editions).[31] These two clearly Renaissance works had deep medieval roots running back at least to Pope Gregory's *Book of Pastoral Care* with its compilation of the modes for counselling the arrogant and the despairing. But with it the still surviving Roman Stoic influence became tangible, and Petrarch's renewal of it in more explicitly rhetorical and Senecan terms was patently also a return to patristic Christianity. Its form, function and content were the cure of souls by the therapy of the word, both divine and human, though Petrarch's aims were existential as much as salvational.

The question then arises of how much the renewal of authentic understanding of ancient rhetoric contributed to a transformation of the medieval-Christian theme of the *conditio hominis* from a consolatory context to the assertion of a powerful vision of the capacities and cultural dominance of man. Actually, it seems to have led more to a deepening of a consolatory rhetoric in a lay and existential context (though clearly Christian in its content), whereas the enhanced vision of the powers of man, contemporary in origin, found inspiration in the traditional exegesis of Genesis 1:26–8.

Petrarch had put forth a very strong statement of confidence in the curative powers of rhetoric, drawn from both Cicero and Seneca and reviving in his *De remediis* the para-medical, or at least mental-hygienic, aspect of rhetoric. This function has been neglected by scholars who have tended to see only the forensic, political, epideictic and literary-theoretical sides of rhetoric. Yet it seems to have flourished among the Greek sophists and even to have had some links with Hippocratic medicine, was reflected in Plato's and Aristotle's concern with *catharsis,* and experienced a revival in Roman Stoicism.[32] A sequel to the consolatory usage of the dignity-of-man theme for the cure of souls, was the Ficinian combination of certain humanist conceptions of the power of language with a new metaphysic and theurgic conception of the cosmos on which a therapeutic 'spiritual magic' was based. Further study of both are needed.[33]

Neither Boccaccio, Salutati nor Valla, who contributed so much to the formation of a humanist philosophy of action and will, wrote directly on the dignity-of-man theme, although they made scattered references to the concept. While Salutati's *De seculo et religione* has certain affinities with the *de miseria* theme, his *De nobilitate legum et medicinae* is an affirmation of the role of human will and reason in regulating the affairs of men. As a humanist Boccaccio seems to have had a major concern with building bridges between his earlier medieval literary culture and the Petrarchan classicism he admired, but he certainly shared Petrarch's admiration of man's moral autonomy and his expectation that, under given circumstances, it could become realized. In his *Repastinatio dialecticae et philosophiae* Valla developed the central analogy of the dignity-of-man theme, that between the persons of the Trinity and the faculties of the soul, into the theoretical base for his opposition of Quintilian's rhetorical categories of substance, quality and action to Aristotle's naturalistic epistemology and ontology. They all moved, in other words, toward the activist, creationist vision of human dignity that was to challenge the older, more traditional employment of the theme for consolatory rhetoric. We shall speak further of Valla and Salutati in our discussion of a *theologia rhetorica*.

Besides this distinction of a consolatory and a celebratory treatment of the dignity theme, best exemplified by Petrarch and Manetti respectively, another important distinction was that between the versions which stressed the theological features of man's dignity, with immortality as its ultimate attainment, and the versions which, while retaining the former ingredients, add to them an emphasis on man's worldly achievements and powers. Admittedly these two distinctions overlap, and it would be wrong to characterize either polarity as 'transcendent/immanent' as all four emphasize man's deification. But the second type of each distinction finds man's potential divinity exemplified by his operative reconstructing of this world, besides retaining the gift of immortality. One finds Manetti breaking away from the conception that man's dignity is the rhetorical complement of man's misery: directly combating Lotario's topics, he stressed that man can achieve dignity and also escape misery. Fazio, da Barga and Brandolini, on the other hand, keep misery as the normal condition of earthly existence. Counter to the establishment of the theme of dignity, in separation from the polemic against misery, there was also a corresponding selection of the miserable and pessimistic aspects of man's existence promulgated in separation from, and even opposition to, any notion of dignity and autonomy. Poggio Bracciolini in his pessimism most clearly and self-consciously represents this tendency.[34]

A cynical doubter of the effectiveness and sincerity of both the politically powerful and the professionally pious, Poggio saw misery everywhere as the inherent condition of life after the fall of man. Seemingly Stoic in his attitude, he was essentially sceptical of the affirmative and reconstructive rationalism of Stoicism as well, perhaps in a deeper and more violent sense than his enemy Valla. Right reason cannot alleviate human misery which is universal and overwhelming but it can contribute to an idealistic illusion of goodness in those favoured few with sufficient material goods to practise charity. Human motivation is ineluctably sinful whatever its nominal conception of itself: grace alone can redeem. Moral action, even for worldly ends, is a Pelagian illusion.

Poggio's view of human motivation and behaviour brought him closer in his outlook to some of the darker views of the Reformation than almost any other pre-Reformation humanist, even though—despite all his anticlerical jibes and his contempt for the mendicant orders—he thought of himself as fully orthodox and religiously conservative. He lacked Petrarch's and Fazio's confidence in reason and rhetoric. These lacked for him the potency and charm so many of his contemporaries saw and admired. Poggio thus represented a voice of doubt concerning the basic values of his own culture and was close in this to the cynical despair which, as Eugenio Garin has recently shown, expressed a persisting side of Leon Battista Alberti's consciousness.[35]

The strongest contrast existed between the views of Manetti, who developed the optimistic side of Petrarch's bipolar remedies, and Poggio's total rejection of consolatory rhetoric and of every bridge between earthly behaviour and salvation. Curiously, however, those humanists who seem to have gone furthest in emphasizing the creative or the civic sides of man's eminence and his manifestation of a divine image, followed Stoic, Ciceronian or Aristotelian lines of argument—curiously because, as is well known, Lorenzo Valla polemicized throughout his career against Stoicism and Aristotle and made a point of preferring Quintilian to Cicero; and Valla's only nominally Epicurean anthropology strongly encouraged bold human actions and the assertion of man's creative powers over the natural and historical worlds.[36] Valla's opposition to the classical mentors, however, was more tactical than fundamental; for him they represented the tokens of an allegiance to a regrettable, unnecessary and incorrect reliance on classical philosophical precedents by Christian thinkers, both old and contemporary. Yet in certain ways both Poggio and Valla found themselves on the same side in their scepticism concerning the views of classical philosophy on the condition of man. Both also relied ultimately on grace to guide man's behaviour, regarding the play of natural motives as almost too powerful to be directed rationally. One may also note a similar ambivalence in Petrarch, although less emphatic. For these three important figures man's capacity to manifest the divine image through his direction of nature and creation of a human world of second nature, was more problematical than it was for Manetti, Morandi and, in certain of his writings, Alberti. Alberti's ambivalence might be mentioned precisely here, as he does not elect one or the other of the polar themes on the condition of man but takes emphatically each position at various and clearly overlapping times. Nevertheless we shall use his more constructivist writings, with Manetti's and

Morandi's, to illustrate this important humanist stress on human creativity and productivity as a realization of man's potential divinity, but we do not forget the brilliant yet puzzled passages in which Eugenio Garin explores Alberti's ambivalence and even his stance against the argument for the dignity of man.

Whatever Manetti's debts to Bartolomeo Fazio or Antonio da Barga, and despite his bald and lengthy citations of Cicero, Lactantius and so many others, his treatise, none the less, reveals independent and powerful thought.[37] His caution and dependence on citation occurs primarily in his first two books where he dealt with the excellences of the body and soul. In the second book on the soul he followed the medieval not the Augustinian order in naming the divine image of the Trinity in man as intellect, memory and will, and, in keeping with the analogy, emphasized man's intelligence but slid easily over memory and will. This was, perhaps, an unintended reversion to the scholastic Aristotle in a Christian context, but he interpreted intelligence in a clearly Renaissance mode as the operation of human inventiveness and creativity throughout human history—man's 'many, great and remarkable instruments or machines marvellously invented and comprehended'.[38]

These civilizing works of man were classified in an ascending hierarchy: navigation, building, painting, sculpture, poetry (which begins the *altiora et liberaliora*), history, oratory and jurisprudence, philosophy, medicine, astronomy and theology. He offered examples from all these categories, and all are ancient ones except those from the first four, the mechanical arts, which come before the higher liberal arts. For these he gave as examples the Portuguese and Italian navigations into the glacial and the Moorish oceans, Brunelleschi's dome, Giotto's paintings and Ghiberti's bronze doors.

Manetti stressed operational intelligence in book two, preparing the way for his third book on the whole man where he fully asserted his own characteristic encomium of man as possessing all the qualities that we like to believe were most admired in the Renaissance. Man's divine creation determines his thought. What, then, of the making of man? he asked. Should we not say that he was most beautifully and admirably and divinely made? But why did God make man? Was it in order to achieve a work of true perfection? The questions are traditional, transmitted to him by the Olivetan Prior, Antonio da Barga. But the rhetoric, as da Barga hoped, is new. Thus he asked in what manner God made man, and answered 'God created man as the most beautiful, most ingenious, most wise, most opulent and finally most powerful' of creatures.[39]

The concept of man as the guardian of the original creation and the creator of the second nature of the human world is reflected in Manetti's treatment of each of these categories. Man's beauty is best shown in his own sense of beauty which leads him to beautify the world with his works:

> Finally, what should we say about mankind who, established as cultivators of the earth, does not permit it to be rendered wild by the cruelty of beasts nor to be made into wasteland by the harshness of plants; mankind by whose works fields, islands and shores are made into countrysides and cities and brightly shine? Indeed, if we were able to see all this with our eyes, just as in our minds, what a marvellous spectacle would appear to those of us living and looking.[40]

Man's ingenuity of inventiveness—the prime quality itself—is manifested in his lengthy listing of the works of man:

> Everything after that first, new and rude creation of the world seems to have been invented, constructed and perfected by us by means of a certain, singular and special sharpness of the human mind. They are ours, that is human, because they are seen to have been made by men.[41]

There follows his lengthy listing. Then:

> These things, certainly, and other things as many and as great, can be examined everywhere, so that the world and all its beauties seems to have been first invented and established by Almighty God for the use of men, then received by them and rendered much more beautiful and much more ornate and far more refined.[42]

Man's wisdom is expressed in his capacity to order and govern the world and himself, and this itself has led to the knowledge and understanding of the true God and His providence. Man's riches consist in all the parts of nature at his disposal (which are listed and classified at great length). Does this not suggest to us that the great work in natural history of the early modern centuries, especially its explorations and cataloguing of nature, is rooted in this Renaissance conception of man and his role in the world? Finally, Manetti asserts, man's power consists in both his natural and supernatural capacities.

If this was the quality or mode of man's creation, then his function or duty, it follows, is to understand the universe given him by God and to operate in it—*intelligere et agere*—as Garin so effectively argued years ago. All that Manetti previously said of man's excellences has led up to this Renaissance insight, firmly based on Genesis 1:28—'Be fruitful and multiply, and replenish the earth, and subdue it; and have dominion over the fish of the sea, and over the fowl of the air, and over every living thing that moveth upon the earth'—which he had cited a little earlier. Manetti's position is clear enough:

So we think and believe the equally right and simple, as well as unique, office of man is such that the world, and especially those things which we see established in this whole earthly sphere, was made for his sake and that he has the knowledge and ability to govern and administer it. He could not do this at all unless he was fully able to perfect and fulfil the task by action and understanding.[43]

This is perhaps as explicit a statement of modern European man's conception of his earthly purpose as being to dominate and control the natural world as one could hope to find at this distance from the Renaissance (when we see today so many of our contemporaries standing appalled at what seems to be the historical consequences of this point of view, so much more strongly asserted and acted upon in the centuries after Manetti's own). Manetti optimistically observed:

Therefore man while alive becomes an inhabitant of the world, and piously dying, he is made into a possessor of heaven, and in this way, both in this present life and in the future one and, indeed, in every time, he is held to be happy and blessed.

But then, as if aware of the perils more recently seen in this position, he added the following warning:

And from this so great and so sublime dignity and excellence of man, as though from the very root, envy, pride, indignation, lust for domination, and ambition, as well as other disturbances of the soul of this sort, not unjustly arise and flow. For whoever thinks himself to have been made so worthy that he seems to excel and dominate all created things certainly will not suffer to be surpassed by others, which is the vice of envy, but worse, longs most of all to excel others, which is thought and believed to be the proper vice of pride and ambition. But if, perchance, it happens that anyone is spurned, or neglected and despised, he is offended to such an extent that he will pursue his humiliators as none other than his capital and bitterest enemies and certain specific violators and detractors of his excellences strenuously even unto death. And I, considering this again and again, and wishing to describe and define man, have explained him, not wrongly in my opinion, as an animal filled with indignation.[44]

Unable, perhaps, fully to accept the moral and religious implications of this condemnation of man as *homo indignabundus,* Manetti went on to claim that it would not be fitting and agreeable for man, who was created in such excellence, to remain perpetually damned. Hence God sent His Son to take on human flesh and suffer the ignominious death of the Cross to redeem mankind. But even if our first parents had not sinned, Christ would have descended, not to redeem mankind, but 'in order that man through this humble assumption of human flesh might be marvellously and unbelievably honoured and glorified'.[45] Many learned and holy men seemed to have believed this, he added, perhaps referring here to Duns Scotus' famous doctrine that the Incarnation was predestined and the elect elected before the creation of Adam, so that salvation was not due to the Advent, but he named no names. More to the point, he asserted the doctrine of man's deification as the final completion of man's dignity, which lacked nothing else 'except that through admixture with divinity itself it would not only become conjoined with divinity in that person of Christ but also would be made one and the same with the divine nature'.[46]

How difficult it is to classify Manetti as a thinker according to any of the existing intellectual traditions! He ranged through so many classical and Christian sources—Aristotelian, Stoic and Ciceronian, patristic and medieval—and even within these groupings paid his respects to different and opposing levels and views. In the end he seemed to have woven out of his amazing erudition a fabric that integrates as warp and woof the Christian creation myth in Genesis 1 of man's role as governor and provider over the natural world in the 'image' of divine providence, with the classical rhetorical (Protagorean-Ciceronian) myth of man as the creator of peace, order and civilization through the invention of the liberal arts, and especially language, in the midst of the savagery of the primitive generations of mankind which bound them to their *bestialitas* and kept them from realizing their *humanitas.* But into the fabric formed of the conjunction of these two traditions Manetti poured the dye of his own experience as a Florentine merchant, citizen and admired governor and orator, who in his own pride of achievement and humanistic study (*agere et intelligere*) carried these classical Christian visions of man into a conceptual and rhetorical definitiveness that went far beyond their original more fragmentary projection. In this way Manetti made his work into a paradigm of the Renaissance genre of the dignity of man.

A brief comment may also be made about Benedetto Morandi's less well-known treatise *De felicitate humana,* in which progress and human civilization is also stressed. Morandi's thinking remained far more encased than Manetti's within traditional Aristotelian terminology, as would not be unexpected in Bologna, still a stronghold of scholastic education despite an increasing humanistic presence. It was the Aristotelian who clashed with the far more conservative, though humanistic, physician, Giovanni Garzoni. Morandi, in brief, argued that the conditions of human existence in this world, quite apart from the higher beatitude of the next life (which he did not deny), could be considered generally favourable to mankind. Although they varied with time, place and culture, these conditions of life are the result of the operation of human industry upon nature, and they lift mankind far above what the natural gifts of animals can give them. The latter, 'compared to the things which human industry invented, are most sordid and abject. And it would have been needless for nature, who does nothing otiose, to have conferred them on man, since by his inventiveness and reason man prepares better things for himself than nature grants to the brutes'.[47]

It did not trouble him that man's superiority was that of *homo viator:*

> Nor do I regard mortals as miserable because the most benign Creator-God said to man, 'In the sweat of thy brow shall ye eat your bread'. In these words he tacitly warned man that not in robbery but in sparing the goods of others, not in enfeebling leisure but in always doing something, he should live his life. And if hands, feet, tongue, eyes and the other organs of the body have their proper functions, will the whole man have none? Therefore what does it profit a man to know, to feel, to believe, to wish, to remember, to compare past with present and through that judge the future, if there was nothing to be done by man?[48]

Again, he rejected the fall of man as a cause for human misery:

> That mortals are not miserable due to the Fall of our parents contaminating all posterity is shown by the words which pious Mother Church for that reason sings, namely, 'O happy guilt which merited to have so great and such a Redeemer', speaking of our saviour Jesus Christ.[49]

As for man's creation in God's image, this too did not seem to make him miserable:

> Certainly the human mind can by no reasoning understand that God made man in his image and made him lord of all things which are in the air, on the land or in the sea, possessed of all the disciplines and a little less than the angels . . . so that at length man would be miserable and calamitous and the divine efforts, the nativity and passion and resurrection of Christ for the salvation of man, would be in vain.[50]

Life for man was a struggle, but in this struggle man made a decent existence for himself. Like Manetti's *intelligere et agere,* Morandi offers something he calls *actio studiosa.* But Garzoni, his opponent, says:

> 'Labour is unending'. Hence there is greater merit in fighting than in yielding ground. . . . Philosophers say that the first perfection is that he is learned in the good arts; the second they place in studious action. The wise man, moreover, if he is leisurely differs not at all from the

slothful, or at least the somnolent. . . . Therefore he will be happy when he is engaged in studious action.[51]

Leon Battista Alberti wrote no specific treatise on man. Yet, as Garin has argued, all his moral essays deal with the condition of human existence. In the discourse of his uncle Lionardo in the second *Libro della famiglia*, and in his work of old age, *De iciarchia*, Alberti expressed a philosophy closely akin to Manetti's and Morandi's. We must be aware, however, that the constructivist vision of human possibility in these works are matched by his complementary pessimism and despair concerning man's lot and his powers, which Garin has so brilliantly expounded. Although the humanistic genre of the dignity of man dealt predominantly with the theological origins, status and destiny of man in general, with where man stood in comparison with animals and divinity and with what was characteristically human, *humanitas*, Alberti in these two works focuses on the historical reality of the process of becoming a man of dignity. Here and now, in the midst of, and against the current of, the enormous mass of human recalcitrance to anything but man's immediate gratification, Alberti projects his vision. It is true that in the treatises not all men reached the level of dignity of which the species was capable, and that Alberti is offering his idealization of the dignified man as he viewed him in early manhood and again in ripe old age. But like Poggio he despaired of most men and thus presented but the dialectical possibility of another mode of existence, which gives still another humanist version of the ideal of the activist life. In both works the evils of *ozio* are opposed by *operosità*. The true conception of man, as of all life, in Lionardo's view and in Alberti's in *De iciarchia*, is that he should be constantly acting: 'Therefore it seems to me, and I so believe, that man was certainly not born to pine away in indolence but to stand up and do things'.[52]

Lionardo proceeded to support this view by presenting a series of traditional *topoi* from the genre of the dignity of man. It would be stupid to argue that the divine force of man's soul, mind, intellect, judgement, memory, virtues and passions, 'with which he overcomes the strength, swiftness and ferocity of any other animal, were given for not wishing to work much'. He did not like Epicurus' view that 'in God supreme happiness consists in doing nothing'. Anaxagoras' stress on man's erect posture for studying 'the marvellous works of God', and that of the Stoics, who held man is by nature 'the contemplator and activator of things', pleased him more. He liked Protagoras' opinion that 'man is the measure of all things'. He could, if he wished, quote other ancients and many sayings of our theologians. Especially pleasing was Aristotle, 'who demonstrated that man is happy like a mortal god in understanding and acting with reason and *virtù*'.[53] Here, again, is the Aristotelian *intelligere et agere* used by Manetti.

The many beautiful and useful things placed in the world to fill man's needs prove his divine origin:

> Here add to this how much man must render service to God in order to satisfy Him with good works for the gift of such great powers which he has given the soul of man, something which is far beyond the scope of other earthly animated creatures.

There follows his depiction of the greatness of man's nature given him by God:

> Nature, that is God, made man as composed of a celestial and divine part, something that is most beautiful and most noble beyond anything mortal . . .

possessing a beautiful and agile body, keen senses, discourse and judgement for learning all necessary things, the mental qualities needed for investigating and understanding all things, the moral restraint necessary for living with other men.

> God also established a strong bond in human souls to hold human society together—justice, equity, liberality and love, with which a man can merit gratitude and praise among other mortals, and pity and mercy before God.

God strengthened the breast of man so that he could sustain every labour, adversity and turn of fortune, so that he could overcome difficulties, conquer suffering, and not fear death. With

> firmness, stability, constancy and strength, and with contempt for perishable things . . . with justice, piety, temperance, and with every other perfect and highly laudable action.

Finally, he concluded:

> I am persuaded, therefore, that man was not born to sorrow in leisure but to become active in magnificent and large affairs, with which one can please and honour God, in the first place, and, through having the use of perfect virtue in oneself, acquire the fruit of felicity.[54]

We cannot follow his long amplification of the importance of virtue and *operosità* and finally of *onestà* in this book. Nor can we, because of space, discuss *De iciarchia,* where this image of the operative man comes through even more strongly from Alberti in his own *persona.* The vision of man as born to manage himself, the world of nature and mankind is asserted by Alberti as an ideal of how man should strive to live well, greatly and humanly in his own environment of the Renaissance city. Yet Alberti's example also reveals the dissidence and tension in urban culture between this optimistic, constructivist view and Alberti's cynical observations of man's wolf-like behaviour to his fellows and the rest of nature.

Held though it was with much ambivalence, a new conception of man was clearly emerging in the Renaissance out of a synthesis of the Stoic view found in Cicero's *De natura deorum* and Augustine's Trinitarian anthropology. Man, in this view, was emphatically active, operative, directive and managerial. Aristotle's three categories of production, action and speculation also exerted a less precisely conceptualized influence. There were also elements of detachment and passivity in Stoic thought and of asceticism and other-worldliness in Augustine. Yet it is remarkable how these three— Manetti, Morandi and more ambiguously Alberti—along with other thinkers of the period, drew upon their own sense of the values embedded in Italian urban culture to construct a vivid and empirical conception of man as a creator. However rhetorical and self-serving of their own way of life this conception was, it none the less succeeded in projecting the basic structure and motivation of Renaissance anthropological thought in a vision of man making his own history and triumphing over nature and fortune. The elements of historical realism that emerge in this transformed literary genre, prompted by so much concern with how Christian man can cope with the actualities and complexities of late medieval society, should not be obscured by the clearly religious modalities that characterized this way of thinking. Yet it is essential that the religious framings of Renaissance anthropological thought are not eliminated but fully appreciated. We turn now to an examination of them.

Theologia Rhetorica

The views put forth in the humanists' discussions of *humanitas* and treatises on the condition of man had profound theological presuppositions and implications, not always clearly articulated but loosely present. It would have been impossible in an intellectual movement generated within the historical context of late medieval Christian Europe for it to have been otherwise. Indeed, a fundamental motivation for the revival of ancient thought and letters was a need to discover a convergence between Christian religious beliefs and the cultural and intellectual problems generated by life in the Italian cities. The availability, both immediate and researched, of the thought and expression of antiquity made it inevitable that ancient culture would provide models and insights for the identification and communication of contemporary problems. But these could be conceived in no other framework than Christian.

Let us take, for example, the case of Petrarch. His sensitivity to the needs of his contemporaries for a more responsible management of their emotional responses to the pressures of urban living than scholastic and canonistic culture provided, led him straight to Seneca's *Epistulae* and Cicero's *Tusculans*. It also led him to find the Christian solution, not in scholastic theology, but in that most poignant ancient confrontation of classical and Christian value, the *Confessions* of St Augustine. And led him to his first great formulations in the *Secretum* and *De vita solitaria,* and to the more profound meditation of the experiential problems of sin, free will, justification and grace found in the *De otio religioso.*[55] The Stoic anthropology of divine rational mind immanent in each individual who is at the same time distracted by the false images of reality imposed by the senses is adapted to Christian ends. The role of the sage pointing to the true and rational way is transformed into that of the saint counselling the deep meditation of death, hell and the horrors of sins. In this way a Christian structuring of reality replaces the superficial lure of sensuality in which the ordinary man, including Petrarch himself, feels trapped. Scholars have fussed over Augustinus' Stoicism, but for Petrarch the greater emotional profundity of Christian experience, mediated by the *Confessions,* triumphs over Stoic rationalistic formula.

The *De otio religioso* sees him in the role of religious counsellor and takes his reader (monastic or lay) through the drama of despair at human insignificance and fear of perdition to the great emotional relief of salvation *gratia sola.* Petrarch's is our first, and perhaps best, example of a humanistic *theologia rhetorica* which defines the elements of Christian theology as embedded in the experience and feelings of living individuals. We might today call it 'existential' if the misplacement of such borrowed terms were not both unnecessary and confusing. But if the direct pastoral confrontation of confessor and confessant is crucial in the medieval Christian experience, Petrarch's literary employment of the situation is a vivid, and for him more experientially valid and hence 'true' statement of Christian doctrine, which scholastic theology as 'science' had succeeded in removing from the context of everyday Christian living.

Yet Petrarch, despite his insights into the affective nature of faith, remained ambivalent on the issue of reason, even leaving *Ratio* as spokesman in imitation of Seneca in the later *De remediis*. His endorsement of *gratia sola* of the *De otio* certainly placed salvation beyond reason, beyond free will, but not entirely beyond will. The ambiguity of the role of will in rhetoric is inherent, as appeals to reason were part of the Ciceronian-Senecan tradition taken up from the Stoics. Yet will was seen as affective and nonrational, and rhetoric as such seeks to move, and to move towards action carrying out a transformed inner purpose or will, as Augustine affirmed in the *De doctrina Christiana*. An Augustinian position necessarily sees the ultimate moment of conversion as suprarational resolution of conflicting wills, which Petrarch recognized in the *Secretum*. Petrarch's endorsement of Latin rhetoric over Aristotelian science in *De ignorantia* also put him on the side of will—'It is better to will the good than to know the truth'.[56] One need not see any Franciscan or Scotist influence in those humanists who endorse the primacy of the will, because in so many ways their own rhetorical arts and purposes demand it. However, the Augustinian influence from the OESA (*Ordo fratrum eremitorum sancti Augustini*), from Dionigio da Borgo San Sepolcro, from Luigi Marsili and others, is not to be dismissed.

Salutati exhibited much of the same ambivalence about will and reason as Petrarch had.[57] But he also made far-reaching statements of the primacy of the will in human existence and its command over both the intellect and the senses. He seems to have been confronted by some of the same moral and theological dilemmas as the nominalist scholastics of the fourteenth-century faced, although there is no doubt that he chose a different path. The problem again for him was one of exhortation both to himself and his fellows, as against the need felt by Ockhamists (whose influence in Italy, and especially in Florence, was still meagre in Salutati's day) for careful analysis of the logical inconsistencies in theological statements and between them and the scriptures. We should recognize that both rhetoric and dialectic in the fourteenth and fifteenth centuries could lead to a new kind of theology containing a new anthropology. There was perhaps in the case of both types of intellectual practitioners, a common dissatisfaction with the heroic efforts of the twelfth- and thirteenth-century paladins of a theological 'science' to bind Christianity to Hellenic, and primarily to Aristotelian, metaphysics.

Salutati, perhaps more than most humanists, wrote specifically about theological questions. Though he did not sermonize, he addressed consolatory and hortatory letters to his friends and justified his viewpoint in his treatises. Will became uppermost in the context of deciding to embark on a certain way of life, to cultivate certain virtues. Salutati affirmed the primacy of the will most emphatically in *De nobilitate legum et medicinae* (one of the most important of the many important humanist statements made available by Eugenio Garin).[58] The principle of man acting upon the world in keeping with, and justified by, God's command in Genesis 1:28–30, underlies Salutati's forceful statements:

> The first action does not even come into the intellect without the counsel and command of the will. The natural desire of knowing is not an attribute of the intellect but of the will. . . . Although the soul may be nobler than exterior things, intellection is a movement from them into the soul, whereas in what is volition the movement is from the soul into things themselves.[59]

Nothing moves in the soul unless the will commands:

> whose strength is so great and its rule over the other powers of the soul

so mighty, that even though the instruments of the senses are the recipients of the sensible species (images), the effect of such a reception scarcely proceeds further without the orders of the will.[60]

These statements occur within the conventional Aristotelian epistemology from the *De anima* he presents, and although, like some of the Ockhamists, he emphasized that man can only know particulars, he clearly retained the notion of the 'real existence' of genera and species preserved within the individual object. In epistemology he was no nominalist here, though later he endorsed a poetic epistemology of the metaphorical character of all human knowledge and statement concerning God and spiritual beings. On the other hand, it is interesting that Ockham most definitely played down the Scotist emphasis on the primacy of the will and insisted upon a bivalence of these two functional aspects of the soul, whereas it is the humanist, prompted by the needs and implications of rhetoric, who carries voluntarism further. Humanism and nominalism are not fully congruous.

Salutati's conception of his intellectual role and purpose is also to be seen in the relatively late directly theological treatise, *De fato, fortuna et casu*. Strongly Augustinian and also apparently influenced by such thirteenth-century figures as Aegidius of Rome, Salutati affirmed a conception of man as highly active, operating in a world of contingencies—natural, economic, social and political. At the same time he sought a mode of harmonizing man's will with divine providence and the network of natural causation, identified and elaborated by philosophy with divine freedom—each of them problems of central concern to contemporary nominalist theology. Theological in format, the treatise's literary form and position were humanistic, especially in its drive to assert man as co-operator with God in making and directing the universe, a viewpoint that supports and is totally consistent with the later, more literary genre of the dignity of man. Salutati saw the humanist's role as one of providing leadership in binding the *studia humanitatis* and the *studia divinitatis* (his name for the older theological writings) into a mutually supporting unity and certainly had a conception of *humanitas* as concerned with the nature and destiny of mankind in this world and the next.

The work of Lorenzo Valla[61] was of fundamental importance in projecting a Christian-rhetorical conception of man—one which marked a break of the most radical kind from both the medieval Hellenic-Aristotelian metaphysics, and from the naiveté and sentimentality of the Renaissance humanist hope of synthesizing a classical *praeparatio evangeliae* with conventional Christianity. The recent important studies of Valla by Fois, Di Napoli and Camporeale all affirm this.[62] It is difficult to have any certainty as to exactly where Valla's doctrines led historically: whether to Erasmus, or Luther, or the more radical anti-Trinitarian and Socinian heresies, if genuinely to any of them. There seems no question of his own desire, at least, to be a loyal and orthodox Catholic Christian as this was conceived in the fifteenth century. We know that in his own lifetime, Valla was considered doctrinally dangerous (if not a heretic) but at the same time was befriended by cardinals and popes. We also know that he was in post-Tridentine disrepute, admired by Luther, followed by Erasmus in some respects but rejected in others, cited on the Trinity by Servetus, and so on. We cannot deny that there was a reformist impulse in him, and that he wished to straighten out the thinking and doctrinal confusion of his contemporaries, but in this aim he did not depart far from his friends Nicholas of Cusa, the German cardinal, Bessarion, or Pope Nicholas V, or possibly from certain other humanists such as Alberti or Manetti. He had perhaps more in common with Giovanni Gioviano Pontano, the young Neapolitan humanist he seems to have befriended but who rejected and criticized him. Pontano thought of Valla as following only one line of authority, his own, but also recalled his personal kindness. For Pontano he was the perfect example of a *homo contentiosus*.[63] I believe that in all three judgements Pontano was right. Valla was totally anti-Aristotelian, but in many instances primarily for the sake of opposing the scholastics' great authority. Pontano was strongly pro-Aristotle, for he recognized the very strengths of practical insight into human behaviour and linguistic usage that Valla stubbornly ignored. But in the final analysis Pontano's position was as fundamentally anti-metaphysical as Valla's. Or, at least, both men thoroughly undermined the topical metaphysics of Hellenism, preferring an historical conception of thought as springing from cultural experience and linguistic usage. Whatever historical precedents there are here for contemporary analytical linguistic philosophy, or for historicism in general, the implications of his drastic linguistic critique of the nature and origins of human culture for the Christian religion were crucial for Valla. He might well have claimed that his critique itself grew from the implications of Christianity, specifically of its creationist vision of God, with man in the divine image making and shaping his own culture on the model of God creating nature. But on the other hand the Christian Gospel was scripturally based and linguistic, a message presented to us by Christ and his apostles, coming from God but in form a literary text to be understood grammatically, rhetorically, historically and poetically.

Clearly Valla's philological and grammatical studies of classical texts and the New Testament have been stressed by scholars because (*pace* Manetti) he was the founder of biblical humanism and exerted a profound (though contradictory) influence on Erasmus and Luther, as well as on the Latin cultures. However, Valla's anthropology—his conception of human thought and action and of the relation of man's status to that of the animal and the divine—simultaneously led to his seizing upon all that he thought was valid in ancient thought and a transformation of medieval-Renaissance thinking about man into a radically new perspective. The ancients generally conceived of man as part of a graduated scale of animal, human and divine with each segment overlapping with the next. Man was, in his physiology and lower psychology, animal, in his intellectuality or spirituality, semidivine and potentially divine. But Antiquity also offered an alternative conception through the rhetorical tradition. Valla grasped the anthropological implications of the rhetorical tradition which were rooted in Greek sophist (Gorgian-Protagorean) thought. These were in Valla's view the subjectivity of man, the impossibility of the individual transcending his own perceptions except by interpreting another's and incorporating these into his own, and the primarily affective and voluntarist character of this condition, which reduced thinking and communication to provisional convention between two or more humans, all of which made it impossible for mankind to differentiate itself from animal kind on the basis of its psychic and intellectual powers. In many of these powers the animals also excelled. In this way Valla carried the sophistic argument farther than the ancients and destroyed the presupposition of natural hierarchy on which classical ontology was based.

Moreover, Valla's and the sophistic conception of the human condition rendered the concept of nature, or the natural, otiose, since the concept itself was seen as a human product. Men differentiated themselves from animals in so far as they utilized their capacities, which differed from animals only in degree and not in kind, to gain a greater quantity or intensity of pleasure and to avoid pain and trouble more effectively. Man was not animal in body and semi-divine in spirit; he was animal both in body and spirit. Man was not born (i.e. naturally) divine; he encountered phenomena which he interpreted as manifesting divinity. The ancient philosophers (and those Latin rhetoricians influenced by them) inflated man's mental and spiritual powers into something godlike, but this Valla believed was illusory. Instead, man, if he had faith, believed that accounts of God given by men in the scriptures were true and that man had at his beginning as a species encountered his Creator directly and had retained a dim recollection of this afterward. According to Valla faith was not generically different from knowledge since all knowledge and truth was simply any man's sincere affirmation that he thought something was true, and therefore truth itself was a faith that a certain judgement was correct. A man of faith would, after the coming of Christ and the founding of his Church reported in the New Testament, have a far greater knowledge of divinity than those ancients who lost their initial knowledge of God but, dimly recalling it, sought to make themselves gods by transcending their own animal natures through the veneration of intellect and virtue. A Christian who believed that God had returned as Christ would also believe that immortality and resurrection awaited mankind after death. It was only by faith in the truth of Christianity, as revealed in the scriptures, that man could differentiate himself from the animal generically and could then anticipate the possibility of immortality, beatitude and deification in the afterlife.

Such, summarily stated, is Valla's Christian vision of man and God as put forth primarily in his *De vero bono,* but supplemented by readings of his *Repastinatio philosophiae et dialecticae* (first redaction).[64] What he offered, if I have read him correctly, was a resolution of the problem of double consciousness inherited from Antiquity, wherein Petrarch and other humanists, and notably Il Galateo as described above, wrestled with the contradictions between a knowledge of the world gained from personal and shared historical experience, and another one derived from an ultimately divinely inspired intellection of an absolute and rational truth.

This double consciousness, clearly enunciated in Plato's confrontation of Protagoras and Socrates of the *Theatetus,*[65] continued through the syntheses and contrasts of rhetoric and philosophy of the pagan and Christian Latin thinkers on into the Renaissance. There the notion of a lower truth of rhetorical verisimilitude sufficient for politics and everyday life, and a higher truth of philosophy, rational demonstration or mystical intuition necessary for orthodoxy and science, was sometimes incorporated into more conventional humanist thinking, but more often it was utilized by scholastic philosophers to subordinate rhetoric, and the understanding of daily life and political affairs, to their own so-called higher learning. Valla in fact reduced the latter to the former.[66] There is no truth but what is subjectively entertained as true, and our collective faith is Christianity.

In doing so, without direct knowledge of the sophists or *Theatetus* (though with minute and precise knowledge of the Latin texts drawing upon them), Valla affirmed the same preference for will over intellect which Petrarch somewhat ambiguously declared in his 'It is better to will the good than to know the truth' and 'Therefore they wander far who put their time into knowing, not loving God'.[67] But Petrarch's and also Salutati's emphasis on the primacy of will, thoroughgoing as we have seen the latter to be, fell short of Valla's radical denial of any autonomy to thought and his simultaneous subordination of ratiocination to verbal usage and to affect.

Valla, moreover, broke sharply from the tradition of scholastic discussions of the problem of human nature. Will, of course, had been brought into it from an Augustinian rather than an Aristotelian provenance. But Valla went further than either Franciscans or Augustinians, or earlier humanists, in his development of Augustinianism. Making no effort to discover a mode of reconciliation with the Aristotelian hierarchy of vegetative, sensitive and rational souls, he fully assimilated the conception of man as an image of the Trinity, consisting, as Augustine had expounded, of the coequal trinity of memory, intellect and will. Yet for Valla it was clear that primacy was given to affect, to non-rational will, even though he formally kept the equistasis of the three faculties. In the end his transformation of Augustinianism, in which the passions were made equally licit with intellectual virtues and the latter equally culpable, determined his position. In *De vero bono,* just as Augustine saw the pagan virtues as splendid vices, Valla made pagan passion (his eroticized 'Epicureanism' of Vegio or Beccadelli) into Christian charity, and pleasure into beatitude. The pagan world, in which Stoic debates Epicurean on behalf of *honestas* or *voluptas,* is transcended in the Christian one where the heroic virtue of fortitude is the same as charity and the means to Christian fulfilment; divine love of God for the sake of the passion of love is the end. But means and end differ only in time; both are charity, one in the present, the other future; or the first passing and the second becoming eternally present.

However, in Valla's Renaissance version, trinitarian man becomes creative and activist. Virtue is *fortezza/carità* because man is a force (*vis*) acting upon the world. Virtue is infused into man by grace but effused out of man. It is therefore not a *habitus.* Rather prudence, the intellect, the arts and all the disciplines are slowly acquired by training, and are habits. Man is born with his passions but painstakingly acquires his intellectual skills. Man with his trinitarian nature is likened to a flame:

> Just as a flame seizes and devours and renders into ashes the material by which it is fed, so the soul is nourished in learning and hides what it perceives within itself and transfigures it in its own heat and light, so that it paints others rather than being painted by others. And as the sun paints its image in polished and smooth things and does not receive their images in itself, so the soul, advancing into exterior things by its own light, projects and depicts a certain image of its memory, intellect and will.[68]

Man, therefore, is part of nature in sharing the same kinds of capacities with animals. But in so far as he discovers that his trinitarian nature is of divine origin and is in the image and likeness of God, man transcends his nature and diverts his pursuit of pleasure from the limited things of this life to the eternal pleasure of beatitude. In this he simultaneously creates a higher Christian culture and transcends nature, or becomes divine. Pagan man sought to create culture with the acquisition of virtues as his chief end of life, but in this he remained one with nature and the animals, and all his creations (as in fact ancient philosophers believed) are merely extensions of nature. Only Christian man becomes a true creator in this world by fulfilling his divinely assigned role of providential manager of nature.

Three closely related themes—free will, pleasure, deification—are also involved in humanist discussions of providentiality, and for all three, which were widely discussed by other humanists, Valla provided a paradig-matic clarity and relevance of interpretation. Humanists not only affirmed the power of will but discussed the necessity of *liberum arbitrium* as an inherent quality of will. Rhetoric assumes this freedom of choice, for otherwise its appeals are futile. Will became a problem both in the context of secular actions and in that of salvation. In the former there was never any question of man's providential freedom to govern nature or human affairs, the only obstacles being physical recalcitrance, fortune and human inca-pacity to act wisely due to the complexity of man's psychic nature. Howev-er, it has to be assumed that by rhetorical appeal he could be aroused to clarity of perception and thought, and propriety of action in the secular realm. The real debate occurred over the question of whether man could attain salvation by the merits of his freely chosen actions or psychic states. Here we cannot review the vast question of ecclesiastical discussions of which many humanists were well aware. And although their importance is obvious we are compelled by reason of space to omit treatment of Petrarch and Salutati. Because they qualify more as formal philosophers than hu-manists, we also do not deal with Ficino and Giovanni Pico della Mirandola and the entire development of Platonism and Hermetism.

Whereas Petrarch and Salutati had emphasized grace and providence but also necessarily affirmed human freedom of choice, Valla's famous position seems even more contradictory. But it is not. Freedom of the will is asserted as an undeniable quality of human experience, which is the first great source of truth for Valla. But divine foreknowledge and predestina-tion are also affirmed on the basis of his faith in the Pauline passages in Romans. The scriptures were, of course, the other great source of truth for Valla. It was clear to him that they were contradictory, but because man's understanding was limited to experience and faith he could not resolve their contradiction but had to accept them both as a *mysterium*.[69] He was closer to Petrarch in standing on experience and faith and avoiding philosophical complexities, but was not unsympathetic to Salutati's desire to affirm a vision of God and man, despite the *ventosa sophistica* of dialectical theology.

Pleasure and sensuality were also subject to humanist praise and blame, particularly as far as the pursuit of pleasure seemed to divert man from God and salvation, and reduce him abjectly to an animal state. Hence a variety of opinions is to be found among the humanists which, again, we cannot deal with here. Valla was not the only one to endorse pleasure as central to human experience, but let us see how he interpreted it in its secular and religious contexts.

Valla's position was important because he stressed, in his antiphiloso-phism, the continuity between the psychic natures of animals and men when outside the realm of salvation. The power of will and of affectivity which he stressed, he saw as closely linked to the senses. *Voluptas,* as the gratificatory goal of animal/human life in Books 1 and 2 of *De vero bono,* is made the equivalent of love and charity in Book 3. Love of God is the ultimate pleasure, but not for the sake of God but because God is the efficient cause of human pleasure and of the human capacity to love. God creates the lovable objects of the world and the human capacities of sensory recipience and loving—*amatio.*

> In God both of these concur, for He produced us from nothing, fit for enjoying good things, so that we ought to love him more than ourselves, and He supplied those very goods which we perceive. Moreover God is these goods Himself, but is distinguished from them by a certain property. For our beatitude is not God Himself but descends from God, as the joy which I take in seeing brightness, or hearing a mellow voice, is not the same as the brightness or the voice, but these things offered to my senses cause me to enjoy. Thus from the vision and knowledge of God, beatitude itself is generated. It should also be noticed that although I say pleasure or delight is the only good, nevertheless, I love not pleasure but God. Pleasure itself is love, but what makes pleasure is God. The recipient loves, the received is loved; loving (*amatio*) is delight itself, or pleasure, or beatitude, or happiness, or charity, which is the ultimate end and on account of which all other things are made.[70]

This is clearly a crucial passage, since Valla speaks as a Christian but endorses pleasure, and by his great power of penetrating to the heart of an experience, sees the identity of pleasure and charity or love. Pleasure of loving is both the ultimate human experience and the great motivator of human thought and action.

Another important humanist theme was that of 'deification'. In the context of image-and-likeness theology, salvation was traditionally seen as *theosis* or *deificatio,* for through this man regained his lost original dignity and even, through Christ's work of redemption, surpassed it. The conception gained a special significance in the Renaissance through its linkage with the new vision of man's creativity on the model of divine creativity. The special qualities of man expounded by Manetti found a more explicit parallel in Ficino's list of the qualities of divinity which men emulated in their eagerness to attain deification. These can be found in the first eight chapters of Book 14 of his *Theologia Platonica*—'That the soul attempts to become God we show by twelve signs according to the twelve gifts of God.' But, as indicated above, we shall not carry our analysis into Renaissance Platonism but simply allude to the tremendous importance of the deification theme in figures such as Ficino and Pico, and perhaps even more in Nicholas of Cusa's conception of man as the creator of culture in the image of God as Creator of reality.[71]

Valla set forth his own vision of deification in his sermon on the Eucharist and in his imagined journey of a soul to Christ in *De vero bono.*[72] But more importantly, one should see in his treatment of affect and virtue an embattled conception of human energy that approaches the notion of divine power. An admirer of combat and struggle, a *miles Christianus* who considered his life and writing as in the service of the Church Militant, his identification of *fortezza* and *carità* as *virtù* in its purest form combines elements drawn from Homeric *arêtè* and from medieval Christian *virtus.* Each pointed toward divinization, the hero emulating the gods by his fortitude, the Christian through his charity manifesting the infusion of divine grace. Though Valla spurned the notion of a *habitus gratiae,* the acquisition of virtue, which he saw as poured in and poured out, remained inexplicable. If acquired, it betokened strength of mind, for to sin is to be conquered by weakness toward that which a man should conquer. Fortitude is the ardour of love which renders animals fierce in the protection of their young, but:

> as we speak more magnificently and aptly, this is why the Apostles, receiving the Holy Spirit, which is the charity of the Father and the Son, were made strong for preaching the Word of God, which previously the Lord had promised to them.[73]

Filled with the Holy Spirit, the *miles Christianus* battles for the right, and in this struggle he approaches the beatification of the other life.

Valla represents, then, the most thorough synthesis of certain patristic-Christian, principally Augustinian, ideas with classical language and rhetorical theory. Within this synthesis of rhetorical and Pauline perspectives, Valla developed a philosophy of man that assimilated the widespread striving for power in Renaissance culture. This power has usually been portrayed by historians as secular and political. Yet it was also a generic human power which not only searched for a certain religious licitness in its possession but was, in its very form and conception, drawn from the Christian tradition of man as created in the divine image. Just as hero or saint was held to approach divinity, so true power was conceived as divine power. This striving for religious and religiously sanctioned power is related as an historical phenomenon to the amazing efflorescence of magic in this period, both natural and spiritual.

But to the humanists power also had a more empirical and naturalistic basis. Language, words and discourse had come to be grasped as something greater than a medium for communicating mental concepts and logical demonstrations. The humanist investigators of classical poetry and rhetoric discovered that language possessed both charm and potency that was activistic and moved men in an organized struggle for existence. Although their classical sources were permeated with philosophic rationalism, the more thorough students of rhetoric—notably Valla and Pontano—discerned the irrational power elements even in the rhetorical writings of Aristotle, Cicero and Quintilian. It was possibly for this reason that Valla was so insistent that ancient rhetoric and grammar had much to offer Christians as means for the promotion of Christ's cause, whereas the ancient philosophical schools were the seedbeds of disunity and heresy. In his own conception of language (he constantly speaks of *vis verbi*) and of the central place of *virtus* (read as 'force' or 'power') in man's existence, there is a recovery of that ancient sophistic recognition of rhetoric as an instrument of power like a magical charm or a potent drug administered by a physician such as is found in Gorgias' *Defence of Helen*. Petrarch, also, argued forcefully for the curative power of language both in his *Contra medicum* and his *De remediis*.[74]

If the above is a valid interpretation of humanist thought, it suggests at the very least that the 'potency' of Renaissance humanism cannot be comprehended in the view of it as a pedantic group of classicizing literary scholars. Indeed the literary and philological studies of the humanists led them to important insights concerning the historical character of human thought and culture. It suggests, furthermore, that the humanists' conceptions of man and his role in the universe had, not at all surprisingly, a profound rapport with the basic trends of Renaissance Italian political, economic and social history and even more with its artistic, cultural and religious history. Finally, one might argue that in the depth, sharpness and range of understanding of their views of human nature and its societal, political and religious ramifications, the humanists clearly laid the foundations for early modern discussions of man, such as have provided a basis for modern anthropological thought. One thinks of Hobbes and Descartes, of Vico and Mandeville among others. But we should also not forget that we should view their anthropological-religious thought anthropologically, and within that context we cannot avoid recognizing how much of the characteristic attitudes and motivations of the men of the Renaissance themselves this body of writing contains—unless, perchance, we have in fact constructed our own neo-Burckhardtian conceptions of Renaissance culture from it!

NOTES

1. Modern study of Renaissance philosophy of man (or philosophical anthropology) begins with Giovanni Gentile, 'Il concetto dell'uomo nel Rinascimento', of 1916, reprinted in his *Il pensiero italiano del Rinascimento* (most recently Florence, 1968), and with Ernst Cassirer, *Individuum und Kosmos in der Philosophie der Renaissance* (1927), Eng. trans. by Mario Domandi (Oxford, 1963).

Both were neo-Burckhardtian and neo-Hegelian or neo-Kantian. For more modern studies see Eugenio Garin, 'La "Dignitas Hominis" e la letteratura patristica', *La Rinascita,* I (1938), 102–46, and many of his other writings; P. O. Kristeller, *Renaissance Concepts of Man and Other Essays* (New York, 1972); Giovanni di Napoli, '"Contemptus Mundi" e "Dignitas Hominis" nel Rinascimento', *Rivista di filosofia neoscolastica,* XLVIII (1956), 9–41, and his *L'immortalità dell'anima nel Rinascimento* (Turin, 1963); Charles Trinkaus, *In Our Image and Likeness: Humanity and Divinity in Italian Humanist Thought* (London-Chicago, 1970) (hereafter cited as *IOIAL*) and 'The Renaissance idea of the dignity of man', *Dictionary of the History of Ideas,* IV (New York, 1973), 136–47. Extensive further bibliographies in Kristeller, Di Napoli, Trinkaus.

2. See Werner Jaeger, *Paideia: The Ideals of Greek Culture,* 3 vols (Oxford, 1939–44); Henri-I. Marrou, *Histoire de l'éducation dans l'antiquité,* 6th edn (Paris, 1965), 151–60 ('La civilisation de la "Paideia" '). For *humanitas* and Renaissance see Kristeller's classical statement, 'Humanism and Scholasticism in the Italian Renaissance', *Byzantion,* XVII (1944/5), 346–74, reprinted in *Studies in Renaissance Thought and Letters* (Rome, 1956), 553–83 and elsewhere. Also see Gioacchino Paparelli, *Feritas, Humanitas, Divinitas (L'essenza umanistica del Rinascimento)* (Naples, 1973).

3. See Garin, Di Napoli, Trinkaus as above.

4. See Jaeger, op. cit., I, xiii–xxix, for important discussion of the ancient conception of culture and the way it differs from modern relativistic anthropology.

5. Cf. Paparelli, op. cit., 124–6.

6. Thus the Renaissance emphasis on *humanitas* as a product of custom and education, rather than nature, introduced an explicit relativism into the universalism received from Antiquity. See S. N. Stever, *Philology and Historical Thought in Early Italian Humanism* (Ann Arbor, University Microfilms, 1976. Diss. Univ. of Michigan).

7. G. G. Pontano, *De sermone libri sex,* ed. by S. Lupi and A. Riscato (Lugano, 1954), I.i.3: *'Ut autem ratio ipsa dux est ac magistra ad actiones quasque dirigendas, sic oratio illorum ministra est omnium quae mente concepta ratiocinandoque agitata depromuntur in medium, cum sociabiles, ut dictum est, nati simus sitque vivendum in multitudine; quae quo maior est ac frequentior, eo in illa huberior est copia eorum omnium quibus vita indigeat, quando nascentibus hominibus inopia data est comes; qua re vita ipsa longe aptior redditur atque habilior tum ad assequandas virtutes tum ad felicitatem comparandam.'*

8. ibid., I.iii.1: *'populosissimis in civitatibus amplissimisque in administrationibus.'*

9. ibid. I.iii.2: *'Sed nos hac in parte de ea, quae oratoria sive vis facultasque sive ars dicitur, nihil omnino loquimur, verum de oratione tantum ipsa communi, quaque homines adeundis amicis, communicandis negociis in quotidianis praecipue utuntur sermonibus, in conventibus, consessionibus, congressibus familiaribusque ac civilibus consuetudinibus. Qua a re alia quadam hi ratione commendantur quam qui oratores dicuntur atque eloquentas.'*

10. ibid., I.iv.1–2: *'Nec vero natura in hoc quoque a se ipsa discessit aut ab ea, quae sua ipsius propria est, varietate ac dissimilitudine. Cum aliorum sermones severi sint ac*

subtristes, aliorum iucundi et lepidi, huius blanda sit elocutio atque ornata, illius inculta et aspera, atque alius in loquendo prae se ferat urbis mores, alius vero ruris, est videri qui velit facetus et comis, contra qui austerus et rigidus, qui maxime verus omnique a simulatione alienus, secus autem cui dissimulatio placeat aut ea quae Graece est "ironia". Itaque loquendi genus tum cuiusque naturam tum etiam mores sequi potissimum videtur. Quid? quod populi gentesque, sive nature ab ipsa sive ab institutione et usu quodque alia alibi magis probantur suntque in pretio maiori, aliae taciturniores sunt, contra loquaciores aliae? Magniloquentia delectat Hispanos, fucatus ac compositus sermo Graecos, Romanorum gravis fuit oratio, Lacedaemoniorum brevis et horrida, Atheniensium multa et studiosa, at Carthaginiensium Afrorumque callida et vafra, de natura illorum sic dicta. Quo fit, ut genus colloquendi alibi aliud magis probetur aut minus.'

11. ibid., I.vii.2: *'quae susceptorum laborum honestum sit levamen relaxatioque maxime laudabilis a curis ac molestis . . . quae hominem ipsum ita constituat ut per eam constet humana conciliatio vigeatque in civitate fides, penes quam actionum nostrarum omnium ac negotiationum vinculum existat ac promissorum doctorumque observatio.'*

12. ibid., I.vii.1: *'adulatores et quasi verborum mercaturam faciant, oratione ubique utuntur secunda et blanda.'*

13. ibid., I.xviii.1–2: *'Et quam alii a natura concessam elocutionem exercent in conservanda hominum societate, in conciliandi amicitiis, in solandis demulcendisque molestiis, laboribus ac moeroribus aliorum, ea ipsi in adversum utantur vel abutantur potius ad odia contrahenda litesque excitandas ac serenda discordiarum semina. . . . Odiosum sane genus hominum et muscarum maxime simile, ut nati hi omnino videantur ad turbas, vexationes, inquietudinem vitaeque ad universae turbationem ac taedia.'*

14. ibid., I.xxx.3: *'quacumque in actione ac vitae genere humanum: . . . nihil superbe agit, nihil arroganter; in incessu, in sermone, in consuetudine aequalem se cunctis exhibet; aegre fert ubi in quempiam agi viderit insolentius, fert gravate et amicorum et civium adversos casus; solatur moerentes, laborantibus qua potest succurrit, adest, opitulatur, operam suam confert; astat ubique comes ei mansuetudo ac facilitas.'*

15. ibid., I.xxx.4: *'a comitate non uno modo differt humanitas. Etenim, qui aliorum moveatur damnis, incommodis, captivitate, orbitate, inopia, exilio malisque aliis, humanum hunc dicimus, nequaquam in hoc tamen comem. . . . Inest tamen utrique quaedam quasi communitas vivendi quacumque in actione ac negocio, sive eam facilitatem vocare volumus sive tractabilitatem.'*

16. G. Manetti, *De dignitate et excellentia hominis*, ed. by E. R. Leonard (Padua, 1976), III.20; 78: *'Nam cum primi illi homines et vetusti eorum successores sine mutuis quibusdam et vicissitudinariis favoribus per se solos nequaquam vivere posse animadvertent, subtile quoddam et acutum loquendi artificium adinvenerunt ut per linguam intercedentibus verbis abstrusa queque atque intime mentis sensa cunctis audientibus innotescerent. Cum deinde, tractu ut fit temporis, genus humanum mirum in modum multiplicaretur ad diversas orbis regiones provinciasque incoleret, necessarium fuit ut elementarum caracteres invenirentur . . . Unde tam varia linguarum genera et tam diverse litterarum figure emanasse et profluxisse cernuntur.'*

17. *Epistole*, critical edn by A. Altamura (Lecce, 1959), 104–20.

18. ibid., 104–5: *'gymnosophistae, magi, chaldei, sacerdotes, vates. Apud Arabes etiam,*

nostrae aetati proximis saeculis, multi et excellentes viri in sapientiae floruerunt. Nos Christiani habuimus quondam nostros, qui veram sapientiam secuti sunt, quam et nos docuerunt, apostolos et evangelistas.'

19. ibid., 105: *'et hoc nomen homo aequivocum esse et non secundum eandem rationem de omnibus praedicari, ut de homine picto et de homine vero.'*

20. ibid., 106: *'pulcherrimum putant ostentare sapientiam, ostentare sanctissimos mores, occultare scelera.'*

21. ibid., 108: *'Magna in rebus humanis ac potentissima res est educatio, primaque illa pabula teneris animis adhibita multum habent in tota vita momenti.'*

22. ibid., 110: *'Sed quum nihil facilius sit quam seipsum fallere nihilque in vita divinius quam seipsum cognoscere, saepenumero, cum homines simus, fallimor; sed nunquam superbius aut arrogantius quam cum eorum, quorum vix discipuli esse meremur, consilia atque actiones corrigimus atque damnamus.'*

23. Cf. my *Adversity's Noblemen, The Italian Humanists on Happiness* (New York, 1965), 47–63 and *passim;* Francesco Tateo, 'La disputa della nobiltà', in *Tradizione e realtà nell'Umanesimo italiano* (Bari, 1967), 355–421.

24. Op. cit., 112: *'beatos nos esse cum maledixerint nobis homines et cum persecutionem patimur propter iustitiam. . . . cum vilissima plebs nos insanos iudicaverit. . . . conscia stultitae et malitiae suae, . . . "Hi sunt, quos habuimus aliquando in derisum. . . . Nos insensati vitam illorum existimabamus insaniam, et finem illorum sine honorem. Ecce quomodo computati sunt inter filios Dei! . . . Ergo erravimus a via veritatis . . ." . . . Quis enim, nisi inscius rerum humanarum et verae nobilitatis, Horatium plebeium aut ignobilem appellaverit?'*

25. ibid., 111: *'Quae quanti sit et quam beata, siqua est, vita otiosa, qui philosophi non sunt non noverunt. . . . Ocium apud sapientes beatum habetur; apud barbaros, hoc est apud indoctos et plebeios, ut ignavum contemptui ac dedecori. Soli igitur philosophi . . . laborant ut quiescant et ocientur; populares vero laborant quotidie, ut magis et magis laborent et agantur.'*

26. Pontano, op. cit., I.xii.4: *'perinde ut cessatio omnis quiesque conceditur relaxandi gratia utque reditus ad labores ac negocia non sit gravis, sic iocos, dicta, sales, lepores facetiasque concedi, ne vitam cogitationesque nostras omnis studiaque in iis collacasse aut in ocio desidiaque aut in marcescentia potius nos appareat.'*

27. *IOIAL,* part II, 'The human condition in humanist thought', provides background for this section but the treatment is independent, more considered and, I hope, more developed. My discussion of Petrarch is based on more extended treatment in my *The Poet as Philosopher, Petrarch and the Formation of Renaissance Consciousness* (New Haven, 1979), but, again, it considers Renaissance anthropological thought in general.

28. Cf. *IOIAL,* 179–80, 190–6.

29. Cf. *IOIAL,* ch. V for da Barga.

30. Lotharius Cardinalis, *De miseria humanae conditionis,* ed. by Michele Maccarrone (Lugano, 1955), 3: *'Si vero paternitas vestra suggesserit, dignitatem humane nature Christo favente describam, quatinus ita per hoc humilietur elatus ut per illud humilis exaltetur.'*

31. Maccarrone, x–xx; Nicholas Mann, 'The manuscripts of Petrarch's *De remediis,* a checklist', *Italia medioevale e umanistica,* 14 (1971), 57–90; W. Fiske, *Francis*

Petrarch's Treatise De remediis utriusque fortunae, Text and Versions, Bibliographical Notices, III (Florence, 1888).

32. Cf. P. L. Entralgo, La Curación por la Palabra en la Antigüedad Clásica (Madrid, 1958), Eng. trans. L. Rather and J. Sharp (New Haven, 1970).

33. Cf. D. P. Walker, Spiritual and Demonic Magic from Ficino to Campanella (London, 1958), ch.I. See now G. W. McClure, The Renaissance Vision of Solace and Tranquillity (Ann Arbor, University Microfilms, 1981. Diss. Univ. of Michigan).

34. See IOIAL, 258–70 for Poggio arguments.

35. In his 'Studi su Leon Battista Alberti', in Rinascite e Rivoluzioni: Movimenti culturali dal XIV al XVII secolo (Rome-Bari, 1975), 133–96.

36. Cf. Salvatore I. Camporeale, Lorenzo Valla, Umanesimo e teologia (Florence, 1972), ch. I; Mario Fois, Il pensiero cristiano di Lorenzo Valla (Rome, 1969), ch.XIII.

37. The discussion of Manetti which follows, while dependent on IOIAL, cap. VI, 230–58, develops further an emphasis on human creativity. For his text I now follow the recent edition of Elizabeth R. Leonard, Giannozzo Manetti, De dignitate et excellentia hominis (Padua, 1976). Cited as 'Leonard'.

38. Lib. II, paragraph 36; Leonard, 57–8 (paragraph numbering is by Leonard): 'plera magna et ingentia vel facinora vel machinamenta admirabiliter inventa et intellecta.'

39. III, 11; Leonard, 71: 'Deus . . . hominem formosissimum, ingeniosissimum sapientissimum, opulentissimum ac denique potentissimum efficeret'.

40. Quoting Cicero, De nat. deorum, II, 39; III, 12; Leonard, 73: 'Quid denique de humano genere dicemus? qui quasi cultores terre constituti non patiuntur eam nec immanitate beluarum efferari nec stirpium asperitate vastari, quorumque operibus agri, insule littoraque collucent distincta terris et urbibus? Que quidem omnia, si ut animis sic oculis uno aspectu videre et conspicere possemus quale et quam mirabile spectaculum nobis ita viventibus et conspicientibus appareret.'

41. III, 20; Leonard, 77: 'cuncta queque post primam illam novam ac rudem mundi creationem ex singulari quodam et precipuo humane mentis acumine a nobis adinventa ac confecta et absoluta fuisse videantur. Nostra namque hoc est humana sunt, quoniam ab hominibus effecta cernuntur.'

42. III, 21; Leonard, 78: 'Hec quidem et cetera huiusmodi tot ac tales undique conspiciuntur ut mundus et cuncta eius ornamenta ab omnipotenti Deo ad usus hominum primo inventa institutaque et ab ipsis postea hominibus gratanter accepta multo pulchriora multoque ornatiora ac longe politiora effecta fuisse videantur.'

43. III, 45; Leonard, 91: 'sic pariter rectum et simplex atque unicum offitium suum tale esse existimamus et credimus, ut mundum eius causa factum ac presertim cuncta que in hoc universo terrarum orbe constituta videmus gubernare et administrare cognoscat et valeat, quod nequaquam nisi cum agendo tum intelligendo penitus perficere et omnino adimplere poterit.'

44. III, 55–6; Leonard, 97: 'Proinde et homo vivens mundi incola fit et pie moriens celi possessor efficitur, ac per hunc modum et in hac presenti et in futura vita semper et omni quidem tempore felix beatusque habetur. Et ex hac igitur tanta ac tam sublimi hominis dignitate et excellentia velut ab ipsa radice invidia, superbia, indignatio, dominandi

libido et ambitio, atque cetere huiusmodi animi perturbationes non iniuria oriuntur et profluunt. Nam qui se se ita dignum factum fuisse considerat, ut cunctis rebus creatis preesse ac dominari videatur, profecto non modo ab aliis superari non patietur, quod est invidie, sed potius ceteros excellere vel maxime concupiscet, quod superbie et ambitionis proprium vitium existimatur et creditur. At si forte contigerit ut aliquando spernatur, negligatur, et contemnatur, usque adeo indignatur ut contemptores suos non secus quam capitales ac acerrimos hostes ac proprios quosdam excellentiarum suarum violatores et detractores enixe usque ad necem persequatur. Quod ego etiam atque etiam considerans atque hominem noviter describere et diffinire volens, ipsum animal indignabundum mea quidem sententia non iniuria explicavi.'

45. III, 58; Leonard, 98: *'ut hominem per hanc humilem humane carne susceptionem mirabiliter et incredibiliter honoraret glorificaretque.'*

46. III, 59; Leonard, 98: *'nisi ut ea per admixtionem cum ipsa divinitate non solum coniuncta in illa Christi persona cum divina, sed etiam ut cum divina natura et sola efficeretur.'*

47. Urb. lat. 1245, f. 28r; Ottob. lat. 1828, f. 176r.: *'comparata his quae humana invenit industria, sordidissima et abiectissima sunt. Ea etiam contulisse homini naturam supervacaneum fuisset, quae nihil agit otiosum, quoniam ingenio et ratione sibi meliora parat homo quam quae brutis natura concessit.'* Cf. IOIAL, 281, 438 n. 33.

48. ibid., f. 22v; f. 127r: *'Nec miseros esse mortales autumno, licet Creator benignissimus Deus homini dixerit, "In sudore vultus tui visceris pane tuo." In quibus verbis tacite monuit, non praedandum, rebus parcendum alienis, non otio marcescendum sed agendum semper aliquid. An si erit manus, pedes, linguae, oculi caeterorumque corporis organorum munus proprium totius hominis nullum erit? Quid igitur illi profuit intelligere, quid sentire, quid opinari, velle, memorari, quid praeterita cum presentia conferre ac per ea futuris iudicare si nihil agendum homini fuerat?'* Cf. IOIAL, 281, 438 n. 34.

49. ibid., f. 20r; f. 169v: *'De parentum nostrorum labe omnem posteritatem inquinatem quod non sint mortales idcirco miseria, hoc satis sit dixisse quod pia mater ecclesia propterea canit, videlicet, "O felix culpa quae tantam ac talem meruit habere redemptorem." de Jesu salvatore nostro intelligens.'* Cf. IOIAL, 288, 441, n. 48.

50. ibid., f. 25v; f. 174v: *'Profecto nulla ratione humanum capere ingenium potest quod Deus hominem ad imaginem sui dominumque rerum omnium, quae in aere, quae in terra, quae in mari sunt, compotum disciplinarum omnium et paulo inferiorem fecerit angelis . . . ut demum miser et calamitosus esset homo, irritque forent divini conatus, nativitas Christi, passio et resurrectio pro salute humana.'* Cf. IOIAL, 289, 441 n. 50.

51. ibid., ff. 15v, 16v; 166r–v: *'At dicet labor est indeficiens. Maius hinc stat meritum pugnanti quam cedenti locum. . . . Primam hominis perfectionem philosophantes esse dicunt quod sit bonis artibus eruditus, secundam vero in actione studiosa collocant. Sapients autem si fuerit otiosus nihil a segni vel saltem dormiente differt. . . . Felix erit igitur dum fuerit in actione studiosa.'* Cf. IOIAL, 286, 441 n. 48.

52. *I libri della famiglia* in Cecil Grayson (ed.), *Opere volgari*, I (Bari, 1960); *De iciarchia*, ibid., II (Bari, 1966). Passage I, 131: *'Pertanto cosi mi pare da credere sia l'uomo nato, certo non per marcire giacendo, ma per stare faccendo.'*

53. ibid., I, 131–2: *'. . . colle quali l'uomo vince la forza, velocità e ferocità d'ogni*

altro animale . . . esserci date per nolle molto adoperare. . . . in Dio somma felicità el far nulla. . . . maravigliose opere divine. . . . speculatore e operatore delle cose. . . . l'uomo essere modo e misura di tutte le cose. . . . el quale constitui l'uomo essere quasi come un mortale iddio felice, intendendo e faccendo con ragione e virtù.'

54. ibid., I, 133–4: *'Aggiugni qui a queste quanto l'uomo abbia a rendere premio a Dio, a satisfarli con buone opere per e'doni di tanta virtù quanta Egli diede all'anima dell'uomo sopra tutti gli altri terreni animanti grandissima e prestantissima. Fece la natura, cioè Iddio, l'uomo composto parte celeste e divino, parte sopra ogni mortale cosa formosissimo e nobilissimo. . . . Statui ancora Iddio negli animi umani un fermo vinculo e contenere la umana compagnia, iustizia, equità, liberalità e amore, colle quali l'uomo potesse apresso gli altri mortali meritare grazia e lode, e apresso el Procreatore suo pietà e clemenza . . . fermezza, stabilità, constanza e forza, e spregio delle cose caduche . . . con giustizia, pietà moderanza e con ogni altri perfetta e lodatissima operazione. Sia adunque persuaso che l'uomo nacque non per atristirsi in ozio, ma per adoperarsi in cose magnifice e ampie, colle quali e' possa piacere e onorare Iddio in prima, e per avere in sé stessi come uso di perfetta virtù, così frutto di felicità.'*

55. For the ensuing discussion of Petrarch see my *IOIAL*, ch. 1 and *The Poet as Philosopher*, chs 3–5.

56. *'Satius est autem bonum velle quam veram nosse.'* In G. Martellotti *et al.* (eds), *Prose* (Milan-Naples, 1955), 748.

57. For a fuller discussion see *IOIAL*, ch. 2.

58. Ed. E. Garin (Florence, 1947), cited as 'Garin'.

59. Garin, 192: *'etiam ad intellectum non perveniat actus primus sine consensu vel imperio voluntatis. Naturale quidem sciendi desiderium non est intellectus sed voluntatis. . . . licet anima sit nobilior exterioribus rebus a quibus intelligere motus est ad animam; et in hoc quod est velle sit ab anima in res ipsas.'* Cf. *IOIAL*, 64, 349 n. 37.

60. Garin, 184: *'cuius quidem tanta vis est tantusque super alias anime potentias principatus, quod etiam licet sensuum instrumenta recipiunt sensibilium species, talis receptionis effectus sine voluntatis iussibus ulterius vix procedat.'* Cf. *IOIAL*, 67, 350 n. 46.

61. For fuller discussion see *IOIAL*, ch. 3.

62. For Fois and Camporeale see n. 36 above. G. Di Napoli, *Lorenzo Valla, Filosofia e religione nell'Umanesimo italiano* (Rome, 1971).

63. Pontano, op. cit., I.xviii.6.

64. Cf. my earlier discussion in *IOIAL*, ch. 3, *passim* and 146–50, 167–70. While Camporeale, Fois, Di Napoli and myself all have different emphases, we seem to approach a consensus as to Valla's great importance as a religious thinker.

65. See *The Poet as Philosopher*, ch. 2, and my 'Protagoras in the Renaissance, an exploration', in E. P. Mahoney (ed.), *Philosophy and Humanism* (Leiden, 1976), 119–213.

66. I believe that the scholarly study of this debate of humanists and scholastics over 'truth' is only now beginning. But see J. E. Seigel, *Rhetoric and Philosophy in Renaissance Humanism* (Princeton, 1968), ch. 5; and C. Vasoli, *Studi sulla cultura del Rinascimento* (Manduria, 1968), 257–344. See also my 'The Question of Truth in Renaissance Rhetoric and Anthropology' in *Renaissance Elo-*

quence: *Studies in the Theory and Practice of Renaissance Rhetoric*, ed. James J. Murphy (Berkeley and Los Angeles, 1983), 207–20.

67. *Itaque longe errant qui . . . in cognoscendo, non amando Deo tempus ponunt.* See n. 56 above.

68. Urb. lat. 1207, f. 76v: *'sicut flamma ignis materiam qua ali apprehendit, devorat, et in prunas convertit, sic anima alitur discendo et ea quae percipit in se recondit, suoque calore ac sua luce transfigurat ut ipsa potius pingit alia quam pingatur ab aliis. Et ut sol in rebus politis ac levibus imaginem suam pingit non illarum in se accipit, sic anima fulgore suo in exteriora prodiens memoriae, intellectus, voluntatisve velut quandam obiicit, et depingit imaginem.'* Cf. *IOIAL*, 164, 386 n. 147.

69. Cf. *IOIAL*, 165–8.

70. Ottob. lat. 2075, f. 219₄; *De vero falsoque bono*, ed. by M. de P. Lorch (Bari, 1970), 114: *'In deum haec ambo concurrunt, qui et nos producit ex nihilo, aptos bonis fruendis, ut se plus quam nos amare debeamus; et haec ipsa suppeditavit bona. Haec autem bona Deus ipse est, sed quadam proprietate distinguitur. Nam beatitudo nostra non est ipsemet Deus sed a Deo descendit, ut gaudium quod capio videnda claritate, aut audienda suavi voce non idem est quod claritas aut vox, sed haec sensibus meis oblata faciunt ut gaudeam. Ita ex visione et notitia Dei beatitudo ipsa generatur. Illud quoque animadvertendum, licet dicam voluptatem, sive delectationem esse solum bonum, non tamen voluptatem amo sed Deum. Voluptas ipsa amor est quod autem voluptatem facit Deus. Recipiens amat; receptum amatur; amatio ipsa delectatio est, sive voluptas, sive beatitudo, sive felicitas, sive charitas; qui est finis ultimus et propter quem fiunt cetera,'* Cf. *IOIAL*, 138, 376 n. 86.

71. *'Quod anima nitatur Deus fieri, ostendimus signis duodecim secundum duodecim Dei dotes.'* Cf. Marsilio Ficino, *Théologie Platonicienne de l'Immortalité des Ames*, ed. R. Marcel (Paris, 1964), II, 246–79. I.e. 'God is and man strives to be (1) one, true and good; (2) everything; (3) the creator of the universe; (4) above all; (5) in all; (6) always. God does and man strives to: (7) provide for all; (8) administer justly; (9) persevere with fortitude in his state of being; (10) deal temperately and smoothly; (11) live richly and joyously; (12) see, admire and worship himself' (*IOIAL*, 487). For Nicholas of Cusa see Pauline Moffitt Watts, *Nicolaus Cusanus, A Fifteenth-Century Vision of Man* (Leiden, 1982), chs 3, 4 and 5.

72. See *IOIAL*, 144–6, 633–8.

73. Urb. lat. 1207, f. 73v: *'ut magnificentius ac pro materia aptius loquamur hinc est quod apostoli accepto spiritu sancto qui est caritas patris et filii effecti sunt fortes ad loquendum verbum Dei, id quod autem Dominus eis futurum promiserat.'* Cf. *IOIAL*, 160, 385 n. 139.

74. Cf. *The Poet as Philosopher*, chs 4 and 5.

Luther's Hexameral Anthropology

The following essay examines Luther's views of human nature and the conditions of human existence as he manifested them in his *Lectures on Genesis,* chapters 1–3.[1] Although Luther dealt with man in many writings and contexts, the *Vorlesungen über 1 Mose* is particularly appropriate for study because of the long Christian tradition of treatment of man in the context of both his creation *ad imaginem et similitudinem Dei* of Genesis 1:26 and man's Fall and Curse of chapter 3. Scholarly interest in this work has seemed to focus more on Luther's conceptions and practice of Biblical exegesis and on his theologically crucial conception of the Word than on what it reveals of Luther's views of man. My interest will center on Luther's anthropology and how it compares with the humanistic traditions of the "dignity of man" rather than on his exegetical sources or on the scholastic traditions emphasized by Gerhard Ebeling in his study (now still in progress) of Luther's *Disputatio de homine.*[2]

It should be no surprise that on the topic of man, and here in this single work, Luther seems to present more than one point of view, and, as is also usual, it will be our task to compare them and seek to unify them, if that is possible. Although his first significant statement occurs on 1:14, we shall look first at the *locus classicus* for discussions on human dignity: *Faciamus hominem ad imaginem et similitudinem nostram* of Genesis 1:26.[3]

In the exegetical traditions concerning this verse there are three basic questions that are almost always discussed: why the special differentiation in the creation of man of the use of a first person imperative instead of the third person: "Let us"?; why the use of the plural *"Faciamus"*; and the large and extended question of what are the meanings of *imago* and *similitudo* and how they are applied to man.[4] For Luther the use of first person by God indicates a deliberate taking of counsel by God, adding a notable and significant difference between the creation of man and others. The animals have a great similarity to man in that men and animals live together, eat, sleep and rest. "But here the text emphatically separates man since it says God had conceived of making man in a definite deliberation, and not only this but of making man in the image of God."[5]

This article deals with Luther's conceptions of the earthly condition of man as revealed in the Genesis accounts of creation and man's fall. It was written for *Continuity and Discontinuity in Church History, Essays Presented to George Hunston Williams,* ed. F. Forrester Church and Timothy George (Leiden: E. J. Brill, 1979), 150–68.

Luther immediately expands on the meaning of this differentiation in a significant way. He sets forth what would have been the condition of man if his nature had remained unimpaired by the Fall. At a definite time, when the human population had grown to the desired fullness, mankind would have been translated to an eternal and spiritual life. At the same time the physical side of man's life, in which he was similar to the animals (nutrition and reproduction), would have been a pleasing service to God, carried on without lust, sin or fear of death. "This certainly would have been a pleasant and delightful life about which we may indeed think but it may not be realized in this life."[6] Man may still look forward to the spiritual life in paradise through the merit of Christ. This is an important statement of Luther's to which we shall shortly return. Meanwhile, he takes up the second question of the plurality of *Faciamus,* emphasizing against various Jewish views, the traditional orthodox Christian interpretation that it represented the involvement of the entire Trinity and was an affirmation of the Trinity.[7]

It is in taking up the third traditional question: "What is that image of God according to which Moses said man was made?" that Luther's break with the tradition takes place, and out of this his own position more clearly emerges. The western theological tradition, as Gerhart Ladner has demonstrated,[8] found its classical statement in Saint Augustine's *De Trinitate,* his *De Genesi ad litteram* and other writings.[9] Stressing *imago* rather than *'omoiosis* as the Greek Fathers had tended, Augustine, as is well known, sought a replication of the divine Trinity in an image in the human soul, with a variety of correspondences between Father, Son and Spirit and memory, intellect and will and a number of their equivalences.[10] For Luther, who first spells out the development of this doctrine in some detail (erring only in identifying Augustine's position with Aristotle's),[11] this will not do: "But just as these not unpleasant speculations point to sharp and otiose minds, so they do hardly anything in rightly explaining the image of God."[12] The trouble is that what started out with Augustine as a likely analogy to make the Trinity understandable ended up with other theologians extending this interpretation into a defense of free will which is born from that image: "For they speak as follows: 'God is free, therefore since man is created according to the image of God, he also has a free memory, mind and will.' In this way much comes out which is either spoken improperly or afterwards taken impiously. Thus the dangerous opinion is born in which it is asserted that God governs men in such a way that He allows them to act on their own impulse . . . From this the conclusion is made that free will concurs as a precedent and efficient cause of salvation. Not unlike these is the more dangerous position of Dionysius when he said, 'Although the demons and man fell, yet the natural powers remained unimpaired, such as mind, memory and will, etc.' But if this is true, it follows that man can so act by the powers of nature that he is saved."[13]

It is clear that Luther, although he sees some good in it, cannot accept this traditional conception of the divine image in the creation of man because it opened the doors to the kind of Pelagian soteriology he regarded as most dangerous. It is also clear that on the same grounds he could not accept the Renaissance notions of the dignity of man, which, almost without exception, were either based on, or included as a central ingredient, this conception of the trinitarian powers of the soul. He adds: "I also fear that, after this image has been lost through sin, we are unable properly to understand it. We, indeed, have memory, will and mind, but most corrupted and seriously weakened, indeed, to speak clearly, entirely leperous and unclean. If those powers are the image of God, Satan, it also follows, was created in the image of God, and he has far stronger natural powers than we have."[14]

For Luther, the image of God in man was the general condition of man at his creation before the Fall and Curse, namely: "That Adam had it in his substance, that he not only knew God and believed that He is good but that he also lived a life that was plainly divine, that is that he was without fear of death and of all dangers and was content in the grace of God." It was as though God said: "This is my image by which you will live just as God lives. But if you sin, you will lose this image and you will die."[15] The significance lies in man's faith and trust in God and the psychological security which accompanies it. It followed that when Adam and Eve sinned out of distrust and loss of faith, they instantly lost the image of God. It was only before the Fall that man could have been godlike, not afterwards as Satan falsely told them.

Before the Fall man indeed had the traditional natural powers of memory, intellect and will "in most beautiful security without any fear of death and without any anxiety whatsoever."[16] But this condition, which was lost, did not constitute man's entire possession of the divine image. "To these interior faculties was also added that most beautiful and excellent power of the body and all its members by which man conquered all other animate natures. For plainly I believe that before sin Adam's eyes were so sharp and clear that he excelled the lynx and the eagle. Moreover, he forcefully dealt with lions and bears, whose strength is the greatest, no differently than we deal with kittens."[17] Luther never neglects the animal-like capacities and qualities of man, in which he excelled before the Fall as part of the divine image. But after the Fall "all experience how great is the rage of the flesh which is not only furious in lusting but also in scorning after it has had what it wished. Thus in both we see neither reason nor a will that is whole, but a fury more than beastlike."[18]

After the Fall there is no question of a human dignity resting on man's creation in the divine image. Within its own premises, however, the post-lapsarian life was later characterized as not entirely devoid of advantages.[19] Rather, now, the human condition is described in terms opposite to what Luther conceived was the pre-lapsarian image of God in man: "Now therefore we see how many dangers, how many deaths and occasions of death this wretched nature is driven to experience and sustain, besides the filthy lust and the other furies of sin and the excessive emotion which are contained in the souls of all men. Never are we secure in God; terror and fright also torture us in dreams. These and similar evils are the image of the Devil who impresses them into us."[20]

He goes on to argue that the divine image is something "really unknown, which not only we do not experience but we instead perpetually experience the contrary and hear nothing of it besides the bare word."[21] Earlier in discussing the beginnings of creation in Genesis 1:2 he argued the incomprehensibility of the divine. "It is madness to dispute concerning God outside and before time because that would be to wish to understand bare divinity or the bare divine essence. Because this is impossible, God involves himself in works and certain images, just as today he involves himself in Baptism and Forgiveness, etc."[22] We have to accept God in and through his wrappings and manifestations, and the Anthropomorphites were not wrong to conceive of God in human terms, but these must clearly be understood as metaphors. "Therefore such figures of speech are pleasing to the Holy Spirit and the works of God are put before us which we may apprehend."[23] On the basis of this limited knowledge, he can present the pre-lapsarian life of Adam, which he will soon argue lasted hardly a single day, as knowable only in its contrast to the life we now know. An important part of it was its fruitfulness, and Adam's strength to dominate over the beasts and to cause any crop he wished for to grow. But as of the following (seventh) day, after the primal sin, nature itself underwent a change; man was physically weakened in his former natural powers; animals became stronger and more dangerous to man; spines and weeds appeared and increased the difficulty of farming;[24] still later the flood was to make things even worse.[25] Therefore, the dignity of man arising out of his creation in the divine image was something that Luther had to adumbrate from what scriptural hints he had and entertain as an act of faith. It could no longer be fully known.

Similarly, the reformation of the divine image in man through Christ and the Gospel had to be taken on faith. "But now the Gospel has brought about the restoration of that image. Intellect and will indeed have remained, but both very much impaired. And so the Gospel brings it about that we are formed once more according to that indeed better image, because we are borne again into eternal life or rather into the hope of eternal life by faith . . ."[26] Not only eternal life is restored but also justice.

It should be noted that he states that intellect and will do remain, though much impaired. As he continues this declaration he refers specifically to the trinitarian qualities of memory, intellect and will that he had spurned above as the elements of the divine image of man. Now in the reformed image he admits these qualities: "In this manner that image of the new creature begins to be repaired through the Gospel in this life, but it is not perfected in this life. But when it is perfected in the kingdom of the Father, then the will will be truly free and good, the mind truly illumined and the memory constant; then also it will happen that all the other creatures will be more subject to us than they were in Adam's Paradise."[27]

As he seems frequently to do, he denies a particular interpretation because it seems to have unacceptable theological implications, only to readmit it later in a different context. The restored image centrally includes man's psychic trinity imaging the divine Trinity, along with immortality and renewed domination of the animal kingdom. But man can only dimly know he possesses this restored image before he enters the heavenly life. "Moreover, this which we say, faith and the Word teach, which show, as though from a great distance, that glory of the divine image."[28] Thus Luther manages both to reject and to reaffirm the traditional argument on behalf of human dignity as based on man's possession of the image of the Trinity. But this possession of the image is reserved for man's brief primeval moment of paradisiac life and for his future restoration through Christ in this world, dimly now and only in faith and hope. Yet in the next life, truly and fully realized, and better than in man's beginning.

But he had also extolled the glory of man earlier in his exposition of the creation of the lights and the division of day and night on the fourth day. Taking up the second part of chapter 1, verse 14: "And let them be for signs and for seasons and for days and years," Luther points out that the value of the heavenly lights for mankind indicated in this verse depends on the invention of number and counting, something which children and animals lack and which has to be learned. "Therefore," he says, "counting indicates that man is an extraordinary creature of God." But what man has added through experience and sciences, such as astrology, is more uncertain. Man's interest in the heavenly bodies and their movements and his acquisition of counting and his measuring of time which the scriptures here enjoin upon him are seen as indicators of the immortality of human souls. Such activities reflect glory on man, because the other animals cannot do this.[29]

He develops this thought into a rounded vision of the course of human existence from creation to salvation. "The first human being was made from a clod by God. Thenceforth the human race was propagated from male and female seed from which, little by little, the embryo is formed in the uterus through its single parts and grows until finally through birth it is brought forth into the light of heaven. Afterwards begins the sensitive life and soon that of action and motion. When the body has gained strength, and mind and reason thrive in a healthy body, then that life of the intellect begins to shine, which does not exist in other earthly creatures, so that by the aid of the mathematical disciplines, which no one can deny are divinely revealed, man in his mind soars on high and, leaving behind earthly things, concerns himself with the heavenly and investigates them. Neither cows, nor pigs nor any other animals do this; only man does it. Therefore, man is a creature created to inhabit the celestial regions, leaving the earth behind at some time, and to live an eternal life. For this is why he not only can speak and make judgments (which pertains to Rhetoric and Dialectic) but thoroughly learns all the mathematical disciplines. Now, therefore, from this fourth day our glory begins to be revealed: that God thought of making such a creature who might understand the movements of those bodies which were created on the fourth day and who would delight in such knowledge as though it was proper to his own nature. They should arouse us to give thanks that, as if its citizens, we may belong to that Fatherland which we now see, admire and understand, though as pilgrims and exiles, but which after this life we may examine more closely and understand more perfectly."[30]

Just as he denies that the mental trinity of memory, intellect and will is what Moses meant by the divine image yet reverts to this standard exegesis for the condition of man before the Fall and after his restoration, so also he takes up here the ancient eulogy of man as master of the liberal arts with explicit reference to the trivium and the quadrivium. Moreover, he talks of God making the world in terms analogous to the human arts, asserting that "the Holy Spirit also has His own language and way of expression, namely, that God, by speaking, created all things and worked through the Word, and that all His works are some words of God, created by the uncreated Word." I do not intend in this essay to enter into the intricacies of Luther's central theological conception of the Word but wish rather only to point out that he has deliberately constructed it on the analogy of the human languages which, he says, exist within each profession. Each profession has its own vocabulary, and the religious meaning of the scriptural account of the creation parallels but does not either affirm or deny the scientific meaning. "Every science should use its own terminology. . . . and they should put their achievements at one another's disposal" just as the various crafts "do to maintain the whole city."[31]

I believe that Luther has revealed here an important echo of the Renaissance (as well as ancient) genre of the dignity of man. In this genre there were two principal arguments supporting man's excellence: first, the magnitude of his mental endowments, reinforced in the Christianizing of the tradition by seeing them (memory, intellect and will), as Augustine did, as the image of the divine Trinity; and second, the accomplishments of the human arts, both the mechanical arts of the craftsman and the liberal arts of the intellectual that, as acquired faculties, differentiate man from the animals. Luther does not explicitly or literally follow this tradition but in a round-about way he brings out both of these two major elements of it, though desiring overtly to deny any dignity to man after the Fall for fear of encouraging a false reliance on free will.

On the other hand, man's relationship to animals plays a major role in Luther's thinking. Before the Fall "naked man without arms and fortifications, indeed, also without any clothing, in his naked flesh only, ruled over the birds, the beasts and the fish." He also had a perfect knowledge of all nature over which he was to rule. Moreover, man knew his Creator, his origin and his destination. Whereas "the other animals entirely lacked this knowledge." "Therefore, they entirely lacked that likeness to God."[32] After the Fall there is still a great difference between man and the other animals but it was much greater before. "The things which we accomplish in life are not now done by means of dominion which Adam had but through industry and art." And man because he now has to work for his living becomes more like the animals and overcomes his physical differences by such invention and labor. Also like the animals, man today is prey to the fury of his emotions, whereas before the Fall "there was also a great unity of minds and wills."[33] When Luther comes to the second account of the creation of man in Genesis chapter 2, which he regards as simply an amplification of what is said in chapter 1,[34] he emphasizes the deliberate action of God in shaping man out of earth and breathing into him a living soul. Here again man is seen as like the animals in his physical life but differentiated by the gift of immortality, which today, through Christ, we have in hope.[35]

Lorenzo Valla, the Italian humanist whom Luther so much admired, had also depicted man as in all ways similar to animals except for his gift of immortality. Man and animals both had similar psychic makeups with the emotions predominating over the intellect, though man's mind was obviously sharper. It was the theological gift that made the difference.[36] So also Luther after his text has described man as placed in the Garden of Eden and provided with the tree of life speaks of his pre-lapsarian life as a physical one to which the spiritual is to be added. Also like Valla Luther emphasized man's pleasure and his enjoyment of both eating and procreation, only in Eden, thanks to the tree of life, he would not have aged as the other animals.[37]

Then the tree of knowledge of good and evil is introduced as a form of religious worship. "Adam was created in such a way that if anything troublesome to his nature had happened he would have a protection against it in the tree of life, which preserved his powers and perfect health at all times. And so, completely surrounded as he was by the goodness of the Creator, if he had remained in the state of innocence, he would have acknowledged God as his Creator and would have governed the beasts according to His will without any inconvenience, in fact with extreme joy. For all things were such that they could not harm man but could delight him in the highest degree. And so when Adam had been created in such a way that he was, as it were, intoxicated with rejoicing toward God and was delighted also with all other creatures, there is now created a new tree for the distinguishing of good and evil, so that Adam might have a definite way to express his worship and reverence toward God."[38]

In distinguishing in this way between two aspects of human life, the secular animal side and the religious, Luther sees Moses as in accord with the established intellectual disciplines: "Therefore, what Moses has said up to now has to do with natural philosophy, economic matters, politics, juridical affairs of medicine. What this statement proposes to Adam about the tree is theological, so that also according to his animality (*animalitatem*) he would have a certain external sign for worshipping God and for yielding obedience in an external work."[39] As he would further develop in great detail in his commentary on chapter 3, Luther regarded the primal sin which ignored the command concerning this tree to be a combination of disobedience to a superior being Who had created man and a reliance by man on his own powers going beyond the bounds of the commanded rule over the animals and guardianship of the garden: "Therefore, let us learn that some external form of worship and a definite work of obedience were necessary for man, who was created to have all other living creatures under his control, to know his Creator, and to thank Him. If, therefore, Adam had not fallen this tree would have been like a common temple and basilica to which people would have streamed." And it would also mark man's acceptance of his limitations and subjection to God.[40]

When he comes to verse 15: "Therefore, the Lord God took man and placed him in the garden of Eden that he might work it and guard it," again Luther speaks of the physical life and the spiritual. But now the former was divided into two functions: "Moreover, God assigns to Adam a twofold duty, namely, to work or cultivate the garden and furthermore to watch and guard it." Vestiges of these duties remain today and give us much trouble and inconvenience. "But if you should wish to discuss the matter of food, not only do the animals have [the need for] it in common with us, but men snatch it away from other men and steal it with fraud. Therefore, there is also need for walls, hedges and other defenses, and yet what you have raised with great trouble can be preserved but feebly."[41] Moreover, now, after the Fall, the earth yields its crops only with labor and sweat and is crowded with thorns and weeds when it would have produced easily and with abundance for Adam if he had not sinned. "Work, which in the state of innocence was a game and a pleasure, is a punishment. And now in this wretched state of nature, if anyone has a pleasant garden it is no labor to sow or plant or dig, but it is done with zeal and a certain pleasure! . . . Moreover, this is a good place to admonish that man was not created for leisure but for labor, even in the state of innocence. Therefore, a life of idleness, such as that of the monks and nuns, is to be condemned."[42]

This is another important statement that aligns Luther with such humanists as Leon Battista Alberti who condemned "ozio" as the greatest of sins and praised a life of activity as the only one fitting for a man of conscience and dignity who wished to fulfill the purpose for which God had created him.[43] It is notable that Luther also made work a duty to be performed in the state of innocence and, though it formally became a punishment after the Fall, it was also a morally desirable and even at times a pleasant state.

Luther's conception of the institutionalizing of human society emerges very specifically in his comments on Genesis 2:16–17: "From every tree of Paradise you shall eat; but from the tree of the knowledge of good and evil you shall not eat." This verse is taken to represent the establishment of the Church, "before there was either an economy or a polity, for Eve was not yet created."[44] The economy is added with the creation of Adam's companion, Eve, and by this he means the household economy, or home, using the term in its old Greek sense. It is the beginning of human society. "Thus the temple is prior to the home just as it is also more important. Moreover, there was no polity before sin, and there was no need for it, for the polity is the necessary remedy against corrupted nature. It is necessary for lust and greed to be constrained by the bonds of law and punishments so that they do not freely wander about. Therefore, you rightly call Polity the kingdom of sin."[45]

Luther's views of the nature of government seem to have changed little here since his treatise on secular government.[46] It is purely protective of the individual home against the rapacious instincts of the others. On the previous verse (2:15) he spoke of the government as a vestige of the guard duty commanded by God in Eden. There "it would have been most pleasant." On the other hand: "We have protection today, but it is obviously horrible. It requires swords, spears, cannons, walls, redoubts and trenches; and yet we can hardly be sage with our families."[47] And he adds on the next verse (16): "Therefore, if men had not become evil through sin, there would have been no need for a Polity. . . . What need would there have been for laws or a Polity, which is like a cauterizing iron and horrible medicine by which harmful limbs are cut off that the rest might be preserved."[48]

Luther does not seem to have too much confidence in a juridical system where laws are largely self-enforced for mutual benefits, even though he sees that exchange of this sort does take place with the products of craftsmen. He relies far more on the Church and its use of moral exhortation in preaching, which is a remnant of what he considers to be God's sermon to Adam at his entrance into Eden. He relies also on the domestic bonds of the family for a softening of the asperities of life after the Fall.[49] Here he makes his usual comparison of what might have happened in Eden and what the relations of the sexes have become. There is a seeming paradox in the contrast between the strict punitiveness of his views of government, and his desire to enhance trust and affection in man's relation to God and in his family. "But who can describe in words the glory of the innocence we have lost? There still remains in nature the longing of the male for the female, likewise the fruit of procreation; but these are combined with the awful hideousness of lust and the frightful pain of birth. Shame, ignominy, and embarrassment arise even among married people when they wish to enjoy their legitimate intercourse. . . . The creation indeed is good and the blessing is good; but through sin they are so corrupted that married people cannot make use of them without shame."[50]

In commenting on the psychological consequences of the original sin in chapter 3, Luther makes some remarkable statements concerning human nudity and the genitalia. He is refuting the claim of the scholastics that man's original justice was not part of his nature and is regained with Christ. Meanwhile, man's natural endowments survive. For Luther it was evidence to the contrary that: "Just as to go nude was of the nature of man, full of trust and security toward God and thus to please God and men, so now after the sin man feels that this nudity of innocent nature displeases God, himself and all creatures. . . . Thus the same members remain in nature, but what were seen to be nude with glory before, now are covered over as though shameful and evil."[51] Adam and Eve "made girdles for covering over that part of the body which by its nature is the most honorable and dignified of all. For what is more noble in nature than the work of generation?"[52] "Should we not therefore feel at last how filthy and horrible sin is, if lust alone can be cured by no remedy, not even marriage which is ordained as a remedy for weak nature?"[53] "Moreover, it is marvellous that no writing by any writer in any language has been found which shows that nudity which was once most virtuous was made shameful through sin. Therefore, we have this one unique master, Moses, who, yet in the briefest words, shows that man fallen from faith was confused and that that glory of the genitals was turned into the greatest ignominy, so that man was forced to cover them over with girdles!"[54]

But before we examine Luther's extraordinarily perceptive analysis of the psychology of sinning and of subsequent guilt as paradigmatically illuminated by the story of the Fall and the Expulsion in chapter 3, there are certain relevant passages still in chapter 2, particularly in connection with the creation of Eve. He finds it necessary to argue against the Aristotelian view of the eternity of the world and consequential rejection of any creation *ex nihilo*. Aristotle explains the new creation of reproduction only in terms of its material and formal causes, how one thing reproduces itself. A Christian looks at the efficient and final causes, what brought something into existence and for what purpose or end. From the point of view of reason and philosophy all of this is absurd. "But why does the creation of Adam and Eve seem so unbelievable and miraculous, while man's propagation, which all men know and see, does not seem so miraculous?"[55] Because endlessly repeated, miracles do not seem miraculous, as Augustine more than once pointed out.[56] "Thus it is a great miracle (*magnum miraculum*) that a small seed is planted and that out of it grows a very tall oak." Describing the development of the human fetus, its birth and nourishment by its mother's milk, Luther exclaims: "All these developments afford the fullest occasion for wonderment and are wholly beyond our understanding, but because of their continued recurrence they have come to be regarded as commonplace, and we have verily become deaf to this lovely music of nature. But if we regarded these wonders in true faith and appraised them for what they actually are, they surely would not be inferior to what Moses says here: that a rib was taken from the side of Adam as he slept and that Eve was created from it." It is the greater miracle of man's creation by the Word, a miracle which lifts him above the merely natural such as Aristotle and the other scientists regard him and shows man his divine end: "that man is created according to the likeness of God; in eternity, therefore, he is to live with God, and while he is here on earth, he is to preach God, thank Him, and patiently obey His Word."[57]

It would seem not unlikely that in this passage Luther was echoing "Hermes Trismegitus" in the *Asclepius* and Pico della Mirandola[58] in his playing upon the miraculous in man, projecting an ideal of human life transcending nature which had great appeal in the Renaissance.[59] It would also seem, therefore, that Luther, himself, felt some attraction toward the latent theme of man's deification contained in the literature on the dignity of man. But for Luther the aspiration toward deification would have been unnecessary if man had only been able to accept the godlikeness in which he had been created and had followed the commandments of his Maker. It was, ironically, man's striving to emulate the deity (rather than patiently awaiting his elevation to immortality) that led to his downfall. Therefore, we shall appropriately turn now to Luther's comment on chapter 3 of Genesis where he acutely and brilliantly analyzes the motivation and behavior of Adam and Eve in their succumbing to temptation, disobedience, and guilty flight from God.

Luther early on in his discussion of the effect of Adam's and Eve's sin in Genesis 3 attacks the doctrine that man's original justice was extrinsic to his natural endowments (which are referred to above in relation to man's shame about nudity) and that man, therefore, had retained the image of God. This is also why in chapter 1 he had rejected the notion of memory, intellect and will as the trinitarian image of God, as we saw above. He wished to stress that man possessed his dignity in his original creation but lost it with the primal sin and will regain it only through Christ, if he has faith in Christ's work, in the next life. For this reason, man's Fall had best be seen as the loss of faith and trust in God. "Just as reason is overwhelmed by many kinds of ignorance, so the will has not only been confused but has been turned away from God and is an enemy of God. It enjoys rushing to evil, when the opposite should have happened. Therefore, this manifold corruption of our nature should not be weakened but should be amplified. From the image of God, from the knowledge of God, from the knowledge of all the other creatures, and from a very honorable nudity man has fallen into blasphemy, into hatred, into contempt of God, indeed, into what is even more, into enmity against God."[60]

Correspondingly, as he moves to discuss the serpent's temptation, he argues that: "the serpent directs its attack at God's good will and makes it its business to prove from the prohibition of the tree that God's will toward man is not good. Therefore, it launches its attack against the very image of God and the most excellent powers in the uncorrupted nature."[61] Satan's purpose is to destroy man's trust and faith in God by insinuating that there is deception and inconsistency in His command about the tree. "Therefore, Satan here attacks Adam and Eve in this way to deprive them of the Word and their trust in God. . . . Truly, therefore, this temptation is the sum of all temptations; it brings with it the ruin or the destruction of the entire Decalogue. Disbelief is the source of all sins. (*Fons enim omnium peccatorum est incredulitas.*) When Satan aroused this disbelief by driving out or corrupting the Word, there was nothing that would not be easy for him."[62] As he says a little below: "For truly the source of all sin is disbelief and doubt when one departs from the Word. Because the world is full of these [departures], it remains in idolatry, denies the truth of God, and invents a new God."[63]

Luther pursues this theme, describing with great subtlety of psychological insight the steps by which Eve is led to the act of plucking the apple. The sin of disbelief, loss of faith led the way. The act, itself, like a good work, automatically followed.[64] Commenting on Adam's confrontation with God, he continues to project a brilliant literary interpretation of the sparse passage, delineating the psychology of guilt. Parenthetically, it might be said that whatever the merits or shortcomings of Erik Erikson's effort to detect a personal psychological crisis in Luther which was paradigmatic for his vast following,[65] there can be no denial of the deeply psychological quality of his religious thought, and in a certain sense the human condition was typified for Luther by man denying his guilt. I believe a viable interpretation of his entire theology could be constructed around this existential situation. Here he depicts it as follows: "Thus when man has been accused of sin by God, he does not acknowledge his sin but rather accuses God and transfers his guilt from himself to the Creator. The outcome is that in this way sin grows endlessly unless God through His mercy grants His help. This wickedness and utmost stupidity Adam regards as supreme wisdom. He has become so confused by his fright that he does not realize what he is saying or what is doing, and by excusing himself he accuses himself most seriously and enormously increases his sin. However, we must not think that this happened to Adam alone. We, each one of us, do the same thing; our nature does not permit us to act otherwise after we have become guilty of sin."[66]

Behind his denial of free will lies Luther's vision of guilt-ridden man. Moreover, Luther sees in his denial of free will no lack of activism on the part of the individual man but rather this pathological and paralyzed state of unreadiness to accept an accusation of guilt, this refusal of responsibility for his motives and actions which drives the individual to all sorts of displacements and covering-over modes of behavior. The only cure for this panic is a trust which cannot possibly be self-engendered. Religiously it must come from God. But man's sin and guilt still remains. Thus Luther's "enslaved will" is so conceived because it is the common condition of man to be in such a state of guilty panic as Luther here describes in Adam that he is incapable of moral choice. Thus also there follows his doctrine of *simul justus et peccator*.[67] Luther clearly acknowledges the centrality of this conception for his whole religious reform striving: "This is the last step of sin, to insult God and to charge Him with being the originator of sin. Unless hearts are given courage through trust in mercy, this nature cannot be urged on beyond this point if there are successive steps of sin. That is why the state of the Church was horrible under the Pope. For then nothing was seen or heard which could encourage a heart in such distress, except that each year the history of the Passion was feebly taught, which weakly showed whence forgiveness could be sought. Everything else led away from the promise of remission of sins to one's own righteousness. . . . Thus these miserable people wasted away without hope, without counsel, and without any help, in deepest sorrows of soul. Were these conditions not full of terror?"[68] It is, I believe, Luther's sense of the psychological disaster of striving for holiness and self-justification that underlies his denial of the divine image to fallen man, as well as unimpaired natural endowments. It is this psychology which explains his anthropology.

The compensating mercy that was to come with Christ is seen by Luther as already co-present in Adam's confrontation with God in his interpretation of the seed of woman, who will crush the serpent's head, as Christ: "There is not that terrible sight as on Mt. Sinai, where trumpet blasts were mingled with flashes of lightning and peals of thunder. But God comes in a very soft breeze to indicate that the reprimand will be fatherly. . . . This shows that even then Christ, our Deliverer, had placed Himself between God and man as a Mediator. It is a very great measure of grace that after Adam's sin God does not remain silent but speaks, and in many words indeed, in order to show signs of His fatherly disposition. . . . And so, although the promise concerning Christ is not yet there, it is already noticeable in the thought and counsel of God."[69]

Passing over his remarkable and sympathetic discussion of the fallen state of women,[70] his discussion of chapter 3 fittingly ends with what might be entitled a description of "The Misery of the Human Condition," although he does not deny there are certain compensations such as "the glory of motherhood" and physical pleasures. This, of course, was the medieval and Renaissance counterpart of works on "The Dignity of Man."[71] Luther clearly seems to have the separate stages of his theological vision of the condition of man continuously present in his narration. The time before the Fall, when man was briefly in possession of his dignity (by Luther's calculation hardly a single day) is followed by the Fall and the Expulsion, to be followed in the fullness of time with the coming of Christ and the eventual otherworldly destinies of all men. But in the present, where we and Luther both live, the miserable condition of man in his loss of dignity is brightened both by the retrospective dream of what might have been done through the glorious potential of his one day of innocence and by the hope of future salvation in the time between Adam and Christ. Yet the available redemption brought by Christ in these latter days of Christendom is shadowed both by the future conditionality of salvation and the harsh continuation of man's sin-ridden exile. In this simultaneity of the ages, therefore, mankind lives, reminded of the great dignity of the pleasurable and immortal life they might have had, frightened and terrified by the enormity of their ancestral crimes and the burden of guilt that they retain, cheered on, if they have faith, by the promise of salvation and the assurance that their restored dignity will be finer than the original possibility lost. Such are the theological components of Luther's hexameral anthropology.

But encased within this shifting frame were certain elements of historical actuality: the psychology of guilt, self-esteem, dependence and trust; the family and the relationship of husband and wife as the chief scene of our earthly life, inflamed and wounded by pain, anxieties, passion and love, but noble and honorable in Luther's eyes; the state with its harsh punitive function but necessary for the peace of everyman; the learned disciplines and professions by which mankind struggled to make these earthly actions more rational and fulfilling; and finally the Church, with its profession of pastors preaching and guiding the faithful and would-be faithful toward deepened faith and trust in God until they reached their heavenly kingdom.

And round about, the idolators, the idlers, the furtive, the larcenous, the murderous who knowingly or unknowingly marched in the hosts of Satan. Here in these lectures on Genesis, chapter 1 to 3, Luther provides this more than usually panoramic view of human destiny. It was a vision which recoiled from the optimism of the Renaissance humanists and Platonists, because, he feared, this very dream of deification (so openly manifested in the writings of Manetti, Ficino and Pico,[72] not likely to have been known to Luther but the substance of similar ideas well known to him) would once again incite men to Adam's sin, namely: "that when he was deprived of his mind by Satan and believed that he would be like God, he became like Satan himself."[73] But Adam, he believed, could have become godlike if he had trusted God in paradise, and now, after Christ, any man could regain the divine image and likeness in his future heavenly home if he believed the divine promises, trusted God's mercy and had faith that Christ had died for him.

NOTES

1. My credentials for this study derive from past efforts to inter-relate Renaissance and Reformation themes and not from the study-in-depth of a life-long Luther scholar. My approach to Luther has been conditioned by study of such works as his *Treatise on Christian Liberty, Secular Government to What Extent Should It Be Obeyed?, The Enslaved Will.* Perhaps more importantly a number of scholars, not necessarily agreeing, have had a syncretistic influence on my understanding of Luther, figures such as: Roland Bainton, F. Edward Cranz, Gerhard Ebeling, B. A. Gerrish, Heiko A. Oberman, Steven E. Ozment, Benjamin N. Nelson, Jaroslav Pelikan, James Samuel Preus, Gordon Rupp, Lewis W. Spitz, Ernst Troeltsch and Max Weber. I have not been able to consult Franz Lau, *"Ausserliche Ordnung" und "Weltlich Ding" in Luthers Theologie.* (Göttingen, 1933). I have used the *Lectures on Genesis* in the following edition and translation: *D. Martin Luthers Werke,* Kritische Gesamtausgabe, 42 Band (Weimar, 1911), hereafter WA 42; and in *Luther's Works,* ed. Jaroslav Pelikan, vol. 1 (St. Louis, 1958), hereafter LW 1. Due to limitations of space Luther's Latin text will not be given, but citations will give page and line numbers of WA 42 and page numbers of LW 1. Translations will be based on those of George V. Schick in LW 1. I have introduced occasional variations where a more literal version seemed stylistically preferable. I have found no places where I would differ with Schick in accuracy of interpretation.

2. Gerhard Ebeling, *Lutherstudien,* Band II: *Disputatio de Homine,* Erster Teil, *Text und Traditionshintergrund* (Tübingen, 1977). I find Luther's doctrines on man consistent in these two works.

3. See below, notes 29, 30, 31.

4. See my *"In Our Image and Likeness:" Humanity and Divinity in Italian Humanist*

Thought (London and Chicago, 1970), 173–99; and "Renaissance Idea of the Dignity of Man," *Dictionary of the History of Ideas* (New York, 1973), IV, 136–47.

5. WA 42: 42, 14–16; LW 1: 56.

6. WA 42: 42, 31–32; LW 1: 57.

7. WA 42: 43–44; LW 1: 57–59.

8. Gerhart Ladner, *The Idea of Reform, Its Impact on Christian Thought and Action in the Age of the Fathers* (rev. ed. New York, 1967), Part II, Chap. 5.

9. *Ibid.*

10. *De Trinitate,* IX–XII.

11. WA 42: 45, 3–4; LW 1: 60.

12. WA 42: 45, 22–23; LW 1: 60.

13. WA 42: 44, 27–39; LW 1: 61.

14. WA 42: 46, 4–9; LW 1: 61.

15. WA 42: 47, 8–17; LW 1: 62–63.

16. WA 42: 46, 20–21; LW 1: 62.

17. WA 42: 46, 21–26; LW 1: 62.

18. WA 42: 46/31–47/2; LW 1: 62.

19. E.g. WA 42: 157; LW 1: 210.

20. WA 42: 47, 18–22; LW 1: 63.

21. WA 42: 47, 31–33; LW 1: 63.

22. WA 42: 10, 3–6; LW 1: 11.

23. WA 42: 37–38; LW 1: 15.

24. E.g. WA 42: 59; LW 1: 77–78.

25. *Ibid.*

26. WA 42: 48, 11–15; LW 1: 64.

27. WA 42: 48, 27–31; LW 1:65.

28. WA 42: 48, 33–35; LW 1: 65.

29. WA 42: 33, 15–16—34; LW 1: 44–46.

30. WA 42: 33–35, 14; LW 1: 46.

31. WA 42: 35, 37–38, 36, 12–15; LW 1: 47–48.

32. WA 42: 49, 27–28, 50, 13–15; LW 1: 66–67.

33. WA 42: 50, 25–26, 20; LW 1: 67.

34. See WA 42: 62, 24–25; LW 1: 82; also see WA 42: 91, 8–9; LW 1: 120. "Totum itaque secundum caput consumit in explicatione conditionis hominis."

35. WA 42: 63–64; LW 1: 83–84

36. *In Our Image,* 125, 131–32, 155–56.

37. WA 42: 70; LW 1: 92.

38. WA 42: 71, 24–34; LW 1: 93–94.

39. WA 42: 71, 39–41—72, 1–2; LW 1: 94.

40. WA 42: 72, 28–32; LW 1: 95.

41. WA 42: 77, 29–31, 78, 9–12; LW 1: 102.

42. WA 42: 78, 21–28; LW 1: 103.

43. Leon Battista Alberti, *I libri della famiglia, Opere volgari,* ed. Cecil Grayson, I (Bari, 1960), 130: "Chi mai stimasse potere asseguire pregio alcuno o digni-

tate sanza ardentissimo studio di perfettissime arti, sanza assiduissimo opera, senza molto sudare in cose virilissime e faticossime? . . . Nulla si truova onde tanto facile surga disonore e infamia quanto dall'ozio."

44. WA 42: 79, 2; LW 1: 103.

45. WA 42: 79, 7–12; LW 1: 103–04.

46. Cf. my "The Religious Foundations of Luther's Social Views," *Essays in Medieval Life and Thought,* ed. John Mundy et al. (New York, 1955).

47. WA 42: 78, 30–34; LW 1: 103.

48. WA 42: 79, 13–19; LW 1: 104.

49. WA 42: 148–149; LW 1: 199.

50. WA 42: 79, 30–36; LW 1: 104–05.

51. WA 42: 125, 23–30; LW 1: 167.

52. WA 42: 125, 35–38; LW 1: 167.

53. WA 42: 126, 7–9; LW 1: 168.

54. WA 42: 125, 20–30; 168.

55. WA 42: 93–94, 94, 29–31; LW 1: 124–26. Cf. *De homine,* theses 12–16, Ebeling, *op. cit.,* 17–18.

56. E.g. *De civ. Dei,* XXI, capp. 7, 8.

57. WA 42: 95, 5–6, 12–17; 98, 20–22; LW 1: 126–27, 131

58. *Asclepius* I, 6 in *Hermetica,* ed. W. Scott, I, 294; Giovanni Pico della Mirandola, *Oratio* [*de dignitate hominis*], (Indianapolis, 1965), 3.

59. I refer to Frances Yates' stress on the *"Magus,"* in *Giordano Bruno and the Hermetic Tradition* (Chicago, 1964) and elsewhere.

60. WA 42: 107, 1–9; LW 1: 142. The actual polemic begins on 123 and 164. The reference to the theological need for rhetoric in the passage cited should be noted.

61. WA 42: 110, 9–12; LW 1: 146.

62. WA 42: 110–11, 38–41, 1–3; LW 1: 147.

63. WA 42: 112, 20–22; LW 1: 149.

64. WA 42: 112–122; LW 1: 149–162.

65. *Young Man Luther, A Study of Psychoanalysis and History* (New York, 1962). In other words I find Luther's own religious-psychological insights vastly important but wonder whether his personal psychogenesis is very relevant to understanding the historical movement.

66. WA 42: 131, 9–16; LW 1: 175.

67. Cf. Steven E. Ozment, *Homo Viator, Luther and Late Medieval Theology,* in *The Reformation in Medieval Perspective,* ed. S. E. Ozment, 142–54, espec. 148–52 and n. 22. My point is that, according to Luther, only in the recognition of man's sinfulness and loss of godlike qualities which flows from a *fides* conceived as a total trust in God can human righteousness be restored.

68. WA 42: 134, 8–21; LW 1: 179–80.

69. WA 42: 135, 8–11, 17–22; LW 1: 180–81.

70. WA 42: 148–51; LW 1: 198–203.

71. Adam's curse. WA 42: 152–63; LW 1: 203–19. For discussion and exposition of the inter-relationship of the dignity of man and the misery of human conditions as themes in the Renaissance, see my *In Our Image,* Part II, *passim.*

Also see Giovanni di Napoli, " 'Contemptus Mundus' e 'Dignitas Hominis' nel Rinascimento," *Rivista di filosofia neoscolastica,* XLVIII (1956), 9–41.
72. For analysis see *In Our Image,* chapters VI, IX and X.
73. See Luther's comments on verse 22 in general: WA 42: 166–68, citation: 166, 29–31; LW 1: 222–25, citation: 223.

Thomas More and the Humanist Tradition: Martyrdom and Ambiguity

This essay is an effort to pay tribute to a man of penetrating intellect, tireless devotion to his fellows, unyielding protection of his faith, and matchless sensitivity to the meaning of word and act. The collective tokens of contemporary admiration for More are manifold. Hardly one of us sees in him exactly what another has, but in all modern students of More there is a unanimity of respect and warmth of regard that responds to the relics of his life and mind as they reach to us across the centuries. We are a generation who in many senses has found in Thomas More the qualities we have missed in ourselves. We have made him embody our own ideals by the ways in which we have sought to interpret him, varied and clashing, yet ultimately agreeing. There was clearly something exceptional and large in him that could evoke such a unity out of plurality, such a coincidence of opposites.

It was my hope in trying to familiarize myself with some of the details of the magnificent Yale edition of the complete works of Thomas More that I might find something approaching an interpretive consensus developing, a consensus that clearly did not exist thirty years ago. But I have come gradually to conclude that however many the symposia, however many times scholars gather to exchange their thoughts and views of More, this will never be. Yet my humility before the scholarly and interpretive achievement of this past generation, both of the makers of the Yale edition and of the many others who have continued to be fascinated, study, and write, is vast, almost rivalling my humility before Thomas More himself. For this reason this paper will, for the most part, leave the discussion of More to others and retreat to a few observations on the humanist tradition from which he came, emphasizing two aspects of this tradition that can be identified in Thomas More. Somewhat arbitrarily, therefore, and yet with a

---

The following paper, completed June 4, 1978, was originally presented to a symposium commemorating the 500th anniversary of the birth of Thomas More, and honoring the late Richard S. Sylvester, held in Washington, D.C., June 22, 1978. Since the paper's two main themes seek to affiliate Thomas More to the Renaissance humanist tradition by stressing the presence of a secular martyrology among the humanists and by emphasizing their awareness of ambiguity and complementarity in their conceptions of cultural and moral values, it seemed entirely appropriate to dedicate this paper to the memory of Benjamin Nelson, a man to whom I owe very much in the development of my own vision of history, culture, and morality. This paper will appear in a memorial volume for Professor Nelson.

strong conviction of their validity, I am going to offer two broader approaches than the usual academic conception of the humanist tradition that seem relevant to this man: the presence of elements of martyrdom and of ambiguity in the tradition.

Martyrdom

Humanism, which is after all a term of our own modern invention, includes not only its meaning of admiration for and education in the ancient classics as first defined but comprehends the entire sweep of learning in the *studia humanitatis* of the Renaissance. [1] But far more than being a series of studies it was also a movement that, starting out from a scholarly and intellectual base, had a profound impact on the thought and action of that entire age. [2] Moreover, these Renaissance humanists who sought to influence their fellows of other professions and their secular and ecclesiastical rulers, also cheered themselves on and enlivened their onlookers and prospective listeners by reciting the lives and merits of the ancients. Petrarch with his *De viris illustribus* was only the first. The humanist tradition in a very literal (and literary) sense then was the rekindled memory of the great figures of the past who had sought somehow to bring their wisdom and learning to bear on the affairs of men. We shall, therefore, as a first broadening of our conception of a humanist tradition, review some of these ancient and early Christian figures with whom Renaissance humanists identified.

Ancient tradition itself was repeated by Cicero in his *Tusculans,* that "Socrates was the first who brought down philosophy from the heavens, placed it in the cities, introduced it into families, and obliged it to examine into life and morals, and good and evil."[3] In thinking of their own kind of learning as important in the lives of men, the Renaissance humanists always returned to this statement of Cicero's and others like it. Socrates, the martyr to the cause of the "examined life," is unquestionably evoked when we think of More, the martyr for his faith. But the connection of Socrates with More and humanism is deeper still. The "philosophy" that Cicero is talking about was that moral philosophy conceded with its qualities as the last of the *studia humanitatis,* and the term "philosophy" was used by Petrarch also to describe his own role of moral and cultural guidance. We are in fact engaged in a quarrel reaching over the centuries for the right to use that word, *philosophy,* and my remarks above show that it is still going on. But the quarrel over *philosophy* and *rhetoric* and the use of the words in a historically valid sense does indeed begin with Plato and his dispute with those who professed to teach wisdom, the *sophistai.* And it is at the end of his *Phaedrus*[4] in which Plato embraces so much of the rhetorical art that he has Socrates express his admiration for the young "rhetor," Isocrates, as the possible future "lover of wisdom" or "philosopher" who will combine the study of wisdom with the art and gift of speech. Similarly it was the mature Isocrates, the gifted and influential educator and advocate of Panhellenism, who spoke always of his philosophical rivals, Plato and Aristotle, as "sophists" and of himself and his friends as "philosophers." And again in the Renaissance the scholastics are charged with windy sophistry (*ventosa sophistica*), beginning with Petrarch, and including emphatic charges by Erasmus and our Thomas.

It was, then, a growing view among Renaissance humanists (Petrarch had not fully shared it, but Salutati certainly had) that the humanist tradition rightly began with Socrates, and who is to say they were wrong. But we, of course, know Socrates by no writings but only by Plato's and Xenophon's accounts, and other echoes which differ sufficiently for us to claim that we know him only by hearsay. Taking our hearsay from Plato, however, we might ask what sort of a man Socrates was and whether he could be seen as a paradigm for Thomas More. The legend is good for our case if we accept, as Aristotle does,[5] that he was the true author of those ideas Plato presents as Socrates's in the *Republic*. And though we can agree with J. H. Hexter[6] that More's use of the *Republic* in *Utopia* was idiosyncratic and that his position was different from Plato's, I think we must also agree that the central question in both works was whether there can be any justice in our private dealings unless there is first justice in the structure of society as a whole. And if we come now to Plato's own views of justice there is the most fundamental disagreement between Plato and More: *justice* clearly meaning *equality* for More, (whether disguised as himself or as "Hythloday"), whereas Plato's definition for it was *proportion*. Moreover, another problem that deeply concerned More throughout his entire life was critical for Plato/Socrates as well: a concern basic to our notion of humanism, that of the role of the morally wise man in the affairs of the public and as a ruler of the state.

The story begins for Plato/Socrates, not in earlier but in different dialogues, namely the *Protagoras* and the *Theatetus,* where the sophist vision of man and moral behavior as represented by Protagoras is directly confronted by Socrates. We in our historical sophistication are inclined to follow Werner Jaeger[7] and Kristeller[8] and see in Protagoras (along with Gorgias and his pupil, Isocrates) the founders of a rival rhetorical tradition to Plato's and Socrates' philosophical one. But we can also see that, as viewed by another age, perhaps the two do not differ that much, and certainly in Renaissance humanist eyes they were differing not in their major purpose, which was to bring learning to bear on public affairs, but about the proper educational means. While Protagoras denies that any man can know other than what he senses and experiences, he also believes that man possesses an innate sense of justice and piety and can be taught to respect what his own society defines as justice. And here is the whole premise of the humanist tradition throughout its history—that most men can be taught to be virtuous, both the peasant and the king—whereas the Platonic/Socratic view is that God, not man, is the measure of all things and that only the philosopher who has achieved an insight into the divine form or structure of things can guide mankind toward justice, best of all when the philosopher himself is the king. And this is a higher (because cosmic) justice than that pragmatic human kind which is wrought in the law courts, taught in the classroom, or preached in the assembly. In this confrontation there are poignant problems for the Renaissance figures we know, be they humanists or other. But before we seek to untangle them we had better take a look at two other paradigms of humanism, better known to most in the Renaissance, Cicero and Seneca.

Let us remember that three of these figures—Socrates, Cicero, and Seneca—paid with their lives when the morality they so famously represented proved an obstacle to the ambition of rulers, and that the fourth, Plato, was deceived and misused by Dionysius, the tyrant of Syracuse. There was something in the Renaissance view (sharply expressed by More's "Hythloday") that a humanist would fare badly in the halls of power (however much he ought to be there). It is difficult to think of Cicero as a martyr because he has seemed in his private letters so manifestly crass and self-serving about his public career even though he wanted it never to be forgotten that he had "saved the state." He brought through his writings more of Greek rhetorical wisdom to the Latin West than anyone but Quintilian, and certainly more of Greek philosophy than anyone excepting only Boethius and Scotus Eriugena until the medieval translations from Greek and Arabic and the Renaissance translations of the Greek. But as one of the world's most renowned lawyers and orators, and however ambivalent and vacillating he was in his devotion to political action on behalf of public freedom and welfare, his contribution to the moral and political thought of the Renaissance was ubiquitous. Justice for Cicero came down to the fulfillment of a man's rationally projected roles in the great society—as a participant in common humanity, as a member of a nation, as a citizen of a city, and as an individual in a family. Although Petrarch was able to misread Cicero as writing on behalf of retirement from public affairs (as in his last days it was forced upon him), Renaissance humanists more generally favored his forthright endorsement of action and civic participation: "No man has any right to permit his intellectual exercises to interfere with his performance of the duties of an active life, for it is by its activity that virtue earns the highest praise. And yet respites come frequently and bring with them abundant opportunities for a return to study; moreover, the mind, which never rests, is quite capable of keeping us, all unwitting, at the task of seeking knowledge."[9]

Cicero was an ancient humanist. With that no one has quarrelled. But to be so conceived, by both himself and by the humanists of the Renaissance, his mastery of rhetoric (theoretical and practical) needed to be linked in some way to philosophy. His allegiance to the practical realm over the theoretical was plain enough. But did he profess philosophy only as a prestigious adjunct to an effective rhetorical career, as some of his statements suggest, or did he have a more genuine commitment? Jerrold Seigel has stressed the importance of Cicero's philosophical side, but seems to leave it, indeed, adjunctive, not genuinely integrated.[10] Cicero does declare allegiance to the Academic school and sometimes takes over the Stoic point of view as his own. He draws loosely and certainly eclectically on a variety of sources. I believe his authentic position can be reconstructed, something as follows: Religiously, he has no doubt concerning the existence of phenomena that were beyond human understanding, and he offered the traditional Roman ways of worshipping and relating to religious reality his utmost reverence and care. He saw this as something apart from philosophy, which he comprehended almost entirely as the pursuit of wisdom in the conduct of human affairs. Natural philosophy seemed useful but secondary to the study of ethics. A serious man should be careful not to commit himself to any one point of view as the various schools and philosophers seemed to contradict themselves and also to overlap and repeat too much. Hence Academicism in the end had the greatest appeal for him with its declaration that any formulation of truth could be matched by a contrary one, so that verisimilitude—probability—was the most for which one could hope. As a lawyer and an orator Cicero and others of similar profession would necessarily deal with a constantly fluctuating situation and a human constituency of the greatest variety. There the rhetorical commonplace, reaching a mixed audience, would indeed provide a basis for the only possible kind of loose unity of which the collective life of man was capable. But talent, practice of the art, experience, expanding knowledge leading to wisdom—all were essential. I believe that an image of Cicero as an orator and a philosopher such as this comes close to the way in which many Renaissance humanists read and judged him, and that this throws light on their own conceptions of their role in relation to philosophy. I believe also that behind Cicero's outlook was the serious grappling with the problem of collective wisdom and virtue by the Greek sophists, particularly Protagoras whom Plato respected sufficiently to confront in two different dialogues. Cicero also learned from the writings of Isocrates and from the rhetorical and moral works of Aristotle, but it is of especial interest that he actually translated Plato's *Protagoras,* a version that has been lost. I do not know if he ever quoted the *Theatetus,* but the point of view in the "Apology of Protagoras"[11] composed by Plato in this dialogue seems appropriate also to Cicero.

Until the fifteenth century Seneca was thought by some humanists to be a Nicodemite, or concealed Christian. And even as late as 1532 Lefèvre d'Étaples was still publishing a commentary on the forged correspondence between Seneca and St. Paul.[12] What Renaissance humanists saw in Seneca, some accepting and some doubting his Christianity, was the great moral counselor and guide to inwardness and tranquillity in the face of life's disturbances and distractions. But Seneca also was a man of public affairs and a counselor of emperors. To many modern commentators his attitude has seemed ambiguous and problematic. In the end he committed suicide at Nero's order. Justice for this Stoic lay in the universal rational order of fate, *heimarmene,* and could be found only by resignation and acceptance. Yet he could counsel humanity and responsibility and offer highly practical psychological advice.

Seneca was important, especially in the early Renaissance, as the paradigm of the lay moral counselor. Petrarch modelled his figure of *Ratio* in the *De remediis* on the authentic Senecan *Epistulae ad Lucillium* as well as on the probably pseudo-Senecan *De remediis fortuitarum.* Seneca's influence on More seems to the outsider to be fairly limited. For instance, there are relatively few citations or allusions to him in *A Dialogue of Comfort.*[13] We shall see a reason for Seneca's diminishment presently.

We come to the interesting question of the extent to which the Church Fathers were regarded as predecessors by Renaissance humanists, and this involves the latters' attitudes toward the non-Christianity of their pagan models of wisdom—not a question to be hastily answered in a short paper. An answer can be approached only by examining the individual complexity found in the cases of each Renaissance writer, and I offer simply this observation: most Renaissance humanists were neither members of religious orders nor churchmen, or if they were, some, like Petrarch and Erasmus, did their best to live as laymen.[14] It was, perhaps, easier for them as laymen to identify with the non-Christian ancient humanist than with the venerable patristic figures who were in many instances saints. Yet Jerome and Augustine both attracted the interest of humanists powerfully and, to my reading, influenced a wide range of Renaissance humanists more deeply and persistently than the pagans. But again the differences of individuals is crucial. In the case of Augustine the Italian humanists played a major role in his late medieval and Renaissance rehabilitation prior to the Reformation. Because of Luther's and Calvin's overt Augustinianism a sectarian problem developed in the sixteenth century. But there were also influential Augustinians at least among the early Catholic Reformers.

For many of the humanists Augustine was the father who admired Plato and, even more significantly, one who became a philosopher on reading Cicero's *Hortensius.* I would not want to argue that the Ciceronian elements were stronger than the Platonic in the formation of Augustine's theology (he refutes and praises them both as the best of the pagans). In the

De doctrina Christiana we have a most influential handbook on the use of lay learning, particularly the language arts and rhetoric, in the service of religion. Other fathers with whom Italian humanists closely identified were Lactantius and Jerome of course, and Eusebius, Basil, and Chrysostom among the Greeks. It should not be overlooked in late antiquity, both in the Latin and Greek worlds, how many men of rhetorical training, orators or *sophistai*, were converted and became Christian writers. Renaissance humanists gladly reported their examples and statements in support of classical studies and a more rhetorical theology. Since not all humanists were concerned with theology it was easier to admire the pastoral writings of the fathers and their pulpit oratory. Only as an interest in theology developed with Lorenzo Valla and the Florentine Platonists, and after them with Erasmus and other so-called Christian humanists of the North, did such philosophical theologians as Origen come to the fore. On the other hand, proponents of the powerful Renaissance theme of the dignity of man early found the theological base for their assertions in Augustine's emphasis on a human mental trinity mirroring the divine Trinity.

More's attachment to St. Augustine is well known, but as Father Surtz declared in his introductory section to the Yale translation of *Utopia,* the exact connection of *Utopia* with the *De civitate Dei* remains to be worked out. [15] Humanists such as Valla and Erasmus did not hesitate to polemicize with many of Augustine's positions. But it should never be forgotten that what were perhaps the pivotal issues of both the Renaissance and the Reformation had found their monumental exposition in the *De civitate Dei,* namely whether the world of man could be truly Christian and how much could mankind save itself from its own impulses to self-destruction apart from grace? Moreover book 19 of the *De civitate Dei* set the terms for the discussion of the great Erasmian-Morean problem of finding peace in a world where there was no peace. There were some who would have argued, not long ago, that to see the Church fathers as central to the thinking of the Renaissance was a contradiction in terms. But I cannot think that it is so anymore. Rather the Church fathers provided the frame within which Renaissance humanists in great preponderance viewed the antique past, explored the great pagan works in a new objectivity and depth, and were able to criticize them for their inappropriateness while admiring their historical actuality.

It would seem then that in speaking of the humanist tradition in the Renaissance we should recognize, as the Renaissance humanists did, that they had had their historical predecessors—seminal writers and thinkers of the classical and early Christian past whose intellectual and literary influence on all subsequent ages has been strong, but who had something special to offer the Renaissance. For the latter they offered examples of the possible social and cultural role of the man of learning, and powerful thinking concerning human nature and a just society. Some of them, at least, presented a model of a certain life-style: that of the intellectual who believed he could and should provide counsel and guidance to the mighty of this world, whether the emperor or the *demos,* only to arouse their ire in an especially vindictive way that could lead to execution, proscription, or commanded suicide. I would not want to suggest that here was the origin of the modern alienated intellectual any more than that Thomas More sought his own martyrdom. But the inner conviction of personal rightness ran strong in Socrates, at least as Plato represents him, as it also did in Cicero and Seneca. At the same time we have some evidence on which to question the absolute purity of motives of all of them. They were in certain respects antiheroes as well as heroes. But I would claim that for most of the individuals comprising the Renaissance phase of the humanist tradition, (though not many had the clean courage to risk and accept martyrdom), there was a sense of exclusion from the seats of power which they simultaneously coveted and despised. In Italy this was true even for those humanists who came from the leading families or the nobility. The motives of idealism—religious, moral, social—and those of self-advancement were never far apart nor totally distinguishable. When I think of the intelligence and integrity and confidence of More, I think of Coluccio Salutati and Lorenzo Valla and even Machiavelli more than of other Italians.

Ambiguity

I shall not try now to justify such an allegation of similarity of life-style between Renaissance and ancient humanists but wish to look at that other broad feature of the humanist tradition I proposed at the beginning of this essay. Thinking primarily of Italian humanist culture and its eventual influences upon a developing northern humanist culture, several interconnected anthropological themes may be identified. Although I will make general statements concerning these themes, it should be understood that I would not wish it to be thought that all humanists engaged in speculation and argumentation concerning these issues or that they always agreed. Indeed, they were frequently presented in dialogue as multisided controversy and debated between individuals. As themes they exhibit complementary positions rather than polarity, and are ordinarily seen as reflecting that exasperating humanist sense of ambiguity that still sets the teeth of scholarly dialecticians on edge.

The first such theme is the question of faith and knowledge, and of the right road toward acquisition of either: linguistic and historical studies or dialectic? From the perspective of purely intellectual history, here is the central issue between humanism and scholasticism, well elaborated in

More's crucial letter to Dorp.[16] It is infrequently noticed that there was a certain agreement between most humanist critics of nominalism and their supposed enemies. Both rejected metaphysical realism. Both assumed the necessity of faith. Could one then speak about God and divine things? Both agreed that one could, provided such speech was seen to have a suppositious, "as if" status. What then was the issue? For the *nominales* of the *via moderna,* theology became the substitution of dialectical analysis of the terms used to speak about God in order to determine whether a logically consistent statement had been made for metaphysical speculation on the statement's correspondence to divine reality. The scriptures were to be accepted as the Word of God, but they were subject to the one grand nominalist assumption that God's power, barring violation of the law of contradiction, was absolute and He could do anything. What God actually did do, therefore, was not naturally necessary but contingent upon His will. What God had wrought and made known through scripture and nature had the authority of divine ordinance and the security of a divine covenant. It was theology's function to support what was divinely established within the world, not to determine its ultimate character by analogy to the science of nature.

For the humanist man could speak about God metaphorically, only as he imagined Him, and of invisible things only through the visible things of this world. But in this he had a model in Biblical poetics. Theology was necessarily poetic and concealed a higher truth behind its figures of speech, as did the scriptures. Such was the viewpoint of Petrarch, Boccaccio, and Salutati. To this was added the philological analysis of scripture by Valla and Manetti, followed later by Erasmus, based on the collation of Vulgate translation with Greek and Hebrew original. From it came a more literal acceptance of the bare scriptural meaning which sometimes had to be seen as concealing a mystery. Faith was a matter of trust and obedience and even more of imaginative inspiration, and the resources of languages were to be deployed by mankind for its mutual persuasion in joyous acceptance of divine mercy and truth.[17] It does seem clear, at least to this scholar, that an important element of reform was central to humanist religious reflection in its desire to circumvent the aridity and artificiality of a formalistic fidelity to church and sacraments, and to reinforce a necessary inwardness. Hence humanists led the way toward a reformation of letter into spirit which Protestants carried much farther, sometimes reverting to literalism, repudiating the authority of the historical church and changing the conception of sacrament. But it also seems clear that for earlier Italian humanism through to More and Erasmus, the aim was to restore authentic belief to Christian obedience and spiritual depth to the sacramental life, for both were part of the historical continuum and interpretive dialogue by which mankind collectively lived. Other and later humanists saw things in Protestant ways as well as also remaining Catholics. Ultimately, of course, it was the humanist way of dialogue and persuasion that failed in the violence of religious persecution and conflict.

The second complementary theme, which was also inherited from the scholastic past, was that of the relationship of intellect and will, reason and affect. Petrarch said, "It is better (*satius*) to love the good than to know the truth."[18] Will was inflamed and aroused by words. In his *De remediis*, on the other hand, *Ratio* is his spokesman. But *Ratio* did not speak in the syllogisms which he had ridiculed in his *Contra medicum*. It offered to *Gaudium* and *Dolor* pithy quotations, anecdotes from the classics, exhortations, all the arsenal of the rhetor's art. *Ratio* is really *Oratio* or Speech, and each chapter is the occasion for a humanistic sermon. It is, as the *Secretum* and the *De otio religioso* reveal, man's affects that he is addressing, but in order to transform, not suppress them.

Behind will is power, as Salutati clearly saw. Theologically the debate over the primacy of the intellect or will, when it moved with Duns Scotus emphatically to the side of the will, reinforced the conception of God as a subjective power, as pure and absolute subjectivity, as He was perceived through the fourteenth century and on up through the Reformation. But correspondingly, human will meant human power; it was the faculty by which man asserted himself, either in obedience or living conformity to God or in defiance. What we see as the statist power dynamics of the age was already spelled out in the theology and political philosophy of the closing medieval centuries.

But could rhetoric, the humanist's reason, temper the fury of the affects? Salutati saw will as commanding and distorting the intellect. Valla saw man as all affect with virtue as *caritas* and *fortitudo*, vice as hate and cowardice. Prudence or malignity, faith or distrust, were merely intellectual instruments of the passions. Behind this debate, or rather sometimes fronting for it, was the question of grace and free will. It should be noted that the action and its moral character belonged to man, whether springing from free will or grace, human power or divine power. Power and love are linked in Franciscan theology and humanist psychology—fortitude and *caritas*, as Valla argued. Erasmus seemingly disagreed with Valla, who actually affirmed both free will and predestination leaving the reconciliation as a mystery beyond man. Luther seemingly agreed.

Action and contemplation, an ancient and medieval theme, acquires a new emphasis in the Renaissance. The speculative life was closest to that of the gods and the happiest for Aristotle. In the Middle Ages contemplation was often identified with the monastic way to salvation, but even more frequently contemplation was the way of the mystic. The old attitude lived on in Petrarch's connection of contemplation, meditation, and *otium* and in the *Secretum* and the *De vita solitaria*. But meditation has become a form of psychic concentration focusing on the last things. It draws the soul back together from its distraction by the trivial moments of daily experience. Already in the *De remediis,* Petrarch praises action as a cure for melancholy, though the greater stress is upon attitudinal change brought on by contemplation. Meditation is ego-directed, not ego-exhausting; it is an internal dialogue, a focusing of rhetoric on the self.

Renaissance activism begins with Salutati's *De vita activa et operosa,* a work planned but never written. There is ample evidence of his views, however, in his letters and other writings. The value of activity is strongly affirmed by Leon Battista Alberti in the *Libri della famiglia* and again in *De iciarchia. Ozio* becomes the worst vice, even a sin, because God did not create man to live in idleness, but in order to employ his faculties. *Industria* is a leading virtue. For Valla, too, God was not quiescent but active and creative. So should be man, whose soul is not a *tabula rasa* painted by his sensations of the exterior world but a flame that casts its light and heat upon the world and uses it. In the emergent genre of "the dignity and excellence of man" Giannozo Manetti affirms that man's creation in the divine image and likeness is actualized by asserting his godlike qualities—beauty, intelligence, inventiveness, power, and opulence. Man's function is to understand and act—*intelligere et agere.* The Renaissance Platonists, Ficino and Pico, take this humanist vision of human activism and rebuild it into a Neoplatonic metaphysics, with especially Ficino stressing man's natural emulation of God. How much this emphasis is stressed in More is matter for discussion. It is certainly strongly projected in *Utopia* and is present in *A Dialogue of Comfort,* while, on the other hand, the question of a special Renaissance mode of meditation surely rises in the Tower works.

A fourth theme develops out of the others. It starts as the polarity of virtue and fortune but grows into a major new insight of the Renaissance. It might be called the "contextuality of character." Human free will is not only bathed in an aura of divine grace in the matter of justification but is both enfranchized and restricted by the social environment itself. The ideas of Machiavelli and More, likely the two greatest social thinkers to appear in the Renaissance, emerge from the earlier humanist discussions of this question and represent a break with the humanist tradition, if they do in fact break, because they aspire to go beyond.

The development begins, again, with that strangely neglected masterwork of Petrarch, *On the Remedies for Both Kinds of Fortune,* (neglected since 1752 by us, that is, though widely copied, translated, printed, and read for the previous four centuries). There has been no printed edition in any language since then; moreover modern scholarly discussion, with a few recent exceptions, has been fragmentary. Petrarch's *Fortuna* turns out to be not simply a depiction of the unpredictable spinning of the wheel of chance but a panoramic overview of late medieval society and its typical life histories differentiated according to geographic, social, and cultural status. The countervailing virtues, as Heitmann[19] has shown, are intended as more effective prudential strategies for individual coping with the general exigencies of earthly life than the depressed shuddering and elated shouting that character-shaping circumstances too often evoke. If Petrarch was a Pelagian, it was in this realm of moral behavior; grace, he also thought, was essential for salvation. But the achievement of a degree of moral autonomy was an inescapable precondition for the trusting acceptance of the creation which might allow an infusion of grace. The parallel question, which Hexter[20] has raised concerning the Utopians, was whether More saw them as more grace-worthy than Christian Europeans of his day. Hexter said "Yes," and I am inclined to agree, but must leave it to the Moreans.

Lorenzo Valla, suspicious not only of the Pelagians of his day, especially the *nominales,* but also of the humanists too enamored of Stoicism (including Petrarch), would have demurred. As in the *Utopia* later, Valla's *De voluptate* or *De vero falsoque bono* declares itself an irony and discusses through the *personae* of some contemporary humanists what a "natural," i.e., pre-Christian morality would be like. Valla's Epicurean, who has no knowledge of Christ, is presented in terms of individual psychology and morality. He is not embedded in a carefully devised economic and social structure as in the case of More, nor in a political structure, as in Machiavelli's case. Epicurean man lives as his everyday experience dictates his needs and not according to abstract moral formulas as did Stoic man. Virtue, or the qualification and specification of motivation and behavior, grows out of experience and the social environment. But virtue is affect, and a form of object-oriented love. Pre-Christian man's love is self-directed or family-directed and pleasure-determined as in the case of animals. Natural man is not different from the animals except for variations in intellectual and emotional powers. Only with Christ does mankind transcend the animal kingdom with man's gift of immortality of soul. Christian man has transferred his love to Christ and seeks his pleasure in beatification. In fact, "pleasure," "charity," "love," and "beatification" are no more than contextually differentiated words meaning the same thing. Just as affect is human emotional power, language is man's intellectual power, and is qualified and differentiated in the active give-and-take of existence.

Giovanni Gioviano Pontano carries the analysis farther still. A major portion of his writings was devoted to a detailed analysis of the socially contextual character of the virtues. He saw these in terms of linguistic usage which he derived from observing self-motivation and the behavior of others. In his *De sermone,*[21] or *On Speech,* he developed a *logos* doctrine for everyday social intercourse, just as Erasmus, following Valla, insisted that Greek New Testament *logos* should be translated as *sermo* not *verbum*— Christ in His entire life and His sayings of the gospels as the "speech" of

God.[22] What Valla and Erasmus sought to make sacred was left secular by Pontano, though he was not at all unaware of its religious implications. Declaring that *De sermone* was a study of the rhetoric of daily human relations, comparable to the more formal and traditional rhetoric of the law court and assembly, Pontano analyzes such positive qualities as *comitas, facetitas, humanitas*—affability or courtesy, merriment or wittiness, gentility or kindness—as character types that he designated by adjectival nouns: *comis, facetus, humanus*. Such men are essential to the well-being of society and make earthly life pleasant, joyful, and bearable. Notable is his use of "humanity" not merely as higher culture but closer to our use of it in a philanthropic sense, contrary to Aulus Gellius's declaration. Equally essential to holding society together in mutual concord and trust are veracity and the truthful man. On the other side are the social vices and evil character types, brilliantly and savagely depicted by Pontano. Pontano combined his studies of classical literary and moral works with his experience as counselor and chancellor in the Neapolitan court and diplomatic service, and there is an important parallelism of career between Pontano and More as well as a carry-over of insight.

Pontano is regarded as an important immediate predecessor to Machiavelli in his social and historical realism. Other humanists such as Alberti, Poggio, and Valla have also been signaled in a more fragmentary sense for this "honor." I will not enter into the hazardous debate as to whether Machiavelli was a humanist (though I would argue he was one). Also, Hexter has made the classical comparison of Machiavelli and More.[23] But I do have a single point to make, which I share with Hexter. Machiavelli's realism (so-called) was not only a realism of external observation but a realism of rhetoric and advocacy. He wanted to change things by showing princes and statesman how to behave in order not to be entrapped in the concatenation of circumstances that was called "fortune" but was in actuality what we would call the political structure and history. But here I would recall that the most serious problem for Machiavelli (apart from the lack of a militia or some other effective organization for war), and one leading to political failure and/or social disaster, was that men's characters were formed by their experience, so that when circumstances changed, they themselves did not change. Machiavelli's recommendations, though admired by many, can also seem in some ways as paltry and certainly ineffective. He advocated forceful, determined, even impulsive action, on the basis of at least some calculation of the structurally determined balance of forces and some sense of ancient and modern precedents for success and failure. As More and Erasmus knew, princes and rulers were already behaving this way and, as we know, they still are today. To what avail?

More well knew the limits of political action and power even in achieving its only possible goal, the retention or expansion of power. And he knew the human consequences of this system well, even though, whether fatuously or not we cannot say, he lent himself to it. In his *Utopia* More set up the classical issues over which good men have differed since then, especially that of the intellectuals and the humanists participating in power (only to then illustrate both sides of the argument in his own life). More also, (and here I agree with Hexter),[24] saw in property the root of all evil, or perhaps more accurately, the root of all sin, and he devised his Utopian communism as a mental experiment outlining an alternative. He did this in all seriousness and not simply to show how a people who had never heard of Christ were more Christian than Christians. As again Hexter insists, he was thinking of his own world and its problems. Nor was he totally naive about the consequences, costs, and problems of such a solution, imaginatively creating fully totalitarian and authoritarian institutions for its maintenance.

If, however, More was actually proposing Utopian communism as a programmatic solution, he would have departed from the humanist tradition. I believe he did see the problematic character of his solution; through his character of "Morus," he genuinely expressed rejection of it at the end of the dialogue. He saw even more clearly and dramatically the tragedy of the opposite failure of mankind to rise above its institutions because he lived with them and directly observed the consequences. In possessing this double vision, More preserved the essential dialogic ambiguity of the humanist tradition.

NOTES

1. See Paul Oscar Kristeller's basic statement, his "Humanism and Scholasticism in the Italian Renaissance," *Byzantion* XVII (1944–45), 346–74, reprinted in his *Studies in Renaissance Thought and Letters* (Rome, 1956), 553–83 and in his *Renaissance Thought, the Classic, Scholastic and Humanist Strains* (New York, 1961), 92–119, reasserted and elaborated in a sequel of other writings.
2. See Eugenio Garin, *Der italienische Humanismus* (Bern, 1947) Eng. trans. by Peter Munz (Oxford and New York, 1965).
3. *Tusc.* V, iv.
4. *Phdr.* 278c–279a.
5. Aristotle cites Socrates in all references to the *Republic* in his *Politics.*
6. *The Complete Works of Thomas More* (hereafter *CW*) IV, *Utopia,* Ed. Edward Surtz, S. J. and J. H. Hexter, Introduction, cix–cx. And see especially Hexter's comments, cvi–cviii.
7. *Paideia: the Ideals of Greek Culture* (New York, 1945) I, 298–321.
8. *Renaissance Thought, cit.,* 11–12.
9. *De officiis,* I, 6.

10. *Rhetoric and Philosophy in Renaissance Humanism, The Union of Eloquence and Wisdom* (Princeton, 1968), espec. 11–18.
11. *Tht.* 166a–168b.
12. See Letizia A. Panizza, "Gasparino Barzizza's Commentaries on Seneca's Letters," *Traditio* XXXIII (1977), 297–341 for a survey of humanist conceptions of Seneca. For Lefèvre d'Étaples, 339.
13. *CW* XII, Index s.v. Seneca. Clearly, however, More was saturated with Stoic notions, whatever their provenance.
14. On the other hand, the number of ecclesiastics involved with humanism was remarkable. See Kristeller's "The Contribution of Religious Orders to Renaissance Thought and Learning," *The American Benedictine Review* XXI (1970): 1–55 and espec. Appendix B, "Humanists and Scholars of the Religious Orders."
15. *CW* IV, clxvi.
16. *The Correspondence of Sir Thomas More,* ed. Elizabeth F. Rogers (Princeton, 1947), letter 15, 17–74. See Salvatore I. Camporeale's study of the possible influence of Lorenzo Valla on More, finding at least extensive parallels of position between the Letter to Dorp and certain texts by Valla, *Da Lorenzo Valla a Tommaso Moro, Lo Statuto Umanistico della Teologia* (Pistoia, 1973), *Memorie Domenicane,* n. 4.
17. See the quotation from Coluccio Salutati in *IOIAL,* 62–63.
18. Francesco Petrarca, *Prose,* ed. G. Martellotti et al. (Milan/Naples, 1955), 748.
19. Klaus Heitmann, *Fortuna und Virtus, Eine Studie zu Petrarcas* Lebensweisheit (Köln/Graz, 1958), II. "Fortuna und Virtus in der Auseinandersetzung."
20. *CW* IV, lxxiv–v *et seq. et passim.* I take it Hexter does say, "yes," in his paragraph lxxvi–lxxvii.
21. *Ioannis Ioviani Pontani de sermone libri sex,* ed. S. Lupi and A. Riscato (Lugano/Padua, 1954).
22. See Marjorie O'Rourke Boyle, *Erasmus on Language and Method in Theology* (Toronto and Buffalo, 1977), espec. chap. 1, "Sermo" and 2, "Oratio."
23. *The Vision of Politics on the Eve of the Reformation* (New York, 1973), chap. 4.
24. *CW* IV, cv–cxxiv, "The Radicalism of *Utopia.*"

The Question of Truth in
Renaissance Rhetoric and Anthropology

La querelle des rhetores et des philosophes dans la renaissance has become almost as notorious to modern scholars as that between ancients and moderns. Generated by criticisms of scholastic dialectic as lacking eloquence on the part of humanists and by the reciprocal criticism of the contentlessness of mere poetry and mere rhetoric on the part of scholastic apologists,[1] it was a Renaissance of Plato's "ancient quarrel of poets and philosophers."[2] Today it has become a battlefield of modern scholars enacting in some large or small ways their participation in C. P. Snow's conflict between scientific and literary cultures.

Once and for all a truce should be declared in this war, with some mutually agreeable concessions so that we may free the study of the Renaissance from the needless burden of a partisanship within the humanities. The importance of Renaissance scholasticism should be conceded—particularly that of the Aristotelianism of the Italian universities—and the continuation of the far more intensive study of its figures and phases begun in this country by the students of Paul Oskar Kristeller and John H. Randall, Jr., should be encouraged, on the one hand. On the other, the importance of such Renaissance philologists as were concerned with the precise interpretation of ancient philosophical and scientific and mathematical texts should also be conceded for the contributions they made to the history of philosophy and science. It should be recognized that the Renaissance of Platonism, despite its deep roots in medieval theology and philosophy, began under the auspices of the long humanist nostalgia for Aristotle's greatest rival, known through the pages of Cicero, Macrobius, and Augustine. The revival of Platonism continued through the sixteenth century with many friendly associations of humanists and Platonists. But it should be reaffirmed that the Renaissance Platonists, too, were genuine philosophers, and that however much individual ones may, like some of the

This paper was prepared for the Newberry Library Renaissance Conference in April 1979 on Renaissance Rhetoric. It was presented in a session on Rhetoric and Philosophy, and although the paper argues the concern of humanists for such philosophical questions as that of truth, it also stresses the anthropological and social-contextual nature of this concern. Hence it is located in part three of this volume. The paper appeared in *Renaissance Eloquence: Studies in the Theory and Practice of Renaissance Rhetoric,* ed. James J. Murphy (Berkeley: University of California Press, 1983) pp. 207–20, a volume containing the papers of the conference.

humanists, have been at odds with scholastic Aristotelianism, many others sought a synthesis or a reconciliation of Plato and Aristotle, commencing with Giovanni Pico della Mirandola. It may be mentioned that Paolo Beni not only taught natural philosophy at the *Sapienza* in Rome in 1595, but that, on becoming professor of the humanities at Padua in 1598, he declared that Plato and Cicero were the two founders of the *studia humanitatis* and that it was difficult to decide whether Plato's eloquence or his wisdom was the greater. He later prepared a volume of extracts from Plato's writings, which he titled *Rhetorica Platonis*.[3]

Paolo Beni may well be a late and extreme example of a humanist who also possessed credentials as a philosopher and a theologian. There were, however, other humanists, beginning with Petrarch, who encountered and discussed genuine problems of philosophy as a necessary part of their functioning as rhetoricians, particularly those who were concerned with the theoretical foundations of their discipline. It is well known that many humanists in their apologetic defenses of their studies claimed to have a more comprehensive (or a more appropriate, or more usable) command of philosophy than the university-trained philosophers, but these claims, which were frequently not serious, are not at issue. Rather it is a legitimate claim that humanists, in the very pursuit of rhetorical goals and methods, could become philosophical in the questions they handled. There definitely were genuinely "philosophical humanists," although this does not mean that they should be called, or confused with, philosophers.

I will attempt to show how the critique of dialectic by three Italian humanists derived from and contributed to their own rhetorically determined need to investigate and understand human motivation and behavior, and how in the pursuit of such understanding they were compelled to take positions on questions concerning truth that must at least be considered para-philosophical. Committed by their art to generating intention and action in their audience and public, Renaissance humanists attempted to become more precise in determining what kind of language and what kind of reasoning would produce meaningful persuasion, that is, a state of mind that would lead to the corresponding appropriate action. Pragmatic and, perhaps, opportunistic, such considerations also involved the establishment of certain norms concerning human nature that, if they were not strictly determined by the precedents of ancient philosophy, at least may be called "anthropological."

In our concern with rhetoric as an art and its employment by the rhetorician, we sometimes forget the recipient of rhetoric, the reader and the audience. There is tendency to assume that Renaissance humanists identified only with the deliverers of rhetoric, with their classical models, Isocrates and Demosthenes, Cicero and Quintilian, Augustine and Jerome. We forget that the humanists were in many cases readers if not hearers of rhetoric and famous as critics and interpreters of texts. They viewed the rhetorical relationship certainly as much from the viewpoint of the recipient as of the deliverer, both in their actuality as living citizens and theoretically as critics and analyzers of eloquence.

A question of major concern to the humanists that links rhetoric to philosophy, however much the two traditions might differ in its discussion, was that of truth. It has bothered and outraged some of our colleagues to encounter Petrarch's famous quip in the *De suiipsius et multorum ignorantia:* "It is better to love the good than to know the truth."[4] This is a clear sign, it is alleged, of his anti-intellectualism, or at best what could be expected of a devotee of the rhetorical tradition who would place an emotional attachment ahead of the knowledge of reality. What is forgotten is that this was an age in which what had for long been held to be philosophical reality was being reduced to the status of mere names by the philosophers of the new dispensation of the *via moderna,* call them "nominalists" or what you will. Petrarch also had a role in these philosophical debates, as is evidenced by his invectives against the physicians and the young Venetian students of natural philosophy who provoked his work.

But it is an earlier work (at least in inception) that best provides his fundamental position, though this is not always recognized. In the prologue to the first book of the *Secretum,* first written in 1347 but much revised in 1349 and 1353, as it is now thought, Petrarch presented the spirit of Truth, who will silently watch and listen while the human figure of "Saint Augustine" endeavors to persuade "Franciscus" of the right path. It is not enough to suggest that there are echoes of Beatrice, Virgil, and Dante in these three of whom Petrarch declares that "Franciscus's" "steps had gone astray" and that he knew "not the gravity of his disease."[5] Petrarch is undoubtedly signalling that his dialogue is concerned with the Truth, with man's capacity to grasp the Truth, with his susceptibility to be transformed by knowledge of the Truth and to live his life in accordance with it. The argument between "Augustinus" and "Franciscus" in this first part of the dialogue develops over whether a man who knows his misery by deep meditation and wishes to remove it can do what he wishes. The recollection of Saint Augustine's agony and conversion under the famous fig tree is to provide example for the wavering and doubting "Franciscus." The saint's own final conflict of will, which held him back from emotional acceptance of his intellectual conviction of the Truth of catholic Christianity, it is agreed, was resolved, by divine grace.[6] In Petrarch's similar case, not a miracle but an intellectual exercise, intensive meditation on man's last ends, is proposed.

It is at exactly this juncture that the definition of man as an animal but one which is rational and mortal is put forth, and Petrarch turns to an attack on scholastic dialectic. As "Augustinus" puts it: "although a host of

little pinpricks play upon the surface of your mind, nothing yet has penetrated the center. The miserable heart is hardened by long habit, and
becomes like some indurable stone; impervious to warning however sa-
lubrious, you will find few people considering with any seriousness the fact
that they will die." "Franciscus" immediately responds: "Then few people
are aware of the very definition of man, which nevertheless is so hackneyed
in the schools, that it ought not merely to weary the ears of those who hear
it, but is now long since scrawled upon the walls and pillars of every
room."[7] It is, of course, this existential condition of the *vulgus* (in which he
includes himself) that is the true barrier to comprehending the Truth, but
Petrarch makes its persistence the special fault of the defective methodology
of the scholastic dialectician who plays with mere words with the resulting
educational shambles. As "Augustinus" puts it: "This prattling of the
Dialecticians will never come to an end; it throws up summaries and
definitions like bubbles, matter indeed for endless controversies but for the
most part they know nothing of the real truth of the things they talk about
(*plerunque autem, quid ipsum vere sit quod loquuntur, ignorant*). . . . Against
this kind of men, so fastidiously negligent and vainly curious, they should
be questioned as follows: Why this everlasting labor for nothing, this
exercise of wit on silly subtleties? Why in total oblivion of reality do you
grow old conversant only with words, and with whitening hair and
wrinkled brows do you spend all your time on childish ineptitudes" (*Quid,
obliti rerum, inter verba senescitis . . . ?*).[8]

It is in the context of this discussion of the epistemological failure of
scholasticism that "Augustinus" presents his description of what it is really
like to live according to reason and his long exposition of death and dying
graphically depicting the powerful physical and emotional effects the wit-
nessing of a horrible death-bed scene and meditation upon it can produce.
Then, and only then, can a man understand the truth of the standard
definition of man as a rational and mortal animal that is bandied about in
the schools. "Augustinus" adds: "This then is what I meant by sinking
down deeply into the soul—not while, perchance by force of habit you
name 'death' or reiterate 'nothing more certain than death, nothing more
uncertain than the hour of death' and other sayings of this kind in daily use.
For these fly right by and do not sink in."[9] Moreover, meditation is
translated into written language and may be seen as a form of rhetoric
practiced on the self and upon one's readers.

Dialectical philosophy, as here and in the probably contemporary
group of letters in *Le familiari,*[10] and Aristotelian natural philosophy and
moral philosophy, as argued in the *De ignorantia,* fail for Petrarch not
because he despises the intellect, knowledge, and truth but because they are
inadequate roads to the Truth, based as they seem to him on too shallow a
conception of human nature. Poetry and rhetoric, which he learned from

his own practice and from Cicero, Seneca, Horace, Virgil, and Saint Augustine (the *De doctrina Christiana* and the *Contra academicos*), are better instruments for acquiring the deep knowledge of the truth that reaches and moves the will. Only this and not mere verbalizing is sufficient. Hence Petrarch avers, "Satius est autem bonum velle quam verum nosse."[11]

His is a different conception of learning that involves a new integration of the self and a discovery of the road to God. Man, however, is rational (as well as mortal) as the definition held, but man's rationality is only a potential until he has truly learned to direct his life by reason. *Ratio,* moreover, along with *oratio,* is the faculty by which he impersonates himself and guides the reader to the transcendence of fortune and its excessive effects in the *De remediis.*[12] Hence truth for Petrarch becomes not the conclusion of an externally correct, logical proposition (a syllogism), but an authentic internal commitment to a conception of reality brought about by deeply meditated personal experience or by contemplation of a powerful poetic or rhetorical statement. As such it has become a virtue.

For Lorenzo Valla truth was only definable subjectively. Valla says in his *Repastinatio:* "The true or the truth is a quality present in the sense of the mind and in speech, as in 'Does he truly feel that?' 'Does he speak truly?' For when we inquire whether there is one world or many, we do not ask thus whether it is true that there is one world but out of the contradiction, either the alternative [position], 'Does he truly believe there are many worlds?' or ours, as when we set up two or more sides among us as we do in deliberating. For there is no investigation of the true before a controversy over the matter arises. Therefore truth is knowledge of a disputed subject, and falsity lack of knowledge concerning the same; that is a species of prudence or imprudence, or wisdom or folly. Or we may say truth is both the knowledge of the mind concerning some matter and the signification of a speech derived from the knowledge of the mind. For the speech is taken in two ways: one whether anyone speaks true when he speaks thus as he feels; the other whether he speaks forth what he feels or something different through simulation or dissimulation. Therefore there may be a double falsehood in the statement, the one out of ignorance, the other out of malice; the first of imprudence, the other of injustice because in actions, as will appear in the sequel."[13]

The passage above is translated as literally as I am able from Valla's first book of his *Repastinatio dialecticae et philosophiae* in a chapter where he argues that the transcendentals of ancient philosophy—the good, the true, and the one—are qualities derived from human linguistic usage and are not metaphysical entities. As the last two sentences quoted indicate, Valla closely links the question of truth and falsehood with that of virtue and vice. Both are qualities of the soul, one pertaining to the intellect or reason, and the other to will or love.[14]

Following Saint Augustine's *De Trinitate,* Valla sets up a parallel between the divine Trinity and the human soul. But the relationship and character of Father, Son, and Spirit are differently stated by Valla, who introduces Quintilian's three categories of controversy—*An sit? Quid sit?* and *Quale sit?*—into his exposition. *An sit?* of course is an axiomatic affirmation that God exists. *Quid sit?* raises the question of the divine substance.[15] But Valla has already set forth his own notion that the orator's subject matter—*res*—is the only transcendental, and it is divided threefold into "substance," "quality" and "action."[16] To describe a thing or to speak of God, it is necessary to recognize that there are only two basic substances—matter and spirit—and their possible combinations. But matter and spirit, including God and the human soul (as well as animal souls) in the latter, are too abstracted for usage in relation to any actually existing *res,* such as God, so that Valla proposes the use of the term *consubstantial* as a better and more inclusive term than *substance.*[17]

The divine consubstantial (as all others) should include the threesome of substance, quality, and action. The divine three-in-one then, following Valla's rhetorical or Quintilianic mode of reasoning, consists of the Father, who "is probably the life, power and eternity of God," the Son, who "is the wisdom of God, born from the power itself," and the Holy Spirit, "who is the love of God." All three have one substance but different qualities, as just described, and actions: the Father gives forth power, creates and emanates; the Son shines with wisdom; the Spirit burns with holy love—all on the analogy of the sun.[18]

Made in the image of God, the human soul is also compared to the vibration, light, and heat of the sun: "in the soul or substance of the soul there are three perpetual qualities: memory, which is the life of the soul, intellect, which is the same as reason, and . . . love." As for its actions: "the soul comprehends and retains other things by memory, examines and judges by the intellect whether things are, what they are and how they are (*an sit, quid sit, quale sit?*), and embraces or rejects them by the affect."[19]

In accordance with this conception of the soul, Valla thinks of the moral virtues, in contrast to the prevailing Aristotelian notions, as emanating only from the affects and as reducible to one, strength of soul, manifested in the vigor of love or hate, joy or sorrow (past, present, and future). Again, he follows Augustine's criticism of the Stoic conception of the virtues in book 14 of *The City of God.* Prudence, so favored by Cicero and many of the humanists, is regarded as a purely intellectual virtue, or rather, as Valla would have it, as knowledge of virtue. Cato and Catiline used their knowledge, the one for justice and the other for injustice. "Therefore [prudence's] praise is for justice, not knowledge." Prudence, if called by its right name of knowledge or cognition, should not be praised or blamed, "but action proceeding from cognition and understanding through good will." In fact, for Valla the whole range of intellectual powers or virtues is removed from the realm of rhetoric, which is reserved for stimulating the actions of the will or for the moral virtues and vices. Hence he carefully distinguishes between *right* (*ius*), which is the knowledge of justice and law, and *justice,* which is "action, right, good and equitable." "That quality [right] is part of prudence. . . . From adhering to right and doing what right orders, this quality [justice] is named. That quality [right] emanates from truth, this [justice] from will."[20]

Moral action follows from knowledge of what is moral, and a man can sin out of ignorance or out of ill will toward an object of his hate. But ignorance is also censurable as a symptom or a consequence of a weakness of soul that prevents the necessary effort and study to discover right reason or truth. Magnanimity and pusillanimity are the paramount virtue and vice, and are manifested in fortitude and charity or their absence. Man is for the most part driven by his passions but also can sometimes exercise free will. "Fortitude," he says, "is a certain resistance against the harsh or the pleasant things which prudence has declared to be evils. Is not such action justice? Yes, except that justice seems to be the result of a freer will and to occur mostly in easier circumstances."[21] There is, then, a realm for instruction and a realm for rhetorical appeal. Since man is motivated by the desire for the experience of loving, which can be reduced to mere pleasure or elevated to holy beatitude, epideictic rhetoric would be the most potent type of appeal for Valla, though there is also room for the judicial and the deliberative.

As sin is from weakness and virtue from strength, he has a vision of man impressing himself on the exterior world rather than being moulded by externals or written upon as on a *tabula rasa.* The mind is not a *tabula rasa* but is more like a flame or the sun: "And to stay with the same comparison, just as a flame seizes and devours and renders into ashes the material by which it can be fed, so the soul is nourished by learning and hides what it perceives within itself and transfigures it in its own heat and light: hence it paints others rather than is painted by others; . . . the soul, advancing into exterior things by its own light, projects and paints upon them a certain image of its memory, intellect and will."[22]

Rhetoric and the study of language and literature are for Valla the key to man's discovery of rightness and wrongness and truth. Hence it is Valla's project to reform dialectic within a Quintilianic context in the remaining two books of his work. But the intellectual virtues, which include faith and hope, are subordinate to charity, or goodness of the will, in their striving for fulfillment in the act of *amatio,* or loving. "As charity is located in the ultimate part of the soul, so faith and hope are in the prior ones where knowledge, wisdom and truth dwell. For to know, or be wise, or understand, is nothing except to believe and feel about things just as they are held to be (*credere ac sentire de rebus ita ut sese habent*), and this is called truth."[23]

Should Valla be called a philosopher? Since he did his best to dissociate himself from philosophy, ancient, medieval, and Renaissance, it would probably be wrong so to consider him. But if it is asked whether by virtue of his consideration of philosophical problems he was a systematic thinker who constructed an orderly and coherent theory of knowledge derived from the study of rhetoric and linguistic usage and a conception of human nature and motivation based on his conception of man's experience as an image and likeness of the divine, an honest reader, it seems to me, would have to say "Yes."

Gioviano Pontano, another ardent student of ancient rhetoric and ethics, visualized the overall structure of human society as determined by the formation of linguistic character types. Developing the ancient sophistic and Ciceronian vision of rhetoric as calling men together into cities and families from an original wild existence, Pontano in his *De sermone* sees the bonds of social existence as growing out of discourse. "Just as reason," he says, "is the guide and mistress for directing actions, so speech (*oratio*) is the manager of all those things which, conceived in the mind and activated by thinking, are pushed forth into the public world, for, as it is said, we are born social and must live in multitudes. Wherever discourse is greater and more frequent, there is a richer supply of all those things in which life is naturally lacking (since need is present as a companion to all men at their birth). By means of speech life itself is rendered far more adaptable as well as more capable of acquiring virtues and of attaining happiness."[24]

What he has in mind is not formal oratory and rhetoric by which, he says, "men who are especially distinguished in elocution establish the greatest position and the highest authority for themselves in the most populous cities and the largest enterprises." "For," he adds, "we are not at all referring to that part of rhetoric which is called the oratorical power or faculty or art, but only to that common discourse itself by which men, in approaching friends, in carrying on their daily tasks, use language in get-togethers, conversations, family and civic meetings and practices. For this reason those who are engaged in such matters are to be commended according to a quite different criterion than those who are called orators and the eloquent."[25]

Within this wider context of universal discourse, Pontano finds that urbanity and truth are specific qualities that especially contribute to the enhancement of society and the good life for man. The latter quality, truth, is of special interest to us because to Pontano truth becomes a moral virtue—*veracitas*. "Because right reason should preside in handling and managing affairs and truth is its special friend," it is held to be of the highest value by all men. "Through truthfulness human conciliation is established and faith flourishes in the city and a kind of bonding of all our actions and affairs takes place as well as the observance of promises and statements. That this is so Christ, both God and at the same time man, has intimated to us, since He has professed himself to be the Truth."[26]

As was just seen, the virtue corresponding to truth is *veracitas*. Since habitual virtues lead to distinctive character types, on the one hand, there results the *verax* or the truthful man. On the other hand, a considerable number of unpleasant types result from the lying, opposite kind of man, and much of Pontano's disquisition will be about the various forms of *ostentatio, simulatio,* and *dissimulatio.* But truth and veracity also have their cognates. "It follows, therefore, that the study of truth is that virtue which is named *veridicentia* [truthsaying], and those who use it are *veridici;* hence those who prophesy truly are *vates* or soothsayers (*harioli*), truthsayers likewise and true-speakers." Truthful men "engage in investigations of things and natural causes or of right and wrong and either in forensic affairs or in physical and mathematical researches." Speaking well of something (*benedicentia*) also follows from speaking truly (*veridicentia*), for it is the part of an upright man to speak well and to be a truthspeaker and to be himself an especially upright and good man and citizen. And if any crime ought to be disparaged, the veracious man will not spare the truth but he will speak in such a way that he does not seem to do it out of zeal for speaking ill or detracting but in order that honesty (uprightness, *honestas*) may be vigorous in the city itself and at the same time there may be liberty and the common good of all citizens, and in order that crime and wickedness will be driven far away.[27]

In the course of developing his exposition of truthfulness, Pontano projects an ideal of a scholarly man and professor (*studiosus, professor*) who in every action and speech assumes in his own person the role of defending truth. "Moreover," he says, "since all virtue is voluntary (*gratuita*) and sought for its own sake, and veracity is laudable among the very first of the virtues and is very helpful for maintaining and expanding human society, no wonder that the truthful men (*veraces*) themselves are scholars (*studiosi*) of the true itself solely for the sake of the truth; and they both cultivate truth for its own sake and, because they understand it to be an especially durable bond of human society, they know that they themselves have been born for cultivating it."[28] Surely this is a fine and, to us, early acknowledgment of the existence and the moral and social necessity of the man of learning and science. Pontano proceeds to enumerate the duties or *officia* of the truthful man: he should speak freely and openly and never deceptively about himself when this is needed, and he should invent nothing concerning himself beyond what he is and has, and not subtract anything, remaining modest all the while. He will not twist the truth or distort by words in any way and will not be windy or intemperate or frigid in tone and manner. "He will be straightforward and true to himself and no different in explaining and speaking of the affairs of others. These he will refer to and expound in circles and councils and gatherings in such a way that he will not seem merely to speak graciously and in order to please the ears but in zeal for and for the sake of the truth alone."[29]

Pontano's discussions of modes of speech as types of virtue and character here and elsewhere are full of descriptions of the shadier and less admirable habits and stratagems he knew well and presented with sharp and telling insight. Side by side with the humanist-scholar was the courtier-civil servant-counselor, a role Pontano also successfully fulfilled. One must guess, however, that when he wrote the passage above it was not without some conflict between the two ideals, and especially with that of the companionable, facetious type he also so patently admired. At any rate he asks whether the truthful man can ever be permitted to shade the truth, to simulate, or to invent, for the pressure of the times on the person who acts in their circumstances is very great. "Now," he says, "they invent much, now on the contrary conceal in adverse and dangerous circumstances—those wise men who are administrators of public affairs, commanders of armies. So also do many learned physicians in the most perilous disease, and not a few priests who are called preachers where they add their own authority to the facts; nor yet are they held to be liars from this, or less than truthsayers, when their purpose is not to lie or deceive but to help in this manner and to avert danger, which is entirely the practice and duty of prudent men."[30]

Pontano's concerns, like Petrarch's and Valla's, are highly moral but are projected from a quite different social context, more secular, public, and courtly, perhaps. Like the others, Pontano is highly original, though his ancient sources were Aristotelian and Ciceronian in contrast to Petrarch's employment of Cicero, Seneca, and Augustine and Valla's overt promotion of the concepts of Quintilian and his tacit Augustinianism and pretended Epicureanism. But in each of the three cases, the question of truth is expounded in a self-consciously grasped nexus of relationships among God, man, nature, history, and society, a nexus which seemed more crucial to these humanists for the discovery and implementation of truth than the institutional isolation and methodological purity of the scholastic philosophers of their day. These broader, more experiential and anthropological modes of conceptualization and motivation can in great part be understood as a consequence of Renaissance humanist study of ancient ethics and rhetoric. The importance of rhetorical humanism in the history of Western thought thus needs to be conceded regardless of whether any humanist is granted a niche in the hall of famous philosophers.

NOTES

1. See, above all, Paul Oskar Kristeller's classic essay "Humanism and Scholasticism in the Italian Renaissance," printed in a number of places, perhaps most

available in *Renaissance Thought, The Classic, Scholastic and Humanist Strains* (New York, 1961), pp. 92–119. For a survey of humanist critique of scholastic dialectic see Cesare Vasoli, *La dialettica e la retorica dell'Umanesimo* (Milan, 1968). For the controversy between Giovanni Pico della Mirandola and Ermolao Barbaro and the adjoinders of Philip Melanchthon, see Quirinus Breen's "Three Renaissance Humanists on the Relation of Philosophy and Rhetoric," chap. 1 of his *Christianity and Humanism, Studies in the History of Ideas* (Grand Rapids, Mich., 1968), pp. 1–68.

2. Plato, *Respub.* X (607B).

3. Although his interpretation is debatable, see on Beni the article of Giancarlo Mazzacurati in *Dizionario biografico degli italiani*, s.v. Beni's comment on Plato and Cicero in his *Oratio . . . quibus omnibus Perfectus Humanitatis Doctor decribitur ac fingitur, Habita Patavii in Publico Gymnasio XVI Kal. Aprilis Anno MDC,* in his *Quinquagintae orationes* (Padua, 1613), p. 17: "Nam Plato, quem elegantiae, urbanitatis, eloquentiae Humanitatis ipsius sive fontem sive Magistrum merito appellaveris, sine quo nostra haec studia in squalore ac situ iacerent, e cuius spatiis (ut multa complectar paucis) extitit noster Cicero, difficile est iudicare an eloquentia magic excellat quam sapientia, disputandi suavitate quam subtilitate, orationis ubertate et copia, quam doctrinae magnitudine et varietate." On the rhetoric of Plato, see his *Oratoriae disputationes, seu Rhetoricae controversiae, Et Platonis Rhetorica subjicitur, ex variis locis excerpta.* Venetiis. Apud Io. Guerilium. 1625. *In Platonis Rhetorica* begins at p. 111.

4. *Francisci Petrarce De sui ipsius et multorum ignorantia liber,* ed. Pier Giorgio Ricci, in *Francesco Petrarca Prose,* eds. G. Martellotti, P. G. Ricci, E. Carrara, E. Bianchi (Milan and Naplesa, 1955), p. 748, "Satius est autem bonum velle quam verum nosse." Translation by Hans Nachod, in *The Renaissance Philosophy of Man,* eds. E. Cassirer, Paul Oskar Kristeller, J. H. Randall, Jr. (Chicago, 1948), p. 105. Subsequent citations will be to *Prose.*

5. *De secreto conflictu curarum mearum libri tres,* ed. E. Carrara, in *Prose,* pp. 22–215; translation by W. H. Draper, *Petrarch's Secret, or the Soul's Conflict with Passion* (London, 1911), hereafter Draper. See *Prose,* 24–26; Draper, 4–5. Latin passages will not be given in subsequent notes on the *Secretum* because of the accessibility of this edition. Translations will sometimes vary from Draper's. The old dating of 1443 has been all but disposed of by Francisco Rico. See his *Vida u obras de Petrarca, I, Lectura del Secretum* (Padua, 1974), pp. 453–535, and esp. pp. 468–71; and his "Precisazioni di cronologia Petrarchesca; Le 'Familiares' VIII ii–v, e i rifacimenti del 'Secretum,'" *Giornale storico della letteratura italiana* 105 (1978), 481–525.

6. *Prose,* 40; Draper, 19–20.

7. *Prose,* 50; Draper, 29.

8. *Prose,* 52; Draper, 29–30.

9. *Prose,* 56; Draper, 33–34.

10. *Rer. fam.,* 1.7–10.

11. See note 4, above.

12. See Klaus Heitmann's discussion in his *Fortuna und Virtus, Eine Studie zu Petrarcas Lebensweisheit* (Cologne and Graz, 1958), passim. On Petrarch's moral philosophy in general, see my *The Poet as Philosopher: Petrarch and the Formation of Renaissance Consciousness* (New Haven, Conn., 179), chaps. 3, 4, and 5.

13. Lorenzo Valla, *Repastinatio dialectice et philosophiae,* Biblioteca Apostolica Vaticana, Cod. urb. lat. 1207 (hereafter Urb. lat. 1207), ff. 50ᵛ–51ʳ: "Verum sive veritas . . . qualitas est quae sensui mentis inest et orationi, ut 'vere ne ille sentit?' 'vere ne hic loquitur?' Nam quom quaerimus an unus mundus sit an plures, non ita quaerimus an verum sit unum mundum esse, sed ex contradictione aut alterius, ut 'vere ne ille sentit plures mundos esse?' aut nostra quom ipsi apud nos duas pluresve partes sicut in deliberando suscipimus. Nec ante veri inquisitio quam rei controversia nascitur. Itaque veritas est notitia rei controversae, falsitas vero eiusdem inscitia; quae est speties prudentiae aut imprudentiae, seu sapientiae aut insapientiae. Seu dicamus: Veritas est tum notitia animi de aliqua re tum orationis ex notitia animi profecta significatio. Nam orationem duobus modis accipi volo: uno an quis verum loquatur quum ita loquatur ut sentit: altero an quod sentit proloquatur, an diversum per simulationem dissimulationemve. Ideoque duplex erit in oratione mendacium: illud ex ignorantia, hoc ex malitia; illud imprudentie, hoc iniustitie, quia in actis ut in sequentibus apparebit."

14. Urb. lat. 1207, 51ʳ⁻ᵛ.

15. See section of book one of his *Repastinatio,* titled "Quid sit Deus?" Urb. lat. 1207, ff. 66⁴–69ᵛ, followed by "Quid sit anima hominis et bruti?" Urb. lat. 1207, ff. 69ᵛ–76ᵛ.

16. See first and second sections of book one of *Repastinatio:* "Omnia tribus elementis sive predicamentis comprehendi" (i.e., substance, quality and action), Urb. lat. 1207, ff. 42ᵛ–rrʳ; "Nec ens nec aliquid esse transcendens, sed tantum res," Urb. lat. 1207, ff. 44ʳ–46ʳ.

17. See sections "De distributione substantiae," Urb. lat. 1207, ff. 58ʳ–59ʳ and "De substantia," Urb. lat. 1207, ff. 65ᵛ–66ʳ.

18. Urb. lat. 1207. ff. 67ᵛ–68ᵛ.

19. Urb. lat. 1207. f. 71ʳ: ". . . in anima seu substantia animae tres perpetuae qualitates: memoria quae vita animi est; intellectus eadem est ratio . . . [et] amor . . . ; . . . anima res alias memoria comprehendit et retinet, intellectu examinat et iudicat an sit, quid sit, quale sit, affectu amplectitur vel repellit."

20. Urb. lat. 1207, ff. 71ʳ–72ᵛ: "Laus ergo iustitiae fuit non cognitionis. . . . Sed actio ex cognitione et scientia prodiens per bonam voluntatem. . . . Iustitia vero non scientia neque ars, sed actio recta, bona, et aequa. Illud prudentiae est. . . . Haec a stando iuri et ab agendo quod iubet ius nominat. Illud a veritate manat; hoc a voluntate."

21. Urb. lat. 1207, f. 72ᵛ: "Est enim fortitudo reluctatio quaedam contra aspera et blanda quae mala esse prudentia dictaverit. An non talis iustitia? nisi quod et liberioris arbitrii videtur et plerunque versari in facilioribus."

22. Urb. lat. 1207, f. 76ʳ⁻ᵛ: "Atque ut eadem in similitudine versemur, sicut flamma ignis materiam qua ali potest apprehendit, devorat et in prunas convertit, sic anima alitur discendo et ea quae percipit in se recondit, suoque calore ac sua luce transfigurat ut ipsa potius pingat alia quam pingatur ab aliis. . . . anima fulgore suo in exteriora prodiens memoriae, intellectus, voluntatisve quandam obiicit et depingit imaginem."

23. Urb. lat. 1207, f. 74ᵛ: ". . . ut caritatem in ultima parte animae ita fidem et

spem in prioribus sitas ubi scientia et sapientia et veritas habitant. Nihil est enim scire et sapere et intelligere, nisi credere ac sentire de rebus ita ut sese habent, et haec vocatur veritas." For a discussion of this, as yet, unpublished work of Valla with a somewhat different emphasis, see my *In Our Image and Likeness, Humanity and Divinity in Italian Humanist Thought* (Chicago, 1970), pp. 150–65.

24. *Ioannis Ioviani Pontani De Sermone Libri Sex,* eds. S. Lupi and A. Riscato (Lugano: 1954), 1.1.3. Latin quotations will not be given because of the availability of this excellent edition. Hereafter *De serm.*

25. *De serm.* 1.3.3–4.

26. *De serm.* 1.7.8.

27. *De serm.* 2.2.52–53.

28. *De serm.* 2.2.53–54.

29. *De serm.* 2.2.54.55.

30. *De serm.* 2.2.57–58.

Italian Humanism and the Problem of "Structures of Conscience"

I

Scholars have shown a high degree of interest in the medieval penitential system which, together with the pastoral "cure of souls," sought to guide and assist the individual in living in accord with his "conscience" and with the theological truths and moral requirements of the Christian religion. Moreover, many historians and sociologists since the time of Max Weber and including today especially Benjamin Nelson, who is both historian and sociologist,[1] have claimed that a basic breakaway from the medieval moral-guidance system occurred as a consequence of the Protestant Reformation, replacing it with essentially the kind of internalized moral and social sanctions which is held to prevail in "modern" society. Although since the time of Burckhardt, and particularly in Italy, the Renaissance has often been studied from the point of view of its "modernity" (or lack of "modernity"), it has not been regarded recently as notably important in the process of historical generation of new modes of "structuring" conscience and forming internalized moral-guidance systems. The history of conscience has been viewed by its students as primarily medieval and Reformational, but not Renaissance.

More recently Professor Nelson has begun to stress a relationship between a "Protestant" quest for moral certitude of conscience, stemming from a conviction of one's divine predestination or a desire to "prove" one's justification, and a rational, natural-scientific pursuit of a certainty of knowledge concerning the universe, such as was manifested in the great seventeenth-century figures, Galileo, Descartes, and Newton. In eventual combination these two movements constitute for him motive, means, and substance of "modernization." And again the humanist-rhetorical Renaissance is not considered to have played a major role.[2]

This playing down of the historical role of the Renaissance in any

---

This paper, as is explained in note 1, was a commentary on the major paper by Benjamin Nelson in a session dedicated to changing "Structures of Conscience" in the process of transition from the medieval to the modern world. Because it asserts an hypothesis concerning the moral influence of Renaissance humanism in the cultural ideals of our own times, it seemed an appropriate piece with which to close this volume on the scope of Renaissance humanism—this time in its meaning for the present age. It was previously published in *The Journal of Medieval and Renaissance Studies* 2 (1972): 19–33.

process of "modernization" has not been characteristic of other groups of recent scholars, who have, however, emphasized several different aspects of the period and conceptions of "modernization." There have been some recent efforts, of course, to bring the Renaissance in line with the Weber-Tawney-Nelson approach by reviving Werner Sombart's characterization of Leon Battista Alberti as a forerunner of Benjamin Franklin (something which Nelson apparently regards as quaint).[3] But more seriously and convincingly a number of scholars have stressed the innovative and "modernizing" qualities of "civic humanism," with particular reference to its middle-class, "enlightened" republicanism—scholars such as Hans Baron, William Bouwsma, Eugenio Garin, Peter Gay, and George Holmes, with intermittent and partial support from Marvin Becker, Gene A. Brucker, Lauro Martines and others.[4] Except for Becker's look at "The Quest for Identity in the Early Renaissance,"[5] and Garin's studies on religious aspects of humanism, the emphasis in this school has been manifestly and predominantly on the public and political aspects of the problem of morals, so that it seems at times to beg the question of the internal thrust of private convictions and conscience (if these can be historically determined). And it has also operated on the basis of rationalistic conceptions both of human nature and motivation, and of what constitutes the characteristically "modern."

Another important approach of Renaissance scholars, principally art historians and historians of philosophy, to the problem of "modernization" has been the exploration of the implications of the "perceptual revolution" that came with the development of naturalistic perspective in Giotto and some of his contemporaries, and then later with Brunelleschi, Masaccio, Alberti, Piero, and others. Ernst Cassirer and Erwin Panofsky led the way in underlining the importance of this new "consciousness of space" and subject-object relationship. Joan Gadol's recent notable study of Leon Battista Alberti has further elaborated the "modernizing" implications of this new vision of man in relation to nature.[6] Since Cassirer and Gadol specifically link it to Galileo and the seventeenth-century scientific and philosophical developments, it has, of course, implications for Nelson's conception of the cultural and psychological importance of the Scientific Revolution. However, it is questionable whether they really agree on fundamentals.

My own studies of humanist religious and moral thought, which have focused on self-perceptions of man in relation to the divine, are closer to the traditional interests of those who follow or criticize the Weberian hypothesis, but lead, I think, to a different outcome. And my most recent work has brought me right up against the critical question of the relationship of the Renaissance to the Reformation.[7] It has also provided most of the interpretive judgments and most of the material expounded in Section II below. Primarily I will argue on behalf of a more pluralistic and open-ended (i.e., nondeterministic) view of the modern world and the influence of the Renaissance on its emergence. The "mysterious" lack of any emphasis on a new "structure of conscience" is no mystery at all. Rather, in contrast with the medieval ecclesiastical situation of an "external forum" of conscience, and the post-Protestant or scientific stances of "interiorized" quests for "certitude" and "certainty" (Weber's *innerweltliche Askese*, the scientist's "intellectual honesty"), the unstructured character of the humanists' conceptions of moral direction was in itself an important cultural and historical mode of addressing the problem of morality. Thanks to flexibility and viability, the humanist approach to conscience managed to survive in the midst of tighter and more fanatical orientations as an equally important paradigm of moral behavior in the modern world.

On the general question, my views approach but do not entirely coincide with those of Frances Yates in her recent study of the Hermetic tradition in the Renaissance.[8] Although I wish to investigate the question further in the future, I do not believe that Quattrocento humanism, or sixteenth-century "Erasmianism" for that matter, found logical fulfillment in either Calvinism (as Trevor-Roper has argued) or in Counter-Reformation Catholicism (as Toffanin, Montano, and sometimes Benjamin Nelson seem to argue). But note how the whole ground of the argument has been shifted from that of the genesis of capitalism to what is now being called modernization. I do not wish to get into the question of "capitalism" and Weber's "capitalist spirit," which still concerns Trevor-Roper in his otherwise excellent analysis of the empirical weakness of the Weber-Nelson positions.[9] (Nelson wisely has substituted the problem of "modernization" for that of the origins of "capitalism," as have Eisenstadt and his collaborators.) For one thing, a more sophisticated view of the modern world sees that many of its problems, particularly of attitude, ethics, and "spirit," are as much a part of "socialism" as of "capitalism." Moreover, the hunt for the genesis of the "spirit of capitalism" imposes a stereotype on the historian to which he attempts to make his data conform. Trevor-Roper argues this brilliantly against Weber's identification of Calvinism as the matrix of the "capitalist spirit" and shows that, so far as the late-sixteenth and seventeenth centuries are concerned, the facts simply do not fit. But he reverts to a stereotype in identifying "Erasmianism" as the typical religious position of the sixteenth-century capitalist entrepreneur, who, forced to flee to the more tolerant Calvinist areas whenever the religious persecution of the Counter-Reformation or the bureaucratism of the princely state became too oppressive, brought his traditional capacity for economic enterprise with him. The problem of the nature and development of modern European culture thus remains before us, both its definition and its study. To structure it only in terms of the "capitalist spirit" and the bourgeois would be to reduce the Renaissance, at least, from the epoch of the "universal" to that of the "one-dimensional" man.

II

Although it has seldom been specifically discussed, the Renaissance occupies a peculiar and important position in the history of "conscience."[10] The moral conceptions of the Italian humanists were formulated after a period when there had been massive efforts to develop a viable system for the regulation of Christian morals, and at a time when the intersecting ecclesiastical systems seeking to determine the requirements of a Christian life and to induce compliance with these requirements were both omnipresent and increasingly ineffective. The medieval Church, no matter how much some of its popes and reformers had sought to make it a monolithic institution, had in fact never become one. The failure was due not merely to the recalcitrance of human nature and the success of secular authorities in resisting these efforts, but more importantly to the plurality and diversity of the efforts themselves.

Even within the confines of the Church there came about a parallel development of separately constituted systems of authority. First of all there was the vocation of preaching, which by various modes of exhortation sought to cajole or frighten the Christian into conformity with his conscience and which provided guidance as to what was required both for life in this world and for salvation in the next. Then there was the central sacrament of penance which allowed the sinner, having first begun to grieve and regret his departures from what God seemingly demanded, to achieve reconciliation with the visible Church through confession and satisfaction. Then there were the ecclesiastical courts, both ordinary episcopal and special inquisitorial, which sought not only to enforce external compliance with the canons of faith and morals but to discover whether there was an internal conformity of conscience. Then there were the interpreters of the canon law itself, whose commentaries were meant to provide guidance both as to its substance and as to its application in given circumstances, both to confessors and judges. Then there were the theologians, who elaborated rival systems of moral theology in some relationship both to the collections and summaries of Church doctrine in the *sententiae* and *summae* and to the insights that could be gleaned from classical moralists such as Cicero and Seneca and above all Aristotle in his *Nicomachean Ethics*.

All of these ecclesiastical systems varied enormously in interpretation and application, each within its own purview and one from another. However, all agreed in the assumption of a single divine truth to which the individual in his conscience and behavior should conform, and all agreed that some form of external and visible guidance was essential to aid the

Christian and to protect him from the wiles of God's enemies. Moreover, though these moral systems competed in practice, they were conceived as mutually supporting within the common body of the Church, which had been divinely appointed to fulfill this task. There was, then, a situation of seeming orthodox unity of vision, but a high degree of diversity of both interpretation and application.

In view of so much pre-existing plurality, it should not be a matter of great surprise that in reviving a classically oriented rhetorical tradition the Italian humanists should simultaneously revive the ancient claims of rhetoric to both a theoretical and a practical role in the direction of human morality. Indeed, Latin patristic and early medieval moral theology was strongly rhetorical in outlook and methodology, granting rhetoric a scope and a role which, as McKeon has shown, [11] in the course of the centuries had withered away. Italian humanism sought to restore this widened moral role for rhetoric. What is important and different in the new moral guidance offered by the humanists, however, is that, as an essentially lay group of intellectuals, and informally and privately even when they were clerics, the humanists began to act as lay moral counselors on their own and outside of formal ecclesiastical direction.

Although it is true that in the course of the fourteenth and fifteenth centuries there were some efforts to inaugurate a new kind of moral discipline on the part of certain humanists—sometimes in pursuit of a secular ideal, as in the case of Leon Battista Alberti's *Omo civile*—I think it should be stressed that the main import of the humanist moral treatises was to lift the burden of an oppressive and negative conception of conscience and to simplify the confusion of the multiplicity of moral imperatives thrust at their readers. Along with a renewal of emphasis on the infinitude of divine mercy that was beyond human measure, there was projected an ideal of divine permissiveness and even encouragement to action which placed before the Christian the image of his Creator, infinite in power, wisdom, and love, after which man had been created, and toward which he might strive, both to make himself similar to his divine model and, by so doing, to fulfill his own nature as a man.

It would therefore be wrong to claim that a total restructuring of human values occurred in the Renaissance of the kind that Nelson suggests took place as cause and consequence of the Reformation and the Scientific Revolution. On the other hand, a more pluralistic and methodologically modest version of the modern world might leave room for other models of modernity besides the Protestant and natural-scientific ones he has affirmed. And in certain ways the Renaissance offered a different and more open-ended paradigm for relating our values to our circumstances and natures, and one which found its sustenance in the very human subjectivity the Protestant and Scientific models are said to have fled. The humanists in their paradigm had no need to avoid or to embrace moral probabilism, because they saw in the very openness of divine creativity an image for human creativity and for variability of behavior. They had no need to resort to or shy away from the horrors of hypothetical fictionalism, because they accepted the world of nature, including man's psychophysical nature itself, as less than perfect to begin with, and regarded them as objects subject to spiritual domination, whether that of divine providence or human purpose. By generating a new vision of the creative use and shaping of the world and the self, developed out of their own reading of the classical and patristic visions of spirit and nature, the humanists, in a piecemeal and pluralistic way, were able to bypass the conflict of conscience with nature and the world. In the course of doing this they managed to project, here and there, statements of this new vision which sought to avoid overt rejection, though not criticism, of the varied systems of ecclesiastical authority. Theirs was the subtler and less revolutionary path of spiritualization, of pouring ever new wine into both old and new bottles.

Let me offer one or two examples. For Petrarch the greatest danger facing man was his tendency to misread both his external situation or "fortune" and his own capacities. The "virtue" he wished man to acquire was based upon taking a more realistic view of the world and of history in those moments when all things seemed to go well and a man triumphantly felt himself eternally favored by God or "fortune" in a fit of self-deluding elation. A more rational restraint and harvesting of his own powers for the time when circumstances would surely change would stand him in good stead. On the other hand, when "fortune" piled blow on blow, the blackness of despair was perhaps the most dangerous condition into which a man could drift. Moreover, the bitterness of despair over disastrous earthly circumstances seemed to lead to a sense of moral guilt and of spiritual feebleness that denied the possibility of divine mercy, since so great an apparent gulf existed between God and miserable man. Worldly despair generated religious guilt, and we have other evidence that this may have been true in the troubled times before and after the Black Death and that preachers sought to exploit these fears to reinforce their older disciplines of conscience. But at this very time when Tuscan artists were making very small the figures of men pictured next to those of divinity in the art of the late Trecento, Petrarch began setting forth a counterimage to despair in the notion of the dignity of man. Man's dignity lay in his trinitarian soul made in the image of God, in the honor shown man in the Incarnation, in man's mechanical and intellectual ingenuity and inventiveness. [12] It is indeed significant that this idea, the symbol of *homo triumphans* in the later Renaissance, should first be voiced as a remedy and alternative spiritual strategy for the moral sickness of a guilt-ridden, overburdened conscience.

Another example is Lorenzo Valla. For him the Gospel message of infinite divine grace was a releasing one, which, entertained by faith in the declarations of Scripture, strengthened and freed the human will. The rationalism of the Stoics, or that of scholastic Aristotelianism, built around conformity to a clearly structured but complex and artificial vision of the universe, imposed the burden and anxiety of a frantic struggle to live rationally in the pursuit of virtue. Without faith in revelation and the truth of God's promises of fulfillment, fruition, and redemption contained there, no philosophical system could overcome man's natural pursuit of utility and pleasure, and the more learned a man became, the more he set up a conflict of conscience and nature within himself. Faith released man's sense of his own divinity and spirituality and transferred his eudemonistic pursuit of joy and love from the things of this world to God and the supreme reward of the joy of loving God in the next. Freely, then, firmly, passionately, and joyfully man could act virtuously in fulfillment of his deeply affective and erotic nature. To the casuistry of monks, canonists, and scholastics Valla opposed a countercasuistry based on a rhetorical analysis of motives, in order to free man from dependence on external circumstances rather than bind him to them. And we are beginning to learn how much of this Christian Epicureanism of Valla was absorbed by Erasmus into his own religious thought. [13]

There were, of course, other and different humanist voices. Leonardo Bruni with true humanist eclecticism managed to praise "the good man" who "is joyful and gay from good conscience of his deeds and from good hope which no fear of punishment disturbs" and to portray the fearful quality of the internal judgment of conscience: "This judge knows all, was present at every crime, and one is not judged one time only but often and frequently. The condemnation of this internal judge forces tears from you and compels you to weep among sacred things. But believe me . . . this is a game and a joke compared with that eternal and ineffable judgment of God which awaits you after death." He wrote thus in his oration against hypocrisy, an attack on the externality and false airs of self-righteousness put on by members of the mendicant orders. They represented the older, formal system of a codified and externally manifested discipline of conscience, which could therefore be simulated. Bruni's defense of conscience made it informal and personal, guided by that bland blend of Stoicism, Epicureanism, and Peripateticism which he put forth in his *Isagogicon moralis disciplinae.* [14]

Poggio and others also ranted against the clerical hypocrites, though Poggio showed little hope of any other system of morals sufficiently powerful to restrain the rapacious and greedy behavior of mankind. Faith and grace alone remained. [15] Moreover Bartolomeo della Fonte praised the spontaneous quality of repentance as a moral virtue that was a prerequisite to and greater than all the other moral virtues in an amazing neglect of the ecclesiastical sacrament of penance and its parts of contrition, confession, and satisfaction, which he merely mentions. Again, individuality and informality are the road to the moral life.[16] On the other hand, we must suppose that many humanists never faced the question of conscience, or did so in a thoroughly conventional manner, like Sicco Polenton, who composed in the form of a humanist dialogue a rehash of the traditional canonist analysis of the sacrament of penance and of the sins, in all its infinite detail of distinction.[17]

Besides all these, there is Leon Battista Alberti, who some have supposed forged a new conception of morality and conscience that corresponded to the emerging new social order. The shadow of Max Weber's "spirit of capitalism" seems to cast itself backward into the sunlight of the Renaissance, or so it has seemed to some. We are coming to know an Alberti quite as versatile as Burckhardt considered him to be and possibly even more resourceful. But we have not yet fully come to terms with his moral philosophy, despite Joan Gadol's and other notable recent studies.[18] Moreover Alberti's concern for the great family as the peer group and social nucleus for individual morality (rather than the political order) has sometimes seemed an exception to the rule of "civic humanism," but is possibly more consistent with Gene Brucker's recent depiction of the centrality of the great household in the urban scene.[19] What we can be sure about, however, is that Alberti projected an activist, operationalist vision of the ideal human life, whose goal was fame and eternal glory in the eyes of God and his fellow citizens, but even more the internal sense of high moral worth within the man himself. And it is here that his new view of conscience enters the situation. The idle man (*ozioso*) suffers the pangs of self-hatred and penitence like the sinner of old, while the industrious, creating man has the satisfied knowledge that he is realizing his true nature as a man in his striving for accomplishment (*l'uomo nacque non per essere simile a una bestia, ma in prima per adoperarsi in quelle cose quale sono proprie all'omo*).[20] Let me give you one passage out of many which makes this clear:

> Many consider the greatest pleasure is to live without doing anything, without thinking, the greatest happiness to need to do nothing. They err. . . . For idleness [*L'ozio*] carries off a man's useful days and leaves in his soul a habit of being useless for anything and caring about nothing himself, full of perpetual and incurable penitence. O penitence, my young friends, what a hard and bitter reviewer of past life it is! Repentance if you think about it, you will see is a species of self-hatred. . . . It would be better to be a statue carved in the image of a man than an idler who is similar to a tree trunk shaped like a man. In seeing that statue you are pleased by the genius and craftsmanship of the man who created it. How can this idler be pleasing to you when he

is disgusting and hateful to himself? The fisherman, the merchant, and similar men, if they return without a catch or a profit, regret nothing so much as the time lost. You, a scholar, born to be as honored and outstanding a man among your fellow citizens as you choose, do not bring about through indolence and neglect a situation in which you will need to lament and say, "Today I have learned nothing, today I have acquired no good grace, today I have performed no useful action for any friend, nor have I done anything helpful to myself."[21]

One can, if one wishes, see in this and similar statements an anticipation of the familiar *Wirtschaftsethik des Kapitalismus,* or the emergence of what Nelson, referring to the Protestants, has called "integrated characters with a full sense of responsibility." I prefer, however, to think of it as closer to Burckhardt's vision of the "modern" man than that of Weber or Sombart. Alberti viewed the world as an arena in which one could prove by his achievements the validity of the Renaissance vision of the dignity of man— man realizing his nature by acting and creating in the image and likeness of a now active and operative deity. Thereby one became a civilized man and a man of dignity, *un omo civile, un omo di degnità.* By passivity and self-indulgence one fell out of the human world into that of *bestialità.* Such was one outlook, which increasingly in the Italian Renaissance was rejecting the negativity and passivity of the older "structures" of conscience for a structureless ideal of personal autonomy where the individual was daily challenged to establish his dignity i ι world of chance, nature, history, and the inscrutable operation of divine providence.

Finally, I should like to speak briefly of the Platonists who extended and systematized these new conceptions of the humanists. Marsilio Ficino, more explicit in his statements than Pico, gave a theological basis to Pico's great vision of man acting outside of the cosmos, as a *mikrotheos* rather than *mikrokosmos,* and choosing freely to live on any metaphysical level. It was conscience itself that was the divine element in man and a gift of grace which gave man his moral freedom to transcend both the laws of nature and the written laws of human societies. Ficino in his commentary on the Epistle to the Romans declares:

> Finally, no law, whether natural or written, has efficacy for justice and salvation unless divine grace, along with the intellect, also moves the affects; and it moves them in such a way that the grace of God, Himself, is served by the precept of the law. . . . Certainly that true light illumining all men coming into this world infuses the light of truth into the mind of man. . . . Like a judge [conscience] sits in the soul and takes the place of God in man.[22]

To this conception of conscience and the divinity of its origin and power should be juxtaposed Ficino's enormous vision of man as regulating, shaping, and transforming the natural and historical worlds. Of the many hortatory passages concerning man's powers over the world, let me quote but this one:

> The other animals either live without art, or have each one single art to the use of which they do not turn by their own power but are dragged by a law of fate. The sign of this is that they gain nothing from time for the work of making things. On the contrary men are the inventors of innumerable arts which they practice according to their own decision. This is shown by the fact that individuals practice many arts, change, and become more expert by extensive exercise, and what is marvellous, human arts make by themselves whatever nature itself makes, so that we seem not to be servants of nature but competitors.[23]

Did the Italian humanists, then, in departing gently and diversely, personally and inwardly, from the confusing multiplicity and externality of the late-medieval moral systems, erect a new structure of conscience of their own? Or did they anticipate in any way the savage compulsion toward moral certitude and epistemological certainty that Nelson discerns in Protestantism and the New Science? I do not think so. Believing deeply in the need for grace and its ever-availability, they were also openly Pelagian in their stress on man's educable freedom of will. Stressing the subjective and inward in man's spiritual life, they did not question or challenge the role of the clergy or the validity of the sacraments. Perhaps, with Protestant hindsight, we may argue that they should have, as in Luther's day it was argued that Erasmus should have. But he and they did not. Was this great period, then, the time of the neither-nors, the age of the halfhearted who should be made to share with Pope Celestine the outer circle of Dante's *Inferno* for their refusal to confront the great issues of history? Those such as Nelson has presented them? Again I think not.

In two respects, it seems to me, the humanist Renaissance, both Italian and Northern, left an important legacy to the modern world that worked in their day and in the succeeding centuries among some men. It offered and continues to offer a *tertium quid,* not a *via media,* but a true alternative to Nelson's ideal-type of modern Catholic ecclesiastical pragmatism and "hypothetical fictionalism" and to his opposing construct of a vision of the compulsions of conscience of the Protestant and rationalist questers for certitude, moral and scientific. The first respect in which the humanist movement continues to be paradigmatic is in its combination of personalism with the notion of a social realm of discourse where men through the arts of visual and verbal communication persuade each other to the minimal wisdom and agreement of a civilized polity. The world of rhetoric and the humanities is both a private and a public world where the two spheres overlap in mutual respect and esteem. It is a humanly wrought *unitas in pluralitate*. In its second respect, humanist unity in diversity is also sacral and religiously inspired. The world of man is seen as a plural world of variety and otherness. Its truths, though individual and particular, are nonetheless truths. They find their unity and certainty in the recognition of the universal spirituality of all mankind: *una religio in varietate rituum*, to quote Cusanus a second time. Their positions were not the same as those of Counter-Reformation Catholicism. Neither moral probabilism nor hypothetical fictionalism contained the vision of the humanists. Within the confines of the rhetorical tradition, which was indeed relativistic as far as morals and knowledge are concerned, the humanists wrought a fluid conception of the world of man as shaped by politics and art. In it each individual, bearing within himself a vestige of the divine Creator, was viewed as a creator both in his own individual existence and in his participation in the wider collective world of politics and society.

NOTES

1. Max Weber's *Die protestantische Ethik und der Geist des Kapitalismus* first appeared in the *Archiv für Sozialwissenschaft und Sozialpolitik,* Vols. 20 and 21 (1904–5), reprinted in *Gesammelte Aufsätze zur Religionssoziologie,* 3 vols. (Tübingen, 1922–23); English translation by Talcott Parsons, *The Protestant Ethic and the Spirit of Capitalism* (New York, 1930). Nelson has dealt with this theme in one monograph and numerous supplementary papers in which he enlarges and revises his views. See *The Idea of Usury: From Tribal Brotherhood to Universal Otherhood* (Princeton, 1949; new and enlarged ed., Chicago, 1969, with extensive bibliographies of both the older and more recent literature). For the views of other historians and sociologists who take the Weber thesis seriously, see *The Protestant Ethic and Modernization: A Comparative View,* ed. S. N. Eisenstadt (New York, 1968).—The present article is a preliminary essay and a partial study of the broader cultural and historical significance of Italian humanist modes of moral exhortation. It was occasioned by the need to comment on a paper presented by Professor Nelson at the annual meeting of the American Historical Association in December 1970. The general title of the session was Structures of Conscience from Abelard to Galileo, and Professor Nelson's paper was called "On the Roads to Modernity: 'Conscience,' Casuistry, and the Quests for Certitude." Professor Karl F. Morrison also commented on Nelson's paper. I mention this circumstance not only to explain that Section II of the present article is essentially my comments on that occasion but in order to make clear, in the absence of Nelson's paper, the intellectual context and the historical problems to which it is addressed.

2. See his " 'Probabilists,' 'Anti-Probabilists,' and the Quest for Certitude in the 16th and 17th Centuries," *Proceedings of the Xth International Congress for the History of Science,* (1965), I, 269–73; and his "Scholastic Rationales of 'Conscience,' Early Modern Crises of Credibility, and the Scientific-Technocultural Revolutions of the 17th and 20th Centuries," *Journal for the Scientific Study of Religion,* 7 (1968), 157–77.

3. Cf. Joan Gadol's remarks, *Leon Battista Alberti, Universal Man of the Early Renaissance* (Chicago, 1969), pp. 225–27; and those of Renée Watkins in her Introduction to her translation of Alberti's *I libri della famiglia, The Family in Renaissance Florence* (Columbia, S.C., 1969), pp. 12–14, 16–20—the latter passage labeled "Elements of a Burgeois Ethic." Sombart's views are set forth in Chap. 7 of his *Der Bourgeois*—in the English translation *The Quintessence of Capitalism* (New York, 1967), pp. 103–24. Nelson's most recent rejection of the significance of the Italian Renaissance for his conception of modernization is "The Medieval Canon Law of Contracts, Renaissance 'Spirit of Capitalism,' and the Reformation 'Conscience': A Vote for Max Weber," in *Philomathes: Studies and Essays in the Humanities in Memory of Philip Merlan,* ed. R. B. Palmer and R. Hamerton-Kelly (The Hague, 1971), Sec. D, "Law, Moral Sentiment, and the 'Spirit of Capitalism' in Renaissance Italy," pp. 542–46. A more classical statement, which he has not improved upon, is his older essay "The Usurer and the Merchant Prince: Italian Businessmen and the Ecclesiastical Law of Restitution, 1100–1500," *The Tasks of Economic History,* Supplement VII (1947) to the *Journal of Economic History,* pp. 104–22. Perhaps the most comprehensive but still not entirely conclusive effort to examine the economic ethic of Florentine businessmen is Christian Bec, *Les Marchands écrivains: Affaires et humanisme à Florence, 1375–1434* (Paris and The Hague, 1967). Weber's thesis has prompted two other recent studies, both in *Action and Conviction in Early Modern Europe,* ed. Theodore K. Raab and Jerrold E. Seigel (Princeton, 1969): Richard M. Douglas, "Talent and Vocation in Humanist and Protestant Thought," pp. 261–98; and Lynn White, Jr., "The Iconography of *Temperantia* and the Virtuousness of Technology," pp. 197–219.

4. Cf. esp. Hans Baron, *The Crisis of the Early Italian Renaissance,* rev. ed. (Princeton, 1966); William Bouwsma, *Venice and the Defense of Republican Liberty* (Berkeley, 1968), Chap. 1, "Renaissance Republicanism and the *Respublica Christiana*"; Eugenio Garin, *Science and Civic Life in the Italian Renaissance* (New York, 1969); Peter Gay, *The Enlightenment: An Interpretation,* Vol. I, *The Rise of Modern Paganism* (New York, 1966), Chap. 5, "The Era of Pagan Christianity," pp. 256–321; George Holmes, *The Florentine Enlightenment, 1400–50* (New York, 1969). Always excepting Garin, this group tends to operate on eighteenth-century enlightenment preconceptions concerning the process of history and modernization, whereas the following show, to my mind at least, greater psychological, political, or social realism: Marvin Becker, *Florence in Transition,* 2 vols. (Baltimore, 1967, 1968); Gene A. Brucker, *Renaissance Florence* (New York, 1969); Lauro Martines, *The Social World of the Florentine Humanists, 1390–1460* (Princeton, 1963).

462 / The Scope of Renaissance Humanism

5. Becker in *Florilegium Historiale: Essays Presented to Wallace K. Ferguson* (Toronto, 1971), pp. 294–312.

6. Ernst Cassirer, *The Individual and the Cosmos in Renaissance Philosophy* (New York, 1964), English translation of original German edition of 1927. Erwin Panofsky recapitulated his previous studies on this theme in *Renaissance and Renascences in Western Art* (Stockholm, 1960; New York, 1969). And Gadol, *Alberti*.

7. Cf. Trinkaus, *"In Our Image and Likeness": Humanity and Divinity in Italian Humanist Thought,* 2 vols. (London and Chicago, 1970). I have an essay in preparation, "The Religious Thought of the Italian Humanist, and the Reformers, Autonomy or Anticipation," but the problem is far from solved.

8. *Giordano Bruno and the Hermetic Tradition* (London and Chicago, 1964; paper edition, New York, 1969). Cf. Trinkaus, *Image,* pp. 498–504 for discussion of our views, agreements and disagreements.

9. H. R. Trevor-Roper, *Religion, the Reformation and Social Change, and Other Essays* (London, 1967), also issued as *The Crisis of the Seventeenth Century and Other Essays* (New York, 1968), Chap. 1, "Religion, the Reformation and Social Change."

10. K. E. Kirk, *Conscience and Its Problems: An Introduction to Casuistry* (London, 1927), a work that has deeply influenced Nelson, does not refer to the Renaissance or to humanism. John T. McNeill, who has written extensively on the medieval penitential systems, does give to Chap. 7 of his *History of the Cure of Souls* (New York, 1951) the title "Three Centuries of Enrichment and Deterioration from the Coming of the Friars to the Renaissance." However, no Italian of the period, nor any other Renaissance figure, is included unless Caxton be counted. Indeed, the literature of our subject is exceedingly sparse, outside of the treatment of individual figures and of the attempts to seek something of the Protestant ethic, or of an alleviation of the usury ban, in the Weberian literature referred to above. Heiko Oberman in his *The Harvest of Medieval Theology* (Cambridge, Mass., 1963) discusses Gabriel Biel's views in relation to late scholastic thought at length.

11. Richard McKeon, "Rhetoric in the Middle Ages," *Speculum,* 17 (1942), pp. 1–32.

12. Cf. Trinkaus, *In Our Image,* Chap. 1, "Petrarch: Man Between Despair and Grace," and Chap. 4, "The Dignity of Man . . . in Petrarch," pp. 179–80, 190–99. Klaus Heitmann, *Fortuna und Virtus: eine Studie zu Petrarcas Lebensweisheit, Studi italiani,* I (Cologne and Graz, 1958).

13. Trinkaus, *In Our Image,* Chap. 3.

14. Ibid., pp. 673–74, 857 n. 94; L. Bruni, *Isagogicon,* ed. Hans Baron, *Humanistischphilosophische Schriften* (Leipzig-Berlin, 1928), pp. 20–41.

15. Trinkaus, *In Our Image,* pp. 673 and 269–70.

16. Ibid., pp. 626–33.

17. Ibid., pp. 616–26.

18. Gadol, *Alberti,* Chap. 5; and see Cecil Grayson's comments in reviewing Gadol's book, *Renaissance Quarterly,* 24 (1971), p. 53.

19. Brucker, *Renaissance Florence,* Chap. 3, "The Patriciate."

20. Leon Battista Alberti, *De Iciarchia,* pp. 187–286, in *Opere volgari,* ed. Cecil Grayson, Vol. 2 (Bari, 1966), p. 212.

21. Grayson, II, 240: Molti reputano summa voluttà el vivere senza faccende, senza pensiere; summa felicità bisognarli far nulla. Errano. Dicemmo e dell'ozio e della voluttà ne' ragionamenti di sopra, ma quel che bisognava continuo provedervi, non e superfluo spesso ricordarlo. L'ozio se ne porta i giorni utili, e lascia nell'anima uno uso d'essere inutile a ogni cosa e nulla curar sé stessi pieno di perpetuo e irrecuperibile pentimento. O duro e acerbo riprenditore della vita passata, giovani, el pentimento! El pentirsi, pensatevi, vederete ch'egli è spezie d'odio contro a te stessi. Dall'ozio, adonque, segue oltre agli altri seco innati mali, odio contro a te stessi. E sarebbe meglio essere una statua figurata simile all'omo, che ozioso simile a un tronco fatto in forma d'omo. A veder quella statua ti piacerà lo 'ngegno e artificio di chi la figurò. Questo ozioso, come può piacere e te quando lui a sé stessi è fastidioso e odioso? El pescatore, el mercante e simili, se torna senza preda e guadagno, di nulla tanto si duole quanto del tempo perduto. Tu studioso, tu nato a essere fra' tuoi cittadini quanto tu desideri omo onorato e primario, non commettere per tua desidia e negligenza che ti bisogni dolerti e dire: oggi imparai nulla, oggi acquistai niuna bona grazia, oggi non dedi opera utile ad alcuno amico, né feci cosa qual giovi a me.

22. Trinkaus, *In Our Image,* pp. 748–49, 883 n. 85.

23. Ibid., pp. 482, 784 n. 44.

Index